# SOCIOLOGICAL THEORY:
# A Book of Readings

The Macmillan Company
Collier-Macmillan Limited, London

THE MACMILLAN COMPANY
COLLIER-MACMILLAN CANADA, LTD., TORONTO, ONTARIO

Printed in the United States of America

3-1303- 00058-1117

# CONTENTS

*v*

# Introduction to the Third Edition

More than a decade has elapsed since the first edition of this book appeared in print. In 1956, these editors thought they were, to some extent, bucking a tide, albeit one that was already markedly receding. A residual suspicion of sociological theory as such, left over from an earlier overcommitment to radical empiricism, could still be felt. By 1964, with a second edition, we seemed to be riding a wave. Very few people by then harbored any doubts about the value and relevance or the indispensable nature of theory. We allowed ourselves to rejoice at the time over a remarkable growth, a creative ferment, a sense of liberation which, in only a few short years, had somewhat transformed our precarious science.

Since then, even more obsolete ideas have been discarded, more of the usable past has been rediscovered, and some needed renovation has taken place.

Like all anthologists, who want others at least to appreciate what they love, we continue to feel maddeningly cramped by limitations of space. This third edition is, nevertheless, and once again, not only a revised but an enlarged version of the original text.

Cuts, apart from those that merely involve trimming and pruning—which in every case were designed to enhance readability—are, of course, our most painful task. Two staple and solid chapters have been eliminated: one on the primary group, certainly not because we think that concept is unimportant, but because beginning students of sociology, as its popularity steadily increases, are so likely to have had heavy exposure to Cooley's brainchild; the final chapter, a discourse on the sociology of knowledge, we have also chosen to omit. It appears, somewhat rewritten, as an entry in the new *International Encyclopedia of Social Sciences,* and thereby becomes available to anyone near a reasonably well-stocked library.

We want to reaffirm part of our introductory statement to the second edition:

> *In searching for the most important theoretical contributions made since 1956 we were governed solely by the criterion of excellence—insofar as two fallible sociologists are capable of recognizing it. After the choices were made (not without anguish) —to our initial surprise and subsequent delight—most of them seemed to form a pattern.*
>
> *The theoretical reflections of Dahrendorf and Wrong, those found in one of Merton's latest essays and Goffman's third book, in articles by Levinson, Gouldner, and Eisenstadt, to mention only these, tend away from a somewhat overdeterministic view of society toward a more flexible conception. Where, for example, earlier theorists saw no alternative to increasing bureaucratization, Eisenstadt and Gouldner consider the possibility of debureaucratization. . . .*

And so on in that vein. Our last paragraph read:

> *Finally, in the broadest sense, Dahrendorf and Wrong urge us to relinquish as inappropriate any relatively static model of society. They point instead to contradictory requirements, conflict, change, and sheer human cussedness and recalcitrance as forces which militate against social stasis, "equilibrium," and the total routinization of life. If what we discern in all this is indeed a new departure in sociological theory, it can only cause us to exult.*

It *was* a new departure, and at the same time, a return, to the recognition that change occupies a place of centrality in all human affairs, that on a theoretical level it should not be merely an afterthought to "stability," from which flux can no more be detached than normality from abnormality—or conformity from nonconformity.

Accordingly, the most substantial addition to this book is a sizeable chapter entitled "Social Change and Social Evolution," harking all the way back to Comte, Marx, and Spencer—not so foolish as those who neglect to read them believe they are, in their allegedly common equation of Change and Progress—but continuing in the work of Parsons—who, along with more and more of his contemporaries and his juniors, not only makes much of change, but endorses evolutionism—followed in their diverse, and yet converging ways, by Sahlins, Eisenstadt, and Moore.

This is probably the most exciting turn that sociological theory has lately taken. But perhaps more important, if less spectacular, is the continuous re-examination of accepted wisdom. We hope by including critical and innovative material from intelligent sociologists like Blau, Homans, Becker, Mizruchi, and Rose Laub Coser, to reflect the fact that, whereas there are no sacred cows in our discipline, the geniuses of old remain an inexhaustible source of inspiration in our discipline.

L. A. C.
B. R.

# Introduction to the First Edition

Alfred North Whitehead may have put the case a little too sharply when he observed that it is a sign of maturity for a science to forget its ancestors. However, it is certainly true that recollection of their work should be selective. One of the weaknesses of traditional histories of sociological thought is that they have attempted to present a synoptic overview of past sociological theory without a conscious effort at selection. Such lack of intellectual discrimination has no place in an ordered perspective. It tends to level figures of very uneven stature and thus to confuse the student who may be feeling his way toward a standard of significance. Attention should be directed here and deflected there. It is our conviction that the student of sociology, as distinct from the historian of ideas, must above all be introduced to those aspects of the works of the past that have proved viable. We know of no better criterion in art or in science, or in a discipline struggling to move from one category to the other.

All writing, however novel, inevitably contains much that is relevant only to the period, place, and society of its compositions, Hence, there should be no reluctance to deal with sociological thought by deliberately choosing from the welter of divergent and antagonistic ideas those which seem most relevant for contemporary research and expanding theory.

We are convinced that sociology as a science can develop only if it is able to point to a genuine accumulation of empirically validated results. Unrelated research findings—the quest for "facts" which, once found, do not speak for themselves—are more likely to produce a miscellany of curiosa than the lineaments of a science. Therefore, we shall attempt, in a necessarily limited and elliptical way, to indicate how large such an accumulation of results interlaced with theory has actually grown up in sociology.

We shall show how certain concepts and theories first suggested by an earlier generation have been developed further at a later date; we shall also be obliged to point out that, in some cases, earlier formulations have been neglected by later theorists who painfully rediscovered what would have been known to them if they had undertaken a careful inventory of their theoretical inheritance. To a small extent this book should serve as such an inventory.

The presentation of texts and the discussion of concepts will differ rather drastically from those found in most books on sociological theory. We shall not be concerned with the assessment of the whole work of any theorists but only with those parts of it which seem most pertinent within the context of present-day inquiry. What once loomed large may by now, in this framework have shriveled to a different dimension. If Ratzenhofer and Gumplowicz can be forgotten completely, Comte and Spencer cannot. Yet neither positivism nor evolutionism is any longer the specter that haunts sociology. Thus, when discussing Herbert Spencer, we shall not have occasion to deal extensively with his evolutionary theories, but deserved weight will be given to his pioneering analysis of structure and function. Similarly, when presenting the work of William Graham Sumner, our emphasis will be on his treatment of different types of controlling norms rather than on the brand of Social Darwinism with which he was historically associated.

The disadvantages of such a method are fairly obvious. The uninitiated reader will not be able to form a fully rounded view of any of the authors we present, although he may be stimulated to do so at his leisure. It seems to us that the advantages of our approach outweigh its disadvantages: instead of being confronted with a jumble of information which he is only too likely to forget in short order, the student will be presented with theoretical conceptions the relevance of which (to current research) will be made apparent to him. Even though he will not receive a complete picture of every writer (which in any case no single book of readings could supply), he will, we hope, attain an integrated view of the development of the science of sociology. This book, then, is not conceived as an exhaustive inventory of sociological ideas, but as a selective and suggestive introduction to those theoretical ideas which inform the work of contemporary sociology. The lines of filiation and mutual influence of the key concepts which sociology utilizes today will, we trust, be made reasonably clear to the student.

The relations between theory and research have been the subject of sustained interest in the last several decades of American sociology. "Rediscovering" certain European theorists such as Max Weber, Emile Durk-heim, and Georg Simmel, and influenced by repeated onslaughts on the part of a younger generation of theoretically oriented sociologists against the busywork of fact gatherers, American sociology has produced what might be called a renaissance of sociological theory. We fear, however, that in the initial exuberance of theoretical discovery there has occasionally been a tendency to revert to some of the most gross errors of an earlier period of theorizing, a tendency to engage in large-scale system-building, the con-struction of imposing theories which contain few if any testable propositions. Such development of generalizations on so high a level of abstraction that their immediate relevance and utility are almost completely obscured is not likely to advance creative research. We feel that such system-building often has led to the unfortunate tendency of epigones to substitute pigeonholing in impressively labeled categories for creative investigation. No insight is gained by translating known facts into new terminology.

It is our intention in the following selections to make clear that leading theorists of the past were concerned with the development of theories *about* relevant aspects of the social reality which they faced, rather than with the building of airtight but empty scholastic systems. Because their theories were constructed in such a way, they were able to survive the tests of time and of usefulness. Thus, William Graham Sumner's distinction between folkways, mores, and institutions still can serve useful purposes, while the impressive generalizations developed by his contemporary Lester Frank Ward are of interest only to specialists in the history of ideas.

Theorists "in the grand manner" fell into disrepute after World War I. With the growth of radical empiricism, social scientists retrenched and pur-sued a will-o'-the-wisp—theory-free investigations of phenomena of less and less consequence. Some old-timers continued to theorize, and for a time they were regarded with a kind of tolerant odium. Today, on the surface at least, this situation has greatly changed. It is generally conceded that theory is an indispensable part of the scientific enterprise. A *sub rosa* cleavage persists, but this has more to do with the absence of sophistication on both sides than with the presence of a philosophical issue. What we can say, with the wisdom of hindsight, is that the revulsion against theory as such was mis-conceived. If such men as Durkheim and Weber still provide us with our best clues, it is because a generation or two of nose counting has supplied us with none that are better. Between their time and ours, *techniques* have been devised, if not perfected, which permit us to pursue lines of investiga-tion programmatically stated by the founders of our science. It is at this point that fruitful lines of continuity can be re-established. We regard it as our principal task to highlight and trace what seem to us such heartening lines as are now in the process of formation.

In the selections that follow the reader will thus not find discussions of integrated systems but only of special propositions, specific concepts, or examples of substantive theorizing. Inevitably an element of personal bias has crept into the process of selection, but we hope we have kept such bias under control.

The editors are aware that much present-day theorizing feeds, though sometimes unconsciously, on theoretical propositions developed long before the rise of formal sociology, or developed independently of it. How can one treat, say, the sociology of power and authority without discussing Machiavelli and Hobbes? How is it possible to touch the sociology of order without reference to de Bonald, de Maistre, and Burke? Yet we have decided to include in our selections only the work of theorists who may be specifically labeled as belonging to sociology, social psychology, and social anthropology. This decision was made on purely pragmatic grounds; it was felt that inclusion of other thinkers would transcend the boundaries which we have set for ourselves and thus burst the limitations of a single volume.

Similar reasons have prompted the decision to include only those European authors whose writings are available in American translation. We deplore the fact that theoretical contributions of great importance, such as the sociological writings of Max Scheler and of Maurice Halbwachs, are as yet not available to American students. We regret that the majority of young sociologists—despite the ritualistic requirements of language examinations—are unable to acquaint themselves with theoretical writings in other languages. But we must accept the fact that by and large only those European works which have been translated have had a decisive influence on American sociological thinking. For this reason, and also because of the space limitations alluded to earlier, we have reluctantly decided to omit—except in one case—all hitherto untranslated works.

A word as to the organization of this book. The reader will note that we have planned in terms of concepts rather than in terms of substantive areas of investigation. Thus he will find chapters dealing with the concept of reference group or the concept of anomie rather than with, say, minority relations or the sociology of the family. We followed this plan because we feel that undue concern with substantive areas of research detracts from the central fact that concepts which are useful in the search for regularities of behavior in one field may also be of import in another seemingly unrelated area. Thus recent investigations have shown that reference-group theory developed in research on military structure may also provide important clues in such seemingly unrelated fields as the sociology of class relations, prejudice, and political behavior, as well as in the sociological interpretation of personality. The customary departmental organization has tended to obscure important interrelations and to hamper the cross-field application of theoretical clues originally developed in one particular area. A student familiar with the central concepts of sociology will be less likely to draw upon *ad hoc* hypotheses to explain a puzzling problem in his own research; he will, we hope, be able to draw upon his conceptual knowledge to explain problems in his particular area—even though these concepts have never as yet been applied to it.

To be sure, a simple array of concepts does not constitute a theory. Concepts, as Robert K. Merton has argued, "constitute the definitions (or prescriptions) of what is to be observed; they are the variables between which empirical relationships are to be sought"; yet it is clear that no theory can be developed without concepts. Only logical interrelations between various concepts may lead to the development of a theory. But for our purposes it seems that the most convenient mode of exposition is to focus on a series of concepts and to observe how various authors have been able, through the utilization of such concepts, to institute theories accounting for uniformities of behavior which these concepts have led them to discover.

A final cautionary word to the student using this volume may be in order. Some of our selections are rather short, while other authors are represented by lengthy excerpts from their work. Such differences are not meant to suggest relative merit. We have often decided to use short excerpts from writings that are easily available in other form, while giving more space to relatively inaccessible material. On the other hand, we often found that, while certain authors have the gift of succinctly stating their main contention, others require more space to develop their train of thought in successive steps.

This book is not meant to help the student pass his examination requirements; it is intended to familiarize him with a heritage of vast knowledge so that he can put it to future use in his own work. The work of the future can be fruitful only if it is informed by the contributions of the past. As T. S. Eliot once wrote: "Someone said 'The dead writers are remote from us because we *know* so much more than they do.' Precisely, and they are that which we know."

## ACKNOWLEDGMENTS

We wish to express our special gratitude to two colleagues. Professor Robert K. Merton of Columbia University read our first draft and made a number of important suggestions which helped shape our orientation and the nature of our final selections. Professor Robert Bierstedt of the College of the City of New York read several drafts of our manuscript and gave us most constructive advice. But for them, what seemed to be an almost unmanageable body of concepts could not have been brought into its present form.

We also wish to thank our wives, Rose Laub Coser and Sarah Helen Rosenberg, who have so graciously contributed to the clarification of our thinking.

Nor are we unmindful of the help given us by students in more than one classroom. The eagerness with which many of them received and entertained general ideas has gladdened us, and suggested more strongly than anything else that American sociological theory may have a bright future.

L. A. C.
B. R.

# 1: Definition of the Field

The precursors of sociological theory are as old as civilization. At least since man attained mastery of the arts of reading and writing, he has speculated about himself, his world, and their relationship to each other. In both Oriental and Occidental antiquity, with the development of high civilization as well as literacy, philosophers often anticipated ideas that required millennia to develop on a "modern" basis. To some extent, there has never been anything new under the sun, and all philosophy *is* but a footnote to Plato. Even physical science may be shorn of its novelty if we remember, for example, that an atomic theory of matter was advanced well before the Christian era by Democritus and Lucretius.

And yet all is flux. Change, transitoriness, impermanence, process are to be seen all around and within us. Applied exclusively to man, the simultaneous presence of fixity and its opposite is summed up by a contemporary philosopher, Kurt Riezler, in the title of his book, *Human Nature: Mutable and Immutable*. Moreover, everything in the present may be traced to something or, more often, to many things in the past which, in their turn, do not spring upon the world *ex nihilo*. As the ancients knew, nothing comes from nothing.

The task we have set ourselves in this chapter is to deal, far from definitively, with what sociological theory is, how the enterprise was conceived and, especially, what motivated a number of men in different parts of the western world to originate it. We have explained in the introduction why, despite our qualms about overlooking early genius, it was not deemed advisable to trace our concepts back through all of history. It would take more than one book, probably more than one small library, to do the job, and even then it would be one for scholars whose competence lies principally in the history of ideas. Also, such a procedure would involve us in an infinite regress. For "X" was influenced by "Y" and "Y" by "Z"—and so on almost into infinity.

So we begin at a point in time when sociology is programmatically freed from social philosophy. That point comes in the nineteenth century; its avatar is a volatile Frenchman named Isidore Auguste François Marie Xavier Comte (1798–1857). To say that sociology as a specific field of inquiry originates with Comte is not to deny that his system was the meeting place of many minds. Harry Elmer Barnes states the case correctly when he points out that Comte's "chief contribution lay in his remarkable capacity for synthesis and organization rather than in the development of new and original social doctrines."[1] Among those from whom Comte derived much, Barnes mentions Aristotle, Bossuet, Kant, Hume, Turgot, Vico, de Maistre, Saint-Pierre, Condorcet, Montesquieu, and Saint-Simon. The list could easily be enlarged. It would demonstrate that Comte was an erudite man with powers of encyclopedic absorption, who greatly benefited from the intellectual labor of others.

However, after all the major sources have been uncovered, there remains a social situation which must be considered if we are to understand Comte's unique synthesis. The founder of sociology lived in a period of tremendous upheaval, of disorganization and reorganization, when many men confidently believed that the world which was collapsing before them could be remade after their hearts' desire. Science had performed wonders in subduing nature. Never before did man know so much about organic and inorganic matter. Only the species itself was proving intractable. What could be more logical than the extension of methods already established as successful in natural science to the one unit of study left untouched by them?

Comte surveyed the history of science. In so doing, he noted its progression: first, astronomy and celestial mechanics, the subject farthest removed from man; then, physics, chemistry, and biology—in that order—gradually approaching man as matter and as an organism. The time now seemed ripe for a science of sciences, something that would embrace man and all his works. Comte saw it as the culmination of trends that had been set in motion a few centuries before. At last disinterested observation and experimentation might be used in a deliberate effort to understand human beings as social animals of a very distinctive sort. Problems of enormous complexity and the possible means of ameliorating or solving them were both at hand.

Comte thought that human intelligence had evolved to the point where social physics or sociology, as a source of knowledge about man, was feasible. With that knowledge, the good society could be created. Clearly, Comte's underlying motivation for the study of sociology was humanitarian. He stated his credo in those words: *"Savoir pour prévoir et prévoir pour pouvoir"* (To know in order to predict and to predict in order to control). Comte felt that only if man was equipped with the necessary knowledge which neither metaphysics nor theology would yield could he hope to deal with his increasingly vexatious problems.

It was one of Comte's firmest beliefs that each branch of knowledge passes through three stages; the theological or fictitious, the metaphysical or abstract, and the scientific or positive. This is the famous Law of the Three Stages. The human mind in its theological state seeks the essential nature of things, first and final causes, absolute truth. It "supposes all phenomena to be produced by the immediate action of supernatural beings." The metaphysical state is merely a modification of the theological. In it, the mind supposes that abstract forces rather than supernatural beings are inherent in and produce all phenomena.

> *In the final, the positive state, the mind has given over the vain search for Absolute notions, the origin and destination of the universe, and the causes of phenomena, and applies itself to the study of their laws—that is, their invariable relations of succession and resemblance. Reasoning and observation, duly combined, are the means of this knowledge . . . There is no science which, having attained the positive stage, does not bear the marks of having passed through the others. Some time since it was (whatever it might be) composed, as we can now perceive, of metaphysical abstractions; and further back in the course of time, it took its form from theological conceptions. We shall have only too much occasion to see, as we proceed, that our most advanced sciences still bear very evident marks of the two earlier periods through which they have passed.*
>
> *The progress of the individual mind is not only an illustration, but an indirect evidence of that of the general mind. The point of departure of the individual and of the race being the same, the phases of the mind of a man correspond to the epochs of the mind of the race. Now, each of us is aware, if he looks back upon his own history, that he was a theologian in his childhood, a metaphysician in his youth, and a natural philosopher in his manhood. All men who are up to their age can verify this for themselves.[2]*

That the individual in his own life cycle relives all of human history is a familiar idea. We find the outstanding Swiss psychologist Jean Piaget expressing it in our own day when he explains socialization, perhaps too optimistically, as a process of moving from theocracy through gerontocracy to democracy.[3] The crux of this idea, stated in surprisingly similar terms by Comte and Piaget, was summed up by nineteenth-century biologists who said that "ontogeny recapitulates phylogeny." The pathfinders of sociological thought were always tempted to use biology as a model for their work. They flourished in an age when every cultivated person had to reckon with the doctrine of evolution and to ponder the theories of men like Lamarck, Cuvier, Wallace, and Darwin.

It is not surprising, therefore, that Comte, Herbert Spencer (1820–1903), his opposite number in Great Britain, and all their American followers, starting with Lester Frank Ward (1841–1913), came to be known as social evolutionists. Like the others, Comte has frequently and justifiably been taxed for his "organicism" (the tendency to see society as an organism, which is less pronounced in Comte than in some other organicists who located a "central sensorium," a medulla oblongata, a cerebrum, and a cerebellum as societal divisions). If sociology is merely biology on a different level of abstraction, then indeed there is little justification for the new and un-pedigreed science. But this aspect of Comte, along with other residues of mysticism, has been abandoned by all sociologists who "are up to their age."

We are the residuary legatees of another vision which Comte saw and inspired others of his time to see. This is the vision of society and the state, not as an organismic but as an *organic* whole. Man had already been viewed from many angles and was to be subjected to more minute analysis. Without questioning the legitimacy of such procedure, Comte proposed that man be viewed sociologically, that is to say, holistically. To see human beings in their total social setting was the peculiar task of sociology as Comte understood it. Although he believed in progress, Comte was convinced that the overview provided by sociology would enable man to plan his future scientifically and thus facilitate what might not otherwise take place so surely or so pointedly. Nothing bespeaks his intention more eloquently than his first book, appropriately entitled *A Program of Scientific Work Required for the Reorganization of Society.*

Herbert Spencer was certainly no radical social reformer; neither was he quite the intransigent enemy of change that his detractors have pictured him to be. Spencer favored intelligent social change and believed that the instrument for such innovation would be sociology. This he emphasizes in

"Our Need for It," which is Chapter One of his famous treatise, *The Study of Sociology.* In opposition to mere common sense, a social science is called for to supply evidence on the basis of which rational decisions can be made. Spencer's books are rich with examples that still give them the ring of contemporaneity. For instance:

> *How obvious it appears that when minds go deranged, there is no remedy but replacing the weak internal control by a strong external control. Yet the "non-restraint system" has had far more success than the system of straight-waistcoats. Dr. Batty Tuke, a physician of much experience in treating the insane, has lately testified that the desire to escape is great when locks and keys are used, but almost disappears when they are disused: the policy of unlocked doors has had 95% of success and 5% of failure. And in further evidence of the mischief often done by measures supposed to be curative, here is Dr. Maudsley, also an authority on such questions, speaking of "asylum-made lunatics." Again, is it not clear that the repression of crime will be effectual in proportion as the punishment is severe? Yet the great amelioration in our penal code, initiated by Romilly, has not been followed by increased criminality but by decreased criminality; and the testimonies of those who have had most experience—Machonochie in Norfolk Island, Dickson in Western Australia, Obermeir in Germany, Montesinos in Spain—unite to show that in proportion as the criminal is left to suffer no other penalty than that of maintaining himself under such restraints only as are needful for public safety, the reformation is great: exceeding indeed, all anticipation.[4]*

It has taken the dominant school of twentieth-century American sociology some time to learn what Spencer kept hammering at a hundred years ago: that common sense is but a poor guide to reality. Men think they know how to go about curing their social ills, although they would never depend on untutored laymen to treat the simpler physical ailments that afflict them. Spencer puts it classically in his *Study:*

> *You see that this wrought-iron plate is not quite flat; it sticks up a little here toward the left—"cockles," as we say. How shall we flatten it? Obviously, you reply, by hitting down on the part that is prominent. Well, here is a hammer, and I give the plate a blow as you advise. Harder, you say. Still no effect. Another stroke: well, there is one, and another, and another. The prominence remains, you see: the evil is as great as ever—greater, indeed. But this is*

> *not all. Look at the warp which the plate has got near the opposite*
> *edge. Where it was flat before it is now curved. A pretty bungle*
> *we have made of it. Instead of curing the original defect, we have*
> *produced a second. Had we asked an artisan practised in "planish-*
> *ing," as it is called, he would have told us that no good was to be*
> *done, but only mischief, by hitting down on the projecting part.*
> *He would have taught us how to give variously—directed and*
> *specially—adjusted blows with a hammer elsewhere: so attacking*
> *the evil not by direct but by indirect actions. The required process*
> *is less simple than you thought. Even a sheet of metal is not to be*
> *successfully dealt with after those common-sense methods in which*
> *you have so much confidence. What, then, shall we say about a*
> *society? "Do you think I am easier to be played upon than a pipe?"*
> *asks Hamlet. Is humanity more readily straightened than an iron*
> *plate?*[5]

The relevance of this statement is made very clear if we place it side by side with some recent observations of Robert K. Merton, who ranks among the two or three greatest contemporary American theorists. When Merton defends his interpretation or "codification" of structural-functionalism (see Chapter 14), he does so in terms similar to those of Spencer. Merton distinguishes between "manifest" and "latent" functions, stressing the latter. "It is precisely the latent functions of a practice or belief which are *not* common knowledge, for these are unintended and generally unrecognized social and psychological consequences. As a result, findings concerning latent functions represent a greater increment in knowledge than findings concerning manifest functions. They represent also greater departure from 'common sense' knowledge about social life,"[6] . . . and therein lies their value.

Spencer must also be credited with having been able to meet the principal objections to sociology as such, objections raised in his time and continuously reiterated thereafter.[7] The complaint is that each man is unique, that the course of his life is unpredictable, and that therefore no generalizations about men can be made. Spencer replies, characteristically, with an analogy:

> *What Biography is to Anthropology, History is to Sociology . . .*
> *The kind of relation which the sayings and doings that make up*
> *the ordinary account of a man's life, bear to an account of his*
> *bodily and mental evolution, structural and functional, is like the*
> *kind of relation borne by that narrative of a nation's actions and*
> *fortunes its historian gives us, to a description of its institutions,*

*regulative and operative, and the ways in which their structures
and functions have gradually established themselves. And if it is
an error to say that there is no Science of Man, because the events
of a man's life cannot be foreseen, it is equally an error to say that
there is no Science of Society, because there can be no prevision
of the occurrences which make up ordinary history.*[8]

There is much more here than mere counterassertion: a cogent argument is
carefully unfolded and repays study even today.

In all probability, Spencer was thinking of Thomas Carlyle when he
declared that a certain class of people was unprepared to interpret sociological phenomena scientifically. Carlyle believed that certain extraordinary
individuals were responsible for the determination of human history. To
Spencer such a philosophy of history corresponded to the mentality of
savages and children. It was precisely to combat Supernaturalism and the
Great-Man Theory of history, that Spencer, like Comte before him, felt the
urgent need for a usable social science. Said Spencer, "If you want roughly
to estimate anyone's mental calibre, you cannot do it better than by observing the ratio of generalities to personalities in his talk—how far simple truths
about individuals are replaced by truths abstracted from numerous experiences of men and things. And when you have thus measured many, you
find but a scattered few likely to take anything more than a biographical
view of human affairs."[9] And it is to the scattered few that he calls for help
in establishing a hitherto neglected, more mature, point of view.

The founders of sociology were actuated by a common dissatisfaction.
They all sensed that something was missing from the armamentarium of
Western scholarship, and each was willing, without deprecating it, to relinquish his original area of interest—history, philology, economics, theology,
chemistry, political science, or psychology—in an effort to transcend the
limitations of all such disciplines. Such men were scattered and few; other
thinkers clung tenaciously to their several specialties. Most scholars were,
and not a few still are, openly disdainful of the sociological upstart. As John
Stuart Mill pointed out to his friend, Auguste Comte, it was, after all, a
bastard science which combined the Latin root *socius* with the Greek *logos*.
Like all illegitimate children, sociology has constantly had to justify its
existence. In providing a *raison d'être*, no one excels the early masters. Only
when sight is lost of their reasoning does the field itself become hazy and
undefinable.

Surely the most persistent criticism sociological theory has had to meet
is that concepts such as "society" are unreal abstractions. Nowadays the

impeachment is somewhat subtilized. Yet it is basically what it was when Georg Simmel (1858–1918) and Emile Durkheim (1858–1917) thought they had laid the ghost. Their argument must be pondered in detail. No more than an inkling can be given here, but for the case in brief or *in extenso,* we are well advised to follow Georg Simmel:

> *Let us grant for the moment that only individuals "really" exist. Even then, only a false conception of science could infer from this "fact" that any knowledge which somehow aims at synthesizing these individuals deals with merely speculative abstractions and unrealities. Quite on the contrary, human thought always and everywhere synthesizes the given into units that serve as subject matters of the sciences. They have no counterpart whatever in immediate reality. Nobody, for instance, hesitates to talk of the development of the Gothic style. Yet nowhere is there such a thing as "Gothic style," whose existence could be shown. Instead, there are particular works of art which, along with individual elements, also contain stylistic elements; and the two cannot be clearly separated. The Gothic style as a topic of historical knowledge is an* intellectual *phenomenon. It is abstracted from reality; it is not itself a given reality. Innumerable times, we do not even want to know how individual things behave in detail; we form new units out of them. When we inquire into the Gothic style, its laws, its development, we do not describe any particular cathedral or place. Yet the* material *that makes up the unit we are investigating— "Gothic style"—we gain only from a study of the details of cathedrals and palaces. Or we ask how the "Greeks" and the "Persians" behaved in the battle of Marathon. If it were true that only individuals are "real," historical cognition would reach its goal only if it included the behavior of each individual Greek and each individual Persian. If we knew his whole life history, we could psychologically understand his behavior during the battle. Yet even if we could manage to satisfy such a fantastic claim, we would not have solved our problem at all. For this problem does not concern this or that individual Greek or Persian; it concerns all of them. The notion, the "Greeks" or the "Persians," evidently constitutes a totally different phenomenon, which results from a certain intellectual synthesis, not from the observation of isolated individuals. To be sure, each of these individuals was led to behave as he did by a development which is somehow different from that*

*of every other individual. In reality, none of them behaved pre-
cisely like any other. And, in no individual, is what he shares with
others clearly separable from what distinguishes him from others.
Both aspects, rather, form the inseparable unity of his personal
life. Yet in spite of all this, out of all these individuals we form the
more comprehensive units, "the Greeks" and "the Persians."*

*Even a moment's reflection shows that similar concepts con-
stantly supersede individual existences. If we were to rob our
cognition of all such intellectual syntheses because only individuals
are "real," we would deprive human knowledge of its least dubious
and most legitimate contents. The stubborn assertion that after
all there exist nothing but individuals which alone, therefore, are
the concrete objects of science, cannot prevent us from speaking
of the histories of Catholicism and Social Democracy, of cities, and
political territories, of the feminist movement, of the conditions of
craftsmen, and of thousands of other synthetic events and collective phenomena—and therefore, of society in general. It
certainly is an abstract concept. But each of the innumerable
articulations and arrangements covered by it is an object that can
be investigated and is worth investigation. And none of them consists of individual existences that are observed in all their details.[10]*

If Simmel sought to dissociate sociology from psychology, so has every
methodologist of the new science since that time. Evidently the battle must
be refought in every generation; as we write, it is far from having subsided.
That social problems should be dealt with on the social level is still a doubtful proposition in many quarters. Let us see how the French genius, Emile
Durkheim, who moved from Kantian philosophy to neo-Comtean sociology,
handled this question in a typical passage from his invaluable book, *The
Rules of Sociological Method:*

*But, it will be said that, since the only elements making up
society are individuals, the first origins of sociological phenomena
cannot but be psychological. In reasoning thus, it can be established just as easily that organic phenomena may be explained by
inorganic phenomena. It is very certain that there are in the living
cell only molecules of crude matter. But these molecules are in
contact with one another, and this association is the cause of the
new phenomena which characterize life, the very germ of which
cannot possibly be found in any of the separate elements. A whole
is not identical with the sum of its parts. . . .*

> *By reason of this principle, society is not a mere sum of individuals. Rather, the system formed by their association represents a specific reality which has its own characteristics. Of course, nothing collective can be produced if individual consciousnesses are not assumed; but this necessary condition is by itself insufficient. These consciousnesses must be combined in a certain way; social life results from this combination and is, consequently, explained by it. . . . The group thinks, feels and acts quite differently from the way in which its members would were they isolated. If, then, we begin with the individual, we shall be able to understand nothing of what takes place in the group. In a word, there is between psychology and sociology the same break in continuity as between biology and the physicochemical sciences.* (Elsewhere in the same treatise, Durkheim admits there is such a thing as biochemistry and there may be such a thing as social psychology. Editors.) *Consequently, every time that a social phenomenon is directly explained by a psychological phenomenon, we may be sure that the explanation is false.*[11]

Durkheim knew that biology, economics, and psychology took up various phases of human activity and shed light upon them. But they only told part of the story. It seemed to him that the older social sciences overlooked those ways of acting, thinking, and feeling which are not mere products of the individual's consciousness. These ways may eventually, and in most cases do, conform to what a person feels subjectively. However, they are not his creations. He inherits them—they are, we would now say, culturally transmitted to him—through formal and informal education. Society provides a large number of predefined conventions which must be obeyed on pain of ridicule, isolation, incarceration, or death. Norms govern our lives, they are exterior to us, and we are constrained to accept them. What follows from these premises is something sociologists have come to know as the normative determination of human behavior.

Thus, the category of facts which interested Durkheim and prompted him to become a sociologist par excellence were those pertaining to an external force whose coercive power largely controls mankind. That force Durkheim identified collectively as society and more particularly as a multitude of habits of thought, modes of dress, languages, and traditions considered appropriate to one's class and country which most men were obliged to accept most of the time. There is always a body of established beliefs and practices that constitutes a social order into which the individual is born.

These are not merely legal and moral regulations, religious faiths, and financial systems. They also include "social currents such as any great movement of indignation, pity or enthusiasm in a crowd."[12] These currents do not originate in any one mind; they carry each person along in spite of himself. In the same class are opinions on religious, political, literary, or general esthetic matters formed either by society as a whole or by certain limited, but influential, circles. There is a continuous effort to impose responses on man that he could not have produced spontaneously. This is most obvious when, during the period of greatest plasticity, the child's views are shaped by education; they are more subtly conditioned when he grows to adulthood. Durkheim saw education, broadly defined, as the means by which social beings are constituted. Their social milieu fashions them in its own image.

It was Durkheim's opinion that collective habits inhere in the successive acts which they determine. These habits receive permanent expression in a formula which is repeated from mouth to mouth and fixed in writing. "Such is the origin and nature of legal and moral rules, popular aphorisms and proverbs, articles of faith wherein religious or political groups condense their beliefs, standards of taste, etc."[13] According to Durkheim, this is also the proper subject matter of sociology.

Durkheim's paramount theoretical problem then became: how can "the proper subject matter of sociology" be isolated from individual, non-social causes? And his answer is altogether relevant, for it was to relate statistical data such as birth rates, marriage rates, or suicide rates to underlying attitudes, to the state of "collective consciousness." This was Durkheim's prescription for neutralizing individual circumstances and disentangling social phenomena from all foreign matter. Durkheim conceded that individual differences are, in a marginal sense, of interest to social psychology. He refused as a sociologist to be preoccupied with them to the exclusion of an anterior collectivity.

If men are constrained by exterior norms that exist prior to, but are ultimately incorporated in, consciousness, then their acts are largely predetermined, and Durkheim believed this to be the case. He by no means considered the individual to lack self-control. His point of view was closer to that of Hegel, who held that freedom consists in the recognition of its nonexistence. To Durkheim this meant the necessity of going "back along the chain of causes and effects until we find a point where the action of man may be effectively brought to bear." In effect, he admonished us to study the regularities in society, and thereby to protect ourselves through our ability to predict, and thus to advance toward a higher state of human development. Durkheim thought that social phenomena down to the most minute ceremonial detail present an astonishing uniformity; if we learn their nature, it will be possible to control them and free ourselves.

By 1917, when the celebrated sociological innovators, William I. Thomas (1863–1947) and Florian Znaniecki published their monumental study, *The Polish Peasant in Europe and America* (2nd ed., 1927) much more was known about the nature of science than could have been apparent in any earlier generation. The widely read "Methodological Note" to Thomas and Znaniecki's famous work reflects a new degree of sophistication. Nevertheless, it faithfully echoes many sound formulations originally set forth by Comte. Thomas and Znaniecki found that the twentieth century even more than the nineteenth urgently needed "a conscious and rational technique" to deal with social processes that tended to get out of hand:

> *The marvelous results attained by a rational technique in the sphere of material reality invite us to apply some analogous procedure to social reality. Our success in controlling nature gives us confidence that we shall eventually be able to control the social world in the same measure.*
>
> *While our realization that nature can be controlled only by treating it as independent of any immediate act of our will or reason is four centuries old, our confidence in "legislation" and "moral suasion" shows that this idea is not generally realized with regard to the social world. But the tendency to rational control is growing in this field also and constitutes at present an insistent demand on the social sciences.*[14]

Thomas and Znaniecki held forty years ago that the moment had arrived for substituting conscious technique for half-conscious routine, although they saw only a halting development of this technique. It was still beset with the weaknesses that Comte had noted, for . . . "even now we find in it many implicit or explicit ideas and methods corresponding to stages of human thought passed hundreds and even thousands of years ago." They observed the continued presence of magic as an anachronism that takes the form of "meeting a crisis by an arbitrary act of will decreeing the disappearance of the undesirable or the appearance of the desirable phenomena, and using arbitrary physical action to enforce the decree."[15] This situation differed but little from the one symbolized by Spencer's wrought-iron plate.

Thomas and Znaniecki take note of a later phase which, while better than the first, is still faulty. This is a phase based upon "common sense" and represented by "practical sociology." The cardinal fallacy of this transitional technique is that it supposes a full knowledge of that social reality with which all human beings have an empirical acquaintance. Such an attitude reminds Thomas and Znaniecki of the ancient assumption "that we know the physical world because we live and act in it, and that therefore we have the right of generalizing without a special and thorough investigation, on the mere basis of 'common sense.' " The illusion of omniscience stems from total reliance upon sense perception and results in such scientific error as the geocentric system in astronomy and the medieval concept of motion. But in the world surveyed by Thomas and Znaniecki men were more willing to deny their senses in defining the inorganic than in understanding the superoganic. They still are.

These pioneer authors who wished to promote sociological theory to a mature state viewed their main problem as that of causal explanation. To them, the determination and systematization of data constituted only a first step in scientific investigation. They boldly faced the task of attempting to understand and control the process of *becoming*, which, they pointed out, must be analyzed into a plurality of facts representing a succession of cause and effect. Therefore, "The idea of social theory is the analysis of the totality of social becoming into such causal processes and a systematization permitting us to understand the connections between these processes."[16] In casting about for the best possible method of causal explanation, Thomas and Znaniecki rejected a fallacy prevalent in their time, according to which science simply takes the facts as they are without any methodological prepossessions "entirely a posteriori from pure experience." However, they declared, "A fact by itself is already an abstraction; we isolate a certain limited aspect of the concrete process of becoming, rejecting, at least provisionally, all its indefinite complexity. The question is only whether we perform this abstraction methodically or not, whether we know what and why we accept and reject or simply take uncritically the old abstractions of "common sense.' "[17] It is a measure of how knowledgeable *they* had become that in 1917 Thomas and Znaniecki could take so advanced a position. Not all of their confrères have yet caught up with it.

Sociology enjoys more general acceptance and academic respectability in the United States at present than in any other part of the world. One reason it has flourished in this country is that from the time of such men as Lester Frank Ward, practicality has made a powerful appeal to American sociologists. The technological side of science—in this case applied sociology or "human engineering"—always had more opportunity to develop in this environment than theory, which was often dismissed contemptuously as abstract, fine-spun and arid. We have suggested that the early European protagonists of sociology usually envisaged practical application of their theories, but they considered such consequences only as ultimate objectives after the development of the science to which they dedicated themselves. In the United States, on the other hand, there was considerable interest in a social science that would provide immediate solutions to complicated problems of the moment. American sociologists could, of course, draw upon a large European reservoir for the analysis of social phenomena. Yet they were more likely to be guided in their investigations by specific problems such as crime, immigration, vice, or feminist unrest. To Thomas and Znaniecki this seemed like putting the cart before the horse. Their insight is all the more remarkable since with their joint study of the *Polish Peasant* they themselves were plunging into the vortex of American social problems. But they were guided in their inquiry by the concepts sociology had already put at their disposal and which they further developed. Their analysis transcends the specific phenomenon under study and through its theoretical elaboration gives us generalizations applicable to a wide range of social situations. Indeed, the "Methodological Note" with which they introduce their major work contains severe strictures against immediate reference to practical aims. It points out the fallacies that result from trying to understand difficult situations without any guiding theoretical framework.

Granting that we should be able to foresee future developments and prepare for them, accumulate a stock of secure and objective information to be applied if the need arises, the authors favored the growth of an exact and empirical science "ready for eventual application. And such a science can be constituted only if we treat it as an end in itself, not as a means to anything else, and if we give it time and opportunity to develop along all the lines of investigation possible, even if we do not see what may be the eventual applications of one or another of its results."[18]

To be sure, there are many urgent social problems which cry out for solution, but, as historians of science (not to mention Thomas and Znaniecki) have often pointed out, practical problems are most often solved in the long run by those who concentrate on most unpractical theoretical work, while those who steep themselves in practicality and common sense remain powerless to make a dent even in those problems which they set out to overcome.

On the other hand, there has been a noticeable tendency to claim with exaggerated and unwarranted enthusiasm that *the* sociological theory is to emerge within a very short time from the development of a master scheme now in the process of elaboration. A certain degree of skepticism seems to be warranted. The speculative mind concerned only with theory in the large is likely to leave behind a system of Byzantine style, a large architectonic scheme admirable perhaps for its logical consistency but otherwise of no relevance to the workaday development of a growing science.

There is a real need today for a science of society, and the features of such a science can by now be perceived rather clearly. But much more difficult theoretical work—in constant interplay with research—is still required to transform into solid achievement what is as yet largely a promise. It seems to us that the pioneers of sociological theory have succeeded in establishing that there *is* a social reality subject to its own partly validated laws of development, a reality which requires analysis on its own terms, and that these terms cannot be reduced to psychology, economics, or any of the other sciences of man. It now remains for us so to codify the results of our research that in the course of time ever more encompassing theories can be initiated to account for uniformities in the social sphere. We heartily concur with Robert K. Merton when he says:

> *Sociological theory must advance on these interconnected planes: through special theories adequate to limited ranges of social data, and the evolution of a more general conceptual scheme adequate to consolidate groups of special theories.*
>
> *To concentrate entirely on the master conceptual scheme for deriving all subsidiary theories is to run the risk of producing twentieth-century equivalents of large philosophical systems of the past, with all their varied suggestiveness, all their architectonic splendor and all their scientific sterility.*[19]

REFERENCES

1. Harry Elmer Barnes, *An Introduction to the History of Sociology*, Chicago, 1948, p. 83.
2. Auguste Comte, *The Postive Philosophy*, London, 1893 (3rd ed.) Vol. 1, p. 2.
3. Jean Piaget, *The Moral Judgment of the Child*, Glencoe, Illinois, 1948.
4. Herbert Spencer, *The Study of Sociology*, New York, 1875, pp. 13–14.
5. *Ibid.*, pp. 270–271.
6. Robert K. Merton, *Social Theory and Social Structure*, Glencoe, Illinois, 1949, p. 68.
7. For a recent example see *The American Scholar Forum*, Spring 1952, and a rejoinder, "Social Science and the Humanists" by Bernard Rosenberg in *The American Scholar*, Spring 1953, pp. 203–214.
8. Spencer, *op. cit.*, p. 58.
9. *Ibid.*, p. 32.
10. Georg Simmel, *The Sociology of Georg Simmel*, translated and edited by Kurt H. Wolff, Glencoe, Illinois, 1950, pp. 4–6.
11. Emile Durkheim, *The Rules of Sociological Method*, Chicago, 1938, pp. 102–104.
12. *Ibid.*, p. 4.
13. *Ibid.*, p. 7.
14. William Isaac Thomas and Florian Znaniecki, *The Polish Peasant in Europe and America*, New York, 1927, p. 1.

15. *Ibid.*, p. 3.
16. *Ibid.*, p. 36.
17. *Ibid.*, p. 37.
18. *Ibid.*, p. 15.
19. Merton, *op. cit.*, p. 10.

# Part I
# General Concepts

# 2: Culture

What distinguishes man from non-man? That, as La Rochefoucauld suggested, he drinks whether thirsty or not and makes love in every season? That he has a soul? That he is a rational animal or a gregarious creature? There are both thoughtful and whimsical answers to this question, but in the cool light of science most of them are seen to be misleading, superficial, or simply erroneous.

All ethnological and sociological reflection begins by asking what differentiates man from other species. Anything that follows from that reflection stands or falls on the validity of a single answer: that man alone is in possession of culture. In *Primitive Culture* Sir Edward Tylor (1832–1917), who, with Herbert Spencer, probably did most to give British social science its special flavor, first advanced the classic definition of culture. It was a simple but inclusive definition which stated or implied that the proper domain of anthropology lay in everything man made and taught to future generations who could also accumulate and transmit their knowledge. This is what Tylor meant by "culture." By reason of his peculiar endowment, man, unlike any other species, is able to recreate the natural environment. Man makes tools and rules and patterns his life according. He becomes at one and the same time a slave to and the master of his own past creations.

The eminent American anthropologist, A. L. Kroeber, in his famous essay on "The Superorganic" in 1917 fully embraced the Tylorian point of view and strongly criticized "biologism" (the reduction of human behavior to biological mechanisms), a major tendency of his day and ours. Tylor's opposite number in the United States, Lewis Henry Morgan (1818–1881), had advanced similar views (which reappear even more forcefully in the contemporary work of a gifted disciple, Leslie White). These premises, in turn, are conceptually identical with those of the great French sociologist, Emile Durkheim (1858–1917), who used "society" to mean what the anthropologists understood by "culture."

In the twentieth century cultural anthropologists such as Bronislaw Malinowski (1884–1942) and Leslie White have stressed the linguistic basis of man's capacity to develop culture. This is most evident in the readings we have selected. Men are organisms in symbolic communication with each other. Therefore, they have culture. We are distinctively a symbol-making and symbol-using species. All else follows from this primary datum, as White has so trenchantly shown us. Neither material culture—which Malinowski brought more to the fore than did Tylor—nor non-material culture—habits, ideas, and beliefs—could exist without the symbol.

Clyde Kluckhohn's valuable summary suggests how far social science has gone in achieving a general acceptance of this key concept.

## CULTURE DEFINED * (*Tylor*)

Culture or Civilization, taken in its wide ethnographic sense, is that complex whole which includes knowledge, belief, art, morals, law, custom, and any other capabilities and habits acquired by man as a member of society. The condition of culture among the various societies of mankind, in so far as it is capable of being investigated on general principles, is a subject apt for the study of laws of human thought and action. On the one hand, the uniformity which so largely pervades civilization may be ascribed, in great measure, to the uniform action of uniform causes; while on the other hand its various grades may be regarded as stages of development or evolution, each the outcome of previous history, and about to do its proper part in shaping the history of the future. To the investigation of these two great principles in several departments of ethnography, with especial consideration of the civilization of the lower tribes as related to the civilization of the higher nations, the present volumes are devoted.

Our modern investigators in the sciences of inorganic nature are foremost to recognize, both within and without their special fields of work, the unity of nature, the fixity of its laws, the definite sequence of cause and

* Reprinted from *Primitive Culture* by Edward B. Tylor, Vol. I, pp. 1–6, John Murray, London, 1891.

effect through which every fact depends on what has gone before it, and acts upon what is to come after it. They grasp firmly the Pythagorean doctrine of pervading order in the universal Kosmos. They affirm, with Aristotle, that nature is not full of incoherent episodes, like a bad tragedy. They agree with Leibnitz in what he calls 'my axiom, that nature never acts by leaps (la nature n'agit jamais par saut),' as well as in his 'great principle, commonly little employed, that nothing happens without its sufficient reason.' Nor, again, in studying the structure and habits of plants and animals, or in investigating the lower functions even of man, are these leading ideas un-acknowledged. But when we come to talk of the higher processes of human feeling and action, of thought and language, knowledge and art, a change appears in the prevalent tone of opinion. The world at large is scarcely prepared to accept the general study of human life as a branch of natural science, and to carry out, in a large sense, the poet's injunction to 'Account for moral as for natural things.' To many educated minds there seems something presumptuous and repulsive in the view that the history of mankind is part and parcel of the history of nature, that our thoughts, wills, and actions accord with laws as definite as those which govern the motion of waves, the combination of acids and bases, and the growth of plants and animals.

The main reasons of this state of the popular judgment are not far to seek. There are many who would willingly accept a science of history if placed before them with substantial definiteness of principle and evidence, but who not unreasonably reject the systems offered to them, as falling too far short of a scientific standard. Through resistance such as this, real knowledge always sooner or later makes its way, while the habit of opposition to novelty does such excellent service against the invasions of speculative dogmatism, that we may sometimes even wish it were stronger than it is. But other obstacles to the investigation of laws of human nature arise from considerations of metaphysics and theology. The popular notion of free human will involves not only freedom to act in accordance with motive, but also a power of breaking loose from continuity and acting without cause,— a combination which may be roughly illustrated by the simile of a balance sometimes acting in the usual way, but also possessed of the faculty of turning by itself without or against its weights. This view of an anomalous action of the will which it need hardly be said is incompatible with scientific argument, subsists as an opinion patent or latent in men's minds, and strongly affecting their theoretic views of history, though it is not, as a rule, brought prominently forward in systematic reasoning. Indeed the definition of human will, as strictly according with motive, is the only possible scientific basis in such enquiries. Happily, it is not needful to add here yet another to the list of dissertations on supernatural intervention and natural causation, on liberty, predestination, and accountability. We may hasten to escape from the regions of transcendental philosophy and theology, to start on a more hopeful journey over more practicable ground. None will deny that, as each man knows by the evidence of his own consciousness, definite and natural cause does, to a great extent, determine human action. Then, keeping aside from considerations of extra-natural interference and causeless spontaneity, let us take this admitted existence of natural cause and effect as our standing-ground, and travel on it so far as it will bear us. It is on this same basis that physical science pursues, with ever-increasing success, its quest of laws of nature. Nor need this restriction hamper the scientific study of human life, in which the real difficulties are the practical ones of enormous complexity of evidence, and imperfection of methods of observation.

Now it appears that this view of human will and conduct, as subject to definite law, is indeed recognized and acted upon by the very people who oppose it when stated in the abstract as a general principle, and who then complain that it annihilates man's free will, destroys his sense of personal responsibility, and degrades him to a soulless machine. He who will say these things will nevertheless pass much of his own life in studying the motives which lead to human action, seeking to attain his wishes through them, framing in his mind theories of personal character, reckoning what are likely to be the effects of new combinations, and giving to his reasoning the crowning character of true scientific enquiry, by taking it for granted that in so far as his calculation turns out wrong, either his evidence must have been false or incomplete, or his judgment upon it unsound. Such a one will sum up the experience of years spent in complex relations with society, by declaring his persuasion that there is a reason for everything in life, and that where events look unaccountable, the rule is to wait and watch in hope that the key to the problem may some day be found. This man's observation may have been as narrow as his inferences are crude and prejudiced, but nevertheless he has been an inductive philosopher 'more than forty years without knowing it.' He has practically acknowledged definite laws of human thought and action, and has simply thrown out of account in his own studies of life the whole fabric of motiveless will and uncaused spontaneity. It is assumed here that they should be just so thrown out of account in wider studies, and that the true philosophy of history lies in extending and improving the methods of the plain people who form their judgments upon facts, and check them upon new facts. Whether the doctrine be wholly or but partly true, it accepts the very condition under which we search for new knowledge in the lessons of experience, and in a word the whole course of our rational life is based upon it.

'One event is always the son of another, and we must never forget the parentage,' was a remark made by a Bechuana chief to Casalis the African missionary. Thus at all times historians, so far as they have aimed at being more than mere chroniclers, have done their best to show not merely succession, but connexion, among the events upon their record. Moreover, they have striven to elicit general principles of human action, and by these to explain particular events, stating expressly or taking tacitly for granted the existence of a philosophy of history. Should any one deny the possibility of thus establishing historical laws, the answer is ready with which Boswell in such a case turned on Johnson: 'Then, sir, you would reduce all history to no better than an almanack.' That nevertheless the labors of so many eminent thinkers should have as yet brought history only to the threshold of science, need cause no wonder to those who consider the bewildering complexity of the problems which come before the general historian. The evidence from which he is to draw his conclusions is at once so multifarious and so doubtful, that a full and distinct view of its bearing on a particular question is hardly to be attained, and thus the temptation becomes all but irresistible to garble it in support of some rough and ready theory of the course of events. The philosophy of history at large, explaining the past and predicting the future phenomena of man's life in the world by reference to general laws, is in fact a subject with which, in the present state of knowledge, even genius aided by wide research seems but hardly able to cope. Yet there are departments of it which, though difficult enough, seem comparatively accessible. If the field of enquiry be narrowed from History as a whole to that branch of it which is here called Culture, the history, not of tribes or nations, but of the condition of knowledge, religion, art, custom, and the like among them, the task of investigation proves to lie within far more moderate compass. We suffer still from the same kind of difficulties which beset the wider argument, but they are much diminished. The evidence is no longer so wildly heterogeneous, but may be more simply classified and compared, while the power of getting rid of extraneous matter, and treating each issue on its own proper set of facts, makes close reasoning on the whole more available than in general history. This may appear from a brief preliminary examination of the problem, how the phenomena of Culture may be classified and arranged, stage by stage, in a probable order of evolution.

# THE SUPERORGANIC * (*Kroeber*)

A way of thought characteristic of our western civilization has been the formulation of complementary antitheses, a balancing of exclusive opposites. One of these pairs of ideas with which our world has been laboring for some two thousand years is expressed in the words *body* and *soul*. Another couplet that has served its useful purpose, but which science is now often endeavoring to rid itself of, at least in certain aspects, is the distinction of the *physical* from the *mental*. A third discrimination is that of the *vital* from the *social*, or in other phraseology, of the *organic* from the *cultural*. The implicit recognition of the difference between organic qualities and processes and social qualities and processes is of long standing. The formal distinction is however recent. In fact the full import of the significance of the antithesis may be said to be only dawning upon the world. For every occasion on which some human mind sharply separates organic and social forces, there are dozens of other times when the distinction between them is not thought of, or an actual confusion of the two ideas takes place.

One reason for this current confusion of the organic and social is the predominance, in the present phase of the history of thought, of the idea of evolution. This idea, one of the earliest, simplest, and also vaguest ever attained by the human mind, has received its strongest ground and fortification in the domain of the organic; in other words, through biological science. At the same time, there is an evolution, or growth, or gradual development, apparent also in other realms than that of plant and animal life. We have theories of stellar or cosmic evolution; and there is obvious, even to the least learned, a growth or evolution of civilization. In the nature of things there is little danger of the carrying over of the Darwinian or post-Darwinian principles of the evolution of life into the realm of burning suns and lifeless nebulae. Human civilization or progress, on the other hand, which exists only in and through living members of the species, is outwardly so similar to the evolution of plants and animals, that it has been inevitable that there should have been sweeping applications of the principles of organic development to the facts of cultural growth. This of course is reasoning by analogy, or arguing that because two things resemble each other in one point they

* Reprinted from *The Nature of Culture* by Alfred Louis Kroeber, pp. 23–30, by permission of The University of Chicago Press. Copyright, 1952, by The University of Chicago.

will also be similar in others. In the absence of knowledge, such assumptions are justifiable as assumptions. Too often, however, their effect is to pre-determine mental attitude, with the result that when the evidence begins to accumulate which could prove or disprove the assumption based on analogy, this evidence is no longer viewed impartially and judiciously, but is merely distributed and disposed of in such a way as not to interfere with the established conviction into which the original tentative guess has long since turned.

This is what has happened in the field of organic and social evolution. This distinction between them, which is so obvious that to former ages it seemed too commonplace to remark upon, except incidentally and indirectly, has been largely obscured in the last fifty years through the hold which thoughts connected with the idea of organic evolution have had on minds of the time. It even seems fair to say that this confusion has been greater and more general among those to whom study and scholarship are a daily pursuit than to the remainder of the world.

And yet many aspects of the difference between the organic and that in human life which is not organic, are so plain that a child can grasp them, and that all human beings, including the veriest savages, constantly employ the distinction. Everyone is aware that we are born with certain powers and that we acquire others. There is no need of argument to prove that we derive some things in our lives and make-up from nature through heredity, and that other things come to us through agencies with which heredity has nothing to do. No one has yet been found to assert that any human being is born with an inherent knowledge of the multiplication table; nor, on the other hand, to doubt that the children of a Negro are born Negroes through the operation of hereditary forces. Some qualities in every individual are however clearly debatable ground; and when the development of civilization as a whole and the evolution of life as a whole are compared, the distinction of the processes involved has too often been allowed to lapse.

Some millions of years ago, it is currently taught, natural selection, or some other evolutionary agency, first caused birds to appear in the world. They sprang from reptiles. Conditions were such that the struggle for existence on the earth was hard; while in the air there were safety and room. Gradually, either by a series of almost imperceptible gradations through a long line of successive generations, or by more marked and sudden leaps in a shorter period, the group of birds was evolved from its reptilian ancestors. In this development, feathers were acquired and scales lost; the grasping faculty of the front legs was converted into an ability to sustain the body in the air. The advantages of resistance enjoyed by a cold-blooded organization were given up for the equivalent or greater compensation of the superior activity that goes with warm-bloodedness. The net result of this chapter of evolutionary history was that a new power, that of aerial locomotion, was added to the sum total of faculties possessed by the highest group of animals, the vertebrates. The verebrate animals as a whole, however, were not affected. The majority of them are without the power of flight as their ancestors were millions of years ago. The birds, in turn, had lost certain faculties which they once possessed, and presumably would still possess were it not for the acquisition of their wings.

In the last few years human beings have also attained the power of aerial locomotion. But the process by which this power was attained, and its effects on the species, are as different from those which characterized the acquisition of flight by the first birds as it is possible for them to be. Our means of flying are outside of our bodies. A bird is born with a pair of wings, but we have invented the aeroplane. The bird renounced a potential pair of hands to get his wings; we, because our new faculty is not part of our congenital make-up, keep all the organs and capacities of our fore-fathers but add to them the new ability. The process of the development of civilization is clearly one of accumulation: the old is retained, in spite of the incoming of the new. In organic evolution, the introduction of new features is generally possible only through the loss or modification of existing organs or faculties.

In short, the growth of new species of animals takes place through, and in fact consists of, changes in their organic constitution. As regards the growth of civilization, on the other hand, the one example cited is sufficient to show that change and progress can take place through an invention with-out any such constitutional alteration of the human species.

There is another way of looking at this difference. It is clear that as a new species originates, it is derived wholly from the individual or individuals that first showed the particular traits distinguishing the new species. When we say that it is derived from these individuals we mean, literally, that it is descended. In other words, the species is composed only of such individuals as contain the "blood"—the germ-plasm—of particular ancestors. Heredity is thus the indispensable means of transmission. When however an invention is made, the entire human race is capable of profiting thereby. People who have not the slightst blood kinship to the first designers of aeroplanes can fly and are flying today. Many a father has used, enjoyed, and profited by the invention of his son. In the evolution of animals, the descendant can build upon the inheritance transmitted to him from his ancestors, and may rise to higher powers and more perfect development; but the ancestor is, in the very nature of things, precluded from thus profiting from his descendant. In short, organic evolution is essentially and inevitably connected with hereditary processes; the social evolution which characterizes the progress of civilization, on the other hand, is not, or not necessarily, tied up with hereditary agencies.

The whale is not only a warm-blooded mammal, but is recognized as the remote descendant of carnivorous land animals. In some few million years, as such genealogies are usually reckoned, this animal lost his legs for running, his claws for holding and tearing, his original hair and external ears that would be useless or worse in water, and acquired fins and fluke, a cylindrical body, a layer of fat, and the power of holding his breath. There was much that the species gave up; more, on the whole, perhaps than it gained. Certainly some of its parts have degenerated. But there was one new power that it did achieve: that of roaming the ocean indefinitely.

The parallel and also contrast is in the human acquistion of the identical faculty. We do not, in gradual alteration from father to son, change our arms into flippers and grow a tail. We do not enter the water at all to navigate it. We build a boat. And what this means is that we preserve our bodies and our natal faculties intact, unaltered from those of our fathers and remotest ancestors. Our means of marine travel is outside of our natural endowment. We make it and use it: the original whale had to turn himself into a boat. It took him countless generations to attain to his present condition. All individuals that failed to conform to type left no offspring; or none that went into the blood of the whales of today.

Again, we may compare human and animal beings when groups of them reach a new and arctic environment, or when the climate of the tract where the race is established slowly becomes colder and colder. The non-human mammal species comes to have heavy hair. The polar bear is shaggy; his Sumatran relative sleek. The arctic hare is enveloped in soft fur; the jack-rabbit in comparison is shabbily thin and moth-eaten. Good furs come from the far north, and they lose in richness, in quality, and in value, in proportion as they are stripped from animals of the same species that inhabit milder regions. And this difference is racial, not individual. The jack-rabbit would quickly perish with the end of summer in Greenland; the caged polar bear suffers from temperature warmth within the massive coat which nature has fastened on him.

Now there are people who look for the same sort of inborn peculiarities in the Arctic Eskimo and Samoyed; and find them, because they look for them. That the Eskimo is furry, no one can assert: in fact, we are hairier than he. But it is asserted that he is fat-protected—like the blubber-covered seal that he lives on; and that he devours quantities of meat and oil because he needs them. The true amount of his fat, compared with that of other human beings, remains to be ascertained. He probably has more than the European; but probably no more than the normal full-blooded Samoan and Hawaiian from under the tropics. And as to his diet, if this is seal and seal and seal all winter long, it is not from any congenital craving of his stomach, but because he does not know how to get himself anything else. The Alaskan miner, and the arctic and antarctic explorer, do not guzzle blubber. Wheat-flour, eggs, coffee, sugar, potatoes, canned vegetables—whatever the exigencies of their vocation and the cost of transportation permit—make up their fare. The Eskimo is only too anxious to join them; and both he and they can thrive on the one diet as on the other.

In fact, what the human inhabitant of intemperate latitudes does, is not to develop a peculiar digestive system, any more than he grows hair. He changes his environment, and thereby is able to retain his original body unaltered. He builds a closed house, which keeps out the wind and retains the heat of his body. He makes a fire or lights a lamp. He skins a seal or a caribou of the furry hide with which natural selection or other processes of organic evolution have endowed these beasts; he has his wife make him a shirt and trousers, boots and gloves, or two sets of them; he puts them on; and in a few years, or days, he is provided with the protection which it took the polar bear and the arctic hare, the sable and the ptarmigan, untold periods to acquire. What is more, his baby, and his baby's baby, and his hundredth descendant are born as naked, and unarmed physically, as he and his hundredth ancestor were born.

That this difference in method of resisting a difficult environment, as followed respectively by the polar bear species and the human Eskimo race, is absolute, need not be asserted. That the difference is deep, is unquestionable. That it is as important as it is often neglected, it is the object of this essay to establish.

It has long been the custom to say that the difference is that between body and mind; that animals have their physiques adapted to their circumstances, but that man's superior intelligence enables him to rise superior to such lowly needs. But this is not the most significant point of difference. It is true that without the much greater mental faculties of man, he could not achieve the attainments the lack of which keeps the brute chained to the limitations of his anatomy. But the greater human intelligence in itself does not cause the differences that exist. This psychic superiority is only the indispensable condition of what is peculiarly human; civilization. Directly, it is

the civilization in which every Eskimo, every Alaskan miner or arctic dis-
coverer is reared, and not any greater inborn faculty, that leads him to build
houses, ignite fire, and wear clothing. The distinction between animal and
man which counts is not that of the physical and mental, which is one of
relative degree, but that of the organic and social which is one of kind. The
beast has mentality, and we have bodies; but in civilization man has something that no animal has.

That this distinction is actually something more than that of the physical and mental, appears from an example that may be chosen from the
non-bodily: speech.

On the surface, human and animal speech, in spite of the enormously
greater richness and complexity of the former, are much alike. Both express
emotions, possibly ideas, in sounds formed by bodily organs and understood
by the hearing individual. But the difference between the so-called language
of brutes and that of men is infinitely great; as a homely illustration will set
forth.

A newly-born pup is brought up in a litter of kittens by a fostering cat.
Familiar anecdotes and newspaper paragraphs to the contrary, the youngster
will bark and growl, not purr or miaow. He will not even try to do the latter.
The first time his toe is stepped on, he will whine, not squeal, just as surely
as when thoroughly angered he will bite as his never-beheld mother did, and
not even attempt to claw as he has seen his foster-mother do. For half his
life seclusion may keep him from sight or sound or scent of another dog. But
then let a bark or a snarl reach him through the restraining wall, and he
will be all attention—more than at any voice ever uttered by his cat associates. Let the bark be repeated, and interest will give way to excitement,
and he will answer in kind, as certainly as, put with a bitch, the sexual
impulses of his species will manifest themselves. It cannot be doubted that
dog speech is ineradicably part of dog nature, as fully contained in it without training or culture, as wholly part of the dog organism, as are teeth
or feet or stomach or motions or instincts. No degree of contact with cats,
or deprivation of association with his own kind, can make a dog acquire cat
speech, or lose his own, any more than it can cause him to switch his tail
instead of wagging it, to rub his sides against his master instead of leaping
against him, or to grow whiskers and carry his drooping ears erect.

Let us take a French baby, born in France of French parents, themselves descended for numerous generations from French-speaking ancestors.
Let us, at once after birth, entrust the infant to a mute nurse, with instructions to let no one handle or see her charge, while she travels by the directest

route to the interior heart of China. There she delivers the child to a Chinese couple, who legally adopt it, and rear it as their son. Now suppose three or ten or thirty years passed. Is it needful to discuss what the growing or grown Frenchman will speak? Not a word of French; pure Chinese, without a trace of accent and with Chinese fluency; and nothing else.

It is true that there is a common delusion, frequent even among educated people, that some hidden influence of his French-talking ancestors will survive in the adopted Chinaman: that it is only necessary to send him to France with a batch of real Chinamen, and he will acquire his mother's tongue with appreciably greater facility, fluency, correctness, and naturalness than this Mongolian companions. That a belief is common, however, is as likely to stamp it a common superstition as a common truth. And a reasonable biologist, in other words, an expert qualified to speak of heredity, will pronounce this answer to this problem in heredity, superstition. He might merely choose a politer phrase.

Now there is something deep-going here. No amount of association with Chinese would turn our young Frenchman's eyes from blue to black, or slant them, or flatten his nose, or coarsen or stiffen his wavy, oval-sectioned hair; and yet his speech is totally that of his associates, in no measure that of his blood kin. His eyes and his nose and his hair are his from heredity; his language is non-hereditary—as much so as the length to which he allows his hair to grow, or the hole which, in conformity to fashion, he may or may not bore in his ears. It is not so much that speech is mental and facial proportions are physical; the distinction that has meaning and use is that human language is non-hereditary and social, eye-color and nose-shape hereditary and organic. By the same criterion, dog speech, and all that is vaguely called the language of animals, is in a class with men's noses, the proportions of their bones, the color of their skin, and the slope of their eyes, and not in a class with any human idiom. It is inherited, and therefore organic. By a human standard, it is not really language at all, except by the sort of metaphor that speaks of the language of the flowers.

It is true that now and then a French child would be found that under the conditions of the experiment assumed, would learn Chinese more slowly, less idiomatically, and with less power of expression, than the average Chinaman. But there would also be French babies, and as many, that would acquire the Chinese language more quickly, more fluently, with richer power of revealing their emotions and defining their ideas, than the normal Chinese. These are individual differences, which it would be absurd to deny, but which do not affect the average, and are not to the point. One Englishman speaks better English, and more of it, than another, and he may also through precocity, learn it much sooner; but one talks English no more and no less truly than the other.

There is one form of animal expression in which the influence of association has sometimes been alleged to be greater than that of heredity. This is the song of birds. There is a good deal of conflicting opinion, and apparently of evidence, on this point. Many birds have a strong inherent impulse to imitate sounds. It is also a fact that the singing of one individual stimulates the other—as with dogs, wolves, cats, frogs, and most noisy animals. That in certain species of birds capable of a complex song the full development will not often be reached in individuals raised out of hearing of their kind, may probably be admitted. But it seems to be clear that every species has a song or call distinctively its own; that this minimum is attainable without association by every normal member of the singing sex, as soon as conditions of age, food, and warmth are proper, and the requisite stimulus of noise, or silence, or sex development, is present. That there has been serious conflict of opinion as to the nature of bird song, will ultimately be found to be chiefly due to the pronouncement of opinions on the matter by those who read their own mental states and activities into animals—a common fallacy that every biological student is now carefully trained against at the outset of his career. In any event, whether one bird does or does not in some degree "learn" from another, there is no fragment of evidence that bird song is a tradition, that like human speech or human music it accumulates and develops from age to age, that it is inevitably altered from generation to generation by fashion or custom, and that it is impossible for it ever to remain the same: in other words, that it is a social thing or due to a process even remotely akin to those affecting the constituents of human civilization.

It is also true that there is in human life a series of utterances that are of the type of animal cries. A man in pain moans without purpose of communication. The sound is literally pressed from him. A person in supreme fright may shriek. We know that his cry is unintended, what the physiologist calls a reflex action. The true shriek is as liable to escape the victim pinned before the approaching engineerless train, as him who is pursued by thinking and planning enemies. The woodsman crushed by a rock forty miles from the nearest human being, will moan like the run-over city dweller surrounded by a crowd waiting for the speeding ambulance. Such cries are of a class with those of animals. In fact, really to understand the "speech" of brutes, we must think ourselves into a condition in which our utterances would be totally restricted to such instinctive cries—"inarticulate" is their general though often inaccurate designation. In an exact sense, they are not language at all.

This is precisely the point. We undoubtedly have certain activities of utterance, certain faculties and habits of sound production, that are truly parallel with those of animals; and we also have something more that is quite different and without parallel among the animals. To deny that something purely animal underlies human speech, is fatuous; but it would be equally narrow to believe that because our speech springs from an animal foundation, and originated in this foundation, it therefore is nothing but animal mentality and utterances greatly magnified. A house may be built on rock; without this base it might be impossible for it to have been erected; but no one will maintain that therefore the house is nothing but improved and glorified stone.

As a matter of fact, the purely animal element in human speech is small. Apart from laughter and crying, it finds rare utterance. Our interjections are denied by philologists as true speech, or at best but half admitted. It is a fact that they differ from full words in not being voiced, generally, to convey a meaning—nor to conceal one. But even these particles are shaped and dictated by fashion, by custom, by the type of civilization to which we belong, in short by social and not by organic elements. When I drive the hammer on my thumb instead of on the head of the nail, an involuntary "damn" may escape me as readily if I am alone in the house, as if companions stand on each side. Perhaps more readily. So far, the exclamation does not serve the purpose of speech and is not speech. But the Spaniard will say "carramba" and not "damn"; and the Frenchman, the German, the Chinaman, will avail himself of still different expression. The American says "outch" when hurt. Other nationalities do not understand this syllable. Each people has its own sound; some even two—one used by men and the other by women. A Chinaman will understand a laugh, a moan, a crying child, as well as we understand it, and as well as a dog understands the snarl of another dog. But he must learn "ouch," or it is meaningless. No dog, on the other hand, ever has given utterance to a new snarl, unintelligible to other dogs, as a result of having been brought up in different associations. Even this lowest element of human speech, then, this involuntary half-speech of exclamations, is therefore shaped by social influences.

Herodotus tells of an Egyptian king, who, wishing to ascertain the parent tongue of humanity, had some infants brought up in isolation from their own kind, with only goats as companions and for sustenance. When the children, grown older, were revisited, they cried the word "bekos," or, subtracting the ending which the normalizing and sensitive Greek could not endure omitting from anything that passed his lips, more probably "bek." The king then sent to all countries to learn in what land this vocable meant something. He ascertained that in the Phrygian idiom it signified bread, and, assuming that the children were crying for food, concluded that they spoke Phrygian in voicing their "natural" human speech, and that this tongue must therefore be the original one of mankind. The king's belief in an inherent and congenital language of man, which only the blind accidents of time had distorted into a multitude of idioms, may seem simple; but naive as it is, inquiry would reveal crowds of civilized people still adhering to it.

This however is not our moral to the tale. That lies in the fact that the one and only word attributed to the children, "bek," was, if the story has any authenticity whatsoever, only a reflection or imitation—as the commentators of Herodotus long since conjectured—of the bleating of the goats that were the children's only associates and instructors. In short, if it is allowable to deduce any inference from so apocryphal an anecdote, what it proves is that there is no natural and therefore no organic human language.

Thousands of years later another sovereign, the Mogul emperor Akbar, repeated the experiment with the intent of ascertaining the "natural" religion of mankind. His band of children were shut up in a house. When, the necessary time having elapsed, the doors were opened in the presence of the expectant and enlightened ruler, his disappointment was great: the children trooped out as dumb as deaf-mutes. Faith dies hard, however; and we may suspect that it would take a third trial, under modern chosen and controlled conditions, to satisfy some natural scientists that speech, for the human individual and for the human race, is wholly an acquired and not a hereditary thing, entirely outward and not at all inward—a social product and not an organic growth.

Human and animal speech, then, though one roots in the other, are in the nature of a different order. They resemble each other only as the flight of a bird and of an aeronaut are alike. That the analogy between them has frequently deceived, proves only the guilelessness of the human mind. The operative processes are wholly unlike; and this, to him who is desirous of understanding, is far more important than the similarity of effect. The savage and the peasant who cure by cleaning the knife and leaving the wound unattended, have observed certain indisputable facts. They know that cleanness aids, dirt on the whole impedes recovery. They know the knife as the cause, the wound as the effect; and they grasp, too, the correct principle that treatment of the cause is in general more likely to be effective than treatment of the symptom. They fail only in not inquiring into the process that may be involved. Knowing nothing of the nature of sepsis, of bacteria, of the agencies of putrefaction and retardation of healing, they fall back on agencies more familiar to themselves, and use, as best they may, the process of magic intertwined with that of medicine. They carefully scrape the knife; they oil it; they keep it bright. The facts from which they work are correct; their logic is sound enough; they merely do not distinguish between two irreconcilable processes—that of magic and that of physiological chemistry—and apply one in place of another. The student of today who reads the civilizationally moulded mind of men into the mentality of a dog or ape, or who tries to explain civilization—that is, history—by organic factors, commits an error which is less antiquated and more in fashion, but of the same kind and nature.

# THE SYMBOL * (White)

## The Origin and Basis of Human Behavior

> "In the Word was the Beginning . . . the beginning of Man and of Culture."

I

In July, 1939, a celebration was held at Leland Stanford University to commemorate the hundredth anniversary of the discovery that the cell is the basic unit of all living tissue. Today we are beginning to realize and to appreciate the fact that the symbol is the basic unit of all human behavior and civilization.

All human behavior originates in the use of symbols. It was the symbol which transformed our anthropoid ancestors into men and made them human. All civilizations have been generated, and are perpetuated, only by the use of symbols. It is the symbol which transforms an infant of Homo sapiens into a human being; deaf mutes who grow up without the use of symbols are not human beings. All human behavior consists of, or is dependent upon, the use of symbols. Human behavior is symbolic behavior; symbolic behavior is human behavior. The symbol is the universe of humanity.

II

The great Darwin declared in *The Descent of Man* that "there is no fundamental difference between man and the higher mammals in their mental faculties," that the difference between them consists "*solely* in his [man's] almost infinitely larger power of associating together the most diversified sounds and ideas . . . the mental powers of higher animals do not differ *in kind*, though greatly *in degree*, from the corresponding powers of man" (Chs. 3, 18; emphasis ours).

This view of comparative mentality is held by many scholars today. Thus, F. H. Hankins, a prominent sociologist, states that "in spite of his large brain, it cannot be said that man has any mental traits that are peculiar to him . . . All of these human superiorities are merely relative or differences of degree." Professor Ralph Linton, an anthropologist, writes in *The Study of Man:* "The differences between men and animals in all these [behavior] respects are enormous, but they seem to be differences in quantity rather than in quality." "Human and animal behavior can be shown to have so much in common," Linton observes, "that the gap [between them] ceases to be of great importance." Dr. Alexander Goldenweiser, likewise an anthropologist, believes that "In point of sheer psychology, mind as such, man is after all no more than a talented animal" and that "the difference between the mentality here displayed [by a horse and a chimpanzee] and that of man is merely one of degree."

That there are numerous and impressive similarities between the behavior of man and that of ape is fairly obvious; it is quite possible that chimpanzees and gorillas in zoos have noted and appreciated them. Fairly apparent, too, are man's behavioral similarities to many other kinds of animals. Almost as obvious, but not easy to define, is a difference in behavior which distinguishes man from all other living creatures. I say "obvious" because it is quite apparent to the common man that the non-human animals with which he is familiar do not and cannot enter, and participate in, the world in which he, as a human being, lives. It is impossible for a dog, horse, bird, or even an ape, to have *any* understanding of the meaning of the sign of the cross to a Christian, or of the fact that black (white among the Chinese) is the color of mourning. No chimpanzee or laboratory rat can appreciate the difference between Holy water and distilled water, or grasp the meaning of *Tuesday, 3,* or *sin.* No animal save man can distinguish a cousin from an uncle, or a cross cousin from a parallel cousin. Only man can commit the crime of incest or adultery; only he can remember the Sabbath and keep it Holy. It is not, as we well know, that the lower animals can do these things but to a lesser degree than ourselves; they cannot perform these acts of appreciation and distinction *at all*. It is, as Descartes said long ago, "not only that the brutes have less Reason than man, but that they have none at all."

But when the scholar attempts to *define* the mental difference between man and other animals he sometimes encounters difficulties which he cannot surmount and, therefore, ends up by saying that the difference is merely one of degree: man has a bigger mind, "larger power of association," wider range of activities, etc. We have a good example of this in the distinguished physiologist, Anton J. Carlson. After taking note of "man's present achievements in science, in the arts (including oratory), in political and social institutions," and noting "at the same time the apparent paucity of such behavior in other animals," he, as a common man "is tempted to conclude that in these capacities, at least, man has a qualitative superiority over other mammals." But, since, as a scientist, Professor Carlson cannot *define* this qualitative difference between man and other animals, since as a physiologist he cannot explain it, he refuses to admit it—" . . . the physiologist does not accept the great development of articulate speech in man as something qualitatively new; . . ."—and suggests helplessly that some day we may find some new "building stone," an "additional lipoid, phosphatid, or potassium ion," in the human brain which will explain it, and concludes by saying that the difference between the mind of man and that of non-man is "probably only one of degree."

The thesis that we shall advance and defend here is that there is a *fundamental* difference between the mind of man and the mind of non-man. This difference is one of kind, not one of degree. And the gap between the two types is of the greatest importance—at least to the science of comparative behavior. Man uses symbols; no other creature does. An organism has the ability to symbol or it does not; there are no intermediate stages.

III

A symbol may be defined as a thing the value or meaning of which is bestowed upon it by those who use it. I say "thing" because a symbol may have any kind of physical form; it may have the form of a material object, a color, a sound, an odor, a motion of an object, a taste.

The meaning, or value, of a symbol is in no instance derived from or determined by properties intrinsic in its physical form: the color appropriate to mourning may be yellow, green, or any other color; purple need not be the color of royalty; among the Manchu rulers of China it was yellow. The meaning of the word "see" is not intrinsic in its phonetic (or pictorial) properties. "Biting one's thumb at" someone might mean anything. The meanings of symbols are derived from and determined by the organisms who use them; meaning is bestowed by human organisms upon physical things or events which thereupon become symbols. Symbols "have their signification," to use John Locke's phrase, "from the arbitrary imposition of men."

All symbols must have a physical form; otherwise they could not enter our experience. This statement is valid regardless of our theory of experiencing. Even the exponents of "Extra-Sensory Perception" who have challenged Locke's dictum that "the knowledge of the existence of any other thing [besides ourselves and God] we can have only by sensation" have been obliged to work with physical rather than ethereal forms. But the meaning of a symbol cannot be discovered by mere sensory examination of its physical form. One cannot tell by looking at an $x$ in an algebraic equation what it stands for; one cannot ascertain with the ears alone the symbolic value of the phonetic compound $si;$ one cannot tell merely by weighing a pig how much gold he will exchange for; one cannot tell from the wave length of a color whether it stands for courage or cowardice, "stop" or "go"; nor can one discover the spirit in a fetish by any amount of physical or chemical examination. The meaning of a symbol can be grasped only by non-sensory, symbolic means.

The nature of symbolic experience may be easily illustrated. When the Spaniards first encountered the Aztecs, neither could speak the language of the other. How could the Indians discover the meaning of santo, or the significance of the crucifix? How could the Spaniards learn the meaning of *calli,* or appreciate Tlaloc? These meanings and values could not be communicated by sensory experience of physical properties alone. The finest ears will not tell you whether *santo* means "holy" or "hungry." The keenest senses cannot capture the value of holy water. Yet, as we all know, the Spaniards and the Aztecs did discover each other's meanings and appreciate each other's values. But not with sensory means. Each was able to enter the world of the other only by virtue of a faculty for which we have no better name than *symbol.*

But a thing which in one context is a symbol is, in another context, not a symbol but a sign. Thus, a word is a symbol only when one is concerned with the distinction between its meaning and its physical form. This distinction *must* be made when one bestows value upon a sound-combination or when a previously bestowed value is discovered for the first time; it *may* be made at other times for certain purposes. But after value has been bestowed upon, or discovered in, a word, its meaning becomes identified, in use, with its physical form. The word then functions as a sign, rather than as a symbol. Its meaning is then grasped with the senses.

We define a *sign* as a physical thing or event whose function is to indicate some other thing or event. The meaning of a sign may be inherent in its physical form and its context, as in the case of the height of a column of mercury in a thermometer as an indication of temperature, or the return of robins in the spring. Or, the meaning of a sign may be merely identified with its physical form as in the case of a hurricane signal or a quarantine flag. But in either case, the meaning of the sign may be ascertained by sensory means. The fact that a thing may be both a symbol (in one context) and a sign (in another context) has led to confusion and misunderstanding.

Thus Darwin says: "That which distinguishes man from the lower animals is not the understanding of articulate sounds, for as everyone knows, dogs understand many words and sentences." (Ch. III, *The Descent of Man*)

It is perfectly true, of course, that dogs, apes, horses, birds, and perhaps creatures even lower in the evolutionary scale, can be taught to respond in a specific way to a vocal command. Little Gua, the infant chimpanzee in the Kelloggs' experiment, was, for a time, "considerably superior to the child in responding to human words." But it does not follow that no difference exists between the meaning of "words and sentences" to a man and to an ape or dog. Words are both signs and symbols to man; they are merely signs to a dog. Let us analyze the situation of vocal stimulus and response.

A dog may be taught to roll over at the command "Roll over!" A man may be taught to stop at the command "Halt!" The fact that a dog can be taught to roll over in Chinese, or that he can be taught to "go fetch" at the command "roll over" (and, of course, the same is true for a man) shows that there is no necessary and invariable relationship between a particular sound combination and a specific reaction to it. The dog or the man can be taught to respond in a certain manner to any arbitrarily selected combination of sounds, for example, a group of nonsense syllables, coined for the occasion. On the other hand, any one of a great number and variety of responses may become evocable by a given stimulus. Thus, so far as the *origin* of the relationship between vocal stimulus and response is concerned, the nature of the relationship, i.e., the meaning of the stimulus, is not determined by properties intrinsic in the stimulus.

But, once the relationship has been established between vocal stimulus and response, the meaning of the stimulus becomes *identified with the sounds;* it is then *as if* the meaning were intrinsic in the sounds themselves. Thus, 'halt' does not have the same meaning as 'hilt' or 'malt,' and these stimuli are distinguished from one another with the auditory mechanism. A dog may be conditioned to respond in a certain way to a sound of a given wave length. Sufficiently alter the pitch of the sound and the response will cease to be forthcoming. The meaning of the stimulus has become identified with its physical form; its value is appreciated with the senses.

Thus in *sign* behavior we see that in *establishing* a relationship between a stimulus and a response the properties intrinsic in the stimulus do not determine the nature of the response. But, *after the relationship has been established* the meaning of the stimulus is *as if* it were *inherent* in its physical form. It does not make any difference what phonetic combination we select to evoke the response of terminating self-locomotion. We may teach a dog, horse, or man to stop at any vocal command we care to choose or devise. But once the relationship has been established between sound and response, the meaning of the stimulus becomes identified with its physical form and is, therefore, perceivable with the senses.

So far we have discovered no difference between the dog and the man; they appear to be exactly alike. And so they are as far as we have gone. But we have not told the whole story yet. No difference between dog and man is discoverable so far as learning to respond appropriately to a vocal stimulus is concerned. But we must not let an impressive similarity conceal an important difference. A porpoise is not yet a fish.

The man differs from the dog—and all other creatures—in that *he can and does play an active role in determining what value the vocal stimulus is to have, and the dog cannot.* The dog does not and cannot play an active part in determining the value of the vocal stimulus. Whether he is to roll over or go fetch at a given stimulus, or whether the stimulus for roll over be one combination of sounds or another is a matter in which the dog has nothing whatever to "say." He plays a purely passive role and can do nothing else. He learns the meaning of a vocal command just as his salivary glands may learn to respond to the sound of a bell. But man plays an active role and thus becomes a creator: let $x$ equal three pounds of coal and it does equal three pounds of coal; let removal of the hat in a house of worship indicate respect and it becomes so. This creative facility, that of freely, actively, and arbitrarily bestowing value upon things, is one of the most commonplace as well as *the* most important characteristic of man. Children employ it freely in their play: "Let's pretend that this rock is a wolf."

The difference between the behavior of man and other animals, then, is that the lower animals may receive new values, may acquire new meanings, but they cannot create and bestow them. Only man can do this. To use a crude analogy, lower animals are like a person who has only the receiving apparatus for wireless messages: he can receive messages but cannot send them. Man can do both. And this difference is one of kind, not of degree: a creature can either "arbitrarily impose signification," can either create and bestow values, or he cannot. There are no intermediate stages. This difference may appear slight, but, as a carpenter once told William James in discussing differences between men, "It's very important." All *human* existence depends upon it and it alone.

The confusion regarding the nature of words and their significance to men and the lower animals is not hard to understand. It arises, first of all, from a failure to distinguish between the two quite different contexts in which words function. The statements, "The meaning of a word cannot be grasped with the senses," and "The meaning of a word can be grasped with the senses," though contradictory, are nevertheless equally true. In the *symbol* context the meaning cannot be perceived with the senses; in the *sign* context it can. This is confusing enough. But the situation has been made worse by using the words 'symbol' and 'sign' to label, not the *different contexts,* but *one and the same thing:* the word. Thus a word is a symbol *and* a sign, two different things—because it may function in two contexts esthetic and commercial.

IV

That man is unique among animal species with respect to mental abilities, that a fundamental difference of kind—not of degree—separates man from all other animals is a fact that has long been appreciated, despite Darwin's pronouncement to the contrary. Long ago, in his *Discourse on Method,* Descartes pointed out that "there are no men so dull and stupid . . . as to be incapable of joining together different words . . . on the other hand, there is no other animal, however perfect . . . which can do the like." John Locke, too, saw clearly that "the power of abstracting is not at all in them [i.e., beasts], and that the having of general ideas is that which puts a perfect distinction between man and brutes, and is an excellency which the faculties of brutes do by no means attain to . . . they have no use of words or any other general signs." The great British anthropologist, E. B. Tylor, remarked upon "the mental gulf that divides the lowest savage from the highest ape . . . A young child can understand what is not proved to have entered the mind of the cleverest dog, elephant, or ape." And, of course, there are many today who recognize the "mental gulf" between man and other species.

Thus, for over a century we have had, side by side, two traditions in comparative psychology. One has declared that man does not differ from other animals in mental abilities except in degree. The other has seen clearly that man is unique in at least one respect, that he possesses an ability that no other animal has. The difficulty of *defining* this difference adequately has kept this question open until the present day. The distinction between *sign* behavior and *symbol* behavior as drawn here may, we hope, contribute to a solution of this problem once and for all.

v

Very little indeed is known of the organic basis of the symbolic faculty: we know next to nothing of the neurology of "symbolling." And very few scientists—anatomists, neurologists or physical anthropologists—appear to be interested in the subject. Some, in fact, seem to be unaware of the existence of such a problem. The duty and task of giving an account of the neural basis of symbolling does not, however, fall within the province of the sociologist or the cultural anthropologist. On the contrary, he should scrupulously exclude it as irrelevant to his problems and interests; to introduce it would bring only confusion. It is enough for the sociologist or cultural anthropologist to take the ability to use symbols, possessed by man alone, as given. The use to which he puts this fact is in no way affected by his, or even the anatomist's, inability to describe the symbolic process in neurological terms. However, it is well for the social scientist to be acquainted with the little that neurologists and anatomists do know about the structural basis of symbolling. We, therefore, review briefly the chief relevant facts here.

The anatomist has not been able to discover why men can use symbols and apes cannot. So far as is known the only difference between the brain of man and the brain of an ape is a quantitative one: ". . . man has no new kinds of brain cells or brain cell connections," as A. J. Carlson has remarked. Nor does man, as distinguished from other animals, possess a specialized "symbol-mechanism." The so-called speech areas of the brain should not be identified with symbolling. The notion that symbolling is identified with, or dependent upon, the ability to utter articulate sounds is not uncommon. Thus, L. L. Bernard lists as "the fourth great organic asset of man . . . his vocal apparatus . . . characteristic of him alone." But this is an erroneous conception. The great apes have the mechanism necessary for the production of articulate sounds. "It seemingly is well established," write R. M. and A. W. Yerkes in *The Great Apes*, "that the motor mechanism of voice in this ape [chimpanzee] is adequate not only to the production of a considerable variety of sounds, but also to definite articulations similar to those of man." And the physical anthropologist, E. A. Hooton, asserts that "all of the anthropoid apes are vocally and muscularly equipped so that they could have an articulate language if they possessed the requisite intelligence." Furthermore, as Descartes and Locke pointed out long ago, there are birds who do actually utter articulate sounds, who duplicate the sounds of human speech, but who of course are quite incapable of symbolling. The "speech areas" of the brain are merely areas associated with the muscles of the tongue, with the larynx, etc. But, as we know, symbolling is not at all confined to the use of these organs. One may symbol with any part of the body that he can move at will.

To be sure, the symbolic faculty was brought into existence by the natural processess of organic evolution. And we may reasonably believe that the focal point, if not the locus, of this faculty is in the brain, especially the forebrain. Man's brain is much larger than that of an ape, both absolutely and relatively. The brain of the average adult human male is about 1500 c.c. in size; brains of gorillas seldom exceed 500 c.c. Relatively, the human brain weighs about $\frac{1}{50}$th of the entire body weight, while that of a gorilla varies from $\frac{1}{150}$th to $\frac{1}{200}$th part of that weight. And the forebrain especially is large in man as compared with the ape. Now in many situations we know that quantitative changes give rise to qualitative differences. Water is transformed into steam by additional quantities of heat. Additional power and speed lift the taxiing airplane from the ground and transform terrestrial locomotion into flight. The difference between wood alcohol and grain alcohol is a qualitative expression of a quantitative difference in the proportions of carbon and hydrogen. Thus a marked growth in size of the brain in many may have brought forth a *new* kind of function.

# THE STUDY OF CULTURE * (*Kluckhohn*)

Culture, as used by American anthropologists, is of course a technical term which must not be confused with the more limited concept of ordinary language and of history and literature. The anthropological term designates those aspects of the total human environment, tangible and intangible, which have been created by men. A "culture" refers to the distinctive way of life of a group of people, their complete "design for living." The Japanese constitute a nation or a society. This entity may be directly observed. "Japa-

* Reprinted from "The Study of Culture" by Clyde Kluckhohn, Chapter V of *The Policy Sciences* edited by Daniel Lerner and Harold D. Lasswell with permission of the publishers, Stanford University Press. Copyright 1951 by the Board of Trustees of Leland Stanford Junior University. Publication assisted by a grant from Carnegie Corporation of New York.

nese culture," however, is an abstraction from observed regularities or trends toward regularity in the modes of response of this people.

Recent anthropological research in the United States has by no means been l⸱⸱⸱ ⸱⸱ ⸱e study of cultures. The community studies of W. Lloyd ⸱⸱⸱⸱⸱ r American anthropologists are well known. There have ⸱⸱⸱ ⸱e pioneer investigations in quantitative comparative soci- ⸱⸱⸱ the theory is drawn from sociology, psychoanalysis, and be- ⸱⸱c psychology as well as from anthropology.[1] An increasing number ⸱rican anthropologists have been concerned with interrelations be- ⸱⸱⸱ltural and the psychological.[2] Others have been developing the ⸱⸱⸱ between biology and anthropology.[3] Still others have con- ⸱⸱⸱ the physical environment as a conditioning and limiting ⸱⸱⸱or in cultural development and function.[4]

Nevertheless, culture remains the master concept of American anthropology, with the partial exception of physical anthropology. For enthnologists, folklorists, anthropological linguists, archaeologists, and social anthropologists, culture is always a point of departure or a point of reference if not invariably the point of central emphasis. During the past fifteen years there have been significant refinements both in the theory of culture and in methods and techniques for the study of cultures.

## Theory

Many different definitions of culture are current. A review of these and their development will shortly be published.[5] They vary in degree of looseness or precision, in the stressing of one conceptual element as opposed to another. There have also been some recent controversies on epistemological and ontological questions.[6] Neglecting, however, the finer details of terminology and some philosophical nuances, most American anthropologists would agree substantially with the following propositions of Herskovits[7] on the theory of culture:

1. Culture is learned;[8]
2. Culture derives from the biological,[9] environmental, psychological, and historical components of human existence;
3. Culture is structured;
4. Culture is divided into aspects;
5. Culture is dynamic;
6. Culture is variable;
7. Culture exhibits regularities that permit its analysis by the methods of science;

8. Culture is the instrument whereby the individual adjusts to his total
setting, and gains the means for creative expression.[10]

A perhaps not unrepresentative brief definition is t⌐ ⌐ ⌐f ⌐luckhohn and
Kelly: "A culture is an historically created system of ⌐⌐licit
designs for living, which tends to be shared by all or s⌐
members of a group at a specified point in time."[11] So⌐
clarify this definition. Each culture is a precipitate of history
terials supplied by human biology and the natural environment ⌐
human organisms must make certain minimal adjustments for surviv⌐
selectivity out of the potentialities afforded by human natu⌐
surroundings and within the limits set by biological and p⌐
channeled by the historical process. The conventional or a⌐
(that is, the purely cultural) arises in part out of the accidents ⌐⌐ ⌐⌐⌐⌐⌐⌐
including both chance internal events and contacts with other peoples. The
word "system" has important implications. The fact that cultures have organization as well as content is now generally recognized. Nor can culture
be used as a conceptual instrument for prediction unless due account is
taken of this systemic property. The word "tends" warns against reifying an
abstraction. One cannot drop a perpendicular from even the most accurate
description of a culture or any specific carrier of that culture. No individual
thinks, feels, or acts precisely as the "blueprints" which constitute a culture
indicate that he will or should. Nor are all the "blueprints" meant by the
society to apply to each individual. There are sex differentials, age differentials, occupational differentials, and the like. The best conceptual model of
the culture can only state correctly the central tendencies of ranges of
variation.

The anthropologist's description of a culture may be compared to a map.
A map is obviously not a concrete bit of land but rather an abstract representation of a particular area. If a map is accurate and one can read it, one
doesn't get lost. If a culture is correctly portrayed, one will realize the existence of the distinctive features of a way of life and their interrelationships.

Culture is omnipresent; it interposes a double screen between, for example, the psychologist and the native or innate or constitutional personality he is trying to discover and describe. One is tempted to paraphrase
Zola's remark that science is nature seen through a temperament and say that
personality is a temperament which is both seen through and screened by a
culture. Because of the mass of tradition and the complexities of human relationships, even the few simple things that people as animals want have
been disguised in cultural patterns. An animal eats when he is hungry—if he
can, but the human animal waits for lunch time. Three daily meals are as

much an artifact as an automobile. Sneezing at first looks like pure biology. But little customs grow up about it, such as saying "excuse me" or "*Gesundheit*." People do not sneeze in exactly the same way in different cultures or in various limited to the same society. Sneezing is a biological act caught in
Warner and othe difficult to point to any activity that is not culturally
been published so.
ology in which people, most of the time, adhere to cultural patterns? We
havioris this question the examination it deserves, but two reasons are
of Amerst by following custom one affirms one's solidarity with one's
tween the a sense of loneliness. Second, patterns are necessary if
interstitial area cial life, with its attendant division of labor. Imagine
centrated upor same home and invariably preparing and eating food in
factory rooms at different times.

The analysis of a culture must encompass both the explicit and the implicit. The explicit culture consists in those regularities in word and deed which may be generalized straight from the evidence of the ear or eye. One has only to observe and to discover the consistencies in one's observations. No arbitrary acts of interpretation on the part of the anthropologist are involved. The implicit culture, however, is an abstraction of the second order. Here the anthropologist infers least common denominators which seem, as it were, to underlie a multiplicity of cultural contents. Only in the most sophisticated and self-conscious of cultures will his attention be called directly to these by carriers of the culture. The implicit culture consists of pure forms. Explicit culture includes both content and structure.

*Culture content.* Description of culture content consists in stating what is done, said, and made—by whom, when, and under what circumstances. A useful system for categorizing culture content has been supplied by Ralph Linton.[12] The most easily isolable elements in designs for living are called culture *traits*. A random list of a few traits in American culture might include listening to news broadcasts at breakfast, the assembly line, and political bosses in large cities. However, each one of these elements can, if the intensity of analysis requires it, be broken down into smaller separable units called *items*. For instance, the interlarding of "commercials" with news in the morning, the fact that news broadcasts are either five minutes or fifteen minutes in length, the fact that each individual or family ordinarily turns to some preferred announcer or commentator—these are some of the items that might be listed when the American trait of "listening to news broadcasts at breakfast" is broken down. Or the culture trait of the crossbow may be analyzed into items: size, materials, details of workmanship, and the like.

On the other hand, lists of traits may be grouped together according to function. The assembly line, collective bargaining, various social services rendered by management to workers, and numerous other traits make up the *trait complex* of the American industrial system. This trait complex, in turn, is linked with various other trait complexes, such as mining, agriculture, and fishing, to make up a total *activity*—economic production.

Linton has also given us a scheme for the description of culture content from the point of view of relative participation of individuals in the various complexes and activities. Those culture elements which apply to all normal adult members of the society are called *universals*. Those which apply only to distinct categories of individuals are *specialties*. Those which are well-known to all adults (or at least to those adults in certain culturally differentiated groups) but with respect to which there is free choice are *alternatives*. *Variants* are elements or complexes "which are shared by certain individuals but which are not common to all members of the society, or even to all the members of any one group of the socially recognized categories."

*Structure.* As Ernst Cassirer and Kurt Lewin, among others, have pointed out, scientific progress frequently depends upon changes in what is regarded as real and amenable to objective study. The development of the social sciences has been impeded by a confusion between the "real" and the concrete. Psychologists, typically, are reluctant to concede reality in the social world to anything but individuals. The greatest advance in contemporary anthropological theory is probably the increasing recognition that there is something more to culture than artifacts, linguistic texts, and lists of atomized traits.

Structural relations are characterized by relatively fixed relations between parts rather than by the parts or elements themselves. That relations are as "real" as things is conceded by most philosophers. It is also clear from ordinary experience that an exhaustive analysis of reality cannot be made within the limitations of an atomistic or narrowly positivistic scheme. Take a brick wall. Its "reality" would be granted by all save those who follow an idealism of Berkeley's sort. Then let us take each brick out of the wall. A radical empiricist would be in all consistency obliged to say that we have destroyed nothing. Yet it is clear that while nothing concrete has been annihilated, a form has been eliminated. Similarly, the student of culture change is forced to admit that forms may persist while content changes or that content remains relatively unaltered but is organized into new structures.

An analogy used by Freud for personality is equally applicable to cultural disintegration. If we throw a crystal to the ground, it breaks; however, its dissolution is not haphazard. The fragmentation accords with lines of cleavage predetermined by the particular structure of the crystal, invisible though it was to the naked eye. So, in culture, the mode in which the parts stand to one another cannot be indifferent from the standpoint of understanding and prediction. If a form ceases to exist, the resultant change is different from that of a purely subtractive operation. Each culture is, among other things, a complex of relations, a multiverse of ordered and interrelated parts. Parts do not cause a whole but they comprise a whole, not necessarily in the sense of being perfectly integrated but in the sense of being separable only by abstraction.

All nature consists of materials. But the manner in which matter is organized into entities is as significant as the substance or the function serviced within a given system. Recent organic chemistry has documented this fact. The selfsame atoms present in exactly the same number may constitute either a medicine or a poison, depending solely upon the fashion in which they are arranged. Contemporary genetics and biology have come to the same conclusion. A famous geneticist has written: "All that matters in heredity is its pattern." An extremely positivistic biologist has observed: "These results appear to demonstrate that statistical features of *organization* can be heritable. . . ."[13] A behavioristic psychologist, Clark Hull, finds that behavior sequences are "strictly patterned" and that it is the pattern which is often determinative of adaptive or nonadaptive behavior.

That organization and equilibrium generally prevail in nature, as they seem to do, is doubtless a matter of balance, economy, or least action of energy. If it is assumed that those aspects of behavior which we call cultural are part of a natural and not of a supernatural order, it is to be expected that exactness of relationship, irrespective of dimensions, must be discovered and described in the cultural realm. One of the most original of anthropological linguists, B. L. Whorf, has put well the approach most suited to cultural studies:

> *In place of apparatus, linguistics uses and develops techniques. Experimental does not mean quantitative. Measuring, weighing, and pointer-reading devices are seldom needed in linguistics, for quantity and number play little part in the realm of pattern, where there are no variables but, instead, abrupt alternations from one configuration to another. The mathematical sciences require exact measurement, but what linguistics requires is, rather, exact "patternment"—an exactness of relation irrespective of dimensions. Quantity, dimension, magnitude are metaphors since they do not*

> *properly belong in this spaceless, relational world. I might use this simile: Exact measurement of lines and angles will be needed to draw exact squares of other regular polygons, but measurement, however precise, will not help us to draw an exact circle. Yet it is necessary only to discover the principle of the compass to reach by a leap the ability to draw perfect circles. Similarly, linguistics has developed techniques which, like compasses, enable it without any true measurement at all to specify exactly the patterns with which it is concerned. Or I might perhaps liken the case to the state of affairs within the atom, where also entities appear to alternate from configuration to configuration rather than to move in terms of measurable positions. As alternants, quantum phenomena must be treated by a method of analysis that substitutes a point in a pattern under a set of conditions for a point in a pattern under another set of conditions—a method similar to that used in analysis of linguistic phenomena.*[14]

There is nothing mystical about saying that cultures have organization as well as content. This point may be driven home by an analogy used by the Gestalt psychologists. Take a musical succession made up of three notes. If one is told that the notes are A, C, and G, one receives information that is fundamental but does not enable one to predict the type of sensation which will be experienced in hearing the notes. One needs further information on relationships. Are the notes to be played in that order? What duration will each receive? How will the emphasis, if any, be distributed? Will the instrument be a piano or a violin?

The analysis of a culture has also only begun when all its items, traits, trait complexes, and activities have been noted. Both the Navaho and the Hopi Indians make dry paintings. In a distribution chart, both of these cultures would be marked "present" as to this trait. Yet the place of this event in the sequence of rites which constitute their great ceremonials is very different. Moreover, the relationship of this trait to the purposes of the whole ceremonial is not envisioned in the same way by the two tribes. In short, the full significance of any single element in a cultural design will be seen only when that element is viewed in the total matrix of its relationship to other elements and indeed to other designs. Naturally, this includes accent or emphasis as well as position. Accent is manifested sometimes through frequency, sometimes through intensity. Both the Navaho and the Diegueno Indians use a certain narcotic plant. Any Navaho, however, can live a full and normal life without ever happening to see this plant used. In contrast, a Diegueno, in former times, could hardly fail to witness the usage many times a year. Both the Navaho and Hopi have an initiation rite for boys wherein the boys are whipped on the naked back by other men with staves of yucca. But the importance of intensity of this occasion is exceedingly different in the two cases. Many adult Navahoes never go through this rite. Among the Hopi, however, this is an absolute prerequisite to full participation in the society. If a Navaho man has been initiated, his references in conversation to this event are likely to be quite casual. The ordinary Hopi will evidence considerable emotion in any discussion of the subject.

If cultural forms are so significant, why has attention to their systematic analysis lagged so far behind the description of culture content? In the first place, some students have overemphasized a consideration in which there is some truth. They have said that what we understand in patterns is the applicability of forms, not the basic meanings. Up to a point, however, motivations need not be sought beyond the border of the pattern itself. An American wants or feels obliged to give at Christmas time. He thinks, "Ah, everyone can use handkerchiefs." The recipient may say to himself, "What will I do with all these handkerchiefs? Oh, well, what did I send him? And anyway it's the spirit that counts. I am glad he thought of me." Giving handkerchiefs at Christmas is often patently absurd from the immediate functional point of view, but it nobly fulfills the pattern. The latent function, of course, is to show that you take your culture seriously.

In the second place, there is probably among Western peoples some resentment of patterns as such. This may be connected with our traditional notions of individualism and of freedom of the will. Americans, at least, dislike grammar because it imposes a pattern (rigidity, determinism) on the medium of expression which most individuals know best. Explicitness with regard to grammar is more than wearying—there is the hint of a personal insult because of interference with the "spontaneity" of personal expression.

In the third place, informants are much less helpful in explaining the patterns of their culture than they are in describing its content. The manner of response has become "second nature." The *structure* of behavior tends to be automatic—one doesn't think about it and one doesn't want to. As Edward Sapir has noted, "There are large sections of culture that act as a bar to the free exercise of rationality. One may observe that adults have compromised rationality with their culture—and they resent a re-examination of these questions by their children." Or, as W. I. Thomas says, "Social habit systems tend to acquire a relatively fixed and unreflective character resembling instinctive reflex responses."

However, during the last twenty years, American anthropologists have been forced—in part by their attempts to make predictions, especially in the field of applied anthropology—to realize that a list of traits never gets beyond the signatory stage. One can say correctly that Plains Indian culture included buffalo food, nomadism, the tipi, the travois, geometric decoration in painting, quill work, the sun dance, and military societies. Such a series of signs is useful, indeed indispensable, in making historical reconstructions from plotted distributions or in determining the influence of geography upon culture content. The travois, for example, is an invaluable clue to such problems. From the internal standpoint, the culture could get along very nicely without the travois. The list does not define adequately the distinctive features of the life of the Plains Indians. Of all the traits catalogued, only the sun dance and the medicine bundle complex are crucial to the emotionally felt structure of the culture. A trait list indicates but does not define. It is like saying, "John Smith is the attorney who lives at 84 Washingon Street." One can have a whole encyclopedia of signatory knowledge and still be unable to answer most of the questions posed by serious students of human life. A trait list, even when sorted as to universals, alternatives, specialties, and variants, is only a relatively objective beginning: it helps one merely to a comparatively superficial and external comprehension.

*Various approaches.* American social scientists have therefore developed ways of conceptualizing cultural structure. They vary in frames of references and in serving different but equally legitimate intellectual interests. When one's attention is directed primarily to the degree of sanction and emotional feeling attached to the following-out of certain sequences in prescribed ways or with prescribed emphasis, one may utilize the well-known categories of Sumner and Keller: folkways and mores. This distinction was one of the earliest systematic discriminations of cultural structure and has proved of considerable utility. But the focal issue is that of *degree* of sanction, and this must often be decided upon extremely arbitrary grounds. Moreover, it is not always clear whether a *mos* or a folkway is established on the basis of behavioral or normative modalities. Finally, mores and folkways tend to imply a static culture.

One can also segregate a complex of patterns in accordance with the varying roles which different patterns play in the total economy of the over-all designs for living. Here one may distinguish situational, instrumental, and integrative patterns.[15] Situational patterns are those which crystallize around the foci supplied by certain invariant "givens" of biological and physical nature. For example, each culture must have patterns that take account of age and sex differences in the members of the society, of the fact of biological kinship, and the like. Instrumental patterns are those that are manifestly functional: those for food production, for the building of shelter, etc. Integrative patterns supply definitions of the situation that rationalize the deeper uncertainties of human existence, such as death. They provide for symbolic and other types of social solidarity. These patterns operate to lessen the potential conflict and obstruction between the various statuses and roles of different individuals. Ideally, these patterns bring it about that all the statuses of the society intermesh like a series of interlocking gears. Without integrative patterns, individuals would, because of mutual obstruction and conflict, be unable to fulfill their roles as defined by the first two groups of patterns.

A. L. Kroeber,[16] with his eye alike upon history, function, and psychology, has distinguished systemic, total-culture, and style patterns. *Systemic patterns* are "nexuses of culture traits which have assumed a definite and coherent structure, which function successfully, and which acquire historic weight and persistence."[17] Kroeber cites plow agriculture, monotheism, and the alphabet as examples:

> *The pattern of plow agriculture comprises the plow itself; animals to draw it; domestication of these beasts; grains of the barley or wheat types sown by broadcast scattering, without attention to the individual seed, seedling, or plant; fields larger than gardens and of some length; and fertilization with dung primarily from draft animals.*[18]

Such a pattern "is modifiable superficially, but modifiable only with difficulty as to its underlying plan." Kroeber compares the concept of mammalian dentition in biology. It is clear that systemic patterns are cross-cultural rather than limited to a single culture.

A *style pattern* is "a way of achieving definiteness and effectiveness in human relations by choosing or evolving one line of procedure out of several possible ones and sticking to it." The style pattern of Greek mathematics was geometric. The style pattern of the modern industrial world includes machine versus manual manufacture but also credit and mass production. "Every style is necessarily prelimited; it is an essential commitment to one manner, to the exclusion of others."

The *total-culture pattern* is similar to the notions of ethos and *Zeitgeist*. It is such a concept which Ruth Benedict used in *Patterns of Culture* and in her description of the Japanese culture-whole, *The Chrysanthemum and the Sword*. Earlier and later nonanthropological attempts to describe total-culture patterns might be cited. Perhaps Burckhardt's *Renaissance* is the most familiar. Kroeber says:

*The pattern or physiognomy of trend of a great civilization is certainly an important thing to know, but it is difficult to formulate accurately and reliably. Such a pattern has in it breadth and complexity, depth and subtlety, universal features but also uniqueness. In proportion as the expression of such a large pattern tends to the abstract, it becomes arid and lifeless; in proportion as it remains attached to concrete facts, it lacks generalization. Perhaps the most vivid and impressive characterizations have been made by frank intuition deployed on a rich body of knowledge and put into skillful words. Yet this does not constitute proof and is at best at the fringe of the approved methods of science and scholarship. These difficulties will explain why the formulation of whole-culture patterns has not progressed farther, though it is surely one of the most important problems that anthropology and related researches face.*[19]

Herskovits has recently presented the interesting concept of *cultural focus*, which

*. . . designates the tendency of every culture to exhibit greater complexity, greater variation in the institutions of some of its aspects than in others. So striking is this tendency to develop certain phases of life, while others remain in the background, so to speak, that in the shorthand of the disciplines that study human societies these focal aspects are often used to characterize whole cultures.*[20]

He points to the changing emphases in Western civilizations: Egypt—economic and politico-religious concerns; Athens—the quest for truth; Rome—the principle of organization; Middle Ages—the other world, with a hierarchical concept of the universe; Renaissance—secular matters, learning, and the arts; etc. He shows the utility of the concept in explaining why a given people accept one new idea or thing and reject another.

In a series of important papers, Morris Opler[21] has developed and applied a concept of *theme:* "a postulate or position, declared or implied, and usually controlling behavior or stimulating activity, which is tacitly approved or openly promoted in a society." These cultural postulates are conceived as arising from and being related to basic human needs and social structure, but as essential to the description and explanation of the patterning and change which go on within this framework. One of Opler's examples is that of the rivalry between the sexes in Jicarilla Apache culture. He shows how the influence of this thematic principle appears in such diverse aspects of culture content as mythology, sexual life, economy, warfare, ceremonials, kinship behavior, and others.

Most of the concepts thus far discussed blur the distinction between explicit and implicit culture in describing structure.[22] It seems necessary for rigor to separate these categories as sharply as possible. There are, first, epistemological and logical reasons. Any statement about implicit culture is a second-order abstraction, and it is only fair that the terminology should warn the reader of this fact. Second, the implicit culture has a different meaning for the culture carriers. Since the implicit culture is largely unverbalized it tends to be taken for granted as a part of the natural order of things and is extraordinarily resistant to change.

*Patterns of the explicit culture.*[23] The explicit culture includes all those features of the designs for living of a group which can be described to an outsider by participants in the culture—though actually the field worker gets his basic data as much or more from observation, from participation, and from listening to informal conversation as he does from questioning informants. Explicit culture includes, of course, manifestations of thought and feeling. In other words, the distinction between explicit and implicit is not that between objective and subjective. Explicit culture comprises culture content and cultural forms. The latter may conveniently be differentiated into *behavioral patterns, normative patterns, orientations, cultural categories,* and *cultural postulates.*

The problem of pattern is the problem of symmetry, of constancies of form irrespective of wide variations in concrete details of actualization. So far as biological and physical possibilities are concerned, a given act can be carried out, an idea stated, or a specific artifact made in a number of different ways. However, in all societies the same mode of disposing of many situations is repeated over and over. There is, as it were, an inhibition alike of the randomness of trial-and-error behavior, of the undifferentiated character of instinctive behavior, and of responses that are merely functional. A determinate organization prevails.

The contrast between behavioral and normative patterns is basically the familiar one between practices and rules, but the word *pattern* is a reminder that one is dealing not merely with regularities but with structural regularities—with a predictable conjunction of words and acts in a fixed order and with definable intensity and emphasis. Behavioral patterns are modes of conduct; normative patterns, modes of standards. Both are inductive generalizations—what a logician would call "class constructs." The anthropologist arrives at behavioral patterns by discovering what people do in fact do—the central tendencies in ranges of behavioral dispersion. The cultural conceptions of how persons of specified status *ought* to behave in given situations (normative patterns) are obtained from regularities in statements and from evidences of approval or disapproval of certain acts. It is clear that a normative pattern may be either positive or negative. The goodness of fit, or lack thereof, between behavior and normative patterns is a sensitive index of the coherence of a culture and of the intensity of culture change at the moment.

For a fine analysis some subsidiary concepts are useful. Normative patterns may be subdivided into *compulsory, preferred, typical, alternative,* and *restricted*. If one were to attempt to obtain a mean average from the facts and state *the* normative patterns, one would often have either to accept a form of statement which was cumbersome and imprecise or to neglect the minor mode or modes entirely and consider the major mode as *the* normative pattern. While the major mode is likely to be the most representative single value in such material, most cultures (since their historical and biological origins have been highly heterogeneous) will strongly tend to give bimodal or multimodal distributions. And a single mode is a notoriously unsatisfactory description of any asymmetrical curve. If the trend of the distributions were markedly regular in the direction of flatness (in which case the mean would doubtless be the most representative value), this fact would in itself signify a lack of patterning of norms (or of behaviors).

It is necessary to distinguish the subtypes of behavioral patterns by different terms. "Compulsory," for instance, plainly refers to a standard of value, and only in the case of an extraordinarily well-integrated culture or a culture where the external sanctions were most efficiently enforced could behavioral patterns be characterized as compulsory. Conversely, one hardly expects the system of normative patterns to encompass patterns which are disapproved or prohibited. There can be cognizance of such patterns in the *idea* patterns of the culture, but not in the normative patterns. *Disapproved* and *prohibited* patterns are inevitably behavioral patterns. For example, adultery is not recognized in the normative patterns of the culture of the Navaho Indians. Behaviorally, however, adultery is common and the carrying out of extramarital relations is most distinctly patterned in ways of which the Navaho are explicitly aware. Prostitution has likewise (at least at some times and places) been a disapproved behavioral pattern of Navaho culture.

Where the anthropologist is interested only in the behavioral patterns or where he has an insufficient knowledge of the normative patterns, the behavioral patterns may be described simply as modalities without in any way begging the question of conformance to the corresponding normative patterns. *Major behavioral pattern* will serve as a label for the behavioral pattern which is unequivocally the major mode of a set of correlative patterns. *Minor behavioral pattern* is suggested for those modes which are definitely minor. Where the interest is in conformance and the necessary information is available, *conformant* and *deviant* behavioral patterns may be distinguished. These latter must not be regarded as synonymous with major and minor, for in a rapidly changing culture the deviant patterns are frequently the major behavioral patterns.

*More diffuse structures of the explicit culture.* Let us now turn to certain aspects of cultural form which, while recognized by the members of the group, are distinct from patterns in that they are more diffuse, more generalized, more all-pervasive. Patterns, whether behavioral or normative, are abstractions having to do with specific series of acts. If we observe and/ or hear repeatedly about a series of marriage ceremonies, scalp dances, and a certain type of feast within the same group, we can abstract designs for specific types of behavior. Each pattern is abstracted not only from the knowledge and habits exhibited in a physical act, but also from the attitudes, values, and ideas associated with the knowledge and habits. All of these data are consciously recognized by the participants and can (to at least some extent) be verbally described by them. There is more to be said of explicit attitudes and values, however, than is strictly attachable to specific pattern forms. The group, as it were, holds a store of "points of view," of generalized ways of feeling, thinking, and believing, that are in some sense independent of physical objects, acts, and speech. This body of "mental" attitudes gives special meaning to new traits, brings about shifts in their function, and places them in their proper position in the hierarchy of cultural values.

## REFERENCES

1. The most impressive example is G. P. Murdock's *Social Structure* (1949).
2. See, for example, Cora Du Bois, *People of Alor* (1944); and Clyde Kluckhohn and Henry A. Murray (eds.), *Personality in Nature, Society, and Culture* (1948).
3. Cf. John Gillin, *The Ways of Men* (1948), pp. 23–175; and Kluckhohn and Murray, *op. cit.,* pp. 107–61 and 377–471.
4. E.g., J. H. Steward, *Basin-Plateau Aboriginal Sociopolitical Groups* (Smithsonian Institution, Bureau of American Ethnology, Bulletin 120 [1938]); A. L. Kroeber, *Cultural and Natural Areas of Native North America* (1939).
5. A. L. Kroeber and C. Kluckhohn, "The Concept of Culture: A Critical Review of Definitions," *Papers of the Peabody Museum* (Harvard University) Vol. XLI (1950). The approximate consensus of these definitions is as follows: "Culture consists in patterned ways of thinking, feeling, and reacting, acquired and transmitted mainly by symbols, constituting the distinctive achievements of human groups, including their embodiments in artifacts; the essential core of culture consists of traditional (i.e., historically derived and selected) ideas and especially their attached values."
6. See D. Bidney, "Human Nature and the Cultural Process," *American Anthropologist,* XLIX, No. 3 (1947), 375–96.

7. Melville J. Herskovits. *Man and His Works* (1940). p. 625.
8. Perhaps it is too obvious to add that while all culture is learned, not all learning is culture: The individual learns a good deal during his own private life-experience which he does not share with others or transmit to others. It might also be commented that some aspects of culture are learned only through the use of symbols, particularly linguistic symbols. Indeed, an argument can be made for R. Bain's definition of culture as "all social behavior which is mediated by symbols."
9. See Claude Lévi-Strauss, *Les Structures Élémentaires de la Parenté* (1949), especially pp. 1–13.
10. Herskovits leaves implicit the fact that participation in a culture or in any part of it is never emotionally neutral. The attitude of the participant may range from hearty acceptance to belligerent revolt, but even what seems to be passive conformance is emotionally tinged.
11. C. Kluckhohn and W. H. Kelly, "The Concept of Culture," in Ralph Linton (ed:), *The Science of Man in the World Crisis* (1945), pp. 78–107.
12. *The Study of Man* (1936).
13. W. J. Crozier and E. Wolf, "Specific Constants for Visual Excitation," *Proceedings of the National Academy of Sciences* XXV, No. 4 (1939), 176–79. Italics mine.
14. B. L. Whorf, "Linguistics as an Exact Science," in United States Department of State, Foreign Institute, *Four Articles on Metalinguistics* (1949), p. 11.
15. See T. Parsons, *Essays in Sociological Theory* (1949), pp. 44–51.
16. *Anthropology* (1948), pp. 312–18, 329–31.
17. This definition is taken from Kroeber's "Structure, Function, and Pattern in Biology and Anthropology," *Scientific Monthly*, LVI (1943), p. 112.
18. *Anthropology* (1948), p. 313.
19. *Ibid.*, p. 317.
20. *Man and His Works*, p. 542.
21. See especially Opler's "Themes as Dynamic Forces in Culture," in *American Journal of Sociology*, LI (1945), 198–206 and "An Application of the Theory of Themes in Culture," in *Journal of the Washington Academy of Sciences*, XXXVI (1946), 137–66.
22. John Gillin in *The Ways of Men* (1948) makes a distinction between overt and internalized (covert) habits and customs. He then distinguishes "behavioral customs" from "mental customs" ("mental" seems a most unfortunate terminology). While Gillin seems to recognize most of the bases for what are here called explicit and implicit culture, he does not follow these considerations through in his analyses of cultural structure. His book, however, makes original and significant contributions to cultural theory. His distinction between actional and representational customs and his Part IV ("Patterning and Coordination of Culture") break some new ground.
23. The system of analysis about to be presented has been partially developed in two papers by C. Kluckhohn: "Patterning as Exemplified in Navaho Culture," in Leslie Spier *et al* (eds), *Language, Culture and Personality* (1941), pp. 109–30; and "Covert Culture and Administrative Problems," *American Anthropologist*, XLV (1943), 213–27. For a critical discussion and a comparison with other American and European explorations into cultural structure see Hans Dietschy, "De Deux Aspects de la Civilisation," *Archives Suisses d'Anthropologie Générale*, XII (1947), 116–31.

# 3: Interaction

The concept of interaction may be said to define the process which constitutes the very core of social life and human behavior. It is one of the tenets of sociology that the behavior of human beings can never be fully understood if one does not realize that the social actions of individuals are always oriented toward other human beings, and that it is the interplay between the action of Self (Ego) and the expected or actual reaction of one or many Others (Alters) which occupies the center of the human stage. Thus, the simplest unit of sociological, as distinct from psychological, analysis consists not of solitary individuals but of at least a pair of individuals mutually influencing each other's behavior.

But were one simply to insist upon the fact that human behavior is behavior in interaction, one would have missed an important part of the story. In a sense interaction seems indeed a universal phenomenon: atoms in a molecule or planets in the solar system react on one another, and within the body cells mutually influence one another and structure the organs by their reciprocal influence. What distinguishes human interaction from other types is above all the fact that this process involves norms, status positions, and reciprocal obligations which always come into play when two or more actors enter into relations with each other. Therefore, sociology is concerned not so much with interaction as such as it is with that form of interaction which is patterned by the social structure within which it takes place.

Georg Simmel (1858–1918), the founder of what has since been called the "formal school" of sociology, was the first to focus the attention of sociologists upon the importance of interactive processes. Simmel contended that it was possible to discover a number of relatively stable forms of interaction underlying the great diversity of concrete social phenomena. Thus it was possible to discover patterned elements of conflict, of cooperation, and of competition in social relationships, though the concrete manifestations of these elements would vary according to the particularities of each concrete social situation. To Simmel it seemed possible to arrive at systematic classification and description of these enduring patterns of reciprocal interaction. This enabled him to counter the claim of those who maintained that no social science was possible since each concrete situation in which individuals were involved was unique and not susceptible of generalization.

Simmel's work has had a deep influence on American social science, especially on the so-called Chicago School. A reading of one of the earliest textbooks in American sociology, the programmatic outline of the field by the Chicago sociologists Robert E. Park (1864–1944) and Ernest W. Burgess, would show this early influence of Simmelian ideas in America.

While Simmel's work thus had an enduring impact in this country, it also proved seminal in his native land. Leopold von Wiese works closely in the Simmelian tradition, especially in his efforts to classify and systematically analyze forms of social interaction. But the influence of Simmel on other German sociologists was also enduring, even though they did not follow Simmel's lead in all respects. The thought of Max Weber (1864–1920), the dean of German sociology, though in crucial ways oriented in quite different directions, was nevertheless based in large part on Simmel's pioneering insistence on the importance of interactive processes. Our selections from Max Weber are meant to indicate this dependence of Weber's thought on Simmelian schemes of analysis.

The great British anthropologist Bronislaw Malinowski (1884–1942) was less directly influenced by Simmel and his successors than the sociologists just mentioned. Yet his conviction that the normative systems of a society as well as its basic obligations and rights must be understood in terms of reciprocal obligations that the members of society have toward each other can be seen as an extension of Simmel's insights. The selections from the French anthropologist Claude Lévi-Strauss and the American sociologists Talcott Parsons and Edward Shils are meant to indicate the extent to which recent anthropological and sociological research re-emphasizes or rediscovers the Simmelian emphasis on interaction.

Our final two selections from two prominent contemporary sociologists, George C. Homans and Peter M. Blau, are intended to provide some perspective on what has been called "exchange theory" in modern sociology. This approach extends the older emphasis on social interaction by stressing similarities between social exchange and economic exchange. The focus is on two-way transfers between interacting persons. We must note that there are also many one-way transfers, *quids* without *quos,* to use Kenneth Boulding's amusing figure of speech, so that this exchange theory can hardly encompass all of social life. But within its restricted field of application, exchange theory seems a very rewarding approach.

# THE DYAD AND THE TRIAD * (*Simmel*)

We see that such phenomena as isolation and freedom actually exist as forms of sociological relations, although they often do so only by means of complex and indirect connections. In view of this fact, the simplest sociological formation, methodologically speaking, remains that which operates between two elements. It contains the scheme, germ, and material of innumerable more complex forms. Its sociological significance, however, by no means rests on its extensions and multiplications only. It itself is a sociation. Not only are many general forms of sociation realized in it in a very pure and characteristic fashion; what is more, the limitation to two members is a condition under which alone several forms of relationship exist. Their typically sociological nature is suggested by two facts. One is that the greatest variation of individualities and unifying motives does not alter the identity of these forms. The other is that occasionally these forms exist as much between two groups—families, states, and organizations of various kinds—as between two individuals.

Everyday experiences show the specific character that a relationship attains by the fact that only two elements participate in it. A common fate or enterprise, an agreement or secret between two persons, ties each of them in a very different manner than if even only three have a part in it. This is perhaps most characteristic of the secret. General experience seems to indicate that this minimum of two, with which the secret ceases to be the property of the one individual, is at the same time the maximum of which its preservation is relatively secure. A secret religious-political society which was formed in the beginning of the nineteenth century in France and Italy, had different degrees among its members.

The real secrets of the society were known only to the higher degrees; but a discussion of these secrets could take place only between any two

* Reprinted from *The Sociology of Georg Simmel,* translated, edited, and with an introduction by Kurt H. Wolff, pp. 122–125, 145–153, by permission of the publisher, The Free Press, Glencoe, Ill. Copyright, 1950, by The Free Press, A Corporation.

members of the high degrees. The limit of two was felt to be so decisive that, where it could not be preserved in regard to knowledge, it was kept at least in regard to the verbalization of this knowledge. More generally speaking, the difference between the dyad and larger groups consists in the fact that the dyad has a different relation to each of its two elements than have larger groups to their members. Although, for the outsider, the group consisting of two may function as an autonomous, super-individual unit, it usually does not do so for its participants. Rather, each of the two feels himself confronted only by the other, not by a collectivity above him. The social structure here rests immediately on the one and on the other of the two, and the secession of either would destroy the whole. The dyad, therefore, does not attain that super-personal life which the individual feels to be independent of himself. As soon, however, as there is a sociation of three, a group continues to exist even in case one of the members drops out.

This dependence of the dyad upon its two individual members causes the thought of its existence to be accompanied by the thought of its termination much more closely and impressively than in any other group, where every member knows that even after his retirement or death, the group can continue to exist. Both the lives of the individual and that of the sociation are somehow colored by the imagination of their respective deaths. And "imagination" does not refer here only to theoretical, conscious thought, but to a part or a modification of existence itself. Death stands before us, not like a fate that will strike at a certain moment but, prior to that moment, exists only as an idea or prophecy, as fear or hope, and without interfering with the reality of this life. Rather, the fact that we shall die is a quality inherent in life from the beginning. In all our living reality, there is something which merely finds its last phase or revelation in our death: we are, from birth on, beings that will die. We are this, of course, in different ways. The manner in which we conceive this nature of ours and its final effect, and in which we react to this conception, varies greatly. So does the way in which this element of our existence is interwoven with its other elements. But the same observations can be made in regard to groups. Ideally, any large group can be immortal. This fact gives each of its members, no matter what may be his personal reaction to death, a very specific sociological feeling. A dyad, however, depends on each of its two elements alone—in its death, though not in its life: for its life, it needs both, but for its death, only one. This fact is bound to influence the inner attitude of the individual toward the dyad, even though not always consciously nor in the same way. It makes the dyad into a group that feels itself both endangered and irreplaceable, and thus into the real locus not only of authentic sociological tragedy, but also of sentimentalism and elegiac problems.

This feeling tone appears wherever the end of the union has become an organic part of its structure. Not long ago, there came news from a city in northern France regarding a strange "Association of the Broken Dish." Years ago, some industrialists met for dinner. During the meal, a dish fell on the floor and broke. One of the diners noted that the number of pieces was identical with that of those present. One of them considered this an omen, and in consequence of it, they founded a society of friends who owed one another service and help. Each of them took part of the dish home with him. If one of them dies, his piece is sent to the president, who glues the fragments he receives together. The last survivor will fit the last piece, whereupon the reconstituted dish is to be interred. The "Society of the Broken Dish" will thus dissolve and disappear. The feeling within that society, as well as in regard to it, would no doubt be different if new members were admitted and the life of the group thereby perpetuated indefinitely. The fact that from the beginning it is defined as one that will die gives it a peculiar stamp—which the dyad, because of the numerical condition of its structure, has always.

## 1. The Sociological Significance of the Third Element

What has been said indicates to a great extent the role of the third element, as well as the configurations that operate among three social elements. The dyad represents both the first social synthesis and unification, and the first separation and antithesis. The appearance of the third party indicates transition, conciliation, and abandonment of absolute contrast (although, on occasion, it introduces contrast). The triad as such seems to me to result in three kinds of typical group formations. All of them are impossible if there are only two elements; and, on the other hand, if there are more than three, they are either equally impossible or only expand in quantity but do not change their formal type.

## 2. The Non-Partisan and the Mediator

It is sociologically very significant that isolated elements are unified by their common relation to a phenomenon which lies outside of them. This applies as much to the alliance between states for the purpose of defense against a common enemy as to the "invisible church" which unifies all the faithful in their equal relation to the one God. The group-forming, mediation function of a third element will be discussed in a later context. In the cases under examination now, the third element is at such a distance from the other two that there exist no properly sociological interactions which concern all three elements alike. Rather, there are configurations of two. In the center of sociological attention, there is either the relation between the two joining elements, the relation between them as a unit and the center of interest that confronts them. At the moment, however, we are concerned with three elements which are so closely related or so closely approach one another that they form a group, permanent or momentary.

In the most significant of all dyads, monogamous marriage, the child or children, as the third element, often has the function of holding the whole together. Among many "nature peoples," only childbirth makes a marriage perfect or insoluble. And certainly one of the reasons why developing culture makes marriages deeper and closer is that children become independent relatively late and therefore need longer care. Perfection of marriage through childbirth rests, of course, on the value which the child has for the husband, and on his inclination, sanctioned by law and custom, to expel a childless wife. But the actual result of the third element, the child, is that it alone really closes the circle by tying the parents to one another. This can occur in two forms. The existence of the third element may directly start or strengthen the union of the two, as for instance, when the birth of a child increases the spouses' mutual love, or at least the husband's for his wife. Or the relation of each of the spouses to the child may produce a new and indirect bond between them. In general, the common preoccupations of a married couple with the child reveal that their union passes through the child, as it were; the union often consists of sympathies which could not exist without such a point of mediation. This emergence of the inner socialization of three elements, which the two elements by themselves do not desire, is the reason for a phenomenon mentioned earlier, namely, the tendency of unhappily married couples not to wish children. They instinctively feel that the child would close a circle within which they would be nearer one another, not only externally but also in their deeper psychological layers, than they are inclined to be.

When the third element functions as a non-partisan, we have a different variety of mediation. The non-partisan either produces the concord of two colliding parties, whereby he withdraws after making the effort of creating direct contact between the unconnected or quarreling elements; or he functions as an arbiter who balances, as it were, their contradictory claims against one another and eliminates what is incompatible in them. Differences between labor and management, especially in England, have developed both forms of unification. There are boards of conciliation where the parties negotiate their conflicts under the presidency of a non-partisan. The mediator, of course, can achieve reconciliation in this form only if each party believes that the proportion between the reasons for the hostility, in short, the objective situation justifies the reconciliation and makes peace advantageous. The very great opportunity that non-partisan mediation has to produce this belief lies not only in the obvious elimination of misunderstandings or in appeals to good will, etc. It may also be analyzed as follows. The non-partisan shows each party the claims and arguments of the other; they thus lose the tone of subjective passion which usually provokes the same tone on the part of the adversary. What is so often regrettable here appears as something wholesome, namely, that the feeling which accompanies a psychological content when one individual has it, usually weakens greatly when it is transferred to a second. This fact explains why recommendation and testimonies that have to pass several mediating persons before reaching the deciding individual, are so often ineffective, even if their objective content arrives at its destination without any change. In the course of these transfers, affective imponderables get lost; and these not only supplement insufficient objective qualifications, but, in practice, they alone cause sufficient ones to be acted upon.

Here we have a phenomenon which is very significant for the development of purely psychological influences. A third mediating social element deprives conflicting claims of their affective qualities because it neutrally formulates and presents these claims to the two parties involved. Thus this circle that is fatal to all reconciliation is avoided: the vehemence of the one no longer provokes that of the other, which in turn intensifies that of the first, and so forth, until the whole relationship breaks down. Furthermore, because of the non-partisan, each party to the conflict not only listens to more objective terms than it would if it confronted the other without mediation. For now it is important for each to win over even the mediator. This, however, can be hoped for only on purely objective grounds, because the mediator is not the arbitrator, but only guides the process of coming to terms; because, in other words, he must always keep out of any decision—whereas the arbitrator ends up by taking sides. Within the realm of sociological techniques, there is nothing that serves the reconciliation of conflicting parties so effectively as does objectivity, that is, the attempt at limiting all complaints and requests to their objective contents. Philosophically speaking, the conflict is reduced to the objective spirit of each partial standpoint, so that the personalities involved appear as the mere vehicles of objective conditions. In case of conflict, the personal form in which objective contents become subjectively alive must pay for its warmth, color, and depth of feeling with the sharpness of the antagonism that it engenders. The diminution of this personal tone is the condition under which the understanding and reconciliation of the adversaries can be attained, particularly because it is only under this condition that each of the two parties actually realizes what the other must insist upon. To put it psychologically, antagonism of the will is reduced to intellectual antagonism. Reason is everywhere the principle of understanding; on its basis can come together what on that of feeling and ultimate decision of the will is irreconcilably in conflict. It is the function of the mediator to bring this reduction about, to represent it, as it were, in himself; or to form a transformation point where, no matter in what form the conflict enters from one side, it is transmitted to the other only in an objective form; a point where all is retained which would merely intensify the conflict in the absence of mediation.

It is important for the analysis of social life to realize clearly that the constellation thus characterized constantly emerges in all groups of more than two elements. To be sure, the mediator may not be specifically chosen, nor be known or designated as such. But the triad here serves merely as a type or scheme; ultimately all cases of mediation can be reduced to this form. From the conversation among three persons that lasts only an hour, to the permanent family of three, there is no triad in which a dissent between any two elements does not occur from time to time—a dissent of a more harmless or more pointed, more momentary or more lasting, more theoretical or more practical nature—and in which the third member does not play a mediating role. This happens innumerable times in a very rudimentary and inarticulate manner, mixed with other actions and interactions, from which the purely mediating function cannot be isolated. Such mediations do not even have to be performed by means of words. A gesture, a way of listening, the mood that radiates from a particular person, are enough to change the difference between two individuals so that they can seek understanding, are enough to make them feel their essential commonness which is concealed under their acutely differing opinions, and to bring this divergence into the shape in which it can be ironed out the most easily. The situation does not have to involve a real conflict or fight. It is rather the thousand insignificant differences of opinion, the allusions to an antagonism of personalities, the emergence of quite momentary contrasts of interest or feeling, which continuously color the fluctuating forms of all living together; and this social life is constantly determined in its course by the presence of the third person, who almost inevitably exercises the function of mediation. This function makes the round among the three elements, since the ebb and flow of social life realizes the form of conflict in every possible combination of two members.

The non-partisanship that is required for mediation has one of two presuppositions. The third element is non-partisan either if he stands above the contrasting interests and opinions and is actually not concerned with them, or if he is equally concerned with both. The first case is the simpler of the two and involves fewest complications. In conflicts between English laborers and entrepreneurs, for instance, the non-partisan called in could be neither a laborer nor an entrepreneur. It is notable how decisively the separation of objective from personal elements in the conflict (mentioned earlier) is realized here. The idea is that the non-partisan is not attached by personal interest to the objective aspects of either party position. Rather, both come to be weighed by him as by a pure, impersonal intellect, without touching the subjective sphere. But the mediator must be subjectively interested in the persons or groups themselves who exemplify the contents of the quarrel which to him are merely theoretical, since otherwise he would not take over his function. It is, therefore, as if subjective interest set in motion a purely objective mechanism. It is the fusion of personal distance from the objective significance of the quarrel with personal interest in its subjective significance which characterizes the non-partisan position. This position is the more perfect, the more distinctly each of these two elements is developed and the more harmoniously, in its very differentiation, each cooperates with the other.

The situation becomes more complicated when the non-partisan owes his position, not to his neutrality, but to his equal participation in the interests in conflict. This case is frequently when a given individual belongs to two different interest groups, one local, and the other objective, especially occupational. In earlier times, bishops could sometimes intervene between the secular ruler of their diocese and the pope. The administrator who is thoroughly familiar with the special interests of his district will be the most suitable mediator in the case of a collision between these special interests and the general interests of the state which employs him. The measure of the combination between impartiality and interest which is favorable to the mediation between two locally separate groups, is often found in persons who come from one of these groups but live with the other. The difficulty of positions of this kind in which the mediator may find himself, usually derives from the fact that his equal interests in both parties, that is, his inner equilibrium, cannot be definitely ascertained and is, in fact, doubted often enough by both parties.

Yet an even more difficult and, indeed, often tragic situation occurs when the third is tied to the two parties, not by specific interests, but by his total personality; and this situation is extreme when the whole matter of the conflict cannot be clearly objectified, and its objective aspect is really only a pretext or opportunity for deeper personal irreconcilabilities to manifest themselves. In such a case, the third, whom love or duty, fate or habit have made equally intimate with both, can be crushed by the conflict—much more so than if he himself took sides. The danger is increased because the balance of his interests, which does not lean in either direction, usually does not lead to successful mediation, since reduction to a merely objective contrast fails. This is the type instanced by a great many family conflicts. The mediator, whose equal distance to both conflicting parties assures his impartiality, can accommodate both with relative ease. But the person who is impartial because he is equally close to the two, will find this much more difficult and will personally get into the most painful dualism of feelings. Where the mediator is chosen, therefore, the equally uninterested will be preferred (other things being equal) to the equally interested. Medieval Italian cities, for instance, often obtained their judges from the outside in order to be sure that they were not prejudiced by inner party frictions.

This suggests the second form of accommodation by means of an impartial third element, namely, arbitration. As long as the third properly operates as a mediator, the final termination of the conflict lies exclusively in the hands of the parties themselves. But when they choose an arbitrator, they relinquish this final decision. They project, as it were, their will to conciliation, and this will becomes personified in the arbitrator. He thus gains a special impressiveness and power over the antagonistic forces. The voluntary appeal to an arbitrator, to whom they submit from the beginning, presupposes a greater subjective confidence in the objectivity of judgment than does any other form of decision. For, even in the state tribunal, it is only the action of the complainant that results from confidence in just decision, since the complainant considers the decision that is favorable to him the just decision. The defendant, on the other hand, must enter the suit whether or not he believes in the impartiality of the judge. But arbitration results only when both parties to the conflict have this belief. This is the principle which sharply differentiates mediation from arbitration; and the more official the act of conciliation, the more punctiliously is this differentiation observed.

This statement applies to a whole range of conflicts; from those between capitalist and worker, which I mentioned earlier, to those of great politics, where the "good services" of a government in adjusting a conflict between two others are quite different from the arbitration occasionally requested of it. The trivialities of daily life, where the typical triad constantly places one into a clear or latent, full or partial difference from two others, offer many intermediary grades between these two forms. In the inexhaustibly varying relations, the parties' appeal to the third person, to his voluntarily or even forcibly seized initiative to conciliate, often gives him a position whose mediating and arbitrating elements it is impossible to separate. If one wants to understand the real web of human society with its indescribable dynamics and fullness, the most important thing is to sharpen one's eyes for such beginnings and transitions, for forms of relationship which are merely hinted at and are again submerged, for their embryonic and fragmentary articulations. Illustrations which exemplify in its purity any one of the concepts denoting these forms, certainly are indispensable sociological tools. But their relation to actual social life is like that of the approximately exact space forms, that are used to illustrate geometrical propositions, to the immeasurable complexity of the actual formations of matter.

After all that has been said, it is clear that from an over-all viewpoint, the existence of the impartial third element serves the perpetuation of the group. As the representative of the intellect, he confronts the two conflicting parties, which for the moment are guided more by will and feeling. He thus, so to speak, complements them in the production of that psychological unity which resides in group life. On the one hand, the non-partisan tempers the passion of the others. On the other hand, he can carry and direct the very movement of the whole group if the antagonism of the other two tends to paralyze their forces. Nevertheless, his success can change into its opposite. We thus understand why the most intellectually disposed elements of a group lean particularly toward impartiality: the cool intellect usually finds lights and shadows in either quarter; its objective justice does not easily side unconditionally with either. This is the reason why sometimes the most intelligent individuals do not have much influence on the decisions in conflicts, although it would be very desirable that such decisions come from them. Once the group has to choose between "yes" and "no" they, above all others, ought to throw their weight into the balance, for then the scale will be the more likely to sink in favor of the right side. If, therefore, impartiality does not serve practical mediation directly, in its combination with intellectuality it makes sure that the decision is not left to the more stupid, or at least more prejudiced, group forces. And in fact, ever since Solon, we often find disapproval of impartial behavior. In the social sense, this disapproval is something very healthy: it is based on the much deeper instinct for the welfare of the whole than on mere suspicion of cowardice—an attack which is frequently launched against impartiality, though often quite unjustifiably.

Whether impartiality consists in the equal distance or in the equal closeness that connects the non-partisan and the two conflicting parties, it is obvious that it may be mixed with a great many other relations between him and each of the two others and their group as a whole. For instance, if he constitutes a group with the other two but is remote from their conflicts, he may be drawn into them in the very name of independence from the parties which already exist. This may greatly serve the unity and equilibrium of the group, although the equilibrium may be highly unstable. It was this sociological form in which the third estate's participation in state matters occurred in England. Ever since Henry III, state matters were inextricably dependent on the cooperation of the great barons who, along with the prelates, had to grant the monies; and their combination had power, often superior power, over the king. Nevertheless, instead of the fruitful collaboration between estates and crown, there were incessant splits, abuses, power shifts, and clashes. Both parties came to feel that these could be ended only by resort to a third element which, until then, had been kept out of state matters; lower vassals, freemen, counties, and cities. Their representatives were invited to councils; and this was the beginning of the House of Commons. The third element thus exerted a double function. First, it helped to make an actuality of government as the image of the state in its comprehensiveness. Secondly, it did so as an agency which confronted hitherto existing government parties objectively, as it were, and thus contributed to the more harmonious employment of their reciprocally exhausted forces for the over-all purpose of the state.

# SOCIAL ACTION AND SOCIAL INTERACTION * (Weber)

1. Social action, which includes both failure to act and passive acquiescence, may be oriented to the past, present, or expected future behaviour of others. Thus it may be motivated by revenge for a past attack, defence against present, or measures of defence against future aggression. The 'others' may be individual persons, and may be known to the actor as such, or may con-

* Reprinted from Max Weber: The Theory of Social and Economic Organization, translated by A. M. Henderson and Talcott Parsons, edited with an introduction by Talcott Parsons, pp. 111–115, 118–120, by permission of the publisher, The Free Press, Glencoe, Ill. Copyright, 1947, by The Free Press, A Corporation.

stitute an indefinite plurality and may be entirely unknown as individuals. Thus 'money' is a means of exchange which the actor accepts in payment because he orients his action to the expectation that a large but unknown number of individuals he is personally unacquainted with will be ready to accept it in exchange on some future occasion.

2. Not every kind of action, even of overt action, is 'social' in the sense of the present discussion. Overt action is non-social if it is oriented solely to the behaviour of inanimate objects. Subjective attitudes constitute social action only so far as they are oriented to the behaviour of others. For example, religious behavior is not social if it is simply a matter of contemplation or of solitary prayer. The economic activity of an individual is only social if, and then only in so far as, it takes account of the behaviour of someone else. Thus very generally in formal terms it becomes social in so far as the actor's actual control over economic goods is respected by others. Concretely it is social, for instance, if in relation to the actor's own consumption the future wants of others are taken into account and this becomes one consideration affecting the actor's own saving. Or, in another connexion, production may be oriented to the future wants of other people.

3. Not every type of contact of human beings has a social character; this is rather confined to cases where the actor's behaviour is meaningfully oriented to that of others. For example, a mere collision of two cyclists may be compared to a natural event. On the other hand, their attempt to avoid hitting each other, or whatever insults, blows, or friendly discussion might follow the collision, would constitute 'social action.'

4. Social action is not identical either with the similar actions of many persons or with action influenced by other persons. Thus, if at the beginning of a shower a number of people on the street put up their umbrellas at the same time, this would not ordinarily be a case of action mutually oriented to that of each other, but rather of all reacting in the same way to the like need of protection from the rain. It is well known that the actions of the individual are strongly influenced by the mere fact that he is a member of a crowd confined within a limited space. Thus, the subject matter of studies of 'crowd psychology,' such as those of Le Bon, will be called 'action conditioned by crowds.' It is also possible for large numbers, though dispersed, to be influenced simultaneously or successively by a source of influence operating similarly on all the individuals, as by means of the press. Here also the behaviour of an individual is influenced by his membership in the crowd and by the fact that he is aware of being a member. Some types of reaction are only made possible by the mere fact that the individual acts as part of a crowd. Others become more difficult under these conditions. Hence it is

possible that a particular event or mode of human behaviour can give rise to the most diverse kinds of feeling—gaiety, anger, enthusiasm, despair, and passions of all sorts—in a crowd situation which would not occur at all or not nearly so readily if the individual were alone. But for this to happen there need not, at least in many cases, be any meaningful relation between the behaviour of the individual and the fact that he is a member of a crowd. It is not proposed in the present sense to call action 'social' when it is merely a result of the effect on the individual of the existence of a crowd as such and the action is not oriented to that fact on the level of meaning. At the same time the borderline is naturally highly indefinite. In such cases as that of the influence of the demagogue, there may be a wide variation in the extent to which his mass clientele is affected by a meaningful reaction to the fact of its large numbers; and whatever this relation may be, it is open to varying interpretations.

But furthermore, mere 'imitation' of the action of others, such as that on which Tarde has rightly laid emphasis, will not be considered a case of specifically social action if it is purely reactive so that there is no meaningful orientation to the actor imitated. The borderline is, however, so indefinite that it is often hardly possible to discriminate. The mere fact that a person is found to employ some apparently useful procedure which he learned from someone else does not, however, constitute, in the present sense, social action. Action such as this is not oriented to the action of the other person, but the actor has, through observing the other, become acquainted with certain objective facts; and it is these to which his action is oriented. His action is then *causally* determined by the action of others, but not meaningfully. On the other hand, if the action of others is imitated because it is 'fashionable' or traditional or exemplary, or lends social distinction, or on similar grounds, it is meaningfully oriented either to the behaviour of the source of imitation or of third persons or of both. There are of course all manner of transitional cases between the two types of imitation. Both the phenomena discussed above, the behaviour of crowds and imitation, stand on the indefinite borderline of social action. The same is true, as will often appear, of traditionalism and charisma. The reason for the indefiniteness of the line in these and other cases lies in the fact that both the orientation to the behaviour of others and the meaning which can be imputed to the actor himself, are by no means always capable of clear determination and are often altogether unconscious and seldom fully self-conscious. Mere 'influence' and meaningful orientation cannot therefore always be clearly differentiated on the empirical level. But conceptually it is essential to distinguish them, even though merely 'reactive' imitation may well have a degree of sociological importance at least equal to that of the type which can be called social action in the strict sense. Sociology, it goes without saying, is by no means confined to the study of 'social action'; this is only, at least for the kind of sociology being developed here, its central subject matter, that which may be said to be decisive for its status as a science. But this does not imply any judgment on the comparative importance of this and other factors.

. . .

The term 'social relationship' will be used to denote the behaviour of a plurality of actors in so far as, in its meaningful content, the action of each takes account of that of the others and is oriented in these terms. The social relationship thus *consists* entirely and exclusively in the existence of a *probability* that there will be, in some meaningful understandable sense, a course of social action. For purposes of definition there is no attempt to specify the basis of this probability.

1. Thus, as a defining criterion, it is essential that there should be at least a minimum of mutual orientation of the action of each to that of the others. Its content may be of the most varied nature; conflict, hostility, sexual attraction, friendship, loyalty, or economic exchange. It may involve the fulfilment, the evasion, or the denunciation of the terms of an agreement; economic, erotic, or some other form of 'competition'; common membership in national or class groups or those sharing a common tradition of status. In the latter cases mere group membership may or may not extend to include social action; this will be discussed later. The definition, furthermore, does not specify whether the relation of the actors is 'solidary' or the opposite.

2. The 'meaning' relevant in this context is always a case of the meaning imputed to the parties in a given concrete case, on the average or in a theoretically formulated pure type—it is never a normatively 'correct' or a metaphysically 'true' meaning. Even in cases of such forms of social organization as a state, church, association, or marriage, the social relationship consists exclusively in the fact that there has existed, exists, or will exist a probability of action in some definite way appropriate to this meaning. It is vital to be continually clear about this in order to avoid the 'reification' of these concepts. A 'state,' for example, ceases to exist in a sociologically relevant sense whenever there is no longer a probability that certain kinds of meaningfully oriented social action will take place. This probability may be very high or it may be negligibly low. But in any case it is only in the sense and degree in which it does exist or can be estimated that the corresponding social relationship exists. It is impossible to find any other clear

meaning for the statement that, for instance, a given 'state' exists or has ceased to exist.

3. The subjective meaning need not necessarily be the same for all the parties who are mutually oriented in a given social relationship; there need not in this sense be 'reciprocity.' 'Friendship,' 'love,' 'loyalty,' 'fidelity to contracts,' 'patriotism,' on one side, may well be faced with an entirely different attitude on the other. In such cases the parties associate different meanings with their actions and the social relationship is in so far objectively 'asymmetrical' from the points of view of the two parties. It may nevertheless be a case of mutual orientation in so far as, even though partly or wholly erroneously, one party presumes a particular attitude toward him on the part of the other and orients his action to this expectation. This can, and usually will, have consequences for the course of action and the form of the relationship. A relationship is objectively symmetrical only as, according to the typical expectations of the parties, the meaning for one party is the same as that for the other. Thus the actual attitude of a child to its father may be at least approximately that which the father, in the individual case, on the average or typically, has come to expect. A social relationship in which the attitudes are completely and fully corresponding is in reality a limiting case. But the absence of reciprocity will, for terminological purposes, be held to exclude the existence of a social relationship only if it actually results in the absence of a mutual orientation of the action of the parties. Here as elsewhere all sorts of transitional cases are the rule rather than the exception.

4. A social relationship can be of a temporary character or of varying degrees of permanence. That is, it can be such a kind that there is a probability of the repeated recurrence of the behaviour which corresponds to its subjective meaning, behaviour which is an understandable consequence of the meaning and hence is expected. In order to avoid fallacious impressions, let it be repeated and continually kept in mind, that it is *only* the existence of the probability that, corresponding to a given subjective meaning complex, a certain type of action will take place, which constitutes the 'existence' of the social relationship. Thus that a 'friendship' or a 'state' exists or has existed means this and only this: that we, the observers, judge that there is or has been a probability that on the basis of certain kinds of known subjective attitude of certain individuals there will result in the average sense a certain specific type of action. For the purposes of legal reasoning it is essential to be able to decide whether a rule of law does or does not carry legal authority, hence whether a legal relationship does or does not 'exist.' This type of question is not, however, relevant to sociological problems.

5. The subjective meaning of a social relationship may change, thus a political relationship, once based on solidarity, may develop into a conflict of interests. In that case it is only a matter of terminological convenience and of the degree of continuity of the change whether we say that a new relationship has come into existence or that the old one continues but has acquired a new meaning. It is also possible for the meaning to be partly constant, partly changing.

6. The meaningful content which remains relatively constant in a social relationship is capable of formulation in terms of maxims which the parties concerned expect to be adhered to by their partners, on the average and approximately. The more rational in relation to values or to given ends the action is, the more is this likely to be the case. There is far less possibility of a rational formulation of subjective meaning in the case of a relation of erotic attraction or of personal loyalty or any other affectual type than, for example, in the case of a business contract.

7. The meaning of a social relationship may be agreed upon by mutual consent. This implies that the parties make promises covering their future behaviour, whether toward each other or toward third persons. In such cases each party then normally counts, so far as he acts rationally, in some degree on the fact that the other will orient his action to the meaning of the agreement as he (the first actor) understands it. In part, they orient their action rationally to these expectations as given facts with, to be sure, varying degrees of subjectively 'loyal' intention of doing their part. But in part also they are motivated each by the value to him of his 'duty' to adhere to the agreement in the sense in which he understands it. This much may be anticipated.

# THE PRINCIPLE OF GIVE
# AND TAKE * (*Malinowski*)

In the foregoing we have seen a series of pictures from native life, illustrating the legal aspect of the marriage relationship, of co-operation in a fishing team, of food barter between inland and coastal villages, of certain ceremonial duties of mourning. These examples were adduced with some detail, in order to bring out clearly the concrete working of what appears to me to

* Reprinted from *Crime and Custom in Savage Society* by Bronislaw Malinowski, pp. 39–45, by permission of the publisher, Routledge & Kegan Paul Ltd.

be the real mechanism of law, social and psychological constraint, the actual forces, motives, and reasons which make men keep to their obligations. If space permitted it would be easy to bring these isolated instances into a coherent picture and to show that in all social relations and in all the various domains of tribal life, exactly the same legal mechanism can be traced, that it places the *binding obligations* in a special category and sets them apart from other types of customary rules. A rapid though comprehensive survey will have to suffice.

To take the economic transactions first: barter of goods and services is carried on mostly within a standing partnership, or is associated with definite social ties or coupled with a mutuality in non-economic matters. Most if not all economic acts are found to belong to some chain of reciprocal gifts and counter-gifts, which in the long run balance, benefiting both sides equally.

I have already given an account of the economic conditions in N. W. Melanesia, in "The Primitive Economics of the Trobriand Islanders" (*Economic Journal,* 1921) and in *Argonauts of the Western Pacific,* 1923. Chapter vi of that volume deals with matters here discussed, i.e., the forms of economic exchange. My ideas about primitive law were not mature at that time, and the facts are presented there without any reference to the present argument—their testimony only the more telling because of that. When, however, I describe a category of offerings as 'Pure Gifts' and place under this heading the gifts of husband to wife and of father to children, I am obviously committing a mistake. I have fallen then, in fact, into the error exposed above, of tearing the act out of its context, of not taking a sufficiently long view of the chain of transactions. In the same paragraph I have supplied, however, an implicit rectification of my mistake in stating that "a gift given by the father to his son is said [by the natives] to be a repayment for the man's relationship to the mother" (p. 179). I have also pointed out there that the 'free gifts' to the wife are also based on the same idea. But the really correct account of the conditions—correct both from the legal and from the economic point of view—would have been to embrace the whole system of gifts, duties, and mutual benefits exchanged between the husband on one hand, wife, children, and wife's brother on the other. It would be found then in native ideas that the system is based on a very complex give and take, and that in the long run mutual services balance.[1]

The real reason why all these economic obligations are normally kept, and kept very scrupulously, is that failure to comply places a man in an intolerable position, while slackness in fulfilment covers him with opprobrium. The man who would persistently disobey the rulings of law in his economic dealings would soon find himself outside the social and economic order—and he is perfectly well aware of it. Test cases are supplied nowadays, when a number of natives through laziness, eccentricity, or a non-conforming spirit of enterprise, have chosen to ignore the obligations of their status and have become automatically outcasts and hangers-on to some white man or other.

The honourable citizen is bound to carry out his duties, though his submission is not due to any instinct or intuitive impulse or mysterious 'group-sentiment,' but to the detailed and elaborate working of a system, in which every act has its own place and must be performed without fail. Though no native, however intelligent, can formulate this state of affairs in a general abstract manner, or present it as a sociological theory, yet every one is well aware of its existence and in each concrete case he can foresee the consequences.

In magical and religious ceremonies almost every act, besides its primary purposes and effects, is also regarded as an obligation between groups and individuals, and here also there comes sooner or later an equivalent repayment or counter-service, stipulated by custom. Magic in its most important forms is a public institution in which the communal magician, who as a rule holds his office by inheritance, has to officiate on behalf of the whole group. Such is the case in the magic of gardens, fishing, war, weather, and canoe-building. As necessity arises, at the proper season, or in certain circumstances he is under an obligation to perform his magic, to keep the taboos, and at times also to control the whole enterprise. For this he is repaid by small offerings, immediately given, and often incorporated into the ritual proceedings. But the real reward lies in the prestige, power, and privileges which his position confers upon him.[2] In cases of minor or occasional magic, such as love charms, curative rites, sorcery, magic of toothache and of pig-welfare, when it is performed on behalf of another, it has to be paid for substantially and the relation between client and professional is based on a contract defined by custom. From the point of view of our present argument, we have to register the fact that all the acts of communal magic are obligatory upon the performer, and that the obligation to carry them out goes with the status of communal magician, which is hereditary in most cases and always is a position of power and privilege. A man may relinquish his position and hand it over to the next in succession, but once he accepts it, he has to carry on the work incumbent, and the community has to give him in return all his dues.

As to the acts which usually would be regarded as religious rather than magical—ceremonies at birth or marriage, rites of death and mourning, the worship of ghosts, spirits, or mythical personages—they also have a legal side clearly exemplified in the case of mortuary performances, described above. Every important act of a religious nature is conceived as a moral obligation towards the object, the ghost, spirit, or power worshipped; it also satisfies some emotional craving of the performer; but besides all this it has also as a matter of fact its place in some social scheme, it is regarded by some third person or persons as due to them, watched and then repaid or returned in kind. When, for example, at the annual return of the departed ghosts to their village you give an offering to the spirit of a dead relative, you satisfy his feelings, and no doubt also his spiritual appetite, which feeds on the spiritual substance of the meal; you probably also express your own sentiment towards the beloved dead. But there is also a social obligation involved: after the dishes have been exposed for some time and the spirit has finished with his spiritual share, the rest, none the worse, it appears, for ordinary consumption after its spiritual abstraction, is given to a friend or relation-in-law still alive, who then returns a similar gift later on.[3] I can recall to my mind not one single act of a religious nature without some such sociological by-play more or less directly associated with the main religious function of the act. Its importance lies in the fact that it makes the act a social obligation, besides its being a religious duty.

I could still continue with the survey of some other phases of tribal life and discuss more fully the legal aspect of domestic relations, already exemplified above, or enter into the reciprocities of the big enterprises, and so on. But it must have become clear now that the detailed illustrations previously given are not exceptional isolated cases, but representative instances of what obtains in every walk of native life.

REFERENCES

1. Compare also the apposite criticism of my expression "pure gift" and of all it implies by M. Marcel Mauss, in L'Année Sociologique, Nouvelle Série, vol. i, pp. 171 sqq. I had written the above paragraph before I saw M. Mauss's strictures, which substantially agreed with my own. It is gratifying to a field-worker when his observations are sufficiently well presented to allow others to refute his conclusions out of his own material. It is even more pleasant for me to find that my maturer judgment has led me independently to the same results as those of my distinguished friend M. Mauss.
2. For further data referring to the social and legal status of the hereditary magician, see Chap. xvii on "Magic," in Argonauts of the Western Pacific, as well as the descriptions of and sundry references to canoe magic, sailing magic, and baloma magic. Compare also the short account of garden magic in "Primitive Economics" (Economic Journ., 1921); of war magic, in Man, 1920 (No. 5 of article); and of fishing magic, in Man, 1918 (No. 53 of article).
3. Comp. the writer's account of the Milamala, the feast of the annual return of the spirits, in "Baloma; the spirits of the dead in the Trobriand Islands" (Journ. of the R. Anthrop. Institute, 1916). The food offerings in question are described on p. 378.

# THE PRINCIPLE OF RECIPROCITY * (*Lévi-Strauss*)

The conclusions of the famous *Essay on the Gift* are well known. In this study which is considered a classic today, Mauss intended to show first of all, that in primitive societies exchange consists less frequently of economic transactions than of reciprocal gifts; secondly, that these reciprocal gifts have a much more important function in these societies than in ours; finally, that this primitive form of exchange is not wholly nor essentially of an economic character but is what he calls "a total social fact," i.e., an event which has at the same time social and religious, magic and economic, utilitarian and sentimental, legal and moral significance. It is known that in numerous primitive societies, and particularly in those of the Pacific Islands and those of the Northwest Pacific coast of Canada and of Alaska, all the ceremonies observed on important occasions are accompanied by a distribution of valued objects. Thus in New Zealand the ceremonial offering of clothes, jewels, arms, food and various furnishings was a common characteristic of the social life of the Maori. These gifts were presented in the event of births, marriages, deaths, exhumations, peace treaties and misdemeanors, and incidents too numerous to be recorded. Similarly, Firth lists the occasions of ceremonial exchange in Polynesia: "birth, initiation, marriage, sickness, death and other social events . . ."[1] Another observer cites the following occasions for ceremonial exchange in a section of the same region: betrothal, marriage, pregnancy, birth and death; and he describes the presents offered by the father of the young man at the celebration of the betrothal: ten baskets of dry fish, ten thousand ripe and six thousand green coco-nuts, the boy himself receiving in exchange two large cakes.[2]

Such gifts are either exchanged immediately for equivalent gifts, or received by the beneficiaries on the condition that on a subsequent occasion they will return the gesture with other gifts whose value often exceeds that of the first, but which bring about in their turn a right to receive later new gifts which themselves surpass the magnificence of those previously given. The most characteristic of these institutions is the potlatch of the Indians in

* Claude Lévi-Strauss. *Les Structures Élémentaires de la Parenté,* chapter v.: "Le Principe de Reciprocité," Presses Universitaires de France, 1949. Abridged and translated by Rose L. Coser and Grace Frazer.

Alaska and in the region of Vancouver. These ceremonies have a triple function: to give back with proper "interest" gifts formerly received; to establish publicly the claim of a family or social group to a title or privilege, or to announce a change of status; finally, to surpass a rival in generosity, to crush him if possible under future obligations which it is hoped he cannot meet, thus taking from him privileges, titles, rank, authority and prestige.

Doubtless the system of reciprocal gifts only reaches such vast proportions with the Indians of the Northwest Pacific, a people who show a genius and exceptional temperament in their treatment of the fundamental themes of a primitive culture. But Mauss has been able to establish the existence of similar institutions in Melanesia and Polynesia. The main function of the food celebrations of many tribes in New Guinea is to obtain recognition of the new "pangua" through a gathering of witnesses, that is to say, the function which in Alaska, according to Barnett, is served by potlatch. . . . Gift exchange and potlatch is a universal mode of culture, although not equally developed everywhere.

But we must insist that his primitive conception of the exchange of goods is not only expressed in well-defined and localized institutions. It permeates all transactions, ritual or secular, in the course of which objects or produce are given or received. Everywhere we find again and again this double assumption, implicit or explicit, that reciprocal gifts constitute a means of transmission of goods; and that these goods are not offered principally or essentially, in order to gain a profit or advantage of an economic nature: "After celebration of birth," writes Turner of the Samoan culture, "after having received and given the *oloa* and the *tonga* (that is the masculine gifts and the feminine gifts) the husband and the wife are not any richer than they were before."

. . .

Exchange does not bring a tangible result as is the case in the commercial transactions in our society. Profit is neither direct, nor is it inherent in the objects exchanged as in the case of monetary profit or consumption values. Or rather, profit does not have the meaning which we assign to it because in primitive culture, there is something else in what we call a "commodity" than that which renders it commodious to its owner or to its merchant. Goods are not only economic commodities but vehicles and instruments for realities of another order: influence, power, sympathy, status, emotion; and the skillful game of exchange consists of a complex totality of maneuvers, conscious or unconscious, in order to gain security and to fortify one's self against risks incurred through alliances and rivalry.

Writing about the Andaman Islanders, Radcliffe-Brown states: "The purpose of the exchange is primarily a moral one; to bring about a friendly feeling between the two persons who participate." The best proof of the supra-economic character of these exchanges is that, in the potlatch, one does not hesitate sometime to destroy considerable wealth by breaking a "copper," or throwing it in the sea and that greater prestige results from the destruction of riches than from its distribution; for distribution, although it may be generous, demands a similar act in return. The economic character exists, however, although it is always limited and qualified by the other aspects of the institution of exchange. "It is not simply the possession of riches which brings prestige, it is rather their distribution. One does not gather riches except in order to rise in the social hierarchy. . . . However, even when pigs are exchanged for pigs, and food for food, the transactions do not lose all economic significance for they encourage work and stimulate a need for cooperation."[3]

The idea that a mysterious advantage is attached to the obtainment of commodities, or at least certain commodities by means of reciprocal gifts, rather than by production or by individual acquisition is not limited to primitive societies.

In modern society, there are certain kinds of objects which are especially well suited for presents, precisely because of their non-utilitarian qualities. In some Iberian countries these objects can only be found, in all their luxury and diversity, in stores especially set up for this purpose and which are similar to the Anglo-Saxon "gift shops." It is hardly necessary to note that these gifts, like invitations (which, though not exclusively, are also free distributions of food and drink) are "returned"; this is an instance in our society of the principle of reciprocity. It is commonly understood in our society that certain goods of a non-essential consumption value, but to which we attach a great psychological aesthetic or sensual value, such as flowers, candies and luxury articles, are obtainable in the form of reciprocal gifts rather than in the form of purchases or individual consumption.

Certain ceremonies and festivals in our society also regulate the periodic return and traditional style of vast operations of exchange. The exchange of presents at Christmas, during one month each year, to which all the social classes apply themselves with a sort of sacred ardor, is nothing else than a gigantic potlatch, which implicates millions of individuals, and at the end of which many family budgets are confronted by lasting disequilibrium. Christmas cards, richly decorated, certainly do not attain the value of the "coppers"; but the refinement of selection, their outstanding designs, their price, the quantity sent or received, give evidence (ritually exhibited on the mantelpiece during the week of celebration), of the recipient's social bonds and the degree of his prestige. We may also mention the subtle techniques which govern the wrapping of the presents and which express in their own way the personal bond between the giver and the receiver: special stickers, paper, ribbon, etc. Through the vanity of gifts, their frequent duplication resulting from the limited range of selection, these exchanges also take the form of a vast and collective destruction of wealth. There are many little facts in this example to remind one that even in our society the destruction of wealth is a way to gain prestige. Isn't it true that the capable merchant knows that a way to attract customers is by advertising that certain high-priced goods must be "sacrificed"? The move is economic but the terminology retains a sense of the sacred tradition.

.    .    .

In the significant sphere of the offering of food, for which banquets, teas, and evening parties are the modern customs, the language itself, e.g., "to give a reception," shows that for us as in Alaska or Oceania, "to receive is to give." One offers dinner to a person whom one wishes to honor, or in order to return a "kindness." The more the social aspect takes precedence over the strictly alimentary, the more emphasis is given to style both of food and of the way in which it is presented: the fine porcelain, the silverware, the embroidered table cloths which ordinarily are carefully put away in the family cabinets and buffets, are a striking counterpart of the ceremonial bowls and spoons of Alaska brought out on similar occasions from painted and decorated chests. Above all, the attitudes towards food are revealing: what the natives of the Northwest coast call "rich food" connotes also among ourselves something else than the mere satisfaction of physiological needs. One does not serve the daily menu when one gives a dinner party. Moreover, if the occasion calls for certain types of food defined by tradition, their apparition alone, through a significant recurrence, calls for shared consumption. A bottle of old wine, a rare liqueur, bothers the conscience of the owner; these are delicacies which one would not buy and consume alone without a vague feeling of guilt. Indeed, the group judges with singular harshness the person who does this. This is reminiscent of the Polynesian ceremonial exchanges, in which goods must as much as possible not be exchanged within the group of paternal relations, but must go to other groups and into other villages. To fail at this duty is called "sori tana" —"to eat from one's own basket." And at the village dances, convention demands that neither of the two local groups consume the food which they have brought but that they exchange their provisions and that each eat the food of the other. The action of the person who, as the woman in the Maori proverb *Kai Kino ana Te Arahe,* would secretly eat the ceremonial food, without offering a part of it, would provoke from his or her relations sentiments which would range, according to circumstances, from irony, mocking and disgust to sentiments of dislike and even rage. It seems that the group confusedly sees in the individual accomplishment of an act which normally requires collective participation a sort of social incest.

But the ritual of exchange does not only take place in the ceremonial meal. Politeness requires that one offer the salt, the butter, the bread, and that one present one's neighbor with a plate before serving oneself. We have often noticed the ceremonial aspect of the meal in the lower-priced restaurants in the south of France; above all in those regions where wine is the main industry, it is surrounded by a sort of mystical respect which makes it "rich food." In those little restaurants where wine is included in the price of the meal each guest finds in front of his plate, a modest bottle of a wine more than often very bad. This bottle is similar to that of the person's neighbor, as are the portions of meat and vegetables, which a waiter passes around. However, a peculiar difference of attitude immediately manifests itself in regard to the liquid nourishment and the solid nourishment: the latter serves the needs of the body and the former its luxury, the one serves first of all to feed, the other to honor. Each guest eats, so to speak, for himself. But when it comes to the wine, a new situation arises; if a bottle should be insufficiently filled, its owner would call good-naturedly for the neighbor to testify. And the proprietor would face, not the anger of an individual victim, but a community complaint. Indeed, the wine is a social commodity whereas the *plat du jour* is a personal commodity. The small bottle can hold just one glass, its contents will be poured not in the glass of the owner, but in that of his neighbor. And the latter will make a corresponding gesture of reciprocity.

What has happened? The two bottles are identical in size, their contents similar in quality. Each participant in this revealing scene, when the final count is made, has not received more than if he had consumed his own wine. From an economic point of view, no one has gained and no one has lost. But there is much more in the exchange itself than in the things exchanged.

The situation of two strangers who face each other, less than a yard apart, from two sides of a table in an inexpensive restaurant (to obtain an individual table is a privilege which one must pay for, and which cannot be awarded below a certain price) is commonplace and episodical. However, it is very revealing, because it offers an example, rare in our society (but prevalent in primitive societies) of the formation of a group for which, doubtless because of its temporary character, no ready formula of integration exists. The custom in French society is to ignore persons whose name, occupation and social rank are unknown. But in the little restaurant, such people find themselves placed for two or three half-hours in a fairly intimate relationship, and momentarily united by a similarity of preoccupations. There is conflict, doubtless not very sharp, but real, which is sufficient to create a state of tension between the norm of "privacy" and the fact of community. They feel at the same time alone and together, compelled to the habitual reserve between strangers, while their respective positions in physical space and their relationships to the objects and utensils of the meal, suggest and to a certain degree call for intimacy. These two strangers are exposed for a short period of time to living together. Without doubt not for as long a time nor as intimately as when one shares a sleeping car, or a cabin on a transatlantic crossing, but for this reason also no clear cultural procedure has been established. An almost imperceptible anxiety is likely to arise in the minds of the two guests with the prospect of small disagreements that the meeting could bring forth. When social distance is maintained, even if it is not accompanied by any manifestation of disdain, insolence or aggression, it is in itself a cause of suffering; for such social distance is at variance with the fact that all social contact carries with it an appeal and that this appeal is at the same  time a hope for response. Opportunity for escape from this trying yet ephemeral situation is provided by an exchange of wine. It is an affirmation of good grace which dispels the reciprocal uncertainty; it substitutes a social bond for mere physical juxtaposition. But it is also more than that; the partner who had the right to maintain reserve is called upon to give it up; wine offered calls for wine returned, cordiality demands cordiality. The relationship of indifference which has lasted until one of the guests has decided to give it up can never be brought back. From now on it must become a relationship either of cordiality or hostilty. There is no possibility of refusing the neighbor's offer of his glass of wine without appearing insulting. Moreover, the acceptance of the offer authorizes another offer, that of conversation. Thus a number of minute social bonds are established by a series of alternating oscillations, in which a right is established in the offering and an obligation in the receiving.

And there is still more. The person who begins the cycle has taken the initiative, and the greater social ease which he has proved becomes an advantage for him. However, the opening always carries with it a risk, namely that the partner will answer the offered libation with a less generous drink, or, on the contrary, that he will prove to be a higher bidder thus forcing the person who offered the wine first to sacrifice a second bottle for the sake of his prestige. We are, therefore, on a microscopic scale, it is true, in the presence of a "total social fact" whose implications are at the same time social, psychological and economic.

This drama, which on the surface seems futile and to which, perhaps, the reader will find that we have awarded a disproportionate importance, seems to us on the contrary to offer material for inexhaustible sociological reflection. We have already pointed out the interest with which we view the non-crystallized forms of social life: the spontaneous aggregations arising from crises, or (as in the example just discussed) simple sub-products of collective life, provide us with vestiges which are still fresh, of very primitive social psychological experiences. In this sense the attitudes of the strangers in the restaurant appear to be an infinitely distant projection, scarcely perceptible but nonetheless recognizable, of a fundamental situation; that in which individuals of primitive tribes find themselves for the first time entering into contact with each other or with strangers. The primitives know only two ways of classifying strangers; strangers are either "good" or "bad." But one must not be misled by a naive translation of the native terms. A "good" group is that to which, without hesitating, one grants hospitality, the one for which one deprives oneself of most precious goods; while the "bad" group is that from which one expects and to which one inflicts, at the first opportunity, suffering or death. With the latter one fights, with the former one exchanges goods.

The general phenomenon of exchange is first of all a total exchange, including food, manufactured objects, as well as those most precious items: women. Doubtlessly we are a long way from the strangers in the restaurant and perhaps it seems startling to suggest that the reluctance of the French peasant to drink his own bottle of wine gives a clue for the explanation of the incest taboo. Indeed, we believe that both phenomena have the same sociological and cultural meaning.

. . .

The prohibition of incest is a rule of reciprocity. It means: I will only give up my daughter or my sister if my neighbor will give up his also. The violent reaction of the community towards incest is the reaction of a community wronged. The fact that I can obtain a wife is, in the last analysis, the consequence of the fact that a brother or a father has given up a woman.

In Polynesia, Firth distinguishes three spheres of exchange according to the relative mobility of the articles concerned. The first sphere concerns food in its diverse forms; the second, rope and fabrics made of bark; the third, hooks, cables, turmeric cakes and canoes. He adds: "Apart from the three spheres of exchange mentioned a fourth may be recognized in cases where goods of unique quality are handed over. Such for instance was the transfer of women by the man who could not otherwise pay for his canoe. Transfers of land might be put into the same category. Women and land are given in satisfaction of unique obligations. . . ."[4]

It is necessary to anticipate the objection that we are relating two phenomena which are not of the same type; it might be argued that indeed gifts may be regarded even in our own culture as a primitive form of exchange but that this kind of reciprocal interaction has been replaced in our society by exchange for profit except for a few remaining instances such as invitations, celebrations and gifts: that in our society the number of goods that are being transferred according to these archaic patterns represents only a small proportion of the objects of commerce and merchandising, and that reciprocal gifts are merely amusing vestiges which can retain the curiosity of the antiquary; and that it is not possible to say that the prohibition of incest, which is as important in our own society as in any other, has been derived from a type of phenomenon which is abnormal today and of purely anecdotical interest. In other words, we will be accused, as we ourselves have accused McLennan, Spencer, Averbury and Durkheim, of deriving the function from the survival and the general case from the existence of an exceptional one.

.     .     .

This objection can be answered by distinguishing between two interpretations of the term "archaic." The survival of a custom or of a belief can be accounted for in different ways: the custom or belief may be a vestige, without any other significance than that of an historical residue which has been spared by chance; but it may also continue throughout the centuries to have a specific function which does not differ essentially from the original one. An institution can be archaic because it has lost its reason for existing or on the contrary because this reason for existing is so fundamental that its transformation has been neither possible nor necessary.

Such is the case of exchange. Its function in primitive society is essential because it encompasses at the same time material objects, social values and women, while in our culture the original function of exchange of goods has gradually been reduced in importance as other means of acquisition have developed; reciprocity as the basis of getting a spouse, however, has maintained its fundamental function; for one thing because women are the most precious property, and above all because women are not in the first place a sign of social value, but a natural stimulant; and the stimulant of the only instinct whose satisfaction can be postponed, the only one consequently, for which, in the act of exchange, and through the awareness of reciprocity, the transformation can occur from the stimulant to the sign and, thereby, give way to an institution; this is the fundamental process of transformation from the conditions of nature to cultural life.

The inclusion of women in the number of reciprocal transactions from group to group and from tribe to tribe is such a general custom that a volume would not suffice to enumerate the instances in which it occurs. Let us note first of all that marriage is everywhere considered as a particularly favorable occasion for opening a cycle of exchanges. The "wedding presents" in our society evidently enter again into the group of phenomena which we have studied above.

In Alaska and in British Columbia, the marriage of a girl is necessarily accompanied by a potlatch; to such a point that the Comox aristocrats organize mock-marriage ceremonies, where there is no bride, for the sole purpose of acquiring privileges in the course of the exchange ritual. But the relation which exists between marriage and gifts is not arbitrary; marriage is itself an inherent part of as well as a central motive for the accompanying reciprocal gifts. Not so long ago it was the custom in our society to "ask for" a young girl in marriage; the father of the betrothed woman "gave" his daughter in marriage; in English the phrase is still used, "to give up the bride." And in regard to the woman who takes a lover, it is also said that she "gives herself." The Arabic word, *sadaqa*, signifies the alm, the bride's price, law and tax. In this last case, the meaning of the word can be explained by the custom of wife buying. But marriage through purchase is an institution which is special in form only; in reality it is only a modality of the fundamental system as analyzed by Mauss, according to which, in primitive society and still somewhat in ours, rights, goods and persons circulate within a group according to a continual mechanism of services and counter-services. Malinowski has shown that in the Trobriand Islands, even after marriage, the payment of mapula represents, on the part of the man, a counter-service destined to compensate for the services furnished by the wife in the form of sexual gratifications.

.    .    .

Even marriage through capture does not contradict the law of reciprocity; it is rather one of the possible institutionalized ways of putting it into practice. In Tikopia the abduction of the betrothed woman expresses in a dramatic fashion the obligation of the detaining group to give up the girls. The fact that they are "available" is thus made evident.

It would then be false to say that one exchanges or gives gifts at the same time that one exchanges or gives women. Because the woman herself is nothing else than one of these gifts, the supreme gift amongst those that can only be obtained in the form of reciprocal gifts. The first stage of our analysis has been directed towards bringing to light this fundamental characteristic of the gift, represented by the woman in primitive society, and to explain the reasons for it. It should not be surprising then to see that women are included among a number of other reciprocal prestations.

.    .    .

The small nomadic bands of the Nambikwara Indians of western Brazil are in constant fear of each other and avoid each other; but at the same time they desire contact because it is the only way in which they are able to exchange, and thereby obtain articles which they are lacking. There is a bond, a continuity between the hostile relations and the provision of reciprocal prestations: exchanges are peacefully resolved wars, wars are the outcome of unsuccessful transactions. This characteristic is evidenced by the fact that the passing of war into peace or at least of hostility into cordiality operates through the intermediary of ritual gestures: the adversaries feel each other out, and with gestures which still retain something of the attitudes of combat, inspect the necklaces, earrings, bracelets, and feathered ornaments of one another with admiring comments.

And from battle they pass immediately to the gifts; gifts are received, gifts are given, but silently, without bargaining, without complaint, and apparently without linking that which is given to that which is obtained. These are, indeed, reciprocal gifts, not commerical operations. But the relationship may be given yet an additional meaning: two tribes who have thus come to establish lasting cordial relations, can decide in a deliberate manner, to join by setting up an artificial kinship relation between the male members of the two tribes: the relationship of brothers-in-law. According to the matrimonial system of the Nambikwara, the immediate consequence of this innovation is that all the children of one group become the potential spouses of the children of the other group and vice-versa; thus a continuous transition exists from war to exchange and from exchange to intermarriage; and the exchange of betrothed women is merely the termination of an uninterrupted process of reciprocal gifts, which brings about the transition from hostility to alliance, from anxiety to confidence and from fear to friendship.

REFERENCES

1. Raymond Firth, *Primitive Polynesian Economy*, London, 1939, p. 321.
2. H. Ian Hogbin, "Sexual life of the natives of Ongton Java." *Journal of the Polynesian Society*, Vol. 40, p. 28.
3. A. B. Deacon, *Malekula . . . A Vanishing People in the New Hebrides*, London, 1934, p. 637.
4. Firth, *op. cit.*, p. 344.

# THE BASIC STRUCTURE OF THE INTERACTIVE RELATIONSHIP * (*Parsons and Shils*)

The interaction of ego and alter is the most elementary form of a social system. The features of this interaction are present in more complex form in all social systems.

In interaction ego and alter are each objects of orientation for the other. The basic differences from orientations to nonsocial objects are two. First, since the outcome of ego's action (e.g., success in the attainment of a goal) is contingent on alter's reaction to what ego does, ego becomes oriented not only to alter's probable *overt* behavior but also to what ego interprets to be alter's expectations relative to ego's behavior, since ego expects that alter's expectations will influence alter's behavior. Second, in an integrated system, this orientation to the expectations of the other is reciprocal or complementary.

Communication through a common system of symbols is the precondition of this reciprocity or complementarity of expectations. The alternatives which are open to alter must have some measure of stability in two respects: first, as realistic possibilities for alter, and second, in their meaning to ego. This stability presupposes generalization from the particularity of the given situations of ego and alter, both of which are continually changing and are never concretely identical over any two moments in time. When such generalization occurs, and actions, gestures, or symbols have more or less the *same* meaning for both ego and alter, we may speak of a common culture existing between them, through which their interaction is mediated.

Furthermore, this common culture, or symbol system, inevitably possesses in certain aspects a normative significance for the actors. Once it is in existence, observance of its conventions is a necessary condition for ego to be "understood" by alter, in the sense of allowing ego to elicit the type of reaction from alter which ego expects. This common set of cultural symbols becomes the medium in which is formed a constellation of the contingent actions of both parties, in such a way that there will simultaneously emerge a definition of a range of *appropriate* reactions on alter's part to each of a

* Reprinted by permission of the publishers from Talcott Parsons and Edward A. Shils, editors, *Toward a General Theory of Action*, pp. 105–107. Cambridge, Mass: Harvard University Press, Copyright, 1952, by The President and Fellows of Harvard College.

range of possible actions ego has taken and vice versa. It will then be a condition of the stabilization of such a system of complementary expectations, not only that ego and alter should *communicate*, but that they should *react appropriately* to each other's action.

A tendency toward consistent appropriateness of reaction is also a tendency toward comformity with a normative pattern. The culture is not only a set of symbols of communication but a *set of norms* for action.

The motivation of ego and alter become integrated with the normative patterns through interaction. The polarity of gratification and deprivation is crucial here. An appropriate reaction on alter's part is a gratifying one to ego. If ego conforms with the norm, this gratification is in one aspect a reward for his conformity with it; the converse holds for the case of deprivation and deviance. The reactions of alter toward ego's conformity with or deviance from the normative pattern thus become sanctions to ego. Ego's expectations vis-à-vis alter are expectations concerning the roles of ego and of alter; and sanctions reinforce ego's motivation to conform with these role-expectations. Thus the complementarity of expectations brings with it the reciprocal reinforcement of ego's and alter's motivation to conformity with the normative pattern which defines their expectations.

The interactive system also involves the process of generalization, not only in the common culture by which ego and alter communicate but in the interpretation of alter's discrete actions vis-à-vis ego as expressions of alter's *intentions* (that is, as indices of the cathectic-evaluative aspects of alter's motivational orientations toward ego). This "generalization" implies that ego and alter agree that certain actions of alter are indices of the *attitudes* which alter has acquired toward ego (and reciprocally, ego toward alter). Since culture and the latter is internalized in ego's need-dispositions, ego is sensitive not only to alter's overt acts, but to his *attitudes*. He acquires a need not only to obtain specific *rewards* and avoid specific *punishments* but to enjoy the favorable attitudes and avoid the unfavorable ones of alter. Indeed, since he is integrated with the same norms, these are the same as his attitudes toward himself as an object. Thus violation of the norm causes him to feel shame toward alter, guilt toward himself.

It should be clear that as an ideal type this interaction paradigm implies *mutuality* of gratification in a certain sense, though not necessarily equal distribution of gratification. As we shall see in the next chapter, this is also the paradigm of the process of the learning of generalized orientations. Even where special mechanisms of adjustment such as dominance and submission or alienation from normative expectations enter in, the process still must be described and analyzed in relation to the categories of this paradigm. It is thus useful both for the analysis of systems of normative expectations and for that of the actual conformity or deviation regarding these expectations in concrete action.

In summary we may say that this is the basic paradigm for the structure of a solitary interactive relationship. It contains all the fundamental elements of the role structure of the social system and the attachment and security system of the personality. It involves culture in both its communicative and its value-orientation functions. It is the modal point of the organization of all systems of action.

# SOCIAL BEHAVIOR AS EXCHANGE * (*Homans*)

Interaction between persons is an exchange of goods, material and non-material. This is one of the oldest theories of social behavior, and one that we still use every day to interpret our own behavior, as when we say, "I found so-and-so rewarding"; or "I got a great deal out of him"; or, even, "Talking with him took a great deal out of me." But perhaps just because it is so obvious, this view has been much neglected by social scientists. So far as I know, the only theoretical work that makes explicit use of it is Marcel Mauss's *Essai sur le don,* published in 1925, which is ancient as social science goes.[1] It may be that the tradition of neglect is now changing and that, for instance, the psychologists who interpret behavior in terms of transactions may be coming back to something of the sort I have in mind.[2]

An incidental advantage of an exchange theory is that it might bring sociology closer to economics—that science of man most advanced, most capable of application, and, intellectually, most isolated. Economics studies exchange carried out under special circumstances and with a most useful built-in numerical measure of value. What are the laws of the general phenomenon of which economic behavior is one class?

In what follows I shall suggest some reasons for the usefulness of a theory of social behavior as exchange and suggest the nature of the propositions such a theory might contain.

* Reprinted from "Social Behavior as Exchange," by George C. Homans, *The American Journal of Sociology,* Vol. 63, No. 6, May 1958, pp. 597–600, by permission of the publisher, The University of Chicago Press.

[1] Translated by I. Cunnison as *The Gift* (Glencoe, Ill.: Free Press, 1954).

[2] In social anthropology D. L. Oliver is working along these lines, and I owe much to him. See also T. M. Newcomb, "The Prediction of Interpersonal Attraction," *American Psychologist,* XI (1956), 575–86.

## An Exchange Paradigm

I start with the link to behavioral psychology and the kind of statement it makes about the behavior of an experimental animal such as the pigeon.[3] As a pigeon explores its cage in the laboratory, it happens to peck a target, whereupon the psychologist feeds it corn. The evidence is that it will peck the target again; it has learned the behavior, or, as my friend Skinner says, the behavior has been reinforced, and the pigeon has undergone *operant conditioning.* This kind of psychologist is not interested in how the behavior was learned: "learning theory" is a poor name for his field. Instead, he is interested in what determines changes in the rate of emission of learned behavior, whether pecks at a target or something else.

The more hungry the pigeon, the less corn or other food it has gotten in the recent past, the more often it will peck. By the same token, if the behavior is often reinforced, if the pigeon is given much corn every time it pecks, the rate of emission will fall off as the pigeon gets *satiated.* If, on the other hand, the behavior is not reinforced at all, then, too, its rate of emission will tend to fall off, though a long time may pass before it stops altogether, before it is *extinguished.* In the emission of many kinds of behavior the pigeon incurs *aversive stimulation,* or what I shall call "cost" for short, and this, too, will lead in time to a decrease in the emission rate. Fatigue is an example of a "cost." Extinction, satiation, and cost, by decreasing the rate of emission of a particular kind of behavior, render more probable the emission of some other kind of behavior, including doing nothing. I shall only add that even a hard-boiled psychologist puts "emotional" behavior, as well as such things as pecking, among the unconditioned responses that may be reinforced in operant conditioning. As a statement of the propositions of behavioral psychology, the foregoing is, of course, inadequate for any purpose except my present one.

We may look on the pigeon as engaged in an exchange—pecks for corn—with the psychologist, but let us not dwell upon that, for the behavior of the pigeon hardly determines the behavior of the psychologist at all. Let us turn to a situation where the exchange is real, that is, where the determination is mutual. Suppose we are dealing with two men. Each is emitting behavior reinforced to some degree by the behavior of the other. How it was in the past that each learned the behavior he emits and how he learned to find the other's behavior reinforcing we are not concerned with. It is enough that

[3] B. F. Skinner, *Science and Human Behavior* (New York: Macmillan Co., 1953)

each does find the other's behavior reinforcing, and I shall call the rein-forcers—the equivalent of the pigeon's corn—*values*, for this, I think, is what we mean by this term. As he emits behavior, each man may incur costs, and each man has more than one course of behavior open to him.

This seems to me the paradigm of elementary social behavior, and the problem of the elementary sociologist is to state propositions relating the variations in the values and costs of each man to his frequency distribution of behavior among alternatives, where the values (in the mathematical sense) taken by these variables for one man determine in part their values for the other.[4]

I see no reason to believe that the propositions of behavioral psychology do not apply to this situation, though the complexity of their implications in the concrete case may be great indeed. In particular, we must suppose that, with men as with pigeons, an increase in extinction, satiation, or aversive stimulation of any one kind of behavior will increase the probability of emission of some other kind. The problem is not, as it is often stated, merely, what a man's values are, what he has learned in the past to find reinforcing, but how much of any one value his behavior is getting him now. The more he gets, the less valuable any further unit of that value is to him, and the less often he will emit behavior reinforced by it.

## The Influence Process

We do not, I think, possess the kind of studies of two-person interaction that would either bear out these propositions or fail to do so. But we do have studies of larger numbers of persons that suggest that they may apply, not-ably the studies by Festinger, Schachter, Back, and their associates on the dynamics of influence. One of the variables they work with they call *co-hesiveness*, defined as anything that attracts people to take part in a group. Cohesiveness is a value variable; it refers to the degree of reinforcement people find in the activities of the group. Festinger and his colleagues con-sider two kinds of reinforcing activity: the symbolic behavior we call "so-cial approval" (sentiment) and activity valuable in other ways, such as doing something interesting.

The other variable they work with they call *communication* and others call *interaction*. This is a frequency variable; it is a measure of the frequency

---

[4] *Ibid*, pp. 297–329. The discussion of "double contingency" by T. Parsons and E. A. Shils could easily lead to a similar paradigm (see *Toward a General Theory of Action* [Cambridge, Mass.: Harvard University Press, 1951], pp. 14–16).

of emission of valuable and costly verbal behavior. We must bear in mind that, in general, the one kind of variable is a function of the other.

Festinger and his co-workers show that the more cohesive a group is, that is, the more valuable the sentiment or activity the members exchange with one another, the greater the average frequency of interaction of the members.[5] With men, as with pigeons, the greater the reinforcement, the more often is the reinforced behavior emitted. The more cohesive a group, too, the greater the change that members can produce in the behavior of other members in the direction of rendering these activities more valuable.[6] That is, the more valuable the activities that members get, the more valuable these that they must give. For if a person is emitting behavior of a certain kind, and other people do not find it particularly rewarding, these others will suffer their own production of sentiment and activity, in time, to fall off. But perhaps the first person has found their sentiment and activity rewarding, and, if he is to keep on getting them, he must make his own behavior more valuable to the others. In short, the propositions of behavioral psychology imply a tendency toward a certain proportionality between the value to others of the behavior a man gives them and the value to him of the behavior they give him.[7]

Schachter also studied the behavior of members of a group toward two kinds of other members, "conformers" and "deviates."[8] I assume that conformers are people whose activity the other members find valuable. For conformity is behavior that coincides to a degree with some group standard or norm, and the only meaning I can assign to *norm* is "a verbal description of behavior that many members find it valuable for the actual behavior of themselves and others to conform to." By the same token, a deviate is a member whose behavior is not particularly valuable. Now Schachter shows that, as the members of a group come to see another member as a deviate, their interaction with him—communication addressed to getting him to change his behavior—goes up, the faster the more cohesive the group. The members need not talk to the other conformers so much; they are relatively satiated by the conformers' behavior: they have gotten what they want out

[5] K. W. Back, "The Exertion of Influence through Social Communication," in L. Festinger, K. Back, S. Schacter, H. H. Kelley, and J. Thibaut (eds.), *Theory and Experiment in Social Communication* (Ann Arbor: Research Center for Dynamics, University of Michigan, 1950), pp. 21–36.

[6] S. Schachter, N. Ellertson, D. McBride, and D. Gregory, "An Experimental Study of Cohesiveness and Productivity," *Human Relations*, IV (1951), 229–38.

[7] Skinner, *op. cit.*, p. 100.

[8] S. Schachter, "Deviation, Rejection, and Communication," *Journal of Abnormal and Social Psychology*, XLVI (1951), 190–207.

of them. But if the deviate, by failing to change his behavior, fails to reinforce the members, they start to withhold social approval from him: the deviate gets low sociometric choice at the end of the experiment. And in the most cohesive groups—those Schachter calls "high cohesive-relevant"—interaction with the deviate also falls off in the end and is lowest among those members that rejected him most strongly, as if they had given him up as a bad job. But, how plonking can we get? These findings are utterly in line with everyday experience.

# THE EXCHANGE OF SOCIAL REWARDS * (*Blau*)

Most human pleasures have their roots in social life. Whether we think of love or power, professional recognition or sociable companionship, the comforts of family life or the challenge of competitive sports, the gratifications experienced by individuals are contingent on actions of others. The same is true for the most selfless and spiritual satisfactions. To work effectively for a good cause requires making converts to it. Even the religious experience is much enriched by communal worship. Physical pleasures that can be experienced in solitude pale in significance by comparison. Enjoyable as a good dinner is, it is the social occasion that gives it its luster. Indeed, there is something pathetic about the person who derives his major gratification from food or drink as such, since it reveals either excessive need or excessive greed; the pauper illustrates the former, the glutton, the latter. To be sure, there are profound solitary enjoyments—reading a good book, creating a piece of art, producing a scholarly work. Yet these, too, derive much of their significance from being later communicated to and shared with others. The lack of such anticipation makes the solitary activity again somewhat pathetic: the recluse who has nobody to talk to about what he reads; the artist or scholar whose works are completely ignored, not only by his contemporaries but also by posterity.

Much of human suffering as well as much of human happiness has its source in the actions of other human beings. One follows from the other, given the facts of group life, where pairs do not exist in complete isolation from other social relations. The same human acts that cause pleasure to some

* Reprinted from *Exchange and Power in Social Life* by Peter M. Blau, John Wiley, New York, 1964, pp. 14–17, by permission of the publishers.

typically cause displeasure to others. For one boy to enjoy the love of a girl who has committed herself to be his steady date, other boys who had gone out with her must suffer the pain of having been rejected. The satisfaction a man derives from exercising power over others requires that they endure the deprivation of being subject to his power. For a professional to command an outstanding reputation in his field, most of his colleagues must get along without such pleasant recognition, since it is the lesser professional esteem of the majority that defines his as outstanding. The joy the victorious team members experience has its counterpart in the disappointment of the losers. In short, the rewards individuals obtain in social associations tend to entail a cost to other individuals. This does not mean that most social associations involve zero-sum games in which the gains of some rest on the losses of others. Quite the contrary, individuals associate with one another because they all profit from their association. But they do not necessarily all profit equally, nor do they share the cost of providing the benefits equally, and even if there are no direct costs to participants, there are often indirect costs born by those excluded from the association, as the case of the rejected suitors illustrates.

Some social associations are intrinsically rewarding. Friends find pleasure in associating with one another, and the enjoyment of whatever they do together—climbing a mountain, watching a football game—is enhanced by the gratification that inheres in the association itself. The mutual affection between lovers or family members has the same result. It is not what lovers do together but their doing it *together* that is the distinctive source of their special satisfaction—not seeing a play but sharing the experience of seeing it. Social interaction in less intimate relations than those of lovers, family members, or friends, however, may also be inherently rewarding. The sociability at a party or among neighbors or in a work group involves experiences that are not especially profound but are intrinsically gratifying. In these cases, all associates benefit simultaneously from their social interaction, and the only cost they incur is the indirect one of giving up alternative opportunities by devoting time to the association.

Social associations may also be rewarding for a different reason. Individuals often derive specific benefits from social relations because their associates deliberately go to some trouble to provide these benefits for them. Most people like helping others and doing favors for them—to assist not only their friends but also their acquaintances and occasionally even strangers, as the motorist who stops to aid another with his stalled car illustrates. Favors make us grateful, and our expressions of gratitude are social rewards that tend to make doing favors enjoyable, particularly if we express our appreciation and indebtedness publicly and thereby help establish a person's reputation as a generous and competent helper. Besides, one good deed deserves another. If we feel grateful and obligated to an associate for favors received, we shall seek to reciprocate his kindness by doing things for him. He in turn is likely to reciprocate, and the resulting mutual exchange of favors strengthens, often without explicit intent, the social bond between us.

A person who fails to reciprocate favors is accused of ingratitude. This very accusation indicates that reciprocation is expected, and it serves as a social sanction that discourages individuals from forgetting their obligations to associates. Generally, people are grateful for favors and repay their social debts, and both their gratitude and their repayment are social rewards for the associate who has done them favors.[1] The fact that furnishing benefits to others tends to produce these social rewards is, of course, a major reason why people often go to great trouble to help their associates and enjoy doing so. We would not be human if these advantageous consequences of our good deeds were not important inducements for our doing them.[2] There are, to be sure, some individuals who selflessly work for others without any thought of reward and even without expecting gratitude, but these are virtually saints, and saints are rare. The rest of us also act unselfishly sometimes, but we require some incentive for doing so, if it is only the social acknowledgment that we are unselfish.

An apparent "altruism" pervades social life; people are anxious to benefit one another and to reciprocate for the benefits they receive. But beneath this seeming selflessness an underlying "egoism" can be discovered; the tendency to help others is frequently motivated by the expectation that doing so will bring social rewards. Beyond this self-interested concern with profiting from social associations, however, there is again an "altruistic" element or, at least, one that removes social transactions from simple egoism or psychological hedonism. A basic reward people seek in their associations is social approval, and selfish disregard for others makes it impossible to obtain this important reward.[3]

---

[1] "We rarely meet with ingratitude, so long as we are in a position to confer favors." François La Rochefoucauld, *The Maxims*, London: Oxford University Press, 1940, p. 101 (#306).

[2] Once a person has become emotionally committed to a relationship, his identification with the other and his interest in continuing the association provide new independent incentives for supplying benefits to the other. Similarly, firm commitments to an organization lead members to make recurrent contributions to it without expecting reciprocal benefits in every instance. The significance of these attachments is further elaborated in subsequent chapters.

[3] Bernard Mandeville's central theme is that private vices produce public benefits because the importance of social approval prompts men to contribute to the welfare of

The social approval of those whose opinions we value is of great significance to us, but its significance depends on its being genuine. We cannot force others to give us their approval, regardless of how much power we have over them, because coercing them to express their admiration or praise would make these expressions worthless. "Action can be coerced, but a coerced show of feeling is only a show."[4] Simulation robs approval of its significance, but its very importance makes associates reluctant to withhold approval from one another and, in particular, to express disapproval, thus introducing an element of simulation and dissimulation into their communications. As a matter of fact, etiquette prescribes that approval be simulated in disregard of actual opinions under certain circumstances. One does not generally tell a hostess, "Your party was boring," or a neighbor, "What you say is stupid." Since social conventions require complimentary remarks on many occasions, these are habitually discounted as not reflecting genuine approbation, and other evidence that does reflect it is looked for, such as whether guests accept future invitations or whether neighbors draw one into further conversations.

---

others in their own self-interest. As he put it tersely at one point, "Moral Virtues are the Political Offspring which Flattery begot upon Pride." *The Fable of the Bees,* Oxford: Clarendon, 1924, Vol. I, 51; see also pp. 63–80.

[4] Erving Goffman, *Asylums,* Chicago: Aldine, 1962, p. 115.

# 4: Social Control

Social control refers to those mechanisms by which society exercises its dominion over component individuals and enforces conformity to its norms and its values. The term was first used by one of the fathers of American sociology, Edward A. Ross (1866–1951), in a series of papers written just before the turn of the century which were later incorporated in the book *Social Control*. It has since become a standard mode of conceptualization in American sociology.

Ross employed the term "social control" in a rather imprecise sense, yet one gathers that he was mainly concerned with those regulative institutions which insure that individual behavior is in conformity with group demands. He showed the important role which belief in the supernatural, ceremonies, public opinion, morals, art, education, law, and related phenomena play in maintaining the normative structure of society.

Ross' contemporary, William G. Sumner (1840–1910), another of the founding fathers of American sociology, attempted in his famous *Folkways* (1906) a somewhat similar task. As the subtitle of the book, "A Study of the Sociological Importance of Usages, Manners, Customs and Morals," indicates, Sumner was primarily concerned with the way in which standardized norms serve to insure individual conformity. "Folkways," in Sumner's terminology, are "habits and customs . . . which become regulative and imperative for succeeding generations . . . they very largely control individual and social undertaking."

These early sociological investigators significantly enlarged our understanding of social control by pointing out that there is a wide range of control mechanisms and that law, which had earlier been seen as the only important mechanism, was one of many, and possibly not even the most important. Yet these analysts never satisfactorily explained the manner in which external control comes to be incorporated into the personality of the individual. When faced with this problem, they tended to use a series of *ad hoc* concepts such as suggestion and imitation. Such concepts not only failed to explain the mechanisms involved; they also proved to be convenient labels for as yet unexplained phenomena.

Further advance came from a number of theorists who, though working independently, arrived at substantially similar results. Emile Durkheim, after first having attempted to explain social control solely in terms of exterior constraints, was led in his later work to emphasize that social norms, far from being imposed on the individual from the outside, became in fact *internalized,* that they are "society living in us." Durkheim now maintained that the essence of control lay in the individual's sense of moral obligation to obey a rule—the voluntary acceptance of duty rather than a simple exterior conformity to outside pressure. The moral demands of society, as Durkheim sees them in his mature work, are constitutive elements of the individual personality itself.

While Durkheim was led to stress internalization of societal demands as the most important element in social control, the American social philosopher, George Herbert Mead (1863–1931), and the Austrian psychiatrist, Sigmund Freud (1856–1939), made further significant contributions to our understanding of the internalization of social norms. Mead argued that a person's self-image, the "me," develops through his social experience as he becomes aware of the expectations and appraisals of others. The attitude of "significant others" becomes internalized and forms the "generalized other," the "conscience" of the individual. In this manner the expectations of others in the society form the character and "conscience" of the individual. Conscience is a societal creation. Sigmund Freud's construct, the superego, which is too well known to require discussion here, though arrived at from a different point of departure and consistent with a different terminology, may nevertheless be said in this respect to dovetail rather closely with Mead's conceptions. It would seem that to Freud, as to Mead, the internalization of societal norms involves a disciplining of impulse through the incorporation of the expectations of others into the psychic structure.

Our reading from the brilliant Swiss psychologist, Jean Piaget, is meant to point toward yet another road, in many respects similar to Mead's, through which the process of internalization of social norms can be approached. It is Piaget's thesis in his work *The Moral Judgment of the Child* that autonomous moral judgments are internalized only on the basis of cooperative social relationships, whereas "authoritarian" social relationships lead only to conformity with heteronomous commands. Types of individual morality are thus seen as deriving genetically from the types of social structure in which individuals are involved.

Dennis Wrong, a talented and constructive critic of his fellow sociologists in America, recently expressed the conviction that they had made too much of social control and too little of human spontaneity. In a broadside, which he has been good enough to rework for us, Wrong protests against the over-socialized conception of man for its failure to accord with human nature as we currently understand that phenomenon.

# SOCIAL CONTROL * (Ross)

Even in a mining camp, the issues are not always between man and man. In the keeping of arms or whiskey from the Indians, or in the limiting of gambling, there comes to light a collective interest which only collective action can protect. There are offences that exasperate the group as well as offences that arouse the ire of the individual. In this common wrath and common vengeance lies the germ of a social control of the person.[1]

So far as the fruits of a common enterprise can be reaped in full by the participants, coöperation may be left entirely free; but when the benefits of a coöperation will redound to the group as a whole and be enjoyed by all alike, it is necessary that all be required to assume their due share of the burden. Among the earliest signs of collective pressure is the endeavor to make kickers, cowards, and shirkers take part in joint undertakings which benefit all. Among the Iowa settlers the first symptom of contractile power in the social tissue appeared in the community defence of cases to test squatter land titles.[2] Along the river building of the levee is the first occasion for compulsory coöperation. In Egypt and China, the early river monarchies, the care of the waters had much to do with forming the state.[3] In new lands, defence against the aborigines is the chief community interest and overrides masterfully the timidity or apathy of individual settlers.

In complex coöperation even the willing need an authority over them, for success implies such a delicate poise of numerous individual performances

* Reprinted from Social Control by Edward Alsworth Ross, pp. 49–50, 59–60, and 411–412 with permission of the publisher, The Macmillan Company. Copyright, 1910, by The Macmillan Company.

that the Word must go forth and with power. This is why warfare, the great primary coöperation, is usually the mother of discipline.

. . .

It is, in fact, impossible to reap the advantages of high organization of any kind—military, political, industrial, commercial, education—save by restraints of one kind or another. If the units of a society are not reliable, the waste and leakage on the one hand, or the friction due to the checks and safeguards required to prevent such loss on the other hand, prove so burdensome as to nullify the advantages of high organization and make complicated social machinery of any kind unprofitable.

Men are therefore in chronic need of better order than the natural moral motives will provide. At this point and at that point they gradually become sensible of a drag on their prosperity. They find themselves in the presence of a degree of discord, collision, and general unreliability which shuts them out of real material advantages. Better order becomes "a long-felt want," and it would be most surprising if this "demand" called forth no "supply." If in their collective capacity men did not find a means of guiding the will or conscience of the individual member of society, they would here betray a lack of enterprise they show nowhere else. The elementary personal struggle threatens the general prosperity just as the swollen river or the wildfire. And if men raise levees and firebreaks against the natural forces, why not against the human passion? Provided it be possible, a group control of conduct is, therefore, just what we should look for. The wonder would be if it were lacking.

Most of us, it is true, are born with a certain fitness for order. Ages of social weathering have allowed a mantle of soft green to creep over the flint of animal ferocity and selfishness. But the layer of soil is too thin. The abundant fruits of righteousness we need to-day must grow on *made* soil. The primitive Teuton is to the modern what the frowning ledges along his Rhine are to the smiling vine-clad terraces into which human labor has transformed them.

An unremitting control is needed, for the moral habit of one generation does not become the instinct of the next.

. . .

In respect to their fundamental character, it is possible to divide most of the supports of order into two groups. Such instruments of control as public opinion, suggestion, personal ideal, social religion, art, and social valuation draw much of their strength from the primal moral feelings. They take their shape from sentiment rather than utility. They control men in many things which have little to do with the welfare of society regarded as a corporation. They are aimed to realize not merely a social order but what one might term a *moral* order. These we may call *ethical*.

On the other hand, law, belief, ceremony, education, and illusion need not spring from ethical feelings at all. They are frequently the means deliberately chosen in order to reach certain ends. They are likely to come under the control of the organized few, and be used, whether for the corporate benefit or for class benefit, as the tools of policy. They may be termed *political*, using the word "political" in its original sense of "pertaining to policy."

Now, the prominence of the one group or the other in the regulative scheme depends upon the constitution of the society. The *political* instruments operating through prejudice or fear will be preferred:

1. In proportion as the population elements to be held together are antipathetic and jarring.
2. In proportion to the subordination of the individual will and welfare by the scheme of control.
3. In proportion as the social constitution stereotypes differences of status.
4. In proportion as the differences in economic condition and opportunity it consecrates are great and cumulative.
5. In proportion as the parasitic relation is maintained between races, classes, or sexes.

In confirmation of these statements, we have but to recall that the chief influences which history recognizes as stiffening State, Church, Hierarchy, Tradition, are conquest, caste, slavery, serfdom, gross inequalities of wealth, military discipline, paternal regimentation, and race antipathies within the bosom of the group. The disappearance of any one of these conditions permits a mellowing and liberalizing of social control.

On the other hand the *ethical* instruments, being more mild, enlightening, and suasive, will be preferred:

1. In proportion as the population is homogeneous in race.
2. In proportion as its culture is uniform and diffused.
3. In proportion as the social contacts between the elements in the population are many and amicable.
4. In proportion as the total burden of requirement laid upon the individual is light.
5. In proportion as the social constitution does not consecrate distinctions of status or the parasitic relation, but conforms to common elementary notions of justice.

REFERENCES

1. Sir Henry Maine shows that in early law only injuries of the community are crimes. The injuries of the individual are torts and can be settled for. Moreover, "When the Roman community conceived itself to be injured the analogy of a personal wrong received was carried out to its consequences with absolute literalness, and the state avenged itself by a single act on the individual wrongdoer. The result was that in the infancy of the commonwealth every offense vitally touching its security or its interests was punished by a separate enactment of the legislature."—"Ancient Law," p. 360.
2. Jesse Macy, "Institutional Beginnings in a Western State." Johns Hopkins University *Studies in Historical and Political Science,* Vol. II.
3. E. J. Simcox. "Primitive Civilizations," Vol. I, pp. 75–76; Vol. II, pp. 9, 63.

# THE MORES * (*Sumner*)

*More exact definition of the mores.* We may now formulate a more complete definition of the mores. They are the ways of doing things which are current in a society to satisfy human needs and desires, together with the faiths, notions, codes, and standards of well living which inhere in those ways, having a genetic connection with them. By virtue of the latter element the mores are traits in the specific character (ethos) of a society or a period. They pervade and control the ways of thinking in all the exigencies of life, returning from the world of abstractions to the world of action, to give guidance and to win revivification. "The mores [*Sitten*] are, before any beginning of reflection, the regulators of the political, social, and religious behavior of the individual. Conscious reflection is the worst enemy of the mores, because mores begin unconsciously and pursue unconscious purposes, which are recognized by reflection often only after long and circuitous processes, and because their expediency often depends on the assumption that they will have general acceptance and currency, uninterfered with by reflection."[1] "The mores are usage in any group, in so far as it, on the one hand, is not the expression or fulfillment of an absolute natural necessity [e.g. eating or sleeping], and, on the other hand, is independent of the arbitrary will of the individual, and is generally accepted as good and proper, appropriate and worthy."[2]

*The ritual of the mores.* The mores are social ritual in which we all participate unconsciously. The current habits as to hours of labor, meal

* Reprinted from *Folkways* by William Graham Sumner, Ginn and Company, 1904, paragraphs 66, 68, 80 and 83.

hours, family life, the social intercourse of the sexes, propriety, amusements, travel, holidays, education, the use of periodicals and libraries, and innumerable other details of life fall under this ritual. Each does as everybody does. For the great mass of mankind as to all things, and for all of us for a great many things, the rule to do as all do suffices. We are led by suggestion and association to believe that there must be wisdom and utility in what all do. The great mass of the folkways give us discipline and the support of routine and habit. If we had to form judgments as to all these cases before we could act in them, and were forced always to act rationally, the burden would be unendurable. Beneficent use and wont save us this trouble.

*The mores have the authority of facts.* The mores come down to us from the past. Each individual is born into them as he is born into the atmosphere, and he does not reflect on them, or criticise them any more than a baby analyzes the atmosphere before he begins to breathe it. Each one is subjected to the influence of the mores, and formed by them, before he is capable of reasoning about them. It may be objected that nowadays, at least, we criticise all traditions, and accept none just because they are handed down to us. If we take up cases of things which are still entirely or almost entirely in the mores, we shall see that this is not so. There are sects of free-lovers amongst us who want to discuss pair marriage (sec. 374). They are not simply people of evil life. They invite us to discuss rationally our inherited customs and ideas as to marriage, which, they say, are by no means so excellent and elevated as we believe. They have never won any serious attention. Some others want to argue in favor of polygamy on grounds of expediency. They fail to obtain a hearing. Others want to discuss property. In spite of some literary activity on their part, no discussion of property, bequest, and inheritance has ever been opened. Property and marriage are in the mores. Nothing can ever change them but the unconscious and imperceptible movement of the mores. Religion was originally a matter of the mores. It became a societal institution and a function of the state. It has now to a great extent been put back into the mores. Since laws with penalties to enforce religious creeds or practices have gone out of use any one may think and act as he pleases about religion. Therefore it is not now "good form" to attack religion. Infidel publications are now tabooed by the mores, and are more effectually repressed than ever before. They produce no controversy. Democracy is in our American mores. It is a product of our physical and economic conditions. It is impossible to discuss or criticise it. It is glorified for popularity, and is a subject of dithyrambic rhetoric. No one treats it with complete candor and sincerity. No one dares to analyze it as he would aristocracy or autocracy. He would get no hearing and would only incur abuse. The thing to be noticed in all these cases is that the masses oppose a deaf ear to every argument against the mores. It is only in so far as things have been transferred from the mores into laws and positive institutions that there is discussion about them or rationalizing upon them. The mores contain the norm by which, if we should discuss the mores, we should have to judge the mores. We learn the mores as unconsciously as we learn to walk and eat and breathe. The masses never learn how we walk, and eat, and breathe, and they never know any reason why the mores are what they are. The justification of them is that when we wake to consciousness of life we find them facts which already hold us in the bonds of tradition, custom, and habit. The mores contain embodied in them notions, doctrines, and maxims, but they are facts. They are in the present tense. They have nothing to do with what ought to be, will be, may be, or once was, if it is not now.

*Inertia and rigidity of the mores.* We see that we must conceive of the mores as a vast system of usages, covering the whole of life, and serving all its interests! also containing in themselves their own justification by tradition and use and wont, and approved by mystic sanctions until, by rational reflection, they develop their own philosophical and ethical generalizations, which are elevated into "principles" of truth and right. They coerce and restrict the newborn generation. They do not stimulate to thought, but the contrary. The thinking is already done and is embodied in the mores. They never contain any provision for their own amendment. They are not questions, but answers, to the problem of life. They present themselves as final and unchangeable, because they present answers which are offered as "the truth." No world philosophy, until the modern scientific world philosophy, and that only within a generation or two, has ever presented itself as perhaps transitory, certainly incomplete, and liable to be set aside to-morrow by more knowledge. No popular world philosophy or life policy ever can present itself in that light. It would cost too great a mental strain. All the groups whose mores we consider far inferior to our own are quite as well satisfied with theirs as we are with ours. The goodness or badness of mores consists entirely in their adjustment to the life conditions and the interests of the time and place (sec. 65). Therefore it is a sign of ease and welfare when no thought is given to the mores, but all coöperate in them instinctively. The nations of southeastern Asia show us the persistency of the mores, when the element of stability and rigidity in them becomes predominant. Ghost fear and ancestor worship tend to establish the persistency of the mores by dogmatic authority, strict taboo, and weighty sanctions. The mores then lose their naturalness and vitality. They are stereotyped. They lose all relation to expediency. They become an end in themselves. They are imposed by imperative authority without regard to interests or conditions (caste, child marriage, widows). When any society falls under the dominion of this disease in the mores it must disintegrate before it can live again. In that diseased state of the mores all learning consists in committing to memory the words of the sages of the past who established the formulae of the mores. Such words are "sacred writings," a sentence of which is a rule of conduct to be obeyed quite independently of present interests, or of any rational considerations.

REFERENCES

1. v. Hartman, *Phänom. des Sittl. Bewusseins*, 73.
2. Lazarus in *Ztsft. für Völkerpsy.*, I., 439.

# THE INTERNALIZATION OF SOCIAL CONTROL I * (*Durkheim*)

What are the distinctive characteristics of a moral fact?

All morality appears to us as a system of rules of conduct. But all techniques are equally ruled by maxims that prescribe the behaviour of the agent in particular circumstances. What then is the difference between moral rules and other rules of technique?

(i) We shall show that moral rules are invested with a special authority by virtue of which they are obeyed simply because they command. We shall reaffirm, as a result of a purely empirical analysis, the notion of duty and nevertheless give a definition of it closely resembling that already given by Kant. Obligation is, then, one of the primary characteristics of the moral rule.

(ii) In opposition to Kant, however, we shall show that the notion of duty does not exhaust the concept of morality. It is impossible for us to carry out an act simply because we are ordered to do so and without consideration of its content. For us to become the agents of an act it must interest our sensibility to a certain extent and appear to us as, in some ways, *desirable*. Obligation or duty only expresses one aspect abstracted from morality. A certain degree of desirability is another characteristic no less important than the first.

* Reprinted from *Sociology and Philosophy* by Emile Durkheim, translated by D. F. Pocock, pp. 35–36 and 40–46, by permission of the publisher. The Free Press, Glencoe, Ill. Copyright, 1953, by The Free Press, A Corporation.

Something of the nature of duty is found in the desirability of morality. If it is true that the content of the act appeals to us, nevertheless its nature is such that it cannot be accomplished without effort and self-constraint. The *élan*, even the enthusiasm, with which we perform a moral act takes us outside ourselves and above our nature, and this is not achieved without difficulty and inner conflict. It is this *sui generis* desirability which is commonly called *good*.

Desirability and obligation are the two characteristics which it is useful to stress, without necessarily denying the existence of others. It will be our main intention to show that all moral acts have these two characteristics, even though they may be combined in different proportions.

.   .   .

Moral reality appears to us under two different aspects that must be clearly distinguished: the objective and the subjective.

Each people at a given moment of its history has a morality, and it is in the name of this ruling morality that tribunals condemn and opinion judges. For a given group there is a clearly defined morality. I postulate, then, supported by the facts, that there is a general morality common to all individuals belonging to a collectivity.

Now, apart from this morality there is an indefinite multitude of others. Each individual moral conscience expresses the collective morality in its own way. Each one sees it and understands it from a different angle. No individual can be completely in tune with the morality of his time, and one could say that there is no conscience that is not in some ways immoral. Each mind, under the influence of its milieu, education or heredity sees moral rules by a different light. One individual will feel the rules of civic morality keenly, but not so strongly the rules of domestic morality, or inversely. Another who feels only very slightly the duties of charity may have a profound respect for contract and justice. The most essential aspects of morality are seen differently by different people.

I do not intend to treat here of both these two sorts of moral reality, but only of the first. I shall deal with objective moral reality, that common and impersonal standard by which we evaluate action. The diversity of individual moral consciences shows how impossible it is to make use of them in order to arrive at an understanding of morality itself. Research into the conditions that determine these individual variations of morality would, no doubt, be an interesting psychological study, but would not help us to reach our particular goal.

Just as I am not concerned with the manner in which this or that particular individual sees morality, I also leave on one side the opinions of philosophers and moralists. I have nothing whatever to do with their systematic attempts to explain or construct moral reality except in so far as one can find in them a more or less adequate expression of the morality of their time. A moralist has a far greater sensibility than the average man to the dominant moral trends of his time, and consequently his consciousness is more representative of the moral reality. But I refuse to accept his doctrines as explanations, as scientific expressions of past or present moral reality.

The subject of my research and the kind of moral reality which I shall study have now been defined. But this reality can be studied in two different ways: (i) We can try to discover and to understand it, or (ii) we can set out to evaluate it at particular times.

Here I do not intend to discuss the second problem. We must begin with the first. Faced with the confusion of present moral ideas, a methodical approach is indispensable. We must begin at the beginning and progress from facts on which common agreement can be reached to see where the divergences occur. In order to judge or appreciate morality, as to evaluate life or nature (for value judgments can apply to the whole realm of reality), one must begin by acquainting oneself with moral reality.

Thus the first condition for the theoretical study of moral reality is to be able to recognize it and to distinguish it from other realities; in brief, to define it. This is not a question of giving it a philosophical definition; that can come when our research has made some headway. All that is possible or profitable is an initial, provisional definition that permits us to agree upon the reality we are dealing with; such a definition is obviously indispensable if we are to know what we are talking about.

The first question that confronts us, as in all rational and scientific research, is: By what characteristics can we recognize and distinguish moral facts?

Morality appears to us to be a collection of maxims, of rules of conduct. But there are also other rules that prescribe our behaviour. All utilitarian techniques are governed by analogous systems of rules, and we must find the distinguishing characteristics of moral rules. If we consider all the rules that govern conduct we shall be able to see whether there are not some that have peculiar and specific characteristics. If we agree that the rules that show these characteristics conform to the popular conception[1] of moral rules we shall be able to apply to them the usual title and to say that here we have the characteristics of moral reality.

To achieve any result at all in this research there is only one method of proceeding. We must discover the intrinsic differences between these moral rules and other rules through their apparent and exterior differences, for at the beginning this is all that is accessible to us. We must find a reagent that will force moral rules to demonstrate their specific character. The reagent we shall employ is this: We shall put these various rules to the test of violation and see whether from this point of view there is not some difference between moral rules and rules of technique.

The violation of a rule generally brings unpleasant consequences to the agent. But we may distinguish two different types of consequence: (i) The first results mechanically from the act of violation. If I violate a rule of hygiene that orders me to stay away from infection, the result of this act will automatically be disease. The act, once it has been performed, sets in motion the consequences, and by analysis of the act we can know in advance what the result will be. (ii) When, however, I violate the rule that forbids me to kill, an analysis of my act will tell me nothing. I shall not find inherent in it the subsequent blame or punishment. There is complete heterogeneity between the act and its consequence. It is impossible to discover *analytically* in the act of murder the slightest notion of blame. The link between act and consequence is here a *synthetic* one.

Such consequences attached to acts by synthetic links I shall call *sanctions*. I do not as yet know the origin or explanation of this link. I merely note its existence and nature, without at the moment going any further.

We can, however, enlarge upon this notion. Since sanctions are not revealed by analysis of the act that they govern, it is apparent that I am not punished *simply because* I did this or that. It is not the intrinsic nature of my action that produces the sanction which follows, but the fact that the act violates the rule that forbids it. In fact, one and the same act, identically performed with the same material consequences, is blamed or not blamed according to whether or not there is a rule forbidding it. The existence of the rule and the relation to it of the act determine the sanction. Thus homicide, condemned in time of peace, is freed from blame in time of war. An act, intrinsically the same, which is blamed today among Europeans, was not blamed in ancient Greece since there it violated no pre-established rule.

We have now reached a deeper conception of sanctions. A sanction is the consequence of an act that does not result from the content of that act, but from the violation by that act of a pre-established rule. It is because there is a pre-established rule, and the breach is a rebellion against this rule, that a sanction is entailed.

Thus there are rules that present this particular characteristic: We refrain from performing the acts they forbid simply because they are forbidden. This is what is meant by the obligatory character of the moral rule. We rediscover by a rigorously empirical analysis the idea of *duty* and obligation almost as Kant understood it.

We have so far only considered negative sanctions (blame, punishment), since in these the characteristic of obligation is most apparent. There are sanctions of another kind. Acts that conform to the moral rule are praised and those who accomplish them are honoured. In this case the public moral consciousness reacts in a different way and the consequence of the act is favorable to the agent, but the mechanism of this social phenomenon is the same. As in the preceding instance the sanction comes not from the act itself, but from its conformity to a rule that prescribes it. No doubt this type of obligation differs slightly from the former in degree, but we have here two varieties of the same group. There are not two kinds of moral rules, negative and positive commands; both are but two classes within the same category.

We have, then, defined moral obligation, and it is a definition not without interest. It shows how far the latest perfected utilitarian moralities have misconceived the problem of morality. Spencer's morality, for example, betrays a complete ignorance of the nature of obligation. For him punishment is no more than the mechanical consequence of an act (this is most apparent in his *Education* on the subject of school punishment).[2] This erroneous idea that punishment arises automatically from the act itself is widespread. In a recent inquiry into godless morality may be found the letter of a scientist who is interested in philosophy and maintains that the only punishment that a secular moralist can consider is the evil consequence of immoral acts (intemperance ruins the health, etc.).

In this way one evades the moral problem, which is precisely to explain duty, to explain its foundations and in what way it is not a hallucination but a reality.

So far we have followed Kant fairly closely. But if his analysis of moral acts is in part correct, it is nevertheless incomplete and insufficient, since it shows us only one aspect of moral reality.

We cannot perform an act which is not in some way meaningful to us simply because we have been commanded to do so. It is psychologically impossible to pursue an end to which we are indifferent—i.e., that does not appear to us as *good* and does not affect our sensibility. Morality must, then, be not only obligatory but also desirable and desired. This *desirability* is the second characteristic of all moral acts.

This desirability peculiar to moral life participates of the preceding characteristic of obligation, and is not the same as the desirability of the objects that attract our ordinary desires. The nature of our desire for the commanded act is a special one. Our *élan* and aspiration are accompanied by discipline and effort. Even when we carry out a moral act with enthusiasm we feel that we dominate and transcend ourselves, and this cannot occur without a feeling of tension and self-restraint. We feel that we do violence to a part of our being. Thus we must admit a certain element of eudemonism and one could show that desirability and pleasure permeate the obligation. We find charm in the accomplishment of a moral act prescribed by a rule that has no other justification than that it is a rule. We feel a *sui generis* pleasure in performing our duty simply because it is our duty. The notion of good enters into those of duty and obligation just as they in turn enter into the notion of good. Eudemonism and its contrary pervade moral life.

Duty, the Kantian Imperative, is only one abstract aspect of moral reality. In fact, moral reality always presents simultaneously these two aspects which cannot, in fact, be isolated. No act has ever been performed as a result of duty alone; it has always been necessary for it to appear in some respect as good. Inversely there is no act that is purely desirable, since all call for some effort.

Just as the idea of obligation, the first characteristic of moral life, gave us the opportunity to criticize utilitarianism, the second characteristic, that of goodness, shows us the insufficiency of Kant's explanation of moral obligation. Kant's hypothesis, according to which the sentiment of obligation was due to the heterogeneity of reason and sensibility, is not easy to reconcile with the fact that moral ends are in one aspect objects of desire. If to a certain extent sensibility has the same end as reason, it cannot be humbled by submitting to the latter.

Are these, then, the only two characteristics of moral reality? They are not, and I could demonstrate others. The two that I have just noted appear to me to be the most important, constant and universal. I know of no moral rule or morality where they are not found. However, in different instances they combine in varied proportions. There are acts which are accomplished almost exclusively by enthusiasm, acts of moral heroism where the element of obligation is at a minimum and where the idea of goodness predominates. There are others also where the idea of duty finds a minimum of support in the sensibility. The relation between these two elements also varies with time; thus in antiquity it would appear that the notion of duty was on the wane; in the systems of morality, and perhaps in the everyday life of the people, the idea of the Sovereign Good predominated. Generally speaking, I believe it is the same wherever morality is essentially religious. In the same epoch the relation of the two elements may vary in the extreme in different individuals. Different persons feel in different degrees the attraction of one or other of these elements, and it is very rarely indeed that both exert an equal attraction. Each one of us has his moral blind spots. There are those for whom moral acts are above all good and desirable; there are those with a greater feeling for the rule itself who enjoy discipline, loathe anything indeterminate, and wish their lives to follow a rigid program and their conduct to be constantly controlled by inflexible rules.

REFERENCES

1. The scientific notion is not he same as the popular notion, which may be erroneous. Popular opinion may deny the qualification *moral* to rules which show all the signs of being moral precepts. All that is necessary is that the difference be not so great as to render the retention of the more usual term inconvenient. Thus the zoologist may speak of 'fish' even though his conception is not identical with the popular one.
2. *Education, Intellectual, Physical and Moral*, Ch. III, London, 1961, D. F. P.

# THE INTERNALIZATION OF SOCIAL CONTROL II * (*Mead*)

We have discussed at length the social foundations of the self, and hinted that the self does not consist simply in the bare organization of social attitudes. We may now explicitly raise the question as to the nature of the "I" which is aware of the social "me." I do not mean to raise the metaphysical question of how a person can be both "I" and "me," but to ask for the significance of this distinction from the point of view of conduct itself. Where in conduct does the "I" come in as over against the "me"? If one determines what his position is in society and feels himself as having a certain function and privilege, these are all defined with reference to an "I," but the "I" is not a "me" and cannot become a "me." We may have a better self and a worse self, but that again is not the "I" as over against the "me," because they are both selves. We approve of one and disapprove of the other, but when we bring up one or the other they are there for such approval as "me's." The "I" does not get into the limelight; we talk to ourselves, but do not see ourselves. The "I" reacts to the self which arises through the taking of the attitudes of others. Through taking those attitudes we have introduced the "me" and we react to it as an "I."

* Reprinted from *Mind, Self and Society* by George H. Mead (edited by Charles W. Morris), pp. 173–178, by permission of The University of Chicago Press. Copyright. 1934, by The University of Chicago.

The simplest way of handling the problem would be in terms of memory. I talk to myself, and I remember what I said and perhaps the emotional content that went with it. The "I" of this moment is present in the "me" of the next moment. There again I cannot turn around quick enough to catch myself. I become a "me" in so far as I remember what I said. The "I" can be given, however, this functional relationship. It is because of the "I" that we say that we are never fully aware of what we are, that we surprise ourselves by our own action. It is as we act that we are aware of ourselves. It is in memory that the "I" is constantly present in experience. We can go back directly a few moments in our experience, and then we are dependent upon memory images for the rest. So that the "I" in memory is there as the spokesman of the self of the second, or minute, or day ago. As given, it is a "me" but it is a "me" which was the "I" at the earlier time. If you ask, then, where directly in your own experience the "I" comes in, the answer is that it comes in as a historical figure. It is what you were a second ago that is the "I" of the "me." It is another "me" that has to take that role. You cannot get the immediate response of the "I" in the process.[1] The "I" is in a certain sense that with which we do identify ourselves. The getting of it into experience constitutes one of the problems of most of our conscious experience; it is not directly given in experience.

The "I" is the response of the organism to the attitudes of the other;[2] the "me" is the organized set of attitudes of others which one himself assumes. The attitudes of the others constitute the organized "me," and then one reacts toward that as an "I." I now wish to examine these concepts in greater detail.

There is neither "I" nor "me" in the conversation of gestures; the whole act is not yet carried out, but the preparation takes place in this field of gesture. Now, in so far as the individual arouses in himself the attitudes of the others, there arises an organized group of responses. And it is due to the individual's ability to take the attitudes of these others in so far as they can be organized that he gets self-consciousness. The taking of all of those organized sets of attitudes gives him his "me"; that is the self he is aware of. He can throw the ball to some other member because of the demand made upon him from other members of the team. That is the self that immediately exists for him in his consciousness. He has their attitudes, knows what they want and what the consequences of any act of his will be, and he has assumed responsibility for the situation. Now, it is the presence of those organized sets of attitudes that constitutes that "me" to which he as an "I" is responding. But what that response will be he does not know and nobody else knows. Perhaps he will make a brilliant play or an error. The response to that situation as it appears in his immediate experience is uncertain, and it is that which constitutes the "I."

The "I" is his action over against that social situation within his own conduct, and it gets into his experience only after he has carried out the act. Then he is aware of it. He had to do such a thing and he did it. He fulfills his duty and he may look with pride at the throw which he made. The "me" arises to do that duty—that is the way in which it arises in his experience. He had in him all the attitudes of others, calling for a certain response; that was the "me" of that situation, and his response is the "I."

I want to call attention particularly to the fact that this response of the "I" is something that is more or less uncertain. The attitudes of others which one assumes as affecting his own conduct constitute the "me," and that is something that is there, but the response to it is as yet not given. When one sits down to think anything out, he has certain data that are there. Suppose that it is a social situation which he has to straighten out. He sees himself from the point of view of one individual or another in the group. These individuals, related all together, give him a certain self. Well, what is he going to do? He does now know and nobody else knows. He can get the situation into his experience because he can assume the attitudes of the various individuals involved in it. He knows how they feel about it by the assumption of their attitudes. He says, in effect, "I have done certain things that seem to commit me to a certain course of conduct." Perhaps if he does so act it will place him in a false position with another group. The "I" as a response to this situation, in contrast to the "me" which is involved in the attitudes which he takes, is uncertain. And when the response takes place, then it appears in the field of experience largely as a memory image.

Our specious present as such is very short. We do, however, experience passing events; part of the process of the passage of events is directly there in our experience, including some of the past and some of the future. We see a ball falling as it passes, and as it does pass part of the ball is covered and part is being uncovered. We remember where the ball was a moment ago and we anticipate where it will be beyond what is given in our experience. So of ourselves; we are doing something, but to look back and see what we are doing involves getting memory images. So the "I" really appears experientially as a part of a "me." But on the basis of this experience we distinguish that individual who is doing something from the "me" who puts the problem up to him. The response enters into his experience only when it takes place. If he says he knows what he is going to do, even there he may be mistaken. He starts out to do something and something happens to interfere. The resulting action is always a little different from anything which he could anticipate. This is true even if he is simply carrying out the process of walking. The very taking of his expected steps puts him in a certain situation which has a slightly different aspect from what is expected, which is in a certain sense novel. That movement into the future is the step, so to speak, of the ego, of the "I." It is something that is not given in the "me."

Take the situation of a scientist solving a problem, where he has certain data which call for certain responses. Some of this set of data call for his applying such and such a law, while others call for another law. Data are there with their implications. He knows what such and such coloration means, and when he has these data before him they stand for certain responses on his part; but now they are in conflict with each other. If he makes one response he cannot make another. What he is going to do he does not know, nor does anybody else. The action of the self is in response to these conflicting sets of data in the form of a problem, with conflicting demands upon him as a scientist. He has to look at it in different ways. That action of the "I" is something the nature of which we cannot tell in advance.

The "I," then, in this relation of the "I" and the "me," is something that is, so to speak, responding to a social situation which is within the experience of the individual. It is the answer which the individual makes to the attitude which others take toward him when he assumes an attitude toward them. Now, the attitudes he is taking toward them are present in his own experience, but his response to them will contain a novel element. The "I" gives the sense of freedom, of initiative. The situation is there for us to act in a self-conscious fashion. We are aware of ourselves, and of what the situation is, but exactly how we will act never gets into experience until after the action takes place.

Such is the basis for the fact that the "I" does not appear in the same sense in experience as does the "me." The "me" represents a definite organization of the community there in our own attitudes, and calling for a response, but the response that takes place is something that just happens. There is no certainty in regard to it. There is a moral necessity but no mechanical necessity for the act. When it does take place then we find what has been done. The above account gives us, I think, the relative position of the "I" and "me" in the situation, and the grounds for the separation of the two in behavior. The two are separated in the process but they belong together in the sense of being parts of a whole. They are separated and yet they belong together. The separation of the "I" and the "me" is not fictitious. They are not identical, for, as I have said, the "I" is something that is never entirely calculable. The "me" does call for a certain sort of an "I" in so far as we meet the obligations that are given in conduct itself, but the "I" is always something different from what the situation itself calls for. So there is always that distinction, if you like, between the "I" and the "me." The "I" both calls out the "me" and responds to it. Taken together they constitute a personality as it appears in social experience. The self is essentially a social process going on with these two distinguishable phases. If it did not have these two phases there could not be conscious responsibility, and there would be nothing novel in experience.

REFERENCES

1. The sensitivity of the organism brings parts of itself into the environment. It does not, however, bring the life-process itself into the environment, and the complete imaginative presentation of the organism is unable to present the living of the organism. It can conceivably present the conditions under which living takes place but not the unitary life-process. The physical organism in the environment always remains a thing (MS).
2. [For the "I" viewed as the biologic individual, see Supplementary Essays II, III.]


# THE INTERNALIZATION OF SOCIAL CONTROL III * (*Piaget*)

The analysis of the child's moral judgments has led us perforce to the discussion of the great problem of the relations of social life to the rational consciousness. The conclusion we came to was that the morality prescribed for the individual by society is not homogeneous because society itself is not just one thing. Society is the sum of social relations, and among these relations we can distinguish two extreme types: relations of constraint, whose characteristic is to impose upon the individual from outside a system of rules with obligatory content, and relations of cooperation whose characteristic is to create within people's minds the consciousness of ideal norms at the back of all rules. Arising from the ties of authority and unilateral respect, the relations of constraint therefore characterize most of the features of society as it exists, and in particular the relations of the child to its adult surrounding. Defined by equality and mutual respect, the relations of cooperation, on the contrary, constitute an equilibrial limit rather than a static system. Constraint, the source of duty and heteronomy, cannot, therefore, be

* Reprinted from *The Moral Judgment of the Child* by Jean Piaget, pp. 401–411, by permission of the publishers, The Free Press, Glencoe, Ill., and Routledge & Kegan Paul Ltd., London. Copyright, 1951, by The Free Press, A Corporation.

reduced to the good and to autonomous rationality, which are the fruits of reciprocity, although the actual evolution of the relations of constraint tends to bring these nearer to cooperation.

In spite of our wish to confine the discussion to the problems connected with child psychology, the reader will not have failed to recognize the affinity of these results with those of the historical or logico-sociological analyses carried out by M. Brunschvicg and M. Lalande. *Le Progrès de la Conscience dans la Philosophie occidentale* is the widest and the most subtle demonstration of the fact that there exists in European thought a law in the evolution of moral judgments which is analogous to the law of which psychology watches the effects throughout the development of the individual. Now to indulge in philosophic enquiry is simply to take increasing cognizance of the currents of thought which enter into and sustain the states of society itself. What the philosopher does is not so much to create something new as to reflect the elaborations of the human mind. It is therefore of the utmost significance that the critical analysis of history which M. Brunschvicg has put to fresh use should have succeeded in bringing to light in the evolution of Western philosophic thought the gradual victory of the norms of reciprocity over those of social conformism.

As to M. Lalande, what he says on "la dissolution" as also on the social character of logical norms, has shown more than any other work on the subject the duality that lies hidden in the word "social." There are, M. Lalande tells us, two societies: existing or organized society, whose constant feature is the constraint which it exercises upon individual minds, and there is the ideal or assimilative society, which is defined by the progressive identification of people's minds with one another. The reader will recognize here the same distinction as we have been led to observe between the relations of authority and the relations of equality.

Some of M. Lalande's minor contentions would, indeed, stand in the way of our complete agreement with his ideas taken as a whole. It does not seem to us at all certain, for example, that "evolution" in the sense of progressive organization is necessarily bound up with a society based on constraint. The passage from the homogeneous to the heterogeneous which M. Lalande agrees with Spencer in taking as the mark of evolution leads no doubt to social differentiation. But this differentiation is precisely, as the sociologists have pointed out, the condition of a break with the conformity due to constraint, and consequently the condition of personal liberation. Moral equality is not the result of an advance towards homogeneity, assuming that agreement can be reached on the meaning of this word, but of a mobility which is a function of differentiation. The more differentiated the society, the better can its members alter their situation is accordance with their aptitudes, the greater will be the opportunity for intellectual and moral cooperation. We cannot, therefore, take the identification of minds, which, for M. Lalande, is the supreme norm, to be the same thing as cooperation. Without attempting to evaluate this "vector," and limiting ourselves to the mere description of psychological facts, what the morality of the good seems to us to achieve is reciprocity rather than identification. The morality of the autonomous conscience does not tend to subject each personality to rules that have a common content: it simply obliges individuals to "place themselves" in reciprocal relationship with each other without letting the laws of perspective resultant upon this reciprocity destroy their individual points of view.

But what do these minor discrepancies matter since it is thanks to M. Lalande's teaching that we are able to dissociate what the sociologists have so often tended to confuse? And above all, what do the concepts that are used in the interpretation of the facts matter, so long as the method employed is the same? For in the work of M. Lalande we have an example of that rare thing—research on the evolution of norms conducted well within the limits of the psycho-sociological method. Without in any way neglecting the demands of rationality, this great logician has been able to discern in intellectual and moral assimilation processes admitting of analysis in terms of social psychology while implying by their very "direction" the existence of ideal norms immanent in the human spirit.

This concordance of ours results with those of historico-critical or logico-sociological analysis brings us to a second point: the parallelism existing between moral and intellectual development. Everyone is aware of the kinship between logical and ethical norms. Logic is the morality of thought just as morality is the logic of action. Nearly all contemporary theories agree in recognizing the existence of this parallelism—from the *a priori* view which regards pure reason as the arbiter both of theoretical reflection and daily practice, to the sociological theories of knowledege and of ethical values. It is therefore in no way surprising that the analysis of child thought should bring to the fore certain particular aspects of this general phenomenon.[1]

One may say, to begin with, that in a certain sense neither logical nor moral norms are innate in the individual mind. We can find, no doubt, even before language, all the elements of rationality and morality. Thus sensorimotor intelligence gives rise to operations of assimilation and construction, in which it is not hard to see the functional equivalent of the logic of classes and of relations. Similarly the child's behaviour towards persons shows signs from the first of those sympathetic tendencies and affective reactions in which one can easily see the raw material of all subsequent moral behaviour. But an intelligent act can only be called logical and a goodhearted impulse moral from the moment that certain norms impress a given structure and rules of equilibrium upon this material. Logic is not co-extensive with intelligence, but consists of the sum-total of rules of control which intelligence makes use of for its own direction. Morality plays a similar part with regard to the affective life. Now there is nothing that allows us to affirm the existence of such norms in the pre-social behaviour occurring before the appearance of language. The control characteristic of sensori-motor intelligence is of external origin: it is things themselves that constrain the organism to select which steps it will take; the initial intellectual activity does actively seek for truth. Similarly, it is persons external to him who canalize the child's elementary feelings, those feelings do not tend to regulate themselves from within.

This does not mean that everything in the *a priori* view is to be rejected. Of course the *a priori* never manifests itself in the form of ready-made innate mechanisms. The *a priori* is the obligatory element, and the necessary connections only impose themselves little by little, as evolution proceeds. It is at the end of knowledge and not in its beginnings that the mind becomes conscious of the laws immanent to it. Yet to speak of directed evolution and asymptotic advance towards a necessary ideal is to recognize the existence of a something which acts from the first in the direction of this evolution. But under what form does this "something" present itself? Under the form of a structure that straightway organizes the contents of consciousness, or under the form of a functional law of equilibrium, unconscious as yet because the mind has not yet achieved this equilibrium, and to be manifested only in and through the multitudinous structures that are to appear later? There seems to us to be no doubt about the answer. There is in the very functioning of sensori-motor operations a search for coherence and organization. Alongside, therefore, of the incoherence that characterizes the successive steps taken by elementary intelligence we must admit the existence of an ideal equilibrium, indefinable as structure but implied in the functioning that is at work Such is the *a priori*: it is neither a principle from which concrete actions can be deduced nor a structure of which the mind can become conscious as such, but it is a sum-total of functional relations implying the distinction between the existing states of disequilibrium and an ideal equilibrium yet to be realized.

How then will the mind extract norms in the true sense from this functional equilibrium? It will form structures by means of an adequate conscious realization (*prise de conscience*). To ensure that the functional search for organization exhibited by the initial sensori-motor and affective activity give rise to rules of organization properly so called, it is sufficient that the mind should become conscious of this search and of the laws governing it, thus translating into structure what till then had been function and nothing more.

But this coming into consciousness or conscious realization is not a simple operation and is bound up with a whole set of psychological conditions. It is here that psycho-sociological research becomes indispensable to the theory of norms and that the genetic parallelism existing between the formation of the logical and of the moral consciousness can be observed.

In the first place it should be noticed that the individual is not capable of achieving this conscious realization by himself, and consequently does not straight away succeed in establishing norms properly so called. It is in this sense that reason in its double aspect, both logical and moral, is a collective product. This does not mean that society has conjured up rationality out of the void, nor that there does not exist a spirit of humanity that is superior to society because dwelling both within the individual and the social group. It means that social life is necessary if the individual is to become conscious of the functioning of his own mind and thus to transform into norms properly so called the simple functional equilibria immanent in all mental and even all vital activity.

For the individual, left to himself, remains egocentric. By which we mean simply this—just as at first the mind, before it can dissociate what belongs to objective laws from what is bound up with the sum of subjective conditions, confuses itself with the universe, so does the individual begin by understanding and feeling everything through the medium of himself before distinguishing what belongs to things and other people from what is the result of his own particular intellectual and affective perspective. At this stage, therefore, the individual cannot be conscious of his own thought, since consciousness of self implies a perpetual comparison of the self with other people. Thus from the logical point of view egocentrism would seem to involve a sort of alogicality, such that sometimes affectivity gains the ascendant over objectivity, and sometimes the relations arising from personal activity prove stronger than the relations that are independent of the self. And from the moral point of view, egocentrism involves a sort of anomie such that tenderness and disinterestedness can go hand in hand with a naive selfishness, and yet the child not feel spontaneously himself to be better in one case than the other. Just as the ideas which enter his mind appear from the first in the form of beliefs and not of hypotheses requiring verification, so do the feelings that arise in the child's consciousness appear to him from the first as having value and not as having to be submitted to some ulterior evaluation. It is only through contact with the judgments and evaluations of others that this intellectual and affective anomie will gradually yield to the pressure of collective logical and moral laws.

In the second place, the relations of constraint and unilateral respect which are spontaneously established between child and adult contribute to the formation of a first type of logical and moral control. But this control is insufficient of itself to eliminate childish egocentrism. From the intellectual point of view this respect of the child for the adult gives rise to an "annunciatory" conception of truth: the mind stops affirming what it likes to affirm and falls in with the opinion of those around it. This gives birth to a distinction which is equivalent to that of truth and falsehood: some affirmations are recognized as valid while others are not. But it goes without saying that although this distinction marks an important advance as compared to the anomie of egocentric thought, it is none the less irrational in principle. For if we are to speak of truth as rational, it is not sufficient that the contents of one's statements should conform with reality: reason must have taken active steps to obtain these contents and reason must be in a position to control the agreement or disagreement of these statements with reality. Now, in the case under discussion, reason is still very far removed from this autonomy: truth means whatever conforms with the spoken word of the adult. Whether the child has himself discovered the propositions which he asks the adult to sanction with his authority, or whether he merely repeats what the adult has said, in both cases there is intellectual constraint put upon an inferior by a superior, and therefore heteronomy. Thus, far from checking childish egocentrism at its source, such a submission tends on the contrary partly to consolidate the mental habits characteristic of egocentrism. Just as, if left to himself, the child believes every idea that enters his head instead of regarding it as a hypothesis to be verified, so the child who is submissive to the word of his parents believes without question everything he is told, instead of perceiving the element of uncertainty and search in adult thought. The self's good pleasure is simply replaced by the good pleasure of a supreme authority. There is progress here, no doubt, since such a transference accustoms the mind to look for a common truth, but this progress is big with danger if the supreme authority be not in its turn criticized in the name of reason. Now, criticism is born of discussion, and discussion is only possible among equals: cooperation alone will therefore accomplish what intellectual constraint failed to bring about. And indeed we constantly have occasion throughout our schools to notice the combined effects of this constraint and of intellectual egocentrism. What is "verbalism," for example, if not the joint result of oral authority and the syncretism peculiar to the egocentric language of the child? In short, in order to really socialize the child, cooperation is necessary, for it alone will succeed in delivering him from the mystical power of the word of the adult.

An exact counterpart of these findings about intellectual constraint is supplied by the observations on the effect of moral constraint contained in the present book. Just as the child believes in the adult's omniscience so also does he unquestioningly believe in the absolute value of the imperatives he receives. This result of unilateral respect is of great practical value, for it is in this way that there is formed an elementary sense of duty and the first normative control of which the child is capable. But it seemed to us clear that this acquisition was not sufficient to form true morality. For conduct to be characterized as moral there must be something more than an outward agreement between its content and that of the commonly accepted rules: it is also requisite that the mind should tend towards morality as to an autonomous good and should itself be capable of appreciating the value of the rules that are proposed to it. Now in the case under discussion, the good is simply what is in conformity with heteronomous commands. And as in the case of intellectual development, moral constraint has the effect of partly consolidating the habits characteristic of egocentrism. Even when the child's behaviour is not just a calculated attempt to reconcile his individual interest with the letter of the law, one can observe (as we had occasion to do in the game of marbles) a curious mixture of respect for the law and of caprice in its application. The law is still external to the mind, which cannot therefore be transformed by it. Besides, since he regards the adult as the source of the law, the child is only raising up the will of the adult to the rank of the supreme good after having previously accorded this rank to the various dictates of his own desires. An advance, no doubt, but again an advance charged with doubtful consequences if cooperation does not come and establish norms sufficiently independent to subject even the respect due to the adult to this inner ideal. And indeed so long as unilateral respect is alone at work, we see a "moral realism." Resting in part on the externality of rules, such a realism is also kept going by all the other forms of realism peculiar to the egocentric mentality of the child. Only cooperation will correct his attitude, thus showing that in the moral sphere, as in matters of intelligence, it plays a liberating and a constructive role.

Hence a third analogy between moral and intellectual evolution: cooperation alone leads to autonomy. With regard to logic, cooperation is at first a source of criticism; thanks to the mutual control which it introduces, it suppresses both the spontaneous conviction that characterizes egocentrism and the blind faith in adult authority. Thus, discussion gives rise to reflection and objective verification. But through this very fact cooperation becomes the source of constructive values. It leads to the recognition of the principles of formal logic in so far as these normative laws are necessary to common search for truth. It leads, above all, to a conscious realization of the logic of relations, since reciprocity on the intellectual plane necessarily involves elaboration of those laws of perspective which we find in the operations distinctive of systems of relations.

In the same way, with regard to moral realities, cooperation is at first the source of criticism and individualism. For by comparing his own private motives with the rules adopted by each and sundry, the individual is led to judge objectively the acts and commands of other people, including adults. Whence the decline of unilateral respect and the primacy of personal judgment. But in consequence of this, cooperation suppresses both egocentrism and moral realism, and thus achieves an interiorization of rules. A new morality follows upon that of pure duty. Heteronomy steps aside to make way for a consciousness of good, of which the autonomy results from the acceptance of the norms of reciprocity. Obedience withdraws in favour of the idea of justice and of mutual service, now the source of all the obligations which till then had been imposed as incomprehensible commands. In a word, cooperation on the moral plane brings about transformations exactly parallel to those of which we have just been recalling the existence in the intellectual domain.

REFERENCE

1. We have further developed this point at the Ninth International Congress of Psychology which met at New Haven (U.S.A.). See *Ninth International Congress of Psychology, Proceedings and Papers*, p. 339.

# THE OVERSOCIALIZED CONCEPTION OF MAN IN MODERN SOCIOLOGY* (Wrong)

I wish briefly to review the answers modern sociological theory offers to one [crucial] question, or rather to one aspect of one question. The question may be variously phrased as, "What are the sources of social cohesion?"; or, "How is social order possible?"; or, stated in social-psychological terms, "How is it that man becomes tractable to social discipline?" I shall call this

*Reprinted from *The American Sociological Review*, XXVI, pp. 184–193, by permission of the publisher, The American Sociological Association, and the author.

question in its social-psychological aspect the "Hobbesian question" and in its more strictly sociological aspect the "Marxist question." The Hobbesian question asks how men are capable of the guidance by social norms and goals that makes possible an enduring society, while the Marxist question asks how, assuming this capability, complex societies manage to regulate and restrain destructive conflicts between groups. Much of our current theory offers an oversocialized view of man in answering the Hobbesian question and an overintegrated view of society in answering the Marxist question.

. . .

Since my view of theory is obviously very different from that of Talcott Parsons and has, in fact, been developed in opposition to his, let me pay tribute to his recognition of the importance of the Hobbesian question— the "problem of order," as he calls it—at the very beginning of his first book, *The Structure of Social Action*.[1] Parsons correctly credits Hobbes with being the first thinker to see the necessity of explaining why human society is not a "war of all against all"; why, if man is simply a gifted animal, men refrain from unlimited resort to fraud and violence in pursuit of their ends and maintain a stable society at all. There is even a sense in which, as Coser and Mills have both noted,[2] Parsons' entire work represents an effort to solve the Hobbesian problem of order.

. . .

The polar terms in Hobbes' theory are the state of nature, where the war of all against all prevails, and the authority of Leviathan, created by social contract. But the war of all against all is not simply effaced with the creation of political authority: it remains an ever-present potentiality in human society, at times quiescent, at times erupting into open violence. Whether Hobbes believed that the state of nature and the social contract were ever historical realities—and there is evidence that he was not that simple-minded and unsociological, even in the seventeenth century—is unimportant; the whole tenor of his thought is to see the war of all against all and Leviathan dialectically, as coexisting and interacting opposites. As R. G. Collingwood has observed, "According to Hobbes . . . *a body politic is a dialectical thing*, a Heraclitean world in which at any given time there is a negative element."[3] The first secular social theorist in the history of Western thought, and one of the first clearly to discern and define the problem of order in human society long before Darwinism made awareness of it a commonplace, Hobbes was a dialectical thinker who refused to separate answers from questions, solutions to society's enduring problems from the conditions creating the problems.

What is the answer of contemporary sociological theory to the Hobbesian question? There are two main answers, each of which has come to be understood in a way that denies the reality and meaningfulness of the question. Together they constitute a model of human nature, sometimes clearly stated, more often implicit in accepted concepts, that pervades modern sociology. The first answer is summed up in the notion of the "internalization of social norms." The second, more commonly employed or assumed in empirical research, is the view that man is essentially motivated by the desire to achieve a positive image of self by winning acceptance or status in the eyes of others.

The following statement represents, briefly and broadly, what is probably the most influential contemporary sociological conception—and dismissal—of the Hobbesian problem: "To a modern sociologist imbued with the conception that action follows institutionalized patterns, opposition of individual and common interests has only a very limited relevance or is thoroughly unsound." From this writer's perspective, the problem is an unreal one: human conduct is totally shaped by common norms or "institutionalized patterns." Sheer ignorance must have led people who were unfortunate enough not to be modern sociologists to ask, "How is order possible?" A thoughtful bee or ant would never inquire, "How is the social order of the hive or ant-hill possible?" for the opposite of that order is unimaginable when the instinctive endowment of the insects ensures its stability and built-in harmony between "individual and common interests." Human society, we are assured, is not essentially different, although conformity and stability are there maintained by non-instinctive processes. Modern sociologists believe that they have understood these processes and that they have not merely answered but disposed of the Hobbesian question, showing that, far from expressing a valid intimation of the tensions and possibilities of social life, it can only be asked out of ignorance.

It would be hard to find a better illustration of what Collingwood, following Plato, calls *eristical* as opposed to dialectical thinking:[4] the answer destroys the question, or rather destroys the awareness of rival possibilities suggested by the question which accounts for its having been asked in the first place. A reversal of perspective now takes place and we are moved to ask the opposite question: "How is it that violence, conflict, revolution, and the individual's sense of coercion by society manage to exist at all, if this view is correct?"[5] Whenever a one-sided answer to a question compels us to raise the opposite question, we are caught up in a dialectic of concepts which reflects a dialectic in things. But let us examine the particular processes sociologists appeal to in order to account for the elimination from human society of the war of all against all.

## The Changing Meaning of Internalization

A well-known section of *The Structure of Social Action*, devoted to the interpretation of Durkheim's thought, is entitled "The Changing Meaning of Constraint."[6] Parsons argues that Durkheim originally conceived of society as controlling the individual from the outside by imposing constraints on him through sanctions, best illustrated by codes of law. But in Durkheim's later work he began to see that social rules do not "merely regulate 'externally' . . . they enter directly into the constitution of the actors' ends themselves."[7] Constraint, therefore, is more than an environmental obstacle which the actor must take into account in pursuit of his goals in the same way that he takes into account physical laws: it becomes internal, psychological, and self-imposed as well. Parsons developed this view that social norms are constitutive rather than merely regulative of human nature before he was influenced by psychoanalytic theory, but Freud's theory of the superego has become the sources and model for the conception of the internalization of social norms that today plays so important a part in sociological thinking. The use some sociologists have made of Freud's idea, however, might well inspire an essay entitled, "The Changing Meaning of Internalization," although, in contrast to the shift in Durkheim's view of constraint, this change has been a change for the worse.

What has happened is that internalization has imperceptibly been equated with "learning," or even with "habit-formation" in the simplest sense. Thus when a norm is said to have been "internalized" by an individual, what is frequently meant is that he habitually both affirms it and conforms to it in his conduct. The whole stress on inner conflict, on the tension between powerful impulses and superego controls the behavioral outcome of which cannot be prejudged, drops out of the picture. And it is this that is central to Freud's view, for in psychoanalytic terms to say that a norm has been internalized, or introjected to become part of the superego, is to say no more than that a person will suffer guilt-feelings if he fails to live up to it, not that he will in fact live up to it in his behavior.

. . .

The main explanatory function of the concept [of the superego] is to show how people repress themselves, imposing checks on their own desires and thus turning the inner life into a battlefield of conflicting motives, no matter which side "wins," by successfully dictating overt action. So far as behavior is concerned, the psychoanalytic view of man is less deterministic than the sociological. For psychoanalysis is primarily concerned with the inner life, not with overt behavior, and its most fundamental insight is that the wish, the emotion, and the fantasy are as important as the act in man's experience.

Sociologists have appropriated the superego concept, but have separated it from any equivalent of the Freudian id. So long as most individuals are "socialized," that is, internalize the norms and conform to them in conduct, the Hobbesian problem is not even perceived as a latent reality.

. . .

Tendencies to deviant behavior are not seen as dialectically related to conformity. The presence in man of motivational forces bucking against the hold social discipline has over him is denied.

Nor does the assumption that internalization of norms and roles is the essence of socialization allow for a sufficient range of motives underlying conformity. It fails to allow for variable "tonicity of the superego," in Kardiner's phrase.[8] The degree to which conformity is frequently the result of coercion rather than conviction is minimized.[9] Either someone has internalized the norms, or he is "unsocialized," a feral or socially isolated child, or a psychopath. Yet Freud recognized that many people, conceivably a majority, fail to acquire superegos. "Such people," he wrote, "habitually permit themselves to do any bad deed that procures them something they want, if only they are sure that no authority will discover it or make them suffer for it; their anxiety relates only to the possibility of detection. Present-day society has to take into account the prevalence of this state of mind."[10] The last sentence suggests that Freud was aware of the decline of "inner-direction," of the Protestant conscience, about which we have heard so much lately. So let us turn to the other elements of human nature that sociologists appeal to in order to explain, or rather explain away, the Hobbesian problem.

## Man the Acceptance-Seeker

The superego concept is too inflexible, too bound to the past and to individual biography, to be of service in relating conduct to the pressures of the immediate situation in which it takes place. Sociologists rely more heavily therefore on an alternative notion, here stated—or, to be fair, overstated—in its baldest form: "People are so profoundly sensitive to the expectations of others that all action is inevitably guided by these expectations."

Parsons' model of the "complementarity of expectations," the view that in social interaction men mutually seek approval from one another by conforming to shared norms, is a formalized version of what has tended to become a distinctive sociological perspective on human motivation. Ralph Linton states it in explicit psychological terms: "The need for eliciting favorable responses from others is an almost constant component of [personality]. Indeed, it is not too much to say that there is very little organized human behavior which is not directed toward its satisfaction in at least some degree."[11]

The insistence of sociologists on the importance of "social factors" easily leads them to stress the priority of such socialized or socializing motives in human behavior. It is frequently the task of the sociologist to call attention to the intensity with which men desire and strive for the good opinion of their immediate associates in a variety of situations, particularly those where received theories or ideologies have unduly emphasized other motives such as financial gain, commitment to ideals, or the effects on energies and aspirations of arduous physical conditions. Thus sociologists have shown that factory workers are more sensitive to the attitudes of their fellow-workers than to purely economic incentives; that voters are more influenced by the preferences of their relatives and friends than by campaign debates on the "issues"; that soldiers, whatever their ideological commitment to their nation's cause, fight more bravely when their platoons are intact and they stand side by side with their "buddies."

It is certainly not my intention to criticize the findings of such studies. My objection is that their particular selective emphasis is generalized—explicitly or, more often, implicitly—to provide apparent empirical support for an extremely one-sided view of human nature. Although sociologists have criticized past efforts to single out one fundamental motive in human conduct, the desire to achieve a favorable self-image by winning approval from others frequently occupies such a position in their own thinking. The following "theorem" has been, in fact, openly put forward by Hans Zetterberg as "a strong contender for the position as the major Motivational Theorem in sociology":[21]

> *An actor's actions have a tendency to become dispositions that are related to the occurence* [sic] *of favored uniform evaluations of the actor and-or his actions in his action system.*[13]

Now Zetterberg is not necessarily maintaining that this theorem is an accurate factual statement of the basic psychological roots of social behavior. He is, characteristically, far too self-conscious about the logic of theorizing and "concept formation" for that. He goes on to remark that "the maximization of favorable attitudes from others would thus be the counterpart in sociological theory to the maximization of profit in economic theory."[14]

But there is a further point to be made. Ralf Dahrendorf has observed that structural-functional theorists do not "claim that order *is based on* a general consensus of values, but that it *can be conceived of in terms of* such consensus and that, if it is conceived of in these terms, certain propositions follow which are subject to the test of specific observations."[15] The same may be said of the assumption that people seek to maximize favorable evaluations by others.

      ·     ·     ·

Yet the question must be raised as to whether we really wish to, in effect, define sociology by such partial perspectives. The assumption of the maximization of approval from others is the psychological complement to the sociological assumption of a general value consensus. And the former is as selective and one-sided a way of looking at motivation as Dahrendorf and others have argued the latter to be when it determines our way of looking at social structure. The oversocialized view of man of the one is a counterpart to the overintegrated view of society of the other.

Modern sociology, after all, originated as a protest against the partial views of man contained in such doctrines as utilitarianism, classical economics, social Darwinism, and vulgar Marxism. All of the great nineteenth and early twentieth century sociologists saw it as one of their major tasks to expose the unreality of such abstraction as economic man, the gain-seeker of the classical economists; political man, the power-seeker of the Machiavellian tradition in political science; self-preserving man, the security-seeker of Hobbes and Darwin; sexual or libidinal man, the pleasure-seeker of the doctrinaire Freudianism; and even religious man, the God-seeker of the theologians. It would be ironical if it should turn out that they have merely contributed to the creation of yet another deified abstraction in socialized man, the status-seeker of our contemporary sociologists.

Of course, such an image of man is, like all the others mentioned, valuable for limited purposes so long as it is not taken for the whole truth. What are some of its deficiencies? To begin with, it neglects the other half of the model of human nature presupposed by current theory: moral man, guided by his built-in superego and beckoning ego-ideal. In recent years sociologists have been less interested than they once were in culture and national character as backgrounds to conduct, partly because stress on the concept of "role" as the crucial link between the individual and the social structure has directed their attention to the immediate situation in which social interaction takes place. Man is increasingly seen as a "role-playing" creature, responding eagerly or anxiously to the expectations of other role-players in the multiple group settings in which he finds himself. Such an approach, while valuable in helping us grasp the complexity of a highly differentiated social structure such as our own, is far too often generalized to serve as a kind of *ad hoc* social psychology, easily adaptable to particular sociological purposes.

But it is not enough to concede that men often pursue "internalized values" remaining indifferent to what others think of them, particularly when, as I have previously argued, the idea of internalization has been "hollowed out" to make it more useful as an explanation of conformity. What of desire for material and sensual satisfactions? Can we really dispense with the venerable notion of material "interests" and invariably replace it with the blander, more integrative "social values"? And what of striving for power, not necessarily for its own sake—that may be rare and pathological —but as a means by which men are able to *impose* a normative definition of reality on others? That material interests, sexual drives, and the quest for power have often been over-estimated as human motives is no reason to deny their reality. To do so is to suppress one term of the dialectic between conformity and rebellion, social norms and their violation, man and social order, as completely as the other term is suppressed by those who deny the reality of man's "normative orientation" or reduce it to the effect of coercion, rational calculation, or mechanical conditioning.

## Social But Not Entirely Socialized

I have referred to forces in man that are resistant to socialization. It is not my purpose to explore the nature of these forces or to suggest how we ought best conceive of them as sociologists—that would be a most ambitious undertaking. A few remarks will have to suffice. I think we must start with the recognition that *in the beginning there is the body*. As soon as the body is mentioned the specter of "biological determinism" raises its head and sociologists draw back in fright. And certainly their view of man is sufficiently disembodied and non-materialistic to satisfy Bishop Berkeley, as well as being de-sexualized enough to please Mrs. Grundy.

Am I, then, urging us to return to the older view of a human nature divided between a "social man" and a "natural man" who is either benevolent, Rousseau's Noble Savage, or sinister and destructive, as Hobbes regarded him? Freud is usually represented, or misrepresented, as the chief modern proponent of this dualistic conception which assigns to the social order the purely negative role of blocking and re-directing man's "imperious biological drives."[16] I say "misrepresented" because, although Freud often said things supporting such an interpretation, other and more fundamental strains in his thinking suggest a different conclusion. John Dollard, certainly not a writer who is oblivious to social and cultural "views" saw this twenty-five years ago: "It is quite clear," he wrote, ". . . that he (Freud) does not regard the instincts as having a fixed social goal; rather, indeed, in the case of the sexual instinct he has stressed the vague but powerful and impulsive nature of the drive and has emphasized that its proper social object is not picked out in advance. His seems to be a drive concept which is not at variance with our knowledge from comparative cultural studies, since his theory does not demand that the 'instinct' work itself out with mechanical certainty alike in every varying culture."[17]

So much for Freud's "imperious biological drives!" When Freud defined psychoanalysis as the study of the "vicissitudes of the instincts," he was confirming, not denying, the "plasticity" of human nature insisted on by social scientists. The drives or "instincts" of psychoanalysis, far from being fixed dispositions to behave in a particular way, are utterly subject to social channelling and transformation and could not even reveal themselves in behavior without social molding any more than our vocal cords can produce articulate speech if we have not learned a langauge. To psychoanalysis man is indeed a social animal; his social nature is profoundly reflected in his bodily structure.[18]

But there is a difference between the Freudian view on the one hand and both sociological and neo-Feudian conceptions of man on the other. To Freud man is a *social* animal without being entirely a *socialized* animal. His very social nature is the source of conflicts and antagonisms that create resistance to socialization by the norms of any of the societies which have existed in the course of human history. "Socialization" may mean two quite distinct things; when they are confused an over-socialized view of man is the result. On the one hand socialization means the "transmission of the culture," the particular culture of the society an individual enters at birth; on the other hand the term is used to mean the "process of becoming human," of acquiring uniquely human attributes from interaction with others.[19] All men are socialized in the latter sense, but this does not mean that they have been completely molded by the particular norms and values of their culture. All cultures, as Freud contended, do violence to man's socialized bodily drives, but this in no sense means that men could possibly exist without culture or independently of society.[20] From such a standpoint, man may properly be called as Norman Brown has called him, the "neurotic" or the "discontented" animal and repression may be seen as the main characteristic of human nature as we have known it in history.[21]

But isn't this psychology, and haven't sociologists been taught to foreswear psychology, to look with suspicion on what are called "psychological variables" in contradistinction to the institutional and historical forces with which they are properly concerned? There is, indeed, as recent critics have complained, too much "psychologism" in contemporary sociology, largely, I think, because of the bias inherent in our favored research techniques. But I do not see how, at the level of theory, sociologists can fail to make assumptions about human nature.[22] If our assumptions are left implicit, we will inevitably presuppose a view of man that is tailor-made to our special needs; when our sociological theory over-stresses the stability and integration of society we will end up imagining that man is the disembodied, conscience-driven, status-seeking phantom of current theory. We must do better if we really wish to win credit outside of our ranks for special understanding of man, that plausible creature[23] whose wagging tongue so often hides the despair and darkness in his heart.

## REFERENCES

1. Talcott Parsons, *The Structure of Social Action*, New York: McGraw-Hill Book Co., 1937, pp. 89–94.
2. Lewis A. Coser, *The Functions of Social Conflict*, Glencoe, Ill.: The Free Press, 1956, p. 21; C. Wright Mills, *The Sociological Imagination*, New York: Oxford University Press, 1959, p. 44.
3. R. G. Collingwood, *The New Leviathan*, Oxford: The Clarendon Press, 1942, p. 183
4. Collingwood, *op. cit.*, pp. 181–182.
5. *Cf.* Mills, op. cit., pp. 32–33, 42.
6. Parsons, *op. cit.*, pp. 378–390.
7. *Ibid.*, p. 382.
8. Abram Kardiner, *The Individual and His Society*, New York: Columbia University Press, 1939, pp. 65, 72–75.
9. Mills, *op. cit.*, pp. 39–41; Dahrendorf, *Class and Class Conflict in Industrial Society*, pp. 157–165.
10. Sigmund Freud, *Civilization and Its Discontents*, New York: Doubleday Anchor Books, 1958, pp. 78–79.
11. Ralph Linton, *The Cultural Background of Personality*, New York: Appleton-Century Co., 1945, p. 91.
12. Hans L. Zetterberg, "Compliant Actions," *Acta Sociologica*, 2 (1957), p. 189.
13. *Ibid.*, p. 188.
14. *Ibid.*, p. 189.
15. Dahrendorf, *Class and Class Conflict in Industrial Society*, p. 158.
16. Robert K. Merton, *Social Theory and Social Structure*, Revised and Enlarged Edition, Glencoe, Ill.: The Free Press, 1957, p. 131. Merton's view is representative of that of most contemporary sociologists. See also Hans Gerth and C. Wright Mills, *Character and Social Structure*, New York: Harcourt, Brace and Company, 1953, pp. 112–113. For a similar view by a "neo-Freudian," see Erich Fromm, *The Sane Society*, New York: Rinehart and Company, 1955, pp. 74–77.
17. John Dollard, *Criteria for the Life History*, New Haven: Yale University Press, 1935, p. 120. This valuable book has been neglected, presumably because it appears to be a purely methodological effort to set up standards for judging the adequacy of biographical and autobiographical data. Actually, the standards serve as well to evaluate the adequacy of general theories of personality or human nature and even to prescribe in part what a sound theory ought to include.
18. One of the few attempts by a social scientist to relate systematically man's anatomical structure and biological history to his social nature and his unique cultural creativity

is Weston La Barre's *The Human Animal,* Chicago: University of Chicago Press, 1954. See especially Chapters 4–6, but the entire book is relevant. It is one of the few exceptions to Paul Goodman's observation that anthropologists nowadays "Commence with a chapter on Physical Anthropology and then forget the whole topic and go on to Culture." See his "Growing up Absurd," *Dissent,* 7 (Spring, 1960), p. 121.

19. Paul Goodman has developed a similar distinction. *Op cit.,* pp. 123–125.
20. Whether it might be possible to create a society that does not repress the bodily drives is a separate question. See Herbert Marcuse, *Eros and Civilization,* Boston: The Beacon Press, 1955; and Norman O. Brown, *Life Against Death,* New York: Random House, Modern Library Paperbacks, 1960. Neither Marcuse nor Brown are guilty in their brilliant, provocative, and visionary books of assuming a "natural man" who awaits liberation from social bonds. They differ from such sociological Utopians as Fromm, in their lack of sympathy for the de-sexualized man of the neo-Freudians. For the more traditional Freudian view, see Walter A. Weisskopf, "The 'Socialization' of Psychoanalysis in Contemporary America," in Benjamin Nelson, editor, *Psychoanalysis and the Future,* New York: National Psychological Association For Psychoanalysis, 1957, pp. 51–56; Hans Meyerchoff, "Freud and the Ambiguity of Culture," *Partisan Review,* 24 (Winter, 1957), pp. 117–130.
21. Norman O. Brown, *Life Against Death,* New York: Random House, Modern Library Paperbacks, 1960, pp. 3–19.
22. "I would assert that very little sociological analysis is ever done without using at least an implicit psychological theory." Alex Inkeles, "Personality and Social Structure," in Robert K. Merton and others, editors, *Sociology Today,* New York: Basic Books, 1959, p. 250.
23. Harry Stack Sullivan once remarked that the most outstanding characteristic of human beings was their "plausibility."

# 5: Power and Authority

Power, that is, broadly speaking, the ability to determine the behavior of others in accord with one's own wishes, is clearly an ubiquitous social phenomenon. There are few social relationships from which the power element is wholly absent. It is therefore all the more remarkable that sociological approaches to the problem of power are of relatively recent origin. Though philosophers and political theorists from the days of Plato and Aristotle have been interested in the social as well as the human consequences of subordination and superordination, sociological contributions marking major departures from earlier perspectives date only from about the turn of the century, more specifically from the writings of Max Weber and Georg Simmel. However, we also owe important insights to Italian sociological theory, especially to the works of Vilfredo Pareto (1848–1923), Roberto Michels (1876–1936) and Gaetano Mosca (1858–1941).

Hence the following pages first present the basic work of Weber and Simmel and then introduce the reader to a sampling of the ways in which their ideas have been utilized and extended by more recent American theorizing.

Many aspects of power relations had already been analyzed by such thinkers as Machiavelli and Hobbes. It has remained for sociologists to point out systematically that the exercise of power, except in marginal cases, involves an element of obedience and that therefore reciprocity is inherent in power relationships. The exercise of social power, though it may rely ultimately upon the ability to apply coercive sanctions in case of non-compliance, involves more than unilateral imposition of will; it also involves acceptance. The excerpts from Georg Simmel's work on subordination and superordination are meant to exemplify this approach and to illustrate Simmel's contention that power relations involve an active reciprocity of orientation.

But if power involves acceptance, such acceptance may be based on a variety of grounds. For example, acceptance of the power of a police official to serve us with a summons and acceptance of the power of a father to discipline children may involve different elements. Hence we must distinguish between different types of voluntary obedience. It is in this respect that the contributions of Max Weber may be considered of crucial relevance. By proposing a classification of types of authority, that is, of ways in which the exercise of power is socially legitimized, he provided us with a method by which different grounds for exacting obedience may be conceptually distinguished. His threefold classification of types of authority—"legal" authority, "traditional" authority, and "charismatic" authority—has been criticized in many respects, yet it remains a fundamental point of entry for later theorizing in this area.

H. Goldhamer and E. Shils, contemporary American sociologists working in a broadly Weberian tradition, attempt here to systematize and refine some of the central insights of Max Weber's sociology of power and authority. The selection from Robert Bierstedt, a perceptive modern analyst of power phenomena, is meant to illustrate the extent to which recent American sociological reflection, while deeply indebted to its European precursors, has succeeded in further clarifying the notion of power. We are now able to distinguish this notion from other concepts, such as leadership and influence. In this connection Bierstedt's observation that authority, as distinct from power, is always attached to statuses, not to persons, and is always institutionalized, may be considered especially valuable.

The selection, from H. Gerth and C. W. Mills, is meant to summarize in a few pithy paragraphs much present theory in the area under consideration.

Finally, Terence K. Hopkins, a young contemporary sociologist, ably shows that two traditions in the analysis of authority, those of Weber and of Chester Barnard, far from being as divergent as has often been asserted, in fact converge in crucial respects. Barnard's stress on the importance of the communication process in the exercise of authority can be integrated into the framework of Weberian analysis if it is realized that the types of communication involved in authority systems are *imperative* communications.

# FORMS OF DOMINATION* (*Simmel*)

## Domination, a Form of Interaction

Nobody, in general, wishes that his influence completely determine the other individual. He rather wants this influence, this determination of the other, to act back upon *him*. Even the abstract will-to-dominate, therefore, is a case of interaction. This will draws its satisfaction from the fact that the acting or suffering of the other, his positive or negative condition, offers itself to the dominator as the product of *his* will. The significance of this solipsistic exercise of domination (so to speak) consists, for the superordinate himself, exclusively in the consciousness of his efficacy. Sociologically speaking, it is only a rudimentary form. By virtue of it alone, sociation occurs as little as it does between a sculptor and his statue, although the statue, too, acts back on the artist through his consciousness of his own creative power. The practical function of this desire for domination, even in this sublimated form, is not so much the exploitation of the other as the mere consciousness of this possibility. For the rest, it does not represent the extreme case of egoistic inconsiderateness. Certainly, the desire for domination is designed to break the *internal* resistance of the subjugated (whereas egoism usually aims only at the victory over his *external* resistance). But still, even the desire for domination has some interest in the other person, who constitutes a value for it. Only when egoism does not even amount to a desire for domination; only when the other is absolutely indifferent and a mere means for purposes which lie beyond him, is the last shadow of any sociating process removed.

The definition of later Roman jurists shows, in a relative way, that the elimination of *all* independent significance of one of the two interacting parties annuls the very notion of society. This definition was to the effect that the *societas leonina*[1] must not be conceived of as a social contract. A comparable statement has been made regarding the lowest-paid workers in modern giant enterprises which preclude all effective competition among rivaling entrepreneurs for the services of these laborers. It has been said that the difference in the strategic positions of workers and employers is so overwhelming that the work contract ceases to be a "contract" in the ordinary

* Reprinted from *The Sociology of Georg Simmel*, translated, edited, and with an introduction by Kurt H. Wolff, 1950, pp. 181–186, by permission of the publisher, The Free Press, Glencoe, Ill. Copyright, 1950, by The Free Press, A Corporation.

sense of the word, because the former are unconditionally at the mercy of the latter. It thus appears that the moral maxim never to use a man as a mere means is actually the formula of every sociation. Where the significance of the one party sinks so low that its effect no longer enters the relationship with the other, there is as little ground for speaking of sociation as there is in the case of the carpenter and his bench.

Within a relationship of subordination, the exclusion of all spontaneity whatever is actually rarer than is suggested by such widely used popular expressions as "coercion," "having no choice," "absolute necessity," etc. Even in the most oppressive and cruel cases of subordination, there is still a considerable measure of personal freedom. We merely do not become aware of it, because its manifestation would entail sacrifices which we usually never think of taking upon ourselves. Actually, the "absolute" coercion which even the most cruel tyrant imposes upon us is always distinctly relative. Its condition is our desire to escape from the threatened punishment or from other consequences of our disobedience. More precise analysis shows that the super-subordination relationship destroys the subordinate's freedom only in the case of direct physical violation. In every other case, this relationship only demands a price for the realization of freedom—a price, to be sure, which we are not willing to pay. It can narrow down more and more the sphere of external conditions under which freedom is clearly realized, but, except for physical force, never to the point of the complete disappearance of freedom. The moral side of this analysis does not concern us here, but only its sociological aspect. This aspect consists in the fact that interaction, that is, action which is mutually determined, action which stems exclusively from personal origins, prevails even where it often is not noted. It exists even in those cases of superordination and subordination—and therefore makes even those cases *societal* forms—where according to popular notions the "coercion" by one party deprives the other of every spontaneity, and thus of every real "effect," or contribution to the process of interaction.

## Authority and Prestige

Relationships of superordination and subordination play an immense role in social life. It is therefore of the utmost importance for its analysis to clarify the spontaneity and co-efficiency of the subordinate subject and and thus to correct their widespread minimization by superficial notions about them. For instance, what is called "authority" presupposes, in a much higher degree than is usually recognized, a freedom on the part of the person subjected to authority. Even where authority seems to "crush" him, it is based not *only* on coercion or compulsion to yield to it.

The peculiar structure of "authority" is significant for social life in the most varied ways; it shows itself in beginnings as well as in exaggerations, in acute as well as in lasting forms. It seems to come about in two different ways. A person of superior significance or strength may acquire, in his more immediate or remote milieu, an overwhelming weight of his opinions, a faith, or a confidence which have the character of objectivity. He thus enjoys a prerogative and an axiomatic trustworthiness in his decisions which excel, at least by a fraction, the value of mere subjective personality, which is always variable, relative, and subject to criticism. By acting "authoritatively," the quantity of his significance is transformed into a new quality; it assumes for his environment the physical state—metaphorically speaking—of objectivity.

But the same result, authority, may be attained in the opposite direction. A super-individual power—state, church, school, family or military organizations—clothes a person with a reputation, a dignity, a power of ultimate decision, which would never flow from his individuality. It is the nature of an authoritative person to make decisions with a certainty and automatic recognition which logically pertain only to impersonal, objective axioms and deductions. In the case under discussion, authority descends upon a person from above, as it were, whereas in the case treated before, it arises from the qualities of the person himself, through a *generatio aequivoca*.[2] But evidently, at this point of transition and change-over [from the personal to the authoritative situation], the more or less voluntary faith of the party subjected to authority comes into play. This transformation of the value of personality into a super-personal value gives the personality something which is beyond its demonstrable and rational share, however slight this addition may be. The believer in authority himself achieves that transformation. He (the subordinate element) participates in a sociological event which requires his spontaneous cooperation. As a matter of fact, the very feeling of the "oppressiveness" of authority suggests that the autonomy of the subordinate party is actually presupposed and never wholly eliminated.

Another nuance of superiority, which is designated as "prestige," must be distinguished from "authority." Prestige lacks the element of super-subjective significance; it lacks the identity of the personality with an objective power or norm. Leadership by means of prestige is determined entirely by the strength of the individual. This individual force always remains conscious of itself. Moreover, whereas the average type of leadership always shows a certain mixture of personal and superadded-objective factors, prestige leadership stems from pure personality, even as authority stems from the objectivity of norms and forces. Superiority through prestige consists in the ability to "push" individuals and masses and to make unconditional followers of them. Authority does not have this ability to the same extent. The higher, cooler, and normative character of authority is more apt to leave room for criticism, even on the part of its followers. In spite of this, however, prestige strikes us as the more voluntary homage to the superior person. Actually, perhaps, the recognition of authority implies a more profound freedom of the subject than does the enchantment that emanates from the prestige of a prince, a priest, a military or spiritual leader. But the matter is difficult in regard to the *feeling* on the part of those led. In the face of authority, we are often defenseless, whereas the *élan* with which we follow a given prestige always contains a consciousness of spontaneity. Here, precisely because devotion is only to the wholly personal, this devotion seems to flow only from the ground of personality with its inalienable freedom. Certainly, man is mistaken innumerable times regarding the measure of freedom which he must invest in a certain action. One reason for this is the vagueness and uncertainty of the explicit conception by means of which we account for this inner process. But in whatever way we interpret freedom, we can say that some measure of it, even though it may not be the measure we suppose, is present wherever there is the feeling and the conviction of freedom.[3]

## Leader and Led

The seemingly wholly passive element is in reality even more active in relationships such as obtain between a speaker and his audience or between a teacher and his class. Speaker and teacher appear to be nothing but leaders; nothing but, momentarily, superordinate. Yet whoever finds himself in such or a similar situation feels the determining and controlling re-action on the part of what seems to be a purely receptive and guided mass. This applies not only to situations where the two parties confront one another physically. All leaders are also led; in innumerable cases, the master is the slave of his slaves. Said one of the greatest German party leaders referring to his followers: "I am their leader, therefore I must follow them."

In the grossest fashion, this is shown by the journalist. The journalist gives content and direction to the opinions of a mute multitude. But he is nevertheless forced to listen, combine, and guess what the tendencies of this multitude are, what it desires to hear and to have confirmed, and whither it wants to be led. While apparently it is only the public which is exposed to *his* suggestions, actually he is as much under the sway of the *public's* suggestion. Thus, a highly complex interaction (whose two, mutually spontaneous forces, to be sure, appear under very different forms) is hidden here beneath the semblance of the pure superiority of the one element and a purely passive being-led of the other.

The content and significance of certain personal relations consist in the fact that the exclusive function of one of the two elements is service for the other. But the perfect measure of this devotion of the first element often depends on the condition that the other element surrenders to the first, even though on a different level of the relationship. Thus, Bismarck remarked concerning his relation to William I: "A certain measure of devotion is determined by law; a greater measure, by political conviction; beyond this, a personal feeling of *reciprocity* is required.—My devotion had its principal ground in my loyalty to royalist convictions. But in the special form in which this royalism existed, it is after all possible only under the impact of a certain reciprocity—the reciprocity between master and servant." The most characteristic case of this type is shown, perhaps, by hypnotic suggestion. An outstanding hypnotist pointed out that in every hypnosis the hypnotized has an effect upon the hypnotist; and that, although this effect cannot be easily determined, the result of the hypnosis could not be reached without it. Thus here, too, appearance shows an absolute influence, on the one side, and an absolute being-influenced, on the other; but it conceals an interaction, an exchange of influences, which transforms the pure one-sidedness of superordination and subordination into a *sociological* form.

REFERENCES

1. "Sociation with a lion," that is, a partnership in which all the advantage is on one side.—Tr.
2. "Equivocal birth" or "spontaneous generation."—Tr.
3. Here—and analogously in many other cases—the point is not to define the concept of prestige but only to ascertain the existence of a certain variety of human interactions, quite irrespective of their designation. The presentation, however, often begins appropriately with the concept which linguistic usage makes relatively most suitable for the discovery of the relationship, because it suggests it. This sounds like a merely definitory procedure. Actually, however, the attempt is never to find the content of a concept, but to describe, rather, an actual content, which only occasionally has the chance of being covered, more or less by an already existing concept.

# TYPES OF AUTHORITY * (*Weber*)

All ruling powers, profane and religious, political and apolitical, may be considered as variations of, or approximations to, certain pure types. These types are constructed by searching for the basis of *legitimacy*, which the ruling power claims. Our modern 'associations,' above all the political ones, are of the type of 'legal' authority. That is, the legitimacy of the power-holder to give commands rests upon rules that are rationally established by enactment, by agreement, or by imposition. The legitimation for establishing these rules rests, in turn, upon a rationally enacted or interpreted 'constitution.' Orders are given in the name of the impersonal norm, rather than in the name of a personal authority; and even the giving of a command constitutes obedience toward a norm rather than an arbitrary freedom, favor, or privilege.

The 'official' is the holder of the power to command; he never exercises this power in his own right; he holds it as a trustee of the impersonal and 'compulsory institution.'[1] This institution is made up of the specific patterns of life of a plurality of men, definite or indefinite, yet specified according to rules. Their joint pattern of life is normatively governed by statutory regulations.

The 'area of jurisdiction' is a functionally delimited realm of possible objects for command and thus delimits the sphere of the official's legitimate power. A hierarchy of superiors, to which officials may appeal and complain in an order of rank, stands opposite the citizen or member of the association. Today this situation also holds for the hierocratic association that is the church. The pastor or priest has his definitely limited 'jurisdiction,' which is fixed by rules. This also holds for the supreme head of the church. The present concept of [papal] 'infallibility' is a jurisdictional concept. Its inner meaning differs from that which preceded it, even up to the time of Innocent III.

The separation of the 'private sphere' from the 'official sphere' (in the case of infallibility: the *ex cathedra* definition) is carried through in the church in the same way as in political, or other, officialdoms. The legal separation of the official from the means of administration (either in natural or in

* From *From Max Weber: Essays in Sociology*, pp. 224–229, edited by H. H. Gerth and C. W. Mills. Copyright 1946 by Oxford University Press, Inc. Reprinted by permission.

pecuniary form) is carried through in the sphere of political and hierocratic associations in the same way as is the separation of the worker from the means of production in capitalist economy: it runs fully parallel to them.

No matter how many beginnings may be found in the remote past, in its full development all this is specifically modern. The past has known other bases for authority, bases which, incidentally, extend as survivals into the present. Here we wish merely to outline these bases of authority in a terminological way.

1. In the following discussions the term 'charisma' shall be understood to refer to an *extraordinary* quality of a person, regardless of whether this quality is actual, alleged, or presumed. 'Charismatic authority,' hence, shall refer to a rule over men, whether predominantly external or predominantly internal, to which the governed submit because of their belief in the extraordinary quality of the specific *person*. The magical sorcerer, the prophet, the leader of hunting and booty expeditions, the warrior chieftain, the so-called 'Caesarist' ruler, and, under certain conditions, the personal head of a party are such types of rulers for their disciples, followings, enlisted troops, parties, et cetera. The legitimacy of their rule rests on the belief in and the devotion to the extraordinary, which is valued because it goes beyond the normal human qualities, and which was originally valued as supernatural. The legitimacy of charismatic rule thus rests upon the belief in magical powers, revelations and hero worship. The source of these beliefs is the 'proving' of the charismatic quality through miracles, through victories and other successes, that is, through the welfare of the governed. Such beliefs and the claimed authority resting on them therefore disappear, or threaten to disappear, as soon as proof is lacking and as soon as the charismatically qualified person appears to be devoid of his magical power or forsaken by his god. Charismatic rule is not managed according to general norms, either traditional or rational, but, in principle, according to concrete revelations and inspirations, and in this sense, charismatic authority is 'irrational.' It is 'revolutionary' in the sense of not being bound to the existing order: 'It is written—but I say unto you . . . !'

2. 'Traditionalism' in the following discussions shall refer to the psychic attitude-set for the habitual workaday and to the belief in the everyday routine as an inviolable norm of conduct. Domination that rests upon this basis, that is, upon piety for what actually, allegedly, or presumably has always existed, will be called 'traditionalist authority.'

Patriarchalism is by far the most important type of domination the legitimacy of which rests upon tradition. Patriarchalism means the authority of the father, the husband, the senior of the house, the sib elder over the members of the household and sib; the rule of the master and patron over bondsmen, serfs, freed men; of the lord over the domestic servants and household officials; of the prince over house- and court-officials, nobles of office, clients, vassals; of the patrimonial lord and sovereign prince (*Landesvater*) over the 'subjects.'

It is characteristic of patriarchical and of patrimonial authority, which represents a variety of the former, that the system of inviolable norms is considered sacred; an infraction of them would result in magical or religious evils. Side by side with this system there is a realm of free arbitrariness and favor of the lord, who in principle judges only in terms of 'personal,' not 'functional,' relations. In this sense, traditionalist authority is irrational.

3. Throughout early history, charismatic authority, which rests upon a belief in the sanctity or the value of the extraordinary, and traditionalist (patriarchical) domination, which rests upon a belief in the sanctity of everyday routines, divided the most important authoritative relations between them. The bearers of charisma, the oracles of prophets, or the edicts of charismatic war lords alone could integrate 'new' laws into the circle of what was upheld by tradition. Just as revelation and the sword were the two extraordinary powers, so were they the two typical innovators. In typical fashion, however, both succumbed to routinization as soon as their work was done.

With the death of the prophet or the war lord the question of successorship arises. This question can be solved by *Kürung*, which was originally not an 'election' but a selection in terms of charismatic qualification; or the question can be solved by the sacramental substantiation of charisma, the successor being designated by consecration, as is the case in hierocratic or apostolic succession; or the belief in the charismatic qualification of the charismatic leader's sib can lead to a belief in hereditary charisma, as represented by hereditary kingship and hereditary hierocracy. With these routinizations, *rules* in some form always come to govern. The prince or the hierocrat no longer rules by virtue of purely personal qualities, but by virtue of acquired or inherited qualities, or because he has been legitimized by an act of charismatic election. The process of routinization, and thus traditionalization, has set in.

Perhaps it is even more important that when the organization of authority becomes permanent, the staff supporting the charismatic ruler becomes routinized. The ruler's disciples, apostles, and followers became priests, feudal vassals and, above all, officials. The original charismatic community lived communistically off donations, alms, and the booty of war: they were thus specifically alienated from the economic order. The community was transformed into a stratum of aids to the ruler and depended upon him for maintenance through the usufruct of land, office fees, income in kind, salaries, and hence, through prebends. The staff derived its legitimate power in greatly varying stages of appropriation, infeudation, conferment, and appointment. As a rule, this meant that princely prerogatives became *patrimonial* in nature. Patrimonialism can also develop from pure patriarchalism through the disintegration of the patriarchical master's strict authority. By virtue of conferment, the prebendary or the vassal has as a rule had a personal *right* to the office bestowed upon him. Like the artisan who possessed the economic means of production, the prebendary possessed the means of administration. He had to bear the costs of administration out of his office fees or other income, or he passed on to the lord only part of the taxes gathered from the subjects, retaining the rest. In the extreme case he could bequeath and alienate his office like other possessions. We wish to speak of *status* patrimonialism when the development by appropriation of prerogatory power has reached this stage, without regard to whether it developed from charismatic or patriarchical beginnings.

The development, however, has seldom stopped at this stage. We always meet with a *struggle* between the political or hierocratic lord and the owners or usurpers of prerogatives, which they have appropriated as status groups. The ruler attempts to expropriate the estates, and the estates attempt to expropriate the ruler. The more the ruler succeeds in attaching to himself a staff of officials who depend solely on him and whose interests are linked to his, the more this struggle is decided in favor of the ruler and the more the privilege-holding estates are gradually expropriated. In this connection, the prince acquires administrative means of his own and he keeps them firmly in his own hands. Thus we find political rulers in the Occident, and progressively from Innocent III to Johann XXII, also hierocratic rulers who have finances of their own, as well as secular rulers who have magazines and arsenals of their own for the provisioning of the army and the officials.

The *character* of the stratum of officials upon whose support the ruler has relied in the struggle for the expropriation of status prerogatives has varied greatly in history. In Asia and in the Occident during the early Middle Ages they were typically clerics; during the Oriental Middle Ages they were typically slaves and clients; for the Roman Principate, freed slaves to a limited extent were typical; humanist literati were typical for China; and finally, jurists have been typical for the modern Occident, in ecclesiastical as well as in political associations.

The triumph of princely power and the expropriation of particular prerogatives has everywhere signified at least the possibility, and often the actual introduction, of a rational administration. As we shall see, however, this rationalization has varied greatly in extent and meaning. One must, above all, distinguish between the *substantive* rationalization of administration and of judiciary by a patrimonial prince, and the *formal* rationalization carried out by trained jurists. The former bestows utilitarian and social ethical blessings upon his subjects, in the manner of the master of a large house upon the members of his household. The trained jurists have carried out the rule of general laws applying to all 'citizens of the state.' However fluid the difference has been—for instance, in Babylon or Byzantium, in the Sicily of the Hohenstaufen, or the England of the Stuarts, or the France of the Bourbons—in the final analysis, the difference between substantive and formal rationality has persisted. And, in the main, it has been the work of *jurists* to give birth to the modern Occidental 'state' as well as to the Occidental 'churches.' We shall not discuss at this point the source of their strength, the substantive ideas, and the technical means for this work.

With the triumph of *formalist* juristic rationalism, the legal type of domination appeared in the Occident at the side of the transmitted types of domination. Bureaucratic rule was not and is not the only variety of legal authority, but it is the purest. The modern state and municipal official, the modern Catholic priest and chaplain, the officials and employees of modern banks and of large capitalist enterprises represent, as we have already mentioned, the most important types of this structure of domination.

The following characteristic must be considered decisive for our terminology: in legal authority, submission does not rest upon the belief and devotion to charismatically gifted persons, like prophets and heroes, or upon sacred tradition, or upon piety toward a personal lord and master who is defined by an ordered tradition, or upon piety toward the possible incumbents of office fiefs and office prebends who are legitimized in their own right through privilege and conferment. Rather, submission under legal authority is based upon an *impersonal* bond to the generally defined and functional 'duty of office.' The official duty—like the corresponding right to exercise authority: the 'jurisdictional competency'—is fixed by *rationally established* norms, by enactments, decrees, and regulations, in such a manner that the legitimacy of the authority becomes the legality of the general rule, which is purposely thought out, enacted, and announced with formal correctness.

REFERENCE

1. *Anstalt.*

# POWER AND STATUS * (*Goldhamer and Shils*)

A person may be said to have *power* to the extent that he influences the behavior[1] of others in accordance with his own intentions. Three major forms
of power may be distinguished in terms of the type of influence brought to
bear upon the subordinated individual. The power-holder exercises *force*
when he influences behavior by a physical manipulation of the subordinated
individual (assault, confinement, etc.); *domination* when he influences behavior by making explicit to others what he wants them to do (command,
request, etc.);[2] and *manipulation* when he influences the behavior of others
without making explicit the behavior which he thereby wants them to perform.[3] Manipulation may be exercised by utilizing symbols or performing
acts. Propaganda is a major form of manipulation by symbols. The under-
mining of confidence in an enterprise by sabotaging its activities may be
taken as an example of manipulation by acts.

Most power-holders claim legitimacy for their acts, i.e., they claim the
"right to rule" as they do. If the legitimacy of the exercise of power is acknowledged by the subordinated individuals we speak of *legitimate power;*
if it is not recognized we call it *coercion* (provided, of course, that the intention of the power-holder is realized). There are three major forms of legitimate power. Legitimate power is regarded as *legal* when the recognition
of legitimacy rests on a belief by the subordinated individuals in the legality
of the laws, decrees, and directives promulgated by the power-holder; *traditional* when the recognition of legitimacy rests on a belief in the sanctity of
traditions by virtue of which the power-holder exercises his power and in the
traditional sanctity of the orders which he issues; and *charismatic* when the
recognition of legitimacy rests on a devotion to personal qualities of the
power-holder. Usually, of course, these personal qualities are, or appear to
the followers to be, extraordinary qualities such as sanctity and heroism.[4]

A person whose general position as a power-holder is recognized as
legitimate may exercise force, domination, or manipulation. But, as far as
the recognition of the legitimacy of individual acts of power is concerned,
it is clear that manipulation cannot be legitimate power, since in the case of

* Reprinted from "Types of Power and Status" by Herbert Goldhamer and Edward
A. Shils, *The American Journal of Sociology*, Vol. XLV, No. 2, September, 1939, pp.
171–182, by permission of The University of Chicago Press.

manipulation there is no recognition by the subordinated individual that an act of power has been effected. Persons who are subject to force (especially as an initial form of influencing behavior and not as a sanction) frequently do not recognize the legitimacy of such acts of power. Generally, therefore, the recognition of a power-holder as a legitimate exerciser of power rests on the recognition of the legitimacy of his acts of domination. However, this need not mean that he may not also exercise force or manipulation.

Attempted domination may meet with obedience or disobedience. The motivation for obedience and disobedience is *instrumental* to the extent that it is based on an anticipation of losses and gains, and *noninstrumental* to the extent that it is based on ethical or affective imperatives of conduct dictating obedience or disobedience to the command. In the case of obedience these imperatives may derive either (*a*) from a belief that the recognition of power as legitimate, i.e., as legal, traditional, or charismatic, imposes obedience as a norm of conduct or (*b*) from norms of conduct (e.g., the mores) which dictate, not obedience to the power-holder but the performance of the particular acts commanded. In the case of disobedience the imperatives will likewise derive either (*a*) from a belief that the recognition of power as nonlegitimate, i.e., coercive, imposes disobedience as a norm of conduct or (*b*) from norms of conduct which dictate not disobedience to the powerholder but the nonperformance of the particular acts commanded.[5] Although one may recognize the legitimacy of power, yet one may also obey or disobey out of instrumental considerations. This signifies in the case of disobedience that the instrumental considerations outweigh the motivation toward conformity arising from the recognition of legitimacy.

If the attempt of a person to exercise power fails, the power act may be followed either by a substitute power act or by a sanction. A *substitute power act* is intended primarily to attain the original aim of the first act. Substitution may take place both within or between types of power. Thus a command may be substituted for a polite request (both forms of attempted domination), or unsuccessful propaganda may be succeeded by an outright command (manipulation and domination). A *sanction* is a power act initiated primarily as a reprisal for nonconformity with a prior act of power; its intent is punitive and not primarily directed toward achieving the goal of the prior unsuccessful power act. Since persons who are subjected to attempted exercise of force or manipulation do not—unlike persons subjected to commands—either obey or disobey, sanctions may most properly be spoken of as a reprisal for disobedience to a command (domination) rather than as nonconformity to other types of power. However, it may be true that an unsuccessful propagandist or unsuccessful exerciser of force may (irrationally) take actions with punitive intent against persons who fail to succumb to his propaganda or to his attempt to exercise force.

A sanction may be either a deprivation of values already possessed or an obstruction to the attainment of values which would have been realized were it not for the punitive intervention of the power-holder. A sanction may be either a physical loss (beating, confinement, etc.) or a nonphysical loss (fining, confiscation, removal from office, ridicule, etc.).

Disobedience to the command of a power-holder may result not only in consciously intended sanctions but also in unintended penalizations (such as guilt feelings, loss of prestige, etc.), the anticipation of which may motivate the individual to conform. Market operations afford an important case of unintended penalizations. The demands of buyers and sellers upon each other produce a collective compromise expressed in the price level. Intransigent buyers and sellers are not necessarily subject to intended losses, but their intransigence is, in fact, likely to squeeze them out of the market. The conformity of the buyers or sellers to the imperatives of market conditions involves, in this case, conformity not only to the immediate demands of those with whom they have direct relations but through them, indirectly, with all other persons in the market. Unintended consequences may also be derivative penalizations, i.e., they may be unintended results from the infliction of an intended sanction. Thus imprisonment may (even after release) result in the loss of job, prestige, and associations.

Sanctions may be exercised either directly by the power-holder himself or indirectly through others in official or nonofficial positions. Most power-holders of any consequence possess a staff of officials to whom the exercise of sanctions is delegated. Although power-holders may instigate persons without official position (mobs, the public, "the consumer," etc.) to take reprisals against nonconformists, the exercise of sanctions by nonofficials is perhaps most important in the case of unintended and derivative penalizations and in the case of intended sanctions without instigation from official power-holders.

A power relation is *unilateral* if only one party to the relationship exercises power over the other and *bilateral* if both parties exercise power over each other. The power relationships between officers and privates in an army are typically unilateral. A major form of bilateral power relation is the case of bargaining power, to the extent that each party influences the behavior of the other in the intended direction. In bargaining each party attempts to influence the behavior of the other either by depriving him of values already possessed or by obstructing the attainment of values not yet possessed but desired. Bilateral power relations exist not only in the case of domination (as when each party is able to make demands on the other) but also in the case of manipulation. That is, each party may influence the behavior of the other party without making explicit what behavior is desired. Thus parties may mutually influence each other's behavior in a desired direction by propaganda or by acts. The outcome of attempted bilateral domination or manipulation may be complete fulfilment of the intentions of both parties (provided they are not incompatible) or a compromise, i.e., a partial success by both parties or the fulfilment (partially or fully) of the intention of only one party or, finally, modes of behavior completely different from the intention of either party.[6]

The exercise of power is *direct* when the power-holder alters the behavior of others without utilizing an intermediary and *indirect* when a chain of direct power acts is initiated by a power-holder who utilizes one or more subordinate power-holders. The control of an army by a general or of factory workers by a large-scale entrepreneur is largely by means of indirect power. The chain of direct power acts constituting the exercise of indirect power may be composed of different types of direct power acts. Thus the initial act may be a command (domination) to a subordinate power-holder who may alter the behavior of others by propaganda (manipulation) in order to instigate mob violence (force) against certain groups, thus attaining the intention of the initiating power-holder. The personnel utilized in the sequence of direct power acts composing indirect power may be both official and nonofficial.

The amount of power exercised by an individual may be measured either by the ratio of his successful power acts to all of his attempted power acts or by certain criteria specified below. These measures may be used as a basis of comparison between different power-holders. The two "amounts" represent not alternative techniques of measurement but differences in what is measured. Amount in these cases does not mean the same thing. Most investigations of power, in so far as they deal with the amount of power, utilize "amount" in the second sense.

Two principal criteria may be used to measure the amount of power exercised by a power-holder: the number of actions of any given person, in each of any number of selected types of behavior, over which control is realized (or potential)[7]; and the number[8] of persons so controlled. The definition of dictatorship as "a form of government where everything that is not forbidden is obligatory" indicates complete power in terms of the spheres of behavior over which control is exercised.

Concentration of power is not diminished if the power-holder acts through many subordinates, provided he is able to exercise control over them. In fact, however, the utilization of a large subordinate staff is very likely to diffuse power, since the chief power-holder is rarely able to control fully the actions of his subordinates who may therefore exercise a certain amount of independent or initiatory, rather than dependent, power. Further the impossibility of maintaining complete control over the subordinate staff and the reliance which the power-holder must place on them tends to set up a bilateral power relation between the chief power-holder and his subordinates, giving the latter power over the chief power-holder in addition to any independent power they may exercise over the mass. Subordinate power-holders, to the extent that they exercise independent power in the sphere claimed by the chief power-holder, will limit the power of the latter, and to that extent lose their character of subordinates. On the other hand, a plurality of independent power-holders (whether partially or completely independent) may not only limit but also reinforce or not at all affect one another's exercise of power. This will be true only to the extent that the power-holders influence the behavior of others in a manner which does not obstruct the intentions of their co-power-holders. With the growing interdependence of all aspects of social life, however, and consequently the increased probabilities that any act will have more extensive repercussions throughout the society than formerly, it becomes more essential for a power-holder both to control many aspects of behavior that formerly might have seemed quite unnecessary for carrying out his intentions and to prevent others from exercising powers that formerly might not have interfered with his intention. Although one finds in contemporary society, both in public and in private spheres, an increasing concentration of power, the necessity, as enterprises increase in size, of exercising power through the utilization of many subordinate power-holders tends to limit the actual if not the formal concentration of power.

The amount and stability of power exercised will be limited by the means which the power-holder has available for influencing the behavior of others by making them want to do what he wants them to do or by the sanctions which they anticipate that he can bring to bear upon them. Large amounts of power cannot be exercised in a purely coercive fashion, for even though the mass of subordinated individuals do not recognize the power-holder as exercising legitimate power, the necessity of utilizing a large staff would introduce other than purely coercive power into the total power system; for the subordinate power-holders, who exercise dependent power and carry out sanctions for cases of nonconformity among the mass, cannot themselves be controlled by coercion alone. The greater the amount of coercive power exercised, the greater is the dependence of the chief power-holder on his staff. For this reason and because the possible supervision over, and sanctions against, the mass often fall short of the requirements for the exercise of coercive power, the latter frequently has to augmented and supported by manipulation. This may serve the purpose not only of getting people to act in a desired manner without exercising coercion but also of developing a belief in the legitimacy of the power exercised and thereby also limiting the need for coercive action.

It is sometimes assumed that a person who uses force or is in a position to impose very drastic sanctions in the event of nonconformity with his commands is somehow more powerful than one who exercises power without the use of these means. But, the amount of power exercised by a legitimate power-holder may be as great as, or greater than, the amount exercised by a coercive power-holder. If, however, we restrict comparison only to coercive power-holders, then it is true, all other things being equal, that power varies directly with the severity of the sanctions, that the power-holder can impose.

Men evaluate the objects, acts, and human attributes with which they come into contact. These evaluations may become systematized into a hierarchy of values. The individual makes judgments of others and ranks them on the basis of his hierarchy of values and his knowledge concerning what characteristics these other persons possess. Such a judgment of rank made about either the total person or relatively stable segments of the person constitutes the *social status* of that person (for the individual making the judgment). Societies and individuals use different gestures to express degrees of deference which they accord to varying ranks of social status. These gestures expressing the status of an individual may be called *deference gestures* or more simply, *deference*.

The deference gestures which a person directs toward or about another person are *genuine* when the deferrer holds them appropriate for expressing the status he ascribes to that other individual, and *spurious* when they are not those which he holds as appropriate for expressing the status he ascribes to the other individual.[9] Spurious deference may be the giving of a deference either higher or lower than that which the deferrer considers appropriate for the status in question (or higher or lower than the deferrer customarily gives to a person with the status in question). The first of these two types of spurious deference constitutes a frequent form of manipulation, the spurious deference being intended to induce a desired form of behavior.

Status judgments are *total* when the evaluation is made of the person as a whole and not of any particular role which he performs or any particular attribute which he possesses and *segmental* when the evaluation is made of the person in terms of a particular role which he performs or of a particular attribute which he possesses.

Deference gestures are *specialized* when they are utilized only toward persons performing certain roles (such as saluting in the case of the army); and *nonspecialized* when they are used equally toward persons of the same status irrespective of their roles (as general terms of respect such as "sir"). People often accord generalized deference gestures to persons to whom they accord segmental status because specialized gestures exist only for a very limited number of roles (such as military or ecclesiastical roles). The use of a nonspecialized deference gesture, such as "sir," does not signify, therefore, that the individual using it necessarily does so because he accords high total status. Persons may, however, intentionally use certain nonspecialized deference gestures in order to create a definite impression that a high total status is being accorded when in fact the status actually accorded is only high segmental status. To the extent that this is successfully used to influence behavior it constitutes manipulation.

Deference gestures frequently become highly conventionalized and hence uniform throughout a society or segments of a society. There may, however, be considerable individuation of deference gestures, i.e., a considerable deviation from the conventional forms. Clearly the more individuated such gestures become, the less they will serve to convey to others the deference being accorded by the person making the gestures. Deference gestures vary not only in their degree of individuation but also in the degree to which they discriminate differences in status. Thus in eighteenth-century Germany Fräulein as a mode of address was a highly discriminatory deference gesture, as it was used only in addressing young women of the upper classes.

In some periods societies or special groups within societies have attempted to level status and deference distinctions, even though they have found it impossible to erase differences in those objective characteristics of persons which usually give rise to status and deference distinctions. Such attempts are often found in the early stages of religious sectarian movements (for the members are equal before God and should therefore be equal before one another) and in the early periods of egalitarian revolutions. It would seem that the attempt to level deference distinctions is usually more successful than the attempt to level status distinctions. Thus leveling terms such as *citoyen* are universally applied to all members of the society, and various honorific terms if retained are universally applied and thus lose their discriminatory value. Because of this one finds that in time new deference gestures are evolved to permit expressions of the different degrees of status developed on the basis of the new revolutionary value system.

The status accorded to a person depends on the value hierarchy held by the individual making the status judgment and the individual's knowledge of the characteristics of the person judged. A status judgment that a person makes of another is *true* if based on an accurate knowledge of the characteristics of the person judged, and *false* if based on an incorrect knowledge of the characteristics of the person judged. Thus if a person ranks wealth very high in his hierarchy of values and if he believes another person to be very wealthy, he will rank the latter high in the status scale. If, in fact, the person judged is wealthy, the status accorded him by the person making the judgment is a true status; but if, in fact, the person judged is poor, then the judgment is a false status. To say that a status judgment concerning an individual is "true" does not imply an objectively true status judgment in the sense that any status judgment deviating from it is false. If persons have different value hierarchies and all have approximately the same correct knowledge of the characteristics of the individual being judged, the various different status judgments will all be true status judgments. As long as the value hierarchies of the persons making the judgments differ, the status judgments must differ if they are true.[10]

The status judgments referred to in this article are privately or subjectively made status judgments. A person may make true status judgments but publicly may state that the individual in question has in his opinion a higher or lower status than he privately judges him to have. Such falsifications may be termed spurious status to distinguish them from status judgments based on incorrect knowledge, i.e., false status judgments. Status judgments are often given expression through deference gestures, and falsification of these constitutes, of course, spurious deference.

The present discussion of status might seem to impute to individuals a high degree of awareness of their own value systems and considerable conscious analysis in the process of assigning status to an individual and according him the appropriate deference gestures. Status judgments and deference gestures are, of course, not usually arrived at in such a fashion, although such a process is likely to occur in the case of some types of persons, such as religious and political sectarian leaders who make all evaluations in terms of a few clearly and fervently held principles. Again, it is possible that an individual may apply different value hierarchies in making status judgments of different types of individuals. The possession of a plurality of value hierarchies is perhaps most likely to exhibit itself in making status judgments of the self and of others with the same objective characteristics. To what extent, however, individuals may have more than one independent value hierarchy is difficult to say. Furthermore, for the entire discussion of social values and social status it is of the highest importance to realize that for some individuals and in some periods for a considerable proportion of the population the value hierarchies may be in a condition of great flux resulting in both ambiguity and ambivalence of status judgments. No investigation of status and deference could afford to ignore the complications mentioned above, but the present discussion does not attempt either to analyze the psychological processes by which status judgments and deference gestures are made or to deal with the manifold consequences resulting from ambiguous and ambivalent value systems.

REFERENCES

1. Behavior is here to be understood as both covert and overt behavior. Influence is to be understood as both an alteration of behavior and a maintenance of behavior as it was, but other than what it would have been without the intervention of the power-holder.
2. "Shoulder arms!" and "Please close the door" are both cases of domination, provided, of course, that these utterances succeed in realizing the intention of the speaker. It may be that everyday associations render "Please close the door" as an example of domination somewhat surprising. A polite request, however, is as much a way of getting people to do what one wants them to do as is the most brutally uttered command. Polite requests often enable a person to exercise power over another where a command containing no elements of deference may fail. The relation between the exercise of power over, and the granting of deference to, subordinated individuals is not treated here.
3. Since the distinction between domination and manipulation rests on the degree to which the power-holder makes his intention explicit to the person whose behavior he wants to influence, the two frequently shade off into each other. It often happens, of course, that the context in which the power-holder's behavior takes place is such as to enable him to assume that his intention is quite clear to the person whom he is attempting to influence. It is desirable to include such cases under domination.

    It is clear that manipulation excludes modifications of behavior following the communication of factual representations in discussion. In the case of discussion the intentions of the discussants are evident to each other. This, of course, does not preclude the possibility of manipulatory elements entering into a discussion. As in the cases discussed in the first paragraph, the line between discussion and manipulation may (in certain concrete cases) be difficult to draw.
4. The classification of types of legitimate power is that of Max Weber (cf. *Wirtschaft und Gesellschaft* [Tübingen, 1925], I, 124).
5. Motivation for conformity with, or rejection of, the expressed wish or demand of the power-holder is here considered only in terms of perceptions by the subordinated person of certain selected characteristics of the power-holder and the commanded act. Clearly a number of other factors would be relevant in a complete analysis of why one individual obeys or disobeys another, e.g., the personality of the obeying person. Such factors are not considered here since the above classification is not being used as a basis for a complete causal explanation of obedience or disobedience.
6. The last case is only an *attempted* bilateral power relation since neither party accomplished his intention. The case in which only one party accomplishes his intention is marginal to the definition of bilateral power and may be characterized as being a case of attempted bilateral power with culmination in unilateral power.

7. It would be extremely dfficult to determine how much control is possible in a given situation unless the power-holder actually attempts to exercise power. Although for some purposes it would be highly desirable to attempt estimates of the potential amount of power that could be wielded, the amount of power actually exercised would in most cases be the primary interest, and of course would involve the sounder empirical procedure. However, the predictions of the power-holder and those subordinate to him as to how much power the power-holder might wield if so inclined may be an important determinant of the behavior of the power-holder and those subordinated to him.

8. "Number" here may be absolute number or the proportion of controlled persons in the total population. It may also be desirable to represent this as the ratio between those who are controlled to the total number over whom control is attempted.

9. Deference gestures toward a particular person may also be said to be genuine or spurious according to whether they conform (genuine deference) or do not conform (spurious deference) with the deference gestures that the deferrer has used toward others of similar status. This assumes, of course, that the majority of his deference gestures have given true expression to his status judgments.

10. Genuine and spurious deference may of course occur either in the case of a correct or an incorrect knowledge of the objective characteristics of the person to whom the deference is being accorded, i.e., they may occur either in the case of true or of false status judgments. The deference accorded a bogus aristocrat may be genuine but would be based on a false status judgment and hence may, for convenience of reference, be called "mistaken deference." If deference is spurious and based on a false status judgment it may be called "deception deference." Since deception deference involves an error concerning the objective characteristics of the individual to whom the deference is accorded and a falsification of the deference gesture by the deferrer, it is conceivable that the two "errors" may cancel each other and that the person giving deception deference may accord the same deference as a person who has correct knowledge and gives genuine deference. The terms "genuine" and "spurious" deference may be taken as implying true status judgments unless otherwise indicated or qualified by the terms "mistaken" and "deception" deference.

# AN ANALYSIS OF SOCIAL POWER* (*Bierstedt*)

Few problems in sociology are more perplexing than the problem of social power. In the entire lexicon of sociological concepts none is more troublesome than the concept of power. We may say about it in general only what St. Augustine said about time, that we all know perfectly well what it is—until someone asks us. Indeed, Robert M. MacIver has recently been induced to remark that "There is no reasonably adequate study of the nature of social power."[1] The present paper cannot, of course, pretend to be a "reasonably adequate study." It aims at reasonableness rather than adequacy and attempts to articulate the problem as one of central sociological concern, to

* Reprinted from *The American Sociological Review*, XV, 6, pp. 730–738, by permission of the publisher. The American Sociological Society, and the author.

clarify the meaning of the concept, and to discover the locus and seek the sources of social power itself.

The power structure of society is not an insignificant problem. In any realistic sense it is both a sociological (*i.e.*, a scientific) and a social (*i.e.*, a moral) problem. It has traditionally been a problem in political philosophy. But, like so many other problems of a political character, it has roots which lie deeper than the *polis* and reach into the community itself. It has ramifications which can be discerned only in a more generalized kind of inquiry than is offered by political theory and which can ultimately be approached only by sociology. Its primitive basis and ultimate locus, as MacIver has emphasized in several of his distinguished books,[2] are to be sought in community and in society, not in government or in the state. It is apparent, furthermore, that not all power is political power and that political power—like economic, financial, industrial, and military power—is only one of several and various kinds of social power. Society itself is shot through with power relations—the power a father exercises over his minor child, a master over his slave, a teacher over his pupils, the victor over the vanquished, the blackmailer over his victim, the warden over his prisoners, the attorney over his own and opposing witnesses, an employer over his employee, a general over his lieutenants, a captain over his crew, a creditor over a debtor, and so on through most of the status relationships of society.[3] Power, in short, is a universal phenomenon in human societies and in all social relationships. It is never wholly absent from social interaction, except perhaps in the primary group where "personal identification" (Hiller) is complete and in those relations of "polite acquaintance" (Simmel) which are "social" in the narrowest sense. All other social relations contain components of power. What, then, is this phenomenon?

Social power has variously been identified with prestige, with influence, with eminence, with competence or ability, with knowledge (Bacon), with dominance, with rights, with force, and with authority. Since the intension of a term varies, if at all, inversely with its extension—*i.e.*, since the more things a term can be applied to the less precise its meaning—it would seem to be desirable to distinguish power from some at least of these other concepts. Let us first distinguish power from prestige.

The closest association between power and prestige has perhaps been made by E. A. Ross in his classic work on social control. "The immediate cause of the location of power," say Ross, "is prestige." And further, "The class that has the most prestige will have the most power."[4] Now prestige may certainly be construed as one of the sources of social power and as one of the most significant of all the factors which separate man from man and group from group. It is a factor which has as one of its consequences the complex stratification of modern societies, to say nothing of the partial stratification of non-literate societies where the chief and the priest and the medicine-man occupy prestigious positions. But prestige should not be identified with power. They are independent variables. Prestige is frequently unaccompanied by power and when the two occur together power is usually the basis and ground of prestige rather than the reverse. Prestige would seem to be a consequence of power rather than a determinant of it or a necessary component of it. In any event, it is not difficult to illustrate the fact that power and prestige are independent variables, that power can occur without prestige, and prestige without power. Albert Einstein, for example, has prestige but no power in any significant sociological sense of the word. A policeman has power, but little prestige. Similarly, on the group level, the Phi Beta Kappa Society has considerable prestige—more outside academic circles than inside, to be sure—but no power. The Communist Party in the United States has a modicum of power, if not the amount so extravagantly attributed to it by certain Senators, but no prestige. The Society of Friends again has prestige but little power.

Similar observations may be made about the relations of knowledge, skill, competence, ability, and eminence to power. They are all components of, sources of, or synonyms of prestige, but they may be quite unaccompanied by power. When power does accompany them the association is incidental rather than necessary. For these reasons it seems desirable to maintain a distinction between prestige and power.

When we turn to the relationship between influence and power we find a still more intimate connection but, for reasons which possess considerable cogency, it seems desirable also to maintain a distinction between influence and power. The most important reason, perhaps, is that influence is persuasive while power is coercive. We submit voluntarily to influence while power requires submission. The mistress of a king may influence the destiny of a nation, but only because her paramour permits himself to be swayed by her designs. In any ultimate reckoning her influence may be more important than his power, but it is inefficacious unless it is transformed into power. The power a teacher exercises over his pupils stems not from his superior knowledge (this is competence rather than power) and not from his opinions (this is influence rather than power), but from his ability to apply the sanction of failure, *i.e.*, to withhold academic credit, to the student who does not fulfill his requirements and meet his standards. The competence may be unappreciated and the influence may be ineffective, but the power may not be gainsaid.

Furthermore, influence and power can occur in relative isolation from each other and so also are relatively independent variables. We should say, for example, that Karl Marx has exerted an incalculable influence upon the twentieth century, but this poverty-stricken exile who spent so many of his hours immured in the British Museum was hardly a man of power. Even the assertion that he was a man of influence is an ellipsis. It is the ideas which are influential, not the man. Stalin, on the other hand, is a man of influence only because he is first a man of power. Influence does not require power, and power may dispense with influence. Influence may convert a friend, but power coerces friend and foe alike. Influence attaches to an idea, a doctrine, or a creed, and has its locus in the ideological sphere. Power attaches to a person, a group, or an association, and has its locus in the sociological sphere. Plato, Aristotle, St. Thomas, Shakespeare, Galileo, Newton, and Kant were men of influence, although all of them were quite devoid of power. Napoleon Bonaparte and Abraham Lincoln were men of both power and influence. Genghis Khan and Adolf Hitler were men of power. Archimedes was a man of influence, but the soldier who slew him at the storming of Syracuse had more power. It is this distinction which gives point to Spengler's otherwise absurd contention that this nameless soldier had a greater impact upon the course of history than the great classical physicist.

When we speak, therefore, of the power of an idea or when we are tempted to say that ideas are weapons or when we assert, with the above-mentioned Bonaparte, that the pen is mightier than the sword, we are using figurative language, speaking truly as it were, but metaphorically and with synecdoche. Ideas are influential, they may alter the process of history, but for the sake of logical and sociological clarity it is preferable to deny to them the attribute of power. Influence in this sense, of course, presents quite as serious and as complex a problem as power, but it is not the problem whose analysis we are here pursuing.

It is relatively easy to distinguish power from dominance. Power is a sociological, dominance a psychological concept. The locus of power is in groups and it expresses itself in inter-group relations; the locus of dominance is in the individual and it expresses itself in inter-personal relations. Power appears in the statuses which people occupy in formal organization; dominance in the roles they play in informal organization. Power is a function of the organization of associations, of the arrangement and juxtaposition of groups, and of the structure of society itself. Dominance, on the other hand, is a function of personality or of temperament; it is a personal trait. Dominant individuals play roles in powerless groups; submissive individuals in powerful ones. Some groups acquire an inordinate power, especially in the political sense, because there are so many submissive individuals who are easily persuaded to join them and who meekly conform to the norms which membership imposes. As an example, one need mention only the growth of the National Socialist Party in Germany. Dominance, therefore, is a problem in social psychology; power a problem in sociology.[5]

It is a little more difficult to distinguish power from "rights" only because the latter term is itself so ambiguous. It appears indeed in two senses which are exactly contradictory—as those privileges and only those which are secured by the state and as those which the state may not invade even to secure. We do not need to pursue the distinctions between various kinds of rights, including "natural rights," which are elaborated in the history of jurisprudence and the sociology of law to recognize that a right always requires some support in the social structure, although not always in the laws, and that rights in general, like privileges, duties, obligations, responsibilities, perquisites, and prerogatives, are attached to statuses both in society itself and in the separate associations of society. One may have a right without the power to exercise it,[6] but in most cases power of some kind supports whatever rights are claimed. Rights are more closely associated with privileges and with authority than they are with power. A "right," like a privilege, is one of the perquisites of power and not power itself.[7]

We have now distinguished power from prestige, from influence, from dominance, and from rights, and have left the two concepts of force and authority. And here we may have a solution to our problem. Power is not force and power is not authority, but it is intimately related to both and may be defined in terms of them. We want therefore to propose three definitions and then to examine their implications: (1) power is latent force; (2) force is manifest power; and (3) authority is institutionalized power. The first two of these propositions may be considered together. They look, of course, like circular definitions and, as a matter of fact, they are. If an independent meaning can be found for one of these concepts, however, the other may be defined in terms of it and the circularity will disappear.[8] We may therefore suggest an independent definition of the concept of force. Force, in any significant sociological sense of the word, means the application of sanctions. Force, again in the sociological sense, means the reduction or limitation or closure or even total elimination of alternatives to the social action of one person or group by another person or group. "Your money or your life" symbolizes a situation of naked force, the reduction of alternatives to two. The execution of a sentence to hang represents the total elimination of alternatives. One army progressively limits the social action of another until only two alternatives remain for the unsuccessful contender—to surrender or die. Dismissal or demotion of personnel in an association similarly, if much less drastically, represents a closure of alternatives. Now all these are situations of force, or manifest power. Power itself is the predisposition or prior capacity which makes the application of force possible. Only groups which have power can threaten to use force and the threat itself is power. Power is the ability to employ force, not its actual employment, the ability to apply sanctions, not their actual application.[9] Power is the ability to introduce force into a social situation; it is the presentation of force. Unlike force, incidentally, power is always successful; when it is not successful it is not, or ceases to be, power. Power symbolizes the force which *may* be applied in any social situation and supports the authority which *is* applied. Power is thus neither force nor authority but, in a sense, their synthesis.

The implications of these propositions will become clearer if we now discuss the locus of power in society. We may discover it in three areas, (1) in formal organization, (2) in informal organization, and (3) in the unorganized community. The first of these presents a fairly simple problem for analysis. It is in the formal organization of associations that social power is transformed into authority. When social action and interaction proceed wholly in conformity to the norms of the formal organization, power is dissolved without residue into authority. The right to use force is then attached to certain statuses within the association, and this right is what we ordinarily mean by authority.[10] It is thus authority in virtue of which persons in an association exercise command or control over other persons in the same association. It is authority which enables a bishop to transfer a priest from his parish, a priest with his "power of the keys" to absolve a sinner, a commanding officer to assign a post of duty to a subordinate officer, a vice-president to dictate a letter to his secretary, the manager of a baseball team to change his pitcher in the middle of an inning, a factory superintendent to demand that a certain job be completed at a specified time, a policeman to arrest a citizen who has violated a law, and so on through endless examples. Power in these cases is attached to statuses, not to persons, and is wholly institutionalized as authority.[11]

In rigidly organized groups this authority is clearly specified and formally articulated by the norms (rules, statutes, laws) of the association. In less rigidly organized groups penumbral areas appear in which authority is less clearly specified and articulated. Sometimes authority clearly vested in an associational status may not be exercised because it conflicts with a moral norm to which both members and non-members of the association adhere in the surrounding community. Sometimes an official may remove a subordinate from office without formal cause and without formal authority because such action, now involving power, finds support in public opinion. Sometimes, on the contrary, he may have the authority to discharge a subordinate, but not the power, because the position of the latter is supported informally and "extra-associationally" by the opinion of the community. An extreme case of this situation is exemplified by the inability of the general manager, Ed Barrow, or even the owner, Colonel Jacob Ruppert, to "fire" Babe Ruth from the New York Yankees or even, when the Babe was at the height of his fame, to trade him.

Sometimes these power relations become quite complicated. In a university organization, for example, it may not be clear whether a dean has the authority to apply the sanction of dismissal to a professor, or, more subtly, whether he has the authority to abstain from offering an increase in salary to a professor in order indirectly to encourage him to leave, or, still more subtly, whether, when he clearly has this authority of abstention, he will be accused of maladministration if he exercises it.[12] It is similarly unclear whether a Bishop of the Episcopal Church has the authority to remove a rector from his parish when the latter apparently has the support of his parishioners.[13] In other words, it sometimes comes to be a matter of unwise policy for an official to exercise the authority which is specifically vested in his position, and it is in these cases that we can clearly see power leaking into the joints of associational structure and invading the formal organization.[14]

It may be observed that the power implied in the exercise of authority does not necessarily convey a connotation of personal superiority. Leo Durocher is not a better pitcher than the player he removes nor, in turn, is he inferior to the umpire who banishes him from the game. A professor may be a "better" scholar and teacher than the dean who dismisses him, a lawyer more learned in the law than the judge who cites him for contempt, a worker a more competent electrician than the foreman who assigns his duties, and so on through thousands of examples. As MacIver has written, "The man who commands may be no wiser, no abler, may be in no sense better than the average of his fellows; sometimes, by any intrinsic standard he is inferior to them. Here is the magic of government."[15] Here indeed is the magic of all social organization.

Social action, as is well known, does not proceed in precise or in absolute conformity to the norms of formal organization. Power spills over the vessels of status which only imperfectly contain it as authority. We arrive, therefore, at a short consideration of informal organization, in which the prestige of statuses gives way to the esteem for persons and in which the social interaction of the members proceeds not only in terms of the explicit norms of the association but also in terms of implicit extra-associational norms whose locus is in the community and which may or may not conflict, at strategic points, with the associational norms. Our previous examples have helped us to anticipate what we have to say about the incidence and practice of power in informal organization. No association is wholly formal, not even the most rigidly organized. Social organization makes possible the orderly social intercourse of people who do not know each other—the crew of a ship and their new captain, the faculty of a university department and a new chairman, the manager of a baseball team and his new recruit, the citizen and the tax collector, the housewife and the plumber, the customer and the clerk. But in any association the members do become acquainted with each other and begin to interact not only "extrinsically" and "categorically," in terms of the statuses they occupy, but also "intrinsically" and "personally," in terms of the roles they play and the personalities they exhibit.[16] Sub-groups arise and begin to exert subtle pressures upon the organization itself, upon the norms which may be breached in the observance thereof, and upon the authority which, however firmly institutionalized, is yet subject to change. These sub-groups may, as cliques and factions, remain within the association or, as sects and splinter groups, break away from it. In any event, no formal organization can remain wholly formal under the exigencies of time and circumstance. Power is seldom completely institutionalized as authority, and then no more than momentarily. If power sustains the structure, opposing power threatens it, and every association is always at the mercy of a majority of its own members. In all associations the power of people acting in concert is so great that the prohibition against "combinations" appears in the statutes of all military organizations and the right of collective petition is denied to all military personnel.

Power appears, then, in associations in two forms, institutionalized authority in the formal organization and uninstitutionalized as power itself in the informal organization. But this does not exhaust the incidence of power with respect to the associations of society. It must be evident that power is required to inaugurate an association in the first place, to guarantee its continuance, and to enforce its norms. Power supports the fundamental order of society and the social organization within it, wherever there is order. Power stands behind every association and sustains its structure. Without power there is no organization and without power there is no order. The intrusion of the time dimension and the exigencies of circumstance require continual re-adjustments of the structure of every association, not excepting the most inelastically organized, and it is power which sustains it through these transitions.[17] If power provides the initial impetus behind the organization of every association, it also supplies the stability which it maintains throughout its history. Authority itself cannot exist without the immediate support of power and the ultimate sanction of force.

   As important as power is, however, as a factor in both the formal and informal organization of associations, it is even more important where it reigns, uninstitutionalized, in the interstices between associations and has its locus in the community itself. Here we find the principal social issues of contemporary society—labor vs. capital, Protestant vs. Catholic, CIO vs. AFL, AMA vs. FSA, Hiss vs. Chambers (for this was not a conflict between individuals), Republican vs. Democrat, the regents of the University of California vs. the faculty, Russia vs. the United States, and countless others throughout the entire fabric of society. It is not the task of our present analysis to examine these conflicts in detail but rather to investigate the role of power wherever it appears. And here we have two logical possibilities— power in the relations of like groups and power in the relations of unlike groups. Examples of the former are commercial companies competing for the same market, fraternal organizations of the same kind competing for members, religious associations competing for adherents, newspapers competing for readers, construction companies bidding for the same contracts, political parties competing for votes, and so on through all the competitive situations of society. Examples of the latter are conflicts between organized labor and organized management, between the legislative and executive branches of government, between different sub-divisions of the same bureaucracy (*e.g.*, Army vs. Navy), between university boards of trustees and an association of university professors, and so on through an equally large number of instances. Power thus appears both in competition and in conflict and has no incidence in groups which neither compete nor conflict, *i.e.*, between groups which do not share a similar social matrix and have no social relations, as for example the American Council of Learned Societies and the American Federation of Labor. Power thus arises only in social opposition of some kind.

   It is no accident that the noun "power" has been hypostatized from the adjective "potential." It may seem redundant to say so, but power is always potential; that is, when it is used it becomes something else, either force or authority. This is the respect which gives meaning, for example, to the concept of a "fleet in being" in naval strategy. A fleet in being represents power, even though it is never used. When it goes into action, of course, it is no longer power, but force. It is for this reason that the Allies were willing to destroy the battleship *Richelieu,* berthed at Dakar, after the fall of France, at the price of courting the disfavor of the French. Indeed, the young officer attending his introductory lectures on naval strategy, is sometimes surprised to hear what he may consider an excessive and possibly even a perverse emphasis upon the phrase, "Protect the battleships." Why should the battleship, the mightiest engine of destruction afloat, require such care in assuring its protection with sufficient cruiser, destroyer, and air support? The answer is that a battleship is even more effective as a symbol of power than it is as an instrument of force.

If power is one of the imperatives of society it may also be partly a pretense and succeed only because it is inaccurately estimated, or unchallenged. This, of course, is a familiar stratagem in war. But it occurs in the majority of power relationships in society. The threat of a strike may succeed when the strike will not. Blackmail may have consequences more dire than the exposure of the secret. The threat of a minority to withdraw from an association may affect it more than an actual withdrawal. The threat of a boycott may achieve the result desired when the boycott itself would fail. As an example of this last, movie exhibitors sometimes discover that if they ignore a ban imposed upon a picture by a religious censor, the ban not only does not diminish the attendance figures but increases them. In poker parlance—and indeed it is precisely the same phenomenon—a "bluff" is powerful, but the power vanishes when the bluff is called.

We may, in a comparatively brief conclusion, attempt to locate the sources of power. Power would seem to stem from three sources: (1) numbers of people, (2) social organization, and (3) resources. In a previous paper we have discussed in some detail the role of majorities in both unorganized and organized social groups, and in both the formal and informal aspects of the latter, and arrived at the conclusion, among others, that majorities constitute a residual locus of social power. It is neither necessary nor desirable to review this proposition here, beyond reiterating an emphasis upon the power which resides in numbers. Given the same social organization and the same resources, the larger number can always control the smaller and secure its compliance. If majorities, particularly economic and political majorities, have frequently and for long historical periods suffered oppression, it is because they have not been organized or have lacked resources. The power which resides in numbers is clearly seen in elections of all kinds, where the majority is conceded the right to institutionalize its power as authority—a right which is conceded because it can be taken. This power appears in all association, even the most autocratic. It is the power of a majority, even in the most formally and inflexibly organized associations, which either threatens or sustains the stability of the associational structure.[18]

As important as numbers are as the primary source of social power, they do not in themselves suffice. As suggested above, majorities may suffer oppression for long historical periods, they may, in short, be powerless or possess only the residual power of inertia. We arrive therefore at the second source of social power—social organization. A well organized and disciplined body of marines or of police can control a much larger number of unorganized individuals. An organized minority can control an unorganized majority. But even here majorities possess so much residual power that there are limits beyond which this kind of control cannot be exercised. These limits appear with the recognition that the majority may organize and thus reverse the control. And an organized majority, as suggested in the paper previously referred to, is the most potent social force on earth.

Of two groups, however, equal or nearly equal in numbers and comparable in organization, the one with access to the greater resources will have the superior power. And so resources constitute the third source of social power. Resources may be of many kinds—money, property, prestige, knowledge, competence, deceit, fraud, secrecy, and, of course, all of the things usually included under the term "natural resources." There are also supernatural resources in the case of religious associations which, as agencies of a celestial government, apply supernatural sanctions as instruments of control. In other words, most of the things we have previously differentiated from power itself may now be re-introduced as among the sources of power. It is easily apparent that, in any power conflict, they can tip the balance when the other sources of power are relatively equal and comparable. But they are not themselves power. Unless utilized by people who are in organized association with one another they are quite devoid of sociological significance.

It may finally be of more than incidental interest to note that there is one, and only one, kind of social situation in which the power of opposing groups is completely balanced. The numbers on each "side" are equal, their social organization is identical, and their resources are as nearly the same as possible. This situation reveals itself in games and contests in which power components are cancelled out and the victory goes to the superior skill. Whether the game be baseball or bridge there is insistence, inherent in the structure of the game itself, upon an equalization of power and this is the universal characteristic of all sports and the basis of the conception "fair play."[19] It would be foolish, of course, to assert that resources are always equal. The New York Yankees, for example, have financial resources which are not available to the St. Louis Browns and one bridge partnership may have better cards than its opponent. But such inequalities excite disapproval because they deny the nature of sport. The franchise of the Browns may be transferred from St. Louis for this reason, and tournament bridge is duplicate bridge so that all teams will play the same hands. When resources cannot be equalized, the situation ceases to be a game and sentiment supports the "underdog." We thus have here a most familiar but nevertheless peculiar power situation, one in which power is so balanced as to be irrelevant. Sport may be a moral equivalent for war, as William James wanted to believe, but it can never be a sociological equivalent. The two situations are only superficially similar. The difference between a conflict and a contest is that the former is a power phenomenon and the latter is not.

In this paper we have taken a somewhat vague and ambiguous concept, the concept of social power, and have attempted to sharpen the edges of its meaning. Among the proposals offered, the following may serve as a summary: (1) power is a social phenomenon *par excellence,* and not merely a political or economic phenomenon; (2) it is useful to distinguish power from prestige, from influence, from dominance, from rights, from force, and from authority; (3) power is latent force, force is manifest power, and authority is institutionalized power; (4) power, which has its incidence only in social opposition of some kind, appears in different ways in formal organization, in informal organization, and in the unorganized community; and (5) the sources and necessary components of power reside in a combination of numbers (especially majorities), social organization, and resources. All of these are preliminary and even primitive propositions. All of them require additional analysis.

## REFERENCES

1. *The Web of Government,* New York: Macmillan, 1947, p. 458. MacIver goes on to say "The majority of the works on the theme are devoted either to proclaiming the importance of the role of power, like those of Hobbes, Gumplowicz, Ratzenhofer, Steinmetz, Treitschke, and so forth, or to deploring that role, like Bertrand Russell in his *Power." Ibid.* One might make the additional comment that most of the discussions of power place it specifically in a political rather than a sociological context and that in the latter sense the problem has attracted almost no attention.
2. See especially *The Modern State,* London: Oxford University Press, 1926, pp. 221–231, and *The Web of Government, op. cit.,* pp. 82–113, *et passim.*
3. It will be noted that not all of these examples of power exhibit the support of the state. To some of them the state is indifferent, to one it is opposed.
4. *Social Control,* New York: Macmillan, 1916, p. 78.
5. This distinction, among others, illustrates the impropriety of associating too closely the separate disciplines of psychology and sociology. Many psychologists and, unfortunately, some sociologists profess an inability to see that individual and group

phenomena are fundamentally different in character and that, for example, "the tensions that cause wars" have little to do with the frustrations of individuals. Just as the personal frustrations of soldiers interfere with the fighting efficiency of a military unit, so the personal frustrations of individuals reduce and sometimes destroy the efficiency of any organized action. Heller has an interesting comment in this connection: "The objective social function of political power may be at marked variance with the subjective intentions of the individual agents who give concrete expression to its organization and activities. The subjective motivations which induce the inhabitant to perform military service or to pay taxes are of minor importance. For political power, no less than every other type of social power, is a cause and effect complex, revolving about the objective social effect and not, at least not exclusively, about the subjective intent and attitude." See his article "Power, Political," *Encyclopaedia of the Social Sciences,* Vol. VI, p. 301. In other words, the subjective factors which motivate an individual to indulge in social action, the ends he seeks and the means he employs, have nothing to do, or at best very little to do, with the objective social consequences of the action. A man may join the army for any number of reasons—to achieve financial security and early retirement, to conform with the law, to escape a delicate domestic situation, to withdraw from an emotional commitment, to see the world, to escape the pressure of mortgage payments, to fight for a cause in which he believes, to wear a uniform, or to do as his friends are doing. None of these factors will affect very much the army which he joins. Similarly, people do not have children because they wish to increase the birth rate, to raise the classification of the municipal post office, or to contribute to the military strength of the state, although the births may objectively have all of these consequences.

6. An example will subsequently be supplied.

7. There is, of course, a further distinction between rights and privileges. Military leave, for example, is a privilege and not a right; it may be requested but it may not be demanded. It may be granted but, on the other hand, it may not.

8. As a matter of purely technical interest, it may be observed that all definitions are ultimately circular. Every system of inference must contain undefined or "primitive" terms in its initial propositions because, if it were necessary to define every term before using it, it would be impossible ever to begin talking or writing or reasoning. An undefined term in one system is not necessarily an indefinable term, however, particularly in another system, and furthermore this kind of circularity is no legal deficiency if the circle, so to speak, *nicht zu klein ist.* This engaging phrase comes from Herbert Feigl, a logician who has examined this problem in a paper on Moritz Schlick, *Erkenntnis* Band 7, 1937–1938, pp. 406. Ralph Eaton also discusses this problem in his *General Logic,* p. 298, as do Whitehead and Russell in the Introduction to *Principia Mathematica.*

9. Sanctions, of course, may be positive or negative, require or prohibit the commission of a social act.

10. Authority appears frequently in another sense as when, for example, we say that Charles Goren is an authority on bridge or Emily Post on etiquette. Here it carries the implication of superior knowledge or skill or competence and such persons are appealed to as sources of information or as arbiters. In this sense authority is related to influence but not to power.

11. This is what Max Weber called *legitime Herrschaft,* which Parsons translates as "authority." See *The Theory of Social and Economic Organization,* Parsons editor, New York: Oxford University Press, 1947, p. 152, n. 83.

12. As in a case at the University of Illinois.

13. As in the Melish case in Brooklyn, which is currently a subject for litigation in the courts.

14. That even the most highly and rigidly organized groups are not immune from these invasions of power has been illustrated, in a previous paper, with respect to the Roman Catholic Church, the United States Navy, and the Communist Party. See Robert Bierstedt, "The Sociology of Majorities," *American Sociological Review,* 13 (December, 1948), 700–710.

**15.** *The Web of Government, op. cit.,* p. 13.

**16.** The terms in quotation marks are E. T. Hiller's. See his *Social Relations and Structures,* New York: Harper, 1947, Chapters 13, 14, 38.

**17.** If the power of the members, informally exercised, supports an association through changes in structure, it is the structure itself which supports it through changes in personnel.

**18.** For an elaboration of this theme see "The Sociology of Majorities," *op. cit.*

**19.** The game of poker is an exception. Here, unless there are betting limits, resources are not initially equalized among the contestants. In this situation, as in war, deceit is encouraged and becomes a part of the structure of the game. It is for this reason, probably, that poker sometimes carries a connotation of immorality.

# POWER AND AUTHORITY: A SUMMARY * (*Gerth and Mills*)

The political order, we have said, consists of those institutions within which men acquire, wield, or influence distributions of power. We ascribe "power" to those who can influence the conduct of others even against their will.

Where everyone is equal there is no politics, for politics involves subordinates and superiors. All institutional conduct, of course, involves distributions of power, but such distributions are the essence of politics. In so far as it has to do with "the state," the political order is the "final authority"; in it is instituted the use of final sanctions, involving physical force, over a given territorial domain. This trait marks off political institutions, such as the state, from other institutional orders.

Since power implies that an actor can carry out his will, power involves obedience. The general problem of politics accordingly is the explanation of varying distributions of power and obedience, and one basic problem of political psychology is why men by their obedience accept others as the powerful. Why do they obey?

A straightforward, although inadequate, answer is given by those who see men in the large as herd animals who must be led by a strong man who stays out in front. The explanation of power and obedience in terms of the strong man may hold in some primitive contexts in which only the strong fighter has a chance to become a military and political chieftain;[1] it may also hold in the "gang," where awe of the strongest holds the others to obedience, and contests over power are decided by fist fights. Beyond such situations, however, the problem of power cannot be reduced to a problem of simple physical might.

In Bernard Shaw's *Saint Joan,* the dauphin dryly remarks that he lacked a great deal in almost everything because his ancestors had used it all up. Yet, despite such personal weaknesses, other men looked up to the dauphin and obeyed him. Physical and mental weaklings are often found ruling proud and strong men. We cannot therefore always explain authority and obedience in terms of the characteristics of the power holder. Although Bismarck once said that you can do all sorts of things with bayonets except sit on them, obviously power and obedience involve more than differences in the biological means and the physical implements of violence.[2]

The incongruity of strong men willingly obeying physical weaklings leads us to ask: Why are there stable power relations which are *not* based on the direct and physical force of the stronger? The question has been answered by political scientists and philosophers in terms of a consensus between the subordinates and the powerful. This consensus has been rationally formulated in theories of "contract," "natural law," or "public sentiment."[3] For the social psychologist, such approaches are valuable in that they emphasize the question of voluntary obedience, for from a psychological point of view the crux of the problem of power rests in understanding the origin, constitution, and maintenance of voluntary obedience.

There is an element of truth in Laud's assertation: "There can be no firmness without law; and no laws can be binding if there is no conscience to obey them; penalty alone could never, can never do it."[4] In any given political order, we may expect to find both "conscience" and "coercion," and it is the element of conscience, of voluntary obedience, that engages our attention, even though we keep in mind the fact that regardless of the type and extent of conscience, all states practice coercion.

An adequate understanding of power relations thus involves a knowledge of the grounds on which a power holder claims obedience, and the terms in which the obedient feels an obligation to obey. The problem of the grounds of obedience is not a suprahistorical question; we are concerned rather with reconstructing those central ideas which in given institutional structures in fact operate as grounds for obedience. Often such ideas are directly stated and theoretically elaborated; often they are merely implied, left inarticulate and taken for granted. But, in either case, different reasons for obedience prevail in different political institutions.

In terms of the publicly recognized reasons for obedience—"legitimations" or symbols of justification[5]—the core of the problem of politics consists in understanding "authority." For it is authority that characterizes enduring political orders. The power of one animal over another may occur in terms of brute coercion, accompanied by grunts and growls, but man, as Suzanne Langer has written, can "control [his] inferiors by setting up symbols of [his] power, and the mere idea that words or images convey stands there to hold our fellows in subjection even when we cannot lay our hands on them. . . . Men . . . oppress each other by symbols of might."[6]

*Power* is simply the probability that men will act as another man wishes. This action may rest upon fear, rational calculation of advantage, lack of energy to do otherwise, loyal devotion, indifference, or a dozen other individual motives. *Authority*, or legitimated power, involves voluntary obedience based on some idea which the obedient holds of the powerful or of his position. "The strongest," wrote Rousseau, "is never strong enough to be always master, unless he transforms his strength into right, and obedience into duty."[7]

Most political analysts have thus come to distinguish between those acts of power which, for various reasons, are considered to be "legitimate," and those which are not. We speak of "naked power" as, for instance, during warfare, after which the successful tries to gain "authority" over the defeated; and we speak of "authority" in cases of legitimate acts of power, and thus, of "public authorities," or "ecclesiastic" or "court authority" and so on. In order to become "duly authorized," power needs to clothe itself with attributes of "justice," "morality," "religion," and other cultural values which define acceptable "ends" as well as the "responsibilities" of those who wield power. Since power is seen as a means, men ask: "Whose power and for what ends?" And most supreme power holders seek to give some sort of answer, to clothe their power in terms of other ends than power for power's sake.

REFERENCES

1. "And when Saul stood among the people, he was higher than any of the people from his shoulders and upward" (I Sam., 10:23).
2. The extent of violence in political orders varies. Thus thirteen out of fourteen nineteenth-century presidents of Bolivia died by violence, but only four out of thirty-three presidents of the United States. Cf. P. A. Sorokin, "Monarchs and Rulers," *Social Forces*, March 1926.
3. See Chapter X: Symbol Spheres, especially Section 1: Symbol Spheres in Six Contexts
4. Cited by John N. Figgs, *The Divine Right of Kings* (rev. ed.; Cambridge: University Press, 1934), p. 265.
5. See Chapter X: Symbol Spheres.
6. *Fortune*, January 1944, p. 150. See also her *Philosophy in a New Key* (Cambridge: Harvard Univ. Press, 1942), pp. 286–87.
7. J. J. Rousseau, *Social Contract*, rev. tr. by Charles Frankel (New York: Hafner, 1947).

# BUREAUCRATIC AUTHORITY:
# THE CONVERGENCE OF
# WEBER AND BARNARD * (*Hopkins*)

Organizational theory today contains two different views of systems of bureaucratic authority. In one, which has its source in the writings of Max Weber, they are power structures operating in a quasi-judicial fashion: rational values legitimate them, trained experts run them, and the principle of hierarchy, prescribing a positive relation between the rank of a unit and its power, defines their shape. In the other, developed most fully by Chester I. Barnard, they are communications processes. Here they function to apprise decision makers of relevant matters of fact and to inform those who execute the decisions of their responsibilities. In this conception neither legitimacy nor hierarchy plays a particularly central role. Both occur, but individual self-interests rather than shared moral commitments provided the main motivations, and the lateral extension of the system in physical space is more salient than its vertical extension in stratified social space. If the first view suggests the image of a pyramid, the second suggests a wheel, with the lines of communication as so many spokes radiating from the few persons at the organization's center who make the decisions to the many along the outer rim who finally carry the decisions out. In one, then, the outstanding elements are power, hierarchy, and legitimacy; in other, decision making, communication, and rational self-interest. Taken together, they comprise the major concepts currently used in the study of bureaucratic authority.

In point of fact, however, they are seldom taken together. Either one view or the other is used but not usually the two in combination. In consequence, many studies of communication systems read as though the exercise of authority depended up on the good will and rationality of the participants, and many studies emphasizing power leave the impression that, so far as the effectiveness of the system is concerned, the processes through which authority is exercised are of little consequence. So much is more implicit than explicit, of course—few proponents of one point of view would actually deny the relevance of the other—but since the researcher usually takes a part for the whole to begin with, it is not surprising that he sometimes ends up with incomplete, and to that extent misleading, conclusions.

* Reprinted from *Complex Organizations, A Sociological Reader*, edited by Amitai Etzioni, copyright © 1962, Holt, Rinehart and Winston, Inc.

Moreover, the two types of findings, once in, remain unrelated—conclusions about power structures and communication systems are rarely seen to have implications for one another—with the result that theoretical developments have been relatively few and far between and, when they do occur, limited to commentaries on the views or additions to them.[1] In short, partly owing to their separation from one another, neither conception has developed very far in the direction of a coherent propositional theory of bureaucratic authority. Rather, each has remained in this respect largely as it was when originally formulated—a loosely related set of assumptions, concepts, and implicit propositions.

It therefore seems reasonable to attempt to integrate the two views of bureaucratic authority. One way of doing this is to turn back to Weber and Barnard, systematically compare their accounts, and then outline the resulting composite picture of bureaucratic authority structures. This paper attempts to carry out such a review. It first demonstrates that, so far as both the definition of authority and the explanation of the stability of bureaucratic authority structures are concerned, Weber and Barnard develop similar ideas. Their convergence on these two points gives the essay its title. Subsequently it suggests where and in what degree their explanations of the effectiveness of authority systems differ. The principal propositions of their theories, and thus the main sources for the two views of bureaucratic authority just described, occur in these explanations, and for this reason only a summary of them is given here. The essay concludes with an outline of their combined conceptions.

## The Definition of Bureaucratic Authority

For Weber, authority of any kind is exercised when a given order is obeyed, when the recipient's action "follows in essentials such a course that the content of the command may be taken to have become the basis of action for its own sake."[2] For Barnard bureaucratic authority is exercised when a communication is accepted, which occurs when the communication governs "the action he (the recipient) contributes" or determines "what he does or does not do so far as the organization is concerned."[3] Both men, then, see the problem of authority as primarily a problem of compliance, they define compliance in the same general way, and, in consequence, their theories are addressed to the same range of problems, the determinants of stable structures of compliant actions.

The setting within which this compliance takes place, and which gives it its specifically bureaucratic character is, in Weber, the rationally organized "corporate group" and, in Barnard, the formally organized "cooperative system."[4] These are not equivalent concepts, since corporate groups by definition have both a restricted membership and rules enforced by specific persons, whereas neither is a necessary feature of cooperative systems. But if the corporate group and the cooperative system have rational, formalized, and complex organizations, they are sufficiently alike to permit the remaining differences to be ignored here because, first, both theories focus on the internal structure and operation of units—their organization— not on their particular goals or social contexts, and, second, both assume, so far as these rationally organized units are concerned, that the grounds for compliance and the qualities that make a system of authority effective are in principle everywhere the same. Owing to this focus and its parallel assumption, Weber and Barnard use the same criterion to judge the effectivents of bureaucratic authority systems, namely, the extent to which those subject to the organization's formalized rules and orders actually obey them.[5]

The concern with compliance further restricts the scope of the theories. Because of it one might think these authors slight the part of authority that pertains to its exercise. In their theories, however, the giving of orders or the sending of communications are themselves forms of compliance, because the orders a participant gives are assumed to derive directly from those he receives. True, in a rationally organized system this sort of chain of command ends eventually in a set of established general rules or policies and a policy-making body. But at this point both theories cease to have relevance. Neither includes as part of its subject matter the actions by which general rules are initially established or intentionally changed. Both pertain only to the command-obedience sequences by which already formulated policies are translated into routine operations and continually maintained in effect.

So much, then, for the subject matter and scope of the theories, the further development of which thus falls naturally into two parts, one dealing with the grounds for compliance in a general way and the second, with the properties of social structure which presumably affect the degrees of compliance and therefore serve to distinguish between authority systems that are more and less effective.

### The Grounds for Compliance: Motives and Values

The "motivation" to obey seemingly receives a good deal of attention, for Weber begins with a discussion of it and Barnard talks about it in various places. But in point of fact neither says anything important about the social psychology of compliance.[6] Instead, both introduce the element of shared values and conclude, each in his own way, that the participants in an organization must to some extent hold in common certain "legitimating" beliefs or "fictions" if obedience is to occur regularly and the chain of command to prove stable.

## LEGITIMACY

As was said, Weber begins his discussion of authority by mentioning a number of motives that may come into play in particular circumstances. But almost immediately he turns from these to "the belief in legitimacy." This, he holds, provides the only "sufficiently reliable basis" for a stable and effective system of authority.[7] Different types of value system provide this belief and so enable different systems of authority to exist.

For bureaucratic authority, the value system providing the required legitimation is rational-legal and contains, *inter alia,* the following ideas: obedience is an obligation of statuses, not of persons as such; an issued command is an interpretation or application of a general rule; such rules (whether established unilaterally by the governing group or voted into being by a majority of the participants) apply in principle to all participants, no one being above the law; the rules may be changed.[8]

This concept of legitimacy designates an essentially moral element. By introducing it Weber is claiming that, in general, people obey when they do because they feel a moral obligation to do so, because, specifically, they and everyone else define the statuses they occupy as allowing or requiring them to do so. To put it in contemporary terms, a system of authority has the property of legitimacy to the extent that the statuses and roles are institutionalized: an act of commanding and its reciprocal act of obeying do not form a specific and stable pattern unless both are appropriate actions within a well-defined role relation.[9]

## THE FICTION OF SUPERIOR AUTHORITY

When Barnard discusses "motives" he does not move directly to the sphere of values but first introduces the concept, "zone of indifference." Among all the orders a person in a particular position in an organization might conceivably receive, some he would consider unacceptable, some would be on the borderline of acceptability, and some would be "unquestionably acceptable." These last fall within that particular person's "zone of indifference," and these he will readily obey.[10]

The "zone," then, is a characteristic of the person. Its scope is determined, not by characteristics distinctive to him as an individual, however, but by characteristics common to all who occupy a similar position in the organization's structure. Turning first to the order itself, Barnard says an acceptable order is usually one which

> . . . *lies within the range that in a general way was anticipated [by the person] at the time of undertaking the connection with the organization.*[11]

These anticipations, he next suggests, are socially determined and form elements of a normative consensus:

> *The common sense of the community informally arrived at affects the attitude of individuals, and makes them, as individuals, loath to question authority that is within or near the [community's] zone of indifference.*[12]

What begins conceptually as a personal zone of indifference becomes in this way part of the definition of the person's status in the organization: he can usually be counted upon to accept any communications or to obey any orders which, because of this status, he both expects to accept and is expected by others to accept. Barnard then introduces the rank structure and the rational-legal ideology and thus arrives at the position taken by Weber:

> *The formal statement of this common sense is the fiction that authority comes down from above, from the general to the particular. This fiction merely establishes a presumption among individuals in favor of the acceptability of orders from superiors. . . . [It] makes it possible normally to treat a personal question impersonally.*[13]

Basic to both men's conceptions, then, are shared values. In effect, each applies to a particular class of actions, the giving and obeying of orders, the general theorem that motivational and cultural elements of action are integrated.[14] Their conceptions thus contain at this point, besides the earlier definitions, the proposition that in a rational and complex organization compliance with the rules varies with the institutionalization of the roles through which commands are issued and obeyed. This statement should be regarded, not as an hypothesis within the theory, however, but as the basis for a further restriction of its subject matter: in order to apply the theory in particular cases, one must be able to assume that compliance is to some extent an institutionalized pattern; otherwise no authority system exists, and therefore no question of its effectiveness arises.

The two views of bureaucratic authority are alike, then, in the following ways. Both define the exercise of authority in terms of compliance; locate the compliant actions within social systems that exhibit a rationalized, formalized, and complex type of organization; define the effectiveness of authority systems as the extent to which those subject to the organization's rules in fact comply with them; assume that for all such systems the grounds for compliance and the qualities that make an authority system effective are in principle the same; and postulate that an authority system exists in so far as compliance is an aspect of the actions of institutionalized roles.

## Bureaucratic Structures of Authority

By definition, all authority structures are institutionalized at least to some extent; presumably, therefore, a system with an authority structure exhibits a higher degree of compliance than a system without one, other things being equal. In addition, though, some authority structures secure higher degrees of compliance than others do, and it is differences of this latter kind, differences in the relative effectiveness of authority structures, that both theories attempt to explain.

The explanations are not so much alike as complementary, however, a fact which accounts for the two views of bureaucratic authority described briefly in the introduction to this paper. Weber and Barnard analyze social structures in somewhat different ways and predicate properties of somewhat different structual units, and in consequence their hypotheses also differ. Weber examines the status of administrator (the office), attributes authority to this unit, and explains the effective exercise of authority mainly in terms of other attributes of the office or in terms of attributes brought to it by officials. Barnard, in contrast, examines the role relation (channel of communication), attributes authority to communications (which thus become more or less authoritative), and explains effectiveness in terms of other attributes of communications or in terms of attributes of role relations that transmit communications. In principle, what is true of a role relation should be translatable into something that is true of a status, and vice versa. The necessary definitions have yet to be formulated, however, and the two conceptions thus appear to differ more than they actually do.

### THE ADMINISTRATIVE OFFICE

From the first Weber employs the principle of hierarchy to divide the participants in the corporate group into three ranked strata: there are the rulers who establish the rules, the administrators who interpret and apply them, and the "subjects" or subordinates (so far as the authority system is concerned) who only comply with them.[15] In the theory of legal authority he pays little attention to the first and third strata and concerns himself instead with the administrative staff. This he describes in two ways, first, in terms of the organizational features that are necessary if the staff as a unit is to perform effectively in its pivotal position between the rulers and the subjects and, second, in terms of the characteristics of officials that make it likely they will do what they are supposed to do as staff members and nothing else.

With respect to the first list, Weber claims in effect that subjects who hold to a rationalistic ideology obey more readily and frequently if the administrative staff's organization can be described by "the fundamental categories of rational-legal authority."[16] These include the following: an explicit and specific statement of the purposes of the corporate group; a set of well-defined statuses differentiated in the light of these purposes; and the arrangement of the statuses in a single hierarchy in which "each lower (ranking) office is under the control and supervision of a higher (ranking) one."[17] Despite the language in which these statements are couched, they constitute a complex proposition, not a definition, and so could conceivably be wrong in part.

In the second set of statements Weber deliberately confines analysis to the structure of authority *within* the administrative staff itself.[18] Officials who are personally free, subject to organizational authority only within specified spheres, appointed according to their technical qualifications, contractually related to the organization, free to resign, and paid by salary; who treat the office as their primary occupation, view it as integral to their careers, and work without owning or appropriating the means of administration—officials in such a system, Weber asserts, are more likely to comply with the organization's rules than officials in systems that lack one or more of these characteristics.[19] Again, this is a complex proposition, not a definition, and could be wrong in whole or in part.

Weber's detailed attention to the structure of the administrative staff seems justified, since the extent to which those lowest in the full hierarchy comply with the rules, and hence the effectiveness of the authority system, depends directly on the administrators' compliance with the rules. However, his neglect of the lowest stratum suggests what surely is not so, that the effectiveness of an authority system is unaffected by the type of social structure among those only subject to it. Substantial differences in organization distinguish the clients or publics of a government agency from the students of a college or the workers of a factory, for example, and such differences, it would seem, can hardly help affecting the degree of compliance typically found in each case. Barnard's approach has in this respect a distinct advantage over Weber's, because it prevents the analyst from committing just this sort of error of omission.

THE CHANNELS OF COMMUNICATION

Basic to Barnard's idea of organizational structure is the concept, "unit of organization."[20] Composed of one superior and several subordinates, these units are in other respects much like Weber's offices. They have clearly defined and specific purposes within the total organization; are marked out as part of the rational division of labor; and, in particular, are arranged hierarchically. Moreover, in Barnard's view *all* activities of the organization take place within the context of one or another of its units, and so *all* participants, whatever their place in the authority system, occupy definite positions in relation to one another. The analyst is thus unlikely to overlook the type of social structure found among those lowest (or highest, for that matter) in the hierarchy he is examining.

These units form a coherent whole in Barnard's scheme because of the double location of their higher-ranking positions. That is, ranked pairs of units have in common one status which in the subordinate unit has high rank and in the superior unit low rank.[21] The foreman, for instance, is simultaneously located in a lower managerial unit and a work unit. A status so located is Barnard's equivalent of Weber's office, and the aggregate of such statuses is the equivalent of the administrative staff. But at this point an important difference between the two modes of analysis shows up.

Because he pictures a structure divided into three distinct strata, Weber is able to isolate his administrative staff, to view it as if it were a detachable part of a total organization. Barnard cannot do this. Exactly this sort of abstraction is precluded by his view of organizational structure. For if one looks at the total organization as a set of interlocking units of organization, neither an administrative status nor an administrative staff so stands out that it can be easily separated from the structure as a whole. What Barnard does abstract, what for him is a relatively free element of structure, is the role relation between two positions within a unit, e.g., the foreman-supervisor relation of the lower managerial unit or the foreman-worker relation of the work unit. These relations taken collectively, however, constitute, not one particular stratum of participants, but the communications structure of the total organization. (In turn, therefore, the organization may be viewed as a network of such relations.) In effect, authority here "flows" to those subject to it through the communications system; it is not exercised "over them" by a well-defined administrative staff.[22]

As might be expected, Barnard describes first what he takes to be the characteristics of an acceptable communication (an order that will be obeyed). These, he says, are four: from the recipient's point of view the communication must be understandable, consistent with the purpose of the organization, compatible with his personal interests, and capable of being executed.[23] Later he adds that the communication must also be authenticated: the recipient must believe that it comes from a particular position and that this position has the right to send such a communication.[24] Since this whole topic receives no attention from Weber, it is worth pointing out that the characteristics listed by Barnard fit well with Weber's characterization of the office. For example, trained officials should be more capable of understanding and executing orders than untrained officials should; and officials who are dependent on the office for their income and style of life should find a wider range of orders compatible with their personal interests than less dependent officials should. Nevertheless, whether or not Barnard's characteristics are considered to derive from Weber's, they are, like his, parts of hypotheses about effective authority structures, not parts of a definition. That orders "consistent" with the purposes of the organization are more readily or more often obeyed than those which are not, for example, is a statement of fact in the present context, not a definition.

Barnard next concerns himself with the "channels of communication" or "lines of authority."[25] Here his analysis is less compact, but again there are several places where his assertions directly parallel statements by Weber, as, for example, in his claim that ". . . individuals are able to exercise authority only when they are acting officially."[26] At the same time, though, owing to his concern with the processes on which the exercise of authority depends, he is able to suggest an important property of office which Weber fails to mention: "Objective authority is only maintained if the positions or leaders continue to be adequately informed."[27] With respect to the lines of authority proper, Barnard lists six properties. Two of these are like two of Weber's: that the persons serving as "communications' centers" must be "competent"[28] corresponds directly to Weber's similar statement; and that the "channels of communication should be definitely known"[29] is similar in content, though not in phrasing, to Weber's requirement that each office consist of a "specified sphere of competence."[30] In addition, Barnard asserts that effective channels formally connect every participant to the organization; that they are as short as possible between any two positions but once set up are never "jumped" by a "communication from the head of an organization to the bottom"; and that they are not broken by a temporary or permanent absence while the organization is in operation.[31]

In summary, then, although they focus on different units of social structure, Weber and Barnard list properties of effective authority systems that are either similar or complementary but never contradictory. Their versions of effective systems are, however, different, because Barnard describes primarily the process through which such a system operates, and Weber, primarily its structure.

## A Composite View

The following outline of a theory of bureaucratic authority systems is directly based on what has gone before, but it necessarily departs in several respects from the two views taken separately. There are three parts to it, the concept of an authority system, the concept of bureaucratic authority systems, and some propositions about the latter. The usual qualifications that precede an attempt such as this apply here: the approach taken is only one of several that could be followed; only a few of the more important parts of the theory are discussed and these only sketchily; a more satisfactory formulation would emphasize the matters of fact for which there is systematic evidence on hand.

THE CONCEPT OF AUTHORITY SYSTEMS

This concept can be described in four steps.

*The exercise of authority* consists of one person issuing a command and a second complying with it, and thus it is a form of interaction. This statement holds whether the interaction is a specific command-and-obedience sequence, or the more enduring and inclusive kind of sequence where one party establishes general rules which the other continually conforms to. Proclaiming a general policy and issuing a single piece of advice are thus equally "commands," and the appropriate responses, equally "compliance."

*Authoritative role relations.* A role relation is authoritative to the degree that it exhibits a stable distribution of commanding actions to one role and the reciprocal complying actions to the other.[32] Relations so differentiated are of two primary types: simple, which do not directly implicate third parties (most professional-client authority relations), and complex, in which a command from A to B implies a subsequent command from B to C (most bureaucratized authority relations).

*Complex structures of authority.* Ordered sets of complex relations form complex structures of authority, and the interactions within them (or, more precisely, with respect to them) constitute the operation of authority systems. Such structures normally include three principal classes of participants, although in concrete circumstances it may not always be easy to distinguish them clearly: a ruling group from which general orders issue forth, an administrative staff which interprets and transmits the orders, and "subjects," that is, those who only comply. (This, of course, is an extremely simplified formulation, but there is not space to qualify or to expand these statements.)

*Legitimation.* A structure of authority of this complex sort is always embedded in some kind of group, at least in part.[33] Expressed otherwise, an authority system is only an abstracted aspect of some concrete social system.[34] The principal significance of this embeddedness is the "legitimation" of the authority system: the members of the group share various values and norms, among which are the values that justify the existence of the authority system and the norms that define its roles and interactions. The same general condition that largely determines the stability of any type of social structure therefore determines also the stability of authority structures, namely, their degree of institutionalization.

Not all who occupy statuses in an authority system, however, need be members of the group whose values legitimate it.[35] Aliens are not "members" (citizens) of the country they are visiting, but they nevertheless occupy a definite status in relation to those who enforce its laws. Again, Weber comments in passing that those subject to an authority system may not even consider it legitimate; in this event the ruling group and the administrative staff alone comprise the membership of the group whose values legitimate it.[36] From the point of view of nonmembers, then, the structure may or may not be legitimate. If it is not, it is less highly institutionalized (and so will probably prove less stable and less effective) than if it were. But the concept requires only that some group's values legitimate the authority system, not that all who occupy positions in the hierarchy consider it legitimate, much less that they be members of that group.

*Bureaucratic systems of authority.* In principle any form of group may provide values legitimating an authority structure. Bureaucratic systems of authority occur in the context of groups having a certain type of value system and a certain type of organization and are themselves in turn characterized by certain distinctive structural features.

*Rational-legal values.* The values legitimating the bureaucratic system of authority conform to Weber's description of the rational-legal ideology and have the effect noted by Barnard, that they "make it possible normally to treat a personal question impersonally."[37]

*Formal organization.* Correspondingly, the group has a relatively specific and explicit set of aims; a body of explicit rules intentionally established in order to realize these aims (or rationalized as being in support of them); and several specialized units of organization, which together contain all the activities deemed necessary to achieve the aims. Universities, factories, hospitals, modern armies, these are all in this sense formally organized groups.

*Bureaucratic structures of authority.* The authority system itself is a product of this rational allocation of labor. The actions which compose it are among those formally assigned to the units and, within the units, to the roles. That is, the units of the rationally organized group are differentiated with respect to responsibility for coordinating the activities carried on within or by the group as a whole; and within each unit the roles are differentiated with respect to coordinating the activities carried on within or on behalf of the unit. Paralleling this is the differentiation of both units and roles with respect to rank: in general, the higher the rank, the greater the coordinating responsibility, and vice versa. (This is the principle of hierarchy.)

A higher-ranking unit is joined to each of the units immediately subordinate to it by a common status: the highest-ranking status within each subordinate unit is at the same time a low-ranking status within the superior unit.[38] The set of these linking statuses constitutes the group's administrative stratum, and it is the activities of these administrators which constitute the heart of the authority system. For, in bureaucratically organized systems, neither the making of policy decisions, which is the specific task of the ruling group, nor the patterns of compliance among those who are only subject to authority (and who may perform any of a very large number of activities), is as such central to the authority system.

Bureaucratic authority thus always operates relative to a given set of rules and produces compliance with them; its systematic exercise is specifically unidirectional;[39] and the measure of its effectiveness is the degree of compliance with the group's formal rules or with the administrators' interpretations of them.

TWO TYPES OF PROPOSITION

Not all actual formal organizations exhibit structures conforming to this model, of course. For concrete systems which do, Weber's and Barnard's conceptions contain a number of propositions which, because they assert matters of fact, can in principle be tested. One kind refers to the authoritative role relation and describes the characteristics of acceptable orders and of effective superior-subordinate lines of communication. A second kind describes the characteristics exhibited by the administrative position or its occupants in effective bureaucratic systems of authority.

## Conclusion

Current studies of formal organizations tend to fall into two groups, those in which the authority system is viewed as a power structure and those in which it is viewed as a communications process, a division which this essay has tried to show is neither useful nor necessary. The principal theorists for each view, Weber on the one hand and Barnard on the other, converge in their ideas about the nature of bureaucratized systems of authority, and their explanations of effectiveness are mutually supporting, not mutually exclusive. Together they develop a conception of bureaucratic authority built around the important tautology that every imperative communication is both imperative and a communication.

REFERENCES

1. Perhaps the best of these are Robert K. Merton, "Bureaucratic Structure and Personality," in *Social Theory and Social Structure* (Glencoe, Ill.: Free Press, 1957), pp. 195–206; Talcott Parsons' discussion of authority in his "Introduction" to Max Weber, *The Theory of Social and Economic Organization*, trans. A. M. Henderson and Talcott Parsons (New York: Oxford, 1947), especially n. 4, pp. 58–60; and Talcott Parsons, "Authority, Legitimation, and Political Action," in Carl J. Friedrich (ed.), *Authority* (Cambridge, Mass.: Harvard, 1958), Chap. 12.
2. Weber, *op. cit.*, p. 327. A certain difficulty attends the interpretation of Weber's theory. In its original version it applies to whole societies, and states that differences in the way control is exercised result from differences in beliefs about the nature of authority. Naturally only a part of this theory is employed in current organizational studies, the part that describes the rational-legal conception of authority and its organizational form, bureaucracy: focusing on particular, concrete organizations, located in societies where this conception is highly institutionalized, these studies use Weber's categories as approximate descriptions of the organizations being examined. But owing to these shifts—from societies to organizations as the units being analyzed, and from cross-cultural comparisons to detailed studies of a particular organizational form—Weber's theory has acquired a second set of meanings and so can now be read in two broadly different ways. For this reason it should be said explicitly that its interpretation here reflects its use in current organizational research, not its original use.
3. Chester I. Barnard, *The Functions of the Executive* (Cambridge, Mass: Harvard, 1938), p. 163.
4. On corporate group, see Weber, *op. cit.*, Chap. 1, Sections 12–17. On cooperative systems, see Barnard, *op. cit.*, pp. 65 ff. Barnard attempts to distinguish between

the concept of "organization" and the concept of "group" (e.g., p. 112). A number of difficulties beset this distinction; but it does catch up one very important point, namely, that the edges ("boundaries") of the organization, as marked out by the line between participants and nonparticipants, does not necessarily coincide with the edges ("boundaries") of the group anchoring the organization, as marked out by the line between group member and nonmember. (On "group" and "member," see Merton, loc. cit., pp. 285–286.) Generally, the organization is the more inclusive; there are participants who are not members, but not usually vice versa. This distinction, between the concepts of participant and member, has an important bearing on the "legitimation" of particular authority structures.

5. Some confusion may arise here because neither writer consistently distinguishes between the effectiveness of the authority system and the effectiveness of the total organization. In Weber, the criterion of the latter is the extent to which the substantive goals of the corporate group are achieved. In Barnard, it is this attainment of goals plus the extent to which personnel are motivated to continue participating in the cooperative system.

6. Compare either's writings with, say, the rigorous paper by Hans Zetterberg, "Compliant Actions," Acta Sociologica, 2 (1957), 179–201.

7. Weber, op. cit., p. 325.

8. Ibid., pp. 329–330. Since the point has been misunderstood on at least one occasion, it bears emphasizing that these are not Weber's own ideas about legal authority but the ideas that, in the typical case, the people subject to a system of legal authority must hold if it is to prove stable and effective.—Ibid., p. 329. For the misunderstanding, see Alvin W. Gouldner, Patterns of Industrial Bureaucracy (Glencoe, Ill.: Free Press, 1954), pp. 19–20.

9. On the concept of institutionalization, see Talcott Parsons, The Social System (Glencoe, Ill.: Free Press, 1951), pp. 36–45. For a more exact rendering of "legitimacy," and a distinction between "legitimation" and "institutionalization," see Parsons, "Authority, Legitimation, and Political Action," loc. cit.

10. Barnard, op. cit., pp. 168–169.

11. Ibid., p. 169.

12. Ibid.

13. Ibid., pp. 169–170. "Fiction," it might be noted, means here a nonlogical construct in Pareto's sense, one which participants use to explain their behavior and which they believe in. Hence the ideas this "fiction" contains "have validity" for those in the system. Barnard himself notes in this regard, "Either as a superior officer or as a subordinate, . . . I know nothing I actually regard as more 'real' than 'authority.' "—Ibid., p. 170, n. 5.

14. Parsons, The Social System, pp. 36–45.

15. Weber does not say so, but these should be conceived as roles or statuses, not concrete persons. Especially in analyzing political systems is this important, because in the democratic type there is in principle a reversibility of the ruler-subject roles, just as in the perfect market there is a reversibility of buyer-seller roles. See below, n. 39.

16. Weber, op. cit., pp. 330–331.

17. Ibid., p. 331. "Office" may mean "unit organization" in Barnard's sense, for Weber speaks in this context of "administrative organs," but he is usually interpreted as referring to a status. For example, see Merton, loc. cit., pp. 195–196.

18. Weber, op. cit., p. 332.

19. Ibid., pp. 333–334.

20. Barnard, op. cit., pp. 109 ff.

21. Ibid., pp. 111–112.

22. Neither Weber's nor Barnard's approach to structures is in general the better one. Weber provides a more useful scheme for depicting structure as such; Barnard, for depicting process. If one wants to characterize the relatively stable differences among the units of a social system on the (complex) dimension of authority, then Weber's is the more useful. If one wants to examine the process(es) through which

these differences are continually re-created—through which "authority" is, so to speak, continually redistributed among the units—then Barnard's is the more useful. It is only a special case of the more general choice between viewing the units of a system as having constant (differential or equal) degrees of a property for the period of the analysis, or viewing them as having degrees of it that vary over this period. For many sociological problems this formal difference becomes the difference between using status as the unit of the system, or using role. See, for example, Talcott Parsons, "A Revised Analytical Approach to the Theory of Social Stratification," in Reinhard Bendix and Seymour Martin Lipset (eds.), *Class, Status, and Power* (Glencoe, Ill., Free Press, 1953), esp. p. 97.

23. *Ibid.*, pp. 165–166.
24. *Ibid.*, pp. 180–181. Before "authenticity" can become a property of communications, participants must view "authority" as a property of positions; the "fiction of superior authority" leads them to take such a view.
25. *Ibid.*, p. 175.
26. *Ibid.*, p. 172.
27. *Ibid.*, p. 174.
28. *Ibid.*, pp. 178–179. On the matter of "competence," Weber and Barnard emphasize somewhat different contents, but the gist of what each says is similar.
29. *Ibid.*, pp. 175–176.
30. Weber, *op. cit.*, p. 330.
31. Barnard, *op. cit.*, pp. 176–180.
32. Predicated of a role, then, authority is always relational: a role "has" a certain degree of authority only in virtue of the relation which defines it. If one predicates authority of a position independently of its relational context, as for example Parsons seems sometimes to do, then what is here called "authority" is equal to the *difference* between the two positions' degrees of authority *in relation to* one another. I do not think it especially useful, however, to conceive of every position in a structure as "having" *some* authority.
33. "Group" is used here as defined by Merton, *loc. cit.*, pp. 285–286. It refers "to a number of people who interact with one another in accord with established patterns" (p. 285), who define themselves as members, and who are defined as members by others.
34. Actually, the authority system is at least at two removes from the concrete group. At the first level of abstraction is the type of social system which best "fits" the group. The authority system is, in turn, an abstract aspect of this social system. It enters as one of the important ways in which units of the system differ from one another, but it is only one; and as one of the important processes constituting the operation of the system, but again as only one. In short, no type of social system is composed of "pure" authority roles; rather, social systems are composed of roles of which authority is only one of the properties or basic dimensions. Thus the roles of student and professor differ on the dimension of authority, but they contain much more; the "commanding" and "complying" aspects of the actions of each role hardly exhaust the significant content of the roles.
35. For the basis for this distinction, see above, n. 4.
36. Under certain conditions, says Weber, an authority structure ". . . can afford to drop even the pretense of a claim to legitimacy. But even then the mode of legitimation of the relation between the chief and his staff may vary widely according to the type of basis of the relation of authority between them . . ."—Weber, *op. cit.*, p. 327. See also the opening paragraph of David Hume's "Of the First Principles of Government."
37. Barnard, *op. cit.*, p. 170.
38. "This is clearly seen in practice, it being customary to recognize a foreman, or a superintendent of a shop section, or a captain, at one time or from one point of view as a 'member' of his gang, shop crew, or company, at another time or from another point of view as a member of a 'district management group,' or the 'shop executives' group,' or the 'regimental organization.'"—Barnard, *op. cit.*, p. 111.
39. Unidirectionality marks "democratic" systems, it might be noted, as much as it

does authoritarian systems, although it may not appear to at first. To make the point briefly, as an aside here, it is necessary to phrase it in an overly simple form. In democratic systems the ideology states that there exists a fourth and highest stratum, the citizenry, from which ultimate authority flows. Of course, for the most part this authority is latent as a structural matter, but at certain times (elections, referenda, and the like), the system changes phases: the "subject" status becomes temporarily latent, and the citizenry collectively issues "commands" to the next echelon, the ruling group. Consequently, in this sense, democratic processes are not the opposite of authority processes, as they are sometimes made to seem, but a particular kind of authority process.

# 6: Cohesion and Conflict

What makes for social order? What accounts for a condition of social cohesion among members of societies or groups? This was one of the earliest questions that sociology attempted to answer. The problem was clearly in the center of Auguste Comte's preoccupations when he formulated the principles of the science which he was the first to call sociology. Comte lived in a society which had been intensely disorganized by the series of social convulsions which began with the French Revolution; hence his quest for a science of order which could help recreate the lost cohesion of French society.

Comte's work now has but little impact on ongoing research (though more careful perusal of the texts might prove rewarding even to present-day researchers), but its impact on the other great pioneer of French sociology, Emile Durkheim, whose work is still of great import today, was considerable. Durkheim began to write after another great disintegrating crisis in French society: defeat in the war with Germany in 1870–71, the Commune, and the birth pangs of the Third Republic. Once again the problem of social cohesion in the face of threatening breakdown was very much the order of the day, and Durkheim's sociology was centrally concerned with this problem. But rather than speculate widely, and often vaguely, as Comte had been wont to do, Durkheim chose to investigate more carefully a series of variables which could be controlled with relative ease. His classic study of suicide is not simply a study of a "social problem" but is an attempt to show how differential suicide rates may be explained in terms of variations in the social cohesion—or solidarity—of different groups. Social solidarity is shown by Durkheim to constitute a key variable in different types of social action. If solidarity is weak, a number of "pathological" consequences—suicide being only one of them—are likely to occur. Inversely, high rates of such "pathological" behavior can be taken as an index of insufficient cohesion in total societies or their sub-groups. It was thus Durkheim's contention that a strong "collective conscience"—or moral integration—among members of a society indicates a degree of societal health, while a weak "collective conscience," a lack of cohesion and integration, indicates that the society suffered from some serious ailment. Social cohesion, Durkheim reasoned, provides psychic support to group members in the various crises of life; it relieves stresses and anxieties and thus cushions the impact of crisis on the individual. Those groups, then, which have little social cohesion cannot adequately protect their members from the impact of such anxieties and tend to have higher suicide rates.

The work of Durkheim has been under attack in various quarters for over half a century. It is easy, for example, to demonstrate the conservative bias in his writings. But his pinpointing of the importance of social cohesion as a sociological variable has been generally recognized as an important center of growth in sociological theorizing.

Our next two selections from the British anthropologists A. R. Radcliffe-Brown (1881–1956) and Bronislaw Malinowski have been placed in this section, though they do in part return to topics which have already been treated in the section on social control. Though these authors dealt with somewhat different phenomena—social sanctions and reciprocal obligations of group members respectively—both were concerned with essentially the same problem that intrigued Durkheim. They attempted to make us see how, and under what conditions, society succeeds in imposing some sort of order upon and cohesion between its members—how, in other words, these members "stick together."

The selections from Karl Marx (1818–1883), George Sorel (1847–1922), and Georg Simmel, as well as the final selections, might seem at first glance to deal with subjects far removed from those treated in the beginning of this section. They discuss social conflict, a phenomenon which might appear to be the very opposite of cohesion. Yet such a common-sense view, certain conservative thinkers to the contrary notwithstanding, is quite mistaken. Indeed, as the excerpts from the work of Karl Marx indicate, social conflict with some brings in its wake social cohesion with others. Social conflict, while seemingly a negative phenomenon which simply "tears down," is seen upon inspection to increase the cohesion of conflicting groups within a society. The modern bourgeoisie, as well as the modern working class, Marx contends, owe their historical existence to the struggle which they conducted against other classes and strata.

To this basic insight George Sorel, the brilliant French social theorist, adds the amplification that a decrease in conflict between classes leads to a decrease of cohesion within those classes, so that a lessening of the violence of class struggle may lead to a weakening of the boundaries between classes and, in the extreme case, to the complete loss of class cohesion and class identity.

Our selections from the classic work *Conflict* by Georg Simmel and from recent work by the British anthropologist, Max Gluckman, as well as by one of the authors of this volume, further extend the ideas already partly adumbrated in the Marxian approach, by pointing out that conflict may be a precondition for the orderly functioning of society. These authors see stability as a temporary balance of conflicting forces.

Rounding out the discussion, Ralf Dahrendorf, a young German sociologist, argues that static models of society recently in vogue cannot account for social change, and that only a conflict model can do justice to the dynamic elements within society.

# SUICIDE AND SOCIAL COHESION * (*Durkheim*)

The aptitude of Jews for suicide is always less than that of Protestants; in a very general way it is also, though to a lesser degree, lower than that of Catholics. Occasionally however, the latter relation is reversed; such cases occur especially in recent times. Up to the middle of the century, Jews killed themselves less frequently than Catholics in all countries but Bavaria; only towards 1870 do they begin to lose their ancient immunity. They still very rarely greatly exceed the rate for Catholics. Besides, it must be remembered that Jews live more exclusively than other confessional groups in cities and are in intellectual occupations. On this account they are more inclined to suicide than the members of other confessions, for reasons other than their religion. If therefore the rate for Judaism is so low, in spite of this aggra-

* Reprinted from *Suicide: A Study in Sociology* by Emile Durkheim, translated by George Simpson, pp. 156–161, 169–170, and 208–212, by permission of the publishers, The Free Press, Glencoe, Ill., and Routledge & Kegan Paul Ltd., London. Copyright, 1951, by The Free Press, A Corporation.

vating circumstance, it may be assumed that other things being equal, their religion has the fewest suicides of all.

These facts established, what is their explanation?

If we consider that the Jews are everywhere in a very small minority and that in most societies where the foregoing observations were made, Catholics are in the minority, we are tempted to find in these facts the cause explaining the relative rarity of voluntary deaths in these two confessions. Obviously, the less numerous confessions, facing the hostility of the surrounding populations, in order to maintain themselves are obliged to exercise severe control over themselves and subject themselves to an especially rigorous discipline. To justify the always precarious tolerance granted them, they have to practice greater morality. Besides these considerations, certain facts seem really to imply that this special factor has some influence. In Prussia, the minority status of Catholics is very pronounced, since they are only a third of the whole population. They kill themselves only one third as often as the Protestants. The difference decreases in Bavaria where two thirds of the inhabitants are Catholics; the voluntary deaths of the latter are here only in the proportion of 100 to 275 of those of Protestants or else of 100 to 238, according to the period. Finally, in the almost entirely Catholic Empire of Austria, only 155 Protestant to 100 Catholic suicides are found. It would seem then that where Protestantism becomes a minority its tendency to suicide decreases.

But first, suicide is too little an object of public condemnation for the slight measure of blame attaching to it to have such influence, even on minorities obliged by their situation to pay special heed to public opinion. As it is an act without offense to others, it involves no great reproach to the groups more inclined to it than others, and is not apt to increase greatly their relative ostracism as would certainly be the case with a greater frequency of crime and misdemeanor. Besides, when religious intolerance is very pronounced, it often produces an opposite effect. Instead of exciting the dissenters to respect opinion more, it accustoms them to disregard it. When one feels himself an object of inescapable hostility, one abandons the idea of conciliating it and is the more resolute in his most unpopular observances. This has frequently happened to the Jews and thus their exceptional immunity probably has another cause.

Anyway, this explanation would not account for the respective situation of Protestants and Catholics. For though the protective influence of Catholicism is less in Austria and Bavaria, where it is in the majority, it is still considerable. Catholicism does not therefore owe this solely to its minority status. More generally, whatever the proportional share of these two confessions in the total population, wherever their comparison has been possible from the point of view of suicide, Protestants are found to kill themselves much more often than Catholics. There are even countries like the Upper Palatinate and Upper Bavaria, where the population is almost wholly Catholic (92 and 96 per cent) and where there are nevertheless 300 and 423 Protestant suicides to 100 Catholic suicides. The proportion even rises to 528 per cent in Lower Bavaria where the reformed religion has not quite one follower to 100 inhabitants. Therefore, even if the prudence incumbent on minorities were a partial cause of the great difference between the two religions, the greatest share is certainly due to other causes.

We shall find these other causes in the nature of these two religious systems. Yet they both prohibit suicide with equal emphasis; not only do they penalize it morally with great severity, but both teach that a new life begins beyond the tomb where men are punished for their evil actions, and Protestantism just as well as Catholicism numbers suicide among them. Finally, in both cults these prohibitions are of divine origin; they are represented not as the logical conclusion of correct reason, but God Himself is their authority. Therefore, if Protestantism is less unfavorable to the development of suicide, it is not because of a different attitude from that of Catholicism. Thus, if both religions have the same precepts with respect to this particular matter, their dissimilar influence on suicide must proceed from one of the more general characteristics differentiating them.

The only essential difference between Catholicism and Protestantism is that the second permits free inquiry to a far greater degree than the first. Of course, Catholicism by the very fact that it is an idealistic religion concedes a far greater place to thought and reflection than Greco-Latin polytheism or Hebrew monotheism. It is not restricted to mechanical ceremonies but seeks the control of the conscience. So it appeals to conscience, and even when demanding blind submission of reason, does so by employing the language of reason. None the less, the Catholic accepts his faith ready made, without scrutiny. He may not even submit it to historical examination since the original texts that serve as its basis are proscribed. A whole hierarchical system of authority is devised, with marvelous ingenuity, to render tradition invariable. All *variation* is abhorrent to Catholic thought. The Protestant is far more the author of his faith. The Bible is put in his hands and no interpretation is imposed upon him. The very structure of the reformed cult stresses this state of religious individualism. Nowhere but in England is the Protestant clergy a hierarchy; like the worshippers, the priest has no other source but himself and his conscience. He is a more instructed guide than the run of worshippers but with no special authority for fixing dogma. But what best proves that this freedom of inquiry proclaimed by the founders of the Reformation has not remained a Platonic affirmation is the increasing multiplicity of all sorts of sects so strikingly in contrast with the indivisible unity of the Catholic Church.

We thus reach our first conclusion, that the proclivity of Protestantism for suicide must relate to the spirit of free inquiry that animates this religion. Let us understand this relationship correctly. Free inquiry itself is only the effect of another cause. When it appears, when men, after having long received their ready made faith from tradition, claim the right to shape it for themselves, this is not because of the intrinsic desirability of free inquiry, for the latter involves as much sorrow as happiness. But it is because men henceforth need this liberty. This very need can have only one cause: the overthrow of traditional beliefs. If they still asserted themselves with equal energy, it would never occur to men to criticize them. If they still had the same authority, men would not demand the right to verify the source of this authority. Reflection develops only if its development becomes imperative, that is, if certain ideas and instinctive sentiments which have hitherto adequately guided conduct are found to have lost their efficacy. Then reflection intervenes to fill the gap that has appeared, but which it has not created. Just as reflection disappears to the extent that thought and action take the form of automatic habits, it awakes only when accepted habits become disorganized. It asserts its rights against public opinion only when the latter loses strength, that is, when it is no longer prevalent to the same extent. If these assertions occur not merely occasionally and as passing crises, but become chronic; if individual consciences keep reaffirming their autonomy, it is because they are constantly subject to conflicting impulses, because a new opinion has not been formed to replace the one no longer existing. If a new system of beliefs were constituted which seemed as indisputable to everyone as the old, no one would think of discussing it any longer. Its discussion would no longer even be permitted; for ideas shared by an entire society draw from this consensus an authority that makes them sacrosanct and raises them above dispute. For them to have become more tolerant, they must first already have become the object of less general and complete assent and been weakened by preliminary controversy.

Thus, if it is correct to say that free inquiry once proclaimed, multiplies schisms, it must be added that it presupposes them and derives from them, for it is claimed and instituted as a principle only in order to permit latent or half-declared schisms to develop more freely. So if Protestantism concedes a greater freedom to individual thought than Catholicism, it is because it has fewer common beliefs and practices. Now, a religious society cannot exist without a collective *credo* and the more extensive the *credo* the more unified and strong is the society. For it does not unite men by an exchange and reciprocity of services, a temporal bond of union which permits and even presupposes differences, but which a religious society cannot form. It socializes men only by attaching them completely to an identical body of doctrine and socializes them in proportion as this body of doctrine is extensive and firm. The more numerous the manners of action and thought of a religious character are, which are accordingly removed from free inquiry, the more the idea of God presents itself in all details of existence, and makes individual wills converge to one identical goal. Inversely, the greater concessions a confessional group makes to individual judgment, the less it dominates lives, the less its cohesion and vitality. We thus reach the conclusion that the superiority of Protestantism with respect to suicide results from its being a less strongly integrated church than the Catholic Church.

This also explains the situation of Judaism. Indeed, the reproach to which the Jews have for so long been exposed by Christianity has created feelings of unusual solidarity among them. Their need of resisting a general hostility, the very impossibility of free communication with the rest of the population, has forced them to strict union among themselves. Consequently, each community became a small, compact and coherent society with a strong feeling of self-consciousness and unity. Everyone thought and lived alike; individual divergences were made almost impossible by the community of existence and the close and constant surveillance of all over each. The Jewish church has thus been more strongly united than any other, from its dependence on itself because of being the object of intolerance. By analogy with what has just been observed apropos of Protestantism, the same cause must therefore be assumed for the slight tendency of the Jews to suicide in spite of all sorts of circumstances which might on the contrary incline them to it. Doubtless they owe this immunity in a sense to the hostility surrounding them. But if this is its influence, it is not because it imposes a higher morality but because it obliges them to live in greater union. They are immune to this degree because their religious society is of such solidarity. Besides, the ostracism to which they are subject is only one of the causes producing this result; the very nature of Jewish beliefs must contribute largely to it. Judaism, in fact, like all early religions, consists basically of a body of practices minutely governing all the details of life and leaving little free room to individual judgment.

Several facts confirm this explanation.

First, of all great Protestant countries, England is the one where suicide is least developed. In fact, only about 80 suicides per million inhabitants are found there, whereas the reformed societies of Germany have from 140 to 400; and yet the general activity of ideas and business seems no less great there than elsewhere. Now, it happens at the same time that the Anglican church is far more powerfully integrated than other Protestant churches. To be sure, England has been customarily regarded as the classic land of individual freedom; but actually many facts indicate that the number of common, obligatory beliefs and practices, which are thus withdrawn from free inquiry by individuals, is greater than in Germany. First, the law still sanctions many religious requirements: such as the law of the observance of Sunday, that forbidding stage representations of any character from Holy Scripture; the one until recently requiring some profession of faith from every member of political representative bodies, etc. Next, respect for tradition is known to be general and powerful in England: it must extend to matters of religion as well as others. But a highly developed traditionalism always more or less restricts activity of the individual. Finally, the Anglican clergy is the only Protestant clergy organized in a hierarchy. This external organization clearly shows an inner unity incompatible with a pronounced religious individualism.

Besides, England has the largest number of clergymen of any Protestant country. In 1876 there averaged 908 church-goers for every minister, compared with 932 in Hungary, 1,100 in Holland, 1,300 in Denmark, 1,440 in Switzerland and 1,600 in Germany. The number of priests is not an insignificant detail nor a superficial characteristic but one related to the intrinsic nature of religion. The proof of this is that the Catholic clergy is everywhere much more numerous than the Protestant. In Italy there is a priest for every 267 Catholics, in Spain for 419, in Portugal for 536, in Switzerland for 540, in France for 823, in Belgium for 1,050. This is because the priest is the natural organ of faith and tradition and because here as elsewhere the organ inevitably develops in exact proportion to its function. The more intense religious life, the more men are needed to direct it. The greater the number of dogmas and precepts the interpretation of which is not left to individual consciences, the more authorities are required to tell their meaning; moreover, the more numerous these authorities, the more closely they surround and the better they restrain the individual. Thus, far from weakening our theory, the case of England verifies it. If Protestantism there does not produce the same results as on the continent, it is because religious society there is much more strongly constituted and to this extent resembles the Catholic Church.

Secondly, we see why, generally speaking, religion has a prophylactic effect upon suicide. It is not, as has sometimes been said, because it condemns it more unhesitatingly than secular morality, nor because the idea of God gives its precepts exceptional authority which subdues the will, nor because the prospect of a future life and the terrible punishments there awaiting the guilty give its proscriptions a greater sanction than that of human laws. The Protestant believes in God and the immortality of the soul no less than the Catholic. More than this, the religion with least inclination to suicide, Judaism, is the very one not formally proscribing it and also the one in which the idea of immortality plays the least role. Indeed, the Bible contains no law forbidding man to kill himself and, on the other hand, its beliefs in a future life are most vague. Doubtless, in both matters, rabbinical teaching has gradually supplied the omissions of the sacred book; but they have not its authority. The beneficent influence of religion is therefore not due to the special nature of religious conceptions. If religion protects man against the desire for self-destruction, it is not that it preaches the respect for his own person to him with arguments *sui generis;* but because it is a society. What constitutes this society is the existence of a certain number of beliefs and practices common to all the faithful, traditional and thus obligatory. The more numerous and strong these collective states of mind are, the stronger the integration of the religious community, and also the greater its preservative value. The details of dogmas and rites are secondary. The essential thing is that they be capable of supporting a sufficiently intense collective life. And because the Protestant church has less consistency than the others it has less moderating effect upon suicide.

.    .    .

We have thus successively set up the three following propositions:

> *Suicide varies inversely with the degree of integration of religious society.*
> *Suicide varies inversely with the degree of integration of domestic society.*
> *Suicide varies inversely with the degree of integration of political society.*

This grouping shows that whereas these different societies have a moderating influence upon suicide, this is due not to special characteristics of each but to a characteristic common to all. Religion does not owe its efficacy to the special nature of religious sentiments, since domestic and political societies both produce the same effects when strongly integrated. This, moreover, we have already proved when studying directly the manner of action of different religions upon suicide. Inversely, it is not the specific nature of the domestic or political tie which can explain the immunity they confer, since religious society has the same advantage. The cause can only be found in a single quality possessed by all these social groups, though perhaps to varying degrees. The only quality satisfying this condition is that they are all strongly integrated social groups. So we reach the general conclusion: suicide varies inversely with the degree of integration of the social groups of which the individual forms a part.

But society cannot disintegrate without the individual simultaneously detaching himself from social life, without his own goals becoming preponderant over those of the community, in a word without his personality tending to surmount the collective personality. The more weakened the groups to which he belongs, the less he depends on them, the more he consequently depends only on himself and recognizes no other rules of conduct than what are founded on his private interests. If we agree to call this state egoism, in which the individual ego asserts itself to excess in the face of the social ego and at its expense, we may call egoistic the special type of suicide springing from excessive individualism.

But how can suicide have such an origin?

First of all, it can be said that, as collective force is one of the obstacles best calculated to restrain suicide, its weakening involves a development of suicide. When society is strongly integrated, it holds individuals under its control, considers them at its service and thus forbids them to dispose wilfully of themselves. Accordingly it opposes their evading their duties to it through death. But how could society impose its supremacy upon them when they refuse to accept this subordination as legitimate? It no longer then possesses the requisite authority to retain them in their duty if they wish to desert; and conscious of its own weakness, it even recognizes their right to do freely what it can no longer prevent. So far as they are the admitted masters of their destinies, it is their privilege to end their lives. They, on their part, have no reason to endure life's sufferings patiently. For they cling to life more resolutely when belonging to a group they love, so as not to betray interests they put before their own. The bond that unites them with the common cause attaches them to life and the lofty goal they envisage prevents their feeling personal troubles so deeply. There is, in short, in a cohesive and animated society a constant interchange of ideas and feelings from all to each and each to all, something like a mutual moral support, which instead of throwing the individual on his own resources, leads him to share in the collective energy and supports his own when exhausted.

But these reasons are purely secondary. Excessive individualism not only results in favoring the action of suicidogenic causes, but it is itself such a cause. It not only frees man's inclination to do away with himself from a protective obstacle, but creates this inclination out of whole cloth and thus gives birth to a special suicide which bears its mark. This must be clearly understood for this is what constitutes the special character of the type of suicide just distinguished and justifies the name we have given it. What is there then in individualism that explains this result?

It has been sometimes said that because of his psychological constitution, man cannot live without attachment to some object which transcends and survives him, and that the reason for this necessity is a need we must have not to perish entirely. Life is said to be intolerable unless some reason for existing is involved, some purpose justifying life's trials. The individual alone is not a sufficient end for his activity. He is too little. He is not only hemmed in spatially; he is also strictly limited temporally. When, therefore, we have no other object than ourselves we cannot avoid the thought that our efforts will finally end in nothingness, since we ourselves disappear. But annihilation terrifies us. Under these conditions one would lose courage to live, that is, to act and struggle, since nothing will remain of our exertions. The state of egoism, in other words, is supposed to be contradictory to human nature and, consequently, too uncertain to have chances of permanence.

In this absolute formulation the proposition is vulnerable. If the thought of the end of our personality were really so hateful, we could consent to live only by blinding ourselves voluntarily as to life's value. For if we may in a measure avoid the prospect of annihilation we cannot extirpate it; it is inevitable, whatever we do. We may push back the frontier for some generations, force our name to endure for some years or centuries longer than our body; a moment, too soon for most men, always comes when it will be nothing. For the groups we join in order to prolong our existence by their means are themselves mortal; they too must dissolve, carrying with them all our deposit of ourselves. Those are few whose memories are closely enough bound to the very history of humanity to be assured of living until its death. So, if we really thus thirsted after immortality, no such brief perspectives could ever appease us. Besides, what of us is it that lives? A word, a sound, an imperceptible trace, most often anonymous, therefore nothing comparable to the violence of our efforts or able to justify them to us. In actuality, though a child is naturally an egoist who feels not the slightest craving to survive himself, and the old man is very often a child in this and so many other respects, neither ceases to cling to life as much or more than the adult; indeed we have seen that suicide is very rare for the first fifteen years and tends to decrease at the other extreme of life. Such too is the case with animals, whose psychological constitution differs from that of men only in degree. It is therefore untrue that life is only possible by its possessing its rationale outside of itself.

Indeed, a whole range of functions concern only the individual; these are the ones indispensable for physical life. Since they are made for this purpose only, they are perfected by its attainment. In everything concerning them, therefore, man can act reasonably without thought of transcendental purposes. These functions serve by merely serving him. In so far as he has no other needs, he is therefore self-sufficient and can live happily with no other objective than living. This is not the case, however, with the civilized adult. He has many ideas, feelings and practices unrelated to organic needs. The roles of art, morality, religion, political faith, science itself are not to repair organic exhaustion nor to provide sound functioning of the organs. All this supra-physical life is built and expanded not because of the demands of the cosmic environment but because of the demands of the social environment. The influence of society is what has aroused in us the sentiments of sympathy and solidarity drawing us toward others; it is society which, fashioning us in its image, fills us with religious, political and moral beliefs that control our actions. To play our social role we have striven to extend our intelligence and it is still society that has supplied us with tools for this development by transmitting to us its trust fund of knowledge.

Through the very fact that these superior forms of human activity have a collective origin, they have a collective purpose. As they derive from society they have reference to it; rather they are society itself incarnated and individualized in each one of us. But for them to have a raison d'être in our eyes, the purpose they envisage must be one not indifferent to us. We can cling to these forms of human activity only to the degree that we cling to society itself.

# SOCIAL SANCTION * (Radcliffe-Brown)

In any community there are certain modes of behavior which are usual and which characterize that particular community. Such modes of behavior may

---

* By A. R. Radcliffe-Brown, reprinted from *Encyclopaedia of the Social Sciences*, Vol. XIII, pp. 531–534, with permission of the publisher, The Macmillan Company. Copyright, 1934, by The Macmillan Company.

be called usages. All social usages have behind them the authority of the society, but among them some are sanctioned and others are not. A sanction is a reaction on the part of a society or of a considerable number of its members to a mode of behavior which is thereby approved (positive sanctions) or disapproved (negative sanctions). Sanctions may further be distinguished according to whether they are diffuse or organized; the former are spontaneous expressions of approval or disapproval by members of the community acting as individuals, while the latter are social actions carried out according to some traditional and recognized procedure. It is a significant fact that in all human societies the negative sanctions are more definite than the positive. Social obligations may be defined as rules of behavior the failure to observe which entails a negative sanction of some sort. These are thus distinguished from non-obligatory social usages, as, for example, customary technical procedures.

The sanctions existing in a community constitute motives in the individual for the regulation of his conduct in conformity with usage. They are effective, first, through the desire of the individual to obtain the approbation and to avoid the disapprobation of his fellows, to win such rewards or to avoid such punishments as the community offers or threatens; and, second, through the fact that the individual learns to react to particular modes of behavior with judgments of approval and disapproval in the same way as do his fellows, and therefore measures his own behavior both in anticipation and in retrospect by standards which conform more or less closely to those prevalent in the community to which he belongs. What is called conscience is thus in the widest sense the reflex in the individual of the sanctions of the society.

It is convenient to begin a discussion of sanctions by a consideration of the diffuse negative sanctions, comprising reactions toward the particular or general behavior of a member of the community which constitute judgments of disapproval. In such reactions there are not only differences of degree—for disapproval is felt and expressed with different degrees of intensity—but also differences of kind. Such differences are difficult to define and classify. In the English language, for example, there are a large number of words which express disapproval of individual behavior; these vary from discourteous, unmannerly, unseemly and unworthy, through improper, discreditable, dishonorable and disreputable, to outrageous and infamous. Every society or culture has its own ways of judging behavior and these might conveniently be studied in the first instance through the vocabulary. But until comparative study of societies of different types has proceeded further no systematic classification of the kinds of diffuse negative sanction is possible. Provisionally the negative moral or ethical sanction may be defined as a reaction of reprobation by the community toward a person whose conduct is disapproved; moral obligations may thus be considered as rules of conduct which, if not observed, bring about a reaction of this kind. Another distinguishable sanction is that whereby the behavior of an individual is met with ridicule on the part of his fellows; this has been called the satirical sanction. The varieties of diffuse positive sanctions, being less definite than negative sanctions, are therefore still more difficult to classify.

From the diffuse sanctions already described there should be distinguished what may be called (by a wide extension of the term) religious sanctions; these have also been named supernatural sanctions and mystic sanctions, but both these terms have unsatisfactory connotations. The religious sanctions are constituted in any community by the existence of certain beliefs which are themselves obligatory; it is therefore only within a religious community that these sanctions exist. They take the form that certain deeds by an individual produce a modification in his religious condition, in either a desirable (good) or an undesirable (evil) direction. Certain acts are regarded as pleasing to gods or spirits or as establishing desirable relations with them, while others displease them or destroy in some way the desirable harmonious relations. The religious condition of the individual is in these instances conceived to be determined by his relation to personal spiritual beings. The change in the religious condition may elsewhere be regarded as the immediate effect of the act itself, not mediated by its effects on some personal god or spirit, a view common not only in many of the simpler societies, but also found in a special form in Buddhism and in other advanced Indian religions. Sin may be defined as any mode of behavior which falls under a negative religious sanction; there is no convenient term for the opposite of sin, that is, an action which produces religious merit or a desirable ritual condition.

The religious sanctions involve the belief that most unsatisfactory ritual or religious conditions (pollution, uncleanness, sinfulness) can be removed or neutralized by socially prescribed or recognized procedures, such as lustration, sacrifice, penance, confession and repentance. These expiatory rites are also considered to act either immediately, or mediately through their effects on gods or spirits, depending upon whether the sin is regarded as acting in the one way or the other.

While in modern western civilization a sin is usually regarded as necessarily a voluntary action or thought, in many simple societies an involuntary action may fall within the given definition of sin. Sickness—for example, leprosy among the Hebrews—is often regarded as similar to ritual or religious pollution and as therefore requiring expiation or ritual purification. A condition of ritual or religious impurity is normally considered as of immediate or ultimate danger to the individual; it may be believed that he will fall sick and perhaps die unless he can be purified. In some religions the religious sanction takes the form of a belief that an individual who sins in this life will suffer some form of retribution in an after life. In many instances an individual who is ritually unclean is looked upon as a source of danger not only to himself but also those with whom he comes in contact or to the whole community. He may therefore be more or less excluded for a time or even permanently from participation in the social life of the community. Frequently if not always therefore an obligation rests upon the sinner, or unclean person, to undertake the necessary process of purification.

Thus the religious sanctions differ from the other diffuse sanctions by reason of the beliefs and conceptions indicated above, which cannot be defined or described in any simple way. Somewhat similar beliefs underlie magical practises and procedures in relation to luck, but whereas religious observances and the beliefs associated with them are obligatory within a given religious community, the former are comparable with technical procedures, customary but not obligatory.

Organized sanctions are to be regarded as special developments of the diffuse sanctions, frequently under the influence of the beliefs belonging to religion. Organized positive sanctions, or premial sanctions, are rarely developed to any great extent. Honors, decorations, titles, and other rewards for merit, including monetary rewards such as special pensions, given to individuals by a community as a whole, are characteristic of modern societies. In preliterate societies a man who has slain an enemy may be given the right to distinguish himself by wearing some special decoration or in other ways.

Organized negative sanctions, important among which are the penal sanctions of criminal law, are definite recognized procedures directed against persons whose behavior is subject to social disapproval. There are many varieties of such procedures, the most important and widespread being the following: subjection to open expression of reprobation or derision, as, for example, through forcible public exposure by confinement in stocks; partial exclusion, permanent or temporary, from full participation in social life and its privileges, including permanent or temporary loss of civil or religious rights; specific loss of social rank, or degradation, the exact contrary of the positive sanction of promotion; infliction of loss of property by imposition of a fine or by forcible seizure or destruction; infliction of bodily pain; mutilation or branding in which pain is incidental to permanent exposure to reprobation; permanent exclusion from the community, as by exile; imprisonment; and punishment by death. These sanctions are legal sanctions when they are imposed by a constituted authority, political, military or ecclesiastic.

In any given society the various primary sanctions form a more or less systematic whole which constitutes the mechanism of social control. There is an intimate relation between the religious sanctions and the moral sanctions, which varies, however, in different societies, and cannot be stated in any brief formula. The primary legal sanctions of criminal law, in all societies except the highly secularized modern states, show a close connection with religious beliefs.

Besides these primary social sanctions and resting upon them there are certain sanctions which may be termed secondary; these are concerned with the actions of persons or groups in their effects upon other persons or groups. In modern civil law, for example, when an individual is ordered by a court to pay damages, the primary sanction behind the order is the power of the court to make forcible seizure of his property or to imprison or otherwise punish him for contempt of court if he fails to obey. Thus secondary sanctions consist of procedures carried out by a community, generally through its representatives, or by individuals with the approval of the community, when recognized rights have been infringed. They are based upon the general principle that any person who has suffered injury is entitled to satisfaction and that such satisfaction should be in some way proportioned to the extent of the injury.

One class of such procedures consists of acts of retaliation, by which is meant socially approved, controlled and limited acts of revenge. Thus in an Australian tribe when one man has committed an offense against another, the latter is permitted by public opinion, often definitely expressed by the older men, to throw a certain number of spears or boomerangs at the former or in some instances to spear him in the thigh. After he has been given such satisfaction he may no longer harbor ill feelings against the offender. In many preliterate societies the killing of an individual entitles the group to which he belongs to obtain satisfaction by killing the offender or some member of his group. In regulated vengeance the offending group must submit to this as an act of justice and must not attempt further retaliation. Those who have received such satisfaction are felt to have no further grounds for ill feeling.

Satisfaction for injury may be obtained also through the duel, a recognized and controlled combat between individuals, or through similar combats between two groups. Among Australian tribes dueling with spears, boomerangs, clubs and shields or stone knives, with the bystanders ready to interfere if they think things are going too far, is a frequently adopted alternative to one-sided retaliation. In these same tribes there are similar regulated combats between two groups, sometimes in the presence of other groups who see that there is fair play. It is often difficult to draw a dividing line between such group combats and warfare; in fact they may possibly be regarded as a special form of warfare characteristic of primitive rather than of civilized societies. Frequently therefore war may be regarded as a secondary social sanction similar to the duel. A political group maintains recognition of its rights by the threat of war if those rights should be infringed. Even in the simplest societies it is recognized that certain acts are right in war and others are wrong and that a declaration of war may be just in certain circumstances and in others unjust, so that the conduct of warfare is to some extent controlled by diffuse sanctions.

Indemnification is often found as an alternative to retaliation as a means of giving and receiving satisfaction. An indemnity is something of value given by a person or group to another person or group in order to remove or neutralize the effects of an infringement of rights. It may be distinguished from a propitiatory gift by the fact that it is obligatory (i.e., subject to a negative sanction, diffuse or organized) in the particular circumstances. A payment made in anticipation of an invasion of rights with the consent of the person or persons receiving it may be regarded as an indemnity. Thus in many societies taking a woman in marriage is regarded as an invasion of the rights of her family and kin, so that before they consent to part with her they must receive an indemnity or the promise of such. In these cases the process of indemnification bears some similarity to that of purchase, which is a transfer of rights of property for a consideration.

In many preliterate societies procedures of indemnification are carried out under the diffuse sanction of public opinion, which compels an individual to indemnify one whose rights he has infringed. In some societies there is a recognized right of an injured person to indemnify himself by forcible seizure of the property of the offender. When society becomes politically organized, procedures of retaliation and indemnification backed by diffuse sanctions give place to legal sanctions backed by the power of judicial authorities to inflict punishment. Thus arises civil law, by which a person who has suffered an infringement of rights may obtain reparation or restitution from the person responsible.

In a consideration of the functions of social sanctions it is not the effects of the sanction upon the person to whom they are applied that are most important but rather the general effects within the community applying the sanctions. For the application of any sanction is a direct affirmation of social sentiments by the community and thereby constitutes an important, possibly essential, mechanism for maintaining these sentiments. Organized negative sanctions in particular, and to a great extent the secondary sanctions, are expressions of a condition of social dysphoria brought about by some deed. The function of the sanction is to restore the social euphoria by giving definite collective expression to the sentiments which have been affected by the deed, as in the primary sanctions and to some extent in the secondary sanctions, or by removing a conflict within the community itself. The sanctions are thus of primary significance to sociology in that they are reactions on the part of a community to events affecting its integration.

# RECIPROCITY AS THE BASIS OF SOCIAL COHESION * (*Malinowski*)

Again, recasting our whole perspective and looking at matters from the sociological point of view, i.e. taking one feature of the constitution of the tribe after another, instead of surveying the various types of their tribal activities, it would be possible to show that the whole structure of Trobriand society is founded on the principle of *legal status*. By this I mean that the claims of chief over commoners, husband over wife, parent over child, and vice versa, are not exercised arbitrarily and one-sidedly, but according to definite rules, and arranged into well-balanced chains of reciprocal services.

Even the chief, whose position is hereditary, based on highly venerable mythological traditions, surrounded with semi-religious awe, enhanced by a princely ceremonial of distance, abasement, and stringent taboos, who has a great deal of power, wealth, and executive means, has to conform to strict norms and is bound by legal fetters. When he wants to declare war, organize an expedition, or celebrate a festivity, he must issue formal summons, publicly announce his will, deliberate with the notables, receive the tribute, services and assistance of his subjects in a ceremonial manner, and finally repay them according to a definite scale.[1] It is enough to mention here what has been previously said about the sociological status of marriage, of the relations between husband and wife, and of the status between

* Reprinted from *Crime and Custom in Savage Society* by Bronislaw Malinowski, pp. 46–49, with permission of the publisher, Routledge & Kegan Paul, Ltd., London.

relatives-in-law.[2] The whole division into totemic clans, into sub-clans of a local nature and into village communities, is characterized by a system of reciprocal services and duties, in which the groups play a game of give and take.

What perhaps is most remarkable in the legal nature of social relations is that reciprocity, the give-and-take principle, reigns supreme also within the clan, nay within the nearest group of kinsmen. As we have seen already, the relation between the maternal uncle and his nephews, the relations between brothers, nay the most unselfish relation, that between a man and his sister, are all and one founded on mutuality and the repayment of services. It is just this group which has always been accused of 'primitive communism.' The clan is often described as the only legal person, the one body and entity, in primitive jurisprudence. "The unit is not the individual, but the kin. The individual is but part of the kin," are the words of Mr. Sidney Hartland. This is certainly true if we take into consideration that part of social life in which the kinship group—totemic clan, phratry, moiety, or class —plays the reciprocity game against co-ordinate groups. But what about the perfect unity within the clan? Here we are offered the universal solution of the "pervading group-sentiment, if not group-instinct," which is said to be specially rampant in the part of the world with which we are concerned, inhabited by "a people dominated by such a group-sentiment as actuates the Melanesian" (Rivers). This, we know, is quite a mistaken view. Within the nearest kinship group rivalries, dissensions, the keenest egotism flourish and dominate indeed the whole trend of kinship relations. To this point I shall have to return presently, for more facts and more definitely telling ones are necessary finally to explode this myth of kinship-communism, of the perfect solidarity within the group related by direct descent, a myth recently revived by Dr. Rivers, and in some danger therefore of gaining general currency.

REFERENCES

1. Comp. for more detail, the various aspects of chieftainship I have brought out in art. cit. "Primitive Economics," op. cit. (*Argonauts*), and the articles on "War" and on "Spirits," also referred to previously.
2. Here again I must refer to some of my other publications, where these matters have been treated in detail, though not from the present point of view. See the three articles published in *Psyche* of October, 1923 ("The Psychology of Sex in Primitive Societies"); April, 1924 ("Psycho-Analysis and Anthropology"); and January, 1925 ("Complex and Myth in Mother-Right"), in which many aspects of sexual psychology, of the fundamental ideas and customs of kinship and relationship, have been described. The two latter articles appear uniform with this work in my *Sex and Repression in Savage Society* (1926).

# CLASS COHESION THROUGH CONFLICT * (Marx)

The organisation of strikes, combinations, trade unions, marches simultaneously with the political struggles of the workers, who now constitute a great political party under the name of Chartists.

It is under the form of these combinations that the first attempts at association among themselves have always been made by the workers.

The great industry masses together in a single place a crowd of people unknown to each other. Competition divides their interests. But the maintenance of their wages, this common interest which they have against their employer, unites them in the same idea of resistance—combination. Thus combination has always a double end, that of eliminating competition among themselves while enabling them to make a general competition against the capitalist. If the first object of resistance has been merely to maintain wages, in proportion as the capitalists in their turn have combined with the idea of repression, the combinations, at first isolated, have formed in groups, and, in face of constantly united capital, the maintenance of the associations became more important and necessary for them than the maintenance of wages. This is so true that the English economists are all astonished at seeing the workers sacrifice a good part of their wages on behalf of the associations which, in the eyes of these economists, were only established in support of wages. In this struggle—a veritable civil war—are united and developed all the elements necessary for a future battle. Once arrived at that point, association takes a political character.

The economic conditions have in the first place transformed the mass of the people of a country into wageworkers. The domination of capital has created for this mass of people a common situation with common interests. Thus this mass is already a class, as opposed to capital, but not yet for itself. In the struggle, of which we have only noted some phases, this mass unites, it is constituted as a class for itself. The interests which it defends are the interests of its class. But the struggle between class and class is a political struggle.

In the bourgeoisie we have two phases to distinguish, that during which it is constituted as a class under the régime of feudalism and absolute

---

* Reprinted from *Poverty of Philosophy* by Karl Marx, translated by H. Quelch, Charles H. Kerr & Company, Chicago, Ill., 1910.

monarchy, and that wherein, already constituted as a class, it overthrew feudalism and monarchy in order to make of society a bourgeois society. The first of these phases was the longest and necessitated the greatest efforts. That also commenced with partial combination against the feudal lords.

Many researches have been made to trace the different historical phases through which the bourgeoisie has passed from the early commune to its constitution as a class.

But when it becomes a question of rendering an account of the strikes, combinations, and other forms in which before our eyes the proletarians effect their organisation as a class, some are seized with fear while others express a transcendental disdain.

# CLASS IDENTITY AND CONFLICT * (Sorel)

According to Marx, capitalism, by reason of the innate laws of its own nature, is hurrying along a path which will lead the world of to-day, with the inevitability of the evolution of organic life, to the doors of the world of to-morrow. This movement comprises a long period of capitalistic construction, and it ends by a rapid destruction, which is the work of the proletariat. Capitalism creates the heritage which Socialism will receive, the men who will suppress the present régime, and the means of bringing about this destruction, at the same time that it preserves the results obtained in production.[1] Capitalism begets new ways of working; it throws the working class into revolutionary organisations by the pressure it exercises on wages; it restricts its own political basis by competition, which is constantly eliminating industrial leaders. Thus, after having solved the great problem of the organisation of labour, to effect which Utopians have brought forward so many naive or stupid hypotheses, capitalism provokes the birth of the cause which will overthrow it, and thus renders useless everything that Utopians have written to induce enlightened people to make reforms; and it gradually ruins the traditional order, against which the critics of the idealists had proved themselves to be so deplorably incompetent. It might therefore be said that capitalism plays a part analogous to that attributed by Hartmann to The Unconscious in nature, since it prepares the coming of social reforms which it did not intend to produce. Without any coordinated plan, without any

* Reprinted from *Reflections on Violence* by Georges Sorel, authorized translation by T. E. Hulme and J. Roth, 1915, pp. 84–91, by permission of the publishers. The Free Press, Glencoe, Ill., and George Allen & Unwin Ltd., London.

directive ideas, without any ideal of a future world, it is the cause of an inevitable evolution; it draws from the present all that the present can give towards historical development; it performs in an almost mechanical manner all that is necessary, in order that a new era may appear, and that this new era may break every link with the idealism of the present times, while preserving the acquisitions of the capitalistic economic system.[2]

Socialists should therefore abandon the attempt (initiated by the Utopians) to find a means of inducing the enlightened middle class to prepare the *transition to a more perfect system of legislation;* their sole function is that of explaining to the proletariat the greatness of the revolutionary part they are called upon to play. By ceaseless criticism the proletariat must be brought to perfect their organisations; they must be shown how the embryonic forms which appear in the unions[3] may be developed, so that, finally, they may build up institutions without any parallel in the history of the middle class; that they may form ideas which depend solely on their position as producers in large industries, and which owe nothing to middle-class thought; and that they may acquire *habits of liberty* with which the middle class nowadays are no longer acquainted.

This doctrine will evidently be inapplicable if the middle class and the proletariat do not oppose each other implacably, with all the forces at their disposal; the more ardently capitalist the middle class is, the more the proletariat is full of a warlike spirit and confident of its revolutionary strength, the more certain will be the success of the proletarian movement.

The middle class with which Marx was familiar in England was still, as regards the immense majority, animated by their conquering, insatiable, and pitiless spirit, which had characterised at the beginning of modern times the creators of new industries and the adventurers launched on the discovery of unknown lands. When we are studying the modern industrial system we should always bear in mind this similarity between the capitalist type and the warrior type; it was for very good reasons that the men who directed gigantic enterprises were named *captains of industry.* This type is still found to-day in all its purity in the United States: there are found the indomitable energy, the audacity based on a just appreciation of its strength, the cold calculation of interests, which are the qualities of great generals and great capitalists.[4] According to Paul de Rousiers, every American feels himself capable of "trying his luck" on the battlefield of business,[5] so that the general spirit of the country is in complete harmony with that of the multi-millionaires; our men of letters are exceedingly surprised to see these latter condemning themselves to lead to the end of their days a galley-slave existence, without ever thinking of leading a nobleman's life for themselves, as the Rothschilds do.

In a society so enfevered by the passion for the success which can be obtained in competition, all the actors walk straight before them like veritable automata, without taking any notice of the great ideas of the sociologists; they are subject to very simple forces, and not one of them dreams of escaping from the circumstances of his condition. Then only is the development of capitalism carried on with that inevitableness which struck Marx so much, and which seemed to him comparable to that of a natural law. If, on the contrary, the middle class, led astray by the *chatter* of the preachers of ethics and sociology, return to an *ideal of conservative mediocrity,* seek to correct the *abuses* of economics, and wish to break with the barbarism of their predecessors, then one part of the forces which were to further the development of capitalism is employed in hindering it, an arbitrary and irrational element is introduced, and the future of the world becomes completely indeterminate.

This indetermination grows still greater if the proletariat are converted to the ideas of social peace at the same time as their masters, or even if they simply consider everything from the corporative point of view; while Socialism gives to every economic contest a general and revolutionary colour.

Conservatives are not deceived when they see in the compromises which lead to collective contracts, and in corporative particularism,[6] the means of avoiding the Marxian revolution;[7] but they escape one danger only to fall into another, and they run the risk of being devoured by Parliamentary Socialism.[8] Jaurès is as enthusiastic as the clericals about measures which turn away the working classes from the idea of the Marxian revolution; I believe he understands better than they do what the result of social peace will be; he founds his own hopes on the simultaneous ruin of the capitalistic and the revolutionary spirit.

It is often urged, in objection to the people who defend the Marxian conception, that it is impossible for them to stop the movement of degeneration which is dragging both the middle class and the proletariat far from the paths assigned to them by Marx's theory. They can doubtless influence the working classes, and it is hardly to be denied that strike violences do keep the revolutionary spirit alive; but how can they hope to give back to the middle class an ardour which is spent?

It is here that the role of violence in history appears to us as singularly great, for it can, in an indirect manner, so operate on the middle class as to awaken them to a sense of their own class sentiment. Attention has often been drawn to the danger of certain acts of violence which compromised *admirable social works,* disgusted employers who were disposed to arrange the happiness of their workmen, and developed egoism where the most noble sentiments formerly reigned.

To repay with *black ingratitude* the *benevolence* of those who would protect the workers,[9] to meet with insults the homilies of the defenders of human fraternity, and to reply by blows to the advances of the propagators of social peace—all that is assuredly not in conformity with the rules of the fashionable Socialism of M. and Mme. Georges Renard,[10] but it is a very practical way of indicating to the middle class that they must mind their own business and only that.

I believe also that it may be useful to thrash the orators of democracy and the representatives of the Government, for in this way you insure that none shall retain any illusions about the character of acts of violence. But these acts can have historical value only if they are the *clear and brutal expression of the class war:* the middle classes must not be allowed to imagine that, aided by cleverness, social science, or high-flown sentiments, they might find a better welcome at the hands of the proletariat.

The day on which employers perceive that they have nothing to gain by works which promote social peace, or by democracy, they will understand that they have been ill-advised by the people who persuaded them to abandon their trade of creators of productive forces for the noble profession of educators of the proletariat. Then there is some chance that they may get back a part of their energy, and that moderate or conservative economics may appear as absurd to them as they appeared to Marx. In any case, the separation of classes being more clearly accentuated, the proletarian movement will have some chance of developing with greater regularity than to-day.

The two antagonistic classes therefore influence each other in a partly indirect but decisive manner. Capitalism drives the proletariat into revolt, because in daily life the employers use their force in a direction opposed to the desire of their workers; but the future of the proletariat is not entirely dependent on this revolt; the working classes are organised under the influence of other causes, and Socialism, inculcating in them the revolutionary idea, prepares them to suppress the hostile class. Capitalist force is at the base of all this process, and its action is automatic and inevitable.[11] Marx supposed that the middle class had no need to be incited to employ force, but we are to-day faced with a new and very unforeseen fact—a middle class which seeks to weaken its own strength. Must we believe that the Marxian conception is dead? By no means, for proletarian violence comes upon the scene just at the moment when the conception of social peace is being held up as a means of moderating disputes; proletarian violence confines employers to their role of producers, and tends to restore the separation of the classes, just when they seemed on the point of intermingling in the democratic marsh.

Proletarian violence not only makes the future revolution certain, but it seems also to be the only means by which the European nations—at present stupefied by humanitarianism—can recover their former energy. This kind of violence compels capitalism to restrict its attentions solely to its material role and tends to restore to it the warlike qualities which it formerly possessed. A growing and solidly organised working class can compel the capitalist class to remain firm in the industrial war; if a united and revolutionary proletariat confronts a rich middle class, eager for conquest, capitalist society will have reached its historical perfection.

## REFERENCES

1. This notion of *revolutionary preservation* is very important; I have pointed out something analogous in the passage from Judaism to Christianity (*Le système historique de Renan*, pp. 72–73, 171–172, 467).
2. Cf. what I have said on the transformation which Marx wrought in Socialism, *Insegnamenti sociali*, pp. 179–186.
3. [The French is *sociétés de résistance*. What is meant is the syndicate, considered principally as a means of combining workmen against the employers.—*Trans. Note.*]
4. I will come back to this resemblance in Chapter VII. iii.
5. P. de Rousiers, *La Vie américaine, l'éducation et la société*, p. 19. "Fathers give very little advice to their children, and let them learn for themselves, as they say over there" (p. 14). "Not only does (the American) wish to be independent, but he wishes to be powerful" (*La Vie américaine: ranches, fermes et usines*, p. 6).
6. [This refers to the conduct of former syndicates which limited their ambitions to the interests of their own handicraft without concerning themselves with the general interests of the working classes.—*Trans. Note.*]
7. There is constant talk nowadays of organising labour, *i.e.* of utilising the corporative spirit by giving it over to the management of well-intentioned, *very serious* and responsible people, and liberating the workers from the yoke of *sophists*. The responsible people are de Mun, Charles Benoist (the amusing specialist in constitutional law), Arthur Fontaine, and the band of democratic *abbés*, . . . and lastly Gabriel Hanotaux!
8. Vilredo Pareto laughs at the simple middle class who are happy, because they are no longer threatened by intractible Marxians, and who have fallen into the snare of the conciliatory Marxians (*Systèmes socialistes*, tome ii. p. 453).
9. Cf. G. Sorel, *Insegnamenti sociali*, p. 53.
10. Mme. G. Renard has published in the *Suisse* of July 26, 1900, an article full of lofty psychological considerations about the workers' fete given by Millerand (Léon de Seilhac, *Le Monde socialiste*, pp. 307–309). Her husband has solved the grave question as to who will drink Clos-Vougeot in the society of the future (G. Renard, *Le Régime socialiste*, p. 175).
11. In an article written in September 1851 (the first of the series published under the title: *Revolution and Counter-revolution*), Marx established the following parallelism

between the development of the middle class and of the proletariat: To a numerous, rich, concentrated, and powerful middle class corresponds a numerous, strong, concentrated and intelligent proletariat. Thus he seems to have thought that the intelligence of the proletariat depends on the historical conditions which secured power in society to the middle classes. He says, again, that the true characters of the class war only exist in countries where the middle class has recast the Government in conformity with its needs.

# CONFLICT AS SOCIATION * (*Simmel*)

The sociological significance of conflict (*Kampf*) has in principle never been disputed. Conflict is admitted to cause or modify interest groups, unifications, organizations. On the other hand, it may sound paradoxical in the common view if one asks whether irrespective of any phenomena that result from conflict or that accompany it, it itself is a form of sociation.[1] At first glance, this sounds like a rhetorical question. If every interaction among men is a sociation, conflict—after all one of the most vivid interactions, which, furthermore, cannot possibly be carried on by one individual alone—must certainly be considered as sociation. And in fact, *dis*sociating factors—hate, envy, need, desire—are the *causes* of conflict; it breaks out because of them. Conflict is thus designed to resolve divergent dualisms; it is a way of achieving some kind of unity, even if it be through the annihilation of one of the conflicting parties. This is roughly parallel to the fact that it is the most violent symptom of a disease which represent the effort of the organism to free itself of disturbances and damages caused by them.

But this phenomenon means much more than the trivial "*si vis pacem para bellum*" [if you want peace, prepare for war]; it is something quite general, of which this maxim only describes a special case. Conflict itself resolves the tension between contrasts. The fact that it aims at peace is only one, an especially obvious, expression of its nature: the synthesis of elements that work both against and for one another. This nature appears more clearly when it is realized that both forms of relation—the antithetical and the convergent—are fundamentally distinguished from the mere indifference of two or more individuals or groups. Whether it implies the rejection or the termination of sociation, indifference is purely negative. In contrast to such pure negativity, conflict contains something positive. Its positive and nega-

---

* Reprinted from *Conflict* by Georg Simmel, translated by Kurt H. Wolff, pp. 13–17, by permission of the publisher, The Free Press, Glencoe, Ill. Copyright by The Free Press. A Corporation.

tive aspects, however, are integrated; they can be separated conceptually, but not empirically.

## The Sociological Relevance of Conflict

Social phenomena appear in a new light when seen from the angle of this sociologically positive character of conflict. It is at once evident then that if the relations among men (rather than what the individual is to himself and in his relations to objects) constitute the subject matter of a special science, sociology, then the traditional topics of that science cover only a subdivision of it: it is more comprehensive and is truly defined by a principle. At one time it appeared as if there were only two consistent subject matters of the science of man: the individual unit and the unit of individuals (society); any third seemed logically excluded. In this conception, conflict itself—irrespective of its contributions to these immediate social units— found no place for study. It was a phenomenon of its own, and its subsumption under the concept of unity would have been arbitrary as well as useless, since conflict meant the negation of unity.

A more comprehensive classification of the science of the relations of men should distinguish, it would appear, those relations which constitute a unit, that is, social relations in the strict sense, from those which counteract unity.[2] It must be realized, however, that both relations can usually be found in every historically real situation. The individual does not attain the unity of his personality exclusively by an exhaustive harmonization, according to logical, objective, religious, or ethical norms, of the contents of his personality. On the contrary, contradiction and conflict not only precede this unity but are operative in it at every moment of its existence. Just so, there probably exists no social unit in which convergent and divergent currents among its members are not inseparably interwoven. An absolutely centripetal and harmonious group, a pure "unification" ("Vereinigung"), not only is empirically unreal, it could show no real life process. The society of saints which Dante sees in the Rose of Paradise may be like such a group, but it is without any change and development; whereas the holy assembly of Church Fathers in Raphael's *Disputa* shows if not actual conflict, at least a considerable differentiation of moods and directions of thought, whence flow all the vitality and the really organic structure of that group. Just as the universe needs "love and hate," that is, attractive and repulsive forces, in order to have any form at all, so society, too, in order to attain a determinate shape, needs some quantitative ratio of harmony and disharmony, of association and competition, of favorable and unfavorable tend-encies. But these discords are by no means mere sociological liabilities or negative instances. Definite, actual society does not result only from other social forces which are positive, and only to the extent that the negative factors do not hinder them. This common conception is quite superficial: society, as we know it, is the result of both categories of interaction, which thus both manifest themselves as wholly positive.[3]

## Unity and Discord

There is a misunderstanding according to which one of these two kinds of interaction tears down what the other builds up, and what is eventually left standing is the result of the subtraction of the two (while in reality it must rather be designated as the result of their addition). This misunder-standing probably derives from the twofold meaning of the concept of unity. We designate as "unity" the consensus and concord of interacting individuals, as against their discords, separations, and disharmonies. But we also call "unity" the total group-synthesis of persons, energies, and forms, that is, the ultimate wholeness of that group, a wholeness which covers both strictly-speaking unitary relations and dualistic relations. We thus account for the group phenomenon which we feel to be "unitary" in terms of functional components considered *specifically* unitary; and in so doing, we disregard the other, larger meaning of the term.

This imprecision is increased by the corresponding twofold meaning of "discord" or "opposition." Since discord unfolds its negative, destructive character between particular individuals, we naively conclude that it must have the same effect on the total group. In reality, however, something which is negative and damaging between individuals if it is considered in isolation and as aiming in a particular direction, does not necessarily have the same effect within the total relationship of these individuals. For, a very different picture emerges when we view the conflict in conjunction with other inter-actions not affected by it. The negative and dualistic elements play an entirely positive role in this more comprehensive picture, despite the de-struction they may work on particular relations. All this is very obvious in the competition of individuals within an economic unit.

REFERENCES

1. "*Vergesellschaftungsform.*" "*Vergesellschaftung*" will be rendered as "sociation." On the term and its various translations, see *The Sociology of Georg Simmel, loc. cit.,* pp. lxiii–lxiv.—Tr.

2. "Einheit" is both "unit" and "unity," and Simmel uses the term promiscuously in both senses—Tr.

3. This is the sociological instance of a contrast between two much more general conceptions of life. According to the common view, life always shows two parties in opposition. One of them represents the positive aspect of life, its content proper, if not its substance, while the very meaning of the other is non-being, which must be subtracted from the positive elements before they can constitute life. This is the common view of the relation between happiness and suffering, virtue and vice, strength and inadequacy, success and failure—between all possible contents and interruptions of the course of life. The highest conception indicated in respect to these contrasting pairs appears to me different: we must conceive of all these polar differentiations as of *one* life; we must sense the pulse of a central vitality even in that which, if seen from the standpoint of a particular ideal, ought not to be at all and is merely something negative; we must allow the total meaning of our existence to grow out of *both* parties. In the most comprehensive context of life, even that which as a single element is disturbing and destructive, is wholly positive; it is not a gap but the fulfillment of a role reserved for it alone. Perhaps it is not given to us to attain, much less always to maintain, the height from which all phenomena can be felt as making up the unity of life, even though from an objective or value standpoint, they appear to oppose one another as pluses and minuses, contradictions, and mutual elimination. We are too inclined to think and feel that our essential being, our true, ultimate significance, is identical with one of these factions. According to our optimistic or pessimistic feeling of life, one of them appears to us as surface or accident, as something to be eliminated or subtracted, in order for the true and intrinsically consistent life to emerge. We are everywhere enmeshed in this dualism (which will presently be discussed in more detail in the text above)—in the most intimate as in the most comprehensive provinces of life, personal, objective, and social. We think we have, or are, a whole or unit which is composed of two logically and objectively opposed parties, and we identify this totality of ours with one of them, while we feel the other to be something alien which does not properly belong and which denies our central and comprehensive being. Life constantly moves between these two tendencies. The one has just been described. The other lets the whole really *be* the whole. It makes the unity, which after all comprises both contrasts, alive in each of these contrasts and in their juncture. It is all the more necessary to assert the right of this second tendency in respect to the sociological phenomenon of conflict, because conflict impresses us with its socially destructive force as with an apparently indisputable fact.

# THE PEACE AND THE FEUD * (*Gluckman*)

Whenever an anthropological study is made of a whole society or of some smaller social group, it emphasizes the great complexity which develops in the relations between human beings. Some of this complexity arises from human nature itself, with its varied organic and personality needs. But the customs of each society exaggerate and complicate this complexity. Differences of age, sex, parentage, residence, and so on, have to be handled somehow. But customary forms for developing relations of kinship, for

*Reprinted from *Custom and Conflict in Africa* by Max Gluckman, pp. 1–4, by permission of the publishers, The Free Press, Glencoe, Ill., and Basil Blackwell, London.

establishing friendships, for compelling the observance through ritual of right relations with the universe, and so forth—these customary forms first divide and then reunite men. One might expect that a small community, of just over a thousand souls, could reside together on an isolated Pacific island with a fairly simple social organization. In fact, such a community is always elaborately divided and cross-divided by customary allegiances; and the elaboration is aggravated by what is most specifically a production of man in society: his religion and his ritual. In this *Notes towards the Definition of Culture*, Mr. T. S. Eliot saw the importance of these divisions. He wrote: 'I . . . suggest that both class and region, by dividing the inhabitants of a country into two different kinds of groups, lead to a conflict favourable to creativeness and progress. And . . . these are only two of an indefinite number of conflicts and jealousies which should be profitable to society. Indeed, the more the better: so that everyone should be an ally of everyone else in some respects, and an opponent in several others, and no one conflict, envy or fear will predominate. . . .'

'I may put the idea of the importance of conflict within a nation more positively', he goes on, 'by insisting on the importance of various and sometimes conflicting loyalties.' This is the central theme of my lectures—how men quarrel in terms of certain of their customary allegiances, but are restrained from violence through other conflicting allegiances which are also enjoined on them by custom. The result is that conflicts in one set of relationships, over a wider range of society or through a longer period of time, lead to the re-establishment of social cohesion. Conflicts are a part of social life and custom appears to exacerbate these conflicts: but in doing so custom also restrains the conflicts from destroying the wider social order. I shall exhibit this process through the working of the feud, of hostility to authority, of estrangements within the elementary family, of witchcraft accusations and ritual, and even in the colour-bar, as anthropologists have studied these problems in Africa.

All over the world there are societies which have no governmental institutions. That is, they lack officers with established powers to judge on quarrels and to enforce their decisions, to legislate and take administrative action to meet emergencies, and to lead wars of offence and defence. Yet these societies have such well-established and well-known codes of morals and law, of convention and ritual, that even though they have no written histories, we may reasonably assume that they have persisted for many generations. They clearly do not live in unceasing fear of breaking up in lawlessness.

We know that some of them have existed over long periods with some kind of internal law and order, and have successfully defended themselves against attacks by others. Indeed, they include turbulent warriors who raided and even terrorized their neighbours. Therefore when anthropologists came to study these societies, they were immediately confronted with the problem of where social order and cohesion lay.

I myself have not had the good fortune to study in detail such a society, in which private vengeance and self-help are the main overt sanctions against injury by others, and where this exercise of self-help is likely to lead to the waging of feuds. Both my own main fields of research have lain in powerful African kingdoms, where the processes of political control are akin to those patently observable in our own nation. But this lack of personal experience of a feuding society does enable me, without vanity, to bring to your attention what I consider to be one of the most significant contributions which social anthropological research has made to our understanding of social relations. Anthropologists have studied the threatened outbreak of feuds—I say 'threatened outbreak,' because nowadays the presence of European governments usually prevents open fighting. But these anthropologists have been able to see the situations which give rise to internecine fights, and, more importantly, to examine the mechanisms which lead to settlements. The critical result of their analysis is to show that these societies are so organized into a series of groups and relationships, that people who are friends on one basis are enemies on another. Herein lies social cohesion, rooted in the conflicts between men's different allegiances. I believe that it would be profitable to apply these analyses to those long-distant periods of European history when the feud was still apparently the main instrument for redress of injury.

But the analysis of feuding societies does not exhaust its interest when we see feud working as a specific institution where there is no government. As I have said, I myself have done research in African kingdoms; and I found it greatly illuminated my analyses of these kingdoms, when I sought in them the processes which my colleagues had disentangled from feuding. Underneath the patent framework of governmental control which organized the state, I found feud and the settlement of feud at work. Permanent states of hostility, like feuds, existed between sections of the nation. These hostilities were redressed by mechanisms similar to those which prevent feuds from breaking out in perpetual open fighting. The same processes go on around us within our own nation-state, and international relations.

# THE FUNCTIONS OF SOCIAL CONFLICT* (*Coser*)

Conflict within a group, we have seen, may help to establish unity or to re-establish unity and cohesion where it has been threatened by hostile and antagonistic feelings among the members. Yet, we noted that not *every* type of conflict is likely to benefit group structure, nor that conflict can subserve such functions for *all* groups: Whether social conflict is beneficial to internal adaptation or not depends on the type of issues over which it is fought as well as on the type of social structure within which it occurs. However, types of conflict and types of social structure are not independent variables.

Internal social conflicts which concern goals, values or interests that do not contradict the basic assumptions upon which the relationship is founded tend to be positively functional for the social structure. Such conflicts tend to make possible the readjustment of norms and power relations within groups in accordance with the felt needs of its individual members or subgroups.

Internal conflicts in which the contending parties no longer share the basic values upon which the legitimacy of the social system rests threaten to disrupt the structure.

One safeguard against conflict disrupting the consensual basis of the relationship, however, is contained in the social structure itself: it is provided by the institutionalization and tolerance of conflict. Whether internal conflict promises to be a means of equilibration of social relations or readjustment of rival claims, or whether it threatens to "tear apart," depends to a large extent on the social structure within which it occurs.

In every type of social structure there are occasions for conflict, since individuals and subgroups are likely to make from time to time rival claims to scarce resources, prestige or power positions. But social structures differ in the way in which they allow expression to antagonistic claims. Some show more tolerance of conflict than others.

Closely knit groups in which there exists a high frequency of interaction and high personality involvement of the members have a tendency to sup-

* Reprinted from *The Functions of Social Conflict* by Lewis A. Coser, pp. 151–156, by permission of the publisher, The Free Press, Glencoe, Ill. Copyright, 1956, by The Free Press, A Corporation.

press conflict. While they provide frequent occasions for hostility (since both sentiments of love and hatred are intensified through frequency of interaction), the acting out of such feelings is sensed as a danger to such intimate relationships, and hence there is a tendency to suppress rather than to allow expression of hostile feelings. In close-knit groups, feelings of hostility tend, therefore, to accumulate and hence to intensify. If conflict breaks out in a group that has consistently tried to prevent expression of hostile feelings, it will be particularly intense for two reasons: First, because the conflict does not merely aim at resolving the immediate issue which led to its outbreak; all accumulated grievences which were denied expression previouly are apt to emerge at this occasion. Second, because the total personality involvement of the group members makes for mobilization of all sentiments in the conduct of the struggle.

Hence, the closer the group, the more intense the conflict. Where members participate with their total personality and conflicts are suppressed, the conflict, if it breaks out nevertheless, is likely to threaten the very root of the relationship.

In groups comprising individuals who participate only segmentally, conflict is less likely to be disruptive. Such groups are likely to experience a multiplicity of conflicts. This in itself tends to constitute a check against the breakdown of consensus: the energies of group members are mobilized in many directions and hence will not concentrate on one conflict cutting through the group. Moreover, where occasions for hostility are not permitted to accumulate and conflict is allowed to occur wherever a resolution of tension seems to be indicated, such a conflict is likely to remain focused primarily on the condition which led to its outbreak and not to revive blocked hostility; in this way, the conflict is limited to "the facts of the case." One may venture to say that multiplicity of conflicts stands in inverse relation to their intensity.

So far we have been dealing with internal social conflict only. At this point we must turn to a consideration of external conflict, for the structure of the group is itself affected by conflicts with other groups in which it engages or which it prepares for. Groups which are engaged in continued struggle tend to lay claim on the total personality involvement of their member so that internal conflict would tend to mobilize all energies and affects of the members. Hence such groups are unlikely to tolerate more than limited departures from the group unity. In such groups there is a tendency to suppress conflict; where it occurs, it leads the group to break up through splits or through forced withdrawal of dissenters.

Groups which are not involved in continued struggle with the outside are less prone to make claims on total personality involvement of the membership and are more likely to exhibit flexibility of structure. The multiple internal conflicts which they tolerate may in turn have an equilibrating and stabilizing impact on the structure.

In flexible social structures, multiple conflicts crisscross each other and thereby prevent basic cleavages along one axis. The multiple group affiliations of individuals makes them participate in various group conflicts so that their total personalties are not involved in any single one of them. Thus segmental participation in a multiplicity of conflicts constitutes a balancing mechanism within the structure.

In loosely structured groups and open societies, conflict, which aims at a resolution of tension between antagonists, is likely to have stabilizing and integrative functions for the relationship. By permitting immediate and direct expression of rival claims, such social systems are able to readjust their structures by eliminating the sources of dissatisfaction. The multiple conflicts which they experience may serve to eliminate the causes for dissociation and to re-establish unity. These systems avail themselves, through the toleration and institutionalization of conflict, of an important stabilizing mechanism.

In addition, conflict within a group frequently helps to revitalize existent norms; or it contributes to the emergence of new norms. In this sense, social conflict is a mechansim for adjustment of norms adequate to new conditions. A flexible society benefits from conflict because such behavior, by helping to create and modify norms, assures its continuance under changed conditions. Such mechanism for readjustment of norms is hardly available to rigid systems: by suppressing conflict, the latter smother a useful warning signal, thereby maximizing the danger of catastrophic breakdown.

Internal conflict can also serve as a means for ascertaining the relative strength of antagonistic interests within the structure, and in this way constitute a mechanism for the maintenance or continual readjustment of the balance of power. Since the outbreak of the conflict indicates a rejection of a previous accommodation between parties, once the respective power of the contenders has been ascertained through conflict, a new equilibrium can be established and the relationship can proceed on this new basis. Consequently, a social structure in which there is room for conflict disposes of an important means for avoiding or redressing conditions of disequilibrium by modifying the terms of power relations.

Conflicts with some produce associations or coalitions with others. Conflicts through such associations or coalitions, by providing a bond between the members, help to reduce social isolation or to unite individuals and groups otherwise unrelated or antagonistic to each other. A social structure in which there can exist a multiplicity of conflicts contains a mechanism for bringing together otherwise isolated, apathetic or mutually hostile parties and for taking them into the field of public social activities. Moreover, such a structure fosters a multiplicity of associations and coalitions, whose diverse purposes crisscross each other, we recall, thereby preventing alliances along one major line of cleavage.

Once group and associations have been formed through conflict with other groups, such conflict may further serve to maintain boundary lines between them and the surrounding social environment. In this way, social conflict helps to structure the larger social environment by assigning position to the various subgroups within the system and by helping to define the power relations between them.

Not all social systems in which individuals participate segmentally allow the free expression antagonistic claims. Social systems tolerate or institutionalize conflict to different degrees. There is no society in which any and every antagonistic claim is allowed immediate expression. Societies dispose of mechanisms to channel discontent and hostility while keeping intact the relationship within which antagonism arises. Such mechanisms frequently operate through "safety-valve" institutions which provide substitute objects upon which to displace hostile sentiments as well as means of abreaction of aggressive tendencies.

Safety-valve institutions may serve to maintain both the social structure and the individual's security system, but they are incompletely functional for both of them. They prevent modification of relationships to meet changing conditions and hence the satisfaction they afford the individual can be only partially or momentarily adjustive. The hypothesis has been suggested that the need for safety-valve institutions increases with the rigidity of the social structure, i.e., with the degree to which it disallows direct expression of antagonistic claims.

Safety-valve institutions lead to a displacement of goal in the actor: he need no longer aim at reaching a solution of the unsatisfactory situation, but merely at releasing the tension which arose from it. Where safety-valve institutions provide substitute objects for the displacement of hostility, the conflict itself is channeled away from the original unsatisfactory relationship onto one in which the actor's goal is no longer the attainment of specific results, but the release of tension.

# OUT OF UTOPIA: TOWARD A REORIENTATION OF SOCIOLOGICAL ANALYSIS* (*Dahrendorf*)

> *Then I may now proceed to tell you how I feel about the society we have just described. My feelings are much like those of a man who has beheld superb animals in a drawing, or, it may be, in real life, but at rest, and finds himself longing to behold them in motion, executing some feat commensurate with their physique. That is just how I feel about the city we have described.—Socrates in* PLATO's Timaios.

## I

All utopias from Plato's Republic to George Orwell's brave new world of 1984 have had one element of construction in common: they are all societies from which change is absent. Whether conceived as a final state and climax of historical development, as an intellectual's nightmare, or as a romantic dream, the social fabric of utopias does not, and perhaps cannot, recognize the unending flow of the historical process.[1] For the sociologist it would be an intellectual experiment both rewarding and entertaining to try and trace in, say, the totalitarian universe of 1984 potential sources of conflict and change and to predict the directions of change indicated in Big Brother's society. Its originator, of course, did not do this: his utopia would not make sense unless it was more than a passing phase of social development.

It is no accident that the catchwords of Huxley's Brave New World—"Community, Identity, Stability"—could be applied with equal justice to most other utopian constructions. Utopian societies have (to use a term popular in contemporary sociological analysis) certain structual requisites; they must display certain features in order to be what they purport to be. First, utopias do not grow out of familiar reality following realistic patterns of development. For most authors, utopias have but a nebulous past and no future; they are suddenly there, and there to stay, suspended in mid-time or, rather, somewhere beyond the ordinary notions of time. Our own society

* Reprinted from *The American Journal of Sociology*, LXIV, pp. 115–127, by permission of the publisher, The University of Chicago Press, and the author.

is, for the citizens of 1984, hardly more than a fading memory. Moreover, there is an unexplained gap, a kind of mutation somewhere between 1948 and 1984, interpreted in the light of arbitrary and premanently adapted "documents" prepared by the Ministry of Truth. The case of Marx is even more pertinent. It is well known how much time and energy Lenin spent in trying to link the realistically possible event of the proletarian revolution with the image of a Communist society in which there are no classes, no conflicts, no state, and, indeed, no division of labor. Lenin, as we know, failed, in theory as in practice, to get beyond the "dictatorship of the proletariat," and somehow we are not surprised at that. It is hard to link, by rational argument or empirical analysis, the wide river of history—flowing more rapidly at some points, more slowly at others, but always moving—and the tranquil village pond of utopia.

Nor are we surprised that in social reality the "dictatorship of the proletariat" soon turned out to be more and more of the former, involving less and less of the latter.

A second structural characteristic of utopias seems to be the uniformity of such societies or, to use more technical language, the existence of universal consensus on prevailing values and institutional arragements. This, too, will prove relevant for the explanation of the impressive stability of all utopias. Consensus on values and institutions does not necessarily mean that utopias cannot in some ways be democratic. Consensus can be enforced—as it is for Orwell—or it can be spontaneous, a kind of *contrat social*—as it is for some eighteenth-century utopian writers, and, if in a perverted way, i.e., by conditioned spontaneity, again for Huxley. One might suspect, on closer inspection, that, from the point of view of political organization, the result would in both cases turn out to be rather similar. But this line of analysis involves critical interpretation and will be postponed for the moment. Suffice it to note that the assumption of universal consensus seems to be built into most utopian constructions and is apparently one of the factors explaining their stability.

Universal consensus means, by implication, absence of structurally generated conflict. In fact, many builders of utopias go to considerable lengths to convince their audience that in their societies conflict about values or institutional arrangements is eiher impossible or simply unnecessary. Utopias are perfect—be it perfectly agreeable or perfectly disagreeable—and consequently there is nothing to quarrel about. Strikes and revolutions are as conspicuously absent from utopian societies as are parliaments in which organized groups advance their conflicting claims for power. Utopian societies may be and, indeed, often are caste societies; but they are not class societies in which the oppressed revolt against their oppressors. We may note, third, that social harmony seems to be one of the factors adduced to account for utopian stability.[2]

Some writers add to their constructions a particularly clever touch of realism: they invent an individual who does not conform to the accepted values and ways of life. Orwell's Winston Smith or Huxley's Savage are cases in point—but it is not difficult to imagine a surviving capitalist in Communist society or similar villains of the peace in other utopias. For exigencies of this kind, utopias usually have varied, though effective, means at their disposal to do away with the disturbers of unity. But how did they emerge in the first place? That question is rather more difficult to answer. Characteristically, utopian writers take refuge in chance to carry off this paradox. Their "outsiders" are not (and cannot be) products of the social structure of utopia but deviants, pathological cases infected with some unique disease.

In order to make their constructions at all realistic, utopians must, of course, allow for some activities and processes in their societies. The difference between utopia and a cemetery is that occasionally some things do happen in utopia. But—and this is the fourth point—all processes going on in utopian societies follow recurrent patterns and occur within, and as part of, the design of the whole. Not only do they not upset the status quo: they affirm and sustain it, and it is in order to do so that most utopians allow them to happen at all. For example, most writers have retained the idea that men are mortal, even in utopia.[3] Therefore, some provisions have to be made for the reproduction, both physical and social, of society. Sexual intercourse (or at least artificial fertilization), the upbringing and education of children, and selection for social positions have to be secured and regulated—to mention only the minimum of social institutions required simply because men are mortal.[4] In addition to this, most utopian constructions have to cope in some way with the division of labor. These regulated processes are, however, no more than the metabolism of society; they are part and parcel of the general consensus on values, and they serve to uphold the existing state of affairs. Although some of its parts are moving in predetermined, calculable ways, utopia as a whole remains a *perpetuum immobile*.

Finally, to add a more obvious observation, utopias generally seem to be curiously isolated from all other communities (if such are indeed assumed to exist at all). We have already mentioned isolation in time, but usually we also find isolation in space. Citizens of utopia are seldom allowed to travel, and, if they are, their reports will serve to magnify, rather than bridge, the differences between utopia and the rest of the world. Utopias are monolithic and homogeneous communities, suspended not only in time but also in space, shut off from the outside world, which might, after all, present a threat to the cherished immobility of the social structure.

There are other features which most utopian constructions have in common, and which it might be interesting for the sociologist to investigate. Also, the question might be asked, Just how pleasant would it be to live in even the most benevolent of utopias? Karl Popper, in his *Open Society and Its Enemies,* has explored these and other aspects of closed and utopian societies at considerable detail, and there is little to add to his incisive analyses.[5] In any case, our concern is of a rather more specific nature than the investigation of some common structural elements of utopia. We now propose to ask the seemingly pointless, and even naïve, question whether we actually encounter all or any of these elements in *real* societies.

One of the advantages of the naiveté of this question is that it is easily answered. A society without history? There are, of course, "new societies" like the United States in the seventeenth and eighteenth centuries; there are "primitive societies" in a period of transition from pre-literate to literate culture. But in either case it would be not only misleading but downright false to say that there are no antecedents, no historical roots, no developmental patterns linking these societies with the past. A society with universal consensus? One without conflict? We know that without the assistance of a secret police it has never been possible to produce such a state and that even the threat of police persecution can, at best, prevent dissensus and conflict from finding expression in open struggles for limited periods of time. A society isolated in space and devoid of processes upsetting or changing its design? Anthropologists have occasionally asserted that such societies do exist, but it has never taken very long to disprove their assertions. In fact, there is no need to discuss these questions very seriously. It is obvious that such societies do not exist—just as it is obvious that every known society changes its values and institutions continuously. Changes may be rapid or gradual, violent or regulated, comprehensive or piecemeal, but it is never entirely absent where human beings create organizations to live together.

These are commonplaces about which even sociologists will hardly disagree. In any case, utopia means Nowhere, and the very construction of a utopian society implies that it has no equivalent in reality. The writer building his world in Nowhere has the advantage of being able to ignore the commonplaces of the real world. He can populate the moon, telephone to Mars, let flowers speak and horses fly, he can even make history come to a standstill—so long as he does not confound his imagination with reality, in which case he is doomed to the fate of Plato in Syracuse, Owen in Harmony, Lenin in Russia.

Obvious as these observations may be, it is at this point that the question arises which explains our interest in the social structure of utopia and which appears to merit some more detailed examination: If the immobility of utopia, its isolation in time and space, the absence of conflict and disruptive processes, is a product of poetic imagination divorced from the common-places of reality—how is it that so much of recent sociological theory has been based on exactly these assumptions and has, in fact, consistently oper-ated with a utopian model of society?[6] What are the reasons and what the consequences of the fact that every one of the elements we found charac-teristic of the social structure of utopia reappears in the attempt to system-atize our knowledge of society and formulate sociological propositions of a generalizing nature?

It would evidently be both misleading and unfair to impute to any sociologist the explicit intention to view society as an unmoving entity of eternal stability. In fact, the commonplace that wherever there is social life there is change can be found at the outset of most sociological treatises. I contend, however, in this paper that (1) recent theoretical approaches, by analyzing social structure in terms of the elements characteristic of immobile societies, have, in fact, assumed the utopian image of society; that (2) this assumption, particularly if associated with the claim to being the most gen-eral, or even the only possible, model, has been detrimental to the advance-ment of sociological research; and that (3) it has to be replaced by a more useful and realistic approach to the analysis of social structure and social process.

## II

Much of the theoretical discussion in contemporary sociology reminds me of a Platonic dialogue. Both share an atmosphere of unrealism, lack of controversy, and irrelevance. To be sure, I am not suggesting that there is or has been a Socrates in our profession. But, as with Plato's dialogues, somebody selects for essentially arbitrary reasons a topic or, more often, a general area of inquiry and, at the same time, states his position. Then there is some initial disagreement. Gradually disagreement gives way to an ap-plauding, but disengaged and unconvincing, murmur of "Indeed," or "You don't say." Then the topic is forgotten—it has nothing to do with anything in particular anyway—and we move on to another one, starting the game all over again (or else we turn away in disgust from the enterprise of theory altogether). In this process, Plato at least managed to convey to us a moral and metaphysical view of the world; we, the scientists, have not even been able to do that.

I am reminded of Plato in yet a more specific sense. There is a curious similarity between the *Republic*—at least from the second book onward[7]— and a certain line of sociological reasoning rather prominent in these days and by no means associated with only one or two names. In the *Republic*, Socrates and his partners set out to explore the meaning of δικανοόνγη, "justice." In modern sociological theory we have set out to explore the meaning of "equilibrium" or, as it is sometimes called, "homoeostasis." Socrates soon finds out that justice really means το ἑαυτοῦ πραττενγ, that everybody does what is incumbent upon him. We have discovered that equilibrium means that everybody plays his role. To illustrate this point, Socrates and his friends go about the business of constructing a theoretical—and presumably ideal—πόλιυς. We have constructed the "social system." In the end, both Plato and we are left with a perfect society which has a structure, is functioning, is in equilibrium, and is therefore just. However, what are we going to do with it? With his blueprint in mind, Plato went to the assistance of his friend Dion in Syracuse and tried to realize it. He failed miserably. Plato was wise, he admitted defeat. Without abandoning his idea of the best of all possible worlds, he decided that perhaps, so far as real human beings and real circumstances were concerned, democracy with all its shortcomings was a more effective way to proceed.[8] We have not yet been quite as wise. Although what we still tend to call "theory" has failed as miserably in tackling real problems as Plato's blueprint, we have so far not admitted defeat.

The social system, like utopia, has not grown out of familiar reality. Instead of abstracting a limited number of variables and postulating their relevance for the explanation of a particular problem, it represents a huge and allegedly all-embracing superstructure of concepts that do not describe, propositions that do not explain, and models from which nothing follows. At least they do not describe or explain (or underlie explanations of) the real world with which we are concerned. For much of our theorizing about social systems the same objection holds that Milton Friedman raised against Lange's "Economic System":

> [He] *largely dispenses with the initial step of theory—a full and comprehensve set of observed and related facts to be generalized—and in the main reaches conclusions no observed facts can contradict. His emphasis is on the formal structure of the*

*theory, the logical interrelations of the parts. He considers it largely unnecessary to test the validity of his theoretical structure except for conformity to the canons of formal logic. His categories are selected primarily to facilitate logical analysis, not empirical application or test. For the most part, the crucial question, "What observed facts would contradict the generalization suggested and what operations could be followed to observe such critical facts?" is never asked; and the theory is so set up that it could seldom be answered if it were asked. The theory provides formal models of imaginary worlds, not generalizations about the real world.*[9]

Consensus on values is one of the prime features of the social system. Some of its advocates make a slight concession ot reality and speak of "relative consensus," thereby indicating their contempt for both the canons of scientific theory (in the models of which there is no place for "relatives" or "almosts") and the observable facts of reality (which show little evidence of any more than highly formal—and tautological—consensus). That societies are held together by some kind of value consensus seems to me either a definition of societies or a statement clearly contradicted by empirical evidence—unless one is concerned not so much with real societies and their problems as with social systems in which anything might be true, including the integration of all socially held values into a religious doctrine. I have yet to see a problem for the explanation of which the assumption of a unified value system is necessary, or a testable prediction that follows from this assumption.

It is hard to see how a social system based on ("almost") universal consensus can allow for structurally generated conflicts. Presumably, conflict always implies some kind of dissensus and disagreement about values. In Christian theology original sin was required to explain the transition from paradise to history. Private property has been no less a *deus ex machina* in Marx's attempt to account for the transition from an early society, in which "man felt as much at home as a fish in the water," to a world of alienation and class struggles.[10] Both these explanations may not be very satisfactory; they at least permit recognition of the hard and perhaps unpleasant facts of real life. Modern sociological theory of the structural-functional variety has failed to do even that (unless one wants to regard the curiously out-of-place chapter on change in Talcott Parsons' *Social System* as the original sin of this approach). By no feat of the imagination, not even by the residual category of "dysfunction," can the integrated and equilibrated social system be made to produce serious and patterned conflicts in its structure.

What the social system can produce, however, is the well-known villain of the peace of utopia, the "deviant." Even he requires some considerable argument and the introduction of a chance, or at least an undetermined variable—in this case, individual psychology. Although the system is perfect and in a state of equilibrium, individuals cannot always live up to this perfection. "Deviance is a motivated tendency for an actor to behave in contravention of one or more institutionalized normative patterns" (Parsons).[11] Motivated by what, though? Deviance occurs either if an individual happens to be pathological, or, if, *"from whatever source* [this, of course, being unspecified], a disturbance is introduced into the system."[12] In other words, it occurs for sociologically—and that means structurally—unknown and unknowable reasons. It is the bacillus that befalls the system from the dark depths of the individual psyche or the nebulous reaches of the outside world. Fortunately, the system has at its disposal certain mechanisms to deal with the deviant and to "re-equilibrate" itself, i.e., the mechanisms of social control.

The striking preoccupation of sociological theory with the related problems of reproduction, socialization, and role allocation or, on the institutional level, with (in this sequence) the family, the educational system, and the division of labor fits in well with our comparison of this type of theory and utopian societies. Plato carefully avoided Justinian's static definition of justice as *suum cuique;* in his definition the emphasis is on πράττειν, on the active and, to apply a much abused term, dynamic aspect. Similarly, the structural-functionalist insists on his concern not with a static but with a moving equilibrium. But what does this moving equilibrium mean? It means, in the last analysis, that the system is a structure not of the building type but of the organism type. Homeostasis is maintained by the regular occurrence of certain patterned processes which, far from disturbing the tranquillity of the village pond, in fact *are* the village pond. Heraclitus' saying, "We enter the same river, and it is not the same," does not hold here. The system is the same, however often we look at it. Children are born and socialized and allocated until they die; new children are born, and the same happens all over again. What a peaceful, what an idyllic, world the system is! Of course, it is not static in the sense of being dead; things happen all the time; but—alas!—they are under control, and they all help to maintain that precious equilibrium of the whole. Things not only happen, but they function, and so long as that is the case, all is well.

One of the more unfortunate connotations of the word "system" is its closure. Although some structural-functionalists have tried, there is no getting away from the fact that a system is essentially something that is—even if only "for purposes of analysis"—self-sufficient, internally consistent, and closed to the outside. A leg cannot be called a system; a body can. Actually, advocates of the system have little reason to be unhappy with this term; abandoning it would rob their analyses of much of their neatness and, above all, would disable them with respect to the "whatever sources"—the villainous outsiders they can now introduce to "account" for unwanted realities. I do not want to go too far in my polemics, but I cannot help feeling that it is only a step from thinking about societies in terms of equilibrated systems to asserting that every disturber of the equilibrium, every deviant, is a "spy" or an "imperialistic agent." The system theory of society comes, by implication, dangerously close to the conspiracy-theory of history—which is not only the end of all sociology but also rather silly.[13] There is nothing logically wrong with the term "system." It begins to give birth to all kinds of undesirable consequences only when it is applied to total societies and is made the ultimate frame of reference of analysis. It is certainly true that sociology deals with society. But it is equally true that physics deals with nature, and yet physicists would hardly see an advance in calling nature a system and trying to analyze it as such. In fact, the attempt to do so would probably—and justly—be discarded as metaphysics.

To repeat, the social system as conceived by some recent sociological theorists appears to be characterized by the same features as those contained in utopian societies. This being so, the conclusion is forced upon us that this type of theory also deals with societies from which historical change is absent and that it is, in this sense, utopian. To be sure, it is utopian not because some of the assumptions of this theory are "unrealistic"—this would be true for the assumptions of almost any scientific theory—but because it is exclusively concerned with spelling out the conditions of the functioning of a utopian social system. Structural-functional theory does not introduce unrealistic assumptions for the purpose of explaining real problems; it introduces many kinds of assumptions, concepts, and models for the sole purpose of describing a social system that has never existed and is not likely ever to come into being.

In thus comparing the social system with utopia, I feel I have done an injustice to the majority of utopian writers which needs to be corrected. With few exceptions, the purpose underlying utopian constructions has been one of criticism, even indictment, of existing societies. The story of utopias is the story of an intensely moral and polemical branch of human thinking, and, although, from a realistic and political point of view, utopian writers may have chosen doubtful means to express their values, they have certainly succeeded in conveying to their times a strong concern with the shortcomings and injustices of existing institutions and beliefs. This can hardly be said of modern sociological theory. The sense of complacency with—if not justification of—the status quo, which, by intention or default, pervades the structural-functional school of social thought is unheard of in utopian literature. Even as utopias go, the social system is rather a weak link in a tradition of penetrating and often radical criticism. I do not want to suggest that sociology should be primarily concerned with uncovering and indicting the evils of society; but I do want to assert that those sociologists who felt that they had to embark on a utopian venture were rather ill-advised in retaining the technical imperfections while at the same time abandoning the moral impulses of their numerous forerunners.

## III

It is easy to be polemical, hard to be constructive, and—at least for me—impossible to be as impressively and happily catholic as those at whom my critical comments are directed. However, I do not propose to evade the just demand to specify whose work I mean when I refer to the utopian nature of sociological theory, to explain why I think that an approach of this kind is useless and even detrimental for our discipline, and to describe what better ways there are in my opinion to deal with our problems.

The name that comes to mind immediately when one speaks about sociological theory in these days is that of Talcott Parsons. Already, in many discussions and for many people, Parsons appears to be more of a symbol than a reality. Let me therefore state quite explicitly that my criticism applies neither to Parsons' total work nor only to his work. I am not concerned with Parsons' excellent and important philosophical analysis of *The Structure of Social Action,* nor am I concerned with his numerous perceptive contributions to the understanding of empirical phenomena. I do think, however, that much of his theoretical work in the last ten years represents an outstanding illustration of what I mean by the utopian bent in sociological theory. The double emphasis on the articulation of purely formal conceptual frameworks and on the social system as the point of departure and arrival of sociological analysis involves all the vices and, in his case, none of the virtues of a utopian approach. But, in stating this, one should not overlook that at some time or other many prominent American sociologists and some British anthropologists have engaged in the same kind of reasoning.

Two main remedies have been proposed in recent years against the malady of utopianism. In my opinion they have both been based on a wrong diagnosis—and by correcting this diagnostic error we may hope to get to the root of the trouble and at the same time to a path that promises to lead us out of utopia.

For some time now it has been quite popular in our profession to support T. H. Marshall's demand for "sociological stepping stones in the middle distance" or Robert K. Merton's plea for "theories of the middle range." I cannot say that I am very happy with these formulations. True, both Marshall and Merton explain at some length what they mean by their formulas. In particular, they advocate something they call a "convergence" of theory and research. But "convergence" is a very mechanical notion of a process that defies the laws of mechanics. Above all, this conception implies that sociological theory and sociological research are two separate activities which it is possible to divide and to join. I do not believe that this is so. In fact, I think that, so long as we hold this belief, our theory will be logical and philosophical, and our research will at best be sociographic, with sociology disappearing in the gorge between these two. The admonitions of Marshall and Merton may actually have led to a commendable rediscovery of empirical problems of investigation, but I venture to assert that, looking purely at their formulations, this has been an unintended consequence, a by-product rather than the content of their statements.[14]

There is no theory that can be divorced from empirical research; but, of course, the reverse is equally true. I have no sympathy with the confusion of the just demand that sociological analysis should be inspired by empirical problems and the unjust demand that it should be based on, or even exclusively concerned with, something called "empirical research." As a matter of fact, the advocates of "empirical research" and the defenders of abstract theory have been strikingly similar in one, to my mind crucial, respect (which explains, by the way, why they have been able to coexist with comparatively little friction and controversy): they have both largely dispensed with that prime impulse of all science and scholarship, with the puzzlement over specific, concrete, and—if this word must be used— empirical problems. Many sociologists have lost the simple impulse of curiosity, the desire to solve riddles of experience, the concern with problems. This, rather than anything else, explains both the success and the danger of the utopian fallacy in sociological thinking and of its smaller brother, the fallacy of empirical research.

It is perhaps fairly obvious that a book like *The Social System* displays but a minimal concern with riddles of experience. But I do not want to be misunderstood. My plea for a reinstatement of empirical problems in the central place that is due to them is by no means merely a plea for greater recognition of "facts," "data," or "empirical evidence." I think that, from the point of view of concern with problems, there is very little to choose between *The Social System* and the ever increasing number of undoubtedly well-documented Ph.D. theses on such subjects as "The Social Structure of a Hospital," "The Role of the Professional Football Player," and "Family Relations in a New York Suburb." "Areas of Investigation," "Fields of Inquiry," "Subjects," and "Topics," chosen because nobody has studied them before or for some other random reason, are not problems. What I mean is that at the outset of every scientific investigation there has to be a fact or set of facts that is puzzling the investigator: children of businessmen prefer professional to business occupations; workers in the automobile industry of Detroit go on strike; there is a higher incidence of suicides among upwardly mobile persons than among others; Socialist parties in predominantly Catholic countries of Europe seem unable to get more than 30 per cent of the popular vote; Hungarian people revolt against the Communist regime. There is no need to enumerate more of such facts; what matters is that every one of them invites the question "Why?" and it is this question, after all, which has always inspired that noble human activity in which we are engaged—science.

There is little point in restating methodological platitudes. Let me confine myself, therefore, to saying that a scientific discipline that is problem-conscious at every stage of its development is very unlikely ever to find itself in the prison of utopian thought or to separate theory and research. Problems require explanation; explanations require assumptions or models and hypotheses derived from such models; hypotheses, which are always, by implication, predictions as well as explanatory propositions, require testing by further facts; testing often generates new problems.[15] If anybody wants to distinguish theory and research in this process, he is welcome to do so; my own feeling is that this distinction confuses, rather than clarifies, our thinking.

The loss of problem-consciousness in modern sociology explains many of the drawbacks of the present state of our discipline and, in particular, the utopian character of sociological theory; moreover, it is in itself a problem worthy of investigation. How was it that sociologists, of all people, could lose touch with the riddles of experience, of which there are so many in the social world? At this point, I think, the ideological interpretation of sociological development which has recently been advanced by a number of authors is pertinent.[16] By turning away from the critical facts of experience, sociologists have both followed and strengthened the trend toward conservatism that is so powerful in the intellectual world today. What is more, their conservatism is not of the militant kind found in the so-called Left Wing of conservative parties in England, France, Germany, and the United States; it is, rather, a conservatism by implication, the conservatism of complacency. I am sure that Parsons and many of those who have joined him in utopia would disclaim being conservatives, and, so far as their explicit political convictions go, there is no reason to doubt their sincerity. At the same time, their way of looking at society or, rather, of not looking at society when they should has promoted a sense of disengagement, of not wanting to worry about things, and has, in fact, elevated this attitude of abstinence to a "scientific theory" according to which there is no need to worry. By thus leaving the job of worrying to the powers that be, sociologists have implicitly recognized the legitimacy of these powers; their disengagement has turned out to be a—however involuntary—engagement on the side of the status quo. What a dramatic misunderstanding of Max Weber's attempt to separate the vocation of politics from that of science!

Let me repeat that I am not advocating a sociological science that is politically radical in the content of its theories. In any case, there would be little sense in trying to do this, since, logically speaking, there can be no such science. I am advocating, however, a sociological science that is inspired by the moral fiber of its forefathers; and I am convinced that if we regain the problem-consciousness which has been lost in the last decades, we cannot fail to recover the critical engagement in the realities of our social world which we need to do our job well. For I hope I have made it quite clear that problem-consciousness is not merely a means of avoiding ideological biases but is, above all, an indispensable condition of progress in any discipline of human inquiry. The path out of utopia begins with the recognition of puzzling facts of experience and the tackling of problems posed by such facts.

There is yet another reason why I think that the utopian character of recent sociological theory has been detrimental to the advancement of our discipline. It is quite conceivable that in the explanation of specific problems we shall at some stage want to employ models of a highly general kind or even formulate general laws. Stripped of its more formal and decorative elements, the social system could be, and sometimes has been, regarded as such a model. For instance, we may want to investigate the problem of why achievement in the educational system ranks so high among people's concerns in our society. The social system can be thought of as suggesting that in advanced industrial societies the educational system is the main, and tends to be the only, mechanism of role allocation. In this case, the social system proves to be a useful model. It seems to me, however, that even in this limited sense the social system is a highly problematic, or at least a very one-sided, model and that here, too, a new departure is needed.

It is perhaps inevitable that the models underlying scientific explanations acquire a life of their own, divorced from the specific purpose for which they have originally been constructed. The *Homo oeconomicus* of modern economics, invented in the first place as a useful, even if clearly unrealistic, assumption from which testable hypotheses could be derived, has today become the cardinal figure in a much discussed philosophy of human nature far beyond the aspirations of most economists. The indeterminacy principle in modern physics, which again is nothing but a useful assumption without claim to any reality other than operational, has been taken as a final refutation of all determinist philosophies of nature. Analogous statements could be made about the equilibrium model of society —although, as I have tried to show, it would unfortunately be wrong to say that the original purpose of this model was to explain specific empirical problems. We face the double task of having to specify the conditions under which this model proves analytically useful and of having to cope with the philosophical implications of the model itself.[17] It may seem a digression for a sociologist to occupy himself with the latter problem; however, in my opinion it is both dangerous and irresponsible to ignore the implications of one's assumptions, even if these are philosophical rather than scientific in a technical sense. The models with which we work, apart from being useful tools, determine to no small extent our general perspectives, our selection of problems, and the emphasis in our explanations, and I believe that in this respect, too, the utopian social system has played an unfortunate role in our discipline.

There may be some problems for the explanation of which it is important to assume an equilibrated, funcioning social system based on consensus, absence of conflict, and isolation in time and space. I think there are such problems, although their number is probably much smaller than many contemporary sociologists wish us to believe. The equilibrium model of society also has a long tradition in social thinking, including, of course, all utopian thinking but also such works as Rousseau's *Contrat social* and Hegel's *Philosophy of Law*. But neither in relation to the explanation of sociological problems nor in the history of social philosophy is it the only model, and I would strongly protest any implicit or explicit claim that it can be so regarded. Parsons' statement in *The Social System* that this "work constitutes a step toward the development of a generalized theoretical system"[18] is erroneous in every respect I can think of and, in particular, insofar as it implies that all sociological problems can be approached with the equilibrium model of society.

It may be my personal bias that I can think of many more problems to which the social system does not apply than those to which it does, but I would certainly insist that, even on the highly abstract and largely philosophical level on which Parsons moves, at least one other model of society is required. It has an equally long and, I think, a better tradition than the equilibrium model. In spite of this fact, no modern sociologist has as yet formulated its basic tenets in such a way as to render it useful for the explanation of critical social facts. Only in the last year or two has there been some indication that this alternative model, which I shall call the "conflict model of society," is gaining ground in sociological analysis.

The extent to which the social system model has influenced even our thinking about social change and has marred our vision in this important area of problems is truly remarkable. Two facts in particular illustrate this influence. In talking about change, most sociologists today accept the entirely spurious distinction between "change within" and "change of societies," which makes sense only if we recognize the system as our ultimate and only reference point. At the same time, many sociologists seem convinced that, in order to explain processes of change, they have to discover certain special circumstances which set these processes in motion, implying that, in society, change is an abnormal, or at least an unusual, state that has to be accounted for in terms of deviations from a "normal," equilibrated system. I think that in both these respects we shall have to revise our assumptions radically. A Galilean turn of thought is required which makes us realize that all units of social organization are continuously changing, unless some force intervenes to arrest this change. It is our task to identify the factors interfering with the normal process of change rather than to look for variables involved in bringing about change. Moreover, change is ubiquitous not only in time but also in space, that is to say, every part of societies is constantly changing, and it is impossible to distinguish between "change within" and "change of," "microscopic" and "macroscopic" change. Historians discovered a long time ago that in describing the historical process it is insufficient to confine one's attention to the affairs of state, to wars, revolutions, and government action. From them we could learn that what happens in Mrs. Smith's house, in a trade union local, or in the parish of a church is just as significant for the social process of history and, in fact, *is* just as much the social process of history as what happens in the White House or the Kremlin.

The great creative force that carries along change in the model I am trying to describe and that is equally ubiquitous is social conflict. The notion that wherever there is social life there is conflict may be unpleasant and disturbing. Nevertheless, it is indispensable to our understanding of social problems. As with change, we have grown accustomed to look for special causes or circumstances whenever we encounter conflict; but, again, a complete turn is necessary in our thinking. Not the presence but the absence of conflict is surprising and abnormal, and we have good reason to be suspicious if we find a society or social organization that displays no evidence of conflict. To be sure, we do not have to assume that conflict is always violent and uncontrolled. There is probably a continuum from civil war to parliamentary debate, from strikes and lockouts to joint consultation. Our problems and their explanations will undoubtedly teach us a great deal about the range of variation in forms of conflict. In formulating such explanations, however, we must never lose sight of the underlying assumption that conflict can be temporarily suppressed, regulated, channeled, and controlled but that neither a philosopher-king nor a modern dictator can abolish it once and for all.

There is a third notion which, together with change and conflict, constitutes the instrumentarium of the conflict model of society: the notion of constraint. From the point of view of this model, societies and social organizations are held together not by consensus but by constraint, not by universal agreement but by the coercion of some by others. It may be useful for some purposes to speak of the "value system" of a society, but in the conflict model such characteristic values are ruling rather than common, enforced rather than accepted, at any given point of time. And as conflict generates change, so constraint may be thought of as generating conflict. We assume that conflict is ubiquitous, since constraint is ubiquitous wherever human beings set up social organizations. In a highly formal sense, it is always the basis of constraint that is at issue in social conflict.

I have sketched the conflict model of society—as I see it—only very briefly. But except in a philosophical context there is no need to elaborate on it, unless, of course, such elaboration is required for the explanation of specific problems. However, my point here is a different one. I hope it is evident that there is a fundamental difference between the equilibrium and the conflict models of society. Utopia is—to use the language of the economist—a world of certainty. It is paradise found; utopians know all the answers. But we live in a world of uncertainty. We do not know what an ideal society looks like—and if we think we do, we are fortunately unable to realize our conception. Because there is no certainty (which, by definition, is shared by everybody in that condition), there has to be constraint to assure some livable minimum of coherence. Because we do not know all the answers, there has to be continuous conflict over values and policies. Because of uncertainty, there is always change and development. Quite apart from its merits as a tool of scientific analysis, the conflict model is essentially nonutopian; it is the model of an open society.

I do not intend to fall victim to the mistake of many structural-functional theorists and advance for the conflict model a claim to comprehensive and exclusive applicability. As far as I can see, we need for the explanation of sociological problems both the equilibrium and the conflict models of society; and it may well be that, in a philosophical sense, society has two faces of equal reality: one of stability, harmony, and consensus and one of change, conflict, and constraint.[19] Strictly speaking, it does not matter whether we select for investigation problems that can be understood only in terms of the equilibrium model or problems for the explanation of which the conflict model is required. There is no intrinsic criterion for preferring one to the other. My own feeling is, however, that, in the face of recent developments in our discipline and the critical considerations offered earlier in this paper, we may be well advised to concentrate in the future not only on concrete problems but on such problems as involve explanations in terms of constraint, conflict, and change. This second face of society may aesthetically be rather less pleasing than the social system—but, if all that sociology had to offer were an easy escape to utopian tranquillity, it would hardly be worth our efforts.

## REFERENCES

1. There are very many utopian constructions, particularly in recent decades. Since these vary considerably, it is doubtful whether any generalization can apply to all of them. I have tried to be careful in my generalizations of this account and to generalize without reservation only where I feel this can be defended. Thus I am prepared to argue the initial thesis of this paper even against such assertions as H. G. Well's: "The Modern Utopia must not be static but kinetic, must shape not as a permanent state but as a hopeful stage, leading to a long ascent of stages" (A Modern Utopia [London: T. Nelson & Sons, 1909], chap. i, sec. 1). It seems to me that the crucial distinction to make here is that between intra-system processes, i.e., changes that are actually part of the design of utopia, and historical change, the direction and outcome of which is not predetermined.
2. R. Gerber states, in his study of Utopian Fantasy (London: Routledge & Paul, 1955): "The most admirably constructed Utopia fails to convince if we are not led to believe that the danger of revolt is excluded" (p. 68).
3. Although many writers have been toying with the idea of immortality as conveyed by either divine grace or the progress of medical science. Why utopian writers should be concerned with this idea may be explained, in part, by the observations offered in this paper.
4. In fact, the subjects of sex, education, role allocation, and division of labor loom large in utopian writing from its Platonic beginnings.
5. Other authors could and should, of course, be mentioned who have dealt extensively

with utopia and its way of life. Sociologically most relevant are L. Mumford, *The Story of Utopias* (New York: P. Smith, 1941); K. Mannheim, *Ideology and Utopia* (New York: Harcourt Brace & Co., 1936 [trans. by L. Wirth and E. Shils]); M. Buber, *Paths in Utopia* (New York: Macmillan, 1950 [trans. by R. F. C. Hull]).

6. In this essay I am concerned mainly with recent sociological theory. I have the impression, however, that much of the analysis offered here also applies to earlier works in social theory and that, in fact, the utopian model of society is one of two models which reappear throughout the history of Western philosophy. Expansion of the argument to a more general historical analysis of social thought might be a task both instructive and rewarding.

7. The first book of the *Republic* has always struck me as a remarkable exception to the general pattern of Plato's Socratic dialogues. (It is, of course, well established that this book was written considerably earlier than the rest of the *Republic*.) Whereas I have little sympathy with the content of Thrasymachus' argument in defense of the "right of the strongest," I have every sympathy with his insistence, which makes this book much more controversial and interesting than any other dialogue.

8. I am aware that this account telescopes the known facts considerably and over-stresses Plato's intention to realize the Ideal State in Syracuse. The education of Dion's son was obviously a very indirect way of doing so. However, there is enough truth even in the overstatement offered here to make it a useful argument.

9. Milton Friedman, "Lange on Price Flexibility and Employment," in *Essays in Positive Economics* (Chicago: University of Chicago Press, 1953), p. 283. The following sentences of Friedman's critique are also pertinent (pp. 283 ff.): "Lange starts with a number of abstract functions whose relevance—though not their form or content—is suggested by casual observations of the world. . . . He then largely leaves the real world and, in effect, seeks to enumerate all possible economic systems to which these functions could give rise. . . . Having completed his enumeration, or gone as far as he can or thinks desirable, Lange then seeks to relate his theoretical structure to the real world by judging to which of his alternative possibilities the real world corresponds. Is it any wonder that 'very special conditions' will have to be satisfied to explain the real world? . . . There are an infinite number of theoretical systems; there are only a few real worlds."

10. Marx tackled this problem in the Paris manuscripts of 1845 on *Economics and Philosophy*. This entire work is an outstanding illustration of the philosophical and analytical problems faced in any attempt to relate utopia and reality.

11. *The Social System* (Glencoe, Ill.: Free Press, 1951), p. 250.

12. *Ibid.*, p. 252; my italics.

13. It could, for instance, be argued that only totalitarian states display one unified value system and that only in the case of totalitarian systems do we have to assume some outside influence ("from whatever source") to account for change—an argument that clearly reduces the extreme structural-functional position to absurdity.

14. Most of the works of Marshall and Merton do display the kind of concern with problems which I am here advocating. My objection to their formulations is therefore not directed against these works but against their explicit assumptions that all that is wrong with recent theory is its generality and that by simply reducing the level of generality we can solve all problems.

15. It is, however, essential to this approach—to add one not so trivial methodological point—that we realize the proper function of empirical testing. As Popper has demonstrated in many of his works since 1935 (the year of publication of *Logik der Forschung*), there can be no verification in science; empirical tests serve to falsify accepted theories, and every refutation of a theory is a triumph of scientific research. Testing that is designed to confirm hypotheses neither advances our knowledge nor generates new problems.

16. I am thinking in particular of the still outstanding articles by S. M. Lipset and R. Bendix on "Social Status and Social Structure," *British Journal of Sociology*, Vol. II (1951), and of the early parts of L. Coser's work, *The Functions of Social Conflict* (Glencoe, Ill.: Free Press, 1956).

17. The approach here characterized by the catchword "social system" has two aspects which are not necessarily related and which I am here treating separately. One is its concentration on formal "conceptual frameworks" of no relevance to particular empirical problems, as discussed in the previous section. The other aspect lies in the application of an equilibrium model of society to the analysis of real societies and is dealt with in the present section. The emphasis of advocates of the social system on one or the other of these aspects has been shifting, and to an extent it is possible to accept the one without the other. Both aspects, however, betray the traces of utopianism, and it is therefore indicated to deal with both of them in an essay that promises to show a path out of utopia.

18. Characteristically, this statement is made in the chapter "The Processes of Change of Social System" (p. 486). In many ways I have here taken this chapter of *The Social System* as a clue to problems of structural-functionalism—an approach which a page-by-page interpretation of the amazingly weak argument offered by Parsons in support of his double claim that (*a*) the stabilized system is the central point of reference of sociological analysis and (*b*) any theory of change is impossible as the present state of our knowledge could easily justify.

19. I should not be prepared to claim that these two are the only possible models of sociological analysis. Without any doubt, we need a considerable number of models on many levels for the explanation of specific problems, and, more often than not, the two models outlined here are too general to be of immediate relevance. In philosophical terms, however, it is hard to see what other models of society there could be which are not of either the equilibrium or the conflict type.

# Part II
# Self—Other Concepts

# 7: Definition of the Situation

That the study of society can never attain the dignity of a science because human behavior is "free," and hence unpredictable, has been a perennial argument of the critics of social science. In an effort to answer this challenge, sociology has responded with two different methodological arguments.

Sociologists within one broad tradition have attempted to show that, no matter what the individual motives may be, it is possible to trace uniformities of behavior in human action. Emile Durkheim pointed out that rates of suicide varied in different types of group structures in relation to the degree of cohesion attained by these groups, and quite irrespective of the particular motives which led individuals to commit suicide. Other investigators have attempted to show that predictable uniformities exist in such diverse fields as birth rates, rates of narcotics addiction, of juvenile delinquency, and the like, which can be profitably investigated without recourse to an analysis of individual motivation.

In the first quarter of this century in the United States and somewhat earlier in Germany, the methodology underlying such studies was countered by an opposing school, which argued that social science deprived itself of its most precious tools if by a self-denying ordinance it abstained from examining the motivational structure of human action. The sociology of a chicken yard, they insisted, could indeed only be undertaken in terms of descriptions of the chickens' behavior, since we are forever barred from understanding the meanings that chickens attach to their activities. But the sociology of human beings could pursue a fundamentally different strategy, since it had the advantage of being able to probe beneath protocols of behavior into the subjective meanings of acting individuals.

This development was stimulated in Germany by such scholars as Wilhelm Dilthey (though certain of its roots can be traced to Hegel, Marx, and even to Vico), but was fully developed as a sociological mode of analysis by Max Weber. It was Weber's contention that the social sciences were concerned with the understanding, as distinct from simple behavioristic reporting, of human action, and that an essential element of the interpretation of human action was the effort to seize upon the subjectively intended meaning of the participants in it. At roughly the same time W. I. Thomas (1863–1947), one of the fathers of American sociology, advanced the theorem that it is essential in our study of man to find out how men define situations in which they find themselves and that "if men define situations as real, they are real in their consequences."

What Weber and Thomas set forth has by now become one of the axioms of sociological research. Stimulated by recent developments in Freudian and non-Freudian social psychology as well as by the trends outlined above, we have come to recognize the fact that men respond to outside stimuli in a selective manner and that such selection is powerfully influenced by the manner in which they define or interpret situations. Anticipatory definitions are likely to have enduring social consequences, even if these definitions seem to an outside observer to be completely devoid of an "objective" truth value. It may be especially relevant in these days to remind ourselves that if men believe in the existence of witches, such beliefs have powerful consequences in political and social relations.

But sociological, as distinct from psychological, analysis of definitions of situations does not rest its case with the study of individual meaning; it attempts to show that intersubjective understanding requires the acquisition of shared meanings. In their analysis of the functions of cultural norms in the rise of group structures, sociologists and anthropologists have emphasized that one of the essential functions of cultural norms is to provide members of a group or society with those shared definitions of the situation without which social living would be impossible.

If the scientific observer is able to penetrate to the typical definitions of the situation prevailing in particular groups, strata, or societies, he is able to make predictions as to the probable response of members of these groups in future situations. Hence the method here outlined, in addition to the method mentioned earlier, serves to validate the contention that sociology is a genuine science.

The further uses of the basic ideas of Weber and Thomas have been extensive and ramified—modern public opinion research, for example, is hardly conceivable without them—but we have limited ourselves to selections from some of the leading social theorists.

Professor Florian Znaniecki was associated with W. I. Thomas in the pioneering study of *The Polish Peasant* (1918–1921) in which the "definition of the situation" approach was first developed. He later extensively developed the initial methodological approaches contained in that study, and our selection is from one of his major theoretical works. Professor MacIver, one of the masters of contemporary American sociology, has in his turn insisted upon the crucial significance of subjective interpretations, "dynamic assessments," as he calls them, in the understanding of human action. His *Social Causation,* from which we print a selection, may be counted among the very few sophisticated approaches to the field of sociological method to have appeared in the last quarter of a century. We are sorry to omit in this edition some specimen from the work of Alfred Schuetz, a disciple of Edmund Husserl, whose phenomenological philosophy has deeply marked European social science. Schuetz combines phenomenological and sociological insights. His essays strongly suggest that insistence on "subjective meaning" or "the definition of the situation" will from now on remain an essential feature of sociological theory.

# THE DEFINITION OF THE SITUATION * (*Thomas*)

One of the most important powers gained during the evolution of animal life is the ability to make decisions from within instead of having them imposed from without. Very low forms of life do not make decisions, as we understand this term, but are pushed and pulled by chemical substances, heat, light, etc., much as iron filings are attracted or repelled by a magnet. They do tend to behave properly in given conditions—a group of small crustaceans will flee as in a panic if a bit of strychnia is placed in the basin containing them and will rush toward a drop of beef juice like hogs crowding around swill—but they do this as an expression of organic affinity for the one substance and repugnance for the other, and not as an expression of choice or "free will." There are, so to speak, rules of behavior but these

* Reprinted from *The Unadjusted Girl* by William I. Thomas, pp. 41–44, with permission from The Social Science Research Council.

represent a sort of fortunate mechanistic adjustment of the organism to typically recurring situations, and the organism cannot change the rule.

On the other hand, the higher animals, and above all man, have the power of refusing to obey a stimulation which they followed at an earlier time. Response to the earlier stimulation may have had painful consequences and so the rule or habit in this situation is changed. We call this ability the power of inhibition, and it is dependent on the fact that the nervous system carries memories or records of past experiences. At this point the determination of action no longer comes exclusively from outside sources but is located within the organism itself.

Preliminary to any self-determined act of behavior there is always a stage of examination and deliberation which we may call *the definition of the situation.* And actually not only concrete acts are dependent on the definition of the situation, but gradually a whole life-policy and the personality of the individual himself follow from a series of such definitions.

But the child is always born into a group of people among whom all the general types of situation which may arise have already been defined and corresponding rules of conduct developed, and where he has not the slightest chance of making his definitions and following his wishes without interference. Men have always lived together in groups. Whether mankind has a true herd instinct or whether groups are held together because this has worked out to advantage is of no importance. Certainly the wishes in general are such that they can be satisfied only in a society. But we have only to refer to the criminal code to appreciate the variety of ways in which the wishes of the individual may conflict with the wishes of society. And the criminal code takes no account of the many unsanctioned expressions of the wishes which society attempts to regulate by persuasion and gossip.

There is therefore always a rivalry between the spontaneous definitions of the situation made by the member of an organized society and the definitions which his society has provided for him. The individual tends to a hedonistic selection of activity, pleasure first; and society to a utilitarian selection, safety first. Society wishes its member to be laborious, dependable, regular, sober, orderly, self-sacrificing; while the individual wishes less of this and more of new experience. And organized society seeks also to regulate the conflict and competition inevitable between its members in the pursuit of their wishes. The desire to have wealth, for example, or any other socially sanctioned wish, may not be accomplished at the expense of another member of the society,—by murder, theft, lying, swindling, black mail, etc.

It is in this connection that a moral code arises, which is a set of rules or behavior norms, regulating the expression of the wishes, and which is built up by successive definitions of the situation. In practice the abuse arises first and the rule is made to prevent its recurrence. Morality is thus the generally accepted definition of the situation, whether expressed in public opinion and the unwritten law, in a formal legal code, or in religious commandments and prohibitions.

The family is the smallest social unit and the primary defining agency. As soon as the child has free motion and begins to pull, tear, pry, meddle, and prowl, the parents begin to define the situation through speech and other signs and pressures: "Be quiet," "Sit up straight," "Blow your nose," "Wash your face," "Mind your mother," "Be kind to sister," etc. This is the real significance of Wordsworth's phrase, "Shades of the prison house begin to close upon the growing child." His wishes and activities begin to be inhibited, and gradually, by definitions within the family, by playmates, in the school, in the Sunday school, in the community, through reading, by formal instruction, by informal signs of approval and disapproval, the growing member learns the code of his society.

In addition to the family we have the community as a defining agency. At present the community is so weak and vague that it gives us no idea of the former power of the local group in regulating behavior. Originally the community was practically the whole world of its members. It was composed of families related by blood and marriage and was not so large that all the members could not come together; it was a face-to-face group. I asked a Polish peasant what was the extent of an "*okolica*" or neighborhood—how far it reached. "It reaches," he said, "as far as the report of a man reaches— as far as a man is talked about." And it was in communities of this kind that the moral code which we now recognize as valid originated. The customs of the community are "folkways," and both state and church have in their more formal codes mainly recognized and incorporated these folkways.

The typical community is vanishing and it would be neither possible nor desirable to restore it in its old form. It does not correspond with the present direction of social evolution and it would now be a distressing condition in which to live. But in the immediacy of relationships and the participation of everybody in everything, it represents an element which we have lost and which we shall probably have to restore in some form of coöperation in order to secure a balanced and normal society,—some arrangement corresponding with human nature.

# SUBJECTIVE MEANING IN THE
# SOCIAL SITUATION I* (*Weber*)

Sociology (in the sense in which this highly ambiguous word is used here)
is a science which attempts the interpretive understanding of social action
in order thereby to arrive at a causal explanation of its course and effects.
In 'action' is included all human behaviour when and in so far as the
acting individual attaches a subjective meaning to it. Action in this sense
may be either overt or purely inward or subjective; it may consist of
positive intervention in a situation, or of deliberately refraining from such
intervention or passively acquiescing in the situation. Action is social in so
far as, by virtue of the subjective meaning attached to it by the acting individual (or individuals), it takes account of the behaviour of others and
is thereby oriented in its course.[1]

## *The Methodological Foundations of Sociology*[2]

1. 'Meaning' may be of two kinds. The term may refer first to the actual
existing meaning in the given concrete case of a particular actor, or to the
average or approximate meaning attributable to a given plurality of actors;
or secondly to the theoretically conceived *pure type*[3] of subjective meaning
attributed to the hypothetical actor or actors in a given type of action. In
no case does it refer to an objectively 'correct' meaning or one which is
'true' in some metaphysical sense. It is this which distinguishes the empirical
sciences of action, such as sociology and history, from the dogmatic disciplines in that area, such as jurisprudence, logic, ethics, and esthetics, which
seek to ascertain the 'true' and 'valid' meanings associated with the objects
of their investigation.

2. The line between meaningful action and merely reactive behaviour
to which no subjective meaning is attached, cannot be sharply drawn empirically. A very considerable part of all sociologically relevant behaviour,
especially purely traditional behaviour, is marginal between the two. In the
case of many psychophysical processes, meaningful, i.e., subjectively under-

* Reprinted ·from *Max Weber: The Theory of Social and Economic Organization*,
translated by A. M. Henderson and Talcott Parsons, edited by Talcott Parsons, pp.
88–100, with permission of The Free Press, Glencoe, Ill., and William Hodge and
Company Limited, London.

standable, action is not to be found at all; in others it is discernible only by the expert psychologist. Many mystical experiences which cannot be adequately communicated in words are, for a person who is not susceptible to such experiences, not fully understandable. At the same time the ability to imagine one's self performing a similar action is not a necessary prerequisite to understanding 'one need not have been Caesar in order to understand Caesar.' For the verifiable accuracy[4] of interpretation of the meaning of a phenomenon, it is a great help to be able to put one's self imaginatively in the place of the actor and thus sympathetically to participate in his experiences, but this is not an essential condition of meaningful interpretation. Understandable and non-understandable components of a process are often intermingled and bound up together.

3. All interpretation of meaning, like all scientific observation, strives for clarity and verifiable accuracy of insight and comprehension (*Evidenz*). The basis for certainty in understanding can be either rational, which can be further subdivided into logical and mathematical, or it can be of an emotionally empathic or artistically appreciative quality. In the sphere of action things are rationally evident chiefly when we attain a completely clear intellectual grasp of the action-elements in their intended context of meaning. Empathic or appreciative accuracy is attained when, through sympathetic participation, we can adequately grasp the emotional context in which the action took place. The highest degree of rational understanding is attained in cases involving the meanings of logically or mathematically related propositions; their meaning may be immediately and unambiguously intelligible. We have a perfectly clear understanding of what it means when somebody employs the proposition $2 \times 2 = 4$ or the Pythagorean theorem in reasoning or argument, or when someone correctly carries out a logical train of reasoning according to our accepted modes of thinking. In the same way we also understand what a person is doing when he tries to achieve certain ends by choosing appropriate means on the basis of the facts of the situation as experience has accustomed us to interpret them. Such an interpretation of this type of rationally purposeful action possesses, for the understanding of the choice of means, the highest degree of verifiable certainty. With a lower degree of certainty, which is, however, adequate for most purposes of explanation, we are able to understand errors, including confusion of problems of the sort that we ourselves are liable to, or the origin of which we can detect by sympathetic self-analysis.

On the other hand, many ultimate ends or values toward which experience shows that human action may be oriented, often cannot be understood completely, though sometimes we are able to grasp them intellectually. The more radically they differ from our own ultimate values, however, the more difficult it is for us to make them understandable by imaginatively participating in them. Depending upon the circumstances of the particular case we must be content either with a purely intellectual understanding of such values or when even that fails, sometimes we must simply accept them as given data. Then we can try to understand the action motivated by them on the basis of whatever opportunities for approximate emotional and intellectual interpretation seem to be available at different points in its course. These difficulties apply, for instance, for people not susceptible to the relevant values, to many unusual acts of religious and charitable zeal; also certain kinds of extreme rationalistic fanaticism of the type involved in some forms of the ideology of the 'rights of man' are in a similar position for people who radically repudiate such points of view.

The more we ourselves are susceptible to them the more readily can we imaginatively participate in such emotional reactions as anxiety, anger, ambition, envy, jealousy, love, enthusiasm, pride, vengefulness, loyalty, devotion, and appetites of all sorts, and thereby understand the irrational conduct which grows out of them. Such conduct is 'irrational,' that is, from the point of view of the rational pursuit of a given end. Even when such emotions are found in a degree of intensity of which the observer himself is completely incapable, he can still have a significant degree of emotional understanding of their meaning and can interpret intellectually their influence on the course of action and the selection of means.

For the purposes of a typological scientific analysis it is convenient to treat all irrational, affectually determined elements of behaviour as factors of deviation from a conceptually pure type of rational action. For example, a panic on the stock exchange can be most conveniently analysed by attempting to determine first what the course of action would have been if it had not been influenced by irrational affects; it is then possible to introduce the irrational components as accounting for the observed deviation from this hypothetical course. Similarly, in analysing a political or military campaign it is convenient to determine in the first place what would have been a rational course, given the ends of the participants and adequate knowledge of all the circumstances. Only in this way is it possible to assess the causal significance of irrational factors as accounting for the deviations from this type. The construction of a purely rational course of action in such cases serves the sociologist as a type ('ideal type') which has the merit of clear understandability and lack of ambiguity. By comparison with this it is possible to understand the ways in which actual action is influenced by irrational factors of all sorts, such as affects[5] and errors, in that they account for the deviation from the line of conduct which would be expected on the hypothesis that the action were purely rational.

Only in this respect and for these reasons of methodological convenience, is the method of sociology 'rationalistic.' It is naturally not legitimate to interpret this procedure as involving a 'rationalistic bias' of sociology, but only as a methodological device. It certainly does not involve a belief in the actual predominance of rational elements in human life, for on the question of how far this predominance does or does not exist, nothing whatever has been said. That there is, however, a danger of rationalistic interpretations where they are out of place naturally cannot be denied. All experience unfortunately confirms the existence of this danger.

4. In all the sciences of human action, account must be taken of processes and phenomena which are devoid of subjective meaning,[6] in the role of stimuli, results, favouring or hindering circumstances. To be devoid of meaning is not identical with being lifeless or non-human; every artifact, such as for example a machine, can be understood only in terms of the meaning which its production and use have had or will have for human action; a meaning which may derive from a relation to exceedingly various purposes. Without reference to this meaning such an object remains wholly unintelligible.[7] That which is intelligible or understandable about it is thus its relation to human action in the role either of means or of end; a relation of which the actor or actors can be said to have been aware and to which their action has been oriented. Only in terms of such categories is it possible to 'understand' objects of this kind. On the other hand processes or conditions, whether they are animate or inanimate, human or non-human, are in the present sense devoid of meaning in so far as they cannot be related to an intended purpose. That is to say they are devoid of meaning if they cannot be related to action in the role of means or ends but constitute only the stimulus, the favouring or hindering circumstances.[8] It may be that the incursion of the Dollart at the beginning of the twelfth century[9] had historical significance as a stimulus to the beginning of certain migrations of considerable importance. Human mortality, indeed the organic life cycle generally from the helplessness of infancy to that of old age, is naturally of the very greatest sociological importance through the various ways in which human action has been oriented to these facts. To still another category of facts devoid of meaning belong certain psychic or psychophysical phenomena such as fatigue, habituation, memory, etc.; also certain typical states of euphoria under some conditions of ascetic mortification; finally, typical variations in the reactions of individuals according to reaction-time, precision, and other modes. But in the last analysis the same principle applies

to these as to other phenomena which are devoid of meaning. Both the actor and the sociologist must accept them as data to be taken into account.

It is altogether possible that future research may be able to discover non-understandable uniformities underlying what has appeared to be specifically meaningful action, though little has been accomplished in this direction thus far. Thus, for example, differences in hereditary biological constitution, as of 'races,' would have to be treated by sociology as given data in the same way as the physiological facts of the need of nutrition or the effects of senescence on action. This would be the case if, and in so far as, we had statistically conclusive proof of their influence on sociologically relevant behaviour. The recognition of the causal significance of such factors would naturally not in the least alter the specific task of sociological analysis or of that of the other sciences of action, which is the interpretation of action in terms of its subjective meaning. The effect would be only to introduce certain non-understandable data of the same order as others which, it has been noted above, are already present, into the complex of subjectively understandable motivation at certain points. Thus it may come to be known that there are typical relations between the frequency of certain types of teleological orientation of action or of the degree of certain kinds of rationality and the cephalic index or skin colour or any other biologically inherited characteristic.

5. Understanding may be of two kinds: the first is the direct observational understanding[10] of the subjective meaning of a given act as such, including verbal utterances. We thus understand by direct observation, in this sense, the meaning of the proposition $2 \times 2 = 4$ when we hear or read it. This is a case of the direct rational understanding of ideas. We also understand an outbreak of anger as manifested by facial expression, exclamations or irrational movements. This is direct observational understanding of irrational emotional reactions. We can understand in a similar observational way the action of a woodcutter or of somebody who reaches for the knob to shut a door or who aims a gun at an animal. This is rational observational understanding of actions.

Understanding may, however, be of another sort, namely explanatory understanding. Thus we understand in terms of *motive* the meaning an actor attaches to the proposition twice two equals four, when he states it or writes it down, in that we understand what makes him do this at precisely this moment and in these circumstances. Understanding in this sense is attained if we know that he is engaged in balancing a ledger or in making a scientific demonstration, or is engaged in some other task of which this particular act would be an appropriate part. This is rational understanding of motivation, which consists in placing the act in an intelligible and more inclusive context of meaning.[11] Thus we understand the chopping of wood or aiming of a gun in terms of motive in addition to direct observation if we know that the woodchopper is working for a wage or is chopping a supply of firewood for his own use or possibly is doing it for recreation. But he might also be 'working off' a fit of rage, an irrational case. Similarly we understand the motive of a person aiming a gun if we know that he has been commanded to shoot as a member of a firing squad, that he is fighting against an enemy, or that he is doing it for revenge. The last is affectually determined and thus in a certain sense irrational. Finally we have a motivational understanding of the outburst of anger if we know that it has been provoked by jealousy, injured pride, or an insult. The last examples are all affectually determined and hence derived from irrational motives. In all the above cases the particular act has been placed in an understandable sequence of motivation, the understanding of which can be treated as an explanation of the actual course of behaviour. Thus for a science which is concerned with the subjective meaning of action, explanation requires a grasp of the complex of meaning in which an actual course of understandable action thus interpreted belongs.[12] In all such cases, even where the processes are largely affectual, the subjective meaning of the action, including that also of the relevant meaning complexes, will be called the 'intended' meaning.[13] This involves a departure from ordinary usage, which speaks of intention in this sense only in the case of rationally purposive action.

6. In all these cases understanding involves the interpretive grasp of the meaning present in one of the following contexts: (a) as in the historical approach, the actually intended meaning for concrete individual action; or (b) as in cases of sociological mass phenomena the average of, or an approximation to, the actually intended meaning; or (c) the meaning appropriate to a scientifically formulated pure type (an ideal type) of a common phenomenon. The concepts and 'laws' of pure economic theory are examples of this kind of ideal type. They state what course a given type of human action would take if it were strictly rational, unaffected by errors or emotional factors and if, furthermore, it were completely and unequivocally directed to a single end, the maximization of economic advantage. In reality, action takes exactly this course only in unusual cases, as sometimes on the stock exchange; and even then there is usually only an approximation to the ideal type.[14]

Every interpretation attempts to attain clarity and certainty, but no matter how clear an interpretation as such appears to be from the point of view of meaning, it cannot on this account alone claim to be the causally valid interpretation. On this level it must remain only a peculiarly plausible hypothesis. In the first place the 'conscious motives' may well, even to the actor himself, conceal the various 'motives' and 'repressions' which constitute the real driving force of his action. Thus in such cases even subjectively honest self-analysis has only a relative value. Then it is the task of the sociologist to be aware of this motivational situation and to describe and analyse it, even though it has not actually been concretely part of the conscious 'intention' of the actor; possibly not at all, at least not fully. This is a borderline case of the interpretation of meaning. Secondly, processes of action which seem to an observer to be the same or similar may fit into exceedingly various complexes of motive in the case of the actual actor. Then even though the situation appear superficially to be very similar we must actually understand them or interpret them as very different, perhaps, in terms of meaning, directly opposed.[15] Third, the actors in any given situation are often subject to opposing and conflicting impulses, all of which we are able to understand. In a large number of cases we know from experience it is not possible to arrive at even an approximate estimate of the relative strength of conflicting motives and very often we cannot be certain of our interpretation. Only the actual outcome of the conflict gives a solid basis of judgment.

More generally, verification of subjective interpretation by comparison with the concrete course of events is, as in the case of all hypotheses, indispensable. Unfortunately this type of verification is feasible with relative accuracy only in the few very special cases susceptible of psychological experimentation. The approach to a satisfactory degree of accuracy is exceedingly various, even in the limited number of cases of mass phenomena which can be statistically described and unambiguously interpreted. For the rest there remains only the possibility of comparing the largest possible number of historical or contemporary processes which, while otherwise similar, differ in the one decisive point of their relation to the particular motive or factor the role of which is being investigated. This is a fundamental task of comparative sociology. Often, unfortunately, there is available only the dangerous and uncertain procedure of the 'imaginary experiment' which consists in thinking away certain elements of a chain of motivation and working out the course of action which would then probably ensue, thus arriving at a causal judgment.[16]

For example, the generalization called Gresham's Law is a rationally clear interpretation of human action under certain conditions and under the assumption that it will follow a purely rational course. How far any actual course of action corresponds to this can be verified only by the available statistical evidence for the actual disappearance of under-valued monetary units from circulation. In this case our information serves to demonstrate a high degree of accuracy. The facts of experience were known before the generalization, which was formulated afterwards; but without this successful interpretation our need for causal understanding would evidently be left unsatisfied. On the other hand, without the demonstration that what can here be assumed to be a theoretically adequate interpretation also is in some degree relevant to an actual course of action, a 'law,' no matter how fully demonstrated theoretically, would be worthless for the understanding of action in the real world. In this case the correspondence between the theoretical interpretation of motivation and its empirical verification is entirely satisfactory and the cases are numerous enough so that verification can be considered established. But to take another example, Eduard Meyer has advanced an ingenious theory of the causal significance of the battles of Marathon, Salamis, and Platea for the development of the cultural peculiarities of Greek, and hence, more generally, Western, civilization.[17] This is derived from a meaningful interpretation of certain symptomatic facts having to do with the attitudes of the Greek oracles and prophets towards the Persians. It can only be directly verified by reference to the examples of the conduct of the Persians in cases where they were victorious, as in Jerusalem, Egypt, and Asia Minor, and even this verification must necessarily remain unsatisfactory in certain respects. The striking rational plausibility of the hypothesis must here necessarily be relied on as a support. In very many cases of historical interpretation which seem highly plausible, however, there is not even a possibility of the order of verification which was feasible in this case. Where this is true the interpretation must necessarily remain a hypothesis.

7. A motive is a complex of subjective meaning which seems to the actor himself or to the observer an adequate ground for the conduct in question. We apply the term 'adequacy on the level of meaning'[18] to the subjective interpretation of a coherent course of conduct when and in so far as, according to our habitual modes of thought and feeling, its component parts taken in their mutual relation are recognized to constitute a 'typical' complex of meaning. It is more common to say 'correct.' The interpretation of a sequence of events will on the other hand be called *causally* adequate in so far as, according to established generalizations from experience, there is a probability that it will always actually occur in the same way. An example of adequacy on the level of meaning in this sense is what is, according to our current norms of calculation or thinking, the correct solution of an arithmetical problem. On the other hand, a causally adequate

interpretation of the same phenomenon would concern the statistical probability that, according to verified generalizations from experience, there would be a correct or an erroneous solution of the same problem. This also refers to currently accepted norms but includes taking account of typical errors or of typical confusions. Thus causal explanation depends on being able to determine that there is a probability, which in the rare ideal case can be numerically stated, but is always in some sense calculable, that a given observable event (overt or subjective) will be followed or accompanied by another event.

A correct causal interpretation of a concrete course of action is arrived at when the overt action and the motives have both been correctly apprehended and at the same time their relation has become meaningfully comprehensible. A correct causal interpretation of typical action means that the process which is claimed to be typical is shown to be both adequately grasped on the level of meaning and at the same time the interpretation is to some degree causally adequate. If adequacy in respect to meaning is lacking, then no matter how high the degree of uniformity and how precisely its probability can be numerically determined, it is still an incomprehensible statistical probability, whether dealing with overt or subjective processes. On the other hand, even the most perfect adequacy on the level of meaning has causal significance from a sociological point of view only in so far as there is some kind of proof for the existence of a probability[19] that action in fact normally takes the course which has been held to be meaningful. For this there must be some degree of determinable frequency of approximation to an average or a pure type.

Statistical uniformities constitute understandable types of action in the sense of this discussion, and thus constitute 'sociological generalizations,' only when they can be regarded as manifestations of the understandable subjective meaning of a course of social action. Conversely, formulations of a rational course of subjectively understandable action constitute sociological types of empirical process only when they can be empirically observed with a significant degree of approximation. It is unfortunately by no means the case that the actual likelihood of the occurrence of a given course of overt action is always directly proportional to the clarity of subjective interpretation. There are statistics of processes devoid of meaning such as death rates, phenomena of fatigue, the production rate of machines, the amount of rainfall, in exactly the same sense as there are statistics of meaningful phenomena. But only when the phenomena are meaningful is it convenient to speak of sociological statistics. Examples are such cases as crime rates, occupational distributions, price statistics, and statistics of crop acreage. Naturally there are many cases where both components are involved, as in crop statistics.

REFERENCES

1. In this series of definitions Weber employs several important terms which need discussion. In addition to *Verstehen*, which has already been commented upon, there are four important ones: *Deuten*, *Sinn*, *Handeln*, and *Verhalten*. *Deuten* has generally been translated as 'interpret.' As used by Weber in this context it refers to the interpretation of subjective states of mind and the meanings which can be imputed as intended by an actor. Any other meaning of the word 'interpretation' is irrelevant to Weber's discussion. The term *Sinn* has generally been translated as 'meaning'; and its variations, particularly the corresponding adjectives, *sinnhaft, sinnvoll, sinnfremd*, have been dealt with by appropriately modifying the term meaning. The reference here again is always to features of the content of subjective states of mind or of symbolic systems which are ultimately referable to such states of mind.

   The terms *Handeln* and *Verhalten* are directly related. *Verhalten* is the broader term referring to any mode of behaviour of human individuals, regardless of the frame of reference in terms of which it is analysed. 'Behaviour' has seemed to be the most appropriate English equivalent. *Handeln*, on the other hand, refers to the concrete phenomenon of human behaviour only in so far as it is capable of 'understanding,' in Weber's technical sense, in terms of subjective categories. The most appropriate English equivalent has seemed to be 'action.' This corresponds to the editor's usage in *The Structure of Social Action* and would seem to be fairly well established. 'Conduct' is also closely similar and has sometimes been used. *Deuten*, *Versthen*, and *Sinn* are thus applicable to human behaviour only in so far as it constitutes action or conduct in this specific sense.—Ed.

2. Weber's text is organized in a somewhat unusual manner. He lays down certain fundamental definitions and then proceeds to comment upon them. The definitions themselves are in the original printed in large type, the subsidiary comments in smaller type. For the purposes of this translation it has not seemed best to make a distinction in type form, but the reader should be aware that the numbered paragraphs which follow a definition or group of them are in the nature of comments, rather than the continuous development of a general line of argument. This fact accounts for what is sometimes a relatively fragmentary character of the development and for the abrupt transition from one subject to another. Weber apparently did not intend this material to be 'read' in the ordinary sense, but rather to serve as a reference work for the clarification and systematization of theoretical concepts and their implications. While the comments under most of the definitions are relatively brief, under the definitions of Sociology and of Social Action, Weber wrote what is essentially a methodological essay. This makes sec. 1 out of proportion to the other sections of this and the following chapters. It has, however, seemed best to retain Weber's own plan for the subdivision of the material.—Ed.

3. Weber means by 'pure type' what he himself generally called and what has come to be known in the literature about his methodology as the 'ideal type.' The reader may be referred for general orientation to Weber's own essay (to which he himself refers below), *Die Objektivität sozialwissenschaftlicher Erkenntnis;* to two works of Dr. Alexander von Schelting, 'Die logische Theorie der historischen Kulturwissenschaften von Max Weber' (*Archiv fuer Sozialwissenschaft*, vol. xlix), and *Max Webers Wissenschaftslehre;* and to the editor's *Structure of Social Action*, chap. xvi. A somewhat different interpretation is given in Theodore Abel, *Systematic Sociology in Germany*, chap. iv.—Ed.

4. This is an imperfect rendering of the German term *Evidenz*, for which, unfortunately, there is no good English equivalent. It has hence been rendered in a number of different ways, varying with the particular context in which it occurs. The primary meaning refers to the basis on which a scientist or thinker becomes satisfied of the

certainty or acceptability of a proposition. As Weber himself points out, there are two primary aspects of this. On the one hand a conclusion can be 'seen' to follow from given premises by virtue of logical, mathematical, or possibly other modes of meaningful relation. In this sense one 'sees' the solution of an arithmetical problem or the correctness of the proof of a geometrical theorem. The other aspect is concerned with empirical observation. If an act of observation is competently performed, in a similar sense one 'sees' the truth of the relevant descriptive proposition. The term *Evidenz* does not refer to the process of observing, but to the quality of its results, by virtue of which the observer feels justified in affirming a given statement. Hence 'certainty' has seemed a suitable translation in some contexts, 'clarity' in others, 'accuracy' in still others. The term 'intuition' is not usable because it refers to the process rather than to the result.—Ed.

5. A term now much used in psychological literature, especially that of psychoanalysis. It is roughly equivalent to 'emotion' but more precise.—Ed.

6. The German term is *sinnfremd*. This should not be translated by 'meaningless,' but interpreted in the technical context of Weber's use of *Verstehen* and *Sinndeutung*. The essential criterion is the impossibility of placing the object in question in a complex of relations on the meaningful level.—Ed.

7. *Unverstehbar.*

8. Surely this passage states too narrow a conception of the scope of meaningful interpretation. It is certainly not *only* in terms such as those of the rational means-end schema, that it is possible to make action understandable in terms of subjective categories. This probably can actually be called a source of rationalistic bias in Weber's work. In practice he does not adhere at all rigorously to this methodological position. For certain possibilities in this broader field, see the editor's *Structure of Social Action*, chaps. vi and xi.—Ed.

9. A gulf of the North Sea which broke through the Netherlands coast, flooding an area.—Ed.

10. Weber here uses the term *aktuelles Verstehen*, which he contrasts with *erklärendes Verstehen*. The latter he also refers to as *motivationsmaessig*. 'Aktuell' in this context has been translated as 'observational.' It is clear from Weber's discussion that the primary criterion is the possibility of deriving the meaning of an act or symbolic expression from immediate observation without reference to any broader context. In *erklärendes Verstehen*, on the other hand, the particular act must be placed in a broader context of meaning involving facts which cannot be derived from immediate observation of a particular act or expression.—Ed.

11. The German term is *Sinnzusammenhang*. It refers to a plurality of elements which form a coherent whole on the level of meaning. There are several possible modes of meaningful relation between such elements, such as logical consistency, the esthetic harmony of a style, or the appropriateness of means to an end. In any case, however, a *Sinnzusammenhang* must be distinguished from a system of elements which are causally interdependent. There seems to be no single English term or phrase which is always adequate. According to variations in the context, 'context of meaning,' 'complex of meaning,' and sometimes 'meaningful system' have been employed.—Ed.

12. On the significance of this type of explanation for causal relationship. See para. 6, below in the present section.

13. The German is *gemeinter Sinn*. Weber departs from ordinary usage not only in broadening the meaning of this conception. As he states at the end of the present methodological discussion, he does not restrict the use of this concept to cases where a clear self-conscious awareness of such meaning can be reasonably attributed to every individual actor. Essentially, what Weber is doing is to formulate an operational concept. The question is not whether in a sense obvious to the ordinary person such an intended meaning 'really exists,' but whether the concept is capable of providing a logical framework within which scientifically important observation can be made. The test of validity of the observations is not whether their object is immediately clear to common sense, but whether the results of these technical observations can be satisfactorily organized and related to those of others in a systematic body of knowledge.—Ed.

14. The scientific functions of such construction have been discussed in the author's article in the *Archiv für Sozialwissenschaft,* vol. xix, p. 64 ff.
15. Simmel, in his *Probleme der Geschichtsphilosophie,* gives a number of examples.
16. The above passage is an exceedingly compact statement of Weber's theory of the logical conditions of proof of causal relationship. He developed this most fully in his essay *Die Objektivität sozialwissenschaftlicher Erkenntnis,* op. cit. It is also discussed in certain of the other essays which have been collected in the volume, *Gesammelte Aufsätze zur Wissenschaftslehre.* The best and fullest secondary discussion is to be found in Von Schelting's book, *Max Webers Wissenschaftslehre.* There is a briefer discussion in chap. xvi of the editor's *Structure of Social Action.*—Ed.
17. See Eduard Meyer, *Geschichte des Altertums,* Stuttgart, 1901, vol. iii, pp. 420, 444ff.
18. The expression *sinnhafte Adäquanz* is one of the most difficult of Weber's technical terms to translate. In most places the cumbrous phrase 'adequacy on the level of meaning' has had to be employed. It should be clear from the progress of the discussion that what Weber refers to is a satisfying level of knowledge for the particular purposes of the subjective state of mind of the actor or actors. He is, however, careful to point out that *causal* adequacy involves in addition to this a satisfactory correspondence between the results of observations from the subjective point of view and from the objective; that is, observations of the overt course of action which can be described without reference to the state of mind of the actor. For a discussion of the methodological problem involved here, see *Structure of Social Action,* chaps. ii and v.—Ed.
19. This is the first occurrence in Weber's text of the term *Chance* which he uses very frequently. It is here translated by 'probability,' because he uses it as interchangeable with *Wahrscheinlichkeit.* As the term 'probability' is used in a technical mathematical and statistical sense, however, it implies the possibility of numerical statement. In most of the cases where Weber uses *Chance* this is out of the question. It is, however, possible to speak in terms of higher and lower degrees of probability. To avoid confusion with the technical mathematical concept, the term 'likelihood' will often be used in the translation. It is by means of this concept that Weber, in a highly ingenious way, has bridged the gap between the interpretation of meaning and the inevitably more complex facts of overt action.—Ed.

# SUBJECTIVE MEANING IN THE SOCIAL SITUATION II* (*Znaniecki*)

The primary empirical evidence about any cultural human action is the experience of the agent himself, supplemented by the experience of those who react to his action, reproduce it, or participate in it. The action of speaking a sentence, writing a poem, making a horseshoe, depositing money, proposing to a girl, electing an official, performing a religious rite, as empirical datum, is what it is in the experience of the speaker and his listeners, the poet and his readers, the blacksmith and the owner of the horse to be shod, the depositor and the banker, the proposing suitor and the courted girl, the voters and the official whom they elect, the religious believers who participate in the ritual. The scientist who wants to study these actions in-

* Reprinted from *Social Actions* by Florian Znaniecki, pp. 11–17, with permission of the publisher, Rinehart & Company, Inc. Copyright, 1936, by Farrar & Rinehart, Inc.

ductively must take them as they are in the human experience of those agents and reagents; they are his empirical data inasmuch and because they are theirs. I have expressed this elsewhere by saying that such data possess for the student *a humanistic coefficient.* The humanistic coefficient distinguishes cultural data from natural data, which the student assumes to be independent of the experience of human agents.

Every student of culture takes his data with a humanistic coefficient. The philologist studies a language as experienced by the people who speak it and understand it; the economist studies money and the active use of money as experienced by the people who use it; the student of art investigates actions of painting, composing or playing music, writing or reading a poem, as experienced by the artists and those aesthetically interested in their work; the political scientist studies elections as actively experienced by the electors, the politicians, and the candidates. There are various well-known techniques of finding out how other people experience the data which the student investigates: the investigator himself repeats, reproduces fully or vicariously, participates, observes, and supplements the direct information thus gained by whatever other people can tell him about their experiences. His data become finally as reliable as any data can be: nobody can doubt the data which a good philologist collects about speaking a language, or a good economist's data about the functioning of a bank, or a good art student's data about the work of artists.

Now, the orthodox behaviorist rejects this primary empirical evidence as a basis for inductive research. He does this first in studying the behavior of animals and infants, for obvious reasons: as a culturally educated observer, he cannot adequately reproduce their active experiences, nor can those experiences be made secondarily accessible to him by verbal communication. Moreover, the behavior itself at this stage shows to the observer such uniformities and causal relationships as to make the evidence of the agent's experience comparatively unimportant for the establishment of a number of valid theoretic generalizations.

When, however, the behaviorist continues to neglect this evidence in his approach to human activities at later stages of evolution, in spite of its being there fully accessible to him, and in spite of the fact that there are already in the various sciences of culture numerous valid inductive generalizations based upon this evidence, his attitude can be only explained, but not justified, partly by a desire to extend his theories beyond their original range at the cost of very little effort—which can be achieved most easily by avoiding the check of this new evidence; partly by the fear of introducing with the agent's "conscious" experience the old "mind" or "soul." Behavioristic studies do not take the gestures and words used by the agent with reference to the agent's own empirical reality as he experiences it, but reinterpret those words and gestures with reference to the agent's environment as the behavioristic observer views it. We shall have several occasions in later chapters to see how this metaphysical bias revenges itself in obstructing the progress of scientific analysis and generalization. Here we must mention only two essential characteristics of active human experiences which the orthodox behaviorist is prevented by this bias from taking into consideration.

The first of these characteristics belongs to all the experiences of human agents: it is the intrinsic objective meaningfulness of every datum with which the agent deals. Behaviorism reduces the problem of meaning to the meaning of symbols. But for the human agent not only symbols have a meaning, but every datum of his experience in which he is actively interested; every datum stands not only for itself, but for other data which it suggests. At an early stage of mental development this meaning is connected with the possibility of organic experiences suggested by the object; thus, food suggests certain experiences of the organs used in eating and digesting. At this stage it is still possible to substitute for it the concept of "incipient behavior." But gradually the meaning expands, includes suggestions of objects outside the organism, and becomes irreducible—even indirectly—to any definite incipient behavior. Steps heard in the next room to the hungry infant may indirectly mean the approach of food and provoke definite organic responses, but to the grown-up they mean the approach of a person toward whom the possible range of attitudes is almost unlimited. A painting suggests, on the one hand, a fragment of nature or a historical event which we never have and never can experience directly; on the other hand, a multiplicity of paintings in similar or different styles, in comparison with which we define its aesthetic characters.

No object as experienced by an active human individual can be defined merely by its sensory content, for on its meaning rather than on its sensory contact depends its practical significance for human activity. Not because of what it "is" as a natural datum, but because of what it "means" as a humanistic, cultural datum, does an object of activity appear to the agent as "useful" or "harmful," "good" or "bad," "beautiful" or "ugly," "pleasant" or "unpleasant." Since all meaningful objects are potential objects of activity and have a practical significance in somebody's experience, I have for twenty-five years been using the term *values* to distinguish logically meaningful objects as given to an agent from *things*, meaningless objects investigated by a student who takes them not as they are given to agents, but as they are supposed to exist "in themselves," as parts of nature. I call the *axiological significance* of a value that practical significance which it acquires when it is appreciated positively or negatively with reference to other values as a possible object of activity.

The second essential point that behaviorism leaves out of consideration in studying human actions is the existence in the experience of human agents of objects which are not only meaningful, but partly—often almost completely—*non-material* in content and irreducible to sensory perception. Such objects are, for instance, myths and other religious entities, political institutions, contents of literary works, scientific and philosophic concepts. Many words in civilized languages are not used to indicate objects given in sensory experience, but precisely to symbolize non-material, "spiritual" objects, to stabilize and communicate their contents.

The student of actions need not engage in philosophic speculation as to the "true essence" of these objects: in fact, it will be safest or him as a scientist to refrain from such speculations, whether his inclination be toward a radical Platonic "realism," affirming the absolute priority of a non-sensual world, or an equally radical "nominalism," reducing non-sensual objects to infinitely complex combinations of sensory data, or toward a more moderate position, like the "conceptualism" prevailing from the end of the Middle Ages to the end of the last century, or the sociologism of Durkheim's "collective representations."

He must be satisfied with the simple and obvious fact that human agents accept such objects as real and meaningful, ascribe to them a positive or a negative practical significance, are influenced by them and try to influence them, produce and reproduce them, cooperate and fight about them. Indeed, many of their cultural actions would never be performed, if such subjects did not exist in their experience and were not regarded by them as real, though entirely different from the sensory data of their natural environment.

For the student of social actions this is a very important point. The primary objects of social actions are other human beings whom the agent tries to influence. This, as we have already said, is what distinguishes at first glance social actions from other actions such as technical production, economic consumption, aesthetic reproduction and creation, religious sanctification and purification, scientific thinking about nature—which do not bear upon human beings, but upon other objects, material or spiritual. We call therefore human beings, as objects of actions, *primary social values*. And a human being, as he appears to the agent for whom he is a social value, is not reducible to data of the agent's sensory experience. He is indeed a body, but he is also "something else"—"a conscious being," a being who has certain capacities and dispositions commonly called "psychological."

Now, it must be clearly understood that we, the sociologists, need not accept as "true" any ideas human agents may have about the "consciousness," "minds" or "souls," of those human beings with whom they deal actively as social values. From the scientific point of view, all we know and ever can know about human "consciousness" is the simple and obvious fact that other people, like ourselves, experience data and perform activities. In this limited and purely formal sense, we can say that every human individual is a "conscious subject," an "experiencing agent," provided we are aware that our task as scientists is not to speculate, as the metaphysicians with their own special methods do, about what conscious subjects "really are," whether their capacity to experience and to act is rooted in a "substance," a "mind," a "soul," an "organism," a "nervous system," or in a "function," an *actus purus*," a "transcendental ego," a specific kind of "energy," or what not. Ours is simply and unpretentiously to investigate the data which conscious agents experience and the activities which they perform.

But a "social agent," i.e., an agent who deals with a human being as a social value, is not a scientific sociologist: he is interested in this being not theoretically, but practically. And from his practical point of view the fact that this human being can experience and perform activities, just as the agent himself, appears as an exceedingly important, real characteristic of this human being, as essential as the fact that he has a body, or even more so. For there my be human beings whom a social agent never has experienced as bodies, whose bodily characteristics do not interest him, and yet whom he tries to influence as social values, and from whom he expects reactions—as when he mails a written request to a firm, an office, or a board or directors whose very names as individuals are unknown to him.

In so far, now, as social values appear to the agent to be "conscious realities," having a mental as well as a physical existence, they are to him values with a content partly material (like technical instruments) and partly non-material, spiritual (like myths, novels, or scientific concepts). This non-material content may predominate completely over the material content: thus, an institution like the treasury of a state is for the citizens primarily a number of active "minds" (if not a single "collective mind"), that may and do, if necessary, utilize human bodies, e.g., the bodies of policemen, to coerce citizens into paying taxes, but whose own bodily composition is of no importance to the tax-payer as compared with their "mental" capacities and dispositions.

It is impossible to take into account the empirical variety of social actions and to explain their changes, unless we realize this fundamental character of social values as they appear to the agents who deal with them. This is what orthodox behaviorists are afraid to do lest, by admitting that human beings appear to each other as psychological entities, they be led to admit that human beings are "in themselves" psychological entities. We shall see later on how unmotivated is this fear. Studying the origin and development of the social objectivation of men by men in the course of social actions, the sociologist can eliminate once and for ever the traditional assumption that psychological reality originally and irreducibly exists as the foundation of cultural life, by showing it to be a product of cultural activity, like religious myths or literary heroes.

Behaviorism as a theory of actions is thus inapplicable beyond its original range of animal and infant behavior (including incipient symbolization), and particularly inapplicable to social actions. This does not mean that all the monographic work it has done outside of this original range is worthless: on the contrary, some of it is really important. It is not the first time in the history of science that a wrong theory has stimulated valuable investigations. But the positive results of these investigations can be adequately utilized for general scientific purposes only after they are separated from the theory which they were meant to prove, and reinterpreted with reference to sounder theoretic hypotheses. Thus, some studies of the "symbolic process" throw a new light on the hitherto neglected problem of the use of symbols as instruments in social actions; but their true theoretic significance will become apparent only in connection with a better inductive theory of social actions than the one behaviorism now offers. The results of numerous investigations concerning the effects on human conduct of pathological organic changes or of environmental processes will be more valuable scientifically when the empirical characters of the original conduct itself are more thoroughly investigated, when cultural causality is better understood, and the effects of the changes are redefined more exactly than behavioristic preconceptions now permit.

Certain recent developments of behaviorism are already leading away from the narrowness of the theory of actions as organic responses to sensory stimuli. Behaviorism, as expressed by men like Read Bain, Kimball Young, L. L. Bernard, and E. Bogardus, ceases to be a particular doctrine or even a specific and exclusive method, and becomes an intellectual attitude which demands that human actions and their changes as empirical data be studied in the same spirit of scientific objectivity and inductive thoroughness and with the same elimination of useless traditions as chemical or biological data —which does not necessarily imply that they must be the same kind of data as the biologist's or the chemist's. We can but heartily agree with such an intellectual attitude, even though we believe that some of the methods in which it finds expression ought to be changed; but this is a later question.

# SUBJECTIVE MEANING IN THE SOCIAL SITUATION III* (MacIver)

1. A business man sits in his office. He has concluded an important deal. The tension under which he had been working is relaxed. He is back to the everyday routine and it has less savor than before. He is conscious of a vague restlessness. He wants a change of some sort. His days have been too slavishly devoted to the demands of business, he has been missing other things. He has been making money—why shouldn't he spend some, indulge himself a little? Why not take time off and go on a voyage? The business can get along without him for a few weeks. A steamship company's advertisement of a "luxury cruise," which he had read some days before, comes to his mind. "It is just the thing I need," he says to himself, "a complete change of scene." His wife has been warning him against overworking. His family will appreciate him more when he comes back after an absence. The air and sunshine will do him good. He will make new acquaintances. It will be pleasant to visit Rio and Buenos Aires and other places he has merely read about. The more he thinks of the idea the better he likes it. Before the day is over he "makes up his mind" and telephones the steamship company for a reservation.

What has our business man been doing? He has been assessing a situation and arriving at a decision. He has had alternatives before him and has chosen between them. He is going to travel, for recreation or health or adventure. That is the way he puts it to others—or to himself. His statement of objective is necessarily incomplete and is probably a simplification. Anyhow he has reached a decision, probably without any meticulous calculation. He cannot really tell you how he arrived at it. *It is his dynamic assessment of a situation.* Let us take it at that for the present. In the process of making a decision, some desire, some valuation, simple or complex, has become dominant for the time being, as a determinant of action within the individual's scheme of values.

2. Having made his decision, our business man reorganizes his activities in order to attain his objective. He gives instructions for the conduct of his

---

* Reprinted from *Social Causation* by R. M. MacIver, pp. 291–299, with permission of the publisher, Ginn and Company. Copyright, 1942, by Ginn and Company.

affairs during his absence. He makes arrangements for family needs. He foresees certain contingencies and provides against them. He cancels some engagements. He buys some travelling equipment. He turns resources hitherto neutral and undirected, such as the money he pays for his transportation, into specific means, the means for his new objective.

In all conscious behavior there is thus a twofold process of selective organization. On the one hand the value-system of the individual, his active cultural complex, his personality, is focussed in a particular direction, towards a particular objective. (Sometimes, as we previously pointed out, the incentive to the reorganization of activity may be a dominating motive that is not attached to a specific objective.) On the other hand certain aspects of external reality are selectively related to the controlling valuation, are distinguished from the rest of the external world, are in a sense withdrawn from it, since they now become themselves value factors, the means, obstacles, or conditions relevant to the value quest. The inner, or subjective, system is focussed by a dynamic valuation; and the outer, or external, system is "spotlighted" in that focus, the part within the spotlight being *transformed from mere externality into something also belonging to a world of values,* as vehicle, accessory, hindrance, and cost of the value attainment.

3. The traveller sets out on his voyage. He enters into a new system of social relations. He is subjected to new influences. He may be deflected thereby from his original objective, he may find new additional objectives, or he may pursue exclusively the first one. Even in the last event he may fail to attain his goal. The experience of adventure may fall flat, he may not improve his health, he may not achieve whatever other end he sought. His assessment of the situation may have been faulty. He may have miscalculated the chances of success. He may have left out of the reckoning some important considerations. Or it may be that developments of an unforeseen character intervene and make his voyage nugatory.

In all conscious behavior we relate means to ends, but the process of establishing this relationship is contingent and involves an attribution of causality that may or may not be confirmed by experience. Before embarking on his ship our traveller had somehow assessed the situation. This assessment, whether superficial or thorough, involved a reckoning of alternatives. It contained, as do all decisions to act, a speculative element. A dynamic assessment weighs alternatives not yet actualized, sets what would be the consequences if this course were taken over against what would be the consequences if that course were taken. It is in this regard a causal judgment. We pointed out in a previous chapter that the attribution of social causation always contains a speculative factor of this sort. But the dynamic assessment, that is, the judgment that carries a decision to act, differs from the *post mortem* judgment of history or social science in that it is doubly contingent. In the historical attribution we imaginatively construct what would have happened if the historically presented event or act had not occurred, or at the least we postulate that certain happenings would not have occurred but for the event or act in question. One of the alternatives that must be weighed in the process of causal attribution is always imaginatively constructed. But in the practical judgment that unleashes action *both* of the final alternatives are constructs, for both refer to the future. The voyager chose what he thought likely to happen if he travelled in preference to what he thought likely to happen if he stayed at home.

4. Our traveller set out on his voyage without reckoning all the contingencies. No one does or could calculate all the possible combinations of circumstance that may conspire against—or in favor of—his enterprise. When a man decides to act he generally has two or three alternatives before him and he assesses these alternatives in the light of a few expectancies. These alone come within the focus of decision. But "there's many a slip 'twixt the cup and the lip." We can perhaps distinguish three types of contingency that may frustrate the attainment of an objective once decided upon. Two of these we have already suggested. The traveller may "change his mind" while he travels and be diverted to another quest. Or he may carry through his project and at the end find that he had miscalculated the means-end nexus—if he travels for health the voyage may not restore him. The first contingency occurs in the structure of the inner or subjective system; the second in the relationship of the inner and the outer—the relation of means to ends was conceived to be such and such and it turned out to be different. But there is a third type of contingency which has reference to the dynamics of the external order alone. Our traveller probably did not consider the chance that his ship might strike a rock or founder in a storm. He certainly did not consider the chance that he might fall on a slippery deck and break his leg. He thought of the ship as an instrument of his ends and since most ships make the port they sail for he gave no consideration to the fact that the ship, as physical reality, is subjected to forces that are oblivious of its instrumental quality. It enters, like all instruments, into two causal systems, the means-end system of the conscious realm and the neutral system of physical nature. The adjustment of the dependent causality of the first system to the independent causality of the second is imperfect, and thus a new set of contingencies arises. Our traveller did not concern himself with these contingencies. He was content to assess a certain routine of experience that he expected would continue if he stayed at home and a certain alternative

to that routine that he expected would occur if he took the voyage. He foresaw, under the impulse of the emotions congenial to his temperament, a preferable train of consequences as likely to occur if he decided to travel—and decided accordingly.

In all conscious behavior the situation we assess, as preliminary to action, is in no sense the total objective situation. In the first place it is obviously not the situation as it might appear to some omniscient and disinterested eye, viewing all its complex interdependences and all its endless contingencies. In the second place it is not the situation as inclusive of all the conditions and aspects observable, or even observed, by the participant himself. Many things of which he is aware he excludes from the focus of interest or attention. Many contingencies he ignores. The situation he assesses is one that he has selectively defined, in terms of his experience, his habit of response, his intellectual grasp, and his emotional engrossment. The dynamic assessment limits the situation by excluding all the numerous aspects that are not apprehended as relevant to the choice between alternatives. At the same time it includes in the situation various aspects that are not objectively given, that would not be listed in any merely physical inventory. For in the first place it envisages the situation as impregnated with values and susceptible of new potential values; and in the second place the envisagement is dependent on the ever-changing value-system of the individual, charged with memory of past experience, moulded by the impact of previous indoctrination, responsive to the processes of change within his whole psycho-organic being. Thus no two individuals envisage and define a situation in exactly the same way, even when they make a seemingly identical decision and even although social influences are always powerfully at work to merge individual assessments into a collective assessment.

Our simple instance of the traveller has brought out a number of points, which we recapitulate as follows:

1. A preliminary to conscious activity is a decision between alternatives —to do this or to do that, to do or not to do. In the process of decision-making the individual assesses a situation in the light of these alternatives. A choice between values congenial to the larger value-system of the individual is somehow reached.

2. The decision once taken, the other purposes or valuations of the individual are accommodated to it. Preparatory actions follow. In this orientation certain external factors are selectively reorganized and given subjective significance. They are construed as means, obstacles, conditions, and limitations, with reference to the attainment of the dominant desire or value. The dynamic assessment brings the external world selectively into the sub-

jective realm, conferring on it subjective significance for the ends of action.

3. The dynamic assessment involves a type of causal judgment that differs from the *post factum* attribution of causality characteristic of the social sciences, in that it is doubly speculative. It rests always on a predictive judgment of the form: if this is done, this consequence will (is likely to) follow *and* if this is not done or if this other thing is done, this other consequence will (is likely to) follow. We may observe in passing that even the most simple-seeming choice may conceal a subtle and unfathomed subjective process.

4. The selectivity of the dynamic assessment, as it reviews the situation prior to decision and as it formulates the alternatives of action, makes it subject to several kinds of contingency and practical hazard. First, the dominant objective registered in the decision to act may not persist throughout the process leading to its attainment. Second, the means-ends nexus envisaged in the decision to act may be misapprehended. Third, the physical order assumed to be under control as the means and conditions of action may "erupt" into the situation in unanticipated ways. All conscious behaving is an implicit reckoning of probabilities, which may or may not be justified by the event.

Before we take leave of our simple case we may point out that the analysis of it contains already the clue to our main problem. What has particularly troubled us is that the various factors we causally relate to any socio-psychological phenomenon belong to different orders of reality. Yet they must somehow get together, they must somehow become comparable and co-ordinate, since they must operate with or against one another in the determination of the phenomenon. But how does, say, a moral conviction "co-operate" with an empty stomach in determining whether or not a man will steal? How does the prevalence of a particular religion combine with rural conditions in determining a high birthrate? How does the decline of religious authority combine with urban congestion and the improvement of contraceptives in the lowering of the birthrate? The suggested answer is that *in the dynamic assessment all the factors determining conscious behavior are brought into a single order.* The external factors enter not as such, but as considerations affecting or relative to the pursuit of ends. A change of religious attitudes and the expense of bringing up children both affect the value systems of the individuals concerned. At every moment of deliberation or decision the individual is faced with alternatives. He has not one desire but many, and they are not independent but interdependent. He seeks attainment not of one value but of a system of values, for that is what it means to have, or be, a personality. What choice he will make, what end he will here and now pursue, depends on the urgency of particular desires, the intensity of depth of particular valuations, relative to the variant conditions of attainment. The intensity and depth of particular valuations will in turn register a recognition of the different possibilities of attainment. The change in religious attitudes is not wholly independent of the conditions of urban living. In any event, it introduces a change in the individual's scheme of values. But so, indirectly, does the fact of urban congestion. It makes some values easier of attainment, and some harder. Values are values only as calling for attainment or for maintenance—there would be no values in a static world; conditions and means are such only as they make for or against the attaining or the maintaining of values.

# 8: Role-Taking and Reference Group

Ever since the major writings of William James appeared almost eighty years ago, American social psychologists have generally postulated the social origin of the individual's self-image. They have noted that the social self is, in James' terms, the recognition which one receives from his mates. The person's image of self, in other words, is taken over from the images of himself which others present to him, as indicated by their reaction of approval or disapproval. The individual learns to follow models of conduct which are suggested to him by others who are significant to him (see Chapter 4).

But anticipation of the response of "significant others" to himself is possible only if the maturing child learns to perceive the other person's point of view, "to take the role of the other." Hence, the ability imaginatively to enact the role of others is a precondition for the rational anticipation of the responses of others and for adequate perception of one's self. Our selection from George Herbert Mead, the eminent American social philosopher, is meant to illustrate the process sketched above.

Human beings do not act toward each other as isolated individuals; they are parts of larger communities and groups whose members have some common agreement about the various social roles and their "correct" performance. However, the *maturing* member of a society does not merely internalize random attitudes; rather he incorporates the typical and standardized role expectations as they are prevalent in the group or groups to which he belongs. Our selection from William Graham Sumner (1840–1910) is meant to indicate how attitudes to various types of situations are shaped to a large extent by the interiorization of the value-laden appraisals of the in-group.

So far we have still reasoned as if the "generalized other," the "conscience" of particular persons, incorporates the norms of the whole society of which they are a part. Yet recent research has made it clear that the individual incorporates only the norms of those segments of society which have became significant to him. The concept of "reference group" has been developed in recent years by a group of social psychologists and sociologists —as our selection from the social psychologist Muzafer Sherif is meant to show. It has helped to clarify the fact that the individual relates himself to selected groups of which he may not necessarily be a member. In other words, his identification may be with groups of which he is a member or with groups of which he would like to be a member. The work of Robert K. Merton and Alice Kitt on reference group theory indicates that many areas of social behavior in heterogeneous societies are illuminated once it is seen that men orient their behavior in terms of both membership and non-membership groups. Behavior which may be judged conformist from the viewpoint of a large organization such as the army may be considered deviant from the viewpoint of a sub-group with its own norms as distinct from those of the inclusive organization. Certain members of a sub-group may pattern their conduct according to the demands of the larger organization and its authoritative spokesmen. For them these men in authority, rather than their immediate associates, function as reference groups. Therefore, they are likely to exhibit conduct quite at variance with that of the in-group for whom the more specialized norms are a point of reference.

Lately role theory has undergone considerable refinement. Among the newer contributors are Daniel J. Levinson and Erving Goffman. Levinson has successfully challenged the unitary concept of role by pointing to many structural complexities. Of Goffman's contributions, none strikes us as more significant than his shift from a grimly "closed" view of role to the "openness" implicit in "role distance," a valuable addition to the literature.

Our last selection, by Rose Laub Coser, stands in a dialectical relationship to Goffman's; it critically examines Goffman's contribution, rejecting some of his contentions while accepting others, thus attempting to integrate Goffman's work with other aspects of current role theory.

# PLAY, THE GAME, AND THE GENERALIZED OTHER* (*Mead*)

We were speaking of the social conditions under which the self arises as an object. In addition to language we found two illustrations, one in play and the other in the game, and I wish to summarize and expand my account on these points. I have spoken of these from the point of view of children. We can, of course, refer also to the attitudes of more primitive people out of which our civilization has arisen. A striking illustration of play as distinct from the game is found in the myths and various of the plays which primitive people carry out, especially in religious pageants. The pure play attitude which we find in the case of little children may not be found here, since the participants are adults, and undoubtedly the relationship of these play processes to that which they interpret is more or less in the minds of even the most primitive people. In the process of interpretation of such rituals, there is an organization of play which perhaps might be compared to that which is taking place in the kindergarten in dealing with the plays of little children, where these are made into a set that will have a definite structure or relationship. At least something of the same sort is found in the play of primitive people. This type of activity belongs, of course, not to the everyday life of the people in their dealing with the objects about them—there we have a more or less definitely developed self-consciousness—but in their attitudes toward the forces about them, the nature upon which they depend; in their attitude toward this nature which is vague and uncertain, there we have a much more primitive response; and that response finds its expression in taking the role of the other, playing at the expression of their gods and their heroes, going through certain rites which are the representation of what these individuals are supposed to be doing. The process is one which develops, to be sure, into a more or less definite technique and is controlled; and yet we can say that it has arisen out of situations similar to those in which little children play at being a parent, at being a teacher—vague personalities that are about them and which affect them and on which they depend. These are personalities which they take, roles they play, and in so far control the development of their own personality. This outcome is just what the kindergarten works toward. It takes the characters of these various

* Reprinted from *Mind, Self and Society* by George H. Mead, pp. 152–164, by permission of The University of Chicago Press. Copyright 1934 by The University of Chicago.

vague beings and gets them into such an organized social relationship to each other that they build up the character of the little child.[1] The very introduction of organization from outside supposes a lack of organization at this period in the child's experience. Over against such a situation of the little child and primitive people, we have the game as such.

The fundamental difference between the game and play is that in the latter the child must have the attitude of all the others involved in that game. The attitudes of the other players which the participant assumes organize into a sort of unit, and it is that organization which controls the response of the individual. The illustration used was of a person playing baseball. Each one of his own acts is determined by his assumption of the action of the others who are playing the game. What he does is controlled by his being everyone else on that team, at least in so far as those attitudes affect his own particular response. We get then an "other" which is an organization of the attitudes of those involved in the same process.

The organized community or social group which gives to the individual his unity of self may be called "the generalized other." The attitude of the generalized other is the attitude of the whole community.[2] Thus, for example, in the case of such a social group as a ball team, the team is the generalized other in so far as it enters—as an organized process or social activity—into the experience of any one of the individual members of it.

If the given human individual is to develop a self in the fullest sense, it is not sufficient for him merely to take the attitudes of other human individuals toward himself and toward one another within the human social process, and to bring that social process as a whole into his individual experience merely in these terms: he must also, in the same way that he takes the attitudes of other individuals toward himself and toward one another, take their attitudes toward the various phases or aspects of the common social activity or set of social undertakings in which, as members of an organized society or social group, they are all engaged; and he must then, by generalizing these individual attitudes of that organized society or social group itself, as a whole, act toward different social projects which at any given time it is carrying out, or toward the various larger phases of the general social process which constitutes its life and of which these projects are specific manifestations. This getting of the broad activities of any given social whole or organized society as such within the experiential field of any one of the individuals involved or included in that whole is, in other words, the essential basis and prerequisite of the fullest development of that individual's self: only in so far as he takes the attitudes of the organized social group to which he belongs toward the organized, co-operative social activity or set of such activities in which that group as such is engaged, does he develop a complete self or possess the sort of complete self he has developed. And on the other hand, the complex co-operative processes and activities and institutional functionings of organized human society are also possible only in so far as every individual involved in them or belonging to that society can take the general attitudes of all other such individuals with reference to these processes and activities and institutional functionings, and to the organized social whole of experiential relations and interactions thereby constituted—and can direct his own behavior accordingly.

It is in the form of the generalized other that the social process influences the behavior of the individuals involved in it and carrying it on, i.e., that the community exercises control over the conduct of its individual members; for it is in this form that the social process or community enters as a determining factor into the individual's thinking. In abstract thought the individual takes the attitude of the generalized other[3] toward himself, without reference to its expression in any particular other individuals; and in concrete thought he takes that attitude in so far as it is expressed in the attitudes toward his behavior of those other individuals with whom he is involved in the given social situation or act. But only by taking the attitude of the generalized other toward himself, in one or another of these ways, can he think at all; for only thus can thinking—or the internalized conversation of gestures which constitutes thinking—occur. And only through the taking by individuals of the attitude or attitudes of the generalized other toward themselves is the existence of a universe of discourse, as that system of common or social meanings which thinking presupposes at its context, rendered possible.

The self-conscious human individual, then, takes or assumes the organized social attitudes of the given social group or community (or of some one section thereof) to which he belongs, toward the social problems of various kinds which confront that group or community at any given time, and which arise in connection with the correspondingly different social projects or organized co-operative enterprises in which that group or community as such is engaged; and as an individual participant in these social projects or co-operative enterprises, he governs his own conduct accordingly. In politics, for example, the individual identifies himself with an entire political party and takes the organized attitudes of that entire party toward the rest of the given social community and toward the problems which confront the party within the given social situation; and he consequently reacts or responds in terms of the organized attitudes of the party as a whole. He thus enters into a special set of social relations with all the other individuals who belong to that political party; and in the same way he enters into various other special sets of social relations, with various other classes of individuals respectively, the individuals of each of these classes being the other members of some one of the particular organized subgroups (determined in socially functional terms) of which he himself is a member within the entire given society or social community. In the most highly developed, organized, and complicated human social communities—those evolved by civilized man—these various socially functional classes or subgroups of individuals to which any given individual belongs (and with the other individual members of which he thus enters into a special set of social relations) are of two kinds. Some of them are concrete social classes or subgroups, such as political parties, clubs, corporations, which are all actually functional social units, in terms of which their individual members are directly related to one another. The others are abstract social classes or subgroups, such as the class of debtors and the class of creditors, in terms of which their individual members are related to one another only more or less indirectly, and which only more or less indirectly function as social units, but which afford or represent unlimited possibilities for the widening and ramifying and enriching of the social relations among all the individual members of the given society as an organized and unified whole. The given individual's membership in several of these abstract social classes or subgroups makes possible his entrance into definite social relations (however indirect) with an almost infinite number of other individuals who also belong to or are included within one or another of these abstract social classes or subgroups cutting across functional lines of demarcation which divide different human social communities from one another, and including individual members from several (in some cases from all) such communities. Of these abstract social classes or subgroups of human individuals the one which is most inclusive and extensive is, of course, the one defined by the logical universe of discourse (or system of universally significant symbols) determined by the participation and communicative interaction of individuals; for all such classes or subgroups, it is the one which claims the largest number of individual members, and which enables the largest conceivable number of human individuals to enter into some sort of social relation, however indirect or abstract it may be, with one another—a relation arising from the universal functioning of gestures as significant symbols in the general human social process of communication.

I have pointed out, then, that there are two general stages in the full development of the self. At the first of these stages, the individual's self is constituted simply by an organization of the particular attitudes of other individuals toward himself and toward one another in the specific social acts in which he participates with them. But at the second stage in the full development of the individual's self that self is constituted not only by an organization of these particular individual attitudes, but also by an organization of the social attitudes of the generalized other or the social group as a whole to which he belongs. These social or group attitudes are brought within the individual's field of direct experience, and are included as elements in the structure or constitution of his self, in the same way that the attitudes of particular other individuals are; and the individual arrives at them, or succeeds in taking them, by means of further organizing, and then generalizing, the attitudes of particular other individuals in terms of their organized social bearings and implications. So the self reaches its full development by organizing these individual attitudes of others into the organized social or group attitudes, and by thus becoming an individual reflection of the general systematic patterns of social or group behavior in which it and the others are all involved—a pattern which enters as a whole into the individual's experience in terms of these organized group attitudes which, through the mechanism of his central nervous system, he takes toward himself, just as he takes the individual attitudes of others.

The game has a logic, so that such an organization of the self is rendered possible: there is a definite end to be obtained; the actions of the different individuals are all related to each other with reference to that end so that they do not conflict; one is not in conflict with himself in the attitude of another man on the team. If one has the attitude of the person throwing the ball he can also have the response of catching the ball. The two are related so that they further the purpose of the game itself. They are interrelated in a unitary, organic fashion. There is a definite unity, then, which is introduced into the organization of other selves when we reach such a stage as that of the game, as over against the situation of play where there is a simple succession of one role after another, a situation which is, of course, characteristic of the child's own personality. The child is one thing at one time and another at another, and what he is at one moment does not determine what he is at another. That is both the charm of childhood as well as its inadequacy. You cannot count on the child; you cannot assume that all the things he does are going to determine what he will do at any moment. He is not organized into a whole. The child has no definite character, no definite personality.

The game is then an illustration of the situation out of which an organized personality arises. In so far as the child does take the attitude of the other and allows that attitude of the other to determine the thing he is going to do with reference to a common end, he is becoming an organic member of society. He is taking over the morale of that society and is becoming an essential member of it. He belongs to it in so far as he does allow the attitude of the other that he takes to control his own immediate expression. What is involved here is some sort of an organized precess. That which is expressed in terms of the game is, of course, being continually expressed in the social life of the child, but this wider process goes beyond the immediate experience of the child himself. The importance of the game is that it lies entirely inside of the child's own experience, and the importance of our modern type of education is that it is brought as far as possible within this realm. The different attitudes that a child assumes are so organized that they exercise a definite control over his response, as the attitudes in a game control his own immediate response. In the game we get an organized other, a generalized other, which is found in the nature of the child itself, and finds its expression in the immediate experience of the child. And it is that organized activity in the child's own nature controlling the particular response which gives unity, and which builds up his own self.

What goes on in the game goes on in the life of the child all the time. He is continually taking the attitudes of those about him, especially the roles of those who in some sense control him and on whom he depends. He gets the function of the process in an abstract sort of a way at first. It goes over from the play into the game in a real sense. He has to play the game. The morale of the game takes hold of the child more than the larger morale of the whole community. The child passes into the game and the game expresses a social situation in which he can completely enter; its morale may have a greater hold on him than that of the family to which he belongs or the community in which he lives. There are all sorts of social organizations, some of which are fairly lasting, some temporary, into which the child is entering, and he is playing a sort of social game in them. It is a period in which he likes "to belong," and he gets into organizations which come into existence and pass out of existence. He becomes a something which can function in the organized whole, and thus tends to determine himself in his relationship with the group to which he belongs. That process is one which is a striking stage in the development of the child's morale. It constitutes him a self-conscious member of the community to which he belongs.

Such is the process by which a personality arises. I have spoken of this as a process in which a child takes the role of the other, and said that it takes place essentially through the use of language. Language is predominantly based on the vocal gesture by means of which co-operative activities in a community are carried out. Language in its significant sense is that vocal gesture which tends to arouse in the individual the attitude which it arouses in others, and it is this perfecting of the self by the gesture which mediates the social activities that gives rise to the process of taking the role of the other. The latter phrase is a little unfortunate because it suggests an actor's attitude which is actually more sophisticated than that which is involved in our own experience. To this degree it does not correctly describe that which I have in mind. We see the process most definitely in a primitive form in those situations where the child's play takes different roles. Here the very fact that he is ready to pay out money, for instance, arouses the attitude of the person who receives money; the very process is calling out in him the corresponding activities of the other person involved. The individual stimulates himself to the response which he is calling out in the other person, and then acts in some degree in response to that situation. In play the child does definitely act out the role which he himself has aroused in himself. It is that which gives, as I have said, a definite content in the individual which answers to the stimulus that affects him as it affects somebody else. The content of the other that enters into one personality is the response in the individual which his gesture calls out in the other.

We may illustrate our basic concept by a reference to the notion of property. If we say "This is my property, I shall control it," that affirmation calls out a certain set of responses which must be the same in any community in which property exists. It involves an organized attitude with reference to property which is common to all the members of the community. One must have a definite attitude of control of his own property and respect for the property of others. Those attitudes (as organized sets of responses) must be there on the part of all, so that when one says such a thing he calls out in himself the response of the others. He is calling out the response of what I have called a generalized other. That which makes society possible is such common responses, such organized attitudes, with reference to what we term property, the cults of religion, the process of education, and the relations of the family. Of course, the wider the society the more definitely universal these objects must be. In any case there must be a definite set of responses, which we may speak of as abstract, and which can belong to a very large group. Property is in itself a very abstract concept. It is that which the individual himself can control and nobody else can control. The attitude is different from that of a dog toward a bone. A dog will fight any other dog trying to take the bone. The dog is not taking the attitude of the other dog. A man who says "This is my property" is taking an attitude of the other person. The man is appealing to his rights because he is able to take the attitude which everybody else in the group has with reference to property, thus arousing in himself the attitude of others.

What goes to make up the organized self is the organization of the attitudes which are common to the group. A person is a personality because he belongs to a community, because he takes over the institutions of that community into his own conduct. He takes its language as a medium by which he gets his personality, and then through a process of taking the different roles that all the others furnish he comes to get the attitude of the members of the community. Such, in a certain sense, is the structure of a man's personality. There are certain common responses which each individual has toward certain common things, and in so far as those common responses are awakened in the individual when he is affecting other persons he arouses his own self. The structure, then, on which the self is built is this response which is common to all, for one has to be a member of a community to be a self. Such responses are abstract attitudes, but they constitute just what we term a man's character. They give him what we term his principles, the acknowledged attitudes of all members of the community toward what are the values of that community. He is putting himself in the place of the generalized other, which represents the organized responses of all the members of the group. It is that which guides conduct controlled by principles, and a person who has such an organized group of responses is a man whom we say has character, in the moral sense.

It is a structure of attitudes, then, which goes to make up a self, as distinct from a group of habits. We all of us have, for example, certain groups of habits, such as the particular intonations which a person uses in his speech. This is a set of habits of vocal expression which one has but which one does not know about. The sets of habits which we have of that sort mean nothing to us; we do not hear the intonations of our speech that others hear unless we are paying particular attention to them. The habits of emotional expression which belong to our speech are of the same sort. We may know that we have expressed ourselves in a joyous fashion but the detailed process is one which does not come back to our conscious selves. There are whole bundles of such habits which do not enter into a conscious self, but which help to make up what is termed the unconscious self.

After all, what we mean by self-consciousness is an awakening in ourselves of the group of attitudes which we are arousing in others, especially when it is an important set of responses which go to make up the members of the community. It is unfortunate to fuse or mix up consciousness, as we ordinarily use that term, and self-consciousness. Consciousness, as frequently used, simply has reference to the field of experience, but self-consciousness refers to the ability to call out in ourselves a set of definite responses which belong to the others of the group. Consciousness and self-consciousness are not on the same level. A man alone has, fortunately or unfortunately, access, to his own toothache, but that is not what we mean by self-consciousness.

I have so far emphasized what I have called the structure upon which the self is constructed, the framework of the self, as it were. Of course we are not only what is common to all: each one of the selves is different from everyone else; but there has to be such a common structure as I have sketched in order that we may be members of a community at all. We cannot be ourselves unless we are also members in whom there is a community of attitudes which control the attitudes of all. We cannot have rights unless we have common attitudes. That which we have acquired as self-conscious persons makes us such members of society and gives us selves. Selves can only exist in definite relationships to other selves. No hard-and-fast line can be drawn between our own selves and the selves of others, since our own selves exist and enter as such into our experience only in so far as the selves of others exist and enter as such into our experience also. The individual possesses a self only in relation to the selves of the other members of his social group; and the structure of his self expresses or reflects the general behavior pattern of this social group to which he belongs, just as does the structure of the self of every other individual belonging to this social group.

REFERENCES

1. ["The Relation of Play to Education," *University of Chicago Record*, I (1896-97), 140 ff.]
2. It is possible for inanimate objects, no less than for other human organisms, to form parts of the generalized and organized—the completely socialized—other for any given human individual, in so far as he responds to such objects socially or in a social fashion (by means of the mechanism of thought, the internalized conversation of gestures). Any thing—any object or set of objects, whether animate or inanimate, human or animal, or merely physical—toward which he acts, or to which he responds, socially, is an element in what for him is the generalized other; by taking the attitudes of which toward himself he becomes conscious of himself as an object or individual, and thus develops a self or personality. Thus, for example, the cult, in its primitive form, is merely the social embodiment of the relation between the given social group or community and its physical environment—an organized social means, adopted by the individual members of that group or community, of entering into social relations with that environment, or (in a sense) of carrying on conversations with it; and in this way that environment becomes part of the total generalized other for each of the individual members of the given social group or community.
3. We have said that the internal conversation of the individual with himself in terms of words or significant gestures—the conversation which constitutes the process or activity of thinking—is carried on by the individual from the standpoint of the "generalized other." And the more abstract that conversation is, the more abstract thinking happens to be, the further removed is the generalized other from any con-

nection with particular individuals. It is especially in abstract thinking, that is to say, that the conversation involved is carried on by the individual with the generalized other, rather than with any particular individuals. Thus it is, for example, that abstract concepts are concepts stated in terms of the attitudes of the entire social group or community; they are stated on the basis of the individual's consciousness of the attitudes of the generalized other toward them, as a result of his taking these attitudes of the generalized other and then responding to them. And thus it is also that abstract propositions are stated in a form which anyone—any other intelligent individual—will accept.

# IN-GROUPS AND OUT-GROUPS * (Sumner)

*Tradition and Its Restraints.*  It is evident that the "ways" of the older and more experienced members of a society deserve great authority in any primitive group. We find that this rational authority leads to customs of deference and to etiquette in favor of the old. The old in turn cling stubbornly to tradition and to the example of their own predecessors. Thus tradition and custom become intertwined and are a strong coercion which directs the society upon fixed lines, and strangles liberty. Children see their parents always yield to the same custom and obey the same persons. They see that the elders are allowed to do all the talking, and that if an outsider enters, he is saluted by those who are at home according to rank and in fixed order. All this becomes rule for children, and helps to give to all primitive customs their stereotyped formality. "The fixed ways of looking at things which are inculcated by education and tribal discipline, are the precipitate of an old cultural development, and in their continued operation they are the moral anchor of the Indian, although they are also the fetters which restrain his individual will." [1]

*The Concept of "Primitive Society"; We-Group and Others-Group.*  The conception of "primitive society" which we ought to form is that of small groups scattered over a territory. The size of the groups is determined by the conditions of the struggle for existence. The internal organization of each group corresponds to its size. A group of groups may have some relation to each other (kin, neighborhood, alliance, connubium and commercium) which draws them together and differentiates them from others. Thus a differentiation arises between ourselves, the we-group, or in-group, and everybody else, or the others-groups, out-groups. The insiders in a we-group are in a relation of peace, order, law, government, and industry, to

* Reprinted from *Folkways* by William Graham Sumner, Ginn and Company, 1904, sections 12 and 13.

each other. Their relation to all outsiders, or others-groups, is one of war and plunder, except so far as agreements have modified it. If a group is exogamic, the women in it were born abroad somewhere. Other foreigners who might be found in it are adopted persons, guest friends, and slaves.

REFERENCE

1. Globus, LXXXVII, 128.


# REFERENCE GROUPS IN HUMAN RELATIONS * (*Sherif*)

Social psychology, on the whole, has been approached historically in contrasting ways. One approach starts with one or a few sovereign principles, such as imitation, suggestion, instinct, libido, etc. On the other hand, there have been attempts to study empirically every social psychological topic, every specific case of attitude in its own right, as though the results concerning the topic at hand are insulated from other facts in that general area.

The approaches which utilize one or a few sovereign concepts tended to start and end with premature formalizations, resulting in rather "closed-system" schools of social psychology, in spite of claims at being systematic and comprehensive. In view of the diverse problems that have to be considered, it has become evident that especially in social psychology we cannot just sit down and write off all the major principles and concepts in one or a few stretches.

On the other hand, approaches which claim that facts speak for themselves uncontaminated with theorizing end up, or rather scatter around, in almost endless discrete results, in lists, inventories, or unrelated social psychological syllabuses. The main trend of "public opinion" polling and attitude studies of diverse kinds have, on the whole, been of the latter sort until very recently.

Fortunately we do not have to be bound by either of these alternatives. There has been growing concern with attaining concepts which stem from serious preoccupation with persistent problems in social psychology, which are organically related to actual research (experimental and otherwise) and

* By Muzafer Sherif (University of Oklahoma), reprinted from *Group Relations at the Crossroads*, The University of Oklahoma Lectures in Social Psychology, edited by Muzafer Sherif and M. O. Wilson, pp. 203–209, with permission of the publisher, Harper & Brothers, New York. Copyright, 1953, by Harper & Brothers.

which can be utilized for pulling together in a comprehensive way seemingly unrelated facts in a major problem area. The concept of reference groups seems to be such a concept.

Even though this concept has started to spread only during the last four or five years, it has already received varied interpretations and usages. There are incipient signs of its becoming a magic term to explain anything and everything concerning group relations. It may more than pay if we spend some time at this early stage in clarifying our understanding of the concept in terms of the experimental work of which it is an extension, and in terms of its application to problems in group relations.

The general problem is obviously that of individual-group relationship. During the past decades the impact of vital events brought the problem of individual-group relationships into sharp focus, and this trend continues to gain momentum. The major character of this trend, as contrasted with the individualistic emphasis, is the realization that group situations generate differential effects of significant consequence. Group interaction is seen as the major determinant in attitude formation and attitude change, and other phenomena of vital consequence to the individual. During the last decades both sociologists and psychologists, with various approaches, contributed to an ever fuller realization of this trend.

Then what is the use of cluttering the already confusing inventory of concepts relative to the individual-group relationship with another? The necessity of the concept of reference group as differentiated from the more general term, group, needs justification. For concepts are not mere constructs which people, even scientists, can posit at will. Nor does consensus of opinion among professionals in an area make the use of a concept valid. As we look historically, consensus of opinion has been abandoned a good many times because, I suspect, it did not do justice to the understanding of events dealt with.

Two sets of events in particular have forced some such specified group concept as reference group to the foreground. One is related to socio-economic conditions; the other set is on the psychological side.

In a stable, integrated and relatively less differentiated society, there would probably be little necessity for the use of reference group as a separate concept. Modern man, especially in Western societies, is caught in the throes of vertical mobility, in the "dilemmas and contradictions of statuses," and the painful predicament of marginality created by the demands and goals originating in diverse groups. He finds himself betwixt and between situations as he carries on the business of living in different roles in relation to diverse groups which not infrequently demand contradictory adjustment of his experience and behavior. He is exposed through actual face-to-face contacts, through the mass media of communication, to pressures, demands, goals of diverse trends and ideologies. These are some of the many aspects of the setting in which he operates, through which he becomes indoctrinated, forms his identifications, faces a great variety of alternatives to choose from in line with his special needs, etc. If his psychological level of functioning were restricted largely to the impact of immediate stimulus situations and his behavior were regulated solely in terms of the immediate ups and downs of his biogenic motives and conditionings on that basis, he would probably not be troubled so much by the demands of overlapping and contradictory groups.

This leads to the second consideration, which relates to man's conceptual level of functioning. As he passes from one group situation to another from time to time, he reacts to the demands, pressures and appeals of new group situations in terms of the person he has come to consider himself to be and aspires to be. In other words, he reacts in terms of more or less consistent ties of belongingness in relation to his past and present identifications and his future goals for security of his identity, and also his status and prestige concerns. In short, this conceptual level of functioning makes possible regulation of experience and behavior in relation to values and norms that lie at times far beyond immediate group situations.

The conceptual level of functioning is, on the whole, taken too much for granted. We may be gaining a great deal if this conceptual level of functioning is deliberately brought into the discussion of motives and goals in relation to group situations. Of course, this idea is tied up with the notion of *levels* so cogently stressed by Schneirla, Lindesmith and Strauss, and others.[1-3]

It is apparent, then, that the groups to which the individual relates himself need not always be the groups in which he is actually moving. His identifications need not always be with groups in which he is registered, is seen to be, or announced to be a member. The concept of reference groups forces itself through such facts. The concept becomes almost indispensable in dealing with the relation of individuals to groups in highly differentiated and poorly integrated societies, in societies in the process of acculturation and high tempo of transition.

With the above considerations in mind, reference groups can be characterized simply as *those groups to which the individual relates himself as a part or to which he aspires to relate himself psychologically.* It is apparent that the characterization of reference groups just presented is a psychological one, that is, it is made from the standpoint of the individual in the individual-group relationship.

In many cases, of course, the individual's reference groups are at the same time his membership groups.[4] However, in cases where the individual's membership groups are not his reference groups, it does not follow that the groups in which the individual actually interacts will not have an effect on him. On the contrary, this creates important psychological problems for him to which we shall have occasion to refer later when we deal with *marginality* as one instance of being caught between the positive attractions of one's reference group, which is not the membership group of the individual at the time, and demands and pressures of the membership group, which is not his reference group.

Numerous studies coming both from psychologists and from sociologists have shown that the major sources of the individual's weighty attitudes are the values or norms of the groups to which he relates himself, that is, of his reference groups. In fact, the values or norms of his reference groups constitute the major anchorages in relation to which his experience of self-identity is organized. This conception enables us to pull together a host of discrete data in various areas. At this point, we shall mention just one illustration. Textbooks on adolescence used to give rather lengthy lists of adolescent interests and attitudes which include some items that appear as oddities. All such lists of adolescent attitudes and interests can be pulled together under a unified conceptual scheme if they are related to the adolescent's reference groups. These are, on the whole, cliques spontaneously formed under the motivational stresses to which the youngsters are exposed, especially in societies in a high tempo of transition.[5] Likewise, psychological problems of gang behavior, problems of marginality, problems of status regulation by individuals, etc., acquire conceptual unification when approached with some such concept as reference groups.

Of course, the various facts and problems which are brought to focus through the reference group concept historically pressed for consideration whether or not the term "reference group" was explicitly used. A number of investigators, especially sociologists, as we shall see, provided interesting and valuable analyses of these specific problems.

Among psychological studies, Chapman and Volkmann's 1939 experiment merits attention.[6] The conception of this experiment, which served as a model for numerous others, derived explicitly from the general fact that judgments, perceptions, etc., take place within referential frameworks. Specifically, level of aspiration was conceived as an instance of "the effect upon a judgment of the frame of reference within which it is executed." Goals set in relation to the task in question were lowered or raised as the case might be, as determined by the position of experimentally introduced groups to the subject's own reference group. In short, the position of other groups relative to one's own reference group, which served as the major anchorage, determined the regulation of goals. The theoretical implications of this and related studies, especially Hyman's 1942 study on judgments of status, will be considered shortly.

More recently, the concept of reference group has come to the foreground with varying emphasis in the works of Hyman,[7] Sherif and Cantril,[8] Sherif,[9] Newcomb,[10] Lindesmith and Strauss,[3] Merton and Kitt,[11] Hartley,[12] and Jahoda, Deutsch and Cook,[13] among others. In spite of the short history of its use, the concept is alreday being utilized in somewhat different senses.

In studying the psychology of status, Hyman, who first used the term "reference group," found shifts in judgments of status with changes of the group or individual in terms of which judgment was made. This was seen as a specific case of an anchoring point in the frame of reference determining judgment, and was called "reference group" or "reference individual." Unfortunately, after the appearance of this important study in 1942, Hyman's contributions have not to date utilized the reference group concept.

In dealing with changing attitudes during adolescence, Sherif and Cantril,[8] found the term most valuable. However, the characterization on the concept used in this paper was presented first in 1948.[9]

Newcomb demonstrated the usefulness of the reference group concept by recasting the previously reported results of his important Bennington Study on attitude change in terms of the shifts or resistance to shifts in reference groups. In his *Social Psychology*,[10] he characterized membership and reference groups in the sense they are used in this paper. However, he introduced the notions of positive and negative reference groups. A positive reference group, in Newcomb's terminology, "is one in which a person is motivated to be accepted and treated as a member (overtly or symbolically) whereas a negative reference group is one which the person is motivated to oppose or in which he does not want to be treated as a member." In addition, Newcomb speaks of one group being both a positive and negative reference group for the same person, in the sense that he may willingly conform to some of its norms and not to others.

In line with their stress on conceptual factors in human social behavior, so well expressed especially in their chapter "Men Without Symbols," Lindesmith and Strauss[3] emphasize that the individual's relatedness and identifications with groups need not be in terms of actual face-to-face relations. They found the concept of reference groups useful in dealing with such relatedness in particular. It seems, however, that "reference groups" refers specifically in their discussion to groups with which the individual identifies himself, but is not actually a member.

REFERENCES

1. Schneirla, T. C. Problems in the biopsychology of social organization. *J. Abn. & Soc. Psychol.*, 1946, 41:385–402.
2. Schneirla, T. C. The "levels" concept in the study of social organization in animals. In J. H. Rohrer and M. Sherif (eds.), *Social Psychology at the Crossroads*. New York: Harper, 1951.
3. Lindesmith, A. R., and Strauss, A. L. *Social Psychology*. New York: Dryden, 1949.
4. To make this point clear, our previous treatment of membership and reference groups is introduced under the title "Effects of Membership and Other Reference Groups." (M. Sherif, *An Outline of Social Psychology*, Harper, 1948.)
5. Davis, K. The sociology of parent-youth conflict. *Amer. Sociol. Rev.*, 1940, 5:523–535.
6. Chapman, D. W., and Volkmann, J. A social determinant of the level of aspiration. *J. Abn. & Soc. Psychol.*, 1939, 34:225–238.
7. Hyman, H. H. The psychology of status. *Arch. Psychol.*, 1942, 269.
8. Sherif, M., and Cantril, H. *The Psychology of Ego-Involvements*. New York: Wiley, 1947.
9. Sherif, M. *An Outline of Social Psychology*. New York: Harper, 1948.
10. Newcomb, T. M. *Social Psychology*. New York: Dryden, 1950.
11. Merton, R. K., and Kitt, A. S. Contributions to the theory of reference group behavior. In R. K. Merton and P. F. Lazarsfeld (eds.), *Continuities in Social Research: Studies in the Scope and Method of "The American Soldier."* Glencoe: The Free Press, 1950.
12. Hartley, E. L. Psychological problems of multiple group membership. In J. H. Rohrer, and M. Sherif (eds.), *Social Psychology at the Crossroads*. New York: Harper, 1951.
13. Jahoda, M., Deutsch, M., and Cook, S. W. *Research Methods in Social Relations*. New York: Dryden, 1951.

# REFERENCE GROUPS * (*Merton and Kitt*)

*Theoretical Implications.* In discussing this panel study, we want to bring into the open some of the connections between reference group theory and functional sociology which have remained implicit to this point,—an objective to which this study lends itself particularly well, since the findings of the study can be readily reformulated in terms of both kinds of theory,

* Reprinted from *Continuities in Social Research, Studies in the Scope and Method of "The American Soldier,"* edited by Robert K. Merton and Paul F. Lazarsfeld, pp. 86–95, by Robert K. Merton and Alice S. Kitt, with permission of the publisher, The Free Press, Glencoe, Ill.

and are then seen to bear upon a range of behavior wider than that considered in the study itself.

The value of such reformulation for social theory is perhaps best seen in connection with the independent variable of "conformity." It is clear, when one thinks about it, that the type of attitude described as conformist in this study is at the polar extreme from what is ordinarily called "social conformity." For in the vocabulary of sociology, social conformity usually denotes conformity to the norms and expectations current in the individual's *own* membership-group. But in this study, conformity refers, not to the norms of the immediate primary group constituted by enlisted men but to the quite different norms contained in the official military mores. Indeed, as data in *The American Soldier* make clear, the norms of the in-groups of associated enlisted men and the official norms of the Army and of the stratum of officers were often at odds.[1] In the language of reference group theory, therefore, attitudes of conformity to the official mores can be described as a positive orientation to the norms of a non-membership group that is taken as a frame of reference. Such conformity to norms of an out-group is thus equivalent to what is ordinarily called nonconformity, that is, nonconformity to the norms of the in-group.[2]

This preliminary reformulation leads directly to two interrelated questions which we have until now implied rather than considered explicitly: what are the consequences, functional and dysfunctional, of positive orientation to the values of a group other than one's own? And further, which social processes initiate, sustain or curb such orientations?

*Functions of positive orientation to non-membership reference groups.*    In considering, however briefly, the possible consequences of this pattern of conformity to non-membership group norms, it is advisable to distinguish between the consequences for the individuals exhibiting this behavior, the sub-group in which they find themselves, and the social system comprising both of these.

For the individual who adopts the values of a group to which he aspires but does not belong, this orientation may serve the twin functions of aiding his rise into that group and of easing his adjustment after he has become part of it. That this first function was indeed served is the gist of the finding in *The American Soldier* that those privates who accepted the official values of the Army hierarchy were more likely than others to be promoted. The hypothesis regarding the second function still remains to be tested. But it would not, in principle, be difficult to discover empirically whether those men who, through a kind of *anticipatory socialization,* take on the values of the non-membership group to which they aspire, find readier acceptance by that group and make an easier adjustment to it. This would require the development of indices of group acceptance and adjustment, and a comparison, in terms of these indices, of those newcomers to a group who had previously oriented themselves to the group's values and those who had not. More concretely, in the present instance, it would have entailed a comparative study among the privates promoted to higher rank, of the subsequent group adjustment of those who had undergone the hypothesized preparation for status shifts and those who had previously held fast to the values of their in-group of enlisted men. Indices of later adjustment could be related to indices of prior value-orientation. This would constitute a systematic empirical test of a functional hypothesis.

It appears, further, that anticipatory socialization is functional for the individual only within a relatively open social structure providing for mobility. For only in such a structure would such attitudinal and behavior preparation for status shifts be followed by actual changes of status in a substantial proportion of cases. By the same token, the same pattern of anticipatory socialization would be dysfunctional for the individual in a relatively closed social structure, where he would not find acceptance by the group to which he aspires and would probably lose acceptance, because of his out-group orientation, by the group to which he belongs. This latter type of case will be recognized as that of the marginal man, poised on the edge of several groups but fully accepted by none of them.

Thus, the often-studied case of the marginal man[3] and the case of the enlisted man who takes the official military mores as a positive frame of reference can be identified, in a functional theory of reference group behavior, as special cases of anticipatory socialization. The marginal man pattern represents the special case in a relatively closed social system, in which the members of one group take as a positive frame of reference the norms of a group from which they are excluded in principle. Within such a social structure, anticipatory socialization becomes dysfunctional for the individual who becomes the victim of aspirations he cannot achieve and hopes he cannot satisfy. But, as the panel study seems to indicate, precisely the same kind of reference group behavior within a relatively open social system is functional for the individual at least to the degree of helping him to achieve the status to which he aspires. The same reference group behavior in different social structures has different consequences.

To this point, then, we find that positive orientation toward the norms of a non-membership group is precipitated by a passage between membership-groups, either in fact or in fantasy, and that the functional or dysfunctional consequences evidently depend upon the relatively open or closed character of the social structure in which this occurs. And what would, at first glance, seem entirely unrelated and disparate forms of behavior—the behavior of such marginal men as the Cape Coloured or the Eurasian, and of enlisted men adopting the values of military strata other than their own—are seen, after appropriate conceptualization, as special cases of reference group behavior.

Although anticipatory socialization may be functional for the *individual* in an open social system, it is apparently dysfunctional for the solidarity of the *group* or *stratum* to which he belongs. For allegiance to the contrasting mores of another group means defection from the mores of the in-group. And accordingly, as we shall presently see, the in-group responds by putting all manner of social restraints upon such positive orientations to certain out-group norms.

From the standpoint of the larger social system, the Army as a whole, positive orientation toward the official mores would appear to be functional in supporting the legitimacy of the structure and in keeping the structure of authority intact. (This is presumably what is meant when the text of *The American Soldier* refers to these conformist attitudes as "favorable from the Army's point of view.") But manifestly, much research needs to be done before one can say that this is indeed the case. It is possible, for example, that the secondary effects of such orientations may be so deleterious to the solidarity of the primary groups of enlisted men that their morale sags. A concrete research question might help clarify the problem: are outfits with relatively large minorities of men positively oriented to the official Army values more likely to exhibit signs of anomie and personal disorganization (e.g. non-battle casualties)? In such situations, does the personal "success" of conformists (promotion) only serve to depress the morale of the others by rewarding those who depart from the in-group mores?

In this panel study, as well as in several of the others we have reviewed here—for example, the study of soldiers' evaluations of the justification for their induction into the Army—reference group behavior is evidently related to the legitimacy ascribed to institutional arrangements. Thus, the older married soldier is less likely to think it "fair" that he was inducted; most enlisted men think it "unfair" that promotions are presumably based on "who you know, not what you know"; and so on. In part, this apparent emphasis on legitimacy is of course an artifact of the research: many of the questions put to soldiers had to do with their conception of the legitimate or illegitimate character of their situation or of prevailing institutional arrangements. But the researchers' own focus of interest was in turn the result of their having observed that soldiers were, to a significant degree, actually concerned with such issues of institutional legitimacy, as the spontaneous comments of enlisted men often indicate.[4]

This bears notice because imputations of legitimacy to social arrangements seem functionally related to reference group behavior. They apparently affect *the range of the inter-group or inter-individual comparisons* that will typically be made. If the structure of a rigid system of stratification, for example, is generally defined as legitimate, if the rights, perquisites and obligations of each stratum are generally held to be morally right, then the individuals within each stratum will be the less likely to take the situation of the other strata as a context for appraisal of their own lot. They will, presumably, tend to confine their comparisons to other members of their own or neighboring social stratum. If, however, the system of stratification is under wide dispute, then members of some strata are more likely to contrast their own situation with that of others, and shape their self-appraisals accordingly. This variation in the structure of systems and in the degree of legitimacy imputed to the rules of the game may help account for the often-noticed fact that the degree of dissatisfaction with their lot is often less among the people in severely depressed social strata in a relatively rigid social system, than among those strata who are apparently "better off" in a more mobile social system. At any rate, the *range of groups* taken as effective bases of comparison in different social systems may well turn out to be closely connected with the degree to which legitimacy is ascribed to the prevailing social structure.

Though much remains to be said, this is perhaps enough to suggest that the pattern of anticipatory socialization may have diverse consequences for the individuals manifesting it, the groups to which they belong, and the more inclusive social structure. And through such re-examination of this panel study on the personal rewards of conformity, it becomes possible to specify some additional types of problems involved in a more comprehensive functional analysis of such reference group behavior.

For example:

1. Since only a fraction of the in-group orient themselves positively toward the values of a non-membership group, it is necessary to discover the social position and personality types of those most likely to do so. For instance, are isolates in the group particularly ready to take up these alien values?

2. Much attention has been paid to the processes making for positive orientation to the norms of one's own group. But what are the processes making

for such orientations to other groups or strata? Do relatively high rates of mobility serve to reinforce these latter orientations? (It will be remembered that *The American Soldier* provides data tangential to this point in the discussion of rates of promotion and assessment of promotion chances.) Suitably adapted, such data on actual rates of mobility, aspirations, and anticipatory socialization to the norms of a higher social stratum would extend a functional theory of conformist and deviant behavior.

3. What connections, if any, subsist between varying rates of mobility and acceptance of the legitimacy of the system of stratification by individuals diversely located in that system? Since it appears that systems with very low rates of mobility may achieve wide acceptance, what other interpretative variables need be included to account for the relationship between rates of mobility and imputations of legitimacy?

4. In civilian or military life, are the mobile individuals who are most ready to reaffirm the values of a power-holding or prestige-holding group the sooner accepted by that group? Does this operate effectively primarily as a latent function, in which the mobile individuals adopt these values because they experience them as superior, rather than deliberately adopting them only to gain acceptance? If such orientations are definitely motivated by the wish to belong, do they then become self-defeating, with the mobile individuals being characterized as strainers, strivers (or, in the Army, as brown-nosers bucking for promotion)?

*Social processes sustaining and curbing positive orientations to non-membership groups.* In the course of considering the functions of anticipatory socialization, we have made passing allusion to social processes which sustain or curb this pattern of behavior. Since it is precisely the data concerning such processes which are not easily caught up in the type of survey materials on attitudes primarily utilized in *The American Soldier*, and since these processes are central to any theory of reference group behavior, they merit further consideration.

As we have seen, what is anticipatory socialization from the standpoint of the individual is construed as defection and nonconformity by the group of which he is a member. To the degree that the individual identifies himself with another group, he alienates himself from his own group. Yet although the field of sociology has for generations been concerned with the determinants and consequences of group cohesion, it has given little *systematic* attention to the complementary subject of group alienation. When considered at all, it has been confined to such special cases as second-generation immigrants, conflict of loyalties between gang and family, etc. In large measure, the subject has been left to the literary observer, who could detect the drama inherent in the situation of the renegade, the traitor, the deserter. The value-laden connotations of these terms used to describe identification with groups other than one's own definitely suggest that these patterns of behavior have been typically regarded from the standpoint of the member-ship group. (Yet one group's renegade may be another group's convert.) Since the assumption that its members will be loyal is found in every group, else it would have no group character, no dependability of action, transfer of loyalty to another group (particularly a group operating in the same sphere of politics or economy), is regarded primarily in affective terms of sentiment rather than in detached terms of analysis. The renegade or traitor or climber—whatever the folk-phrase may be—more often becomes an object of vilification than an object for sociological study.

The framework of reference group theory, detached from the language of sentiment, enables the sociologist to identify and to locate renegadism, treason, the assimilation of immigrants, class mobility, social climbing, etc. as so many special forms of identification with what is at the time a non-membership group. In doing so, it affords the possibility of studying these, not as *wholly* particular and unconnected forms of behavior, but as different expressions of similar processes under significantly different conditions. The transfer of allegiance of upper class individuals from their own to a lower class—whether this be in the pre-revolutionary period of 18th century France or of 20th century Russia—belongs to the same family of sociological prob-lems as the more familiar identification of lower class individuals with a higher class, a subject which has lately begun to absorb the attention of sociologists in a society where upward social mobility is an established value. Our cultural emphases notwithstanding, the phenomenon of topdogs adopt-ing the values of the underdog is as much a reference group phenomenon lending itself to further inquiry as the underdogs seeking to become topdogs.

In such defections from the in-group, it may turn out, as has often been suggested, that it is the isolate, nominally in a group but only slightly incor-porated in its network of social relations, who is most likely to become posi-tively oriented toward non-membership groups. But, even if generally true, this is a static correlation and, therefore, only partly illuminating. What needs to be uncovered is the process through which this correlation comes to hold. Judging from some of the qualitative data in *The American Soldier* and from other studies of group defection, there is continued and cumulative interplay between a deterioration of *social relations* within the membership group and positive *attitudes* toward the norms of a non-membership group.

What the individual experiences as estrangement from a group of which he is a member tends to be experienced by his associates as repudiation of the group, and this ordinarily evokes a hostile response. As social relations between the individual and the rest of the group deteriorate, the norms of the group become less binding for him. For since he is progressively seceding from the group and being penalized by it, he is the less likely to experience rewards for adherence to the group's norms. Once initiated, this process seems to move toward a cumulative detachment from the group, in terms of attitudes and values as well as in terms of social relations. And to the degree that he orients himself toward out-group values, perhaps affirming them verbally and expressing them in action, he only widens the gap and reinforces the hostility between himself and his in-group associates. Through the interplay of dissociation and progressive alienation from the group values, he may become doubly motivated to orient himself toward the values of another group and to affiliate himself with it. There then remains the distinct question of the objective possibility of affiliating himself with his reference group. If the possibility is negligible or absent, then the alienated individual becomes socially rootless. But if the social system realistically allows for such change in group affiliations, then the individual estranged from the one group has all the more motivation to belong to the other.

This hypothetical account of dissociation and alienation, which of course only touches upon the processes which call for research in the field of reference group behavior, seems roughly in accord with qualitative data in *The American Soldier* on what was variously called brown-nosing, bucking for promotion, and sucking up. Excerpts from the diary of an enlisted man illustrate the interplay between dissociation and alienation: the outward-oriented man is too sedulous in abiding by the official mores—"But you're *supposed* to [work over there]. The lieutenant said you were supposed to."— this evokes group hostility expressed in epithets and ridicule—"Everybody is making sucking, kissing noises at K and S now"—followed by increasing dissociation within the group—"Ostracism was visible, but mild . . . few were friendly toward them . . . occasions arose where people avoided their company"—and more frequent association with men representing the non-membership reference group—"W, S and K sucked all afternoon; hung around lieutenants and asked bright questions." In this briefly summarized account, one sees the mechanisms of the in-group operating to curb positive orientation to the official mores[5] as well as the process through which this orientation develops among those who take these mores as their major frame of reference, considering their ties with the in-group as of only secondary importance.

Judging from implications of this panel research on conformity-and-mobility, then, there is room for study of the consequences of reference group behavior patterns as well as for study of their determinants. Moreover, the consequences pertinent for sociology are not merely those for the individuals engaging in this behavior, but for the groups of which they are a part. There develops also the possibility that the extent to which legitimacy is accorded the structure of these groups and the status of their members may affect the range of groups or strata which they ordinarily take as a frame of reference in assessing their own situation. And finally, this panel research calls attention to the need for close study of those processes in group life which sustain or curb positive orientations to non-membership groups, thus perhaps leading to a linking of reference group theory and current theories of social organization.

## REFERENCES

1. Although the absolute percentages of men endorsing a given sentiment cannot of course be taken at face value since these percentages are affected by the sheer phrasing of the sentiment, it is nevertheless suggestive that data presented earlier in the volume (e.g., I, 147 ff.) find only a small minority of the samples of enlisted men in this study adhering to the officially approved attitudes. By and large, a significantly larger proportion of officers abide by these attitudes.

2. There is nothing fixed about the boundaries separating in-groups from out-groups, membership-groups from non-membership-groups. These change with the changing situation. Vis-à-vis civilians or an alien group, men in the Army may regard themselves and be regarded as members of an in-group; yet, in another context, enlisted men may regard themselves and be regarded as an in-group in distinction to the out-group of officers. Since these concepts are relative to the situation, rather than absolute, there is no paradox in referring to the officers as an out-group for enlisted men in one context, and as members of the more inclusive in-group, in another context.

3. Qualitative descriptions of the behavior of marginal men, as summarized, for example, by E. V. Stonequist, *The Marginal Man* (New York, Scribner's, 1937), can be analytically recast as that special and restricted case of reference group behavior in which the individual seeks to abandon one membership-group for another to which he is socially forbidden access.

4. For example, in response to the question, "If you could talk with the President of the United States, what are the three most important questions you would want to ask him about war and your part in it?", a substantial proportion of both Negro and white troops evidently raised questions regarding the legitimacy of current practices and arrangements in the Army. The Negro troops of course centered on unjust practices of race discrimination, but 31 per cent of the white troops also introduced "questions and criticisms of Army life." (I, 504, et passim.)

5. An official War Department pamphlet given to new recruits attempted to give "bucking" a blessing: " 'Bucking' implies all the things a soldier can honestly do to gain attention and promotion. The Army encourages individuals to put extra effort into drill, extra 'spit and polish' into personal appearance. At times this may make things uncomfortable for others who prefer to take things easier, but it stimulates a spirit of competition and improvement which makes ours a better Army." I, 264.

# ROLE, PERSONALITY, AND SOCIAL STRUCTURE * (*Levinson*)

My purpose here is to examine role theory primarily as it is used in the analysis of organizations (such as the hospital, business firm, prison, school). The organization provides a singularly useful arena for the development and application of role theory. It is small enough to be amenable to empirical study. Its structure is complex enough to provide a wide variety of social positions and role-standardizing forces. It offers an almost limitless opportunity to observe the individual personality *in vivo* (rather than in the psychologist's usual *vitro* of laboratory, survey questionnaire, or clinical office), selectively utilizing and modifying the demands and opportunities given in the social environment. The study of personality can, I submit, find no setting in which the reciprocal impact of psyche and situation is more clearly or more dramatically evidenced.

## *"Social Role" as a Unitary Concept*

The concept of role is related to, and must be distinguished from, the concept of social position. A position is an element of organizational anatomy, a location in social space, a category of organizational membership. A role is, so to say, an aspect of organizational physiology; it involves function, adaptation, process. It is meaningful to say that a person "occupies" a social position; but it is inappropriate to say, as many do, that one occupies a role.

There are at least three specific senses in which the term "role" has been used, explicitly or implicitly, by different writers or by the same writer on different occasions.

1. Role may be defined as the *structurally given demands* (norms, expectations, taboos, responsibilities, and the like) associated with a given social position. Role is, in this sense, something outside the given individual, a set of pressures and facilitations that channel, guide, impede, support his functioning in the organization.

2. Role may be defined as the member's *orientation* or *conception* of the part he is to play in the organization. It is, so to say, his inner definition of

* Reprinted from the *Journal of Abnormal and Social Psychology*, LVIII, pp. 170–180.

what someone in his social position is supposed to think and do about it. G. H. Mead (1934) is probably the main source of this view of social role as an aspect of the person, and it is commonly used in analyses of occupational roles.

3. Role is commonly defined as the *actions* of the individual members . . . actions seen in terms of their relevance for the social structure (that is, seen in relation to the prevailing norms). In this sense, role refers to the ways in which members of a position act (with or without conscious intention) *in accord with or in violation of a given set of organizational norms.* Here, as in (b), role is defined as a characteristic of the actor rather than of his normative environment.

Often, the term is used in a way that includes all three meanings at once. In this *unitary,* all-embracing conception of role, there is, by assumption, a close fit between behavior and disposition (attitude, value), between societal prescription and individual adaptation. This point of view has its primary source in the writings of Linton, whose formulations of culture, status, and role have had enormous influence. According to Linton (1945), a role "includes the attitudes, values, and behavior ascribed by the society to any and all persons occupying this status." In other words, society provides for each status or position a single mold that shapes the beliefs and actions of all its occupants.

In short, the "unitary" conception of role assumes that there is a 1:1 relationship, or at least a *high degree of congruence,* among the three role aspects noted above. In the theory of bureaucratic organization, the rationale for this assumption is somewhat as follows. The organizationally given requirements will be internalized by the members and will thus be mirrored in their role-conceptions. People will know, and will want to do, what is expected of them. The agencies of role socialization will succeed except with a deviant minority—who constitute a separate problem for study. Individual action will in turn reflect the structural norms, since the appropriate role-conceptions will have been internalized and since the sanctions system rewards normative behavior and punishes deviant behavior. Thus, it is assumed that structural norms, individual role-conceptions and individual role-performance are three isomorphic reflections of a single entity: "the" role appropriate to a given organizational position.

It is, no doubt, reasonable to expect some degree of congruence among these aspects of a social role. Certainly, every organization contains numerous mechanisms designed to further such congruence. At the same time, it is a matter of common observation that organizations vary in the degree of their integration; structural demands are often contradictory, lines of authority may be defective, disagreements occur and reverberate at and below the surface of daily operations. To assume that what the organization requires, and what its members actually think and do, comprise a single, unified whole is severely to restrict our comprehension of organizational dynamics and change.

It is my thesis, then, that the unitary conception of social role is unrealistic and theoretically constricting. We should, I believe, eliminate the single term "role" except in the most general sense, i.e., of "role theory" as an over-all frame of analysis. Let us, rather, give independent conceptual and empirical status to the above three concepts and others. Let us investigate the relationships of each concept with the others, making no assumptions about the degree of congruence among them. Further, let us investigate their relationships with various other characteristics of the organization and or its individual members. I would suggest that the role concepts be named and defined as follows:

## *Organizationally Given Role-Demands*

The role-demands are external to the individual whose role is being examined. They are the situational pressures that confront him as the occupant of a given structural position. They have manifold sources: in the official charter and policies of the organization; in the traditions and ideology, explicit as well as implicit, that help to define the organization's purposes and modes of operation; in the views about this position which are held by members of the position (who influence any single member) and by members of the various positions impinging upon this one; and so on.

It is a common assumption that the structural requirements for any position are as a rule defined with a *high degree of explicitness, clarity*, and *consensus* among all the parties involved. To take the position of hospital nurse as an example: it is assumed that her role-requirements will be understood and agreed upon by the hospital administration, the nursing authorities, the physicians, etc. Yet one of the striking research findings in all manner of hospitals is the failure of consensus regarding the proper role of nurse.[1] Similar findings have been obtained in school systems, business firms, and the like.[2]

In attempting to characterize the role-requirements for a given position, one must therefore guard against the assumption that they are unified and logically coherent. There may be major differences and even contradictions between official norms, as defined by charter or by administrative authority, and the "informal" norms held by various groupings within the organization.

Moreover, within a given status group, such as the top administrators, there may be several conflicting viewpoints concerning long range goals, current policies, and specific role-requirements. In short, the structural demands themselves are often multiple and disunified. Few are the attempts to investigate the sources of such disunity, to acknowledge its frequency, or to take it into conceptual account in general structural theory.

It is important also to consider the specificity or *narrowness* with which the normative requirements are defined. Norms have an "ought" quality; they confer legitimacy and reward-value upon certain modes of action, thought and emotion, while condemning others. But there are degrees here. Normative evaluations cover a spectrum from "strongly required," through various degrees of qualitative kinds of "acceptable," to more or less stringently tabooed. Organizations differ in the width of the intermediate range on this spectrum. That is, they differ in the number and kinds of adaptation that are normatively acceptable. The wider this range—the less specific the norms—the greater is the area of personal choice for the individual. While the existence of such an intermediate range is generally acknowledged, structural analyses often proceed as though practically all norms were absolute prescriptions or proscriptions allowing few alternatives for individual action.

There are various other normative complexities to be reckoned with. A single set of role-norms may be internally contradictory. In the case of the mental hospital nurse, for example, the norm of maintaining an "orderly ward" often conflicts with the norm of encouraging self-expression in patients. The individual nurse then has a range of choice, which may be narrow or wide, in balancing these conflicting requirements. There are also ambiguities in norms, and discrepancies between those held explicitly and those that are less verbalized and perhaps less conscious. These normative complexities permit, and may even induce, significant variations in individual role-performance.

The degree of *coherence* among the structurally defined role-requirements, the degree of consensus with which they are held, and the degree of *individual choice* they allow (the range of acceptable alternatives) are among the most significant properties of any organization. In some organizations, there is very great coherence of role-requirements and a minimum of individual choice. In most cases, however, the degree of integration within roles and among sets of roles appears to be more moderate.[3] This structural pattern is of especial interest from a sociopsychological point of view. To the extent that the requirements for a given position are ambiguous, contradictory, or otherwise "open," the individual members have greater opportunity for selection among existing norms and for creation of new norms. In this process, personality plays an important part. I shall return to this issue shortly.

While the normative requirements (assigned tasks, rules governing authority-subordinate relationships, demands for work output, and the like) are of great importance, there are others aspects of the organization that have an impact on the individual member. I shall mention two that are sometimes neglected.

*Role-Facilities.* In addition to the demands and obligations imposed upon the individual, we must also take into account the techniques, resources, and conditions of work—the means made available to him for fulfilling his organizational functions. The introduction of tranquilizing drugs in the mental hospital, or of automation in industry, has provided tremendous leverage for change in organizational structure and role-definition. The teacher-student ratio, an ecological characteristic of every school, grossly affects the probability that a given teacher will work creatively with individual students. In other words, technological and ecological facilities are not merely "tools" by which norms are met; they are often a crucial basis for the maintenance or change of an organizational form.

*Role-Dilemmas or Problematic Issues.* In describing the tasks and rules governing a given organizational position, and the facilities provided for their realization, we are, as it were, looking at that position from the viewpoint of a higher administrative authority whose chief concern is "getting the job done." Bureaucracy is often analyzed from this (usually implicit) viewpoint. What is equally necessary, though less often done, is to look at the situation of the position-members from their own point of view: the meaning it has for them, the feelings it evokes, the ways in which it is stressful or supporting. From the sociopsychological perspective, new dimensions of role analysis emerge. The concept of role-dilemma is an example. The usefulness of this concept stems from the fact that every human situation has its contradictions and its problematic features. Where such dilemmas exist, there is no "optimal" mode of adaptation; each mode has its advantages and its costs. Parsons in his discussion of "the situation of the patient," explores some of the dilemmas confronting the ill person in our society.[4] Erikson, and Pine and Levinson have written about the dilemmas of the mental hospital patient; for example, the conflicting pressures (from without and from within) toward cure through self-awareness and toward cure through repressive self-control.[5] Role-dilemmas of the psychiatric resident have been studied by Sharaf and Levinson.[6] Various studies have described the problems of the factory foreman caught in the conflicting cross-pressures between the workers he must supervise and the managers to whom he is responsible. The foreman's situation tends to evoke feelings of social marginality, mixed identifications, and conflicting tendencies to be a good "older brother" with subordinates and an obedient son with higher authority.

Role-dilemmas have their sources both in organizational structure and in individual personality. Similarly, both structure and personality influence the varied forms of adaptation that are achieved. The point to be emphasized here is that every social structure confronts its members with adaptive dilemmas. If we are to comprehend this aspect of organizational life, we must conceive of social structure as having intrinsically *psychological* properties, as making complex psychological demands that affect, and are affected by, the personalities of its members.

## Personal Role-Definition

In the foregoing we have considered the patterning of the environment for an organizational position—the kind of sociopsychological world with which members of the position must deal. Let us turn now to the individual members themselves. Confronted with a complex system of requirements, facilities, and conditions of work, the individual effects his modes of adaptation. I shall use the term "personal role-definition" to encompass the individual's adaptation within the organization. This may involve passive "adjustment," active furthering of current role-demands, apparent conformity combined with indirect "sabotage," attempts at constructive innovation (revision of own role or of broader structural arrangements), and the like. The personal role-definition may thus have varying degrees of fit with the role-requirements. It may serve in various ways to maintain or to change the social structure. It may involve a high or a low degree of self-commitment and personal involvement on the part of the individual.[7]

For certain purposes, it is helpful to make a sharp distinction between two levels of adaptation: at a more *ideational* level, we may speak of a role-conception; at a more *behavioral* level, there is a pattern of role-performance. Each of these has an affective component. Role-conception and role-performance are independent though related variables; let us consider them in turn.

*Individual (and Modal) Role-Conceptions.* The nature of a role-conception may perhaps be clarified by placing it in relation to an ideology. The boundary between the two is certainly not a sharp one. However, ideology refers most directly to an orientation regarding the entire organizational (or other) structure—its purposes, its modes of operation, the prevailing forms of individual and group relationships, and so on. A role-conception offers a definition and rationale for one position within the structure. If ideology portrays and rationalizes the organizational world, then role-conception delineates the specific functions, values, and manner of functioning appropriate to one position within it.

The degree of uniformity or variability in individual role-conceptions within a given position will presumably vary from one organization to another. When one or more types of role-conception are commonly held (consensual), we may speak of modal types. The maintenance of structural stability requires that there be at least moderate consensus and that modal role-conceptions be reasonably congruent with role-requirements. At the same time, the presence of incongruent modal role-conceptions may, under certain conditions, provide an ideational basis for major organizational change.

Starting with the primary assumption that each member "takes over" a structurally defined role, many social scientists tend to assume that there is great uniformity in role-conception among the members of a given social position. They hold, in other words, that for every position there is a *dominant modal role-conception corresponding to the structural demands,* and that there is relatively little individual deviation from the modal pattern. Although this state of affairs may at times obtain, we know that the members of a given social position often have quite diverse conceptions of their proper roles.[8] After all, individual role-conceptions are formed only partially within the present organizational setting. The individual's ideas about his occupational role are influenced by childhood experiences, by his values and other personality characteristics, by formal education and apprenticeship, and the like. The ideas of various potential reference groups within and outside of the organization are available through reading, informal contacts, etc. There is reason to expect, then, that the role-conceptions of individuals in a given organizational position will vary and will not always conform to official role-requirements. Both the diversities and the modal patterns must be considered in organizational analysis.

*Individual (and Modal) Role-Performance.* This term refers to the overt behavioral aspect of role-definition—to the more or less characteristic ways in which the individual acts as the occupant of a social position. Because role-performance involves immediately observable behavior, its description would seem to present few systematic problems. However, the formulation of adequate variables for the analysis of role-performance is in fact a major theoretical problem and one of the great stumbling blocks in empirical research.

Everyone would agree, I suppose, that role-performance concerns only those aspects of the total stream of behavior that are structurally relevant. But which aspects of behavior are the important ones? And where shall the boundary be drawn between that which is structurally relevant and that which is incidental or idiosyncratic?

One's answer to these questions probably depends, above all, upon his conception of social structure. Those who conceive of social structure rather narrowly in terms of concrete work tasks and normative requirements, are inclined to take a similarly narrow view of role. In this view, role-performance is simply the fulfillment of formal role-norms, and anything else the person does is extraneous to role-performance as such. Its proponents acknowledge that there are variations in "style" of performance but regard these as incidental. What is essential to *role*-performance is the degree to which norms are met.

A more complex and inclusive conception of social structure requires correspondingly multi-dimensional delineation of role-performance. An organization has, from this viewpoint, "latent" as well as "manifest" structure; it has a many-faceted emotional climate; it tends to "demand" varied forms of interpersonal allegiance, friendship, deference, intimidation, ingratiation, rivalry, and the like. If characteristics such as these are considered intrinsic properties of social structure, then they must be included in the characterization of role-performance. My own preference is for the more inclusive view. I regard social structure as having psychological as well as other properties, and I regard as intrinsic to role-performance the varied meanings and feelings which the actor communicates to those about him. Ultimately, we must learn to characterize organizational behavior in a way that takes into account, and helps to illuminate, its functions for the individual, for the others with whom he interacts, and for the organization.

It is commonly assumed that there is great uniformity in role-performance among the members of a given position. Or, in other words, that there is a *dominant, modal pattern of role-performance corresponding to the structural requirements*. The rationale here parallels that given above for role-conceptions. However, where individual variations in patterns of role-performance have been investigated, several modal types rather than a single dominant pattern were found.[9]

Nor is this variability surprising, except to those who have the most simplistic conception of social life. Role-performance, like any other form of human behavior, is the resultant of many forces. Some of these forces derive from the organizational matrix; for example, from role-demands and the pressures of authority, from informal group influences, and from impending sanctions. Other determinants lie within the person, as for example his role-conceptions and role-relevant characteristics. Except in unusual cases where all forces operate to channel behavior in the same direction, role-performance will reflect the individual's attempts at choice and compromise among diverse external and internal forces.

The relative contributions of various forms of influence to individual or modal role-performance can be determined only *if each set of variables is* defined and measured, independently of the others. That is, indeed, one of the major reasons for emphasizing and sharpening the distinctions among role-performance, role-conception, and role-demands. Where these distinctions are not sharply drawn, there is a tendency to study one element and to assume that the others are in close fit. For example, one may learn from the official charter and the administrative authorities how the organization is supposed to work—the formal requirements—and then assume that it in fact operates in this way. Or, conversely, one may observe various regularities in role-performance and then assume that these are structurally determined, without independently assessing the structural requirements. To do this is to make structural explanations purely tautologous.

More careful distinction among these aspects of social structure and role will also, I believe, permit greater use of personality theory in organizational analysis. Let us turn briefly to this question.

## Role Definition, Personality, and Social Structure

Just as social structure presents massive forces which influence the individual from without toward certain forms of adaptation, so does personality present massive forces from within which lead him to select, create, and synthesize certain forms of adaptation rather than others. Role-definition may be seen from one perspective as an aspect of personality. It represents the individual's attempt to structure his social reality, to define his place within it, and to guide his search for meaning and gratification. Role-definition is, in this sense, an *ego achievement*—a reflection of the person's capacity to resolve conflicting demands to utilize existing opportunities and create new ones, to find some balance between stability and change, conformity and autonomy, the ideal and the feasible, in a complex environment.

The formation of a role-definition is, from a dynamic psychological point of view, an "external function" of the ego. Like the other external (reality-oriented) ego functions, it is influenced by the ways in which the ego carries out its "internal functions" of coping with, and attempting to synthesize, the demands of id, super-ego, and ego. These internal activities—the "psychodynamics" of personality—include among other things: unconscious fantasies; unconscious moral conceptions and the wishes against which they are directed; the characteristic ways in which unconscious processes are transformed or deflected in more conscious thought, feeling, and behavioral striving; conceptions of self and ways of maintaining or changing these conceptions in the face of changing pressures from within and from the external world.

In viewing role-definition as an aspect of personality, I am suggesting that it is, to varying degrees, related to and imbedded within other aspects of personality. An individual's conception of his role in a particular organization is to be seen within a series of wider psychological contexts; his conception of his occupational role generally (occupational identity), his basic values, life-goals, and conception of self (ego identity), and so on. Thus, one's way of relating to authorities in the organization depends in part upon his relation to authority in general, and upon his fantasies, conscious as well as unconscious, about the "good" and the "bad" parental authority. His ways of dealing with the stressful aspects of organizational life are influenced by the impulses, anxieties, and modes of defense that these stresses activate in him.[10]

There are variations in the degree to which personal role-definition is imbedded in and influenced by, deeper-lying personality characteristics. The importance of individual or modal personality for role-definition is a matter for empirical study and cannot be settled by casual assumption. Traditional sociological theory can be criticized for assuming that individual role-definition is determined almost entirely by social structure. Similarly, dynamic personality theory will not take its rightful place as a crucial element of social psychology until it views the individual within his socio-cultural environment. Lacking an adequate recognition and *conceptualization* of the individual's external reality—including the "reality" of social structure—personality researchers tend to assume that individual adaptation is primarily personality-determined and that reality is, for the most part, an amorphous blob structured by the individual to suit his inner needs.

Clearly, individual role-conception and role-performance do not emanate fully formed, from the depths of personality. Nor are they simply mirror images of a mold established by social structure. Elsewhere, I have used the term "mirage" theory for the view, frequently held or implied in the psychoanalytic literature, that ideologies, role-conceptions, and behavior are mere epiphenomena or by-products of unconscious fantasies and defenses.[11] Similarly, the term "sponge" theory characterizes the view, commonly forwarded in the sociological literature in which man is merely a passive mechanical absorber of the prevailing structural demands.

Our understanding of personal role-definition will remain seriously impaired as long as we fail to place it, analytically, in both intrapersonal and structural-environment contexts. That is to say, we must be concerned with the meaning of role-definition both for the individual personality and for the social system. A given role-definition is influenced by, and has an influence upon, the psyche as well as the socius. If we are adequately to understand the nature, the determinants, and the consequences of role-definition, we need the double perspective of personality and social structure. The use of these two reference points is, like the use of our two eyes in seeing, necessary for the achievement of depth in our social vision.

Theory and research on organizational roles must consider relationships among at least the following sets of characteristics: structurally given role-demands and -opportunities, personal role-definition (including conceptions and performance), and personality in its role-related aspects. Many forms of relationships may exist among them. I shall mention only a few hypothetical possibilities.

In one type case, the role requirements are so narrowly defined, and the mechanisms of social control so powerful, that only one form of role-performance can be sustained for any given position. An organization of this type may be able selectively to recruit and retain only individuals who, by virtue of personality, find this system meaningful and gratifying. If a congruent modal personality is achieved, a highly integrated and stable structure may well emerge. I would hypothesize that a structurally congruent modal personality is one condition, though by no means the only one, for the stability of a rigidly integrated system. (In modern times, of course, the rapidity of technological change prevents long-term stability in any organizational structure.)

However, an organization of this kind may acquire members who are not initially receptive to the structural order, that is, who are incongruent in role-conception or in personality. Here, several alternative developments are possible.

1. The incongruent members may change so that their role-conceptions and personalities come better to fit the structural requirements.

2. The incongruent ones may leave the organization, by choice or by expulsion. The high turnover in most of our organizations is due less to technical incompetence than to rejection of the "conditions of life" in the organization.

3. The incongruent ones may remain, but in a state of apathetic con-

formity. In this case, the person meets at least the minimal requirements of role-performance but his role-conceptions continue relatively unchanged, he gets little satisfaction from work, and he engages in repeated "sabotage" of organizational aims. This is an uncomfortably frequent occurrence in our society. In the Soviet Union as well, even after 40 years of enveloping social controls, there exist structurally incongruent forms of political ideology, occupational role-definition, and personality.[12]

4. The incongruent members may gain sufficient social power to change the organizational structure. This phenomenon is well known, though not well enough understood. For example, in certain of our mental hospitals, schools and prisons over the past 20–30 years, individuals with new ideas and personal characteristics have entered in large enough numbers, and in sufficiently strategic positions, to effect major structural changes. Similar ideological and structural transitions are evident in other types of organization, such as corporate business.

The foregoing are a few of many possible developments in a relatively monolithic structure. A somewhat looser organizational pattern is perhaps more commonly found. In this setting, structural change becomes a valued aim and innovation is seen as a legitimate function of members at various levels in the organization. To the extent that diversity and innovation are valued (rather than merely given lip service), variations in individual role-definition are tolerated or even encouraged within relatively wide limits. The role-definitions that develop will reflect various degrees of synthesis and compromise between personal preference and structural demand.

In summary, I have suggested that a primary distinction be made between the structurally given role-demands and the forms of role-definition achieved by the individual members of an organization. Personal role-definition then becomes a linking concept between personality and social structure. It can be seen as a reflection of those aspects of individual personality that are activated and sustained in a given structural-ecological environment. This view is opposed both to the "sociologizing" of individual behavior and to the "psychologizing" of organizational structure. At the same time, it is concerned with both the psychological properties of social structure and the structural properties of individual adaptation.

Finally, we should keep in mind that both personality structure and social structure inevitably have their internal contradictions. No individual is sufficiently all of a piece that he will for long find any form of adaptation, occupational or otherwise, totally satisfying. Whatever the psychic gains stemming from a particular role-definition and social structure, there will also be losses: wishes that must be renounced or made unconscious, values that must be compromised, anxieties to be handled, personal goals that will at best be incompletely met. The organization has equivalent limitations. Its multiple purposes cannot all be optimally achieved. It faces recurrent dilemmas over conflicting requirements: control and freedom; centralization and decentralization of authority; security as against the risk of failure; specialization and diffusion of work function; stability and change; collective unity and diversity. Dilemmas such as these arise anew in different forms at each new step of organizational development, without permanent solution. And perpetual changes in technology, in scientific understanding, in material resources, in the demands and capacities of its members and the surrounding community, present new issues and require continuing organizational readjustment.

In short, every individual and ever sociocultural form contains within itself the seeds of its own destruction—or its own reconstruction. To grasp both the sources of stability and the seeds of change in human affairs is one of the great challenges to contemporary social science.

REFERENCES

1. C. Argyris, *Human Relations in a Hospital*. New Haven: Labor and Management Center, 1955; T. Burling, Edith Lentz, and R. N. Wilson, *The Give and Take in Hospitals*, New York: Putnam, 1956.
2. N. Gross *et al.*, *Explorations in Role Analysis*. New York: Wiley, 1958; A. Kornhauser *et al.*, *Industrial Conflict*. New York: McGraw-Hill, 1954.
3. The reduced integration reflects in part the tremendous rate of technological change, the geographical and occupational mobility, and the diversity in personality that characterize modern society. On the other hand, diversity is opposed by the standardization of culture on a mass basis and by the growth of large-scale organization itself. Trends toward increased standardization and uniformity are highlighted in Whyte's analysis (W. F. Whyte, *The Organization Man*. New York: Simon & Shuster, 1956).
4. T. Parsons, *The Social System*
5. K. T. Erikson, "Patient Role and Social Uncertainty: A Dilemma of the Mentally Ill," *Psychiatry*, 1957, 20, 263–274; F. Pine and D. J. Levinson,* *Problematic Issues in the Role of Mental Hospital Patient*, Mimeographed; Center for Sociopsychological Research, Massachusetts Mental Health Center, 1958. [* rev. & publ. by same authors, as "A Sociopsychological Conception of Patienthood," *Intntl-Journal of Soc. Psychiatry*, 1961, 7:2:106–122.]
6. M. R. Sharaf and D. J. Levinson, "Patterns of Ideology and Role Definition among Psychiatric Residents," in M. Greenblatt, D. J. Levinson, and R. H. Williams (eds.), *The Patient and the Mental Hospital*, Glencoe, Ill.: Free Press, 1957.
7. Philip Selznick, *Leadership and Administration*, Evanston, Ill.: Row, Peterson & Co., 1957.
8. M. Greenblatt, D. J. Levinson, and R. H. Williams (eds.), *The Patient and the Mental Hospital*, Glencoe, Ill.: Free Press, 1957; N. Gross *et al.*, *op. cit.*; L. Reissman and J. J. Rohrer (eds.), *Change and Dilemma in the Nursing Profession*. New York: Putnam, 1957; R. Bendix, *Work and Authority in Industry*, New York: Wiley, 1956.

9. C. Argyris, *Personality and Organization*, New York: Harper, 1957; M. Greenblatt et al., *op. cit.*

10. C. Argyris, *op. cit.*; E. H. Erikson, *Childhood and Society*, New York: Norton, 1950; W. E. Henry, "The Business Executive: The Psychodynamics of a Social Role," *American Journal of Sociology*, 1949, 54, 286–291; F. H. Blum, *Toward a Democratic Work Process*. New York: Harper, 1953; and F. Pine and D. J. Levinson, "Two Patterns of Ideology, Role Conception and Personality among Mental Hospital Aides," in M. Greenblatt et al., *op. cit.*

11. D. J. Levinson, "Idea Systems in the Individual and Society," Paper presented at Boston University, Founder's Day Institute, 1954. Mimeographed: Center for Sociopsychological Research, Massachusetts Mental Health Center.

12. A. Inkeles, Eugenia Hanfmann, and Helen Beier, "Modal Personality and Adjustment to the Soviet Political System," *Human Relations*, 1958, 11, 3–22.

# PERFORMANCES * (*Goffman*)

## Belief in the Part One Is Playing

When an individual plays a part he implicitly requests his observers to take seriously the impression that is fostered before them. They are asked to believe that the character they see actually possesses the attributes he appears to possess, that the task he performs will have the consequences that are implicitly claimed for it, and that, in general, matters are what they appear to be. In line with this, there is the popular view that the individual offers his performance and puts on his show "for the benefit of other people." It will be convenient to begin a consideration of performances by turning the question around and looking at the individual's own belief in the impression of reality that he attempts to engender in those among whom he finds himself.

At one extreme, one finds that the performer can be fully taken in by his own act; he can be sincerely convinced that the impression of reality which he stages is the real reality. When his audience is also convinced in this way about the show he puts on—and this seems to be the typical case—then for the moment at least, only the sociologist or the socially disgruntled will have any doubts about the "realness" of what is presented.

At the other extreme, we find that the performer may not be taken in at all by his own routine. This possibility is understandable, since no one is in quite as good an observational position to see through the act as the person who puts it on. Coupled with this, the performer may be moved to guide the conviction of his audience only as a means to other ends, having no ultimate concern in the conception that they have of him or of the situation. When the individual has no belief in his own act and no ultimate concern with the beliefs of his audience, we may call him cynical, reserving the term "sincere" for individuals who believe in the impression fostered by their own performance. It should be understood that the cynic, with all his professional disinvolvement, may obtain unprofessional pleasures from his masquerade, experiencing a kind of gleeful spiritual aggression from the fact that he can toy at will with something his audience must take seriously.[1]

It is not assumed, of course, that all cynical performers are interested in deluding their audiences for purposes of what is called "self-interest" or private gain. A cynical individual may delude his audience for what he considers to be their own good, or for the good of the community, etc. For illustrations of this we need not appeal to sadly enlightened showmen such as Marcus Aurelius or Hsun Tzu. We know that in service occupations practitioners who may otherwise be sincere are sometimes forced to delude their customers because their customers show such a heartfelt demand for it. Doctors who are led into giving placebos, filling station attendants who resignedly check and recheck tire pressures for anxious women motorists, shoe clerks who sell a shoe that fits but tells the custmer it is the size she wants to hear—these are cynical performers whose audiences will not allow them to be sincere. Similarly, it seems that sympathetic patients in mental wards will sometimes feign bizarre symptoms so that student nurses will not be subjected to a disappointingly sane performance.[2] So also, when inferiors extend their most lavish reception for visiting superiors, the selfish desire to win favor may not be the chief motive; the inferior may be tactfully attempting to put the superior at ease by simulating the kind of world the superior is thought to take for granted.

I have suggested two extremes: an individual may be taken in by his own act or be cynical about it. These extremes are something a little more than just the ends of a continuum. Each provides the individual with a position which has its own particular securities and defenses, so there will be a tendency for those who have traveled close to one of these poles to complete the voyage. Starting with lack of inward belief in one's role, the individual may follow the natural movement described by Park:

> *It is probably no mere historical accident that the word person, in its first meaning, is a mask. It is rather a recognition of the fact that everyone is always and everywhere, more or less consciously, playing a role. . . . It is in these roles that we know each other; it is in these roles that we know ourselves.*[3]

> *In a sense, and in so far as this mask represents the conception we have formed of ourselves—the role we are striving to live up to—this mask is our truer self, the self we would like to be. In the end, our conception of our role becomes second nature and an integral part of our personality. We come into the world as individuals, achieve character, and become persons.*[4]

This may be illustrated from the community of life of Shetland.[5] For the last four or five years the island's tourist hotel has been owned and operated by a married couple of crofter origins. From the beginning, the owners were forced to set aside their own conceptions as to how life ought to be led, displaying in the hotel a full round of middle-class services and amenities. Lately, however, it appears that the managers have become less cynical about the performance that they stage; they themselves are becoming middle class and more and more enamored of the selves their clients impute to them. Another illustration may be found in the raw recruit who initially follows army etiquette in order to avoid physical punishment and eventually comes to follow the rules so that his organization will not be shamed and his officers and fellow soldiers will respect him.

As suggested, the cycle of disbelief-to-belief can be followed in the other direction, stating with conviction or insecure aspiration and ending in cynicism. Professions which the public holds in religious awe often allow their recruits to follow the cycle in this direction, and often recruits follow it in this direction not because of a slow realization that they are deluding their audience—for by ordinary social standards the claims they make may be quite valid—but because they can use this cynicism as a means of insulating their inner selves from contact with the audience. And we may even expect to find typical careers of faith, with the individual starting out with one kind of involvement in the performance he is required to give, then moving back and forth several times between sincerity and cynicism before completing all the phases and turning-points of self-belief for a person of his station. Thus, students of medical schools suggest that idealistically oriented beginners in medical school typically lay aside their holy aspirations for a period of time. During the first two years the students find that their interest in medicine must be dropped that they may give all their time to the task of learning how to get through examinations. During the next two years they are too busy learning about diseases to show much concern for the persons who are diseased. It is only after their medical schooling has ended that their original ideals about medical service may be reasserted.[6]

While we can expect to find natural movement back and forth between cynicism and sincerity, still we must not rule out the kind of transitional point that can be sustained on the strength of a little self-illusion. We find that the individual may attempt to induce the audience to judge him and the situation in a particular way, and he may seek this judgment as an ultimate end in itself, and yet he may not completely believe that he deserves the valuation of self which he asks for or that the impression of reality which he fosters is valid. Another mixture of cynicism and belief is suggested in Kroeber's discussion of shamanism:

> *Next, there is the old question of deception. Probably most shamans or medicine men, the world over, help along with sleight-of-hand in curing and especially in exhibitions of power. This sleight-of-hand is sometimes deliberate; in many cases awareness is perhaps not deeper than the foreconscious. The attitude, whether there has been repression or not, seems to be as toward a pious fraud. Field ethnographers seem quite generally convinced that even shamans who know that they add fraud nevertheless also believe in their powers, and especially in those of other shamans: they consult them when they themselves or their children are ill.*[7]

## REFERENCES

1. Perhaps the real crime of the confidence man is not that he takes money from his victims but that he robs all of us of the belief that middle-class manners and appearance can be sustained only by middle-class people. A disabused professional can be cynically hostile to the service relation his clients expect him to extend to them; the confidence man is in a position to hold the whole "legit" world in this contempt.
2. See Harold Taxel, "Authority Structure in a Mental Hospital Ward" (unpublished Master's Thesis, Department of Sociology, University of Chicago, 1953), p. 4. Harry Stack Sullivan has suggested that the tact of institutionalized performers can operate in the other direction, resulting in a kind of *noblesse-oblige* sanity. See his "Socio-Psychiatric Research," *American Jounrnal of Psychiatry*, X, pp. 987–88.

   "A study of 'social recoveries' in one of our large mental hospitals some years ago taught me that patients were often released from care because they had learned not to manifest symptoms to the environing persons; in other words, had integrated enough of the personal environment to realize the prejudice opposed to their delusions. It seemed almost as if they grew wise enough to be tolerant of the imbecility surrounding them, having fully discovered that it was stupidity and not malice. They could then secure satisfaction from contact with others, while discharging a part of their cravings by psychotic means."
3. Robert Ezra Park, *Race and Culture* (Glencoe, Ill.: The Free Press, 1950), p. 249.
4. *Ibid.*, p. 250.
5. Shetland Isle Study.
6. H. S. Becker and Blanche Greer, "The Fate of Idealism in Medical School," *American Sociological Review*, 23, pp. 50–56.
7. A. L. Kroeber, *The Nature of Culture* (Chicago: University of Chicago Press, 1952), p. 311.

# ROLE DISTANCE * (Goffman)

The occurrence of explanations and apologies as limitations on the expressiveness of role leads us to look again at what goes on in concrete face-to-face activity. I return to our situated example, the merry-go-round.

A merry-go-round horse is a thing of some size, some height, and some movement; and while the track is never wet, it can be very noisy. American middle-class two-year-olds often find the prospect too much for them. They fight their parents at the last moment to avoid being strapped into a context in which it had been hoped they would prove to be little men. Sometimes they become frantic half-way through the ride, and the machine must be stopped so that they can be removed.

Here we have one of the classic possibilities of life. Participation in any circuit of face-to-face activity requires the participant to keep command of himself, both as a person capable of executing physical movements and as one capable of receiving and transmitting communications. A flustered failure to maintain either kind of role poise makes the system as a whole suffer. Every participant, therefore, has the function of maintaining his own poise, and one or more participants are likely to have the specialized function of modulating activity so as to safeguard the poise of the others. In many situated systems, of course, all contingencies are managed without such threats arising. However, there is no such system in which these troubles might not occur, and some systems such as those in a surgery ward, presumably provide an especially good opportunity to study these contingencies.

Just as a rider may be disqualified during the ride because he proves to be unable to handle riding, so a rider will be removed from his saddle at the very beginning of the ride because he does not have a ticket or because, in the absence of his parents, he makes management fear for his safety. There is an obvious distinction, then, between qualifications required for permission to attempt a role and attributes required for performing suitably once the role has been acquired.

At three and four, the task of riding a wooden horse is still a challenge, but apparently a manageable one, inflating the rider to his full extent with demonstrations of capacity. Parents need no longer ride alongside to protect their youngsters. The rider throws himself into the role in a serious way,

* From *Encounters* by Erving Goffman, copyright © 1961, reprinted by permission of the publishers, The Bobbs-Merrill Company, Inc.

playing it with verve and an admitted engagement of all his faculties. Passing his parents at each turn, the rider carefully lets go one of his hands and grimly waves a smile or a kiss—this, incidentally, being an example of an act that is a typical part of the role but hardly an obligatory feature of it. Here, then, doing is being and what was designed as a "playing at" is stamped with serious realization.

Just as "flustering" is a classic possibility in all situated systems, so also is the earnest way these youngsters of three or four ride their horses. Three matters seem to be involved: an admitted or expressed attachment to the role; a demonstration of qualifications and capacities for performing it; an active *engagement* or spontaneous involvement in the role activity at hand, that is, a visible investment of attention and muscular effort. Where these three features are present, I will use the term *embracement*. To embrace a role is to disappear completely into the virtual self available in the situation, to be fully seen in terms of the image, and to confirm expressively one's acceptance of it. To embrace a role is to be embraced by it. Particularly good illustrations of full embracement can be seen in persons in certain occupations: team managers during baseball games; traffic policemen at intersections during rush hours; landing signal officers who wave in planes landing on the decks of aircraft carriers; in fact, any one occupying a directing role where the performer must guide others by means of gestural signs.[1]

An individual may affect the embracing of a role in order to conceal a lack of attachment to it, just as he may affect a visible disdain for a role, thrice refusing the kingly crown, in order to defend himself against the psychological dangers of his actual attachment to it. Certainly an individual may be attached to a role and fail to be able to embrace it, as when a child proves to have no ticket or to be unable to hang on.

Returning to the merry-go-round, we see that at five years of age the situation is transformed, especially for boys. To be a merry-go-round horse rider is now apparently not enough, and this fact must be demonstrated out of a dutiful regard for one's own character. Parents are not likely to be allowed to ride along, and the strap for preventing falls is often disdained. One rider may keep time to the music by clapping his feet or a hand against the horse, an early sign of utter control. Another may make a wary stab at standing on the saddle or changing horses without touching the platform. Still another may hold on to the post with one hand and lean back as far as possible while looking up to the sky in a challenge to dizziness. Irreverence begins, and the horse may be held on to by his wooden ear or his tail. The child says by his actions: "Whatever I am, I'm not just someone who can barely manage to stay on a wooden horse." Note that what the rider is apologizing for is not some minor untoward event that has cropped up during the interaction, but the whole role. The image of him that is generated for him by the routine entailed in his mere participation—his virtual self in the context—is an image from which he apparently withdraws by *actively* manipulating the situation. Whether this skittish behavior is intentional or unintentional, sincere or affected, correctly appreciated by others present or not, it does constitute a wedge between the individual and his role, between doing and being. This "effectively" expressed pointed separateness between the individual and his putative role I shall call *role distance.* A shorthand is involved here: the individual is actually denying not the role but the virtual self that is implied in the role for all accepting performers.

In any case, the term role distance is not meant to refer to all behavior that does not directly contribute to the task core of a given role but only to those behaviors that are seen by someone present as relevant to assessing the actor's attachment to his particular role and relevant in such a way as to suggest that the actor possibly has some measure of disaffection from, and resistance against, the role. Thus, for example, a four-year-old halfway through a triumphant performance as a merry-go-round rider may sometimes go out of play, dropping from his face and manner any confirmation of his virtual self, yet may indulge in this break in role without apparent intent, the lapse reflecting more on his capacity to sustain any role than on his feelings about the present one. Nor can it be called role distance if the child rebels and totally rejects the role, stomping off in a huff, for the special facts about self that can be conveyed by holding a role off a little are precisely the ones that cannot be conveyed by throwing the role over.

At seven and eight the child not only dissociates himself self-consciously from the kind of horseman a merry-go-round allows him to be but also finds that many of the devices that younger people use for this are now beneath him. He rides no-hands, gleefully chooses a tiger or a frog for a steed, clasps hands with a mounted friend across the aisle. He tests limits, and his antics may bring negative sanction from the adult in charge of the machine. And he is still young enough to show distance by handling the task with bored, nonchalant competence, a candy bar languidly held in one hand.

At eleven and twelve, maleness for boys has become a real responsibility, and no easy means of role distance seems to be available on merry-go-rounds. It is necessary to stay away or to exert creative acts of distancy, as when a boy jokingly treats his wooden horse as if it were a racing one; he jogs himself up and down, leans far over the neck of the horse, drives his heel mercilessly into its flanks, and uses the reins for a lash to get more speed, brutally reining in the horse when the ride is over. He is just old enough to achieve role distance by defining the whole undertaking as a lark, a situation for mockery.

Adults who choose to ride a merry-go-round display adult techniques of role distance. One adult rider makes a joke of tightening the safety belt around him; another crosses his arms, giving popcorn with his left hand to the person on his right and a coke with his right hand to the person on his left. A young lady riding sidesaddle tinkles out, "It's cold," and calls to her watching boy friend's boy friend, "Come on, don't be chicken." A dating couple riding adjacent horses holds hands to bring sentiment, not daring, to the situation. Two double-dating couples employ their own techniques: the male in front sits backwards and takes a picture of the other male rider taking a picture of him. And, of course, some adults, riding close by their threatened two-and-a-half-year-old, wear a face that carefully demonstrates that they do not perceive the ride as an event in itself, their only present interest being their child.

And finally there is the adult who runs the machine and takes the tickets. Here, often, can be found a fine flowering of role distance. Not only does he show that the ride itself is not—as a ride—an event to him, but he also gets off and on and around the moving platform with a grace and ease that can only be displayed by safely taking what for children and even adults would be chances.

Some general points can be made about merry-go-round role distance. First, while the management of a merry-go-round horse in our culture soon ceases to be a challenging "developmental task," the task of expressing that it is not continues for a long time to be a challenge and remains a felt necessity. A full twist must be made in the iron law of etiquette: the act through which one can afford to try to fit into the situation is an act that can be styled to show that one is somewhat out of place. One enters the situation to the degree that one can demonstrate that one does not belong.

A second general point about role distance is that immediate audiences figure very directly in the display of role distance. Merry-go-round horsemen are very ingenuous and may frankly wait for each time they pass their waiting friends before playing through their gestures of role distance. Moreover, if persons above the age of twelve or so are to trust themselves to making a lark of it, they almost need to have a friend along on the next horse, since persons who are "together" seem to be able to hold off the socially defining force of the environment much more than a person alone.

A final point: two different means of establishing role distance seem to be found. In one case the individual tries to isolate himself as much as possible from the contamination of the situation, as when an adult riding along to guard his child makes an effort to be completely stiff, affectless, and preoccupied. In the other case, the individual cooperatively projects a childish self, meeting the situation more than halfway, but then withdraws from this castoff self by a little gesture signifying that the joking has gone far enough. In either case the individual can slip the skin the situation would clothe him in.

A summary of concepts is now in order. I have tried to distinguish among three easily confused ideas: *commitment, attachment,* and *embracement.*[2] It is to be noted that these sociological terms are of a different order from that of *engagement,* a psychobiological process that a cat or a dog can display more beautifully than man. Finally, the term *role distance* was introduced to refer to actions which effectively convey some disdainful detachment to the performer from a role he is performing.

REFERENCES

1. Here, as elsewhere, I am indebted to Gregory Stone.
2. A somewhat different and more differentiated analysis may be found in G. P. Stone, "Clothing and Social Relations: A Study of Appearance in the Context of Community Life" (unpublished Ph.D. dissertation, Department of Sociology, University of Chicago, 1959).

# ROLE DISTANCE, SOCIOLOGICAL AMBIVALENCE, AND TRANSITIONAL STATUS SYSTEMS * (Rose Laub Coser)

With the concept of "role distance," Erving Goffman[1] has identified an important aspect of role behavior, namely, that individuals do not always live up to all the behavioral prescriptions regarding their status position. According to Goffman, the concept is meant to refer to the gap between role obligation and role performance and to the ability of the actor to blend the concrete demands of immediate situations with elements derived from a wider repertoire of internalized attitudes.

Goffman has provided a novel formulation for a problem that recently has captured the sociological imagination, that is, that of the actor's social creativity in the predefined situations he finds himself in.[2] Yet, perhaps

* Reprinted from *the American Journal of Sociology,* Vol. 72, No. 2, September 1966, The University of Chicago, with the permission of the publisher and author.
[1] Erving Goffman, *Encounters* (Indianapolis: Bobbs-Merrill Co., 1961), pp. 85–152.
[2] See, e.g., Dennis Wrong, "The Oversocialized Conception of Man in Modern Sociology," *American Sociological Review,* XXVI (April, 1961), 183–93; Alvin Gouldner,

Goffman's more enduring contribution is the one I want to address myself to in this paper: he programmatically, and more implicitly than explicitly, urges us to explore the structural conditions, the normative boundaries, and the social functions of the behavioral pattern he identifies.[3]

If related to the theory of reference-group behavior,[4] what Goffman calls "role distance" turns out to be normative, notwithstanding his statement to the contrary that "it is not part of the normative framework of role."[5] Further, if Goffman's concept is integrated with Merton's theory, it turns out that it is mainly a property of the social structure of transitional status systems. Hence, Goffman's concept will be shown to be a useful element of a theory of socialization in that it will help explain some problems concerned with the transition between various stages of the maturation process.

## Normative Aspects of Role Distance

For Goffman, "role distance" refers to a measure of withdrawal from role expectations, that is, "to actions which effectively convey some disdainful detachment of the performer from a role he is performing."[6] The surgeon who jokes during the operation, the nurse who withdraws into the role of female for a moment, the older boy on the merry-go-round who refuses to sit nicely on his horse as expected, are some of Goffman's illustrations of "role distance" from expected role behavior. The persons who are described are said to be making use of the "leeway" they find in the structure to show that they are not subsumed under it. "Role distance" allegedly allows individualized behavior not actually included within the realm of normative expectations. While this type of behavior, in Goffman's scheme, is not conformist, it is not deviant either. However, I want to challenge the implica-

---

"The Norm of Reciprocity: A Preliminary Statement," *American Sociological Review*, XXV (April, 1960), 161–73; William J. Goode, "A Theory of Role Strain," *American Sociological Review*, XXV (August, 1960), 483–96; Daniel Levinson, "Role, Personality, and Social Structure in the Organizational Setting," *Journal of Abnormal and Social Psychology*, LVIII (1959), 170–80; Lewis A. Coser, "Some Functions of Deviant Behavior and Normative Flexibility," *American Journal of Sociology*, LXVIII (September, 1962), 172–81.

[3] This formulation of Goffman's contribution was suggested to me by Fred Davis in a personal communication.

[4] Goffman is aware of the relevance of this theory for his conceptualization when once, in the beginning of the essay, he refers to Merton's theory of role-set (*op. cit.*, p. 86).

[5] *Ibid.*, p. 115

[6] *Ibid.*, p. 110

tion that "role distance" lies somewhere in "no-man's land" as far as social control is concerned and shall argue that it is normative.

To find out whether a type of behavior is normative, we examine the reactions of others when the behavior fails to occur or when it is exaggerated. When we apply this *social-sanction test* it immediately becomes clear that a person who does not show what Goffman calls "role distance" is accused of being a "stuffed shirt" or of "taking himself too seriously," and in more extreme cases of being a "fanatic." In contrast, a person who can assume "role distance" is congratulated for "having a good sense of humor" and for "showing detachment." Just as with any behavior that is subject to social control, sanctions exist against overconformity to the norm of "role distance" as well, as when a person is accused of being "blasé" or "cynical."

One of Goffman's main examples of "role distance" is that of eight-year-old boys on the merry-go-round who show by clowning their lack of interest in the activity. It would seem that at that age a boy is not expected to have unequivocal pleasure on the merry-go-round. If he did, his friends would ridicule him. Yet, he cannot afford to stand by and refuse to participate, for he would lay claim to a degree of maturity he does not have and would be accused of trying to be a "big shot."[7] Goffman senses the normative aspect of this type of clowning when he describes the behavior of the twelve-year-old "for whom maleness in boys has become a real *responsibility*."[8]

Goffman's main example of what he calls "role distance" is the use of humor in the medical, more specifically the surgical, setting.[9] However, his own description shows that humor here serves to assure role conformity for all members of the team. He correctly notes that in this social setting "role distance is routinely expressed," and he devotes a whole chapter to "The Functions of Role Distance for Surgery."[10] He speaks of the significance of this behavior for the "effective conduct of the operation"[11] and shows that jocular talk helps the chief surgeon to live up to the "obligation" of maintaining the poise of the members of the team as well as his own.[12] It would seem, then, that the surgeon, faced with somewhat contradictory expectations, meets all of them and hence performs his role superbly. One wonders what it is that he takes *distance* from.

Indeed, a person who has a "good sense of humor" is congratulated for

---

[7] Such negative sanctions against the non-participating, "more serious" boys must have been observed, just as the clowning, by many who have taken children to amusement parks or seen them in other settings.

[8] Goffman, *op. cit.*, p. 108; italics mine.

[9] *Ibid.*, pp. 120 ff.

[10] *Ibid.*, p. 120.

[11] *Ibid.*, p. 123.

[12] *Ibid.*, p. 126

handling a difficult situation; he is able to perform his role well by adhering to its demands with flexibility. What is being positively sanctioned in these terms is the fact that through humor a status-holder is able to face and to resolve social ambiguities. The person who does not have this skill is negatively sanctioned by being called a "fanatic," and we know that a fanatic is a person who cannot *tolerate ambiguities*.[13]

The structural sources of ambiguity are to be found in situations in which a status-holder faces contradictory normative expectations. All the illustrations that Goffman gives, no matter how different in content—whether it is the "trivial" merry-go-round or the "dramatic" operating room, whether they refer to boys or girls, children or adults, subordinates or authority holders (and Goffman very astutely gave us such a random sample)—have one important structual element in common: *sociological ambivalence*[14] is built into the structure of statuses and roles. Thus, all of Goffman's various explanations—he speaks of "affiliative crosspressures,"[15] "claims of a multi-situated kind,"[16] identification with one type of structure at the expense of another,"[17] "heterogeneous commitments and attachments"[18]—can be subsumed under the one concept of *sociological ambivalence*.

## Sociological Ambivalence

According to Robert K. Merton and Elinor Barber, sociological ambivalence "refers to incompatible normative expectations of attitudes, beliefs, and behavior assigned to a status or to a set of statuses in a society . . . or incorporated into a single social status."[19] It makes itself felt in those situations in which a status-holder faces contradictory expectations and where the social mechanisms that Merton identified in an earlier paper as securing "some degree of articulation among the roles in the role-set"[20] do not suffice.

---

[13] Cf. the brilliant paper by Else Frenkl-Brunswick, "Intolerance of Ambiguity as an Emotional and Perceptual Personality Variable," *Journal of Personality*, XVIII (1949–50), 109–43.

[14] Robert K. Merton and Elinor Barber, "Sociological Ambivalence," in A. Tiryakin (ed.), *Sociological Theory, Values and Sociocultural Change* (New York: Free Press, 1963), pp. 91–120. See also Robert K. Merton, "Resistance to the Systematic Study of Multiple Discoveries in Science," *Archives européennes de sociologie*, IV, No. 2 (1963), 237–82.

[15] Goffman, *op. cit.*, p. 134.     [16] *Ibid.*, p. 135.
[17] *Ibid.*, p. 137.     [18] *Ibid.*, p. 150.
[19] *Op. cit.*, p. 95.
[20] In Robert K. Merton, *Social Theory and Social Structure* (New York: Free Press, 1957), pp. 371 ff.

In his earlier paper Merton had anticipated that "these mechanisms may not prove sufficient to reduce the [burden of conflicting expectations]."[21] It must be added that, not only may they not suffice, but they may not always operate, either because they are not firmly institutionalized or because the structure inhibits their smooth operation. For example, if graduate students who have a bull session are suddenly *intruded upon* by a faculty member because student and faculty facilities are not sufficiently segregated, there will be embarrassment, sudden silence, and, typically, some joking in response to what is experienced as a *disturbance*. The mechanism of "insulation from observability" by role-partners differently located in the social structure fail to operate because of inadequate segregation of social space, and humor is one way of handling the ambivalence in this situation.

In Goffman's example of the lower-middle-class girls on horseback, each girl was observable by her friends. Each showed the others by clowning and emphasizing her lack of skill that she was not attached to the upper-middle-class activity of horseback riding. I believe that this behavior was called forth by the contradiction between the middle-class values concerning the activity and those of their own group, which would be likely to define horseback riding as "uppity." In full observability by peers, each girl must create the impression that she does not claim a right to a status that the others will not grant her. Goffman's observation that "participation with a group of one's similars can lend strength to the show of role distance"[22] must be understood to mean that it is because the peers are present, because each girl finds herself fully observable by them, that she feels she must show that she is not attached to the role. Were she to show skill and familiarity with the horses, or otherwise too much attachment to the activity, she would be accused of wanting to "pass." Goffman is right when he suspects that "if one of these girls were alone with a thorough-going horsewoman she would be less prone to flourish this kind of distance."[23] She would then not be observed by members of her own group. It is not that "this scene is just what they need in order to create a clear impression of what they choose not to lay claim to."[24] It is because there is a scene, that is, because the girls are observable by significant role-partners, that they have no choice but to deny the claim to a right not granted by their witnessing peers.

It is interesting to speculate what would have happened if some "thorough-going horsewomen" were present *at the same time* as the group of

21 *Ibid.*, p. 380.     22 *Ibid.*, p. 112.
23 *Ibid.*              24 *Ibid.*

peers. This situation would be in one respect similar to that observed by many teachers, when an embarrassed student carries out the assignment of giving a lecture to the class: he faces the contradictory expectations of being a student in relation to the teacher and an instructor in relation to class-mates by whom, moreover, he is ordinarily defined as a peer. The nature of the assignment requires a structure that precludes insulation from simul-taneous observability by his different role-partners and hence calls forth embarrassment.

This example points to yet a third reason for the non-operation of the conflict-reducing mechanisms discussed by Merton. It will be remembered that these are predicated for their operation on the interplay between the status-holder's role-partners: their differential power over him, their differ-ential access to his observability, and their differential involvement with his behavior.[25] How are these mechanisms to operate if contradictory expecta-tions emanate from a single role-partner? In its original meaning, "psychol-ogical ambivalence" refers to contradictory feelings within the same person. Similarly, "sociological ambivalence," which is associated with the status position rather than with the inner feeling state, may also be a result of a contradiction emanating from *one* role-partner. In the above example, the teacher expects the student to handle the class *as if* he were a teacher while yet all the while remaining a student. The latter is faced, therefore, with contradictory expectations emanating from the same role-partner.[26] The lack of availability of mechanisms for reducing sufficiently the burden of conflicting expectations emanating from the same role-partner is testified to, in this example, by the fact that students in this situation typically fail to perform to capacity.

The clowning boys in Goffman's example would seem to find themselves in a similar situation when they are not expected to enjoy the "kid stuff" by the same partners who will yet not grant them a claim to higher status. Similarly, in the operating room the surgeon is expected by the same role-partners and in their full visibility to exercise control "over a subordinate at the same time as he has to help him maintain his poise."[27]

In summary, sociological ambivalence is especially salient when it

[25] Merton, *Social Theory and Social Structure,* pp. 371 ff.

[26] This would seem to be a frequent situation in the modern American middle-class family, in which the structural position of the mother is a source for developing con-tradictory expectations of her children. See my paper, "Authority and Structural Ambivalence in the Middle-Class Family," in Rose Laub Coser (ed.), *The Family, Its Structure and Functions* (New York: St Martins Press, 1964), pp. 370–83.

[27] Goffman, *op. cit.,* p. 122.

emanates from the same role-partner and is most difficult to cope with in his full visibility.

Max Gluckman has suggested that in primitive society the multiple role requirements a person faces in the absence of segmentation of time and place would be overwhelming were they not given social definition through rituals and ceremonies. "I am going to suggest that we may seek to explain this high ritualization of tribal society from the fact that each social relation in a subsistence economy tends to serve manifold purposes."[28] Gluckman goes on to describe a setting that lacks insulation from observability for the group members:

> A man plays most of his roles, as several kinds of productive workers, as consumer, as teacher and pupil, as worshipper, in close association with the people whom he calls father and son and brother, wife and sister; and he shares citizenship with them, that mediated citizenship which is so marked a feature of tribal constitutional law. Moreover, all these roles are played on the same comparatively small stage, of the village and its environs, where shrines are placed about the huts or in the cattle corral, where the baby is born and the dead are buried, where the year's provender is stored. . . . It is from this situation that I see emerging the relatively great development of special customs and stylized etiquette to mark the different roles which a man or woman is playing at any one moment.[29]

If Gluckman is correct, we would find in our own society a greater insistence on rituals and etiquette in settings in which separation of role-partners with their manifold expectations of one another cannot be carried out sufficiently for the articulation of their multiple roles through a proper distribution of space and time. Perhaps this explains the high insistence on ritual dress, taboos, and etiquette in hospitals generally and in the operating room in particular.[30] Yet, in the operating room, in spite of much ritualization, there cannot be, as in a simple society, clear-cut "rituals of avoidance" or "that

[28] Max Gluckman, "Les rites de passage," in Daryll Forde, Meyer Fortes, Max Gluckman, Victor W. Turner, *Essays on the Ritual of Social Relations* (Manchester: Manchester University Press, 1962), p. 26.

[29] *Ibid.*, p. 27. From this perspective the present building boom both in suburban residence and in urban office space, while stemming from manifold economic and social sources and serving a variety of purposes, can be seen also as serving to maximize spatial segregation and spatial extension in a society that grows in complexity.

[30] Cf. Julius A. Roth, "Ritual and Magic in the Control of Contagion," *American Sociological Review*, XXII (June, 1957), 310–14; Robert N. Wilson, "Teamwork in the Operating Room," *Human Organization*, XII (Winter, 1954), 15–20.

exaggerated emphasis on differences between the sexes, to denote clearly their distinction,"[31] because of the combined emphasis on achievement, co-operation, and esprit de corps.[32] The ambivalence, therefore, is not entirely resolved through hospital etiquette.

In contrast to simple societies, in modern complex society the segmentation of roles and the differentiation in time and place where they have to be enacted make the dealing with multiple contradictory demands much easier. This leaves freedom of choice, yet it can be experienced as a burden, especially in those situations where insulating and segregating mechanisms do not operate and where the rites of passage of simpler or traditional societies are much less frequent.[33]

## Resolving Sociological Ambivalence

Once we have identified the sources of sociological ambivalence, we must ask what legitimate means there are available for a status-holder to deal with them. He can withdraw his interest and participation altogether, an act of last resort which Merton discusses in his earlier paper on role-sets.[34] He can avoid acting for the time being, through a momentary withdrawal, a stalling for time. He can bring about some redistribution of his time and space,[35] thus setting into motion one of the above-mentioned mechanisms, that is, creating for himself the "insulation from observability" which the structure fails to provide. He can also "act to make the contradiction manifest" by redirecting "the conflict so that it is one between members of the role-set rather than between them and himself."[36] The extent to which he can do these things, that is, the extent to which he himself can set the conflict-reducing mechanisms into motion, depends, of course, on the power, authority, and influence associated with his position in the structure. But note that in all these cases he makes use of space and time. Yet, sociological ambivalence may have to be dealt with on the spur of the moment, under conditions of dire scarcity of time and space. Humor seems to be a useful means in such situations. A person using humor, by simultaneously high-

---

[31] Gluckman, *op. cit.*, p. 27.

[32] Cf. Wilson, *op. cit.*

[33] I am reminded of a situation in which a group had to come to terms with the sudden death of a colleague. When his friends assembled in consternation, only one of them knew how to act: being religious, he turned to the wall and prayed. Others were nervous, anxious, and soon left. "Free choice," in this case, was paralyzing.

[34] Merton, *Social Theory and Social Structure*, p. 379.

[35] Goode calls this "barriers against intrusion." On this point, and generally on what he calls "ego's manipulation of his role structure," see "A Theory of Role Strain," *op. cit.*

[36] Merton, *Social Theory and Social Structure*, p. 377.

lighting and denying the ambivalence, is said to be "quick."[37] By doing so he unifies through consensual laughter role-partners threatened by the dissociation of contradictory expectations.[38] The resolution of sociological ambivalence has adaptational value. The use of humor, as a means to bring this about, makes better role performance possible. In the absence of humor, in the face of conflict, as in the earlier example of the student conducting a class in the presence of his teacher, performance is more likely to remain inhibited.

It is not surprising that humor is the most frequent form used in Goffman's illustrations of what he calls "role distance." Humor at once highlights and denies the existing ambivalence. Not only does humor help to maintain the level of performance in the operating room; the frequency of its use in a hierarchical setting, as I have shown elsewhere and Goffman also mentions, is associated with status. Senior members have more right to use this device than do junior members.[39] And with the right comes the obligation: in the absence of some other available mechanism for conflict resolution, such as insulation from observability of the team members from one another, the burden of this resolution for himself and for his staff rests on the chief surgeon. If he assumes it, he lives up to the strict expectations surrounding his status position.

If humor brings about better role performance, one is led to ask whether its use is an instance of "role distance" at all. It is not clear in Goffman's essay what the role expectations are that the joking surgeon takes distance from, but I surmise that he sees them as being focused on the serious act of operating. If we were to accept this behavioral definition of role, and if my interpretation, as well as Goffman's, of the role-adequate performance of

[37] On the functions of humor for "social economy," see my paper "Some Social Functions of Laughter," *Human Relations*, XII (May, 1959), 171–82.

[38] On this function of humor, see my paper "Laughter among Colleagues," *Psychiatry*, XXIII (February, 1960), 81–95. Humor in the operating room, as in some measure in all medical settings, helps those present to live up to the ambivalent role prescription of "detached concern" (cf. Robert K. Merton, "Some Preliminaries to a Sociology of Medical Education," in Merton, George G. Reader, and Patricia L. Kendall [eds.], *The Student Physician: Introductory Studies in the Sociology of Medical Education* [Cambridge, Mass.: Harvard University Press, 1957], p. 74; Merton and Barber, *op. cit.*). In the fine words of Henri Bergson: "Here I would point out . . . the absence of feeling which usually accompanies laughter. . . . Try, for a moment, to . . . give your sympathy its widest expression: as though at the touch of a fairy wand you will see the flimsiest of objects assume importance, and a gloomy hue spread over everything. Now step aside, look upon life as a disinterested spectator: many a drama will turn into a comedy" (*Laughter* [New York: Doubleday & Co., 1956], p. 63). On the functions of humor in the medical setting, see also Renée C. Fox, *Experiment Perilous* (N.Y.: Free Press, 1959) pp. 76–85 and 170–77.

[39] R. L. Coser, "Laughter among Colleagues," *op. cit.*

the surgeon is correct, we have to face the logical contradiction that some measure of refusal to live up to role requirements makes for better rather than for worse role performance.[40]

This contradiction seems to stem from some misconception in Goffman, as in some other sociologists, of what "role" refers to.

The concept *"role" always refers to a relationship*. One theoretical advantage of limiting the concept of "role" to refer to relationships is that it makes abstraction and hence comparisons possible. When we analyze the role of patient, for example, we can compare it in some of its aspects to the role of client. Similarly, when we analyze the role of the surgeon in the operating room, we see him in his relation to his team as we see a leader, whether army commander or foreman in industry, who must maintain morale. The sociological ambivalence of the demands upon a leader generally consists in his having to maintain "cheerful submission to authority."[41] To both maintain the subordinates' submission and have them be cheerful are contradictory requirements. Once we are able to locate the sources of structural ambivalence facing the surgeon in his role of leader, it is possible to formulate hypotheses concerning the handling of sociological ambivalence in other leadership roles as well.

Role is the "aspect of what the actor does in his relations with others seen in the context of its functional significance for the social system."[42] We speak of the role of mother because it implies a relationship with her child, of wife because it implies a relationship with her husband, of teacher because it implies a relationship with students, of patients because it implies a relationship with physician or nurse. Parsons' distinction between task performance and role performance provides a useful example: "Somatic illness may be defined in terms of incapacity for relevant task performance . . . mental illness as incapacity for role performance."[43] The following excerpt from my field notes will illustrate this: "A polio patient, paralyzed from the shoulders down, the mother of three school-age children, is confined to a respirator tank. The social worker reports about her home visits that this patient is an excellent mother. The children know that they have to come to the tank before and after school; the mother makes sure they are

[40] Goffman notes this when he says: "We see a paradoxical fact: one of the concerns that prevents the individual from fully accepting his situated self is his commitment to the situated activity system itself" (*op. cit.*, p. 121).

[41] This definition of "morale" is derived from C. Wright Mills in *The Sociological Imagination* (New York: Oxford University Press, 1959), pp. 93–94.

[42] Talcott Parsons, *The Social System* (New York: Free Press, 1951), p. 25.

[43] Talcott Parsons, *Social Structure and Personality* (New York: Free Press, 1964), p. 262.

328 ROLE-TAKING AND REFERENCE GROUP

properly fed and dressed. After school, she listens to what the children come to tell her, and if she does not always hear everything they say, it is because they all talk at once." This woman, who is unable to perform the tasks customarily associated with motherhood, can remain a mother in a way a psychotic patient cannot. A mentally disturbed person cannot be "mother," "wife," "husband," "teacher," in the relational sense that these terms imply.

To be sure, the adequacy of role performance is manifested through behavior. The analytical distinction emphasized here is that between division of labor and role structure. Workers may do different types of work without necessarily having different types of relationships with their foreman or one another. It is the relationships rather than specific behaviors that determine the role structure, and the latter furnishes "the primary focus of the articulation and hence interpenetration between personalities and social systems."[44] *Role requirements, therefore, refer to a set of expected behaviors that are geared toward maintaining or strengthening one or more patterned relationships.*

There is, of course, no strict dichotomy between behavior that is relevant for maintaining a relationship and behavior that is not. The extent to which the division of labor coincides with the role structure depends on the social structure and the cultural setting. In primitive society there would seem to be more overlap, for the division of labor is more often "mechanical" in Durkheim's sense. Tasks are more concretely defined in relation to specific roles."[45] Durkheim sees "organic solidarity" as arising in a network of relationships governed by norms that "do not contract the sphere of action of the individual" but serve to maintain functional interrelationships.[46] We can agree with Talcott Parsons, who reads Durkheim's distinction to mean that in primitive society "there is a minute regulation of the detail of action. With the progress of the division of labor this detailed regulation gradually

[44] *Ibid.*, p. 261.

[45] It would seem that the model of primitive societies informs much of the current theory of role differentiation against which Slater argues cogently: "The main weight of [the] argument rests on the notion that role differentiation occurs because two discriminable types of behavior cannot be performed at the same time. One cannot, for example, work and play at once, although the universality of work songs suggest that even this statement must be qualified. . . . If a special person is required to lead the laughing and playing, . . . then it follows that still another person will be required to lead the weeping, since clearly a person cannot laugh and mourn at the same time. On the instrumental side, this role fragmentation becomes even more complicated. According to this view, the farm family must at all times send two persons to the well, one to lower the bucket and one to raise it up, since the bucket cannot be raised and lowered at the same time" (Philip E. Slater, "Parental Role Differentiation," *American Journal of Sociology*, LXVII (November, 1961), 296–311.

[46] Émile Durkheim, *Division of Labor in Society* (New York: Free Press, 1947), p. 302.

falls away. The sanctions . . . no longer attach to particular acts . . . but only to very general principles and attitudes."[47]

The distinction between "particular acts" or *behavior* and *attitude*[48] is useful here because it helps to specify further the relation between role performance and division of labor. Some roles are maintained through conformity to expectations concerning behavior, others through conformity to expectations concerning attitudes.[49] The woman who admonishes her daughter, "It's not that I mind if you don't do the dishes, it's your attitude I object to" would not make the same statement to her maid. For the latter, the specific behavior is indispensable for role performance.

The relevance of a certain behavior pattern for the maintenance of role relationships may itself be a matter of sociological ambivalence. Driving a car or preparing a meal may be seen by the actors involved in a subsystem as role-irrelevant tasks to be accomplished by whomever is available, yet they may be looked upon as adaptive for the role structure by other role-partners. Or the actors involved in a system may themselves have different definitions of their roles. Thus, in the research reported by Melvin L. Kohn and Eleanor E. Carroll, working-class mothers want their husbands to relate to the children—they want the father to be "more encouraging"—while fathers tend to conceive of concern about children in behavioral terms and assign their behavior to their wives. They "see child rearing as their wives' responsibility."[50]

Whether role performance is defined primarily by behavioral or primarily by attitudinal prescriptions depends to some extent on class position in the society, at least in our own.[51] In comparison with the American middle-class family, in the working-class, family tasks tend to be more specifically prescribed and assigned to one of the spouses. If the family structure is defined

[47] Talcott Parsons, *The Structure of Social Action* (New York: Free Press, 1937), p. 323.

[48] For the relevance of this distinction, see Robert K. Merton, "Discrimination and the American Creed," in R. H. MacIver (ed.), *Discrimination and National Welfare* (New York: Harper & Bros., 1949), pp. 94–126.

[49] On these different types of conformity, see Robert K. Merton, "Conformity, Deviation and Opportunity Structures," *American Sociological Review*, XXIV (April, 1959), 177–88; Rose Laub Coser, "Insulation from Observability and Types of Social Conformity," *American Sociological Review*, XXVI (February, 1961), 28–39.

[50] Melvin L. Kohn and Eleanor E. Carroll, "Social Class and the Allocation of Parental Responsibilities," *Sociometry*, XXIII (December, 1960), 372–92; see also Mirra Komarowsky, *Blue Collar Marriage* (New York: Random House, 1964), *passim* and pp. 122 ff.

[51] Melvin L. Kohn, "Social Class and Parental Values," *American Journal of Sociology*, LXIV (January, 1959), 337–51; *idem*, "Social Class and the Exercise of Parental Authority," *American Sociological Review*, XXIV (June, 1959), 352–66; Kohn and Carroll, *op. cit.*

by the participants as resting on a division of labor based on sex, a taking over by husband and wife of each other's activities would indeed threaten the role structure. In this case, the tasks assigned to each are seen as symbolic of the roles of husband and wife.

The high divorce and separation rates in our society can be related, not so much to the de-differentiation of roles in the modern family, as is often believed, but to the sociological ambivalence concerning behavioral or attitudinal prescriptions for role performance. It must be noted, however, that such ambivalence is a concomitant of a changing society and of social mobility, for only where the association between division of labor and role structure has been established once and for all would such discrepancies in social definitions never occur. It is because of such ambivalence-creating situations, that is, situations where there are contradictory expectations in regard to role-relevant and role-irrelevant behavior, that choices have to be made and that structural changes become possible.

If prescriptions surrounding the relevance of specific behavior for role performance differ in the class structure, it follows that ambivalence is endemic in social mobility within the society at large and, correlatively, in moving up in occupational status. Indeed, in hierarchical organizations, the extent to which behavioral conformity is expected is inversely related to status position.[52] This is another way of stating the familiar observation that the higher the status position in the hierarchy, the more leeway there is in the choice of behavior related to role performance. Not only is there more choice than in lower positions for being deviant,[53] there is a wider range of choice for conformity as well, for behavior is guided not by specific prescriptions but by the actor's conforming attitude.

The scope of a person's inner dispositions is broader than that of specific activities, and it is expected that he bring this broadness to bear upon his choice of behavior. Evidence of this broadness of scope is positively sanctioned. The executive who has a family picture on his desk, rather than taking "role distance" as Goffman implies,[54] could not be more conventional. The picture is a symbol of his good character in another role and can therefore be used as evidence, circumstantial though it is, that "proper" inner dispositions will inform his behavior in his present status position. Thus,

[52] Melvin Kohn has suggested that the emphasis on behavioral conformity in the working-class family is related to the emphasis on behavioral conformity in the workers' occupational roles ("Social Class and Parent-Child Relationships," *American Journal of Sociology*, LXVIII [January, 1963], 471–80).

[53] Cf. L. A. Coser, *op. cit.*; George C. Homans, *Social Behavior: Its Elementary Forms* (New York: Harcourt, Brace & Co., 1961), pp. 339 ff.

[54] *Op. cit.*, pp. 130, 137.

rather than being an example of "role-irrelevant idiosyncrasy of behavior,"[55] it is a functional equivalent to a diploma on the wall.

It should be clear by now that, if the distinction is made between task and role, the sociological conception of living up to role requirements refers to a greater rather than to a lesser degree of freedom of choice. Thus the mother who interrupts her cooking activities in order to play games with her children when they need her most—for example, during the late afternoon lull between their independent activities and father's arrival—makes a choice and decides that her relationship with her children is more important than being on schedule in her task. In addition, her show of "disdain" for cooking and her turning toward her children, rather than being a show of role *distance,* could be called an instance of role *closeness.* The freedom she takes to live up to her role is concomitant with her awareness (an instance of an enlarged ego in psychoanalytic conceptualization) of the nature of the demand made on her. The trait is positively sanctioned by being called "social sensitivity." In contrast, a person who, from the psychological perspective, is said to be "compulsive" is one who, from the sociological perspective, insists on adhering to customary behavior at the expense of weakening role relationships.

If Goffman's assumption were correct, that joking while operating is *taking role distance,* the most role-conforming person would be what Merton calls the "ritualist";[56] yet the notion that this is a deviant social type has been generally accepted.

## Conformity and Non-Conformity: Two Types of Conflict Resolution

If a role were defined by concrete behavior as Goffman implies when he speaks of the "role of merry-go-round rider" or of "merry-go-round role distance,"[57] there would be as many social roles as there are verbs in the language. We would then speak of the eating role, the sleeping role, or the day-dreaming role. Absurd as this sounds, I once actually heard a reputable young sociologist refer to the "non-coping role" when describing a troubled man.

If we reserve the term "role" to express a relationship, it becomes at once clear that it refers to the rights and obligations surrounding a status position.

[55] *Ibid.,* p. 130.

[56] Robert K. Merton, "Social Structure and Anomie," in *Social Theory and Social Structure,* pp. 131–60.

[57] *Op. cit.,* pp. 110 and 109, respectively.

The eight-year-old boys on the merry-go-round, then, do not take distance from the "role of merry-go-round rider" but from the status of the smaller child.[58] Hence "role distance" refers to behavior that takes distance from status position. It would be more accurate to speak of *status distance* which is defined as behavior that lives up to the expectation that a person performing a role associated with a specified status take distance from it.

We must also distinguish between taking distance in order temporarily to relinquish some prerogatives associated with status position, as when one lowers his claims for recognition *the better to maintain his status,* and taking distance from a *status one intends to abandon* or does not have a claim to. The first, as exemplified by humor, occurs in many established status relationships and serves to maintain them as defined by removing the threat posed by sociological ambivalence. The latter occurs in the transition from one status position to another and serves to resolve the sociological ambivalence derived from two roles, the old one and the new. It is typical in situations of social mobility, either with respect to age or with respect to class, and is exemplified by clowning, as in the cases of the eight-year old boys or the lower-class girls. This raises the more general problem of status transition.

## Status Transition, Deviance, and the Process of Socialization

If we view growing up as a continuous change in status and role, it entails some non-conformity either to the requirements of the status that has to be abandoned or to those of the status one aspires to but cannot claim. It follows that some measure of deviant behavior is endemic in the process of growing up.

In learning new roles, a person faces sociological ambivalence twice compounded: he faces different expectations from various reference groups who all have an interest in his growth, yet who define his growth in different ways; at the same time, each reference group expects him to live up to role requirements surrounding his present as well as his future status.

Different role-partners interested in a person's growth, though all expecting signs of abandonment of the earlier status, often differ in their prescriptions or preferences as to the manner in which this is done. For example, social control exercised by parents differs from that exercised by peers, for parents are deeply involved in signs of growing maturity in their

---

[58] Peter M. Blau has called attention to the fact that the behavior of the boys described by Goffman is a display of superior status (see his *Exchange and Power in Social Life* [New York: John Wiley & Sons, 1964], p. 40).

children in a way that peers are not. Although parents as well as peers are interested in the child's giving up some of his "childish behavior," his friends are interested in whether, like them, he gives evidence of giving up "kid stuff" in order to be "one of the gang." His parents, however, are more interested in their children's growth. The manner of assuming distance differs in these situations. A ten-year-old taken to the zoo for the first time in several years may surprise his parents by manifesting restraint from feeding the animals but showing instead an interest in the various types of animals, their origins, and their various behaviors. He takes distance from a previous status by assuming that of observer and judge and thus wins the approval of his parents, who see in his new detachment a sign of his growing maturity.

In order to have his claim granted by his parents in their presence, the youngster must take distance from earlier behavior in a manner that persuades *them* of the legitimacy of his claim. With his peers, however, his "intellectual manner" of taking distance would invite ridicule for being a "smarty." With them, clowning is the way of "getting in," for it makes fun of the type of activity assigned to boys of lower-age status at the same time as it denies the claim to the reasonableness of the older child. Yet, if parents were to witness this behavior, they would criticize the youngster for "acting childish," thus high-lighting the ambivalence by blaming him for behaving in a manner which his clowning is precisely meant to deny.

The advice given to parents "not to meddle in the children's play" appears to be not merely a prescription of etiquette but a preventive of role conflict. Since parents especially in the middle class are more interested in indications of their children's future character, they apply different standards to their behavior than do age peers. Through the separation of various role-partners with different interests in the child, the latter can *take distance* from his former status in the expected normative way in *each* situation.

Following Merton, it can be said that this insulation from simultaneous observability by different role-partners helps the child to articulate his role. But, in addition to helping him articulate his role of child in relation to parents and peers, it helps him articulate his changing role as a growing person.

It is not sufficient to say that the child can make use of available mechanisms for reducing the burden of contradictory expectations in order to articulate his role. It must be added that he himself gradually learns to make such mechanisms operable, as when he allocates time and space to certain activities or actively enlarges or restricts his role-set by seeking out associates or avoiding them. But this the child is likely to learn only in a structural situation that lends itself to manipulation, so that what Goffman calls "role distance" can be achieved, and, what is more, is expected to be achieved.[59]

## Growing Up and Complexity of Role-Set

The process of maturation takes place in an ever extending role-set and consists in the child's increasing obligation as well as ability to differentiate his behavior in relation to his various role-partners. This will enable him to deal with their various demands, even if they are contradictory, provided mechanisms are at work, or provided he can make active use of such mechanisms, for facilitating "role distance."

As the number of the child's role-partners increases,[60] he will have to learn the differences in expectations of teacher, playmates, cub mother, playground attendant, and parents, and the differences in expectations of father and mother. Just as he learns to play more complex games—such as soccer, where he will "be ready to take the attitude of everyone else involved in the game" and to relate the players with one another, where "he must know *what everyone else is going to do* in order to carry out his play," where he "organizes into a sort of unit the attitudes of the other players," and where "that organization controls his response"[61]—the child learns to interact with many role-partners, facing some, turning away from others. His expectations of *what everyone else is going to do* may be contradictory and call forth incompatible responses on his part. In spite, or perhaps because, of the difficulty that this entails, such ambivalence and role conflicts will also provide for him the opportunity to assimilate from his various associations ever more patterns of responses which he can put at the service of conflict resolution.

The very source of conflict also furnishes the means for its creative resolution. In Goffman's example, the twelve-year-old boy on the merry-go-round who wants to abandon his childish status can, in contrast to the younger child, behave like a play actor rather than a clown. Having found

---

59 Cf. Alan F. Blum, "The Study of Socialization Failure: A Review of Sociological Theories of Family Structure and Deviant Behavior" 1964 (mimeographed).

60 Georges Duhamel describes charmingly how a child's broadening of his role-set is ambivalently interpreted by the parent as a sign of growing up. Writing about his little boy, he says: "Quand il se promène au jardin, il adresse la parole à des enfants que nous n'avons jamais vus: 'Bonjour, Jacques! Bonjour, Nelly!' Ce sont des amitiés à lui, des amitiés dont nous sommes exclus. Et pourtant! Pourtant, je vous l'ai dit, il fleure encore le lait maternel" (*Les plaisirs et les jeux* [Paris: Mercure de France, 1931], p. 157).

61 From G. H. Mead, *Mind, Self, and Society: From the Standpoint of a Social Behaviorist* (Chicago: University of Chicago Press, 1934), pp. 151–54; italics mine.

out what would be expected of him were he on a real horse, a symbol of older-age status, he can, in Goffman's words, "exert creative acts of distancy, as when he jokingly treats his wooden horse as if it were a racing one."[62] This boy responds to a situation that he prepares to abandon by adopting a pattern that he hopes to use in another situation. His creativity consists in his ability to take distance through an act of anticipatory socialization.

A growing youngster will develop several identifications; he will adopt new ones as he takes distance from the old and learn to play several roles at once. When he reaches adulthood he will be able to mesh what Goffman calls "a simultaneous multiplicity of selves" into a coherent self-image. He will make use of the attitudes he has developed in his various role relationships for making choices in his behavior with his different role-partners. Thus, the mature individual, in contrast to the person who "does his job," has learned to live up to the demands of his status position with a repertoire of attitudes and inner dispositions which he can call upon freely to solve unexpected and ambiguous situations and in this way to maintain otherwise threatened role relationships.

The ability to use inner resources that were developed through successive resolutions of conflicts with the expectations of various role-partners is the sociological counterpart to what Freud has called sublimation. It is the ability of the individual with a "strong ego" to make use of the accumulated resources developed in manifold patterned role relationships of the past and present in the performance of his various roles. Role relationships, rather than being a source of constraint as some will have it, provide the opportunity for socially creative behavior. He who acknowledges his inner dispositions, crystallized over many years of role-learning, and puts them to the use of role performance is a truly creative individual.

---

[62] Goffman, *op. cit.*, p. 108; italics mine.

# Part III
# Structural Concepts

# 9: Status

The concept of "status," once referred only to *inherited* status, a fixed, usually hereditary, position within the social order. Such was the usage of writers like the distinguished nineteenth century. English evolutionist, Sir Henry Maine (1822–1888) and two vastly important American sociologists, Robert E. Park (1864–1944) and Ernest W. Burgess, who in 1921 coauthored the still valuable, if somewhat dated, *Introduction to the Science of Sociology*. Maine had written of the transition from status to contract; many other writers, even in our own time, have elaborated the dichotomy. For Park and Burgess, as our reading makes clear, the relevant contrast was that between status and competition, the latter being evident even in primitive societies, but eventually eclipsing the former altogether.

With the development of modern anthropology and sociology, status has been broadened to encompass all culturally prescribed rights and duties inherent in social positions, whatever their origin. The individual is now viewed as having a total status which generally combines a large number of subsidiary statuses. The eminent American anthropologist, Ralph Linton (1893–1953) distinguished between ascribed (or inherited) status—which would have been a redundancy to earlier theorists—and achieved status, which results from personal attainment of goals set forth by the culture. This distinction has been all but universally accepted in social science. As such there are certain irreducible bases for the determination of status, among them those mentioned by Linton: age, sex, and occupation. Furthermore, status, whether the by-product of effort or the result of birth, carries with it an image of exemplary behavior, a model of collective expectations. The concept of status is related to the concept of "role," i.e.; what Linton calls the more dynamic aspect of status which we shall discuss both in this context and in relation to reference groups (see Section 8). It is impossible fully to dissociate them.

All of the foregoing applies in equal measure to simple nonliterate societies and to complex civilizations. However, the growth of modern industrial society produces a tremendous differentiation of functions. While age and sex continue to be relevant factors in status ascription, the occupational determination of status and the occupational definition of role assumed unprecedented importance. In the status-role situation there are always meaningful "others" whose approval is sought by conformity to their shared understandings and who in turn provide a variety of gratifications for the well socialized individual. This is the meaning of an omnipresent process that Talcott Parsons has termed the "complimentarity of expectations." Znaniecki, in his subtle analysis of role and status, refers to the same phenomenon in speaking of "social circles," each of which has its own set of values. These are ever-widening circles which in the modern world have tended to produce a bewildering multiplicity of differential standards.

Although the way a man earns his living will decisively affect his status, it does not necessarily *clarify* all his rights and responsibilities. Indeed, the rapidity of social change so typical of our age may create doubt and confusion about appropriate (socially acceptable) conduct in areas where virtual certainty previously obtained. In general, status is problematic when roles are vaguely or ambiguously defined. Thus, women, mothers-in-law, adolescents, and the aged are suspended in a painful and doubtful position across the American social scene. Robert Park, concerned with race mixture, discussed the half-breed, born of two cultures, but not fully accepted by either. He labeled this type of person "the marginal man." Many students of sociology have found Park's phrase suggestive, not the least of them Everett C. Hughes, who has illuminated certain dilemmas and contradictions of status by applying the phrase not so much to racial as to professional relations. His essay is indicative of a productive trend in sociological theory.

Our final selection, Robert K. Merton's seminal paper on *The Role Set,* develops the idea that each social status involves not a single social role but a whole array of such roles. Merton contends that persons occupying a particular status are engaged in a series of role-relationships which together make up their role-set. This notion points up the need for identifying social mechanisms which help to articulate the expectations of those in the role-set, so that the occupant of a status is not confronted with multiple, conflicting, and contradictory demands.

# PERSONAL COMPETITION, SOCIAL SELECTION, AND STATUS *1  (*Park and Burgess*)

The function of personal competition, considered as a part of the social system, is to assign to each individual his place in that system. If "all the world's a stage," this is a process that distributes the parts among the players. It may do it well or ill, but after some fashion it does it. Some may be cast in parts unsuited to them; good actors may be discharged altogether and worse ones retained; but nevertheless the thing is arranged in some way and the play goes on.

That such a process must exist can hardly, it seems to me, admit of question; in fact, I believe that those who speak of doing away with competition use the word in another sense than is here intended. Within the course of the longest human life there is necessarily a complete renewal of the persons whose communication and cooperation make up the life of society. The new members come into the world without any legible sign to indicate what they are fit for, a mystery to others from the first and to themselves as soon as they are capable of reflection: the young man does not know for what he is adapted, and no one else can tell him. The only possible way to get light upon the matter is to adopt the method of experiment. By trying one thing and another and by reflecting upon his experience, he begins to find out about himself, and the world begins to find out about him. His field of investigation is of course restricted, and his own judgment and that of others is liable to error, but the tendency of it all can hardly be other than to guide his choice to that one of the available careers in which he is best adapted to hold his own. I may say this much, perhaps, without assuming anything regarding the efficiency or justice of competition as a distributer of social functions, a matter regarding which I shall offer some suggestions later. All I wish to say here is that the necessity of some selective process is inherent in the conditions of social life.

It will be apparent that, in the sense in which I use the term, competition is not necessarily a hostile contention, nor even something of which the competing individual is always conscious. From our infancy onward through-

---

* Reprinted from *Introduction to the Science of Sociology* by Robert E. Park and Ernest W. Burgess, pp. 708–714, by permission of The University of Chicago Press. Copyright, 1921, by The University of Chicago.

out life judgments are daily forming regarding us of which we are unaware, but which go to determine our careers. "The world is full of judgment days." A and B, for instance, are under consideration for some appointment; the experience and personal qualifications of each are duly weighed by those having the appointment to make, and A, we will say, is chosen. Neither of the two need know anything about the matter until the selection is made. It is eligibility to perform some social function that makes a man a competitor, and he may or may not be aware of it, or, if aware of it, he may or may not be consciously opposed to others. I trust that the reader will bear in mind that I always use the word competition in the sense here explained.

There is but one alternative to competition as a means of determining the place of the individual in the social system, and that is some form of status, some fixed, mechanical rule, usually a rule of inheritance, which decides the function of the individual without reference to his personal traits, and thus dispenses with any process of comparison. It is possible to conceive of a society organized entirely upon the basis of the inheritance of functions, and indeed societies exist which may be said to approach this condition. In India, for example, the prevalent idea regarding the social function of the individual is that it is unalterably determined by his parentage, and the village blacksmith, shoemaker, accountant, or priest has his place assigned to him by a rule of descent as rigid as that which governs the transmission of one of the crowns of Europe. If all functions were handed down in this way, if there were never any deficiency or surplus of children to take the place of their parents, if there were no progress or decay in the social system making necessary new activities or dispensing with old ones, then there would be no use for a selective process. But precisely in the measure that a society departs from this condition, that individual traits are recognized and made available, or social change of any sort comes to pass, in that measure must there be competition.

Status is not an active process, as competition is; it is simply a rule of conservation, a makeshift to avoid the inconveniences of continual readjustment in the social structure. Competition or selection is the only constructive principle, and everything worthy the name of organization had at some time or other a competitive origin. At the present day the eldest son of a peer may succeed to a seat in the House of Lords simply by right of birth; but his ancestor got the seat by competition, by some exercise of personal qualities that made him valued or loved or feared by a king or a minister.

Sir Henry Maine has pointed out that increase of competition is a characteristic trait of modern life, and that the powerful ancient societies of the old world were for the most part non-competitive in their structure.

While this is true, it would be a mistake to draw the inference that status is a peculiarly natural or primitive principle of organization and competition a comparatively recent discovery. On the contrary the spontaneous relations among men, as we see in the case of children, and we may infer from the life of the lower animals, are highly competitive, personal prowess and ascendency being everything and little regard being paid to descent simply as such. The regime of inherited status, on the other hand, is a comparatively complex and artificial product, necessarily of later growth, whose very general prevalence among the successful societies of the old world is doubtless to be explained by the stability and consequently the power which it was calculated to give to the social system. It survived because under certain conditions it was the fittest. It was not and is not universally predominant among savages or barbarous peoples. With the American Indians, for example, the definiteness and authority of status were comparatively small, personal prowess and initiative being correspondingly important. The interesting monograph on Omaha sociology, by Dorsey, published by the United States Bureau of Ethnology, contains many facts showing that the life of this people was highly competitive. When the tribe was at war any brave could organize an expedition against the enemy, if he could induce enough others to join him, and this organizer usually assumed the command. In a similar way the managers of the hunt were chosen because of personal skill; and, in general, "any man can win a name and rank in the state by becoming 'wacuce' or brave, either in war or by the bestowal of gifts and the frequent giving of feasts."

Throughout history there has been a struggle between the principles of status and competition regarding the part that each should play in the social system. Generally speaking the advantage of status is in its power to give order and continuity. As Gibbon informs us, "The superior prerogative of birth, when it has obtained the sanction of time and popular opinion, is the plainest and least invidious of all distinctions among mankind," and he is doubtless right in ascribing the confusion of the later Roman Empire largely to the lack of an established rule for the transmission of imperial authority. The chief danger of status is that of suppressing personal development, and so of causing social enfeeblement, rigidity, and ultimate decay. On the other hand, competition develops the individual and gives flexibility and animation to the social order, its danger being chiefly that of disintegration in some form or other. The general tendency in modern times has been toward the relative increase of the free or competitive principle, owing to the fact that the rise of other means of securing stability has diminished the need for status. The latter persists, however, even in the freest countries, as the method by which wealth is transmitted, and also in social classes, which, so far as they exist at all, are based chiefly upon inherited wealth and the culture and opportunities that go with it. The ultimate reason for this persistence—without very serious opposition—in the face of the obvious inequalities and limitations upon liberty that it perpetuates is perhaps the fact that no other method of transmission has arisen that has shown itself capable of giving continuity and order to the control of wealth.

## Personal Competition and the Evolution of Individual Types[2]

The ancient city was primarily a fortress, a place of refuge in time of war. The modern city, on the contrary, is primarily a convenience of commerce and owes its existence to the market place around which it sprang up. Industrial competition and the division of labor, which have probably done most to develop the latent powers of mankind, are possible only upon condition of the existence of markets, of money and other devices for the facilitation of trade and commerce.

The old adage which describes the city as the natural environment of the free man still holds so far as the individual man finds in the chances, the diversity of interests and tasks, and in the vast unconscious co-operation of city life, the opportunity to choose his own vocation and develop his peculiar individual talents. The city offers a market for the special talents of individual men. Personal competition tends to select for each special task the individual who is best suited to perform it.

> The difference of natural talents in different men is, in reality, much less than we are aware of; and the very different genius which appears to distinguish men of different professions, when grown up to maturity, is not upon many occasions so much the cause, as the effect of the division of labour. The difference between the most dissimilar characters, between a philosopher and a common street porter, for example, seems to arise not so much from nature, as from habit, custom and education. When they came into the world, and for the first six or eight years of their existence, they were perhaps very much alike, and neither their parents nor playfellows could perceive any remarkable difference. About that age, or soon after, they come to be employed in different occupations. The difference of talents comes then to be taken notice of, and widens by degrees, till at last the vanity of the

*philosopher is willing to acknowledge scarce any resemblance. But without the disposition to truck, barter, and exchange, every man must have procured to himself every necessary and conveniency of life which he wanted. All must have had the same duties to perform, and the same work to do, and there could have been no such difference of employment as could alone give occasion to any great difference of talent.*

*As it is the power of exchanging that gives occasion to the division of labour, so the extent of this division must always be limited by the extent of that power, or, in other words, by the extent of the market. . . . There are some sorts of industry, even of the lowest kind, which can be carried on nowhere but in a great town.*

Success, under conditions of personal competition, depends upon concentration, upon some single task, and this concentration stimulates the demand for rational methods, technical devices, and exceptional skill. Exceptional skill, while based on natural talent, requires special preparation, and it has called into existence the trade and professional schools, and finally bureaus for vocational guidance. All of these, either directly or indirectly, serve at once to select and emphasize individual differences.

Every device which facilitates trade and industry prepares the way for a further division of labor and so tends further to specialize the tasks in which men find their vocations.

The outcome of this process is to break down or modify the older organization of society, which was based on family ties, on local associations, on culture, caste, and status, and to substitute for it an organization based on vocational interests.

In the city every vocation, even that of a beggar, tends to assume the character of a profession, and the discipline which success in any vocation imposes, together with the associations that it enforces, emphasizes this tendency.

The effect of the vocations and the division of labor is to produce, in the first instance, not social groups but vocational types—the actor, the plumber, and the lumber-jack. The organizations, like the trade and labor unions, which men of the same trade or profession form are based on common interests. In this respect they differ from forms of associations like the neighborhood, which are based on contiguity, personal association, and the common ties of humanity. The different trades and professions seem disposed to group themselves in classes, that is to say, the artisan, business, and professional classes. But in the modern democratic state the classes have as yet attained no effective organization. Socialism, founded on an effort to create an organization based on "class consciousness," has never succeeded in creating more than a political party.

The effects of the division of labor as a discipline may therefore be best studied in the vocational types it has produced. Among the types which it would be interesting to study are: the shopgirl, the policeman, the peddler, the cabman, the night watchman, the clairvoyant, the vaudeville performer, the quack doctor, the bartender, the ward boss, the strike-breaker, the labor agitator, the school teacher, the reporter, the stockbroker, the pawnbroker; all of these are characteristic products of the conditions of city life; each with its special experience, insight, and point of view determines for each vocational group and for the city as a whole its individuality.

REFERENCES

1. Adapted from Charles H. Cooley, "Personal Competition," in *Economic Studies,* IV (1899), No. 2, 78–86.
2. From Robert E. Park, "The City," in the *American Journal of Sociology,* XX (1915), 584–86.

# STATUS AND ROLE * (*Linton*)

In the preceding chapter we discussed the nature of society and pointed out that the functioning of societies depends upon the presence of patterns for reciprocal behavior between individuals or groups of individuals. The polar positions in such patterns of reciprocal behavior are technically known as *statuses.* The term *status,* like the term *culture,* has come to be used with a double significance. A *status,* in the abstract, is a position in a particular pattern. It is thus quite correct to speak of each individual as having many statuses, since each individual participates in the expression of a number of patterns. However, unless the term is qualified in some way, the *status* of any individual means the sum total of all the statuses which he occupies. It represents his position with relation to the total society. Thus the status of Mr. Jones as a member of his community derives from a combination of all the statuses which he holds as a citizen, as an attorney, as a Mason, as a Methodist, as Mrs. Jones's husband, and so on.

* Reprinted from *The Study of Man* by Ralph Linton, pp. 113–119, with permission of the publisher, Appleton-Century-Crofts, Inc. Copyright, 1936, by Appleton-Century-Crofts, Inc.

A status, as distinct from the individual who may occupy it, is simply a collection of rights and duties. Since these rights and duties can find expression only through the medium of individuals, it is extremely hard for us to maintain a distinction in our thinking between statuses and the people who hold them and exercise the rights and duties which constitute them. The relation between any individual and any status he holds is somewhat like that between the driver of an automobile and the driver's place in the machine. The driver's seat with its steering wheel, accelerator, and other controls is a constant with ever-present potentialities for action and control, while the driver may be any member of the family and may exercise these potentialities very well or very badly.

A *role* represents the dynamic aspect of a status. The individual is socially assigned to a status and occupies it with relation to other statuses. When he puts the rights and duties which constitute the status into effect, he is performing a role. Role and status are quite inseparable, and the distinction between them is of only academic interest. There are no roles without statuses or statuses without roles. Just as in the case of *status*, the term *role* is used with a double significance. Every individual has a series of roles deriving from the various patterns in which he participates and at the same time a *role* in general, which represents the sum total of these roles and determines what he does for his society and what he can expect from it.

Although all statuses and roles derive from social patterns and are integral parts of patterns, they have an independent function with relation to the individuals who occupy particular statuses and exercise their roles. To such individuals the combined status and role represent the minimum of attitudes and behavior which he must assume if he is to participate in the overt expression of the pattern. Status and role serve to reduce the ideal patterns for social life to individual terms. They become models for organizing the attitudes and behavior of the individual so that these will be congruous with those of the other individuals participating in the expression of the pattern. Thus if we are studying football teams in the abstract, the position of quarter-back is meaningless except in relation to the other positions. From the point of view of the quarter-back himself it is a distinct and important entity. It determines where he shall take his place in the line-up and what he shall do in various plays. His assignment to this position at once limits and defines his activities and establishes a minimum of things which he must learn. Similarly, in a social pattern such as that for the employer-employee relationship the statuses of employer and employee define what each has to know and do to put the pattern into operation. The employer does not need to know the techniques involved in the employee's labor, and the employee does not need to know the techniques for marketing or accounting.

It is obvious that, as long as there is no interference from external sources, the more perfectly the members of any society are adjusted to their statuses and roles the more smoothly the society will function. In its attempts to bring about such adjustments every society finds itself caught on the horns of a dilemma. The individual's formation of habits and attitudes begins at birth, and, other things being equal, the earlier his training for a status can begin the more successful it is likely to be. At the same time, no two individuals are alike, and a status which will be congenial to one may be quite uncongenial to another. Also, there are in all social systems certain roles which require more than training for their successful performance. Perfect technique does not make a great violinist, nor a thorough book knowledge of tactics an efficient general. The utilization of the special gifts of individuals may be highly important to society, as in the case of the general, yet these gifts usually show themselves rather late, and to wait upon their manifestation for the assignment of statuses would be to forfeit the advantages to be derived from commencing training early.

Fortunately, human beings are so mutable that almost any normal individual can be trained to the adequate performance of almost any role. Most of the business of living can be conducted on a basis of habit, with little need for intelligence and none for special gifts. Societies have met the dilemma by developing two types of statuses, the *ascribed* and the *achieved*. *Ascribed* statuses are those which are assigned to individuals without reference to their innate differences or abilities. They can be predicted and trained for from the moment of birth. The *achieved* statuses are, as a minimum, those requiring special qualities, although they are not necessarily limited to these. They are not assigned to individuals from birth but are left open to be filled through competition and individual effort. The majority of the statuses in all social systems are of the ascribed type and those which take care of the ordinary day-to-day business of living are practically always of this type.

In all societies certain things are selected as reference points for the ascription of status. The things chosen for this purpose are always of such a nature that they are ascertainable at birth, making it possible to begin the training of the individual for his potential statuses and roles at once. The simplest and most universally used of these reference points is sex. Age is used with nearly equal frequency, since all individuals pass through the same cycle of growth, maturity, and decline, and the statuses whose occupation will be determined by age can be forecast and trained for with accuracy.

Family relationships, the simplest and most obvious being that of the child to its mother, are also used in all societies as reference points for the establishment of a whole series of statuses. Lastly, there is the matter of birth into a particular socially established group, such as a class or caste. The use of this type of reference is common but not universal. In all societies the actual ascription of statuses to the individual is controlled by a series of these reference points which together serve to delimit the field of his future participation in the life of the group.

The division and ascription of statuses with relation to sex seems to be basic in all social systems. All societies prescribe different attitudes and activities to men and to women. Most of them try to rationalize these prescriptions in terms of the physiological differences between the sexes or their different roles in reproduction. However, a comparative study of the statuses ascribed to women and men in different cultures seems to show that while such factors may have served as a starting point for the development of a division the actual ascriptions are almost entirely determined by culture. Even the psychological characteristics ascribed to men and women in different societies vary so much that they can have little physiological basis. Our own idea of women as ministering angels contrasts sharply with the ingenuity of women as torturers among the Iroquois and the sadistic delight they took in the process. Even the last two generations have seen a sharp change in the psychological patterns for women in our own society. The delicate, fainting lady of the middle eighteen-hundreds is as extinct as the dodo.

When it comes to the ascription of occupations, which is after all an integral part of status, we find the differences in various societies even more marked. Arapesh women regularly carry heavier loads than men "because their heads are so much harder and stronger." In some societies women do most of the manual labor; in others, as in the Marquesas, even cooking, housekeeping, and baby-tending are proper male occupations, and women spend most of their time primping. Even the general rule that women's handicap through pregnancy and nursing indicates the more active occupations as male and the less active ones as female has many exceptions. Thus among the Tasmanians seal-hunting was women's work. They swam out to the seal rocks, stalked the animals, and clubbed them. Tasmanian women also hunted opossums, which required the climbing of large trees.

Although the actual ascription of occupations along sex lines is highly variable, the pattern of sex division is constant. There are very few societies in which every important activity has not been definitely assigned to men or to women. Even when the two sexes cooperate in a particular occupation, the field of each is usually clearly delimited. Thus in Madagascar rice culture the men make the seed beds and terraces and prepare the fields for transplanting. The women do the work of transplanting, which is hard and back-breaking. The women weed the crop, but the men harvest it. The women then carry it to the threshing floors, where the men thresh it while the women winnow it. Lastly, the women pound the grain in mortars and cook it.

When a society takes over a new industry, there is often a period of uncertainty during which the work may be done by either sex, but it soon falls into the province of one or the other. In Madagascar, pottery is made by men in some tribes and by women in others. The only tribe in which it is made by both men and women is one into which the art has been introduced within the last sixty years. I was told that during the fifteen years preceding my visit there had been a marked decrease in the number of male potters, many men who had once practised the art having given it up. The factor of lowered wages, usually advanced as the reason for men leaving one of our own occupations when women enter it in force, certainly was not operative here. The field was not overcrowded, and the prices for men's and women's products were the same. Most of the men who had given up the trade were vague as to their reasons, but a few said frankly that they did not like to compete with women. Apparently the entry of women into the occupation had robbed it of a certain amount of prestige. It was no longer quite the thing for a man to be a potter, even though he was a very good one.

The use of age as a reference point for establishing status is as universal as the use of sex. All societies recognize three age groupings as a minimum: child, adult, and old. Certain societies have emphasized age as a basis for assigning status and have greatly amplified the divisions. Thus in certain African tribes the whole male population is divided into units composed of those born in the same years or within two- or three-year intervals. However, such extreme attention to age is unusual, and we need not discuss it here.

The physical differences between child and adult are easily recognizable, and the passage from childhood to maturity is marked by physiological events which make it possible to date it exactly for girls and within a few weeks or months for boys. However, the physical passage from childhood to maturity does not necessarily coincide with the social transfer of the individual from one category to the other. Thus in our own society both men and women remain legally children until long after they are physically adult. In most societies this difference between the physical and social transfer is more clearly marked than in our own. The child becomes a man not when he is physically mature but when he is formally recognized as a man by his society. This recognition is almost always given ceremonial expression in what are technically known as puberty rites. The most important element in these rites is not the determination of physical maturity but that of social maturity. Whether a boy is able to breed is less vital to his society than whether he is able to do a man's work and has a man's knowledge. Actually, most puberty ceremonies include tests of the boy's learning and fortitude, and if the aspirants are unable to pass these they are left in the child status until they can. For those who pass the tests, the ceremonies usually culminate in the transfer to them of certain secrets which the men guard from women and children.

The passage of individuals from adult to aged is harder to perceive. There is no clear physiological line for men, while even women may retain their full physical vigor and their ability to carry on all the activities of the adult status for several years after the menopause. The social transfer of men from the adult to the aged group is given ceremonial recognition in a few cultures, as when a father formally surrenders his official position and titles to his son, but such recognition is rare. As for women, there appears to be no society in which the menopause is given ceremonial recognition, although there are a few societies in which it does alter the individual's status. Thus Comanche women, after the menopause, were released from their disabilities with regard to the supernatural. They could handle sacred objects, obtain power through dreams and practise as shamans, all things forbidden to women of bearing age.

The general tendency for societies to emphasize the individual's first change in age status and largely ignore the second is no doubt due in part to the difficulty of determining the onset of old age. However, there are also psychological factors involved. The boy or girl is usually anxious to grow up, and this eagerness is heightened by the exclusion of children from certain activities and knowledge. Also, society welcomes new additions to the most active division of the group, that which contributes most to its perpetuation and well-being. Conversely, the individual who enjoys the thought of growing old is atypical in all societies. Even when age brings respect and a new measure of influence, it means the relinquishment of much that is pleasant. We can see among ourselves that the aging usually refuse to recognize the change until long after it has happened.

# THE SOCIAL ROLE AND
# THE SOCIAL CIRCLE * (*Znaniecki*)

In recent years the term "social role" has been used by many sociologists to denote the phenomena in question. We say that a priest, a lawyer, a politician, a banker, a merchant, a physician, a farmer, a workman, a soldier, a housewife, a teacher performs a specific social role. Furthermore, the concept (with certain variations) has proved applicable not only to individuals who specialize in certain activities but also to individuals as members of certain groups: thus, an American, a Frenchman, a Methodist, a Catholic, a Communist, a Fascist, a club member, a member of the family (child, father, mother, grandparent) plays a certain social role. An individual in the course of his life performs a number of different roles, successively or simultaneously; the synthesis of all the social roles he has ever performed from birth to death constitutes his social personality.

Every social role presupposes that between the individual performing the role, who may thus be called a "social person," and a smaller or larger set of people who participate in his performance and may be termed his "social circle" there is a common bond constituted by a complex of values which all of them appreciate positively. These are economic values in the case of a merchant or a banker and the circle formed by his clients; hygienic values for the physician and his patients; political values for a king and his subjects; religious values for the priest and his circle of lay believers; aesthetic values for the artist and the circle of his admirers and critics; a combination of various values which fill the content of family life between the child and his family circle. The person is an object of positive valuation on the part of his circle because they believe that they all need his cooperation for the realization of certain tendencies connected with these values. The banker's cooperation is presumably needed by those who tend to invest or borrow money; the physician's cooperation by those who wish to regain or to preserve their own health and the health of the people in whom they are interested; the child's cooperation by other family members for the maintenance of family life. On the other hand, the person obviously cannot perform his role without the cooperation of his circle—though not necessarily the cooperation of any particular individual within the circle. There can be no active banker without clients, no practicing physician without patients, no reigning king without subjects, no child-in-the-family without other family members.

The person is conceived by his circle as an organic and psychological entity who is a "self," conscious of his own existence as a body and a soul and aware of how others regard him. If he is to be the kind of person his social circle needs, his "self" must possess in the opinion of the circle certain qualities, physical and mental, and not possess certain other qualities. For instance, organic "health" or "sickness" affects his supposed capacity to perform most roles, but particularly occupational roles, such as the farmer's, the workman's, the soldier's, and the housewife's, which require certain bodily skills; while lack of training in the "proper" ways of moving and eating may exclude an individual from roles which require "society" manners. Some roles are limited to men, others to women; there are upper or lower age limits for every role; the majority of roles imply certain somatic racial characteristics and definite, though variable, standards of external appearance.

The psychological qualities ascribed to persons performing social roles are enormously diversified: in every Western language there are hundreds of words denoting supposed traits of "intelligence" and "character"; and almost every such trait has, or had in the past, an axiological significance, that is, is positively or negatively valued, either in all persons or in persons performing certain kinds of role. In naive popular reflection, such psychological traits are real qualities of a substantial "mind" or "soul," whose existence is manifested by specific acts (including verbal statements) of the individual.

A person who is needed by a social circle and whose self possesses the qualities required for the role for which he is needed has a definite social *status,* that is, his circle grants him certain rights and enforces those rights, when necessary, against individual participants of the circle or outsiders. Some of those rights concern his bodily existence. For instance, he has an ecological position, the right to occupy a definite space (as home, room, office, seat) where he is safe from bodily injury, and the right to move safely over given territories. His economic position includes rights to use certain material values regarded as necessary for his subsistence on a level commensurate with his role. Other rights involve his "spiritual welfare": he has a fixed moral standing, can claim some recognition, social response, and participation in the nonmaterial values of his circle.

He, in turn, has a social *function* to fulfill; he is regarded as obliged to achieve certain tasks by which the supposed needs of his circle will be satisfied and to behave toward other individuals in his circle in a way that shows his positive valuation of them.

Such are the essential components which we believe, on the basis of previous studies, to be found in all social roles, although of course the specific composition of different kinds of social role varies considerably. But our knowledge of a social role is not complete if we know only its composition, for a role is a dynamic system and its components may be variously interconnected in the course of its performance. There are many different ways of performing a role, according to the dominant active tendencies of the performer. He may, for instance, be mainly interested in one of the components of his role—the social circle, his own self, the status, or the function— and tend to subordinate other components to it. And, whatever his main interest, he may tend to conform with the demands of his circle or else try to innovate, to become independent of those demands. And, again, in either case he may be optimistically confident in the opportunities offered by his role and tend to expand it or else he may mistrust its possibilities and tend to restrict it to a perfectly secure minimum.

The possibility of reaching such general conclusions about all social roles and more specific, though still widely applicable, generalizations about social roles of a certain kind—such as the role of peasant, priest, merchant, factory worker, or artist—points obviously to the existence of essential uniformities and also of important variations among these social phenomena. Social roles constitute one general class of social system, and this class may be subdivided into less general classes, these into subclasses, and so on; for instance, within the specific class of factory worker there are hundreds of subclasses of workers employed in particular trades and there is another line of differentiation according to the economic organization of the factories in which they are employed. Systematic sociology stands before a task similar to that of systematic biology with its still greater complication of classes and subclasses of living organisms; and here, as there, only uniformities of specific systems make possible a further search for static and dynamic laws. But, manifestly, the source of uniformities in the social field is different from that in the field of biology.

Although in both fields differentiation is due to variations of individual systems, biological uniformities are due in the main to heredity; whereas uniformities of social systems, like those of all cultural systems, are chiefly the result of a reflective or unreflective use of the same *cultural patterns* in many particular cases. There is obviously a fundamental and universal, though unreflective, cultural pattern in accordance with which all kinds of lasting relationships between individuals and their social milieus are normatively organized and which we denote by the term "social role." The genesis of this pattern is lost in an inaccessible past, and so are the origins of what are probably its earliest variations, that is, those which everywhere differentiate individual roles according to sex and age.

But most of the patterns which have evolved during the history of mankind can be studied in the course of their becoming and duration. They originated usually by differentiation from older undifferentiated patterns, more seldom by entirely original, though gradual, invention. Many of these new patterns were short-lived or applied only within small collectivities, but some have lasted for thousands of years and spread over whole continents. In modern American society we find a number of patterns of social roles which can be traced back to prehistoric times, some still very vital, like the pattern of the rural housewife, others probably mere survivals destined soon to disappear, such as the patterns of the magician and the fortune teller.

# DILEMMAS AND CONTRADICTIONS OF STATUS * (Hughes)

It is doubtful whether any society ever had so great a variety of statuses or recognized such a large number of status-determining characteristics as does ours. The combinations of the latter are, of course, times over more numerous than the characteristics themselves. In societies where statuses[1] are well defined and are entered chiefly by birth or a few well-established sequences of training or achievement, the particular personal attributes proper to each status are woven into a whole. They are not thought of as separate entities. Even in our society, certain statuses have developed characteristic patterns of expected personal attributes and a way of life. To such, in the German language, is applied the term *Stand.*

Few of the positions in our society, however, have remained fixed long enough for such an elaboration to occur. We put emphasis on change in the system of positions which make up our social organization and upon mobility of the individual by achievement. In the struggle for achievement,

* By Everett Cherrington Hughes, reprinted from *The American Journal of Sociology* Vol. L., July 1944–May 1945, pp. 353–359, by permission of The University of Chicago Press, and the author.

individual traits of the person stand out as separate entities. And they occur in peculiar combinations which make for confusion, contradictions, and dilemmas of status.

Now there may be, for a given status or social position, one or more specifically determining characteristics of the person. Some of them are formal, or even legal. No one, for example, has the status of physician unless he be duly licensed. A foreman is not such until appointed by proper authority. The heavy soprano is not a prima donna in more than temperament until formally cast for the part by the director of the opera. For each of these particular positions there is also an expected technical competence. Neither the formal nor the technical qualifications are, in all cases, so clear. Many statuses, such as membership in a social class, are not determined in a formal way. Other statuses are ill-defined both as to the characteristics which determine identification with them and as to their duties and rights.

There tends to grow up about a status, in addition to its specifically determining traits, a complex of auxiliary characteristics which come to be expected of its incumbents. It seems entirely natural to Roman Catholics that all priests should be men, although piety seems more common among women. In this case the expectation is supported by formal rule. Most doctors, engineers, lawyers, professors, managers, and supervisors in industrial plants are men, although no law requires that they be so. If one takes a series of characteristics, other than medical skill and a license to practice it, which individuals in our society may have, and then thinks of physicians possessing them in various combinations, it becomes apparent that some of the combinations seem more natural and are more acceptable than others to the great body of potential patients. Thus a white, male, Protestant physician of old American stock and of a family of at least moderate social standing would be acceptable to patients of almost any social category in this country. To be sure, a Catholic might prefer a physician of his own faith for reasons of spiritual comfort. A few ardent feminists, a few race-conscious Negroes, a few militant sectarians, might follow their principles to the extent of seeking a physician of their own category. On the other hand, patients who identify themselves with the "old stock" may, in an emergency, take the first physician who turns up.[2]

If the case is serious, patients may seek a specialist of some strange or disliked social category, letting the reputation for special skill override other traits. The line may be crossed also when some physician acquires such renown that his office becomes something of a shrine, a place of wonderful, last-resort cures. Even the color line is not a complete bar to such a reputation. On the contrary, it may add piquancy to the treatment of a particularly enjoyed malady or lend hope to the quest for a cure of an "incurable" ailment. Allowing for such exceptions, it remains probably true that the white, male, Protestant physician of old American stock, although he may easily fail to get a clientele at all, is categorically acceptable to a greater variety of patients than is he who departs, in one or more particulars, from this type.

It is more exact to say that, if one were to imagine patients of the various possible combinations of these same characteristics (race, sex, religion, ethnic background, family standing), such a physician could treat patients of any of the resulting categories without a feeling by the physician, patient, or the surrounding social circle that the situation was unusual or shocking. One has only to make a sixteen-box table showing physicians of the possible combinations of race (white and Negro) and sex with patients of the possible combinations to see that the white male is the only resulting kind of physician to whom patients of all the kinds are completely accessible in our society (see Table I).

*Table 1\**

| | PHYSICIAN | | | |
|---|---|---|---|---|
| PATIENT | WHITE MALE | WHITE FEMALE | NEGRO MALE | NEGRO FEMALE |
| White male | | | | |
| White female | | | | |
| Negro male | | | | |
| Negro female | | | | |

\* I have not used this table in any study of preferences but should be glad if anyone interested were to do so with selected groups of people.

One might apply a similar analysis to situations involving other positions, such as the foreman and the worker, the teacher and the pupil. Each case may be complicated by adding other categories of persons with whom the person of the given position has to deal. The teacher, in practice, has dealings not only with pupils but with parents, school boards, other public functionaries, and, finally, his own colleagues. Immediately one tries to make this analysis, it becomes clear that a characteristic which might not interfere with some of the situations of a given position may interfere with others.

I do not maintain that any considerable proportion of people do consciously put together in a systematic way their expectations of persons of given positions. I suggest, rather, that people carry in their minds a set of expectations concerning the auxiliary traits properly associated with many of the specific positions available in our society. These expectations appear as advantages or disadvantages to persons who, in keeping with American social belief and practice, aspire to positions new to persons of their kind.

The expected or "natural" combinations of auxiliary characteristics become embodied in the stereotypes of ordinary talk, cartoons, fiction, the radio, and the motion picture. Thus, the American Catholic priest, according to a popular stereotype, is Irish, athletic, and a good sort who with difficulty refrains from profanity in the presence of evil and who may punch someone in the nose if the work of the Lord demands it. Nothing could be farther from the French or French-Canadian stereotype of the good priest. The surgeon, as he appears in advertisements for insurance and pharmaceutical products, is handsome, socially poised, and young of face but gray about the temples. These public, or publicity, stereotypes—while they do not necessarily correspond to the facts or determine peoples expectations—are at least significant in that they rarely let the persons in the given position have any strikes against him. Positively, they represent someone's ideal conception; negatively, they take care not to shock, astonish, or put doubts into the mind of a public whose confidence is sought.

If we think especially of occupational status, it is in the colleague-group or fellow-worker group that the expectations concerning appropriate auxiliary characteristics are worked most intricately into sentiment and conduct. They become, in fact, the basis of the colleague-group's definition of its common interests, of its informal code, and of selection of those who become the inner fraternity—three aspects of occupational life so closely related that few people separate them in thought or talk.

The epithets "hen doctor," "boy wonder," "bright young men," and "brain trust" express the hostility of colleagues to persons who deviate from the expected type. The members of a colleague-group have a common interest in the whole configuration of things which control the number of potential candidates for their occupation. Colleagues, be it remembered, are also competitors. A rational demonstration that an individual's chances for continued success are not jeopardized by an extension of the recruiting field for the position he has or hopes to attain, or by some short-cutting of usual lines of promotion, does not, as a rule, liquidate the fear and hostility aroused by such a case. Oswald Hall found that physicians do not like one of their number to become a consultant too soon.[3] Consulting is something for the crowning, easing-off years of a career; something to intervene briefly between high power and high blood-pressure. He who pushes for such practice too early shows an "aggressiveness" which is almost certain to be punished. It is a threat to an order of things which physicians—at least, those of the fraternity of successful men—count upon. Many of the specific rules of the game of an occupation become comprehensible only when viewed as the almost instinctive attempts of a group of people to cushion themselves against the hazards of their careers. The advent of colleague-competitors of some new and peculiar type, or by some new route, is likely to arouse anxieties. For one thing, one cannot be quite sure how "new people"—new in kind—will act in the various contingencies which arise to test the solidarity of the group.[4]

How the expectations of which we are thinking become embodied in codes may be illustrated by the dilemma of a young woman who became a member of that virile profession, engineering. The designer of an airplane is expected to go up on the maiden flight of the first plane built according to the design. He (*sic*) then gives a dinner to the engineers and workmen who worked on the new plane. The dinner is naturally a stag party. The young woman in question designed a plane. Her co-workers urged her not to take the risk—for which, presumably, men only are fit—of the maiden voyage. They were, in effect, asking her to be a lady rather than an engineer. She chose to be an engineer. She then gave the party and paid for it like a man. After food and the first round of toasts, she left like a lady.

Part of the working code of a position is discretion; it allows the colleagues to exchange confidences concerning their relations to other people. Among these confidences one finds expressions of cynicism concerning their mission, their competence, and the foibles of their superiors, themselves, their clients, their subordinates, and the public at large. Such expressions take the burden from one's shoulders and serve as a defense as well. The unspoken mutual confidence necessary to them rests on two assumptions concerning one's fellows. The first is that the colleague will not misunderstand; the second is that he will not repeat to uninitiated ears. To be sure that a new fellow will not misunderstand requires a sparring match of social gestures. The zealot who turns the sparring match into a real battle, who takes a friendly initiation too seriously, is not likely to be trusted with the lighter sort of comment on one's work or with doubts and misgivings; nor can he learn those parts of the working code which are communicated only by hint and gesture. He is not to be trusted, for though he is not fit for stratagems, he is suspected of being prone to treason. In order that men may communicate freely and confidentially, they must be able to take a good deal of each other's sentiments for granted. They must feel easy about their silences as well as about their utterances. These factors conspire to make colleagues, with a large body of unspoken understandings, uncomfortable in the presence of what they consider odd kinds of fellows. The person who is the first of his kind to attain a certain status is often not drawn into the informal brotherhood in which experiences are exchanged, competence built up, and the formal code elaborated and enforced. He thus remains forever a marginal man.

Now it is a necessary consequence of the high degree of individual mobility in America that there should be large numbers of people of new kinds turning up in various positions. In spite of this and in spite of American heterogeneity, this remains a white, Anglo-Saxon, male, Protestant culture in many respects. These are the expected characteristics for many favored statuses and positions. When we speak of racial, religious, sex, and ethnic prejudices, we generally assume that people with these favored qualities are not the objects thereof. In the stereotyped prejudices concerning others, there is usually contained the assumption that these other people are peculiarly adapted to the particular places which they have held up to the present time; it is a corollary implication that they are not quite fit for new positions to which they may aspire. In general, advance of a new group—women, Negroes, some ethnic groups, etc.—to a new level of positions is not accompanied by complete disappearance of such stereotypes but only by some modification of them. Thus, in Quebec the idea that French-Canadians were good only for unskilled industrial work was followed by the notion that they were especially good at certain kinds of skilled work but were not fit to repair machines or to supervise the work of others. In this series of modifications the structure of qualities expected for the most-favored positions remains intact. But the forces which make for mobility continue to create marginal people on new frontiers.

Technical changes also break up configurations of expected status characteristics by altering the occupations about which they grow up. A new machine or a new managerial device—such as the assembly line—may create new positions or break old ones up into numbers of new ones. The length of training may be changed thereby and, with it, the whole traditional method of forming the person to the social demands of a colleague-group. Thus, a snip of a girl is trained in a few weeks to be a "machinist" on a practically foolproof lathe; thereby the old foolproof machinist, who was initiated slowly into the skills and attitudes of the trade, is himself made a fool of in his own eyes or—worse—in the eyes of his wife, who hears that a neighbor's daughter is a machinist who makes nearly as much money as he. The new positions created by technical changes may, for a time, lack definition as a status. Both the technical and the auxiliary qualifications may be slow in taking form. The personnel man offers a good example. His title is perhaps twenty years old, but the expectations concerning his qualities and functions are still in flux.[5]

Suppose we leave aside the problems which arise from technical changes, as such, and devote the rest of this discussion to the consequences of the appearance of new kinds of people in established positions. Every such occurrence produces, in some measure, a status contradiction. It may also create a status dilemma for the individual concerned and for other people who have to deal with him.

The most striking illustration in our society is offered by the Negro who qualifies for one of the traditional professions. Membership in the Negro race, as defined in American mores and/or law, may be called a master status-determining trait. It tends to overpower, in most crucial situations, any other characteristics which might run counter to it. But professional standing is also a powerful characteristic—most so in the specific relationships of professional practice, less so in the general intercourse of people. In the person of the professionally qualified Negro these two powerful characteristics clash. The dilemma, for those whites who meet such a person, is that of having to choose whether to treat him as a Negro or as a member of his profession.

The white person in need of professional services, especially medical, might allow him to act as doctor in an emergency. Or it may be allowed that a Negro physician is endowed with some uncanny skill. In either case, the white client of ordinary American social views would probably avoid any nonprofessional contacts with the Negro physician.[6] In fact, one way of reducing status conflict is to keep the relationship formal and specific. This is best done by walking through a door into a place designed for the specific relationship, a door which can be firmly closed when one leaves. A common scene in fiction depicts a lady of degree seeking, veiled and alone, the address of the fortuneteller or the midwife of doubtful practice in an obscure corner of the city. The anonymity of certain sections of cities allows people to seek specialized services, legitimate but embarrassing as well as illegitimate, from persons with whom they would not want to be seen by members of their own social circle.

Some professional situations lend themselves more than others to such quarantine. The family physician and the pediatrician cannot be so easily isolated as some other specialists. Certain legal services can be sought indirectly by being delegated to some queer and unacceptable person by the family lawyer. At the other extreme is school teaching, which is done in full view of the community and is generally expected to be accompanied by an active role in community activities. The teacher, unlike the lawyer, is expected to be an example to her charges.

For the white colleagues of the Negro professional man the dilemma is even more severe. The colleague-group is ideally a brotherhood; to have within it people who cannot, given one's other attitudes, be accepted as brothers is very uncomfortable. Furthermore, professional men are much more sensitive than they like to admit about the company in which non-professionals see them. The dilemma arises from the fact that, while it is bad for the profession to let laymen see rifts in their ranks, it may be bad for the individual to be associated in the eyes of his actual or potential patients with persons, even colleagues, of so despised a group as the Negro. The favored way of avoiding the dilemma is to shun contacts with the Negro professional. The white physician or surgeon of assured reputation may solve the problem by acting as consultant to Negro colleagues in Negro clinics and hospitals.

For the Negro professional man there is also a dilemma. If he accepts the role of Negro to the extent of appearing content with less than full equality and intimacy with his white colleagues, for the sake of such security and advantage as can be so got, he himself and others may accuse him of sacrificing his race. Given the tendency of whites to say that any Negro who rises to a special position is an exception, there is a strong temptation for such a Negro to seek advantage by fostering the idea that he is unlike others of his race. The devil who specializes in this temptation is a very insinuating fellow; he keeps a mailing list of "marginal men" of all kinds and origins. Incidentally, one of the by-products of American mores is the heavy moral burden which this temptation puts upon the host of Americans who have by great effort risen from (sic) groups which are the objects of prejudice.

There may be cases in which the appearance in a position of one or a few individuals of a kind not expected there immediately dissolves the auxiliary expectations which make him appear odd. This is not, however, the usual consequence. The expectations usually continue to exist, with modifications and with exceptions allowed.

A common solution is some elaboration of social segregation. The woman lawyer may become a lawyer to women clients, or she may specialize in some kind of legal service in keeping with woman's role as guardian of the home and of morals. Women physicians may find a place in those specialties of which only women and children have need. A female electrical engineer was urged by the dean of the school from which she had just been graduated to accept a job whose function was to give the "woman's angle" to design of household electrical appliances. The Negro professional man finds his clients among Negroes. The Negro sociologist generally studies race relations and teaches in a Negro college. A new figure on the American scene is the Negro personnel man in industries which have started employing Negro workers. His functions are to adjust difficulties of Negro workers, settle minor clashes between the races, and to interpret management's policies to the Negro as well as to present and explain the Negro's point of view to management. It is a difficult job. Our interest for the moment, however, is in the fact that the Negro, promoted to this position, acts only with reference to Negro employees. Many industries have had women personnel officials to act with reference to women. In one sense, this is an extension of the earlier and still existing practice of hiring from among a new ethnic group in industry a "straw boss" to look after them. The "straw boss" is the liaison officer reduced to lowest terms.

Another solution, which also results in a kind of isolation if not in segregation, is that of putting the new people in the library or laboratory, where they get the prestige of research people but are out of the way of patients and the public. Recently, industries have hired a good many Negro chemists to work in their testing and research laboratories. The chemist has few contacts with the production organization. Promotion within the laboratory will put the Negro in charge of relatively few people, and those few will be of his own profession. Such positions do not ordinarily lead to the positions of corresponding importance in the production organization. They offer a career line apart from the main streams of promotion to power and prestige.

These solutions reduce the force of status contradiction by keeping the new person apart from the most troublesome situations. One of the consequences is that it adds new stories to the superstructure of segregation. The Negro hospital and medical school are the formal side of this. The Negro personnel man and foreman show it within the structure of existing institutions. There are evidences that physicians of various ethnic groups are being drawn into a separate medical system of hospitals, clinics, and schools, partly because of the interest of the Roman Catholic church in developing separate institutions but also partly because of the factors here discussed. It is doubtful whether women will develop corresponding separate systems to any great extent. In all of these cases, it looks as if the highest point which a member of these odd groups may attain is determined largely by the number of people of his own group who are in a position to seek his services or in a position such that he may be assigned by other authority to act professionally with reference to them. On the other hand, the kind of segregation involved may lead professional people, or others advanced to special positions, to seek—as compensation—monopoly over such functions with reference to their own group.

Many questions are raised by the order of things here discussed. One is that of the place of these common solutions of status conflict in the evolution of the relations between the sexes, the races, and the ethnic groups of our society. In what circumstances can the person who is accepted formally into a new status, and then informally kept within the limits of the kind mentioned, step out of these limits and become simply a lawyer, foreman, or whatever? Under what circumstances, if ever, is the "hen doctor" simply a doctor? And who are the first to accept her as such—her colleagues or her patients? Will the growth of a separate superstructure over each of the segregated bottom groups of our society tend to perpetuate indefinitely the racial and ethnic division already existing, or will these superstructures lose their identity in the general organization of society? These are the larger questions.

The purpose of the paper, however, is not to answer these large questions. It is rather to call attention to this characteristic phenomenon of our heterogeneous and changing society and to suggest that it become part of the frame of reference of those who are observing special parts of the American social structure.

## REFERENCES

1. "Status" is here taken in its strict sense as a defined social position for whose incumbents there are defined rights, limitations of rights, and duties. See the *Oxford Dictionary* and any standard Latin lexicon. Since statuses tend to form a hierarchy, the term itself has—since Roman times—had the additional meaning of rank.
2. A Negro physician, driving through northern Indiana, came upon a crowd standing around a man just badly injured in a road accident. The physician tended the man and followed the ambulance which took him to the hospital. The hospital authorities tried to prevent the physician from entering the hospital for even long enough to report to staff physicians what he had done for the patient. The same physician, in answer to a Sunday phone call asking him to visit a supposedly very sick woman, went to a house. When the person who answered the door saw that the physician was a Negro, she insisted that they had not called for a doctor and that no one in the house was sick. When he insisted on being paid, the people in the house did so, thereby revealing their lie. In the first instance, an apparently hostile crowd accepted the Negro as a physician because of urgency. In the second, he was refused presumably because the emergency was not great enough.
3. Oswald Hall, "The Informal Organization of Medical Practice" (unpublished Ph.D. dissertation, University of Chicago, 1944).
4. It may be that those whose positions are insecure and whose hopes for the higher goals are already fading express more violent hostility to "new people." Even if so, it must be remembered that those who are secure and successful have the power to exclude or check the careers of such people by merely failing to notice them.
5. The personnel man also illustrates another problem which I do not propose to discuss in this paper. It is that of an essential contradiction between the various functions which are united in one position. The personnel man is expected to communicate the

mind of the workers to management and then to interpret management to the workers. This is a difficult assignment. The problem is well stated by William F. Whyte, in "Pity the Personnel Man," *Advanced Management,* October-December, 1944, pp. 154–58. The Webbs analyzed the similar dilemma of the official of a successful trade-union in their *History of Trade-Unionism* (rev. ed.; London: Longmans, Green, 1920).

6. The Negro artist can be treated as a celebrity. It is within the code of social tuft-hunting that one may entertain, with a kind of affected Bohemian intimacy, celebrities who, on all counts other than their artistic accomplishments, would be beyond the pale.


# THE ROLE-SET: PROBLEMS IN SOCIOLOGICAL THEORY * (*Merton*)

## The Problematics of the Role-Set

However much they may differ in other respects, contemporary socio-logical theorists are largely at one in adopting the premise that social statuses and social roles comprise major building blocks of social structure. This has been the case, since the influential writings of Ralph Linton on the subject, a generation ago. By status, and T. H. Marshall has indicated the great diversity of meanings attached to this term since the time of Maine,[1] Linton meant a position in a social system involving designated rights and obligations; by role, the behaviour oriented to these patterned expectations of others. In these terms, status and roles become concepts serving to connect culturally defined expectations with the patterned conduct and relationships which make up a social structure. Linton went on to state the long recognized and basic fact that each person in society inevitably occupies multiple statuses and that each of these statuses has an associated role.

It is at this point that I find it useful to depart from Linton's conception. The difference is initially a small one, some might say so small as not to deserve notice, but it involves a shift in the angle of vision which leads, I believe, to successively greater differences of a fundamental kind. Unlike Linton, I begin with the premise that each social status involves not a single associated role, but an array of roles. This basic feature of social structure can be registered by the distinctive but not formidable term, role-set. To repeat, then, by role-set I mean that complement of role-relationships in which persons are involved by virtue of occupying a particular social status. Thus, in our current studies of medical schools,[2] we have begun with the

* Reprinted by permission from *The British Journal of Sociology,* VIII, June, 1957, and by permission of the author. Copyright, 1957, Routledge & Kegan Paul.

view that the status of medical student entails not only the role of a student *vis-à-vis* his teachers, but also an array of other roles relating him diversely to other students, physicians, nurses, social workers, medical technicians, and the like. Again, the status of school teacher in the United States has its distinctive role-set, in which are found pupils, colleagues, the school principal and superintendent, the Board of Education, professional associations, and, on occasion, local patriotic organizations.

It should be made plain that the role-set differs from what sociologists have long described as "multiple roles." By established usage, the term multiple role refers not to the complex of roles associated with a single social status, but with the various social statuses (often, in differing institutional spheres) in which people find themselves—for illustration, the statuses of physician, husband, father, professor, church elder, Conservative Party member and army captain. (This complement of distinct statuses of a person, each of these in turn having its own role-set, I would designate as a status-set. This concept gives rise to its own range of analytical problems which cannot be considered here.)

The notion of the role-set reminds us, in the unlikely event that we need to be reminded of this obstinate fact, that even the seemingly simple social structure is fairly complex. All societies face the functional problem of articulating the components of numerous role-sets, the functional problem of managing somehow to organize these so that an appreciable degree of social regularity obtains, sufficient to enable most people most of the time to go about their business of social life, without encountering extreme conflict in their role-sets as the normal, rather than the exceptional, state of affairs.

If this relatively simple idea of role-set has any theoretical worth, it should at the least generate distinctive problems for sociological theory, which come to our attention only from the perspective afforded by this idea, or by one like it. This the notion of role-set does. It raises the general problem of identifying the social mechanisms which serve to articulate the expectations of those in the role-set so that the occupant of a status is confronted with less conflict than would obtain if these mechanisms were not at work. It is to these social mechanisms that I would devote the rest of this discussion.

Before doing so, I should like to recapitulate the argument thus far. We depart from the simple idea, unlike that which has been rather widely assumed, that a single status in society involves, not a single role, but an array of associated roles, relating the status-occupant to diverse others. Secondly, we note that this structural fact, expressed in the term role-set, gives rise to distinctive analytical problems and to corresponding questions for empirical inquiry. The basic problem, which I deal with here, is that of identifying social mechanisms, that is, processes having designated effects for designated parts of social structure, which serve to articulate the role-set more nearly than would be the case, if these mechanisms did not operate. Third, unlike the problems centred upon the notion of "multiple roles," this one is concerned with social arrangements integrating the expectations of those in the role-set; it is not primarily concerned with the familiar problem of how the occupant of a status manages to cope with the many, and sometimes conflicting, demands made of him. It is thus a problem of social structure, not an exercise in the no doubt important but different problem of how individuals happen to deal with the complex structures of relations in which they find themselves. Finally, by way of setting the analytical problem, the logic of analysis  exhibited in this case is developed wholly in terms of the elements of social structure, rather than in terms of providing concrete historical description of a social system.

All this presupposes, of course, that there is always a *potential* for differing and sometimes conflicting expectations of the conduct appropriate to a status-occupant among those in the role-set. The basic source of this potential for conflict, I suggest—and here we are at one with theorists as disparate as Marx and Spencer, Simmel and Parsons—is that the members of a role-set are, to some degree, apt to hold social positions differing from that of the occupant of the status in question. To the extent that they are diversely located in the social structure, they are apt to have interests and sentiments, values and moral expectations differing from those of the status-occupant himself. This, after all, is one of the principal assumptions of Marxist theory, as it is of all sociological theory: social differentiation generates distinct interests among those variously located in the structure of the society. To continue with one of our examples: the members of a school board are often in social and economic strata which differ greatly from that of the school teacher; and their interests, values and expectations are consequently apt to differ, to some extent, from those of the teacher. The teacher may thus become subject to conflicting role-expectations among such members of his role-set as professional colleagues, influential members of the school board, and, say, the Americanism Committee of the American Legion. What is an educational essential for the one may be judged as an education frill, or as downright subversion, by the other. These disparate and contradictory evaluations by members of the role-set greatly complicate the task of coping with them all. The familiar case of the teacher may be taken as paradigmatic. What holds conspicuously for this one status holds, in varying degree, for the occupants of all other statuses who are structurally related, through their role-set, to others who themselves occupy diverse positions in society.

This, then, is the basic structural basis for potential disturbance of a role-set. And it gives rise, in turn, to a double question: which social mechanisms, if any, operate to counteract such instability of role-sets and, correlatively, under which circumstances do these social mechanisms fail to operate, with resulting confusion and conflict. This is not to say, of course, that role-sets do invariably operate with substantial efficiency. We are concerned here, not with a broad historical generalization to the effect that social order prevails, but with an analytical problem of identifying social mechanisms which produce a greater degree of order than would obtain, if these mechanisms were not called into play. Otherwise put, it is theoretical sociology, not history, which is of interest here.

## Social Mechanisms Articulating Role-Sets

1. *Relative Importance of Various Statuses.* The first of these mechanisms derives from the oft-noticed sociological circumstance that social structures designate certain statuses as having greater importance than others. Family and job obligations, for example, are defined in American society as having priority over membership in voluntary associations.[3] As a result, a particular role-relationship may be of peripheral concern for some; for others it may be central. Our hypothetical teacher, for whom this status holds primary significance, may by this circumstance be better able to withstand the demands for conformity with the differing expectations of those comprising his role-set. For at least some of these others, the relationship has only peripheral significance. This does not mean, of course, that teachers are not vulnerable to demands which are at odds with their own professional commitments. It means only that when powerful members of their role-set are only little concerned with this particular relationship, teachers are less vulnerable than they would otherwise be (or sometimes are). Were all those involved in the role-set *equally* concerned with this relationship, the plight of the teacher would be considerably more sorrowful than it often is. What holds for the particular case of the teacher presumably holds for the occupants of other statuses: the impact upon them of diverse expectations among those in their role-set is mitigated by the basic structural fact of differentials of involvement in the relationship among those comprising their role-set.

2. *Differences of Power of Those in the Role-Set.* A second potential

mechanism for stabilizing the role-set is found in the distribution of power and authority. By power, in this connection, is meant the observed and predictable capacity to impose one's will in a social action, even against the opposition of others taking part in that action; by authority, the culturally legitimized organization of power.

As a consequence of social stratification, the members of a role-set are not apt to be equally powerful in shaping the behaviour of status-occupants. However, it does not follow that the individuals, group, or stratum in the role-set which are *separately* most powerful uniformly succeed in imposing their demands upon the status-occupant, say, the teacher. This would be so only in the circumstance that the one member of the role-set has either a monopoly of power in the situation or outweighs the combined power of the others. Failing this special but, of course, not infrequent, situation, there may develop *coalitions of power* among some members of the role-set which enable the status-occupants to go their own way. The familiar pattern of a balance of power is of course not confined to the conventionally-defined political realm. In less easily visible form, it can be found in the workings of role-sets generally, as the boy who succeeds in having his father's decision offset his mother's opposed decision has ample occasion to know. To the extent that conflicting powers in his role-set neutralize one another, the status-occupant has relative freedom to proceed as he intended in the first place.

Thus, even in those potentially unstable structures in which the members of a role-set hold contrasting expectations of what the status-occupant should do, the latter is not wholly at the mercy of the most powerful among them. Moreover, the structural variations of engagement in the role-structure, which I have mentioned, can serve to reinforce the relative power of the status-occupant. For to the extent that powerful members of his role-set are not centrally concerned with this particular relationship, they will be the less motivated to exercise their potential power to the full. Within varying margins of his activity, the status-occupant will then be free to act as he would.

Once again, to reiterate that which lends itself to misunderstanding, I do not say that the status-occupant subject to conflicting expectations among members of his role-set is in fact immune to control by them. I suggest only that the power and authority-structure of role-sets is often such that he has a larger measure of autonomy than he would have had if this structure of competing power did not obtain.

3. *Insulation of Role-Activities from Observability by Members of the Role-Set.* People do not engage in continuous interaction with all those in

their role-sets. This is not an incidental fact, to be ignored because familiar, but one integral to the operation of social structure. Interaction with each member of a role-set tends to be variously intermittent. This fundamental fact allows for role-behaviour which is at odds with the expectations of some in the role-set to proceed without undue stress. For, as I elsewhere suggest at some length,[4] effective social control presupposes social arrangements making for the observability of behaviour. (By observability, a conception which I have borrowed from Simmel and tried to develop, I mean the extent to which social norms and role-performances can readily become known to others in the social system. This is, I believe, a variable crucial to structural analysis, a belief which I cannot, unhappily, undertake to defend here.)

To the extent that the social structure insulates the individual from having his activities known to members of his role-set, he is the less subject to competing pressures. It should be emphasized that we are dealing here with structural arrangements for such insulation, not with the fact that this or that person *happens* to conceal part of his role-behaviour from others. The structural fact is that social statuses differ in the extent to which the conduct of those in them are regularly insulated from observability by members of the role-set. Some have a functionally significant insulation of this kind, as for example, the status of the university teacher, insofar as norms hold that what is said in the classroom is privileged. In this familiar type of case, the norm clearly has the function of maintaining some degree of autonomy for the teacher. For if they were forever subject to observation by all those in the role-set, with their often differing expectations, teachers might be driven to teach not what they know or what the evidence leads them to believe, but to teach what will placate the numerous and diverse people who are ostensibly concerned with "the education of youth." That this sometimes occurs is evident. But it would presumably be more frequent, were it not for the relative exemption from observability by all and sundry who may wish to impose their will upon the instructor.

More broadly, the concept of privileged information and confidential communication in the professions has this same function of insulating clients from observability of their behaviour and beliefs by others in their role-set. Were physicians or priests free to tell all they have learned about the private lives of their clients, the needed information would not be forthcoming and they could not adequately discharge their functions. More generally, if all the facts of one's conducts and beliefs were freely available to anyone, social structures could not operate. What is often described as "the need for privacy"—that is, insulation of actions and beliefs from surveillance by others—is the individual counterpart to the functional requirement of social structure that some measure of exemption from full observability be provided. "Privacy" is not only a personal predilection, though it may be that, too. It is also a requirement of social systems which must provide for a measure, as they say in France, of *quant-à-soi,* a portion of the self which is kept apart; immune from observation by others.

Like other social mechanisms, this one of insulation from full observability can, of course, miscarry. Were the activities of the politician or, if one prefers, the statesman, fully removed from the public spotlight, social control of his behaviour would be correspondingly reduced. And as we all know, anonymous power anonymously exercised does not make for a stable social structure meeting the values of a society. So, too, the teacher or physician who is largely insulated from observability may fail to live up to the minimum requirements of his status. All this means only that some measure of observability of role-performance by members of the role-set is required, if the indispensable social requirement of accountability is to be met. This statement does not contradict an earlier statement to the effect that some measure of insulation from observability is also required for the effective operation of social structures. Instead, the two statements, taken in conjunction, imply that there is an optimum zone of observability, difficult to identify in precise terms and doubtless varying for different social statuses, which will simultaneously make both for accountability and for substantial autonomy, rather than for a frightened acquiescence with the distribution of power which happens, at a particular moment, to obtain in the role-set.

4. *Observability of Conflicting Demands by Members of a Role-Set.* This mechanism is implied by what has been said and therefore needs only passing comment here. As long as members of the role-set are happily ignorant that their demands upon the occupants of a status are incompatible, each member may press his own case. The pattern is then many against one. But when it becomes plain that the demands of some are in full contradiction with the demands of others, it becomes, in part, the task of members of the role-set, rather than that of the status-occupant, to resolve these contradictions, either by a struggle for over-riding power or by some degree of compromise.

In such circumstances, the status-occupant subjected to conflicting demands often becomes cast in the role of the *tertius gaudens,* the third (or more often, the *n*th) party who draws advantage from the conflict of the others. Originally at the focus of the conflict, he can virtually become a bystander whose function it is to highlight the conflicting demands being made by members of his role-set. It becomes a problem for them, rather than for him, to resolve their contradictory demands. At the least, this serves to make evident that it is not wilful misfeasance on his part which keeps him from conforming to all the contradictory expectations imposed upon him.[5] When most effective, this serves to articulate the expectations of those in the role-set beyond a degree which would occur, if this mechanism of making contradictory expectations manifest were not at work.

5. *Mutual Social Support among Status-Occupants.* Whatever he may believe to the contrary, the occupant of a social status is not alone. The very fact that he is placed in a social position means that there are others more or less like-circumstanced. To this extent, the actual or potential experience of facing a conflict of expectations among members of the role-set is variously common to all occupants of the status. The particular persons subject to these conflicts need not, therefore, meet them as wholly private problems which must be coped with in wholly private fashion.

It is this familiar and fundamental fact of social structure, of course, which is the basis for those in the same social status forming the associations intermediate to the individual and the larger society in a pluralistic system. These organizations constitute a structural response to the problems of coping with the (potentially or actually) conflicting demands by those in the role-sets of the status.[6] Whatever the intent, these constitute social formations serving to counter the power of the role-set; of being, not merely amenable to its demands, but of helping to shape them. Such organizations— so familiar a part of the social landscape of differentiated societies—also develop normative systems which are designed to anticipate and thereby to mitigate such conflicting expectations. They provide social support to the individuals in the status under attack. They minimize the need for their improvising personal adjustments to patterned types of conflicting expectations. Emerging codes which state in advance what the socially-supported conduct of the status-occupant should be, also serve this social function. This function becomes all the more significant in the structural circumstances when status-occupants are highly vulnerable to pressures from their role-set because they are relatively isolated from one another. Thus, thousands of librarians sparsely distributed among the towns and villages of America and not infrequently subject to censorial pressures received strong support from the code on censorship developed by the American Library Association.[7] This only illustrates the general mechanisms whereby status-peers curb the pressures exerted upon them individually by drawing upon the organizational and normative support of their peers.

6. *Abridging the Role-Set.* There is, of course, a limiting case in the modes of coping with incompatible demands by the role-set. Role-relations

are broken off, leaving a greater consensus of role-expectations among those who remain. But this mode of adaptation by amputating the role-set is possible only under special and limited conditions. It can be effectively utilized only in those circumstances where it is still possible for status-occupants to perform their other roles, without the support of those with whom they have discontinued relations. It presupposes that the social structure provides this option. By and large, however, this option is infrequent and limited, since the composition of the role-set is ordinarily not a matter of personal choice but a matter of the social organization in which the status is embedded. More typically, the individual goes, and the social structure remains.

## *Residual Conflict in the Role-Set*

Doubtless, these are only some of the mechanisms which serve to articulate the expectations of those in the role-set. Further inquiry will uncover others, just as it will probably modify the preceding account of those we have provisionally identified. But, however much the substance may change, I believe that the logic of the analysis will remain largely intact. This can be briefly recapitulated.

First, it is assumed that each social status has its organized complement of role-relationships which can be thought of as comprising a role-set. Second, relationships hold not only the between occupant of the particular status and each member of the role-set, but always potentially and often actually, between members of the role-set itself. Third, to the extent that members of the role-set themselves hold substantially differing statuses, they will tend to have some differing expectations (moral and actuarial) of the conduct appropriate for the status-occupant. Fourth, this gives rise to the sociological problem of how their diverse expectations become sufficiently articulated for the status-structure and the role-structure to operate with a modicum of effectiveness. Fifth, inadequate articulation of these role-expectations tends to call one or more social mechanisms into play, which serve to reduce the extent of patterned conflict below the level which would be involved if these mechanisms were not at work.

And now, sixth, finally and importantly, even when these (and probably other) mechanisms are operating, they may not, in particular cases, prove sufficient to reduce the conflict of expectations below the level required for the social structure to operate with substantial effectiveness. This residual conflict within the role-set may be enough to interfere materially with the effective performance of roles by the occupant of the status in question. Indeed, it may well turn out that this condition is the most frequent one—role-systems operating at considerably less than full efficiency. Without trying to draw tempting analogies with other types of systems, I suggest only that this is not unlike the case of engines which cannot fully utilize heat energy. If the analogy lacks force, it may nevertheless have the merit of excluding the utopian figment of a perfectly effective social system.

We do not yet know some of the requirements for fuller articulation of the relations between the occupant of a status and members of his role-set, on the one hand, and for fuller articulation of the values and expectations among those comprising the role-set, on the other. As we have seen, even those requirements which can now be identified are not readily satisfied, without fault, in social systems. To the extent that they are not, social systems are forced to limp along with that measure of ineffectiveness and inefficiency which is often accepted because the realistic prospect of decided improvement seems so remote as sometimes not to be visible at all.

REFERENCES

1. T. H. Marshall, 'A note on "status"', in K. M. Kapadia (editor), *Professor Ghurye Felicitation Volume* (Bombay: Popular Book Depot, n.d.), 11–19.
2. R. K. Merton, P. L. Kendall, and G. G. Reader, editors, *The Student-Physician: Introductory Studies in the Sociology of Medical Education* (Cambridge, Mass.: Harvard University Press, 1957).
3. Bernard Barber has drawn out the implications of this structural fact in his study of voluntary associations; see his 'Participation and mass apathy in associations', in A. W. Gouldner, ed., *Studies in Leadership* (New York: Harper & Brothers, 1950), 477–504, especially at 486 ff.
4. Robert K. Merton, *Social Theory and Social Structure* (Glencoe, Illinois: The Free Press, rev. ed., 1957), 336–56. This discussion of role-set draws upon one part of Chapter IX, 'Continuities in the Theory of Reference Groups and Social Structures', 368–84.
5. See the observations by William G. Carr, the executive secretary of the National Education Association, who has summarized some of the conflicting pressures exerted upon school curricula by voluntary organizations, such as the American Legion, the Association for the United Nations, the National Safety Council, the Better Business Bureau, the American Federation of Labour, and the Daughters of the American Revolution. His summary may serve through concrete example to indicate the extent of competing expectations among those in the complex role-set of school superintendents and local school boards in as differentiated a society as our own. Sometimes, Mr. Carr reports, these voluntary organizations 'speak their collective opinions temperately, sometimes scurrilously, but always insistently. They organize contests, drives, collections, exhibits, special days, special weeks, and anniversaries that run all year long.

'They demand that the public schools give more attention to Little League baseball, first aid, mental hygiene, speech correction, Spanish in the first grade, military preparedness, international understanding, modern music, world history, American history, and local history, geography and homemaking, Canada and South America, the Arabs and the Israelis, the Turks and the Greeks, Christopher Columbus and Leif Ericsson, Robert E. Lee and Woodrow Wilson, nutrition, care of the teeth, free enterprise, labour relations, cancer prevention, human relationships, atomic energy, the use of firearms, the Constitution, tobacco, temperance, kindness to animals,

Esperanto, the 3 R's, the 3 C's and the 4 F's, use of the typewriter and legible pen-manship, moral values, physical fitness, ethical concepts, civil defence, religious literacy, thrift, law observance, consumer education, narcotics, mathematics, dra-matics, physics, ceramics, and (that latest of all educational discoveries) phonics.

'Each of these groups is anxious to avoid overloading the curriculum. All any of them ask is that the non-essentials be dropped in order to get their material in. Most of them insist that they do not want a special course—they just want their ideas to permeate the entire daily programme. Every one of them proclaims a firm belief in local control of education and an apprehensive hatred of national control.

'Nevertheless, if their national organization programme in education is not adopted forthwith, many of them use the pressure of the press, the radiance of the radio, and all the props of propaganda to bypass their elected school board.' An address at the inauguration of Hollis Leland Caswell, Teachers College, Columbia University, November 21–2, 1955, 10.

6. In this context, see the acute analysis of the formation of the National Union of Teachers by Asher Tropp, *The School Teachers* (London: Heinemann, 1957).

7. See R. P. McKeon, R. K. Merton and W. Gellhorn, *Freedom to Read* (1957).

# 10: Class

"Class" is an ambiguous term which has been used loosely in everyday parlance and not much more rigorously in some of the technical literature. There is nevertheless a common understanding that class pertains to hierarchical position in the social order and differential distribution of prestige based on that position. It refers to one form of stratification by contrast with another major form, usually called "caste." Class implies mobility, i.e., the possibility of movement up and down the social scale, whereas the mark of caste is a hereditary relationship to other castes which is in principle incapable of change. Caste exists by the Weberian criteria (*connubium* and *commensality*) when intermarriage and intimate social intercourse are prohibited. Class permits, if it does not encourage, these relationships. About this much in the realm of social stratification general agreement could be achieved. The rest would probably give rise to divergent views.

In the final paragraphs of the third volume of his *chef d'oeuvre*, Karl Marx (1818–1883) undertook, too late, to define the word "class." We reproduce that tantalizing passage from *Capital* for two reasons: (1) there is no other attempt known to us in all of Marx's writing to be so explicit about class; (2) the fragment from an unfinished classic indicates that whatever inferential meaning one may impute to a concept that is the very cornerstone of Marxism, Marx himself fully understood its complexity.

It should be said that there are many "Marxes"—and unresolved difficulties or "residual categories," to use Talcott Parsons' term, in all of them. We ought to be aware of at least four incarnations: the young Marx, the mature one, the scholar, and the agitator. As the author of *Capital*, he is also the mature scholar, and something less than that as coauthor of *The German*

*Ideology.* Yet our selection from the earlier work foreshadows that conception of class which we fairly associate with Marx. For him class is much more often than not a condition generated by the economic division of labor and shaped thereafter according to what he called the relations of production. There is much more. There are shadings and nuances. There is above all class conflict. *The Communist Manifesto,* promulgated in 1848 by Marx and Friedrich Engels (1820–1895), asserts that, "The history of all hitherto existing society is the history of class struggles . . . Freeman and slave, patrician and plebeian, lord and serf, guildmaster and journeyman, in a word oppressor and oppressed, stood in constant opposition to one another. . . ."

It is not, however, for formulating and fostering the class struggle that sociological theory owes so much to Marx, but rather for his pointing sharply to the objective reality of social stratification. Marx spoke of *class consciousness* as well as class. He recognized the difference between them, but thought that in time one would inevitably come to "reflect" the other. Max Weber, the titan of German sociology, had a somewhat different definition of class, although it was perhaps not so great a departure from Marx as he supposed. Albert Salomon, a profound German-American sociologist who studied with Weber, has said that his teacher whom he has named "the bourgeois Marx" was engaged in a lifelong dialogue with the ghost of Marx. Weber held that class could be defined in exclusively economic or market terms, and in this there is no basic disagreement with Marx. However, it was his merit carefully to have distinguished class, so defined, from other closely related levels of stratification. The subjective or attitudinal side of this phenomenon Weber calls status and it connotes everything that clusters around honor. For him, as for Thorstein Veblen (1857–1929), status suggests the consumption of goods rather than their production.

Until recently, with the major exception of Thorstein Veblen, American theory touched but fleetingly and superficially on the subject of class. Pitirim Sorokin wrote a useful textbook called *Social Mobility* thirty years ago, but its roots were European. From Italy came the powerful challenge of Gaetano Mosca (1858–1941) and Vilfredo Pareto (1848–1923) to whom stratification was a central and ineradicable fact, and from Germany there emerged a great deal of richly suggestive speculation.

In the United States no one has treated class with such mastery as Veblen who not only used it as the basis for twelve remarkable books but inseminated the thought of nearly all who later discussed the subject. That influence is particularly evident in the earliest and still most valuable community study, the *Middletown* of Robert and Helen M. Lynd.

The literature has been enlivened by an ongoing intramural battle between members of the same sociological school. It turns on the question of whether existing class inequality is positively functional. We will let the principals speak for themselves. The discussion promises to take us forward in an area of the greatest theoretical importance that has been static or retrograde for far too long.

Seymour M. Lipset and Hans L. Zetterberg, theorists of our time, deal creatively with the problem of social mobility in its several complex dimensions.

# THE DEFINITION OF CLASS * (Marx)

The owners of mere labor-power, the owners of capital, and the landlords, whose respective sources of income are wages, profit and ground-rent, in other words, wage laborers, capitalists and landlords, form the three great classes of modern society resting upon the capitalist mode of production.

In England, modern society is indisputably developed most highly and classically in its economic structure. Nevertheless the stratification of classes does not appear in its pure form, even there. Middle and transition stages obliterate even here all definite boundaries, although much less in the rural districts than in the cities. However, this is immaterial for our analysis. We have seen that the continual tendency and law of development of capitalist production is to separate the means of production more and more from labor, and to concentrate the scattered means of production more and more in large groups, thereby transforming labor into wage labor and the means of production into capital. In keeping with this tendency we have, on the other hand, the independent separation of private land from capital and labor,[1] or the transformation of all property in land into a form of landed property corresponding to the capitalist mode of production.

The first question to be answered is this: What constitutes a class? And this follows naturally from another question, namely: What constitutes wage laborers, capitalists and landlords into three great social classes?

At first glance it might seem that the identity of their revenues and their sources of revenue does that. They are three great social groups, whose component elements, the individuals forming them, live on wages, profit

---

* Reprinted from *Capital*, Vol. III, by Karl Marx, edited by Frederick Engels, translated from the first German edition by Ernest Untermann, pp. 1031–1032, Charles H. Kerr & Company, Chicago, Ill., 1909.

and ground-rent, or by the utilization of their labor-power, their capital, and their private land.

However, from this point of view physicians and officials would also form two classes, for they belong to the two distinct social groups, and the revenues of their members flow from the same common source. The same would also be true of the infinite dissipation of interests and positions created by the social division of labor among laborers, capitalists and landlords. For instance, the landlords are divided into owners of vineyards, farms, forest, mines, fisheries.

REFERENCE

1. F. List remarks correctly: "Prevalence of self-management in the case of large estates proves only a lack of civilization, of means of communication, of home industries and rich cities. For this reason it is found everywhere in Russia, Poland, Hungary, Mecklenburg. Formerly it prevailed also in England. But with the rise of commerce and industry came their division into medium-sized farms and their occupancy by tenants." (*The Agrarian Constitution, the Petty Farm, and Emigration,* 1842, p. 10.)

# CLASS AND THE DIVISION OF LABOR *   (*Marx and Engels*)

The relations of different nations among themselves depend upon the extent to which each has developed its productive forces, the division of labour and internal intercourse. This statement is generally recognized. But not only the relation of one nation to others, but also the whole internal structure of the nation itself depends on the stage of development reached by its production and its internal and external intercourse. How far the productive forces of a nation are developed is shown most manifestly by the degree to which the division of labour has been carried. Each new productive force, in so far as it is not merely a quantitative extension of productive forces already known (for instance the bringing into cultivation of fresh land) brings about a further development of the division of labour.

The division of labour inside a nation leads at first to the separation of industrial and commercial from agricultural labour, and hence to the separation of town and country and a clash of interests between them. Its further development leads to the separation of commercial from industrial

* Reprinted from *The German Ideology* by Karl Marx and Friedrich Engels, New York, 1939, pp. 8–12.

labour. At the same time through the division of labour there develop further, inside these various branches, various divisions among the individuals co-operating in definite kinds of labour. The relative position of these individual groups is determined by the methods employed in agriculture, industry and commerce (patriarchalism, slavery, estates, classes). These same conditions are to be seen (given a more developed intercourse) in the relations of different nations to one another.

The various stages of development in the division of labour are just so many different forms of ownership; i.e., the existing stage in the division of labour determines also the relations of individuals to one another with reference to the material, instrument, and product of labour.

The first form of ownership is tribal ownership. It corresponds to the undeveloped stage of production, at which a people lives by hunting and fishing, by the rearing of beasts or, in the highest stage, agriculture. In the latter case it presupposes a great mass of uncultivated stretches of land. The division of labour is at this stage still very elementary and is confined to a further extension of the natural division of labour imposed by the family. The social structure is therefore limited to an extension of the family; patriarchal family chieftains; below them the members of the tribe; finally slaves. The slavery latent in the family only develops gradually with the increase of population, the growth of wants, and with the extension of external relations, of war or of trade.

The second form is the ancient communal and State ownership which proceeds especially from the union of several tribes into a city by agreement or by conquest, and which is still accompanied by slavery. Beside communal ownership we already find movable, and later also immovable, private property developing, but as an abnormal form subordinate to communal ownership. It is only as a community that the citizens hold power over their labouring slaves, and on this account alone, therefore, they are bound to the form of communal ownership. It is the communal private property which compels the active citizens to remain in this natural form of association over against their slaves. For this reason the whole structure of society based on this communal ownership, and with it the power of the people, decays in the same measure as immovable private property evolves. The division of labour is already more developed. We already find the antagonism of town and country; later the antagonism between those states which represent town interests and those which represent country, and inside the towns themselves the antagonism between industry and maritime commerce. The class relation between citizens and slaves is now completely developed.

This whole interpretation of history appears to be contradicted by the fact of conquest. Up till now violence, war, pillage, rape and slaughter, etc., have been accepted as the driving force of history. Here we must limit ourselves to the chief points and take therefore only a striking example—the destruction of an old civilization by a barbarous people and the resulting formation of an entirely new organization of society. (Rome and the barbarians; Feudalism and Gaul; the Byzantine Empire and the Turks.) With the conquering barbarian people war itself is still, as hinted above, a regular form of intercourse, which is the more eagerly exploited as the population increases, involving the necessity of new means of production to supersede the traditional and, for it, the only possible, crude mode of production. In Italy it was, however, otherwise. The concentration of landed property (caused not only by buying-up and indebtedness but also by inheritance, since loose living being rife and marriage rare, the old families died out and their possessions fell into the hands of a few) and its conversion into grazing-land (caused not only by economic forces still operative to-day but by the importation of plundered and tribute-corn and the resultant lack of demand for Italian corn) brought about the almost total disappearance of the free population. The very slaves died out again and again, and had constantly to be replaced by new ones. Slavery remained the basis of the whole productive system. The plebeians, mid-way between freemen and slaves, never succeeded in becoming more than a proletarian rabble. Rome indeed never became more than a city; its connection with the provinces was almost exclusively political and could therefore easily be broken again by political events.

With the development of private property, we find here for the first time the same conditions which we shall find again, only on a more extensive scale, with modern private property. On the one hand the concentration of private property, which began very early in Rome (as the Licinian agrarian law proves) and proceeded very rapidly from the time of the civil wars and especially under the Emperors; on the other hand, coupled with this, the transformation of the plebeian small peasantry into a proletariat, which, however, owing to its intermediate position between propertied citizens and slaves, never achieved an independent development.

The third form of ownership is feudal or estate-property. If antiquity started out from the town and its little territory, the Middle Ages started out from the country. This different starting-point was determined by the sparseness of the population at that time, which was scattered over a large area and which received no large increase from the conquerors. In contrast to Greece and Rome, feudal development therefore extends over a much wider field, prepared by the Roman conquests and the spread of agriculture at first associated with it. The last centuries of the declining Roman Empire and its conquest by the barbarians destroyed a number of productive forces; agriculture had declined, industry had decayed for want of a market, trade had died out or been violently suspended, the rural and urban population had decreased. From these conditions and the mode of organization of the conquest determined by them, feudal property developed under the influence of the Germanic military constitution. Like tribal and communal ownership, it is based again on a community; but the directly producing class standing over against it is not, as in the case of the ancient community, the slaves, but the enserfed small peasantry. As soon as feudalism is fully developed, there also arises antagonism to the towns. The hierarchical system of land ownership, and the armed bodies of retainers associated with it, gave the nobility power over the serfs. This feudal organization was, just as much as the ancient communal ownership, an association against a subjected producing class; but the form of association and the relation to the direct producers were different because of the different conditions of production.

This feudal organization of land-ownership had its counterpart in the towns in the shape of corporative property, the feudal organization of trades. Here property consisted chiefly in the labour of each individual person. The necessity for association against the organized robber-nobility, the need for communal covered markets in an age when the industrialist was at the same time a merchant, the growing competition of the escaped serfs swarming into the rising towns, the feudal structure of the whole country: these combined to bring about the guilds. Further, the gradually accumulated capital of individual craftsmen and their stable numbers, as against the growing population, evolved the relation of journeyman and apprentice, which brought into being in the towns a hierarchy similar to that in the country.

Thus the chief form of property during the feudal epoch consisted on the one hand of landed property with serf-labour chained to it, and on the other of individual labour with small capital commanding the labour of journeymen. The organization of both was determined by the restricted conditions of production—the small-scale and primitive cultivation of the land, and the craft type of industry. There was little division of labour in the heyday of feudalism. Each land bore in itself the conflict of town and country and the division into estates was certainly strongly marked; but apart from the differentiation of princes, nobility, clergy and peasants in the country, and masters, journeymen, apprentices and soon also the rabble of casual labourers in the towns, no division of importance took place. In agriculture it was rendered difficult by the strip-system, beside which the cottage industry of the peasants themselves emerged as another factor. In industry there was no division of labour at all in the individual trades themselves, and very little between them. The separation of industry and commerce was found already in existence in older towns; in the newer it only developed later, when the towns entered into mutual relations.

The grouping of larger territories into feudal kingdoms was a necessity for the landed nobility as for the towns. The organization of the ruling class, the nobility, had, therefore, everywhere a monarch at its head.

The fact is, therefore, that definite individuals who are productively active in a definite way enter into these definite social and political relations. Empirical observation must in each separate instance bring out empirically, and without any mystification and speculation, the connection of the social and political structure with production. The social structure and the State are continually evolving out of the life-process of definite individuals, but of individuals, not as they may appear in their own or other people's imagination, but as they really are, i.e., as they are effective, produce materially, and are active under definite material limits, presuppositions and conditions independent of their will.

## ARE THE PEASANTS A CLASS? * (Marx)

The small peasants form a vast mass, the members of which live in similar conditions, but without entering into manifold relations with one another. Their mode of production isolates them from one another, instead of bringing them into mutual intercourse. The isolation is increased by France's bad means of communication and by the poverty of the peasants. Their field of production, the small holding, admits of no division of labour in its cultivation, no application of science and, therefore, no multiplicity of development, no diversity of talents, no wealth of social relationships. Each individual peasant family is almost self-sufficient; it itself directly produces the major part of its consumption and thus acquires its means of life more through exchange with nature than in intercourse with society. The small holding, the peasant and his family; alongside them another small holding, another peasant and another family. A few score of these make up a village, and a few score of villages make up a Department. In this way, the great

* Reprinted from *The Eighteenth Brumaire of Louis Napoleon*, by Karl Marx. English translation, 1898.

mass of the French nation is formed by simple addition of homologous magnitudes, much as potatoes in a sack form a sackful of potatoes. In so far as millions of families live under economic conditions of existence that divide their mode of life, their interests and their culture from those of the other classes and put them in hostile contrast to the latter, they form a class. In so far as there is merely a local interconnection among these small peasants, and the identity of their interests begets no unity, no national union and no political organisation, they do not form a class. They are consequently incapable of enforcing their class interest in their own name, whether through a parliament or through a convention. They cannot represent themselves, they must be represented. Their representative must at the same time appear as their master, as an authority over them, as an unlimited governmental power, that protects them against the other classes and sends them the rain and the sunshine from above. The political influence of the small peasants, therefore finds its final expression in the executive power subordinating society to itself.

.    .    .

After the first Revolution had transformed the peasants from semi-villeins into freeholders, Napoleon confirmed and regulated the conditions on which they could exploit undisturbed the soil of France which had only just come into their possession and slake their youthful passion for property. But what is now causing the ruin of the French peasant is his dwarf holding itself, the division of the land, the form of property which Napoleon consolidated in France. It is precisely the material conditions which made the feudal peasant into a small peasant and Napoleon into an emperor. Two generations have sufficed to produce the inevitable result: progressive deterioration of agriculture, progressive indebtedness of the agriculturist. The "Napoleonic" form of property, which at the beginning of the nineteenth century was the condition for the liberation and enrichment of the French country folk, has developed in the course of this century as the law of their enslavement and pauperisation. And it is just this law which is the first of the "*idées napoléoniennes*" which the second Bonaparte has to uphold. If he still shares with the peasants the illusion that the cause of their ruin is to be sought not in this small holding property itself but outside it in the influence of secondary causes, then his experiments will burst like soap bubbles when they come into contact with the relations of production.

The economic development of this small holding property has turned the relation of the peasants to the remaining classes of society completely upside down. Under Napoleon, the fragmentation of the land in the countryside supplemented free competition and the beginning of big industry in the towns. [Even the favouring of the peasant class was in the interest of the new bourgeois order. This newly-created class was the many-sided extension of the bourgeois regime beyond the gates of the towns, its realisation on a national scale.] This class was the ubiquitous protest against the landed aristocracy which had just been overthrown.

[If it was favoured above all, it, above all, offered the point of attack for the restoration of the feudal lands.]

The roots that this small holding property struck in French soil deprived feudalism of all nutriment. Its landmarks formed the natural fortifications of the bourgeoisie against any *coup de main* on the part of its old overlords. But in the course of the nineteenth century the feudal lords were replaced by urban usurers; the feudal obligation that went with the land was replaced by the mortgage; aristocratic landed property was replaced by bourgeois capital. The small holding of the peasant is now only the pretext that allows the capitalist to draw profits, interest and rent from the soil, while leaving it to the tiller of the soil himself to see how he can extract his wages. The mortgage debt burdening the soil of France imposes on the French peasantry payment of an amount of interest equal to the annual interest on the entire British national debt. Small holding property, in this enslavement by capital to which its development inevitably pushes forward, has transformed the mass of the French nation into troglodytes. Sixteen million peasants (including women and children) dwell in hovels, a large number of which have but one opening, others only two and the most favoured only three. And windows are to a house what the five senses are to the head. The bourgeois order, which at the beginning of the century set the state to stand guard over the newly arisen small holding and manured it with laurels, has become a vampire that sucks out its blood and marrow and throws them into the alchemistic cauldron of capital. The *Code Napoléon* is now nothing but a *codex* of distraints, forced sales and compulsory auctions. To the four million (including children, etc.) officially recognised paupers, vagabonds, criminals and prostitutes in France, must be added five millions who hover on the margin of existence and either have their haunts in the countryside itself or, with their rags and their children, continually desert the countryside for the towns and the towns for the countryside. The interests of the peasants, therefore, are no longer, as under Napoleon, in accord with, but in opposition to the interests of the bourgeoisie, to capital. Hence the peasants find their natural ally and leader in the *urban proletariat* whose task is the overthrow of the bourgeois order. But *strong and unlimited government*—and this is the second "*idée napoléonienne*," which the second Napoleon has to carry out—is called upon to defend by force this "material" order. This "material order" also serves as the catchword in all Bonaparte's proclamations against the rebellious peasants.

# CLASS AND STATUS *(Weber)

## Economically Determined Power and the Social Order

Law exists when there is a probability that an order will be upheld by a specific staff of men who will use physical or psychical compulsion with the intention of obtaining conformity with the order, or of inflicting sanctions for infringement of it.[1] The structure of every legal order directly influences the distribution of power, economic or otherwise, within its respective community. This is true of all legal orders and not only that of the state. In general, we understand by "power" the chance of a man or of a number of men to realize their own will in a communal action even against the resistance of others who are participating in the action.

"Economically conditioned" power is not, of course, identical with "power" as such. On the contrary, the emergence of economic power may be the consequence of power existing on other grounds. Man does not strive for power only in order to enrich himself economically. Power, including economic power, may be valued "for its own sake." Very frequently the striving for power is also conditioned by the social "honor" it entails. Not all power, however, entails social honor: The typical American Boss, as wll as the typical big speculator, deliberately relinquishes social honor. Quite generally, "mere economic" power, and especially "naked" money power, is by no means a recognized basis of social honor. Nor is power the only basis of social honor. Indeed, social honor, or prestige, may even be the basis of political or economic power, and very frequently has been. Power, as well as honor, may be guaranteed by the legal order, but, at least normally, it is not their primary source. The legal order is rather an additional factor that enhances the chance to hold power or honor; but it cannot always secure them.

The way in which social honor is distributed in a community between typical groups participating in this distribution we may call the "social order." The social order and the economic order are, of course, similarly

* From *From Max Weber: Essays in Sociology,* pp. 180–184, 186–188, edited by H. H. Gerth and C. Wright Mills, copyright, 1946, by Oxford University Press, New York. Reprinted by permission.

related to the "legal order." However, the social and the economic order are not identical. The economic order is for us merely the way in which economic good and services are distributed and used. The social order is of course conditioned by the economic order to a high degree, and in its turn reacts upon it.

Now: "classes," "status groups," and "parties" are phenomena of the distribution of power within a community.

## *Determination of Class-Situation by Market-Situation*

In our terminology, "classes" are not communities; they merely represent possible, and frequent, bases for communal action. We may speak of a "class" when (1) a number of people have in common a specific causal component of their life chances, in so far as (2) this component is represented exclusively by economic interests in the possession of goods and opportunities for income, and (3) is represented under the conditions of the commodity or labor markets. [These points refer to "class situation," which we may express more briefly as the typical chance for a supply of goods, external living conditions, and personal life experiences, in so far as this chance is determined by the amount and kind of power, or lack of such, to dispose of goods or skills for the sake of income in a given economic order. The term "class" refers to any group of people that is found in the same class situation.]

It is the most elemental economic fact that the way in which the disposition over material property is distributed among a plurality of people, meeting competitively in the market for the purpose of exchange, itself creates specific life chances. According to the law of marginal utility this mode of distribution excludes the non-owners from competing for highly valued goods; it favors the owners and, in fact, gives to them a monopoly to acquire such goods. Other things being equal, this mode of distribution monopolizes the opportunities for profitable deals for all those who, provided with goods, do not necessarily have to exchange them. It increases, at least generally, their power in price wars with those who, being propertyless, have nothing to offer but their services in native form or goods in a form constituted through their own labor, and who above all are compelled to get rid of these products in order barely to subsist. This mode of distribution gives to the propertied a monopoly on the possibility of transferring property from the sphere of use as a "fortune," to the sphere of "capital goods"; that is, it gives them the entrepreneurial function and all chances to share directly or indirectly in returns on capital. All this holds true within the area in which pure market conditions prevail. "Property" and "lack of property" are, therefore, the basic categories of all class situations. It does not matter whether these two categories become effective in price wars or in competitive struggles.

Within these categories, however, class situations are further differentiated: on the one hand, according to the kind of property that is usable for returns; and, on the other hand, according to the kind of services that can be offered in the market. Ownership of domestic buildings, productive establishments; warehouses; stores; argiculturally usable land, large and small holdings—quantitative differences with possibly qualitative consequences; ownership of mines; cattle; men (slaves); disposition over mobile instruments of production, or capital goods of all sorts, especially money or objects that can be exchanged for money easily and at any time; disposition over products of one's own labor or of others' labor differing according to their various distances from consumability; disposition over transferable monopolies of any kind—all these distinctions differentiate the class situations of the propertied just as does the "meaning" which they can and do give to the utilization of property, especially to property which has money equivalence. Accordingly, the propertied, for instance, may belong to the class of rentiers or to the class of entrepreneurs.

Those who have no property but who offer services are differentiated just as much according to their kinds of services as according to the way in which they make use of these services, in a continuous or discontinuous relation to a recipient. But always this is the generic connotation of the concept of class: that the kind of chance in the *market* is the decisive moment which presents a common condition for the individual's fate. "Class situation" is, in this sense, ultimately "market situation." The effect of naked possession *per se*, which among cattle breeders gives the non-owning slave or serf into the power of the cattle owner, is only a forerunner of real "class" formation. However, in the cattle loan and in the naked severity of the law of debts in such communities, for the first time mere "possession" as such emerges as decisive for the fate of the individual. This is very much in contrast to the agricultural communities based on labor. The creditor-debtor relation becomes the basis of "class situation" only in those cities where a "credit market," however primitive, with rates interest increasing according to the extent of dearth and a factual monopolization of credits, is developed by a plutocracy. Therewith "class struggles" begin.

Those men whose fate is not determined by the chance of using goods or services for themselves on the market, e.g., slaves, are not, however, a "class" in the technical sense of the term. They are, rather, a "status group."

## Communal Action Flowing from Class Interest

According to our terminology, the factor that creates "class" is unambiguously economic interest, and indeed, only those interests involved in the existence of the "market." Nevertheless, the concept of "class-interest" is an ambiguous one: even as an empirical concept it is ambiguous as soon as one understands by it something other than the factual direction of interests following with a certain probability from the class situation for a certain "average" of those people subjected to the class situation. The class situation and other circumstances remaining the same, the direction in which the individual worker, for instance, is likely to pursue his interests may vary widely, according to whether he is constitutionally qualified for the task at hand to a high, to an average, or to a low degree. In the same way, the direction of interests may vary according to whether or not a *communal* action of a larger or smaller portion of those commonly affected by the "class situation," or even an association among them, e.g., a "trade union," has grown out of the class situation from which the individual may or may not expect promising results. [Communal action refers to that action which is oriented to the feeling of the actors that they belong together. Societal action, on the other hand, is oriented to a rationally motivated adjustment of interests.] The rise of societal or even of communal action from a common class situation is by no means a universal phenomenon.

The class situation may be restricted in its effects to the generation of essentially *similar* reactions, that is to say, within our terminology, of "mass actions." However, it may not have even this result. Furthermore, often merely an amorphous communal action emerges. For example, the "murmuring" of the workers known in ancient oriental ethics: the moral disapproval of the work-master's conduct, which in its practical significance was probably equivalent to an increasingly typical phenomenon of precisely the latest industrial development, namely, the "slow down" (the deliberate limiting of work effort) of laborers by virtue of tacit agreement. The degree in which "communal action" and possibly "societal action" emerges from the "mass actions" of the members of a class is linked to general cultural conditions, especially to those of an intellectual sort. It is also linked to the extent of the contrasts that have already evolved, and is especially linked to the *transparency* of the connections between the causes and the consequences of the "class situation." For however different life chances may be, this fact in itself, according to all experience, by no means gives birth to "class action" (communal action by the members of a class). The fact of being conditioned and the results of the class situation must be distinctly recognizable. For only then the contrast of life chances can be felt not as an absolutely given fact to be accepted, but as a resultant from either (1) the given distribution of property, or (2) the structure of the concrete economic order. It is only then that people may react against the class structure not only through acts of an intermittent and irrational protest, but in the form of rational association. There have been "class situations" of the first category (1), of a specifically naked and transparent sort, in the urban centers of Antiquity and during the Middle Ages; especially then, when great fortunes were accumulated by factually monopolized trading in industrial products of these localities or in foodstuffs. Futhermore, under certain circumstances, in the rural economy of the most diverse periods, when agriculture was increasingly exploited in a profit-making manner. The most important historical example of the second category (2) is the class situation of the modern "proletariat."

## Status Honor

In contrast to classes, *status groups* are normally communities. They are, however, often of an amorphous kind. In contrast to the purely economically determined "class situation" we wish to designate as "status situation" every typical component of the life fate of men that is determined by a specific, positive or negative, social estimation of honor. This honor may be connected with any quality shared by a plurality, and, of course, it can be knit to a class situation: class distinctions are linked in the most varied ways with status distinctions. Property as such is not always recognized as a status qualification, but in the long run it is, and with extraordinary regularity. In the subsistence economy of the organized neighborhood, very often the richest man is simply the chieftain. However, this often means only an honorific preference. For example, in the so-called pure modern "democracy," that is, one devoid of any expressly ordered status privileges for individuals, it may be that only the families coming under approximately the same tax class dance with one another. This example is reported of certain smaller Swiss cities. But status honor need not necessarily be linked with a "class situation." On the contrary, it normally stands in sharp opposition to the pretensions of sheer property.

Both propertied and propertyless people can belong to the same status group, and frequently they do with very tangible consequences. This "equality" of social esteem may, however, in the long run become quite precarious. The "equality" of status among the American "gentlemen," for instance, is expressed by the fact that outside the subordination determined by the different functions of "business," it would be considered strictly repugnant—wherever the old tradition still prevails—if even the richest "chief," while playing billiards or cards in his club in the evening, would not treat his "clerk" as in every sense fully his equal in birthright. It would be repugnant if the American "chief" would bestow upon his "clerk" the condescending "benevolence" marking a distinction of "position," which the German chief can never dissever from his attitude. This is one of the most important reasons why in America the German "clubby-ness" has never been able to attain the attraction that the American clubs have.

## Guarantees of Status Stratification

In content, status honor is normally expressed by the fact that above all else a specific *style of life* can be expected from all those who wish to belong to the circle. Linked with this expectation are restrictions on "social" intercourse (that is, intercourse which is not subservient to economic or any other of business's "functional" purposes). These restrictions may confine normal marriages to within the status circle and may lead to complete endogamous closure. As soon as there is not a mere individual and socially irrelevant imitation of another style of life, but an agreed-upon communal action of this closing character, the "status" development is under way.

In its characteristic form, stratification by "status groups" on the basis of conventional styles of life evolves at the present time in the United States out of the traditional democracy. For example, only the resident of a certain street ("the street") is considered as belonging to "society," is qualified for social intercourse, and is visited and invited. Above all, this differentiation evolves in such a way as to make for strict submission to the fashion that is dominant at a given time in society. This submission to fashion also exists among men in America to a degree unknown in Germany. Such submission is considered to be an indication of the fact that a given man *pretends* to qualify as a gentleman. This submission decides, at least *prima facie*, that he will be treated as such. And this recognition becomes just as important for his employment chances in "swank" establishments, and above all, for social intercourse and marriage with "esteemed" families, as the qualification for dueling among Germans in the Kaiser's day. As for the rest: certain families resident for a long time, and, of course, correspondingly wealthy, e.g., "F. F. V., i.e. First Families of Virgina," or the actual or alleged descendants of the "Indian Princess" Pocahontas, of the Pilgrim fathers, or of the Knickerbockers, the members of almost inaccessible sects and all sorts of circles

setting themselves apart by means of any other characteristics and badges
. . . all these elements usurp "status" honor. The development of status is
essentially a question of stratification resting upon usurpation. Such usurpation is the normal origin of almost all status honor. But the road from this
purely conventional situation to legal privilege, positive or negative, is easily
traveled as soon as a certain stratification of the social order has in fact been
"lived in"and has achieved stability by virtue of a stable distribution of
economic power.

REFERENCE

1. *Wirtschaft und Gesellschaft,* part III, chap. 4, pp. 631–40. The first sentence in
   paragraph one and the several definitions in this chapter which are in brackets do
   not appear in the original text. They have been taken from other contexts of
   *Wirtschaft und Gesellschaft.*

# CONSPICUOUS CONSUMPTION *(Veblen)*

In what has been said of the evolution of the vicarious leisure class and its
differentiation from the general body of the working classes, reference has
been made to a further division of labor—that between different servant
classes. One portion of the servant class, chiefly those persons whose occupation is vicarious leisure, come to undertake a new, subsidiary range of duties
—the vicarious consumption of goods. The most obvious form in which this
consumption occurs is seen in the wearing of liveries and the occupation of
spacious servants' quarters. Another, scarcely less obtrusive or less effective
form of vicarious consumption, and a much more widely prevalent one, is
the consumption of food, clothing, dwelling, and furniture by the lady and
the rest of the domestic establishment.

But already at a point in economic evolution far antedating the emergence of the lady, specialized consumption of goods as an evidence of
pecuniary strength had begun to work out in a more or less elaborate
system. The beginning of a differentiation in consumption even antedates
the appearance of anything that can fairly be called pecuniary strength. It is
traceable back to the initial phase of predatory culture, and there is even a
suggestion that an incipient differentiation in this respect lies back of the
beginnings of the predatory life. The most primitive differentiation in the

* Reprinted from *The Theory of the Leisure Class* by Thorstein Veblen, pp. 60–70,
by permission of The Viking Press, Inc. Copyright, 1899, 1912, by The Macmillan
Company.

consumption of goods is like the later differentiation with which we are all so intimately familiar, in that it is largely of a ceremonial character, but unlike the latter it does not rest on a difference in accumulated wealth. The utility of consumption as an evidence of wealth is to be classed as a derivative growth. It is an adaptation to a new end, by a selective process, of a distinction previously existing and well established in men's habits of thought.

In the earlier phases of the predatory culture the only economic differentiation is a broad distinction between an honorable superior class made up of the able-bodied men on the one side, and a base inferior class of laboring women on the other. According to the ideal scheme of life in force at that time it is the office of the men to consume what the women produce. Such consumption as falls to the women is merely incidental to their work; it is a means to their continued labor, and not a consumption directed to their own comfort and fullness of life. Unproductive consumption of goods is honorable, primarily as a mark of prowess and a perquisite of human dignity; secondarily it becomes substantially honorable in itself, especially the consumption of the more desirable things. The consumption of choice articles of food, and frequently also of rare articles of adornment, becomes tabu to the women and children; and if there is a base (servile) class of men, the tabu holds also for them. With further advance in culture this tabu may change into simple custom of a more or less rigorous character; but whatever be the theoretical basis of the distinction which is maintained, whether it be a tabu or a larger conventionality, the features of the conventional scheme of consumption do not change easily. When the quasi-peaceable stage of industry is reached, with its fundamental institution of chattel slavery, the general principle, more or less rigorously applied, is that the base, industrious class should consume only what may be necessary to their subsistence. In the nature of things, luxuries and the comforts of life belong to the leisure class. Under the tabu, certain victuals, and more particularly certain beverages, are strictly reserved for the use of the superior class.

The ceremonial differentiation of the dietary is best seen in the use of intoxicating beverages and narcotics. If these articles of consumption are costly, they are felt to be noble and honorific. Therefore the base classes, primarily the women, practice an enforced continence with respect to these stimulants, except in countries where they are obtainable at a very low cost. From archaic times down through all the length of the patriarchal regime it has been the office of the women to prepare and administer these luxuries, and it has been the perquisite of the men of gentle birth and breeding to consume them. Drunkenness and the other pathological consequences of the free use of stimulants therefore tend in their turn to become honorific, as being a mark, at the second remove, of the superior status of those who are able to afford the indulgence. Infirmities induced by over-indulgence are among some peoples freely recognized as manly attributes. It has even happened that the name for certain diseased conditions of the body arising from such an origin has passed into everyday speech as a synonym for "noble" or "gentle." It is only at a relatively early stage of culture that the symptoms of expensive vice are conventionally accepted as marks of a superior status, and so tend to become virtues and command the deference of the community; but the reputability that attaches to certain expensive vices long retains so much of its force as to appreciably lessen the disapprobation visited upon the men of the wealthy or noble class for any excessive indulgence. The same invidious distinction adds force to the current disapproval of any indulgence of this kind on the part of women, minors, and inferiors. This invidious traditional distinction has not lost its force even among the more advanced peoples of today. Where the example set by the leisure class retains its imperative force in the regulation of the conventionalities, it is observable that the women still in great measure practice the same traditional continence with regard to stimulants.

This characterization of the greater continence in the use of stimulants practiced by the women of the reputable classes may seem an excessive refinement of logic at the expense of common sense. But facts within easy reach of anyone who cares to know them go to say that the greater abstinence of women is in some part due to an imperative conventionality; and this conventionality is, in a general way, strongest where the patriarchal tradition—the tradition that the woman is a chattel—has retained its hold in greatest vigor. In a sense which has been greatly qualified in scope and rigor, but which has by no means lost its meaning even yet, this tradition says that the woman, being a chattel, should consume only what is necessary to her sustenance—except so far as her further consumption contributes to the comfort or the good repute of her master. The consumption of luxuries, in the true sense, is a consumption directed to the comfort of the consumer himself, and is, therefore, a mark of the master. Any such consumption by others can take place only on a basis of sufferance. In communities where the popular habits of thought have been profoundly shaped by the patriarchal tradition we may accordingly look for survivals of the tabu on luxuries at least to the extent of a conventional deprecation of their use by the unfree and dependent class. This is more particularly true as regards certain luxuries, the use of which by the dependent class would detract sensibly from the comfort or pleasure of their masters, or which are held to be of doubtful legitimacy on other grounds. In the apprehension of the great conservative middle class of Western civilization the use of these various stimulants is obnoxious to at least one, if not both, of these objections; and it is a fact too significant to be passed over that it is precisely among these middle classes of the Germanic culture, with their strong surviving sense of the patriarchal proprieties, that the women are to the greatest extent subject to a qualified tabu on narcotics and alcoholic beverages. With many qualifications—with more qualifications as the patriarchal tradition has gradually weakened— the general rule is felt to be right and binding that women should consume only for the benefit of their masters. The objection of course presents itself that expenditure on women's dress and household paraphernalia is an obvious exception to this rule; but it will appear in the sequel that this exception is much more obvious than substantial.

During the earlier stages of economic development, consumption of goods without stint, especially consumption of the better grades of goods—ideally all consumption in excess of the subsistence minimum—pertains normally to the leisure class. This restriction tends to disappear, at least formally, after the later peaceable stage has been reached, with private ownership of goods and an industrial system based on wage labor or on the petty household economy. But during the earlier quasi-peaceable stage, when so many of the traditions through which the institution of a leisure class has affected the economic life of later times were taking form and consistency, this principle has had the force of a conventional law. It has served as the norm to which consumption has tended to conform, and any appreciable departure from it is to be regarded as an aberrant form, sure to be eliminated sooner or later in the further course of development.

The quasi-peaceable gentleman of leisure, then, not only consumes, of the staff of life beyond the minimum required for subsistence and physical efficiency, but his consumption also undergoes a specialization as regards the quality of the goods consumed. He consumes freely and of the best, in food, drink, narcotics, shelter, services, ornaments, apparel, weapons and accoutrements, amusements, amulets, and idols or divinities. In the process of gradual amelioration which takes place in the articles of his consumption, the motive principle and the proximate aim of innovation is no doubt the higher efficiency of the improved and more elaborate products for personal comfort and well-being. But that does not remain the sole purpose of their consumption. The canon of reputability is at hand and seizes upon such innovations as are, according to its standard, fit to survive. Since the consumption of these more excellent goods is an evidence of wealth, it becomes honorific;

and conversely, the failure to consume in due quantity and quality becomes a mark of inferiority and demerit.

This growth of punctilious discrimination as to qualitative excellence in eating, drinking, etc., presently affects not only the manner of life, but also the training and intellectual activity of the gentleman of leisure. He is no longer simply the successful, aggresive male—the man of strength, resource, and intrepidity. In order to avoid stultification he must also cultivate his tastes, for it now becomes incumbent on him to discriminate with some nicety between the noble and the ignoble in consumable goods. He becomes a connoisseur in creditable viands of various degrees of merit, in manly beverages and trinkets, in seemly apparel and architecture, in weapons, games, dances, and the narcotics. This cultivation of the æsthetic faculty requires time and application, and the demands made upon the gentleman in this direction therefore tend to change his life of leisure into a more or less arduous application to the business of learning how to live a life of ostensible leisure in a becoming way. Closely related to the requirement that the gentleman must consume freely and of the right kind of goods, there is the requirement that he must know how to consume them in a seemly manner. His life of leisure must be conducted in due form. Hence arise good manners in the way pointed out in an earlier chapter. High-bred manners and ways of living are items of conformity to the norm of conspicuous leisure and conspicuous consumption.

Conspicuous consumption of valuable goods is a means of reputability to the gentleman of leisure. As wealth accumulates on his hands, his own unaided effort will not avail to sufficiently put his opulence in evidence by this method. The aid of friends and competitors is therefore brought in by resorting to the giving of valuable presents and expensive feasts and entertainments. Presents and feasts had probably another origin than that of naïve ostentation, but they acquired their utility for this purpose very early, and they have retained that character to the present; so that their utility in this respect has now long been the substantial ground on which these usages rest. Costly entertainments, such as the potlatch or the ball, are peculiarly adapted to serve this end. The competitor with whom the entertainer wishes to institute a comparison is, by this method, made to serve as a means to the end. He consumes vicariously for his host at the same time that he is a witness to the consumption of that excess of good things which his host is unable to dispose of singlehanded, and he is also made to witness his host's facility in etiquette.

In the giving of costly entertainments other motives, of a more genial kind, are of course also present. The custom of festive gatherings probably originated in motives of conviviality and religion; these motives are also present in the later development, but they do not continue to be the sole motives. The latter-day leisure-class festivities and entertainments may continue in some slight degree to serve the religious need and in a higher degree the needs of recreation and conviviality, but they also serve an invidious purpose; and they serve it none the less effectually for having a colorable non-invidious ground in these more avowable motives. But the economic effect of these social amenities is not therefore lessened, either in the vicarious consumption of goods or in the exhibition of difficult and costly achievements in etiquette.

As wealth accumulates, the leisure class develops further in function and structure, and there arises a differentiation within the class. There is a more or less elaborate system of rank and grades. This differentiation is furthered by the inheritance of wealth and the consequent inheritance of gentility. With the inheritance of gentility goes the inheritance of obligatory leisure; and gentility of a sufficient potency to entail a life of leisure may be inherited without the complement of wealth required to maintain a dignified leisure. Gentle blood may be transmitted without goods enough to afford a reputably free consumption at one's ease. Hence results a class of impecunious gentlemen of leisure, incidentally referred to already. These half-caste gentlemen of leisure fall into a system of hierarchical gradations. Those who stand near the higher and the highest grades of the wealthy leisure class, in point of birth, or in point of wealth, or both, outrank the remoter-born and the pecuniarily weaker. These lower grades, especially the impecunious, or marginal, gentlemen of leisure, affiliate themselves by a system of dependence or fealty to the great ones; by so doing they gain an increment of repute, or of the means with which to lead a life of leisure, from their patron. They become his courtiers or retainers, servants; and being fed and countenanced by their patron they are indices of his rank and vicarious consumers of his superfluous wealth. Many of these affiliated gentlemen of leisure are at the same time lesser men of substance in their own right; so that some of them are scarcely at all, others only partially, to be rated as vicarious consumers. So many of them, however, as make up the retainers and hangers-on of the patron may be classed as vicarious consumers without qualification. Many of these again, and also many of the other aristocracy of less degree, have in turn attached to their persons a more or less comprehensive group of vicarious consumers in the persons of their wives and children, their servants, retainers, etc.

Throughout this graduated scheme of vicarious leisure and vicarious consumption the rule holds that these offices must be performed in some such manner, or under some such circumstances or insignia, as shall point plainly to the master to whom this leisure or consumption pertains, and to whom therefore the resulting increment of good repute of right inures. The consumption and leisure executed by these persons for their master or patron represents an investment on his part with a view to an increase of good fame. As regards feasts and largesses this is obvious enough, and the imputation of repute to the host or patron here takes place immediately, on the ground of common notoriety. Where leisure and consumption are performed vicari- ously by henchmen and retainers, imputation of the resulting repute to the patron is effected by their residing near his person so that it may be plain to all men from what source they draw. As the group whose good esteem is to be secured in this way grows larger, more patent means are required to indicate the imputation of merit for the leisure performed, and to this end uniforms, badges, and liveries come into vogue. The wearing of uniforms or liveries implies a considerable degree of dependence, and may even be said to be a mark of servitude, real or ostensible. The wearers of uniforms and liveries may be roughly divided into two classes—the free and the servile, or the noble and the ignoble. The services performed by them are likewise divisible into noble and ignoble. Of course the distinction is not observed with strict consistency in practice; the less debasing of the base services and the less honorific of the noble functions are not infrequently merged in the same person. But the general distinction is not on that account to be over- looked. What may add some perplexity is the fact that this fundamental distinction between noble and ignoble, which rests on the nature of he ostensible services performed, is traversed by a secondary distinction into honorific and humiliating, resting on the rank of the person for whom the service is performed or whose livery is worn. So, those offices which are by right the proper employment of the leisure class are noble; such as govern- ment, fighting, hunting, the care of arms and accoutrements, and the like— in short, those which may be classed as ostensibly predatory employments. On the other hand, those employments which properly fall to the industrious class are ignoble; such as handicraft or other productive labor, menial serv- ices and the like. But a base service performed for a person of very high degree may become a very honorific office; as for instance the office of a Maid of Honor or of a Lady in Waiting to the Queen, or the King's Master of the Horse or his Keeper of the Hounds. The two offices last named sug- gest a principle of some general bearing. Whenever, as in these cases, the menial service in question has to do directly with the primary leisure employ- ments of fighting and hunting, it easily acquires a reflected honorific character. In this way great honor may come to attach to an employment which in its own nature belongs to the baser sort.

In the later development of peaceable industry, the usage of employing an idle corps of uniformed men-at-arms gradually lapses. Vicarious consumption by dependents bearing the insignia of their patron or master narrows down to a corps of liveried menials. In a heightened degree, therefore, the livery comes to be a badge of servitude, or rather of servility. Something of an honorific character disappears when the livery becomes the exclusive badge of the menial. The livery becomes obnoxious to nearly all who are required to wear it. We are yet so little removed from a state of effective slavery as still to be fully sensitive to the sting of any imputation of servility. This antipathy asserts itself even in the case of the liveries or uniforms which some corporations prescribe as the distinctive dress of their employees. In this country the aversion even goes the length of discrediting—in a mild and uncertain way—those government employments, military and civil, which require the wearing of a livery or uniform.

With the disappearance of servitude, the number of vicarious consumers attached to any one gentleman tends, on the whole, to decrease. The like is of course true, and perhaps in a still higher degree, of the number of dependents who perform vicarious leisure for him. In a general way, though not wholly nor consistently, these two groups coincide. The dependent who was first delegated for these duties was the wife, or the chief wife; and, as would be expected, in the later development of the institution, when the number of persons by whom these duties are customarily performed gradually narrows, the wife remains the last. In the higher grades of society a large volume of both these kinds of service is required; and here the wife is of course still assisted in the work by a more or less numerous corps of menials. But as we descend the social scale, the point is presently reached where the duties of vicarious leisure and consumption devolve upon the wife alone. In the communities of the Western culture, this point is at present found among the lower middle class.

And here occurs a curious inversion. It is a fact of common observance that in this lower middle class there is no pretense of leisure on the part of the head of the household. Through force of circumstances it has fallen into disuse. But the middle-class wife still carries on the business of vicarious leisure, for the good name of the household and its master. In descending the social scale in any modern industrial community, the primary fact—the conspicuous leisure of the master of the household—disappears at a relatively high point. The head of the middle-class household has been reduced by economic circumstances to turn his hand to gaining a livelihood by occupations which often partake largely of the character of industry, as in the case of the ordinary business man of today. But the derivative fact— the vicarious leisure and consumption rendered by the wife and the auxiliary vicarious performance of leisure by menials—remains in vogue as a conventionality which the demands of reputability will not suffer to be slighted. It is by no means an uncommon spectacle to find a man applying himself to work with the utmost assiduity, in order that his wife may in due form render for him that degree of vicarious leisure which the common sense of the time demands.

The leisure rendered by the wife in such cases is, of course, not a simple manifestation of idleness or indolence. It almost invariably occurs disguised under some form of work or household duties or social amenities, which prove on analysis to serve little or no ulterior end beyond showing that she does not occupy herself with anything that is gainful or that is of substantial use. As has already been noticed under the head of manners, the greater part of the customary round of domestic cares to which the middle-class housewife gives her time and effort is of this character. Not that the results of her attention to household matters, of a decorative and mundificatory character, are not pleasing to the sense of men trained in middle-class proprieties; but the taste to which these effects of household adornment and tidiness appeal is a taste which has been formed under the selective guidance of a canon of propriety that demands just these evidences of wasted effort. The effects are pleasing to us chiefly because we have been taught to find them pleasing. There goes into these domestic duties much solicitude for a proper combination of form and color, and for other ends that are to be classed as æsthetic in the proper sense of the term; and it is not denied that effects having some substantial æsthetic value are sometimes attained. Pretty much all that is here insisted on is that, as regards these amenities of life, the housewife's efforts are under the guidance of traditions that have been shaped by the law of conspicuously wasteful expenditure of time and substance. If beauty or comfort is achieved—and it is a more or less fortuitous circumstance if they are—they must be achieved by means and methods that commend themselves to the great economic law of wasted effort. The more reputable, "presentable" portion of middle-class household paraphernalia are, on the one hand, items of conspicuous consumption, and on the other hand, apparatus for putting in evidence the vicarious leisure rendered by the housewife.

The requirement of vicarious consumption at the hands of the wife continues in force even at a lower point in the pecuniary scale than the requirement of vicarious leisure. At a point below which little if any pretense of wasted effort, in ceremonial cleanness and the like, is observable, and where there is assuredly no conscious attempt at ostensible leisure, decency still requires the wife to consume some goods conspicuously for the reputability of the household and its head. So that, as the latter-day outcome of this evolution of an archaic institution, the wife, who was at the outset the drudge and chattel of the man, both in fact and in theory—the producer of goods for him to consume—has become the ceremonial consumer of goods which he produces. But she still quite unmistakably remains his chattel in theory; for the habitual rendering of vicarious leisure and consumption is the abiding mark of the unfree servant.

This vicarious consumption practiced by the household of the middle and lower classes can not be counted as a direct expression of the leisure-class scheme of life, since the household of this pecuniary grade does not belong within the leisure class. It is rather that the leisure-class scheme of life here comes to an expression at the second remove. The leisure class stands at the head of the social structure in point of reputability; and its manner of life and its standards of worth therefore afford the norm of reputability for the community. The observance of these standards, in some degree of approximation, becomes incumbent upon all classes lower in the scale. In modern civilized communities the lines of demarcation between social classes have grown vague and transient, and wherever this happens the norm of reputability imposed by the upper class extends its coercive influence with but slight hindrance down through the social structure to the lowest strata. The result is that the members of each stratum accept as their ideal of decency the scheme of life in vogue in the next higher stratum, and bend their energies to live up to that ideal. On pain of forfeiting their good name and their self-respect in case of failure, they must conform to the accepted code, at least in appearance.

The basis on which good repute in any highly organized industrial community ultimately rests is pecuniary strength; and the means of showing pecuniary strength, and so gaining or retaining a good name, are leisure and a conspicuous consumption of goods. Accordingly, both of these methods are in vogue as far down the scale as it remains possible; and in the lower strata in which the two methods are employed, both offices are in great part delegated to the wife and children of the household. Lower still, where any degree of leisure, even ostensible, has become impracticable for the wife, the conspicuous consumption of goods remains and is carried on by the wife and children. The man of the household also can do something in this direction, and indeed, he commonly does; but with a still lower descent into the levels of indigence—along the margin of the slums—the man, and presently also the children, virtually cease to consume valuable goods for appearances, and the woman remains virtually the sole exponent of the household's pecuniary decency. No class of society, not even the most abjectly poor, forgoes all customary conspicuous consumption. The last items of this category of consumption are not given up except under stress of the direst necessity. Very much of squalor and discomfort will be endured before the last trinket or the last pretense of pecuniary decency is put away. There is no class and no country that has yielded so abjectly before the pressure of physical want as to deny themselves all gratification of this higher or spiritual need.

# SOME PRINCIPLES OF STRATIFICATION * (Davis and Moore)

In a previous paper some concepts for handling the phenomena of social inequality were presented.[1] In the present paper a further step in stratification theory is undertaken—an attempt to show the relationship between stratification and the rest of the social order.[2] Starting from the proposition that no society is "classless," or unstratified, an effort is made to explain, in functional terms, the universal necessity which calls forth stratification in any social system. Next, an attempt is made to explain the roughly uniform distribution of prestige as between the major types of positions in every society. Since, however, there occur between one society and another great differences in the degree and kind of stratification, some attention is also given to the varieties of social inequality and the variable factors that give rise to them.

Clearly, the present task requires two different lines of analysis—one to understand the universal, the other to understand the variable features of stratification. Naturally each line of inquiry aids the other and is indispensable, and in the treatment that follows the two will be interwoven, although, because of space limitations, the emphasis will be on the universals.

Throughout, it will be necessary to keep in mind one thing—namely, that the discussion relates to the system of positions, not to the individuals occupying those positions. It is one thing to ask why different positions carry different degrees of prestige, and quite another to ask how certain in-

* By Kingsley Davis and Wilbert E. Moore, reprinted from *American Sociological Review*, Vol. X, 1945, No. 2, pp. 242–249, with permission of The American Sociological Society and the authors.

dividuals get into those positions. Although, as the argument will try to show, both questions are related, it is essential to keep them separate in our thinking. Most of the literature on stratification has tried to answer the second question (particularly with regard to the ease or difficulty of mobility between strata) without tackling the first. The first question, however, is logically prior and, in the case of any particular individual or group, factually prior.

## The Functional Necessity of Stratification

Curiously, however, the main functional necessity explaining the universal presence of stratification is precisely the requirement faced by any society of placing and motivating individuals in the social structure. As a functioning mechanism a society must somehow distribute its members in social positions and induce them to perform the duties of these positions. It must thus concern itself with motivation at two different levels: to instill in the proper individuals the desire to fill certain positions, and, once in these positions, the desire to perform the duties attached to them. Even though the social order may be relatively static in form, there is a continuous process of metabolism as new individuals are born into it, shift with age, and die off. Their absorption into the positional system must somehow be arranged and motivated. This is true whether the system is competitive or non-competitive. A competitive system gives greater importance to the motivation to achieve positions, whereas a non-competitive system gives perhaps greater importance to the motivation to perform the duties of the positions; but in any system both types of motivation are required.

If the duties associated with the various positions were all equally pleasant to the human organism, all equally important to societal survival, and all equally in need of the same ability or talent, it would make no difference who got into which positions, and the problem of social placement would be greatly reduced. But actually it does make a great deal of difference who gets into which positions, not only because some positions are inherently more agreeable than others, but also because some require special talents or training and some are functionally more important than others. Also, it is essential that the duties of the positions be performed with the diligence that their importance requires. Inevitably, then, a society must have, first, some kind of rewards that it can use as inducements, and, second, some way of distributing these rewards differentially according to positions. The rewards and their distribution become a part of the social order, and thus give rise to stratification.

One may ask what kind of rewards a society has at its disposal in distributing its personnel and securing essential services. It has, first of all, the things that contribute to sustenance and comfort. It has, second, the things that contribute to humor and diversion. And it has, finally, the things that contribute to self-respect and ego expansion. The last, because of the peculiarly social character of the self, is largely a function of the opinion of others, but it nonetheless ranks in importance with the first two. In any social system all three kinds of rewards must be dispensed differentially according to positions.

In a sense the rewards are "built into" the position. They consist in the "rights" associated with the position, plus what may be called its accompaniments or perquisites. Often the rights, and sometimes the accompaniments, are functionally related to the duties of the position. (Rights as viewed by the incumbent are usually duties as viewed by other members of the community.) However, there may be a host of subsidiary rights and perquisites that are not essential to the function of the position and have only an indirect and symbolic connection with its duties, but which still may be of considerable importance in inducing people to seek the positions and fulfil the essential duties.

If the rights and perquisites of different positions in a society must be unequal, then the society must be stratified, because that is precisely what stratification means. Social inequality is thus an unconsciously evolved device by which societies insure that the most important positions are conscientiously filled by the most qualified persons. Hence every society, no matter how simple or complex, must differentiate persons in terms of both prestige and esteem, and must therefore possess a certain amount of institutionalized inequality.

It does not follow that the amount or type of inequality need be the same in all societies. This is largely a function of factors that will be discussed presently.

## The Two Determinants of Positional Rank

Granting the general function that inequality subserves, one can specify the two factors that determine the relative rank of different positions. In general those positions convey the best reward, and hence have the highest rank, which (a) have the greatest importance for the society and (b) require the greatest training or talent. The first factor concerns function and is a matter of relative significance; the second concerns means and is a matter of scarcity.

*Differential functional importance.* Actually a society does not need to reward positions in proportion to their functional importance. It merely needs to give sufficient reward to them to insure that they will be filled competently. In other words, it must see that less essential positions do not compete successfully with more essential ones. If a position is easily filled, it need not be heavily rewarded, even though important. On the other hand, if it is important but hard to fill, the reward must be high enough to get it filled anyway. Functional importance is therefore a necessary but not a sufficient cause of high rank being assigned to a position.[3]

*Differential scarcity of personnel.* Practically all positions, no matter how acquired, require some form of skill or capacity for performance. This is implicit in the very notion of position, which implies that the incumbent must, by virtue of his incumbency, accomplish certain things.

There are, ultimately, only two ways in which a person's qualifications come about: through inherent capacity or through training. Obviously, in concrete activities both are always necessary, but from a practical standpoint the scarcity may lie primarily in one or the other, as well as in both. Some positions require innate talents of such high degree that the persons who fill them are bound to be rare. In many cases, however, talent is fairly abundant in the population but the training process is so long, costly, and elaborate that relatively few can qualify. Modern medicine, for example, is within the mental capacity of most individuals, but a medical education is so burdensome and expensive that virtually none would undertake it if the position of the M.D. did not carry a reward commensurate with the sacrifice.

If the talents required for a position are abundant and the training easy, the method of acquiring the position may have little to do with its duties. There may be, in fact, a virtually accidental relationship. But if the skills required are scarce by reason of the rarity of talent or the costliness of training, the position, if functionally important, must have an attractive power that will draw the necessary skills in competition with other positions. This means, in effect, that the position must be high in the social scale—must command great prestige, high salary, ample leisure, and the like.

*How variations are to be understood.* In so far as there is a difference between one system of stratification and another, it is attributable to whatever factors affect the two determinants of differential reward—namely, functional importance and scarcity of personnel. Positions important in one society may not be important in another, because the conditions faced by the societies, or their degree of internal development, may be different. The same conditions, in turn, may affect the question of scarcity; for in some societies the stage of development, or the external situation, may wholly obviate the necessity of certain kinds of skill or talent. Any particular system of stratification, then, can be understood as a product of the special conditions affecting the two aforementioned grounds of differential reward.

## Major Societal Functions and Stratification

*Religion.* The reason why religion is necessary is apparently to be found in the fact that human society achieves its unity primarily through the possession by its members of certain ultimate values and ends in common. Although these values and ends are subjective, they influence behavior, and their integration enables the society to operate as a system. Derived neither from inherited nor from external nature, they have evolved as a part of culture by communication and moral pressure. They must, however, appear to the members of the society to have some reality, and it is the role of religious belief and ritual to supply and reinforce this appearance of reality. Through belief and ritual the common ends and values are connected with an imaginary world symbolized by concrete sacred objects, which world in turn is related in a meaningful way to the facts and trials of the individual's life. Through the worship of the sacred objects and the beings they symbolize, and the acceptance of supernatural prescriptions that are at the same time codes of behavior, a powerful control over human conduct is exercised, guiding it along lines sustaining the institutional structure and conforming to the ultimate ends and values.

If this conception of the role of religion is true, one can understand why in every known society the religious activities tend to be under the charge of particular persons, who tend thereby to enjoy greater rewards than the ordinary societal member. Certain of the rewards and special privileges may attach to only the highest religious functionaries, but others usually apply, if such exists, to the entire sacerdotal class.

Moreover, there is a peculiar relation between the duties of the religious official and the special privileges he enjoys. If the supernatural world governs the destinies of men more ultimately than does the real world, its earthly representative, the person through whom one may communicate with the supernatural, must be a powerful individual. He is a keeper of sacred tradition, a skilled performer of the ritual, and an interpreter of lore and myth. He is in such close contact with the gods that he is viewed as possessing some of their characteristics. He is, in short, a bit sacred, and hence free from some of the more vulgar necessities and controls.

It is no accident, therefore, that religious functionaries have been associated with the very highest positions of power, as in theocratic regimes. Indeed, looking at it from this point of view, one may wonder why it is that they do not get *entire* control over their societies. The factors that prevent this are worthy of note.

In the first place, the amount of technical competence necessary for the performance of religious duties is small. Scientific or artistic capacity is not required. Anyone can set himself up as enjoying an intimate relation with deities, and nobody can successfully dispute him. Therefore, the factor of scarcity of personnel does not operate in the technical sense.

One may assert, on the other hand, that religious ritual is often elaborate and religious lore abstruce, and that priestly ministrations require tact, if not intelligence. This is true, but the technical requirements of the professions are for the most part adventitious, not related to the end in the same way that science is related to air travel. The priest can never be free from competition, since the criteria of whether or not one has genuine contact with the supernatural are never strictly clear. It is this competition that debases the priestly position below what might be expected at first glance. That is why priestly prestige is highest in those societies where membership in the profession is rigidly controlled by the priestly guild itself. That is why, in part at least, elaborate devices are utilized to stress the identification of the person with his office—spectacular costume, abnormal conduct, special diet, segregated residence, celibacy, conspicuous leisure, and the like. In fact, the priest is always in danger of becoming somewhat discredited—as happens in a secularized society—because in a world of stubborn fact, ritual and sacred knowledge alone will not grow crops or build houses. Furthermore, unless he is protected by a professional guild, the priest's identification with the supernatural tends to preclude his acquisition of abundant worldly goods.

As between one society and another it seems that the highest general position awarded the priest occurs in the medieval type of social order. Here there is enough economic production to afford a surplus, which can be used to support a numerous and highly organized priesthood; and yet the populace is unlettered and therefore credulous to a high degree. Perhaps the most extreme example is to be found in the Buddhism of Tibet, but others are encountered in the Catholicism of feudal Europe, the Inca regime of Peru, the Brahminism of India, and the Mayan priesthood of Yucatan. On the other hand, if the society is so crude as to have no surplus and little differentiation, so that every priest must be also a cultivator or hunter, the separation of the priestly status from the others has hardly gone far enough for priestly prestige to mean much. When the priest actually has high prestige under these circumstances, it is because he also performs other important functions (usually political and medical).

In an extremely advanced society built on scientific technology, the priesthood tends to lose status, because sacred tradition and supernaturalism drop into the background. The ultimate values and common ends of the society tend to be expressed in less anthropomorphic ways, by officials who occupy fundamentally political, economic, or educational rather than religious positions. Nevertheless, it is easily possible for intellectuals to exaggerate the degree to which the priesthood in a presumably secular milieu has lost prestige. When the matter is closely examined the urban proletariat, as well as the rural citizenry, proves to be surprisingly god-fearing and priest-ridden. No society has become so completely secularized as to liquidate entirely the belief in transcendental ends and supernatural entities. Even in a secularized society some system must exist for the integration of ultimate values, for their ritualistic expression, and for the emotional adjustments required by disappointment, death, and disaster.

*Government.* Like religion, government plays a unique and indispensable part in society. But in contrast to religion, which provides integration in terms of sentiments, beliefs, and rituals, it organizes the society in terms of law and authority. Furthermore, it orients the society to the actual rather than the unseen world.

The main functions of government are, internally, the ultimate enforcement of norms, the final arbitration of conflicting interests, and the overall planning and direction of society; and externally, the handling of war and diplomacy. To carry out these functions it acts as the agent of the entire people, enjoys a monopoly of force, and controls all individuals within its territory.

Political action, by definition, implies authority. An official can command because he has authority, and the citizen must obey because he is subject to that authority. For this reason stratification is inherent in the nature of political relationships.

So clear is the power embodied in political position that political inequality is sometimes thought to comprise all inequality. But it can be shown that there are other bases of stratification, that the following controls operate in practice to keep political power from becoming complete: (a) The fact that the actual holders of political office, and especially those determining top policy must necessarily be few in number compared to the total population. (b) The fact that the rulers represent the interest of the group rather than of themselves, and are therefore restricted in their behavior by rules and mores designed to enforce this limitation of interest. (c) The fact that the holder of political office has his authority by virtue of his office and nothing else, and therefore any special knowledge, talent, or capacity he may claim is purely incidental, so that he often has to depend upon others for technical assistance.

In view of these limiting factors, it is not strange that the rulers often have less power and prestige than a literal enumeration of their formal rights would lead one to expect.

*Wealth, property, and labor.*  Every position that secures for its incumbent a livelihood is, by definition, economically rewarded. For this reason there is an economic aspect to those positions (e.g., political and religious) the main function of which is not economic. It therefore becomes convenient for the society to use unequal economic returns as a principal means of controlling the entrance of persons into positions and stimulating the performance of their duties. The amount of the economic return therefore becomes one of the main indices of social status.

It should be stressed, however, that a position does not bring power and prestige *because* it draws a high income. Rather, it draws a high income because it is functionally important and the available personnel is for one reason or another scarce. It is therefore superficial and erroneous to regard high income as the cause of a man's power and prestige, just as it is erroneous to think that a man's fever is the cause of his disease.[4]

The economic source of power and prestige is not income primarily, but the ownership of capital goods (including patents, good will, and professional reputation). Such ownership should be distinguished from the possession of consumers' goods, which is an index rather than a cause of social standing. In other words, the ownership of producers' goods is, properly speaking, a source of income like other positions, the income itself remaining an index. Even in situations where social values are widely commercialized and earnings are the readiest method of judging social position, income does not confer prestige on a position so much as it induces people to compete for the position. It is true that a man who has a high income as a result of one position may find this money helpful in climbing into another position as well, but this again reflects the effect of his initial, economically advantageous status, which exercises its influence through the medium of money.

In a system of private property in productive enterprise, an income above what an individual spends can give rise to possession of capital wealth. Presumably such possession is a reward for the proper management of one's finances originally and of the productive enterprise later. But as social differentiation becomes highly advanced and yet the institution of inheritance persists, the phenomenon of pure ownership, and reward for pure ownership, emerges. In such a case it is difficult to prove that the position is functionally important or that the scarcity involved is anything other than extrinsic and accidental. It is for this reason, doubtless, that the institution of private property in productive goods becomes more subject to criticism as social development proceeds toward industrialization. It is only this pure, that is, strictly legal and functionless ownership, however, that is open to attack; for some form of active ownership, whether private or public, is indispensable.

One kind of ownership of production goods consists in rights over the labor of others. The most extremely concentrated and exclusive of such rights are found in slavery, but the essential principle remains in serfdom, peonage, encomienda, and indenture. Naturally this kind of ownership has the greatest significance for stratification, because it necessarily entails an unequal relationship.

But property in capital goods inevitably introduces a compulsive element even into the nominally free contractual relationship. Indeed, in some respects the authority of the contractual employer is greater than that of the feudal landlord, inasmuch as the latter is more limited by traditional reciprocities. Even the classical economics recognized that competitors would fare unequally, but it did not pursue this fact to its necessary conclusion that, however it might be acquired, unequal control of goods and services must give unequal advantage to the parties to a contract.

*Technical knowledge.* The function of finding means to single goals, without any concern with the choice between goals, is the exclusively technical sphere. The explanation of why positions requiring great technical skill receive fairly high rewards is easy to see, for it is the simplest case of the rewards being so distributed as to draw talent and motivate training. Why they seldom if ever receive the highest rewards is also clear: the importance of technical knowledge from a societal point of view is never so great as the integration of goals, which takes place on the religious, political, and economic levels. Since the technological level is concerned solely with means, a purely technical position must utimately be subordinate to other positions that are religious, political, or economic in character.

Nevertheless, the distinction between expert and layman in any social order is fundamental, and cannot be entirely reduced to other terms. Methods of recruitment, as well as of reward, sometimes lead to the erroneous interpretation that technical positions are economically determined. Actually, however, the acquisition of knowledge and skill cannot be accomplished by purchase, although the opportunity to learn may be. The control of the avenues of training may inhere as a sort of property right in certain families or classes, giving them power and prestige in consequence. Such a situation adds an artificial scarcity to the natural scarcity of skills and talents. On the other hand, it is possible for an opposite situation to arise. The rewards of technical position may be so great that a condition of excess supply is created, leading to at least temporary devaluation of the rewards. Thus "unemployment in the learned professions" may result in a debasement of the prestige of those positions. Such adjustments and readjustments are constantly occurring in changing societies; and it is always well to bear in mind that the efficiency of a stratified structure may be affected by the modes of recruitment for positions. The social order itself, however, sets limits to the inflation or deflation of the prestige of experts: an over-supply tends to debase the rewards and discourage recruitment or produce revolution, whereas an under-supply tends to increase the reward or weaken the society in competition with other societies.

Particular systems of stratification show a wide range with respect to the exact position of technically competent persons. This range is perhaps most evident in the degree of specialization. Extreme division of labor tends to create many specialists without high prestige since the training is short and the required native capacity relatively small. On the other hand it also tends to accentuate the high position of the true experts—scientists, engineers, and administrators—by increasing their authority relative to other functionally important positions. But the idea of a technocratic social order or a government or priesthood of engineers or social scientists neglects the limitations of knowledge and skills as a basic for performing social functions. To the extent that the social structure is truly specialized the prestige of the technical person must also be circumscribed.

## Variation in Stratified Systems

The generalized principles of stratification here suggested form a necessary preliminary to a consideration of types of stratified systems, because it is in terms of these principles that the types must be described. This can be seen by trying to delineate types according to certain modes of variation. For instance, some of the most important modes (together with the polar types in terms of them) seem to be as follows:

*a. The degree of specialization.* The degree of specialization affects the fineness and multiplicity of the gradations in power and prestige. It also influences the extent to which particular functions may be emphasized in the invidious system, since a given function cannot receive much emphasis in the hierarchy until it has achieved structural separation from the other functions. Finally, the amount of specialization influences the bases of selection. Polar types: *Specialized. Unspecialized.*

   *b. The nature of the functional emphasis.*   In general when emphasis is put on sacred matters, a rigidity is introduced that tends to limit specialization and hence the development of technology. In addition, a brake is placed on social mobility, and on the development of bureaucracy. When the preoccupation with the sacred is withdrawn, leaving greater scope for purely secular preoccupations, a great development, and rise in status, of economic and technological positions seemingly takes place. Curiously, a concomitant rise in political position is not likely, because it has usually been allied with the religious and stands to gain little by the decline of the latter. It is also possible for a society to emphasize family functions—as in relatively undifferentiated societies where high mortality requires high fertility and kinship forms the main basis of social organization. Main types: *Familistic, Authoritarian (Theocratic* or sacred, and *Totalitarian* or secular), *Capitalistic.*

   *c. The magnitude of invidious differences.*   What may be called the amount of social distance between positions, taking into account the entire scale, is something that should lend itself to quantitative measurement. Considerable differences apparently exist between different societies in this regard, and also between parts of the same society. Polar types: *Equalitarian, Inequalitarian.*

   *d. The degree of opportunity.*   The familiar question of the amount of mobility is different from the question of the comparative equality or inequality of rewards posed above, because the two criteria may vary independently up to a point. For instance, the tremendous divergences in monetary income in the United States are far greater than those found in primitive societies, yet the equality of opportunity to move from one rung to the other in the social scale may also be greater in the United States than in a hereditary tribal kingdom. Polar types: *Mobile* (open), *Immobile* (closed).

   *e. The degree of stratum solidarity.*   Again, the degree of "class solidarity" (or the presence of specific organizations to promote class interests) may vary to some extent independently of the other criteria, and hence is an important principle in classifying systems of stratification. Polar types: *Class organized, Class unorganized.*

## External Conditions

What state any particular system of stratification is in with reference to each of these modes of variation depends on two things: (1) its state with reference to the other ranges of variation, and (2) the conditions outside the system of stratification which nevertheless influence that system. Among the latter are the following:

*a. The stage of cultural development.* As the cultural heritage grows, increased specialization becomes necessary, which in turn contributes to the enhancement of mobility, a decline of stratum solidarity, and a change of functional emphasis.

*b. Situation with respect to other societies.* The presence or absence of open conflict with other societies, of free trade relations or cultural diffusion, all influence the class structure to some extent. A chronic state of warfare tends to place emphasis upon the military functions, especially when the opponents are more or less equal. Free trade, on the other hand, strengthens the hand of the trader at the expense of the warrior and priest. Free movement of ideas generally has an equalitarian effect. Migration and conquest create special circumstances.

*c. Size of the society.* A small society limits the degree to which functional specialization can go, the degree of segregation of different strata, and the magnitude of inequality.

## Composite Types

Much of the literature on stratification has attempted to classify concrete systems into a certain number of types. This task is deceptively simple, however, and should come at the end of an analysis of elements and principles, rather than at the beginning. If the preceding discussion has any validity, it indicates that there are a number of modes of variation between different systems, and that any one system is a composite of the society's status with reference to all these modes of variation. The danger of trying to classify whole societies under such rubrics as *caste, feudal,* or *open class* is that one or two criteria are selected and others ignored, the result being an unsatisfactory solution to the problem posed. The present discussion has been offered as a possible approach to the more systematic classification of composite types.

REFERENCES

1. Kingsley Davis. "A Conceptual Analysis of Stratification." *American Sociological Review.* 7:309–21, June, 1942.
2. The writers regret (and beg indulgence) that the present essay, a condensation of a longer study, covers so much in such short space that adequate evidence and qualification cannot be given and that as a result what is actually very tentative is presented in an unfortunately dogmatic manner.
3. Unfortunately, functional importance is difficult to establish. To use the position's

prestige to establish it, as is often unconsciously done, constitutes circular reasoning from our point of view. There are, however, two independent clues: (a) the degree to which a position is functionally unique, there being no other positions that can perform the same function satisfactorily: (b) the degree to which other positions are dependent on the one in question. Both clues are best exemplified in organized systems of positions built around one major function. Thus, in most complex societies the religious, political, economic, and educational functions are handled by distinct structures not easily interchangeable. In addition, each structure possesses many different positions, some clearly dependent on, if not subordinate to, others. In sum, when an institutional nucleus becomes differentiated around one main function, and at the same time organizes a large portion of the population into its relationships, the *key* positions in it are of the highest functional importance. The absence of such specialization does not prove functional unimportance, for the whole society may be relatively unspecialized; but it is safe to assume that the more important functions receive the first and clearest structural differentiation.

4. The symbolic rather than intrinsic role of income in social stratification has been succinctly summarized by Talcott Parsons, "An Analytical Approach to the Theory of Social Stratification," *American Journal of Sociology.* 45: 841–862, May, 1940.

# SOME PRINCIPLES OF STRATIFICATION: A CRITICAL ANALYSIS* (*Tumin*)†

The fact of social inequality in human society is marked by its ubiquity and its antiquity. Every known society, past and present, distributes its scarce and demanded goods and services unequally. And there are attached to the positions which command unequal amounts of such goods and services certain highly morally-toned evaluations of their importance for the society.

The ubiquity and the antiquity of such inequality has given rise to the assumption that there must be something both inevitable and positively functional about such social arrangements.

Clearly, the truth or falsity of such an assumption is a strategic question for any general theory of social organization. It is therefore most curious that the basic premises and implications of the assumption have only been most casually explored by American sociologists.

The most systematic treatment is to be found in the well-known article by Kingsley Davis and Wilbert Moore, entitled "Some Principles of Strati-

* By Melvin W. Tumin reprinted from *American Sociological Review*, Vol. 18, 1953, No. 4, with permission of The American Sociological Society and the author.

† The writer has had the benefit of a most helpful criticism of the main portions of this paper by Professor W. J. Goode of Columbia University. In addition, he has had the opportunity to expose this paper to criticism by the Staff Seminar of the Sociology Section at Princeton. In deference to a possible rejoinder by Professors Moore and Davis, the writer has not revised the paper to meet the criticisms which Moore has already offered personally.

fication." [1] More than twelve years have passed since its publication, and though it is one of the very few treatments of stratification on a high level of generalization, it is difficult to locate a single systematic analysis of its reasoning. It will be the principal concern of this paper to present the beginnings of such an analysis.

The central argument advanced by Davis and Moore can be stated in a number of sequential propositions, as follows:

1. Certain positions in any society are functionally more important than others, and require special skills for their performance.
2. Only a limited number of individuals in any society have the talents which can be trained into the skills appropriate to these positions.
3. The conversion of talents into skills involves a training period during which sacrifices of one kind or another are made by those undergoing the training.
4. In order to induce the talented persons to undergo these sacrifices and acquire the training, their future positions must carry an inducement value in the form of differential, i.e., privileged and disproportionate access to the scarce and desired rewards which the society has to offer. [2]
5. These scarce and desired goods consist of the rights and perquisites attached to, or built into, the positions, and can be classified into those things which contribute to (a) sustenance and comfort, (b) humor and diversion, (c) self-respect and ego-expansion.
6. This differential access to the basic rewards of the society has as a consequence the differentiation of the prestige and esteem which various strata acquire. This may be said, along with the rights and perquisites, to constitute institutionalized social inequality, i.e., stratification.
7. Therefore, social inequality among different strata in the amounts of scarce and desired goods, and the amounts of prestige and esteem which they receive, is both positively functional and inevitable in any society. Let us take these propositions and examine them *seriatim*. [3]

*1. Certain positions in any society are more functionally important than others and require special skills for their performance.*

The key term here is "functionally important." The functionalist theory of social organization is by no means clear and explicit about this term. The minimum common referent is to something known as the "survival value" of a social structure. [4] This concept immediately involves a number of perplexing questions. Among these are: (a) the issue of minimum vs. maximum survival, and the possible empirical referents which can be given to those terms; (b) whether such a proposition is a useless tautology since any *status quo* at any given moment is nothing more and nothing less than everything present in the *status quo*. In these terms, all acts and structures must be judged positively functional in that they constitute essential portions of the *status quo*; (c) what kind of calculus of functionality exists which will enable us, at this point in our development, to add and subtract long and short range consequences, with their mixed qualities, and arrive at some summative judgment regarding the rating an act or structure should receive on a scale of greater or lesser functionality? At best, we tend to make primarily intuitive judgments. Often enough, these judgments involve the use of value-laden criteria, or, at least, criteria which are chosen in preference to others not for any sociologically systematic reasons but by reason of certain implicit value preferences.

Thus, to judge that the engineers in a factory are functionally more important to the factory than the unskilled workmen involves a notion regarding the dispensability of the unskilled workmen, or their replaceability, relative to that of the engineers. But this is not a process of choice with infinite time dimensions. For at some point along the line one must face the problem of adequate motivation for *all* workers at all levels of skill in the factory. In the long run, *some* labor force of unskilled workmen is as important and as indispensable to the factory as *some* labor force of engineers. Often enough, the labor force situation is such that this fact is brought home sharply to the entrepreneur in the short run rather than in the long run.

Moreover, the judgment as to the relative indispensability and replaceability of a particular segment of skills in the population involves a prior judgment about the bargaining-power of that segment. But this power is itself a culturally shaped *consequence* of the existing system of rating, rather than something inevitable in the nature of social organization. At least the contrary of this has never been demonstrated, but only assumed.

A generalized theory of social stratification must recognize that the prevailing system of inducements and rewards is only one of many variants in the whole range of possible systems of motivation which, at least theoretically, are capable of working in human society. It is quite conceivable, of course, that a system of norms could be institutionalized in which the idea of threatened withdrawal of services, except under the most extreme circumstances, would be considered as absolute moral anathema. In such a case, the whole notion of relative functionality, as advanced by Davis and Moore, would have to be radically revised.

*2. Only a limited number of individuals in any society have the talents which can be trained into the skills appropriate to these positions ( i.e., the more functionally important positions).*

The truth of this proposition depends at least in part on the truth of proposition 1 above. It is, therefore, subject to all the limitations indicated above. But for the moment, let us assume the validity of the first proposition and concentrate on the question of the rarity of appropriate talent.

If all that is meant is that in every society there is a *range* of talent, and that some members of any society are by nature more talented than others, no sensible contradiction can be offered, but a question must be raised here regarding the amount of sound knowledge present in any society concerning the presence of talent in the population.

For, in every society there is some demonstrable ignorance regarding the amount of talent present in the population. *And the more rigidly stratified a society is, the less chance does that society have of discovering any new facts about the talents of its members.* Smoothly working and stable systems of stratification, wherever found, tend to build-in obstacles to the further exploration of the range of available talent. This is especially true in those societies where the opportunity to discover talent in any one generation varies with the differential resources of the parent generation. Where, for instance, access to education depends upon the wealth of one's parents, and where wealth is differentially distributed, large segments of the population are likely to be deprived of the chance even to *discover* what are their talents.

Whether or not differential rewards and opportunities are functional in any one generation, it is clear that if those differentials are allowed to be socially inherited by the next generation, then, the stratification system is specifically dysfunctional for the discovery of talents in the next generation. In this fashion, systems of social stratification tend to limit the chances available to maximize the efficiency of discovery, recruitment and training of "functionally important talent." [5]

Additionally, the unequal distribution of rewards in one generation tends to result in the unequal distribution of motivation in the succeeding generation. Since motivation to succeed is clearly an important element in the entire process of education, the unequal distribution of motivation tends to set limits on the possible extensions of the educational system, and hence, upon the efficient recruitment and training of the widest body of skills available in the population. [6]

Lastly, in this context, it may be asserted that there is some noticeable tendency for elites to restrict further access to their privileged positions, once they have sufficient power to enforce such restrictions. This is especially true in a culture where it is possible for an elite to contrive a high demand and a proportionately higher reward for its work by restricting the numbers of the elite available to do the work. The recruitment and training of doctors in modern United States is at least partly a case in point.

Here, then, are three ways, among others which could be cited, in which stratification systems, once operative, tend to reduce the survival value of a society by limiting the search, recruitment and training of functionally important personnel far more sharply than the facts of available talent would appear to justify. It is only when there is genuinely equal access to recruitment and training for all potentially talented persons that differential rewards can conceivably be justified as functional. And stratification systems are apparently *inherently antagonistic* to the development of such full equality of opportunity.

3. *The conversion of talents into skills involves a training period during which sacrifices of one kind or another are made by those undergoing the training.*

Davis and Moore introduce here a concept, "sacrifice" which comes closer than any of the rest of their vocabulary of analysis to being a direct reflection of the rationalizations, offered by the more fortunate members of a society, of the rightness of their occupancy of privileged positions. It is the least critically thought-out concept in the repertoire, and can also be shown to be least supported by the actual facts.

In our present society, for example, what are the sacrifices which talented persons undergo in the training period? The possibly serious losses involve the surrender of earning power and the cost of the training. The latter is generally borne by the parents of the talented youth undergoing training, and not by the trainee themselves. But this cost tends to be paid out of income which the parents were able to earn generally by virtue of *their* privileged positions in the hierarchy of stratification. That is to say, the parents' ability to pay for the training of their children is part of the differential *reward* they, the parents, received for their privileged positions in the society. And to charge this sum up against sacrifices made by the youth is falsely to perpetrate a bill or a debt already paid by the society to the parents.

So far as the sacrifice of earning power by the trainee themselves is concerned, the loss may be measured relative to what they might have earned had they gone into the labor market instead of into advanced training for the "important" skills. There are several ways to judge this. One way is to take all the average earnings of age peers who did go into the labor market for a period equal to the average length of the training period. The total income, so calculated, roughly equals an amount which the elite can, on the average, earn back in the first decade of professional work, over and above the earnings of his age peers who are not trained. Ten years is probably the maximum amount needed to equalize the differential.[7] There remains, on the average, twenty years of work during each of which the skilled person then goes on to earn far more than his unskilled age peers. And, what is often forgotten, there is then still another ten or fifteen year period during which the skilled person continues to work and earn when his unskilled age peer is either totally or partially out of the labor market by virtue of the attrition of his strength and capabilities.

One might say that the first ten years of differential pay is perhaps justified, in order to regain for the trained person what he lost during his training period. But it is difficult to imagine what would justify continuing such differential rewards beyond that period.

Another and probably sounder way to measure how much is lost during the training period is to compare the per capita income available to the trainee with the per capita income of the age peer on the untrained labor market during the so-called sacrificial period. If one takes into account the earlier marriage of untrained persons, and the earlier acquisition of family dependents, it is highly dubious that the per capita income of the wage worker is significantly larger than that of the trainee. Even assuming, for the moment, that there is a difference, the amount is by no means sufficient to justify a lifetime of continuing differentials.

What tends to be completely overlooked, in addition, are the psychic and spiritual rewards which are available to the elite trainees by comparison with their age peers in the labor force. There is, first, the much higher prestige enjoyed by the college student and the professional-school student as compared with persons in shops and offices. There is, second, the extremely highly valued privilege of having greater opportunity for self-development. There is, third, all the psychic gain involved in being allowed to delay the assumption of adult responsibilities such as earning a living and supporting a family. There is, fourth, the access to leisure and freedom of a kind not likely to be experienced by the persons already at work.

If these are never taken into account as rewards of the training period it is not because they are not concretely present, but because the emphasis in American concepts of reward is almost exclusively placed on the material returns of positions. The emphases on enjoyment, entertainment, ego enhancement, prestige and esteem are introduced only when the differentials in these which accrue to the skilled positions need to be justified. If these other rewards were taken into account, it would be much more difficult to demonstrate that the training period, as presently operative, is really sacrificial. Indeed, it might turn out to be the case that even at this point in their careers, the elite trainees were being differentially rewarded relative to their age peers in the labor force.

All of the foregoing concerns the quality of the training period under our present system of motivation and rewards. Whatever may turn out to be the factual case about the present system—and the factual case is moot— the more important theoretical question concerns the assumption that the training period under *any* system must be sacrificial.

There seem to be no good theoretical grounds for insisting on this assumption. For, while under any system certain costs will be involved in training persons for skilled positions, these costs could easily be assumed by the society-at-large. Under these circumstances, there would be no need to compensate anyone in terms of differential rewards once the skilled positions were staffed. In short, there would be no need or justification for stratifying social positions on *these* grounds.

*4. In order to induce the talented persons to undergo these sacrifices and acquire the training, their future positions must carry an inducement value in the form of differential, i.e., privileged and disproportionate access to the scarce and desired rewards which the society has to offer.*

Let us assume, for the purposes of the discussion, that the training period is sacrificial and the talent is rare in every conceivable human society. There is still the basic problem as to whether the allocation of differential rewards in scarce and desired goods and services is the only or the most efficient way of recruiting the appropriate talent to these positions.

For there are a number of alternative motivational schemes whose efficiency and adequacy ought at least to be considered in this context. What can be said, for instance, on behalf of the motivation which De Man called "joy in work," Veblen termed "instinct for workmanship" and which we latterly have come to identify as "intrinsic work satisfaction"? Or, to what extent could the motivation of "social duty" be institutionalized in such a fashion that self interest and social interest come closely to coincide? Or, how much prospective confidence can be placed in the possibilities of institutionalizing "social service" as a widespread motivation for seeking one's appropriate position and fulfilling it conscientiously?

Are not these types of motivations, we may ask, likely to prove most appropriate for precisely the "most functionally important positions"? Especially in a mass industrial society, where the vast majority of positions become standardized and routinized, it is the skilled jobs which are likely to retain most of the quality of "intrinsic job satisfaction" and be most readily identifiable as socially serviceable. Is it indeed impossible then to build these motivations into the socialization pattern to which we expose our talented youth?

To deny that such motivations could be institutionalized would be to overclaim our present knowledge. In part, also, such a claim would seem to derive from an assumption that what has not been institutionalized yet in human affairs is incapable of institutionalization. Admittedly, historical experience affords us evidence we cannot afford to ignore. But such evidence cannot legitimately be used to deny absolutely the possibility of heretofore untried alternatives. Social innovation is as important a feature of human societies as social stability.

On the basis of these observations, it seems that Davis and Moore have stated the case much too strongly when they insist that a "functionally important position" which requires skills that are scarce, "must command great prestige, high salary, ample leisure, and the like," if the appropriate talents are to be attracted to the position. Here, clearly, the authors are postulating the unavoidability of very specific types of rewards and, by implication, denying the possibility of others.

5. *These scarce and desired goods consist of rights and perquisites attached to, or built into, the positions and can be classified into those things which contribute to (a) sustenance and comfort; (b) humor and diversion; (c) self-respect and ego expansion.*

6. *This differential access to the basic rewards of the society has as a consequence the differentiation of the prestige and esteem which various strata acquire. This may be said, along with the rights and perquisites, to constitute institutionalized social inequality, i.e., stratification.*

With the classification of the rewards offered by Davis and Moore there need be little argument. Some question must be raised, however, as to whether any reward system, built into a general stratification system, must allocate equal amounts of all three types of reward in order to function effectively, or whether one type of reward may be emphasized to the virtual neglect of others. This raises the further question regarding which type of emphasis is likely to prove most effective as a differential inducer. Nothing in the known facts about human motivation impels us to favor one type of reward over the other, or to insist that all three types of reward must be built into the positions in comparable amounts if the position is to have an inducement value.

It is well known, of course, that societies differ considerably in the kinds of rewards they emphasize in their efforts to maintain a reasonable balance between responsibility and reward. There are, for instance, numerous societies in which the conspicuous display of differential economic advantage is considered extremely bad taste. In short, our present knowledge commends to us the possibility of considerable plasticity in the way in which different types of rewards can be structured into a functioning society. This is to say, it cannot yet be demonstrated that it is *unavoidable* that differential prestige and esteem shall accrue to positions which command differential rewards in power and property.

What does seem to be unavoidable is that differential prestige shall be given to those in any society who conform to the normative order as against those who deviate from that order in a way judged immoral and detrimental. On the assumption that the continuity of a society depends on the continuity and stability of its normative order, some such distinction between conformists and deviants seems inescapable.

It also seems to be unavoidable that in any society, no matter how literate its tradition, the older, wiser and more experienced individuals who are charged with the enculturation and socialization of the young must have more power than the young, on the assumption that the task of effective socialization demands such differential power.

But this differentiation in prestige between the conformist and the deviant is by no means the same distinction as that between strata of individuals each of which operates *within* the normative order, and is composed of adults. The *latter* distinction, in the form of differentiated rewards and prestige between social strata is what Davis and Moore, and most sociologists, consider the structure of a stratification system. The *former* distinctions have nothing necessarily to do with the workings of such a system nor with the efficiency of motivation and recruitment of functionally important personnel.

Nor does the differentiation of power between young and old necessarily create differentially valued strata. For no society rates its young as less morally worthy than its older persons, no matter how much differential power the older ones may temporarily enjoy.

7. *Therefore, social inequality among different strata in the amounts of scarce and desired goods, and the amounts of prestige and esteem which they receive, is both positively functional and inevitable in any society.*

If the objections which have heretofore been raised are taken as reasonable, then it may be stated that the only items which any society *must* distribute unequally are the power and property necessary for the performance of different tasks. If such differential power and property are viewed by all as commensurate with the differential responsibilities, and if they are culturally defined as *resources* and not as rewards, then no differentials in prestige and esteem need follow.

Historically, the evidence seems to be that every time power and property are distributed unequally, no matter what the cultural definition, prestige and esteem differentiations have tended to result as well. Historically, however, no systematic effort has ever been made, under propitious circumstances, to develop the tradition that each man is as socially worthy as all other men so long as he performs his appropriate tasks conscientiously. While such a tradition seems utterly utopian, no known facts in psychological or social science have yet demonstrated its impossibility or its dysfunctionality for the continuity of a society. The achievement of a full institutionalization of such a tradition seems far too remote to contemplate. Some successive approximations at such a tradition, however, are not out of the range of prospective social innovation.

What, then, of the "positive functionality" of social stratification? Are there other, negative, functions of institutionalized social inequality which can be identified, if only tentatively? Some such dysfunctions of stratification have already been suggested in the body of this paper. Along with others they may now be stated, in the form of provisional assertions, as follows:

1. Social stratification systems function to limit the possibility of discovery of the full range of talent available in a society. This results from the fact of unequal access to appropriate motivation, channels of recruitment and centers of training.
2. In foreshortening the range of available talent, social stratification systems function to set limits upon the possibility of expanding the productive resources of the society, at least relative to what might be the case under conditions of greater equality of opportunity.
3. Social stratification systems function to provide the elite with the political power necessary to procure acceptance and dominance of an ideology which rationalizes the *status quo*, whatever it may be, as "logical," "natural" and "morally right." In this manner, social stratification systems function as essentially conservative influences in the societies in which they are found.
4. Social stratification systems function to distribute favorable self-images unequally throughout a population. To the extent that such favorable self-images are requisite to the development of the creative potential inherent in men, to that extent stratification systems function to limit the development of this creative potential.
5. To the extent that inequalities in social rewards cannot be made fully acceptable to the less privileged in a society, social stratification systems function to encourage hostility, suspicion and distrust among the various

segments of a society and thus to limit the possibilities of extensive social integration.

6. To the extent that the sense of significant membership in a society depends on one's place on the prestige ladder of the society, social stratification systems function to distribute unequally the sense of significant membership in the population.

7. To the extent that loyalty to a society depends on a sense of significant membership in the society, social stratification systems function to distribute loyalty unequally in the population.

8. To the extent that participation and apathy depend upon the sense of significant membership in the society, social stratification systems function to distribute the motivation to participate unequally in a population.

Each of the eight foregoing propositions contains implicit hypotheses regarding the consequences of unequal distribution of rewards in a society in accordance with some notion of the functional importance of various positions. These are empirical hypotheses, subject to test. They are offered here only as exemplary of the kinds of consequences of social stratification which are not often taken into account in dealing with the problem. They should also serve to reinforce the doubt that social inequality is a device which is uniformly functional for the role of guaranteeing that the most important tasks in a society will be performed conscientiously by the most competent persons.

The obviously mixed character of the functions of social inequality should come as no surprise to anyone. If sociology is sophisticated in any sense, it is certainly with regard to its awareness of the mixed nature of any social arrangement, when the observer takes into account long as well as short range consequences and latent as well as manifest dimensions.

## Summary

In this paper, an effort has been made to raise questions regarding the inevitability and positive functionality of stratification, or institutionalized social inequality in rewards, allocated in accordance with some notion of the greater and lesser functional importance of various positions. The possible alternative meanings of the concept "functional importance" has been shown to be one difficulty. The question of the scarcity or abundance of available talent has been indicated as a principal source of possible variation. The extent to which the period of training for skilled positions may reasonably be viewed as sacrificial has been called into question. The possibility has been suggested that very different types of motivational schemes might conceivably be made to function. The separability of differentials in power and property considered as resources appropriate to a task from such differentials considered as rewards for the performance of a task has also been suggested. It has also been maintained that differentials in prestige and esteem do not necessarily follow upon differentials in power and property when the latter are considered as appropriate resources rather than rewards. Finally, some negative functions, or dysfunctions, of institutionalized social inequality have been tentatively identified revealing the mixed character of the outcome of social stratification, and casting doubt on the contention that

> Social inequality is thus an unconsciously evolved device by which societies insure that the most important positions are conscientiously filled by the most qualified persons.[8]

REFERENCES

1. *American Sociological Review*, X (April, 1945), pp. 242–249. An earlier atricle by Kingsley Davis, entitled, "A Conceptual Analysis of Stratification," *American Sociological Review*, VII (June, 1942), pp. 309–321, is devoted primarily to setting forth a vocabulary for stratification analysis. A still earlier atricle by Talcott Parsons, "An Analytical Approach to the Theory of Social Stratification." *American Journal of Sociology*, XLV (November, 1940), pp. 849–862, approaches the problem in terms of why "differential ranking is considered a really fundamental phenomenon of social systems and what are the respects in which such ranking is important." The principal line of integration asserted by Parsons is with the fact of the normative orientation of any society. Certain crucial lines of connection are left unexplained, however, in this article, and in the Davis and Moore article of 1945 only some of these lines are made explicit.
2. The "scarcity and demand" qualities of goods and services are never explicitly mentioned by Davis and Moore. But it seems to the writer that the argument makes no sense unless the goods and services are so characterized. For if rewards are to function as differential inducements they must not only be differentially distributed but they must be both scarce and demanded as well. Neither the scarcity of an item by itself nor the fact of its being in demand is sufficient to aĭlow it to function as a differential inducement in a system of unequal rewards. Leprosy is scarce and oxygen is highly demanded.
3. The arguments to be advanced here are condensed versions of a much longer analysis entitled, *An Essay on Social Stratification*. Perforce, all the reasoning necessary to support some of the contentions cannot be offered within the space limits of this article.
4. Davis and Moore are explicitly aware of the difficulties involved here and suggest two "independent clues" other than survival value. See footnote 3 on p. 244 of their article.
5. Davis and Moore state this point briefly on p. 248 but do not elaborate it.
6. In the United States, for instance, we are only now becoming aware of the amount of productivity we, as a society, lose by allocating inferior opportunities and rewards, and hence, inferior motivation to our Negro population. The actual amount of loss is difficult to specify precisely. Some rough estimate can be made, however, on the assumption that there is present in the Negro population about the same range of talent that is found in the white population.

7. These are only very rough estimates, of course, and it is certain that there is considerable income variation within the so-called elite group, so that the proposition holds only relatively more or less.

8. Davis and Moore, *op. cit.*, p. 243.


# A THEORY OF SOCIAL MOBILITY *
## (*Lipset and Zetterberg*)[1]


## Some Dimensions of Mobility

Max Weber has indicated how useful it is to conceive of stratification along many dimensions.[2] More recently Parsons has suggested that one way of viewing stratification is to conceive of it as "the ranking of units in a social system in accordance with the standards of the common value system."[3] This approach also affords a multitude of cross-cutting stratifications. Of this multitude we would like to single out a few for discussion. They deal with the ranking of occupational and economic statuses, and with the ranking of certain properties of role relationships such as intimacy and power.

OCCUPATIONAL RANKINGS

From Plato to the present occupation has been the most common indicator of stratification. Observers of social life—from novelists to pollsters— have found that occupational class is one of the major factors which differentiate people's beliefs, values, norms, customs and occasionally some of their emotional expressions.

We now have good measures of the prestige ranks of various occupations which can be used as bases for computation of occupational mobility. Occupations are differentially esteemed and studies show a remarkable agreement as to how they rank in esteem. In a well-known survey 90 occupations ranging from "Supreme Court Justice" and "Physician" to "Street Sweeper" and "Shoe Shiner" were ranked by a national sample of the United States.[4] On the whole, there is substantial agreement among the raters from different areas of the country, different sizes of home towns, different age groups, different economic levels, and different sexes. Lenski reports that occupations not mentioned in the survey can be fitted into the

* Reprinted from *Transactions of the Third World Congress of Sociology*, Publication A.185 of the Bureau of Applied Social Research, by permission of the International Sociological Association and the authors.

original rank order with high reliability.[5] Thus it appears that we have available a technique which makes the notion of occupational rank quite feasible for the researcher. Occupations receiving approximately the same rank will be called an *occupational class.* There appears to be a great deal of international consensus about occupational prestige classes.

· · · ·

The above approach to occupational classes in the form of ranking of different occupational titles is theoretically neat and operationally easy. However, one must be aware that it sometimes obscures significant shifts such as those involved in movements from a skilled manual occupation to a low-level white collar position, or from either of these to a modest self-employment. All these occupations might at times fall in the same prestige class. The difficulties inherent in relying solely on this method of classification can be observed most vividly in the fact that many changes in social position which are a consequence of industrialization would *not* be considered as social mobility since they most frequently involve shifts from a low rural to a low urban position. This points to the need of recording not only occupational class but also *occupational setting,* that is, the kind of social system in which the occupation is found. Changes between occupational settings may also be important: white-collar workers behave differently in specified ways from small businessmen or skilled workers although the prestige of their occupational titles may not differ greatly. For example, most researchers in the United States place small business ownership higher than white-collar employment, and the latter, in turn, higher than the blue-collar enclave of the same corporation. When estimating their own social status level, white-collar workers and small businessmen are much more likely to report themselves as members of the "middle class" than are manual workers who may earn more than they do.[6] Studies of occupational aspirations indicate that many manual workers would like to become small businessmen.[7] Political studies suggest that at the same income level, manual workers are more inclined to support leftist parties which appeal to the interests of the lower classes, than are white-collar workers or self-employed individuals.[8]

CONSUMPTION RANKINGS

It is theoretically and empirically useful to separate occupational and economic statuses. For example, economists have for good reasons differentiated between their subjects in their status as "producers" in the occupational structure, and in their status as "consumers." Both statuses might be ranked but it is not necessarily true that those who receive a high rating in their producing capacity would also receive a high consumption rating.

The ranking of consumer status is difficult. Yet it is plain that styles of life differ and that some are considered more "stylish" than others. Those whose style of life carries approximately the same prestige might be said to constitute a *consumption class*. Changes in consumption class may or may not be concomitant with changes along the other stratification dimensions.

At the same occupational income level, men will vary in the extent to which they are oriented toward acting out the behaviour pattern common to different social classes. For example, highly-paid workers may choose to live either in working-class districts or in middle-class suburbs. This decision both reflects and determines the extent to which workers adopt middle-class behaviour patterns in other areas of life. A study of San Francisco longshoremen has indicated that longshoremen who moved away from the docks area after the income of the occupation improved tended to be much more conservative politically than those who remained in the docks area.[9] A British Labour Party canvasser has suggested that one can differentiate between Labour Party and Conservative voters within the working-class by their consumption patterns. The Tory workers are much more likely to imitate middle class styles.

. . . .

It is plain that as an index to consumption class, total income is inadequate, although it obviously sets the ultimate limit for a person's consumption class. It is the way income is spent rather than the total amount, that determines a man's consumption class. The best operational index to consumption class is, therefore, not total income, but amount of income spent on prestigious or cultural pursuits. The fact, however, that lower prestige occupations now often have incomes at the level of white-collar occupations is likely to affect both the style of life and the political outlook of manual workers in a high income bracket and of salaried members of the white-collar class in a relatively lower income position. A comparison of these two groups in terms of their consumption patterns or styles of life is thought to be of particular importance in forecasting future political behaviour, as well as crucial for an understanding of the factors related to other types of mobility in different societies.

It is, of course, difficult to measure the extent of the shift up or down in consumption class. In part, this might be done by comparing the consumption pattern of families at the same income level whose occupational class or income has changed over some particular period of time. Perhaps the best, although most expensive way of dealing with the problem, is to employ a "generational" panel. That is, to interview the parents of a portion of the original random sample, and to compare income in father's and son's family, and their scores on a consumption scale.

SOCIAL CLASS

Much of the research in stratification in America has been concerned with *social class*. This term, as used by American sociologists, refers to roles of intimate association with others. Essentially, social classes in this sense denote strata of society composed of individuals who accept each other as equals and qualified for intimate association. For example, the Social Register Association of American cities considers only candidates for membership after three or more individuals already belonging to the Social Register certify that they accept the candidate as a person with whom they associate regularly and intimately. Men may change their occupational class by changing their job, but they may improve their social class position only if they are admitted to intimacy relationships by those who already possess the criteria for higher rank.

One method of studying social class mobility would be a comparison of the occupational or economic class position of husbands and wives before marriage, or of the respective in-laws.[10] Another index of social class might be obtained by asking respondents in a survey to name the occupational status of their best friends. These latter methods would give us some measure of the extent to which upward or downward mobility in the occupational structure is parallel by upward or downward movement in the social class structure. Such research would be best done in the context of a study which used a "generational" panel.

POWER RANKINGS

Certain role-relationships are also authority or power relationships, that is, they involve subordination on one part and superordination on the other. The extent to which a person's role-relationship affords the means to impose his version of order upon the social system might be ranked as his power, and persons having approximately the same power might be said to constitute a *power class*. It is plain that power classes may be, in part at least, independent of other classes. A labour leader may have a low occupational status and yet wield considerable political influence. A civil servant or parliamentarian whose office is vested with a great deal of political power may enjoy a high occupational and social class, but not be able to meet the consumption standards of these classes. Power as a vehicle for other kinds of social mobility has so far been a neglected area of research.

.   .   .   .

An operational index to power class is difficult to construct. The public debate in Western societies seems rather shy when it comes to matters of power. While there is a fairly freely admitted consensus about the desirability of high occupational consumption and social status, there is less consensus about the loci of power, and less admittance that power might be desirable. Perhaps the best one can do at present is to ask a panel of informed social scientists to list the various types of power positions available to individuals at different class levels. Among workers in the United States, for example, these might include positions in political parties, trade unions, veterans' organizations, and ethnic groups. After collecting the data on all positions held by members of a sample, it should be possible to rank the relative importance of different posts.

The complexity of this problem is of such a magnitude that one cannot anticipate more than fragmental findings on *individual* changes of power class position. The relative power position of various *groups,* however, may change over time, as witnessed, for example, by the return to power of the industrialists in Germany, the decline of the gentry in England, and throughout the Western World the manifest increase in the power of organized labour. It is plain that individuals change in their power class to the extent that they belong to these groups. Such membership (easy to ascertain by survey methods) may reflect itself in different feelings of political involvement and influence; for example, a study of two cities in Sweden by Segerstedt and Lundquist indicates that workers have these feelings to a greater extent than the white-collar class.[11] Likewise, the British worker may experience himself and his class as politically less impotent than, say, the American worker.

This concludes the discussion of the dimensions of social stratification which seems to us theoretically most rewarding and which are accessible by available research techniques. Previous studies of class mobility have, for the most part, ignored the possibility that a society may have a higher rate of mobility on one of these dimensions and a lower one on others. Similarly, an individual may rank high along one dimension while occupying a lower rank along another. We would like to draw attention to the possibility that such a multi-dimensional approach makes it possible to draw more qualified and accurate conclusions about comparative mobility and stratification systems, and above all, might enable us to deal with many interesting problems of intra-society dynamics, particularly in the realm of politics.

．　．　．　．

## Some Causes of Social Mobility

Much of the discussion about the degree of openness of a given society is confused by the failure to distinguish between two different processes, both of which are described and experienced as social mobility. These are:

1. *The supply of vacant statuses.* The number of statuses in a given stratum is not always or even usually constant. For example, the expansion in the proportion of professional, official, managerial, and white-collar positions, and the decline in the number of unskilled labour positions require a surge of upward mobility, providing that these positions retain their relative social standing and income. Demographic factors also operate to facilitate mobility, when the higher classes do not reproduce themselves and hence create a "demographic vacuum".[12]

2. *The interchange of ranks.* Any mobility which occurs in a given social system, which is not a consequence of a change in the supply of statuses and actors must necessarily result from an interchange. Consequently, if we think of a simple model, for every move up there must be a move down. Interchange mobility will be determined in large part by the extent to which a given society gives members of the lower strata the means with which to compete with those who enter the social structure on a higher level. Thus the less emphasis which a culture places on family background as a criterion for marriage, the more class mobility that can occur, both up and down, through marriage. The more occupational success is related to educational achievements, which are open to all, the greater the occupational mobility.

The description of these processes does not, of course, account for *motivational* factors in mobility. If mobility is to occur, individuals need to be motivated to aspire to secure higher positions. The obvious common sense starting point for a discussion of mobility motivation is the observation that people do not like to be downwardly mobile: they prefer to keep their rank or to improve it.

An insightful motivation theory which accounts for men's desire to improve themselves, as well as to avoid falling in social position, may be found in Veblen's analysis of the factors underlying consumption mobility.

> *Those members of the community who fall short of (a) somewhat indefinite, normal degree of prowess or of property suffer in the esteem of their fellowmen; and consequently they suffer also in their own esteem, since the usual basis for self-respect is the respect*

*accorded by one's neighbours. Only individuals with an aberrant temperament can in the long run retain their self-esteem in the face of the dis-esteem of their fellows.*

*"So as soon as the possession of property becomes the basis of popular esteem, therefore, it becomes also a requisite to that complacency which we call self-respect. In any community where goods are held in severality, it is necessary, in order to ensure his own peace of mind, that an individual should possess as large a portion of goods as others with whom he is accustomed to class himself; and it is extremely gratifying to possess something more than others. But as fast as a person makes new acquisitions, and becomes accustomed to the resulting new standard of wealth, the new standard forthwith ceases to afford appreciably greater satisfaction than the earlier standard did. The tendency in any case is constantly to make the present pecuniary standard the point of departure for a fresh increase of wealth; and this in turn gives rise to a new standard of sufficiency and a new pecuniary classification of one's self as compared with one's neighbours. So far as concerns the present question, the end sought by accumulation is to rank high in comparison with the rest of the community in point of pecuniary strength. So long as the comparison is distinctly unfavourable to himself, the normal, average individual will live in chronic dissatisfaction with his present lot; and when he has reached what may be called the normal pecuniary standard of the community, or of his class in the community, this chronic dissatisfaction will give place to a restless straining to place a wider and ever-widening pecuniary interval between himself and this average standard. The invidious comparison can never become so favourable to the individual making it that he would not gladly rate himself still higher relatively to his competitors in the struggle for pecuniary reputability."*[13]

Implicit in this passage seem to be the following hypotheses:
1. The evaluation (rank, class) a person receives from his society determines in large measure his self-evaluation.
2. A person's actions are guided, in part at least, by an insatiable desire to maximize a favourable self-evaluation.

Hence, if the society evaluates a high consumption standard favourably, the individual will try to maximize his consumption level, since he thereby maximizes his self-evaluation. This theory can easily be generalized to any other dimension of class. Since any ranking is an evaluation by the society, it will be reflected in a person's self-evaluation; since any person tries to maximize his self-evaluation, he tries to maximize his rank. This would go for all the rankings we discussed earlier, that is, occupational, consumption, social and perhaps also power classes. The basic idea is that persons like to protect their class positions in order to protect their egos, and improve their class positions in order to enhance their egos. For example, societies with a more visible occupational stratification—for example, Western Europe— are likely to produce stronger ego-needs favouring occupational mobility. Societies which place less emphasis on visible signs of occupational class and stress themes of equality—for example, the United States—are likely to produce less strong ego needs favouring mobility.

We cannot discuss here all the qualifications that modern research must impose on the Veblen theory of motivation for mobility. However, the theory is interesting from the point of view that it does not assume that mobility occurs only as a result of specific social norms pressuring people to be mobile. Instead, the motivations for mobility are placed in the realm of more or less universal ego-needs, operating within stratified societies. This is not to say that the presence of norms to the effect that people *should* be mobile are without effect. It seems to be a general law of social psychology that those who conform to norms are rewarded by more favourable sentiments from their environment.[14] Motivation arising from norms pressuring for mobility might supplement the motivations to rise derived from ego-needs. It is perhaps precisely in societies where these ego-needs are weakest due to cultural themes of equality that mobility norms are most necessary. Thus, the intriguing paradox arises that the United States because of the emphasis on equality must emphasize also mobility norms in order to furnish the motivation necessary to fill higher positions.

This theory, stressing supply of actors and statuses, interchange of rank, and universal ego-needs, goes a long way to explain one of the most in- triguing findings that seems to emerge from comparative mobility research. Popular and academic consensus have long held that occupational mobility in the United States is higher than in Western Europe. Examination of available evidence suggests that this is perhaps not the case.[15] It is now pos- sible to expand the empirical basis for this conclusion. It has been possible to locate data from ten countries which have been collected by survey methods on national samples. The studies comprise Denmark, Finland, Germany (two studies), Great Britain, Italy, Soviet Russia (post-war emigrés), Sweden (two studies), and the United States (three studies). The studies afford only very crude international comparisons, largely using the three categories of manual, non-manual, and farm occupations. In presenting these materials in Table I we make the assumption that a move from manual to non-manual employment constitutes upward mobility among *males*. This assumption may be defended primarily on the grounds that most male non-manual occupations receive higher prestige than most manual occupations, even skilled ones. It is true, of course, that many white-collar positions are lower in income and prestige than the higher levels of skilled manual work. Most of the less rewarded white-collar positions, however, are held by women. The men among them are often able to secure higher level supervisory posts. Consequently, we believe that using the division between manual and non-manual occupations as indicators of low and high occupational status is justified as an approximate dichotomous break of urban male occupations. It is important to recognize, however, that like all single item indicators of complex phenomena, this one will necessarily result in some errors.

When examining the results of these studies, especially the ones for the United States, France, Switzerland and Germany (which are most comparable), there can be little doubt that the advanced European societies for which we have data have "high" rates of social mobility, if by a high rate we mean one which is similar to that of the United States. In each country, a large minority is able to rise above the occupational position of their fathers, while a smaller but still substantial minority falls in occupational status. A British research group, under the direction of David Glass, attempted a quantitative comparison of their data with the findings from the French, Italian and the third American study. Glass and his associates concluded that Britain, the U.S. and France had similar rates of mobility.[16] The Italian and Finnish findings, however, indicate a lower rate of social mobility than in the other countries. It is difficult to make any clear judgment concerning the Finnish data, since father's occupation in the Finnish study is based on the reply to "what class do you consider your father belongs (ed): white-collar, working-class, or farmer?" while the sons are grouped according to their objective occupation.[17] The British, Danish, Italian and second Swedish studies combine urban and rural occupations in the same classes. This has the consequence of increasing downward mobility since many sons of farmers who are middle-class become urban workers. It also reduces upward mobility since children of farm-laborers are less likely to move up than the offspring of manual workers.

The data from these studies tend to challenge the popular conception that America is a land of wide open occupational mobility as compared to Europe, where family background is alleged to play a much more important role in determining the position of sons. It is important to note, however, that the available data should not be treated as if they were a set of quantitatively comparable censuses of mobility in different countries. All that we can say from the existing survey studies is that they do not validate the traditional assumptions. Considerable mobility occurs in every country for which we have data. Furthermore, available historical material tends to indicate that much of Europe had occupational mobility rates from 1900 to 1940 which are similar to the present, and which did not lag behind the American one.[18] Whether there are significant differences among these countries can only be decided after the completion of an integrated comparative research project, which employs the same methods of collecting, classifying, and processing the data. Thus far, no such study exists.

. . . .

## Some Political Consequences of Mobility

Earlier, we called attention to the fact that most studies of social mobility have been descriptive in character and have not attempted to relate findings concerning mobility to other aspects of the society. In this concluding section, we shall discuss the relevance of mobility theory and research to political analysis. Our guiding general assumption is that *many of the major political problems facing contemporary society are, in part, a consequence of the conflict and tensions resulting from the contradictions inherent in the need for both aristocracy and equality.*[19]

Much of the writing in the general area of social stratification has been concerned with the problem of equality. Writers from the time of the Greek civilization on have pointed to the need for tenure in high status positions and the inheritance of social position as requirements for the stability of complex societies. These theorists have suggested that the division of labour require differential rewards in prestige and privilege as the means of motivating individuals to carry out the more difficult leadership or other positions requiring a great deal of intelligence and training. Also, given a system of differetnial rewards, the particularistic values which are a necessary part of family organization require high-statused individuals to attempt to pass their gratifications to their children. The simplest way to assure these rewards for their children is to pass their privileged positions on to them. Thus, a strain towards aristocracy, or the inheritance of rank, is, as Plato indicated, a necessary concomitant of a stratified society.

The legitimation of inherited rank immediately gives rise to another problem, that is the problem of reconciling the legitimation of inherited privilege with the social need to encourage some men born into lower status positions to aspire to and attain higher positions. Thus all economically expanding societies such as the United States, most of Western Europe, India, the Soviet Union, South Africa, and many others, must encourage individuals to aspire to higher or at least different occupational positions from those held by their parents. The dilemma confronting a society in doing this may best be seen in the problems faced by the Soviet Union. Soviet writers have complained that most Russian schoolchildren only desire important bureaucratic and military positions. They have castigated the school system for failing in its obligation of making the children of workers and peasants proud of their fathers' occupations.[20] Yet, while the new ruling class of the Soviet Union attempts on the one hand to reduce the ambitions of lower class youth, its goal of an expanding industrial society forces it to recruit constantly from the ranks of the lower classes.

However, social mobility is not only an issue for the politicians, it is also a force generating political and ideological pressures. There can be little doubt that a system of differential rewards and inherited privilege entails internal strains which make for instability. Such a system requires a large proportion of the population to accept a lower conception of its own worth as compared with others (this follows from the first hypothesis we derived from Veblen). This barrier to the possibility of enhancement of the self may in some cases lead to a rejection of self, described as "self hatred" in the analyses of the personalities of lower-status minority group members. Such a rejection, however, is necessarily difficult to maintain, and in all stratified societies, some men have tended to reject the dominant valuation placed on the upper classes. Sometimes this rejection takes the form of lower class religious values which deny the moral worth of wealth or power; at other times it may take the form of rebellious "Robin Hood" bands, or formal revolutionary or social reform movements; often it may lead to individual efforts to improve one's status through legitimate or illegitimate means.

It is entirely conceivable that the political consequences of class deprivation might be different depending on what dimension of class is challenged. Some recent analysts of the development of rightist extremism in the United States have suggested that this movement is, in part, a response to insecurity about social class position.[21] Essentially, these analyses assume that when the occupational and consumption aspects of stratification are salient, the ideological debate and the political measures will be concerned with the issue of job security, redistribution of property and income. Political movements with this motivation are most common in times of depression when many see their economic position decline. On the other hand, when the social class dimension is challenged or confused, the ideological debate will contain endless discussions of traditional values of ascription, often with elements of irrationality and scape-goating. Political movements with this motivation are likely to occur in times of high occupational and consumption mobility when the old upper class feels itself threatened by *nouveaux arrivées,* and when the latter feel frustrated in not being accepted socially by those who already hold high social position.

The political themes related to threats to social class position, or to frustrations in achieving higher position in the social class structure are likely to be more irrational than those related to the desire for economic security or achievement. Franz Neumann has suggested that the adoption of a conspiracy theory of politics, placing the blame for social evils on a secret group of evil-doers is related to social class insecurity.[22] Groups in this position account for the actual or potential decline which they desire to avert by blaming a conspiracy rather than themselves or their basic social institutions. In doing so, they can continue to believe in the ongoing social structure which accords them their status, while at the same time feel that they are taking action to eliminate the threat to their social status.

It might be interjected at this point that the above is not untestable speculation. We already know how to measure the kinds of mobility which are the independent variables of the hypotheses. The dependent variables— the political themes—can also be measured by the conventional kind of public opinion poll questions. In fact, many already existing questions presumed to measure along a conservatism-liberalism continuum would tap some of the themes, and for the others equally simple items can be constructed. It is also easy to ascertain by survey methods memberships in groups or associations known to embrace any of the above political themes.

Short of having survey data, it is possible to present some impressionistic evidence for the hypothesis that strains introduced by mobility aspirations or anxieties will predispose individuals towards accepting more extreme political views. Political literature knows several suggestions that class discrepancies, e.g. high social class and lower economic position, has this effect. Such hypotheses about rank discrepancies are not strictly hypotheses about social mobility. However, it is plain that whenever social mobility occurs, rank discrepancies are likely to occur, since it is extremely rare that a person would rise or decline at the same rate along all dimensions of class. For example, this hypothesis has been suggested in explaining political behaviour in contemporary Canada. In the province of Saskatchewan, governed since 1944 by a socialist party, it was found that the leaders of the socialist party who were either businessmen or professionals, were largely of non-Anglo-Saxon origin, that is, of low social class. On the other hand, the big majority, over 90 per cent of the middle-class leaders of the Liberal and Conservative Parties, were Anglo-Saxons.

So far, we have reported hypotheses which have predicted a political orientation to the left when a group's social class position is lower than its occupational or economic position, in spite of the fact that the latter normally would predispose to a conservative outlook. It has also been suggested, however, that a rightist orientation also occurs among people in such positions. It has been argued, for example, that *nouveaux riches* are sometimes even more conservative than the old rich, because some of them seek to move up in the social class structure by adapting to the value and behaviour patterns which they believe are common in the class above them, or more simply, perhaps because they have not developed patterns of *noblesse oblige*, characteristic of established upper classes. Riesman and Glazer have argued that the economically successful upwardly mobile Irish in America have become more conservative as a concomitant of their search for higher status.[23]

The political orientation of a group whose social class position is higher than their occupational-economic class should be also affected by this discrepancy in class positions. We have already reported hypotheses which indicate that this may result in rightist political behaviour. On the other hand, however, are suggestions that a discrepancy in status may lead an old but declining upper class to be more liberal in its political orientation. For example, most observers of British politics have suggested that the emergence of Tory Socialism, the willingness to enact reforms which benefited the working-class, was a consequence of the hostility of the old English landed aristocracy toward the rising business class, which was threatening its status and power. W. L. Warner reports a situation in which members of old families in an American city characterized by a high degree of emphasis on ascriptive social class supported the efforts of a radical trade union to organize the plants, which were owned by newly wealthy Jews.[24]

Unfortunately, there is no empirical research and little speculation on the conditions which are related to such varying reactions. Much of the speculation and evidence presented above suggests alternative reactions to seemingly similar social pressures. That is, both rightist and leftist political behaviour has been explained as a reaction to discrepancies in status. Three studies of electoral choice offer a similar dilemma. These studies were made by the Survey Research Centre of the University of Michigan in 1952, by the UNESCO Institute of Social Science in Cologne, Germany, in 1953, and by the Finnish Gallup Poll in 1949. The Finnish and German studies suggest that middle-class individuals of working-class origin are more likely to vote for the more liberal or left-wing party, than are those who are in the same class position as their fathers. The American data, on the other hand, indicate that successfully upward mobile sons of workers are even more conservative in their party choice than those middle-class individuals whose fathers held occupations comparable to their own[25] (Table 1).

**Table 1.** *Left vote of Finnish, German and American middle-class men related to their social origins**

| FATHER'S OCCUPATION | PER CENT BOTH LEFT PARTIES | FIN-LAND— 1949 PER CENT SOCIAL DEMO-CRATIC | PER CENT COM-MUNIST | GERMANY— 1953 PER CENT SOCIAL DEMO-CRATIC | U.S. 1952 PER CENT | U.S. 1948 DEMO-CRATIC |
|---|---|---|---|---|---|---|
| Non-Manual | 23 | 20 | 3 (157) | 32 (200) | 22 (67) | 35 (72) |
| Farm | 6 | 5 | 1 (356) | 20 (142) | 30 (79) | 39 (83) |
| Manual | 10 | 10 | – (183) | 22 (58) | 34 (59) | 49 (61) |

  * The data from which these tables were constructed were furnished by the Finnish Gallup Poll, the UNESCO Institute of Social Science and the Survey Research Center. We would like to express our thanks to them. Non-voters and persons not expressing a party choice are eliminated from this table.

It would be easy to construct some *ex post facto* interpretations for the variations in the consequences of upward social mobility in Finland, Germany and the United States. Rather than do so at this point, we prefer to simply present these results as another illustration of both the complexities and potential rewards inherent in cross-national comparisons.

While the political consequences of upward mobility vary among Germany, Finland and the United States, downward mobility seems to have the same result in the three countries. The working-class sons of middle-class fathers are less likely to back the left parties than are the sons of workers (Table 2).

It is clear from these data that the more consistent the class position of a worker and his father, the more likely he is to accept the dominant political pattern of his class.[26] Also, there can be little doubt that the facts of downward social mobility go at least a part of the way in accounting for conservatives among the working-class.

These two studies like the qualitative and more speculative political analyses reported earlier, only begin to open up the area of the impact of

*Table 2. Left vote of Finnish, German and American workers related to their social origins*

| FATHER'S OCCUPATION | PER CENT BOTH LEFT PARTIES | FIN- LAND— 1949 PER CENT SOCIAL- DEMO- CRATIC | PER CENT COMMUNIST | GERMANY— 1953 PER CENT SOCIAL- DEMOCRATIC | U.S. 1952 PER CENT | U.S. 1948 DEMO- CRATIC |
|---|---|---|---|---|---|---|
| Manual | 81 | 53 | 28 (1017) | 64 (357) | 62 (119) | 82 (101) |
| Non-Manual | 42 | 34 | 8 (50) | 52 (58) | 54 (37) | 64 (36) |
| Farm | 67 | 56 | 11 (378) | 38 (75) | 58 (87) | 89 (64) |

stratification dynamics on political behaviour. The consequences of social mobility, and the determinants of political behaviour are, of course, much more complex than has been hinted above. There is obviously a need for further exploratory research in order to suggest hypotheses that are better than random guesses. From this point of view, it would be gratifying if public opinion surveys concerning political matters see fit to include, in the future, mobility information as a standard category.

REFERENCES

1. The preparation of this paper was facilitated by funds made available by the Bureau of Applied Social Research, Columbia University, from a grant by the Ford Foundation for an inventory of political research, and a grant from the Ida K. Loeb Fund. We are also indebted to the Center for Advanced Study in the Behavioral Sciences for assistance. We would like to acknowledge the advice of Professor Leo Lowenthal, Dr. Natalie Rogoff, Mr. Juan Linz, and Mr. Yorke Lucci. None of these institutions or individuals have any responsibility for the statements made in this article.
   This paper is Publication A.185 of the Bureau of Applied Social Research.
2. Max Weber, *The Theory of Social and Economic Organization* (New York: Oxford University Press, 1947), p. 425, see also pp. 424–429, and Max Weber, *Essays in Sociology* (New York: Oxford University Press, 1946), pp. 180–195.
3. Talcott Parsons, *Essays in Sociological Theory* (Glencoe: The Free Press, 1954), p. 388.
4. National Opinion Research Center, "Jobs and Occupations: A Popular Evaluation," *Opinion News*, September 1, 1947, pp. 3–13.
5. G. E. Lenski, "Status Crystallization: a Non-vertical Dimension of Social Status," *American Sociological Review*, 19 (1954), pp. 405–413.
6. Richard Centers, *The Psychology of Social Class* (Princeton: Princeton University Press, 1949), p. 86.
7. Nancy C. Morse and Robert S. Weiss, "The Function and Meaning of Work and the Job," *American Sociological Review*, 20 (1955), pp. 191–198.
8. S. M. Lipset, *et al.*, "The Psychology of Voting: An Analysis of Political Behaviour," in G. Lindzey, ed., *Handbook of Social Psychology* (Cambridge: Addison-Wesley, 1954), pp. 1139.

9. Unpublished study of Joseph Aymes, former graduate student in the Department of Psychology, University of California at Berkeley.
10. See S. M. Lipset and Natalie Rogoff, "Class and Opportunity in Europe and America," *Commentary*, 19 (1954), pp. 562–568; and David V. Glass, ed., *op. cit.*, pp. 321–338, 344–349.
11. Torgny Segerstedt and Agne Lungquist, *Människan i industrisamhället II: Fritidsliv samhällsliv* (Stockholm: Studieförbundet Näringsliv och Samhälle, 1955), pp. 287–290.
12. See P. Sorokin, *Social Mobility* (New York: Harper and Brothers, 1927), pp. 346–377; and Eldridge Sibley, "Some Demographic Clues to Stratification," *American Sociological Review*, 7, 1942, pp. 322–330.
13. Thorstein Veblen, *The Theory of the Leisure Class* (New York: The Modern Library, 1934), pp. 30–32.
14. H. W. Riecken and G. C. Homas, "Psychological Aspects of Social Structure," in G. Lindzey, ed., *op. cit.*, pp. 787–789.
15. See Lipset and Rogoff, *op. cit.*
16. David V. Glass, ed., *op. cit.*, pp. 260–265.
17. The findings indicating considerable fluidity in the occupational class structure outside of America are buttressed by the results of studies of mobility in individual cities in different countries. A study based on a random sample of the Tokyo population indicates that about one-third of the sons of fathers employed in manual occupations were in non-manual jobs when interviewed, while about thirty per cent of the sons of men in non-manual occupations had become manual workers. (A. G. Ibi, "Occupational Stratification and Mobility in the Large Urban Community: A Report of Research on Social Stratification and Mobility in Tokyo, II," *Japanese Sociological Review*, 4 (1954), pp. 135–149. We describe the results of this study in general terms since close to twenty per cent, of the men were in occupational categories, which we could not fit into the conventional manual—non-manual farm groups without more knowledge about Japanese occupational titles.) A study of mobility among a group of young residents of Stockholm indicates that over half of the sons of manual workers who grew up in Stockholm were in non-manual occupations at the age of twenty-four. (Gunnar Boalt, "Social Mobility in Stockholm: A Pilot Investigation," in *Transactions of the Second World Congress of Sociology*, II, *op. cit.*, pp. 67–73. Two excellent studies of social mobility in a Danish (Geiger, *op. cit.*) and an American (Rogoff, *op. cit.*) provincial city permit an even more detailed comparison of mobility between Europe and America, which is presented in Lipset and Rogoff, *op. cit.* It is clear that there is no substantial difference in the patterns of social mobility in Aarhus and Indianapolis.
18. For example, a study which secured questionnaire data from over 90,000 German workers in the late 1920's reported that almost one-quarter of the males in this group came from manual working-class families. (Gewerkschaftsbund der Angestellten, *Die wirtschaftliche und soziale Lage der Angestellten* (Berlin, 1931), p. 43; see also Hans Speier, *The Salaried Employee in German Society*, Vol. I (New York: Department of Social Science, Columbia University, 1939), pp. 86–98). An early British survey of the social origins of the owners, directors and managers in the cotton industry found that over two-thirds of this group had begun their occupational careers either as manual workers or in low status clerical positions. (S. J. Chapman and F. J. Marquis. "The Recruiting of the Employing Classes from the Ranks of Wage Earners in the Cotton Industry," *Journal of the Royal Statistical Society*, February, 1912, pp. 293–306). Pitirim Sorokin (*op. cit.*) who made an extensive analysis of social mobility research around the world before 1927 also concluded that the assumption that the United States was a more open society in terms of occupational mobility than the industrial sections of Europe was not valid. For early data on mobility in the city of Rome, see Chessa, *op. cit.*
19. See Talcott Parsons, "A Revised Analytical Approach to the Theory of Stratification," in R. Bendix and S. M. Lipset, eds., *Class, Status and Power* (Glencoe: The Free Press, 1953), p. 117; and K. Davis and W. F. Moore, "Some Principles of Stratification," *American Sociological Review*, 10, 1945, pp. 242–249. For a critique of

this position and an answer to it, see H. M. Tumin, "Some Principles of Stratification: a Critical Analysis," *American Sociological Review,* 18, 1953, pp. 387–394; K. Davis, "Reply to Tumin," *ibid.,* pp. 394–397.

20. Alex Inkeles, "Social Stratification and Mobility in the Soviet Union: 1940–1950," in R. Bendix and S. M. Lipset, eds., *op. cit.,* pp. 611–621.

21. See the various essays reprinted in Daniel Bell, ed., *The New American Right* (New York: Criterion Books, 1955); and Richard Hofstadter, *The Age of Reform* (New York: Alfred A. Knopf, 1955), esp. pp. 131–172.

22. Franz Neumann, "Anxiety in Politics," *Dissent,* Spring 1955, pp. 135–141.

23. David Riesman and Nathan Glazer, "The Intellectuals and the Discontented Classes," in D. Bell, ed., *op. cit.,* pp. 66–67.

24. W. L. Warner and J. O. Low, *The Social System of the Modern Factory* (New Haven: Yale University Press, 1947); see also S. M. Lipset and R. Bendix, *op. cit.,* pp. 230–233.

25. Two other American studies suggest similar conclusions. Maccoby found that upward mobile youth in Cambridge were more Republican than non-mobiles in the class to which the upward mobile moved. Eleanor E. Maccoby, "Youth and Political Choice," *Public Opinion Quarterly,* Spring 1954, p. 35. The M.I.T. Center for International Studies interviewed a random sample of 1,000 American business executives in 1955. These data show that only 5 per cent of the children of manual workers are Democrats as compared with 10 per cent Democratic among the executive sons of middle- or upper-class fathers. Hans Speier in his study of white-collar workers in pre-Hitler Germany estimated that 50 per cent of the members of the Socialist white-collar union were the sons of workers, while less than 25 per cent of the members of the two conservative white-collar unions were sons of workers. This finding is similar to the patter in contemporary Germany, see Speier, *op. cit.,* pp. 92–93.

Hence three American studies agree that the upward-mobile are more conservative than the stationary middle-class, while two German and one Finnish study find that the upward-mobile in these countries are more radical than the stationary non-manual workers.

26. Similar patterns are suggested in other American studies. Richard Centers reported that workers who have middle-class fathers are more likely to give conservative responses on questions designed to measure liberalism-conservatism, while the successfully upward mobile sons of manual workers do not differ from those in non-manual occupations whose fathers held similar posts. Centers, *op. cit.,* p. 180. A study of the United Automobile Workers Union found that 78 per cent of the sons of workers were Democrats in 1952 as compared to 60 per cent of the off-spring of middle-class fathers. Arthur Kornhauser, *Why Labor Votes—A Study of Auto Workers* (Boston: Beacon Press, forthcoming). Two studies of trade union membership indicate that mobile individuals are less likely to belong to, or be active in, trade unions. S. M. Lipset and Joan Gordon, "Mobility and Trade Union Membership," in R. Bendix and S. M. Lipset, eds., *op. cit.,* pp. 491–500 and Arnold Tannenbaum, *Participation in Local Unions* (Ann Arbor: University of Michigan Survey Research Center, Mimeo, 1954), p. 292. It is interesting to note that one study based on survey materials, which attempted to relate social mobility to ethnic prejudice in an American city found that both upward and downward mobile persons were more prejudiced than individuals who were in the same social position as their fathers. This result suggests that the socially mobile, whether upward or downward, are more insecure in their dealings with others than those who are stationary in the class structure. It is congruent with our findings that the socially mobile in America are more conservative than the non-mobile at the same level. See Joseph Greenblum and Leonard I. Pearlin, "Vertical Mobility and Prejudice: A Socio-Psychological Analysis," in R. Bendix and S. M. Lipset, eds., *op. cit.,* pp. 480–491.

# 11: Bureaucracy

Bureaucracy may be defined as that type of hierarchical organization which is designed rationally to coordinate the work of many individuals in the pursuit of large-scale administrative tasks. The sociologist uses the term "bureaucracy" in order to designate a certain type of structure, a particular organization of rationally coordinated unequals, and he rejects a popular usage of the term which equates bureaucracy with "red tape," inefficiency, and the like.

The nineteenth century produced a number of brilliantly descriptive and literary accounts of modern bureaucracies. Among the most perceptive were the work of the German sociologist Lorenz von Stein (1815–1890), Balzac's splendid novel, *The Functionaries,* and Dickens' *Bleak House.* All of these teach us much about the origins and working of bureaucracy, but it was Max Weber who began the systematic study of this area. Weber attempted to define a "pure type" of bureaucratic organization by abstracting what he considered the most characteristic features of bureaucracy. He hoped thus to furnish a kind of "measuring rod" which could direct and guide future investigators of specific bureaucratic structures. By providing an ideal construct of the pure form of bureaucracy, Weber sought to permit subsequent research to measure departures from the model. We have chosen two selections from his work. The first is meant to acquaint the reader with the main characteristics of Weber's ideal-type, the second illustrates his more general views about the progressive rationalization and disenchantment of the world which finds the trend toward increasing bureaucratization one of its central manifestations.

Though Weber's work has been seminal, it has frequently been misunderstood. It was often mistakenly assumed that he provided a description of concrete bureaucracies rather than an abstract conceptual scheme. Thus misunderstood, Weber's work of course did not lead to further investigations; it was either accepted or rejected and was not applied to research. Only in the last twenty or so years have his ideas begun to bear fruit in American research. Weber's theory is now neither accepted nor rejected, but it is put to use. Before we consider its influence on younger American theorists, we must turn to that other father of the modern theory of bureaucracy, Robert Michels.

Robert Michels (1876–1936) was a German-Italian sociologist who, though active in many fields of sociological theorizing, will be best remembered for his *Political Parties,* which has exerted considerable influence on both sociological and political theory. While Weber had in the main focused on bureaucratic structures in public and private administration, Michels was concerned with voluntary associations. *Political Parties* was based primarily on the history of European socialist and trade-union organizations before the First World War. If Weber's work was, as we have seen, often unduly simplified by his immediate successors, Michels himself tended to certain oversimplifications. Thus, when he stated his alleged "iron law of oligarchy," i.e., the "law" that all organizations necessarily assume an oligarchical character in the course of their development, his evidence seemed to support only the more moderate view that all organizations have a tendency to develop in the oligarchical forms if this tendency is not counterbalanced by other forces. But Michels' classic analysis of oligarchical tendencies in voluntary associations has, in conjunction with Weber's work, continued to provide the starting point for the bulk of recent investigations into bureaucratic processes.

Robert K. Merton's study of *Bureaucratic Structure and Personality* is a fruitful extension of certain insights provided by Max Weber. Merton's analysis of the ritualistic elements in the role-personality of the bureaucrat has exerted a considerable influence on recent research in the field. While Weber tended to emphasize the positive functions of bureaucracy, Merton allows us to see its dysfunctions as well.

Philip Selznick's book, *T.V.A. and the Grass Roots,* is one of the most important recent works in the empirical analysis of bureaucratic structures. Our selection is taken from a somewhat earlier essay in which Selznick attempted to fuse elements derived from both Weber and Michels into a consistent theory of bureaucracy.

Our last two selections represent efforts to counteract an overly deterministic and, perhaps, overly pessimistic view of bureaucratic developments which has been prevalent until recently. Alvin Gouldner argues against theorists such as Michels and Selznick that the notion of organizational constraints having stacked the cards against democracy flows from a "pathos of pessimism" rather than from the results of scientific analysis. S. N. Eisenstadt, a gifted Israeli sociologist, stresses that the process of bureaucratization is not irreversible, as has often been assumed, but that, on the contrary, historical analysis reveals instances of debureaucratization as well as of bureaucratization.

# CHARACTERISTICS OF
# BUREAUCRACY * (Weber)

Modern officialdom functions in the following specific manner:

I. There is the principle of fixed and official jurisdictional areas, which are generally ordered by rules, that is, by laws or administrative regulations.

1. The reguar activities required for the purposes of the bureaucratically governed structure are distributed in a fixed way as official duties.
2. The authority to give the commands required for the discharge of these duties is distributed in a stable way and is strictly delimited by rules concerning the coercive means, physical, sacerdotal, or otherwise, which may be placed at the disposal of officials.
3. Methodical provision is made for the regular and continuous fulfilment of these duties and for the execution of the corresponding rights; only persons who have the generally regulated qualifications to serve are employed.

In public and lawful government these three elements constitute "bureaucratic authority" In private economic domination, they constitute bureaucratic "management." Bureaucracy, thus understood, is fully developed in political and ecclesiastical communities only in the modern state, and, in the private economy, only in the most advanced insitutions of capitalism. Permanent and public office authority, with fixed jurisdiction, is not the historical rule but rather the exception. This is so even in large political structures such as those of the ancient Orient, the Germanic and Mongolian empires of conquest, or of many feudal structures of state. In all these cases, the ruler executes the most important measures through personal trustees, table-companions, or court-servants. Their commissions and authority are

* From From Max Weber: Essays in Sociology, pp. 196–204, edited by H. H. Gerth and C. Wright Mills, copyright 1946, by Oxford University Press. Reprinted by permission.

not precisely delimited and are temporarily called into being for each case.

II. The principles of office hierarchy and of levels of graded authority mean a firmly ordered system of super- and subordination in which there is a supervision of the lower offices by the higher ones. Such a system offers the governed the possibility of appealing the decision of a lower office to its higher authority, in a definitely regulated manner. With the full development of the bureaucratic type, the office hierarchy is monocratically organized. The principle of hierarchical office authority is found in all bureaucratic structures: in state and ecclesiastical structures as well as in large party organizations and private enterprises. It does not matter for the character of bureaucracy whether its authority is called "private" or "public."

When the principle of jurisdictional "competency" is fully carried through, hierarchical subordination—at least in public office—does not mean that the "higher" authority is simply authorized to take over the business of the "lower." Indeed, the opposite is the rule. Once established and having fulfilled its task, an office tends to continue in existence and be held by another incumbent.

III. The management of the modern office is based upon written documents ("the files"), which are preserved in their original or draught form. There is, therefore, a staff of subaltern officials and scribes of all sorts. The body of officials actively engaged in a "public" office, along with the respective apparatus of material implements and the files, make up a "bureau." In private enterprise, "the bureau" is often called "the office."

In principle, the modern organization of the civil service separates the bureau from the private domicile of the official, and, in general, bureaucracy segregates official activity as something distinct from the sphere of private life. Public monies and equipment are divorced from the private property of the official. This condition is everywhere the product of a long development. Nowadays, it is found in public as well as in private enterprises; in the latter, the principle extends even to the leading entrepreneur. In principle, the executive office is separatd from the household, business from private correspondence, and business assets from private fortunes. The more consistently the modern type of business management has been carried through the more are these separations the case. The beginnings of this process are to be found as early as the Middle Ages.

It is the peculiarity of the modern entrepreneur that he conducts himself as the "first official" of his enterprise, in the very same way in which the ruler of a specifically modern bureaucratic state spoke of himself as "the first servant" of the state.[1] The idea that the bureau activities of the state are intrinsically different in character from the management of private economic offices is a continental European notion and, by way of contrast, is totally foreign to the American way.

IV. Office management, at least all specialized office management— and such management is distinctly modern—usually presupposes thorough and expert training. This increasingly holds for the modern executive and employee of private enterprises, in the same manner as it holds for the state official.

V. When the office is fully developed, official activity demands the full working capacity of the official, irrespective of the fact that his obligatory time in the bureau may be firmly delimited. In the normal case, this is only the product of a long development, in the public as well as in the private office. Formerly, in all cases, the normal state of affairs was reversed: official business was discharged as a secondary activity.

VI. The management of the office follows general rules, which are more or less stable, more or less exhaustive, and which can be learned. Knowledge of these rules represents a special technical learning which the officials possess. It involves jurisprudence, or administrative or business management.

The reduction of modern office management to rules is deeply embedded in its very nature. The theory of modern public administration, for instance, assumes that the authority to order certain matters by decree—which has been legally granted to public authorities—does not entitle the bureau to regulate the matter by commands given for each case, but only to regulate the matter abstractly. This stands in extreme contrast to the regulation of all relationships through individual privileges and bestowals of favor, which is absolutely dominant in patrimonialism, at least in so far as such relationships are not fixed by sacred tradition.

## The Position of the Official

All this results in the following for the internal and external position of the official:

I. Office holding is a "vocation." This is shown, first, in the requirement of a firmly prescribed course of training, which demands the entire capacity of work for a long period of time, and in the generally prescribed and special examinations which are prerequisites of employment. Furthermore, the position of the official is in the nature of a duty. This determines the internal structure of his relations, in the following manner: Legally and actually, office holding is not considered a source to be exploited for rents or emoluments, as was normally the case during the Middle Ages and frequently up to the threshold of recent times. Nor is office holding considered a usual exchange of services for equivalents, as is the case with free labor contracts. Entrance into an office, including one in the private economy, is considered an acceptance of a specific obligation of faithful management in return for a secure existence. It is decisive for the specific nature of modern loyalty to an office that, in the pure type, it does not establish a relationship to a *person*, like the vassal's or disciple's faith in feudal or in patrimonial relations of authority. Modern loyalty is devoted to impersonal and functional purposes. Behind the functional purposes, of course, "ideas of culture-values" usually stand. These are *ersatz* for the earthly or supra-mundane personal master: ideas such as "state," "church," "community," "party," or "enterprise" are thought of as being realized in a community; they provide an ideological halo for the master.

The political official—at least in the fully developed modern state—is not considered the personal servant of a ruler. Today, the bishop, the priest, and the preacher are in fact no longer, as in early Christian times, holders of purely personal charisma. The supra-mundane and sacred values which they offer are given to everybody who seems to be worthy of them and who asks for them. In former times, such leaders acted upon the personal command of their master; in principle, they were responsible only to him. Nowadays, in spite of the partial survival of the old theory, such religious leaders are officials in the service of a functional purpose, which in the present-day "church" has become routinized and, in turn, ideologically hallowed.

II. The personal position of the official is patterned in the following way:

1. Whether he is in a private office or a public bureau, the modern official always strives and usually enjoys a distinct *social esteem* as compared with the governed. His social position is guaranteed by the prescriptive rules of rank order and, for the political official, by special definitions of the criminal code against "insults of officials" and "contempt" of state and church authorities.

The actual social position of the official is normally highest where, as in old civilized countries, the following conditions prevail: a strong demand for administration by trained experts; a strong and stable social differentiation, where the official predominantly derives from socially and economically privileged strata because of the social distribution of power; or where the costliness of the required training and status conventions are binding upon him. The possession of educational certificates—to be discussed elsewhere[2]— are usually linked with qualification for office. Naturally, such certificates or patents enhance the "status element" in the social position of the official.

For the rest this status factor in individual cases is explicitly and impassively acknowledged; for example, in the prescription that the acceptance or rejection of an aspirant to an official career depends upon the consent ("election") of the members of the official body. This is the case in the German army with the officer corps. Similar phenomena, which promote this guild-like closure of officialdom, are typically found in patrimonial and, particularly, in prebendal officialdoms of the past. The desire to resurrect such phenomena in changed forms is by no means infrequent among modern bureaucrats. For instance, they have played a role among the demands of the quite proletarian and expert officials (the *tretyj* element) during the Russian revolution.

Usually the social esteem of the officials as such is especially low where the demand for expert administration and the dominance of status conventions are weak. This is especially the case in the United States; it is often the case in new settlements by virtue of their wide fields for profitmaking and the great instability of their social stratification.

2. The pure type of bureaucratic official is *appointed* by a superior authority. An official elected by the governed is not a purely bureaucratic figure. Of course, the formal existence of an election does not by itself mean that no appointment hides behind the election—in the state, especially, appointment by party chiefs. Whether or not this is the case does not depend upon legal statutes but upon the way in which the party mechanism functions. Once firmly organized, the parties can turn a formally free election into the mere acclamation of a candidate designated by the party chief. As a rule, however, a formally free election is turned into a fight, conducted according to definite rules, for votes in favor of one of two designated candidates.

In all circumstances, the designation of officials by means of an election among the governed modifies the strictness of hierarchical subordination. In principle, an official who is so elected has an autonomous position opposite the superordinate official. The elected official does not derive his position "from above" but "from below," or at least not from a superior authority of the official hierarchy but from powerful party men ("bosses"), who also determine his further career. The career of the elected official is not, or at least not primarily, dependent upon his chief in the administration. The official who is not elected but appointed by a chief normally functions more exactly, from a technical point of view, because, all other circumstances being equal, it is more likely that purely functional points of consideration and qualities will determine his selection and career. As laymen, the governed can become acquainted with the extent to which a candidate is expertly qualified for office only in terms of experience, and hence only after his service. Moreover, in every sort of selection of officials by election, parties quite naturally give decisive weight not to expert considerations but to the services a follower renders to the party boss. This holds for all kinds of procurement of officials by elections, for the designation of formally free, elected officials by party bosses when they determine the slate of candidates, or the free appointment by a chief who has himself been elected. The contrast, however, is relative: substantially similar conditions hold where legitimate monarchs and their subordinates appoint officials, except that the influence of the followings are then less controllable.

Where the demand for administration by trainel experts is considerable, and the party followings have to recognize an intellectually developed, educated, and freely moving "public opinion," the use of unqualified officials falls back upon the party in power at the next election. Naturally, this is more likely to happen when the officials are appointed by the chief. The demand for a trained administration now exists in the United States, but in the large cities, where immigrant votes are "corralled," there is, of course, no educated public opinion. Therefore, popular elections of the administrative chief and also of his subordinate officials usually endanger the expert qualification of the official as well as the precise functioning of the bureaucratic mechanism. It also weakens the dependence of the officials upon the hierarchy. This holds at least for the large administrative bodies that are difficult to supervise. The superior qualification and integrity of federal judges, appointed by the President, as over against elected judges in the United States is well known, although both types of officials have been selected primarily in terms of party considerations. The great changes in American metropolitan administrations demanded by reformers have proceeded essentially from elected mayors working with an apparatus of officials who were appointed by them. These reforms have thus come about in a "Caesarist" fashion. Viewed technically, as an organized form of authority, the efficiency of "Caesarism," which often grows out of democracy, rests in general upon the position of the "Caesar" as a free trustee of the masses (of the army or of the citizenry), who is unfettered by tradition. The "Caesar" is thus the unrestrained master of a body of highly qualified military officers and officials whom he selects freely and personally without regard to tradition or to any other considerations. This "rule of the personal genius," however, stands in contradiction to the formally "democratic" principle of a universally elected officialdom.

3. Normally, the position of the official is held for life, at least in public bureaucracies; and this is increasingly the case for all similar structures. As a factual rule, *tenure for life* is presupposed, even where the giving of notice

or periodic reappointment occurs. In contrast to the worker in a private enterprise, the official normally holds tenure. Legal or actual life-tenure, however, is not recognized as the official's right to the possession of office, as was the case with many structures of authority in the past. Where legal guarantees against arbitrary dismissal or transfer are developed, they merely serve to guarantee a strictly objective discharge of specific office duties free from all personal considerations. In Germany, this is the case for all juridical and, increasingly, for all administrative officials.

Within the bureaucracy, therefore, the measure of "independence," legally guaranteed by tenure, is not always a source of increased status for the official whose position is thus secured. Indeed, often the reverse holds, especially in old cultures and communities that are highly differentiated. In such communities, the stricter the subordination under the arbitrary rule of the master, the more it guarantees the maintenance of the conventional seigneurial style of living for the official. Because of the very absence of these legal guarantees of tenure, the conventional esteem for the official may rise in the same way as, during the Middle Ages, the esteem for the nobility of office[3] rose at the expense of esteem for the freemen and as the king's judge surpassed that of the people's judge. In Germany, the military officer or the administrative official can be removed from office at any time, or at least far more readily than the "independent judge," who never pays with loss of his office for even the grossest offense against the "code of honor" or against social conventions of the salon. For this very reason, if other things are equal, in the eyes of the master stratum the judge is considered less qualified for social intercourse than are officers and administrative officials, whose greater dependence on the master is a greater guarantee of their conformity with status conventions. Of course, the average official strives for a civil-service law, which would materially secure his old age and provide increased guarantees against his arbitrary removal from office. This striving, however, has its limits. A very strong development of the "right to the office" naturally makes it more difficult to staff them with regard to technical efficiency, for such a development decreases the career-opportunities of ambitious candidates for office. This makes for the fact that officials, on the whole, do not feel their dependency upon those at the top. This lack of a feeling of dependency, however, rests primarily upon the inclination to depend upon one's equals rather than upon the socially inferior and governed strata. The present conservative movement among the Badenian clergy, occasioned by the anxiety of a presumably threatening separation of church and state, has been expressly determined by the desire not to be turned "from a master into a servant of the parish."[4]

4. The official receives the regular *pecuniary* compensation of a normally fixed *salary* and the old age security provided by a pension. The salary is not measured like wage in terms of work done, but according to "status," that is, according to the length of service. The relatively great security of the official's income, as well as the rewards of social esteem, make the office a sought-after position, especially in countries which no longer provide opportunities for colonial profits. In such countries, this situation permits relatively low salaries for officials.

5. The official is set for a *"career"* within the hierarchical order of the public service. He moves from the lower, less important, and lower paid to the higher positions. The average official naturally desires a mechanical fixing of the conditions of promotion: if not of the offices, at least of the salary levels. He wants these conditions fixed in terms of "seniority," or possibly according to grades achieved in a developed system of expert examinations. Here and there, such examinations actually form a character *indelebilis* of the official and have lifelong effects on his career. To this is joined the desire to qualify the right to office and the increasing tendency toward status group closure and economic security. All of this makes for a tendency to consider the offices as *"prebends"* of those who are qualified by educational certificates. The necessity of taking general personal and intellectual qualifications into consideration, irrespective of the often subaltern character of the educational certificate, has led to a condition in which the highest political offices, especially the positions of "ministers," are principally filled without reference to such certificates.

REFERENCES

1. Frederick II of Prussia.
2. Cf. *Wirtschaft und Gesellschaft*, pp. 73 ff. and part II. (German Editor.)
3. "Ministerialen."
4. Written before 1914. (German editor's note.)

# SOME CONSEQUENCES OF BUREAUCRATIZATION * (*Weber*)

Imagine the consequences of that comprehensive bureaucratization and rationalization which already to-day we see approaching. Already now,

* Abridged from Max Weber, *Gesammelte Aufsaetze zur Soziologie and Sozialpolitik*, pp. 412 ff. English translation in J. P. Mayer, *Max Weber and German Politics*, 2nd ed., pp. 126–128. Copyright, 1956, by Faber and Faber, Ltd. Reprinted by permission.

throughout private enterprise in wholesale manufacture, as well as in all other economic enterprises run on modern lines, *Rechenhaftigkeit,* rational calculation, is manifest at every stage. By it, the performance of each individual worker is mathematically measured, each man becomes a little cog in the machine and, aware of this, his one preoccupation is whether he can become a bigger cog. Take as an extreme example the authoritative power of the State or of the municipality in a monarchical constitution: it is strikingly reminiscent of the ancient kingdom of Egypt, in which the system of the "minor official" prevailed at all levels. To this day there has never existed a bureaucracy which could compare with that of Egypt. This is known to everyone who knows the social history of ancient times; and it is equally apparent that to-day we are proceeding towards an evolution which resembles that system in every detail, except that it is built on other foundations, on technically more perfect, more rationalized, and therefore much more mechanized foundations. The problem which besets us now is not: how can this evolution be changed?—for that is impossible, but: what will come of it? We willingly admit that there are honourable and talented men at the top of our administration; that in spite of all the exceptions such people have opportunities to rise in the official hierarchy, just as the universities, for instance, claim that, in spite of all the exceptions, they constitute a chance of selection for talent. But horrible as the thought is that the world may one day be peopled with professors (laughter)—we would retire on to a desert island if such a thing were to happen (laughter)—it is still more horrible to think that the world could one day be filled with nothing but those little cogs, little men clinging to little jobs and striving towards bigger ones—a state of affairs which is to be seen once more, as in the Egyptian records, playing an ever-increasing part in the spirit of our present administrative system, and specially of its offspring, the students. This passion for bureaucracy, as we have heard it expressed here, is enough to drive one to despair. It is as if in politics the spectre of timidity—which has in any case always been rather a good standby for the German—were to stand alone at the helm; as if we were deliberately to become men who need "order" and nothing but order, who become nervous and cowardly if for one moment this order wavers, and helpless if they are torn away from their total incorporation in it. That the world should know no men but these: it is in such an evolution that we are already caught up, and the great question is therefore not how we can promote and hasten it, but what can we oppose to this machinery in order to keep a portion of mankind free from this parceling-out of the soul, from this supreme mastery of the bureaucratic way of life. The answer to this question to-day clearly does not lie here.

# BUREAUCRACY AND POLITICAL PARTIES* (*Michels*)

The organization of the state needs a numerous and complicated bureaucracy. This is an important factor in the complex of forces of which the politically dominant classes avail themselves to secure their dominion and to enable themselves to keep their hands upon the rudder.

The instinct of self-preservation leads the modern state to assemble and to attach to itself the greatest possible number of interests. This need of the organism of the state increases *pari passu* with an increase among the multitude, of the conviction that the contemporary social order is defective and even irrational—in a word, with the increase of what the authorities are accustomed to term discontent. The state best fulfils the need for securing a large number of defenders by constituting a numerous caste of officials, of persons directly dependent upon the state. This tendency is powerfully reinforced by the tendencies of modern political economy. On the one hand, from the side of the state, there is an enormous supply of official positions. On the other hand, among the citizens, there is an even more extensive demand. This demand is stimulated by the ever-increasing precariousness in the position of the middle classes (the smaller manufacturers and traders, independent artisans, farmers, etc.) since there have come into existence expropriative capitalism on the grand scale, on the one hand, and the organized working classes on the other—for both these movements, whether they wish it or not, combine to injure the middle classes. All those whose material existence is thus threatened by modern economic developments endeavour to find safe situations for their sons, to secure for these a social position which shall shelter them from the play of economic forces. Employment under the state, with the important right to a pension which attaches to such employment, seems created expressly for their needs. The immeasurable demand for situations which results from these conditions, a demand which is always greater than the supply, creates the so-called "intellectual proletariat." The numbers of this body are subject to great fluctuations. From time to time the state, embarrassed by the increasing demand for positions in its service, is forced to open the sluices of its bureaucratic

* Reprinted from *Political Parties* by Robert Michels, pp. 185–188, with permission of the publisher, The Free Press, Glencoe, Ill. Copyright, 1915, by The Free Press, A Corporation.

canals in order to admit thousands of new postulants and thus to transform these from dangerous adversaries into zealous defenders and partisans. There are two classes of intellectuals. One consists of those who have succeeded in securing a post at the manger of the state, whilst the other consists of those who, as Scipio Sighele puts it, have assaulted the fortress without being able to force their way in.[1] The former may be compared to an army of slaves who are always ready, in part from class egoism, in part for personal motives (the fear of losing their own situations), to undertake the defence of the state which provides them with bread. They do this whatever may be the question concerning which the state has been attacked and must therefore be regarded as the most faithful of its supporters. The latter, on the other hand, are sworn enemies of the state. They are those eternally restless spirits who lead the bourgeois opposition and in part also assume the leadership of the revolutionary parties of the proletariat. It is true that the state bureaucracy does not in general expand as rapidly as do the discontented elements of the middle class. None the less, the bureaucracy continually increases. It comes to assume the form of an endless screw. It grows ever less and less compatible with the general welfare. And yet this bureaucratic machinery remains essential. Through it alone can be satisfied the claim of the educated members of the population for secure positions. It is further a means of self-defence for the state. As the late Amilcare Puviani of the University of Perugia, the political economist to whom we are indebted for an important work upon the legend of the state, expresses it, the mechanism of bureaucracy is the outcome of a protective reaction of a right of property whose legal basis is weak, and is an antidote to the awakening of the public conscience.[2]

The political party possesses many of these traits in common with the state. Thus the party in which the circle of the *élite* is unduly restricted, or in which, in other words, the oligarchy is composed of too small a number of individuals, runs the risk of being swept away by the masses in a moment of democratic effervescence. Hence the modern party, like the modern state, endeavors to give to its own organization the widest possible base, and to attach to itself in financial bonds the largest possible number of individuals.[3] Thus arises the need for a strong bureaucracy and these tendencies are reinforced by the increase in the tasks[4] imposed by modern organization.[5]

As the party bureaucracy increases, two elements which constitute the essential pillars of every socialist conception undergo an inevitable weakening: an understanding of the wider and more ideal cultural aims of socialism, and an understanding of the international multiplicity of its manifestations. Mechanism becomes an end in itself. The capacity for an accurate grasp of the peculiarities and the conditions of existence of the labour movement in other countries diminishes in proportion as the individual national organizations are fully developed. This is plain from a study of the mutual international criticisms of the socialist press. In the days of the so-called "socialism of the émigrés," the socialists devoted themselves to an elevated policy of principles, inspired by the classical criteria of internationalism. Almost every one of them was, if the term may be used, a specialist in this more general and comprehensive domain. The whole course of their lives, the brisk exchange of ideas on unoccupied evenings, the continued rubbing of shoulders between men of the most different tongues, the enforced isolation from the bourgeois world of their respective countries, and the utter impossibility of any "practical" action, all contributed to this result. But in proportion as, in their own country, paths of activity were opened for the socialists, at first for agitation and soon afterwards for positive and constructive work, the more did a recognition of the demands of the everyday life of the party divert their attention from immortal principles. Their vision gained in precision but lost in extent. The more cotton-spinners, boot and shoe operatives, or brushmakers the labour leader could gain each month for his union, the better versed he was in the tedious subtleties of insurance against accident and illness, the greater the industry he could display in the specialized questions of factory inspection and of arbitration in trade disputes, the better acquainted he might be with the system of checking the amount of individual purchases in co-operative stores and with the methods for the control of the consumption of municipal gas, the more difficult was it for him to retain a general interest in the labour movement, even in the narrowest sense of this term. As the outcome of inevitable psychophysiological laws, he could find little time and was likely to have little inclination for the study of the great problems of the philosophy of history, and all the more falsified consequently would become his judgment of international questions. At the same time he would incline more and more to regard every one as an "incompetent," an "outsider," an "unprofessional," who might wish to judge questions from some higher outlook than the purely technical; he would incline to deny the good sense and even the socialism of all who might desire to fight upon another ground and by other means than those familiar to him within his narrow sphere as a specialist. This tendency towards an exclusive and all-absorbing specialization, towards the renunciation of all far-reaching outlooks, is a general characteristic of modern evolution. With the continuous increase in the acquirements of scientific research, the polyhistor is becoming extinct. His place is taken by the writer of monographs. The universal zoologist no longer exists, and we have instead ornithologists and entomologists; and indeed the last become further subdivided into lepidopterists, coleopterists, myrmecologists.

REFERENCES

1. Scipio Sighele, *L'Intelligenza della Folla*, Bocca, Turin, 1903, p. 160.
2. Amilcare Puviani, *Teoria della Illusione finanziaria*, R. Sandron, Milan-Naples-Palermo, 1903, pp. 258 et seq.
3. The governing body of Tammany in New York consists of four hundred persons. The influence of this political association is concentrated in a sub-commitee of thirty persons, the so-called Organization Committee (Ostrogorsky, *La Démocratie etc.*, ed. cit., vol. ii., p. 199).
4. Cf. pp. 33 et seq.
5. Inquiries made by Lask have shown how deeply rooted in the psychology of the workers is the desire to enter the class of those who receive pensions. A very large number of proletarians, when asked what they wished to do with their sons, replied: "To find them employment which would give right to a pension." Doubtless this longing is the outcome of the serious lack of stability characteristic of the social and economic conditions of the workers) Georg v. Schulze-Gaevernitz, *Nochmals: "Marx oder Kant?,"* "Archiv für Sozialwiss.," xxx, fasc. 2, p. 520).

# AN APPROACH TO A THEORY OF BUREAUCRACY * (*Selznick*)

This analysis will consider bureaucracy as a special case of the general theory of purposive organization. Recent sociological research has made explicit several conceptions which must serve as essential background for any analysis such as that to follow. Based upon that research, three hypotheses may be introduced here:

A. *Every organization creates an informal structure.*

B. *In every organization, the goals of the organization are modified (abandoned, deflected, or elaborated) by processes within it.*

C. *The process of modification is effected through the informal structure.*

Three recent sociological studies have elucidated these hypotheses.

1. In an intensive examination of a shop department, Roethlisberger and Dickson found clear evidences of an informal structure. This structure consisted of a set of procedures (binging, sarcasm, ridicule) by means of which control over members of the group was exercised, the formation of cliques

* By Philip Selznick, reprinted from *American Sociological Review*, Vol. VIII, 1943, No. 1, pp. 47–54, with permission of The American Sociological Society and the author.

which functioned as instruments of control, and the establishment of informal leadership. "The men had elaborated, spontaneously and quite unconsciously, an intricate social organization around their collective beliefs and sentiments."[1]

The informal structure of the worker group grew up out of the day-to-day practices of the men as they groped for ways of taking care of their own felt needs. There was no series of conscious acts by which these procedures were instituted, but they were no less binding on that account. These needs largely arose from the way in which the men defined their situation within the organization. The informal organization served a triple *function:* (a) it served to control the behavior of the members of the worker group; (b) within the context of the larger organization (the plant), it was an attempt on the part of the particular group to control the conditions of its existence; (c) it acted as a mechanism for the expression of personal relationships for which the formal organization did not provide. Thus the informal structure provided those avenues of aggression, solidarity, and prestige-construction required by individual members.

The *consequence* of the activity of the men through the informal organization was a deleterious effect upon the professed goal of the organization as a whole: it resulted in the restriction of output. In asserting its control over the conditions of the job, the group wanted above all to protect itself from outside intereference, exhibiting a strong resistance to change.

Thus the facts in this empirical investigation illustrate the hypotheses noted above: the creation of an informal organization, the modification of the professed goal (maximum output), and the effectuation of this modification through the informal structure. In addition, three important characteristics of the informal structure were observed in the study: (a) it arises spontaneously; (b) the bases of the relationships are personal, involving factors of prestige, acceptance within the group, friendship ties, etc.; and (c) the relationships are *power* relationships, oriented toward techniques of *control*. These characteristics are general, and they are important for conceiving of the theory of bureaucratic behavior as a special case of the general theory of organization.

2. C. I. Barnard, in his theoretical analysis of organizational structure, concerned mainly with the problems of the executive discusses explicitly the character and function of informal structures which arise out of the attempts to solve those problems. By informal structures he means "the aggregate of the personal contacts and interactions and the associated groupings of people" which do not have common or joint purposes, and which are, in fact, "indefinite and rather structureless."[2] He says, further, that

"though common or joint purposes are excluded by definition, common or joint results of an important character nevertheless come from such organization."[3]

Barnard lists three functions of informal structures as they operate in formal organizations: (a) as a means of communication, establishing norms of conduct between superordinates and subordinates; (b) "maintenance of cohesiveness in formal organizations through regulating the willingness to serve and the stability of objective authority"; (c) "the maintenance of the feeling of personal integrity, of self-respect, of independent choice."[4] The last mentioned function means simply that the individual's "integrity" is protected by the *appearance* of choice, at the same time that subtle group pressures guarantee control of his actions. Barnard's view of the functions of the informal structure is primarily in terms of the needs of the executive (control through friendship ties, personal authority, a "grape-vine" system, etc.), but it is clear that his analysis agrees with the hypothesis that the informal organization is oriented essentially toward the techniques of control. In the Roethlisberger and Dickson study, it was the worker group which was attempting to control the conditions of its existence; in this case, it is the executive who is doing the same thing.

3. A discussion by Waller and Henderson[5] based on the study of institutions of segregative care, gives further evidence for the theses presented here. The general hypotheses about organizational processes are confirmed by the examination of such structures as private schools, transient camps, prisons, flophouses, reformatories and military organizations. The authors set the problem in this way:

> Each of our institutions has an idea or purposes—most of them have several purposes more or less compatible with one another— and this idea or purpose gives rise to an institutional structure. The institutional structure consists of a system of organized groups. The interaction of these elements is a principal clue to the understanding of institutions of segregative care. Without a structure, the purpose of an institution would be an empty form of words, and yet the process of translating the purpose into an institutional structure always somehow deflects and distorts it.
>
> It is thus the iron necessity of an organizational structure for the achievement of group goals which creates the paradox to which we have referred. The ideals of those who construct the organization are one thing; the "facts of life" operating independently of and often against those ideals are something else again.

*Professed and operational goals.*  Running an organization, as a specialized and essential activity, generates problems which have no necessary (and often an opposed) relationship to the professed or "original" goals of the organization. The day-to-day behavior of the group becomes centered around specific problems and proximate goals which have primarily an internal relevance. Then, since these activities come to consume an increasing proportion of the time and thoughts of the participants, they are—from the point of view of actual behavior—*substituted* for the professed goals.

The day-to-day activity of men is ordered by those specific problems which have a direct relevance to the materials with which they have to deal. "Ultimate" issues and highly abstract ideas which do not specify any concrete behavior have therefore little direct influence on the bulk of human activities. (The general ideas, of course, may influence action by setting its context and, often, defining its limits.) This is true not because men are evil or unintelligent, but because the "ultimate" formulations are not *helpful* in the constant effort to achieve that series of equilibria which represent behavioral solutions to the specific problems which day-to-day living poses. Besides those professed goals which do not specify any concrete behavior, which are analogous to non-procedural formulations in science, there are other professed goals which require actions which conflict with what must be done in the daily business of running an organization. In that conflict the professed goals will tend to go down in defeat, usually through the process of being extensively ignored. This phenomenon may be introduced as a fourth hypothesis in the general theory of organization:

> D.  *The actual procedures of every organization tend to be molded by action toward those goals which provide operationally relevant solutions for the daily problems of the organization as such.*

This hypothesis does not deny that operational goals may be, and very often are, specified in the formulation of the professed goals of the organization. But in any case it is the operational goals which must be looked to for an understanding of the conduct of the organization.

What is meant by the "daily problems"? Consider a boys' reformatory.[6] The institution is organized on the basis of progessive ideals as specified in social work literature. But the processes of constructing and operating the organization create problems and demands, effective daily, to which the general ideals give no adequate answer. Since, however, the existence of the organization depends upon such answers, and since the way of life of everyone concerned depends on the continued existence of the organization, a

set of precedural rules is worked out which *is helpful* in solving these problems. These rules are, in practice, substituted for the professed ideals. "The
social work ideals are fine, but how can we do otherwise than use techniques
of discipline, regimentation, spying, etc.?" This is the cry of those who must
meet daily crises in the institutions of segregative care. "Holiday speech,"
"lip-service," "we've got to be practical" are expressions which confirm from
ordinary experience, repeated over and over again, the validity of this hypothesis.

*The "tragedy of organization."* Beyond such specific sociological investigations as have been mentioned, it is necessary only to point to the fact of organizational frustration as a persistent characteristic of the age of relative
democracy. The tragedy of organization is evident precisely in the fact and
in the consequences of increased participation in associational endeavour.

There have been many critics of democracy, but relatively few have
ventured to support the sweeping judgment of Robert Michels that democracy leads inevitably to oligarchy.[7] It must be admitted, however, that in this
discussion the thesis of Michels finds much comfort. For this theory (taken
in its sociological rather than in its psychological context) stands or falls, in
terms of its lasting significance, with the possibility of establishing that
there are processes inherent in and internal to organization as such which
tend to frustrate action toward professed goals. The burden of research, on
the plane of organizations in general, indicates quite clearly that such is the
case.

Bearing in mind the hypotheses stated above, and the specified character of the informal structure (spontaneity, network of personal relationships, orientation toward control), we may turn to the problem of bureaucracy itself.

*The term bureaucracy.* If the ideas developed above have been clear,
it will be readily evident that the approach which identifies bureaucracy
with any administrative system based on professionalization and on hierarchical subordination is not accepted here. Such a point of view is maintained in the work of Friedrich and Cole[8] on the Swiss Civil Service; the
interest of the authors is clearly in the *formal* structure of the administrative
apparatus as a mechanism of, in this case, popular government. The structure is related to the asserted, professed purposes of the administration; and
*bureaucratization* is conceived of as the tendency toward the complete
achievement of the formal system.

The same point of view is evident in Max Weber's long and careful essay
on bureaucracy—the outstanding work in the literature we have at present:[9]
The main burden of Weber's work is devoted to an examination of the roots,

conditions, and dominant features of the formal organization of an administrative hierarchy. The development of this structure with its dominant features of authoritative jurisdiction, hierarchy of office, specialized training and general abstract rules of procedure, is a process of the *depersonalization* of administrative relationships. Weber's main interest was in the development of rational bureaucratic behaviour as a break from the ties of seignorial leadership set up under the feudal system. The development of centralized hierarchical administration did in fact involve a tendency to vitiate that particular kind of personal influence. But what Weber seems to have only partly understood is that the dynamics of the administrative apparatus itself created new personal influences—those of the administrators themselves seeking their own ends and engaging, as newly powerful participants, in power relationships. That Weber did not overlook the facts of the case is clear from his final pages, in which he discusses the power-role of the bureaucracy. Although recognizing them, he seems to have neglected their theoretical importance.

The use of the term bureaucracy, not as designating an administrative organization as such, but rather some special characteristics of that organization, is common in the literature. Thus Laski's[10] definition of bureaucracy emphasizes the *de facto* power relationships and their consequences. Again, although Dimock and Hyde[11] *define* bureaucracy in terms of the subdivision of jurisdiction, hierarchy and professionalization of personnel, their *use* of the term indicates an interest in such phenomena as "organizational resistance," with the formal structure operating as simply the environment of the bureaucratic tendencies.

The idea of bureaucracy proposed here is consonant although not identical with the usage of Laski and Dimock-Hyde. It will be considered in terms of the hypotheses suggested above. "Bureaucratic behaviour" will designate that behavior of *agents in social action* which:

1. tends to create the organization-paradox, that is, the modification of the professed aims of the organization—aims toward which the agent is formally supposed to strive; this process obtains

2. through such behavior patterns in the informal organization as are centered primarily around the ties of influence among the functionaries, and as tend to concentrate the locus of power in the hands of the officials; and

3. through such patterns as develop through the displacement of the functionaries' motives on the habit level, e.g., routinization.

This does not mean that every situation in which the organization-paradox is found is a bureaucratic one. Bureaucracy is concerned with the behavior of officials, while the action of, say, worker groups, may also lead to deflection of an organization. It is clear from this definition that the emphasis is on the *informal* structure as the mechanism or manifestation of bureaucratic patterns; it does not follow, of course, that those patterns are uninfluenced by the character of the formal organization.

A final point is the question of size. For the most part, the existence of bureaucracy in any sense is associated with large organizations. For Dimock and Hyde, for example, "The broadest structural cause of bureaucracy, whether in business or in government, is the tremendous size of the organization."[12] Indeed, there seems to be little doubt that the factor of sheer size is a very important element in concrete bureaucratic structures. However, because of the patterns exhibited in the behavior of agents in small organized groups and because of the implications for greater generality, the formulation used here does not make the factor of size crucial for the existence of bureaucratic behavior patterns.

*Bureaucratization: a general formulation.* A brief analytical formula stating the general character of the process of bureaucratization may here be introduced:

1. Co-operative effort, under the conditions of increasing number and complexity of functions, requires the *delegation of functions*. Thus action which seeks more than limited, individual results becomes *action through agents*. It is the activity of officials acting as agents with which the discussion of bureaucracy is concerned.

2. The use of intermediaries creates a tendency toward a *bifurcation of interest* between the initiator of the action and the agent employed. This is due to the creation of two sets of problems: for the initiator, the achievement of the goal which spurred him to action, and for the intermediary, problems which are concerned chiefly with his social position as agent. The character of the agent's new values are such as to generate actions whose objective consequences undermine the professed aims of the organization. This conflict need not be between the employer as a person or a group and the agent, for the latter may be able to manipulate the ideas of the former, but between the actual course of the organization and those aims formally asserted, whether the employer recognizes the conflict or not.

3. This bifurcation of interest makes dominant, for initiator and agent alike, the issue of *control*. What is at stake for each is the control of the conditions (the organizational mechanism) which each group will want to manipulate (not necessarily consciously) toward solving its special problems. In this struggle for control, an *informal structure* is created, based largely on relationships involving personal influences rather than formal rules.

4. Because of the concentration of skill and the control of the organizational mechanism in the hands of the intermediaries, it becomes possible for the problems of the officials as such to become those which operate *for the organization*. The action of the officials tends to have an increasingly *internal relevance,* which may result in the deflection of the organization from its original path, which, however, usually remains as the formally professed aim of the organization.

*The bureaucratic leader vs. the rank and file which employs him.*   Utilizing the scheme outlined above, let us examine a concrete type of bureaucratic situation, that which opposes a bureaucratic leader to the rank and file for which he is formally an agent. This situation tends to arise whenever a group of people organize for the attainment of shared objectives, with the additional aim of conducting their organization along democratic lines. Common examples are political parties, trade unions, a national political democracy.

> *1. The need for the delegation of functions to a leader arises from the pressure of the wide range of problems, with which every individual must deal in his social existence, against strictly limited time and ability as well as against the social pressures which limit the exercise of certain functions to only some personality types and to members of only some classes. Even in the small group, individual differences in terms of aptitude for the various functions of organized effort (speaker, writer, record-keeper, etc.) play an important role in creating a leader-ranks relationship.*
>
> *2. Another bifurcation of problems arises from the fact that the problems and interests which impel men to organization are of a quite different kind from those which occur in running the organization. Whenever the ranks are needed to carry out the work of the organization, this gap becomes of real importance. Spurts in organization effort on the part of the members occur when a direct connection can be seen between this organizational work and the reason for allegiance to the organization. Thus a political party can get "activity" when it carries on direct political propaganda—but the day-to-day task of keeping the party together, shaping its character, and strengthening its roots in various centers of power are tasks too far divorced from the original problems to stir most people from their ordinary way of living. In a political democracy, too, only heated contests over broad issues can really "bring out*

the vote," while the day-to-day changes which in the long run are decisive remain uninfluenced by the mass.

3. *There is a hierarchy of values attached to* kinds of work. *Thus even equality between a worker in a unionized plant and the union organizer, in terms of money, does not alter the situation. It is the kind of work involved which is valued above the work of the ordinary members. Not only is there the fact of being well-known (the prestige of bare celebrity), but the fact of having certain powers, however small, of being associated with the incumbent leadership and of being acquainted with the "mysteries" of organization are important. There are always men who* want *to be officials.*

4. *Positive valuation of the office as such raises new problems for the bureaucrat. His interest in the ultimate purpose of the organization, or in the "common good," becomes subordinate to his pre-occupation with the problems involved in the* maintenance *of his post. This is not the same thing as the attempt to hold on to an official sinecure; for in this case, the post is primarily a source of social prestige and power. In many cases, the leaders could obtain better positions financially in another field. The leader of a women's club who,* because she has a following, *is treated with respect by political or other socially important forces, has more than a merely well-paid position. A. J. Muste, in his discussion of factional fights in trades unions*[13] *deals with the problem of why a leadership seeks to maintain its status. He points to reasons such as those already mentioned: the positions are pleasant, the return to the shop is humiliating, the official tends to become less efficient in his old trade. In addition there are motives connected with what they honestly consider to be the good of the union. They feel that they are better (more competent, have a better policy) than the opposition and that they have given more to the union and deserve to be left in power. This is often quite sincere and even* objectively a correct appraisal. *For our purposes that changes nothing: whether honest or corrupt, the tendency is for leaders, to use the same general procedures for the maintenance of their power. This ought not to be surprising: if the question of organizational dominance as such becomes directive in action, and the available means are limited, it is to be expected that the characters of their procedures would converge toward a common type, regardless of their ultimate reasons for desiring dominance.*

5. *The delegation of functions introduces a relation of* dependence. *This is enforced by and perhaps directly dependent upon the
professionalization of the work of the officialdom. To the extent
that the necessary knowledge and skill are increased, the possibilities for replacement of the leadership are diminished. The existence of the organization itself becomes dependent on the
continued functioning of the incumbent leadership. And so long
as this is true, and the ranks still require the organization (or think
they require it), their dependence upon the leaders become firmly
established. This has nothing to do with the existence of formal
(e.g., constitutional) procedures for replacing leaders; these may
continue to exist, but they are relatively harmless to the intrenched
leaders; (because functionless) so long as the ranks fear the consequences of using them.*

6. *In order to be secure in his position, the leader-bureaucrat
must strive to make himself as independent as possible from the
ranks. He must seek a power-base which is not controlled by them.
He may attempt to derive his strength from an electorate more
general than the party or union membership. Thus he will be able
to follow independent policies by claiming that he has a responsibility to a broader base than the party ranks; and the ranks cannot
do without his influence on outside groups. In a nation, an independent politician tends to cultivate those forces, such as a ruling
economic group, which control the instruments which shape mass
opinion as well as the electoral machinery, but which are not themselves controlled by the mass. It is a well-established political
principle that a politician reacts most sensitively to those forces to
which he owes the maintenance of his position; to the extent that
forces can be developed apart from the electorate, he can—and
often must, because he becomes dependent upon the new force—
assert his independence from his formal constituency.*

7. *The leader-bureaucrat must seek a personal base within a
group itself: some mechanism directly dependent on, devoted to,
or in alliance with him which can be used to maintain his organizational fences. A class base in a nation, a political faction in a trade
union, paid gangsters, an elite guard, a secret police force, protégés
and confidants—these are the weapons which he must use in order
to be independent of the shifting sands of public favor.*

8. *Because of this series of problems which the bureaucrat must*

*face, his action in the name of the group, that is, that activity car-*
*ried on to further its professed purposes, comes to have more*
*and more a chiefly* internal relevance. *Actions are taken, policies*
*adopted, with an eye more to the effect of the action or policy on*
*the power-relations inside the organization than to the achievement*
*of its professed goals. An organization drive in a trade union, party*
*activity, legislative action, even the "activities program" of a club*
*—all come to be oriented toward the problem of self-maintenance*
*before possible onslaughts from the membership. Factors of*
*"morale"—the condition wherein the ranks support the incumbent*
*leadership—become dominant.* Bureaucratization is in a sense the
process of transforming this set of procedures from a minor aspect
of organization into a leading consideration in the behavior of the
leadership.

9. *Struggles within a group tend to become exclusively struggles*
between leaders. *The masses (rank and file) play the role of ma-*
*nipulable weapons in the conflict between the controlling groups.*
*The struggle for control between the initiators and the agent-*
*officials is a very complex problem. The rank and file as a group*
*(and in an important sense the leader, too, because he has to build*
*an apparatus which creates new problems for him) cannot ex-*
*ercise* direct *control. Even a struggle against an incumbent leader-*
*ship must be carried on through intermediaries. When a faction*
*is formed, it being an organization too, the relations which operated*
*for the organization as a whole come to be effective within the*
*faction. The faction leaders assert their dominance over their*
*groups and come to grips with one another as leaders whose*
*strength is measured by the forces they can deploy. There are,*
*however, three ways in which the influence of the rank and file is*
*felt in a democratic organization: (a) the threat of spontaneous*
*rank and file action and of a consequent internal revolt makes the*
*construction of bureaucratic power-relationships necessary as a*
*preventive measure; (b) opposing faction leaders tend to champion*
*the professed aim of the organization against the leaders who*
*abandoned it, thus expressing, if temporarily, the desires of the*
*rank and file; and (c) pressure groups, often spontaneous, which*
*do not seek the seizure of the organizational reins, may influence*
*the course of the leadership in directions desired by the mass.*
*This last, however, has usually a limited measure of success pre-*
*cisely because no direct threat to the power of the leadership is*

*offered. It is significant that tolerance of these groups is a function of the extent to which they are interested in "new leadership."*

10. *The bureaucrats, like every other social type with a power-position to maintain,* construct an ideology *peculiar to their social position. The following general characteristics may be noted.*

(*a*) *By the identification of the particular administration with the group as a whole: playing upon the known desire of the ranks for the maintenance of the organization (national, state, party, union, etc.), the leadership attempts to spread the idea that any opposition immediately places the very existence of the organization in jeopardy. In defending itself from attack, it tends to identify its opposition with enemies of the group as such. Thus opponents are "disrupters," "foreign agents," "agent of an alien class," etc.*

(*b*) *An incumbent leadership tends to adopt the ideology of* centralization, *while those out of office call for* autonomy. *The opposition wants to retain its dominance over the local groups or factions which it controls and in general desires to avoid increasing the power of the central authority; the concentration of the control of the organizational mechanism (jobs, equipment, finances) is especially to be avoided, although the minority may not object to that within its own domain. For the ruling group, on the other hand, it is convenient that its power, especially over the organizational mechanism, be increased; it is also desirable that the central powers have the right to step into the affairs of a local group dominated by the opposition, in order to be able to take the offensive against it within the center of its own power. Each side attempts to defend its view by appealing to the professed aims of the group as a whole. In an action organization, the leadership will stress the military aspect and the importance of centralization for discipline action; the opposition will stress the importance of democracy. Although this rule is often broken, there is a tendency for* neither *side to discuss the matter on the basis of the power-motives involved, either in defense of their own view or in criticism of their opponents. This is not surprising, for that would create the danger of exposing the irrelevance of the struggle to the overt aims of the group, which would inevitably result in alienating some of the ranks from both. They therefore sometimes form a pact of silence on these matters, carrying the discussion forward on the level of general principles, at the same time waging furious battle in the shadow-land of informal maneuver.*

(c) The leadership creates the ideology of the "collective submission to the collective will."[14] The obvious necessity for the delegation of certain functions is generalized, and democracy is interpreted sufficiently broadly to include the notion that the group has the democratic right to abdicate its power. The leader, it is proclaimed, represents the "general will," and every action that he takes is justifiable on the ground that he is merely exercising the desires of the collective. Thus the symbol of democracy itself becomes an ideological bulwark of autocracy within the group.

(d) An existing leadership tends to don the mantle of conservatism, with its many variant expressions justifying the maintenance of existing conditions. Since, having the power they are responsible for the exercise of the basic functions of the group or state, they must abandon slogans which are characteristic of irresponsible minorities. The latter need not be considered merely a term of opprobrium; the fact is that a minority can be irresponsible because its function as an opposition is radically different from its function as an administrative leadership, manning and responsible for the conduct of the chief posts of a party or a state. In small groups too, the function of the critic may change, and with that his ideas as well, when he is faced with the new problem of carrying out a program.[15] It is also important to note that a party can be deeply conservative in some aspects and revolutionary in others: thus in the Marxist parties, factors in conservative ideology such as dependence on tradition, depreciation of youth, and rigidity in organizational procedure may go hand in hand with a thoroughly revolutionary program with respect to outside political events. Needless to say, the internal character of such an organization plays an important rôle if that organization achieves any great social influence.

The above discussion emphasizes certain characteristic tendencies in the organization process. These tendencies are, however, analytical: they represent abstractions from concrete organizational patterns. To state these tendencies is merely to *set* a problem, for although they ascribe to organizations in general an *initial presumption of bureaucratic consequence*, it always remains to be determined to what degree the bureaucratic tendencies have become dominant. It may be said, indeed, that this is the way organizations will develop if they are permitted to follow the line of least resistance. That is what does happen, often enough. But in the real world of living organizations there is always the possibility of counter-pressure, of devising techniques for blocking the bureaucratic drift. The study of these techniques, which must be based on a clear understanding of the general nature of the problem involved, is one of the most pressing intellectual tasks of our time.

REFERENCES

1. F. J. Roethlisberger, and W. J. Dickson, *Management and the Worker*, Cambridge: Harvard University Press, 1941, p. 524.
2. C. I. Barnard, *The Functions of the Executive*, Cambridge: Harvard University Press, 1940, p. 115.
3. *Ibid.*
4. *Loc. cit.*, pp. 122–123.
5. W. Waller and W. Henderson, "Institutions of Segregative Care and the Organized Group" (unpublished manuscript), 1941.
6. From a description by Mr. F. E. Robin.
7. *Political Parties*, Hearst's International Library Co., New York, 1915.
8. C. J. Friedrich, and T. Cole, *Responsible Bureaucracy*, Cambridge: Harvard University Press, 1932, p. 84.
9. Max Weber, "Bürokratie," Ch. 7, Pt. 3 of *Wirtschaft und Gesellschaft*. Since translated in *The Theory of Economic and Social Organization*.
10. H. J. Laski, "Bureaucracy" in *Encyclopedia of the Social Sciences*, v. 3, p. 70.
11. M. E. Dimock, and H. Hyde, *Bureaucracy and Trusteeship in Large Corporations*, TNEC Monograph No. 11, p. 31.
12. *Ibid.*, p. 36.
13. "Factional Fights in Trade Unions," *American Labor Dynamics*, ed. by J. B. S. Hardman, New York, Harcourt, Brace, 1928.
14. See Robert Michels' excellent chapter on "Bonapartist Ideology" in his *Political Parties*.
15. For material on the metamorphosis of leaders see Michels, *op. cit.*, and J. B. S. Hardman, "Problems of a Labor Union Somewhere in the U.S.," pp. 163–6, in his *American Labor Dynamics*.

# BUREAUCRATIC STRUCTURE AND PERSONALITY* (*Merton*)

A formal, rationally organized social structure involves clearly defined patterns of activity in which, ideally, every series of actions is functionally related to the purposes of the organization.[1] In such an organization there is integrated a series of offices, of hierarchized statuses, in which inhere a number of obligations and privileges closely defined by limited and specific rules. Each of these offices contains an area of imputed competence and

* Reprinted from *Social Theory and Social Structure* by Robert K. Merton, pp. 151–160, with permission of the publisher, The Free Press, Glencoe, Ill. Copyright, 1949, by The Free Press, A Corporation.

responsibility. Authority, the power of control which derives from an ac-knowledged status, inheres in the office and not in the particular person who performs the official role. Official action ordinarily occurs within the frame-work of preexisting rules of the organization. The system of prescribed relations between the various offices involves a considerable degree of formality and clearly defined social distance between the occupants of these positions. Formality is manifested by means of a more or less complicated social ritual which symbolizes and supports the "pecking order" of the various offices. Such formality, which is integrated with the distribution of authority within the system, serves to minimize friction by largely restricting (official) contact to modes which are previously defined by the rules of the organization. Ready calculability of others' behavior and a stable set of mutual expectations is thus built up. Moreover, formality facilitates the interaction of the occupants of offices despite their (possibly hostile) private attitudes toward one another. In this way, the subordinate is protected from the arbitrary action of his superior, since the actions of both are constrained by a mutually recognized set of rules. Specific procedural devices foster objectivity and restrain the "quick passage of impulse into action."[2]

## The Structure of Bureaucracy

The ideal type of such formal organization is bureaucracy and, in many respects, the classical analysis of bureaucracy is that by Max Weber.[3] As Weber indicates, bureaucracy involves a clear-cut division of integrated activities which are regarded as duties inherent in the office. A system of differentiated controls and sanctions is stated in the regulations. The assign-ment of roles occurs on the basis of technical qualifications which are ascer-tained through formalized, impersonal procedures (e.g., examinations). Within the structure of hierarchically arranged authority, the activities of "trained and salaried experts" are governed by general, abstract, clearly defined rules which preclude the necessity for the issuance of specific in-structions for each specific case. The generality of the rules requires the constant use of *categorization*, whereby individual problems and cases are classified on the basis of designated criteria and are treated accordingly. The pure type of bureaucratic official is appointed, either by a superior or through the exercise of impersonal competition; he is not elected. A measure of flexibility in the bureaucracy is attained by electing higher functionaries who presumably express the will of the electorate (e.g., a body of citizens or a board of directors). The election of higher officials is designed to affect the purposes of the organization, but the technical procedures for attaining these ends are carried out by a continuous bureaucratic personnel.[4]

Most bureaucratic offices involve the expectation of life-long tenure, in the absence of disturbing factors which may decrease the size of the organization. Bureaucracy maximizes vocational security.[5] The function of security of tenure, pensions, incremental salaries and regularized procedures for promotion is to ensure the devoted performance of official duties, without regard for extraneous pressures.[6] The chief merit of bureaucracy is its technical efficiency, with a premium placed on precision, speed, expert control, continuity, discretion, and optimal returns on input. The structure is one which approaches the complete elimination of personalized relationships and non-rational considerations (hostility, anxiety, affectual involvements, etc.).

With increasing bureaucratization, it becomes plain to all who would see that man is to a very important degree controlled by his social relations to the instruments of production. This can no longer seem only a tenet of Marxism, but a stubborn fact to be acknowledged by all, quite apart from their ideological persuasion. Bureaucratization makes readily visible what was previously dim and obscure. More and more people discover that to work, they must be employed. For to work, one must have tools and equipment. And the tools and equipment are increasingly available only in bureaucracies, private or public. Consequently, one must be employed by the bureaucracies in order to have access to tools in order to work in order to live. It is in this sense that bureaucratization entails separation of individuals from the instruments of production, as in modern capitalistic enterprise or in state communistic enterprise (of the 1949 variety), just as in the post-feudal army, bureaucratization entailed complete separation from the instruments of destruction. Typically, the worker no longer owns his tools nor the soldier, his weapons. And in this special sense, more and more people become workers, either blue collar or white collar or stiff shirt. So develops, for example, the new type of the scientific worker, as the scientist is "separated" from his technical equipment—after all, the physicist does not ordinarily own his cyclotron. To work at his research, he must be employed by a bureaucracy with laboratory resources.

Bureaucracy is administration which almost completely avoids public discussion of its techniques, although there may occur public discussion of its policies.[7] This secrecy is confined neither to public nor to private bureaucracies. It is held to be necessary to keep valuable information from private economic competitors or from foreign and potentially hostile political groups. And though it is not often so called, espionage among competitors is perhaps as common, if not as intricately organized, in systems of private economic enterprise as in systems of national states. Cost figures, lists of clients, new technical processes, plans for production—all these are typically regarded as essential secrets of private economic bureaucracies which might be revealed if the bases of all decisions and policies had to be publicly defended.

## The Dysfunctions of Bureaucracy

In these bold outlines, the positive attainments and functions of bureaucratic organization are emphasized and the internal stresses and strains of such structures are almost wholly neglected. The community at large, however, evidently emphasizes the imperfections of bureaucracy, as is suggested by the fact that the "horrid hybrid," bureaucrat, has become an epithet, a *Schimpfwort*.

The transition to a study of the negative aspects of bureaucracy is afforded by the application of Veblen's concept of "trained incapacity," Dewey's notion of "occupational psychosis" or Warnotte's view of "professional deformation." Trained incapacity refers to that state of affairs in which one's abilities function as inadequacies or blind spots. Actions based upon training and skills which have been successfully applied in the past may result in inappropriate responses *under changed conditions*. An inadequate flexibility in the application of skills, will, in a changing milieu, result in more or less serious maladjustments.[8] Thus, to adopt a barnyard illustration used in this connection by Burke, chickens may be readily conditioned to interpret the sound of a bell as a signal for food. The same bell may now be used to summon the "trained chickens" to their doom as they are assembled to suffer decapitation. In general, one adopts measures in keeping with his past training and, under new conditions which are not recognized as *significantly* different, the very soundness of this training may lead to the adoption of the wrong procedures. Again, in Burkes' almost echolalic phrase, "people may be unfitted by being fit in an unfit fitness"; their training may become an incapacity.

Dewey's concept of occupational psychosis rests upon much the same observations. As a result of their day to day routines, people develop special preferences, antipathies, discriminations and emphases.[9] (The term psychosis is used by Dewey to denote a "pronounced character of the mind.") These psychoses develop through demands put upon the individual by the particular organization of his occupational role.

The concepts of both Veblen and Dewey refer to a fundamental ambivalence. Any action can be considered in terms of what it attains or what it fails to attain. "A way of seeing is also way of not seeing—a focus upon object A involves a neglect of object B."[10] In his discussion, Weber is almost exclusively concerned with what the bureaucratic structure attains: precision, reliability, efficiency. This same structure may be examined from another perspective provided by the ambivalence. What are the limitations of the organizations designed to attain these goals?

For reasons which we have already noted, the bureaucratic structure exerts a constant pressure upon the official to be "methodical, prudent, disciplined." If the bureaucracy is to operate successfully, it must attain a high degree of reliability of behavior, an unusual degree of conformity with prescribed patterns of action. Hence, the fundamental importance of discipline which may be as highly developed in a religious or economic bureaucracy as in the army. Discipline can be effective only if the ideal patterns are buttressed by strong sentiments which entail devotion to one's duties, a keen sense of the limitation of one's authority and competence, and methodical performance of routine activities. The efficacy of social structure depends ultimately upon infusing group participants with appropriate attitudes and sentiments. As we shall see, there are definite arrangements in the bureaucracy for inculcating and reinforcing these sentiments.

At the moment, it suffices to observe that in order to ensure discipline (the necessary reliability of response), these sentiments are often more intense than is technically necessary. There is a margin of safety, so to speak, in the pressure exerted by these sentiments upon the bureaucrat to conform to his patterned obligations, in much the same sense that added allowances (precautionary overestimations) are made by the engineer in designing the supports for a bridge. But this very emphasis leads to a transference of the sentiments from the *aims* of the organization onto the particular details of behavior required by the rules. Adherence to the rules, originally conceived as a means, becomes transformed into an end-in-itself; there occurs the familiar process of *displacement of goals* whereby "an instrumental value becomes a terminal value."[11] Discipline, readily interpreted as conformance with regulations, whatever the situation, is seen not as a measure designed for specific purposes but becomes an immediate value in the life-organization of the bureaucrat. This emphasis, resulting from the displacement of the original goals, develops into rigidities and an inability to adjust readily. Formalism, even ritualism, ensues with an unchallenged insistence upon punctilious adherence to formalized procedures.[12] This may be exaggerated to the point where primary concern with conformity to the rules interferes with the achievement of the purposes of the organization, in which case we have the familiar phenomenon of the technicism or red tape of the official.

An extreme product of this process of displacement of goals is the bureaucratic virtuoso, who never forgets a single rule binding his action and hence is unable to assist many of his clients.[13] A case in point, where strict recognition of the limits of authority and literal adherence to rules produced this result, is the pathetic plight of Bernt Balchen, Admiral Byrd's pilot in the flight over the South Pole.

> *According to a ruling of the department of labor, Bernt Balchen . . . cannot receive his citizenship papers. Balchen, a native of Norway, declared his intention in 1927. It is held that he has failed to meet the condition of five years' continuous residence in the United States. The Byrd antarctic voyage took him out of the country, although he was on a ship carrying the American flag, was an invaluable member of the American expedition, and in a region to which there is an American claim because of the exploration and occupation of it by Americans, this region being Little America.*
>
> *The bureau of naturalization explains that it cannot proceed on the assumption that Little America is American soil. That would be* trespass on international questions *where it has no sanction. So far as the bureau is concerned, Balchen was out of the country and* technically *has not complied with the law of naturalization.*[14]

## Structural Sources of Overconformity

Such inadequacies in orientation which involve trained incapacity clearly derive from structural sources. The process may be briefly recapitulated. (1) An effective bureaucracy demands reliability of response and strict devotion to regulations. (2) Such devotion to the rules leads to their transformation into absolutes; they are no longer conceived as relative to a given set of purposes. (3) This interferes with ready adaptation under special conditions not clearly envisaged by those who drew up the general rules. (4) Thus, the very elements which conduce toward efficiency in general produce inefficiency in specific instances. Full realization of the inadequacy is seldom attained by members of the group who have not divorced themselves from the "meanings" which the rules have for them. These rules in time become symbolic in cast, rather than strictly utilitarian.

Thus far, we have treated the ingrained sentiments making for rigorous discipline simply as data, as given. However, definite features of the bureaucratic structure may be seen to conduce to these sentiments. The bureaucrat's official life is planned for him in terms of a graded career, through the organizational devices of promotion by seniority, pensions, incremental salaries, *etc.*, all of which are designed to provide incentives for disciplined action and conformity to the official regulations.[15] The official is tacitly expected to and largely does adapt his thoughts, feelings and actions to the prospect of this career. But *these very devices* which increase the probability of conformance also lead to an over-concern with strict adherence to regulations which induces timidity, conservatism, and technicism. Displacement of sentiments from goals onto means is fostered by the tremendous symbolic significance of the means (rules).

Another feature of the bureaucratic structure tends to produce much the same result. Functionaries have the sense of a common destiny for all those who work together. They share the same interests, especially since there is relatively little competition insofar as promotion is in terms of seniority. In-group aggression is thus minimized and this arrangement is therefore conceived to be positively functional for the bureaucracy. However, the esprit de corps and informal social organization which typically develops in such situations often leads the personnel to defend their entrenched interests rather than to assist their clientele and elected higher officials. As President Lowell reports, if the bureaucrats believe that their status is not adequately recognized by an incoming elected official, detailed information will be withheld from him, leading him to errors for which he is held responsible. Or, if he seeks to dominate fully, and thus violates the sentiment of self-integrity of the bureaucrats, he may have documents brought to him in such numbers that he cannot manage to sign them all, let alone read them.[16] This illustrates the defensive informal organization which tends to arise whenever there is an apparent threat to the integrity of the group.[17]

It would be much too facile and partly erroneous to attribute such resistance by bureaucrats simply to vested interests. Vested interests oppose any new order which either eliminates or at least makes uncertain their differential advantage deriving from the current arrangements. This is undoubtedly involved in part in bureaucratic resistance to change but another process is perhaps more significant. As we have seen, bureaucratic officials affectively identify themselves with their way of life. They have a pride of craft which leads them to resist change in established routines; at least, those changes which are felt to be imposed by co-workers. This nonlogical pride of craft is a familiar pattern found even, to judge from Sutherland's *Professional Thief*, among pickpockets who, despite the risk, delight in mastering the prestige-bearing feat of "beating a left breech" (picking the left front trousers pocket).

In a stimulating paper, Hughes has applied the concept of "secular" and "sacred" to various types of division of labor; "the sacredness" of caste and *Stände* prerogatives contrasts sharply with the increasing secularism of occupational differentiation in our mobile society.[18] However, as our discussion suggests, there may ensue, in particular vocations and in particular types of organization, the *process of sanctification* (viewed as the counterpart of the process of secularization). This is to say that through sentiment-formation, emotional dependence upon bureaucratic symbols and status, and affective involvement in spheres of competence and authority, there develop prerogatives involving attitudes of moral legitimacy which are established as values in their own right, and are no longer viewed as merely technical means for expediting administration. One may note a tendency for certain bureaucratic norms, originally introduced for technical reasons, to become rigidified and sacred, although, as Durkheim would say, they are *laïque en apparence*.[19] Durkheim has touched on this general process in his description of the attitudes and values which persist in the organic solidarity of a highly differentiated society.

## Primary vs. Secondary Relations

Another feature of the bureaucratic structure, the stress on depersonalization of relationships, also plays its part in the bureaucrat's trained incapacity. The personality pattern of the bureaucrat is nucleated about this norm of impersonality. Both this and the categorizing tendency, which develops from the dominant role of general, abstract rules, tend to produce conflict in the bureaucrat's contacts with the public or clientele. Since functionaries minimize personal relations and resort to categorization, the peculiarities of individual cases are often ignored. But the client who, quite understandably, is convinced of the "special features" of *his* own problem often objects to such categorical treatment. Stereotyped behavior is not adapted to the exigencies of individual problems. The impersonal treatment of affairs which are at times of great personal significance to the client gives rise to the charge of "arrogance" and "haughtiness" of the bureaucrat. Thus, at the Greenwich Employment Exchange, the unemployed worker who is securing his insurance payment resents what he deems to be "the impersonality and, at times, the apparent abruptness and even harshness of his treatment by the clerks. . . . Some men complain of the superior attitude which the clerks have."[20]

Still another source of conflict with the public derives from the bureaucratic structure. The bureaucrat, in part irrespective of his position within the hierarchy, acts as a representative of the power and prestige of the entire structure. In his official role he is vested with definite authority. This often leads to an actually or apparently domineering attitude, which may only be exaggerated by a discrepancy between his position within the hierarchy and his position with reference to the public.[21] Protest and recourse to other officials on the part of the client are often ineffective or largely precluded by the previously mentioned esprit de corps which joins the officials into a more or less solidary in-group. This source of conflict *may* be minimized in private enterprise since the client can register an effective protest by transferring his trade to another organization within the competitive system. But with the monopolistic nature of the public organization, no such alternative is possible. Moreover, in this case, tension is increased because of a discrepancy between ideology and fact: the governmental personnel are held to be "servants of the people," but in fact they are usually superordinate, and release of tension can seldom be afforded by turning to other agencies for the necessary service.[22] This tension is in part attributable to the confusion of the status of bureaucrat and client; the client may consider himself socially superior to the official who is at the moment dominant.[23]

Thus, with respect to the relations between officials and clientele, one structural source of conflict is the pressure for formal and impersonal treatment when individual, personalized consideration is desired by the client. The conflict may be viewed, then, as deriving from the introduction of inappropriate attitudes and relationships. Conflict within the bureaucratic structure arises from the converse situation, namely, when personalized relationships are substituted for the structurally required impersonal relationships. This type of conflict may be characterized as follows.

The bureaucracy, as we have seen, is organized as a secondary, formal group. The normal responses involved in this organized network of social expectations are supported by affective attitudes of members of the group. Since the group is oriented toward secondary norms of impersonality, any failure to conform to these norms will arouse antagonism from those who have identified themselves with the legitimacy of these rules. Hence, the substitution of personal for impersonal treatment within the structure is met with widespread disapproval and is characterized by such epithets as graft, favoritism, nepotism, apple-polishing, etc. These epithets are clearly manifestations of injured sentiments.[24] The function of such "automatic resentment" can be clearly seen in terms of the requirements of bureaucratic structure.

Bureaucracy is a secondary group structure designed to carry on certain activities which cannot be satisfactorily performed on the basis of primary group criteria.[25] Hence behavior which runs counter to these formalized norms becomes the object of emotionalized disapproval. This constitutes a functionally significant defence set up against tendencies which jeopardize the performance of socially necessary activities. To be sure, these reactions are not rationally determined practices explicitly designed for the fulfillment of this function. Rather, viewed in terms of the individual's interpretation of the situation, such resentment is simply an immediate response opposing the "dishonesty" of those who violate the rules of the game. However, this subjective frame of reference notwithstanding, these reactions serve the latent function of maintaining the essential structural elements of bureaucracy by reaffirming the necessity for formalized, secondary relations and by helping to prevent the disintegration of the bureaucratic structure which would occur should these be supplanted by personalized relations. This type of conflict may be generically described as the intrusion of primary group attitudes when secondary group attitudes are institutionally demanded, just as the bureaucrat-client conflict often derives from interaction on impersonal terms when personal treatment is individually demanded.[26]

## Problems for Research

The trend towards increasing bureaucratization in Western Society, which Weber had long since foreseen, is not the sole reason for sociologists to turn their attention to this field. Empirical studies of the interaction of bureaucracy and personality should especially increase our understanding of social structure. A large number of specific questions invite our attention. To what extent are particular personality types selected and modified by the various bureaucracies (private enterprise, public service, the quasi-legal political machine, religious orders)? Inasmuch as ascendancy and submission are held to be traits of personality, despite their variability in different stimulus-situations, do bureaucracies select personalities of particularly submissive or ascendant tendencies? And since various studies have shown that these traits can be modified, does participation in bureaucratic office tend to increase ascendant tendencies? Do various systems of recruitment (e.g., patronage, open competition involving specialized knowledge or "general mental capacity," practical experience) select different personality types? Does promotion through seniority lessen competitive anxieties and enhance administrative efficiency? A detailed examination of mechanisms for imbuing the bureaucratic codes with affect would be instructive both sociologically and psychologically. Does the general anonymity of civil service decisions tend to restrict the area of prestige-symbols to a narrowly defined inner circle? Is there a tendency for differential association to be especially marked among bureaucrats?

The range of theoretically significant and practically important questions would seem to be limited only by the accessibility of the concrete data. Studies of religious, educational, military, economic, and political bureaucracies dealing with the interdependence of social organization and personality formation should constitute an avenue for fruitful research. On that avenue, the functional analysis of concrete structures may yet build a Solomon's House for sociologists.

## REFERENCES

1. For a development of the concept of "rational organization," see Karl Mannheim, *Mensch und Gesellschaft im Zeitalter des Umbaus* (Leiden: A. W. Sijthoff, 1935), esp. pp. 28 ff.
2. H. D. Lasswell, *Politics* (New York: McGraw-Hill, 1936), pp. 120–21.
3. Max Weber, *Wirtschaft und Gesellschaft* (Tübingen: J. C. B. Mohr, 1922), Pt. III, chap. 6; pp. 650–678. For a brief summary of Weber's discussion, see Talcott Parsons, *The Structure of Social Action* (Glencoe: The Free Press, 1949), esp. pp. 506 ff. For a description, which is not a caricature, of the bureaucrat as a personality type, see C. Rabany, "Les types sociaux: le fonctionnaire," *Revue générale d'administration*, LXXXVIII (1907), 5–28.
4. Karl Mannheim, *Ideology and Utopia* (New York: Harcourt, Brace, 1936), pp. 18n., 105 ff. See also Ramsay Muir, *Peers and Bureaucrats* (London: Constable, 1910), pp. 12–13.
5. E. G. Cahen-Salvador suggests that the personnel of bureaucracies is largely constituted of those who value security above all else. See his "La situation matérielle et morale des fonctionnaires," *Revue politique et parlementaire* (1926), p. 319.
6. H. J. Laski, "Bureaucracy," *Encyclopedia of the Social Sciences*. This article is written primarily from the standpoint of the political scientist rather than that of the sociologist.
7. Weber, *op. cit.*, p. 671.
8. For a stimulating discussion and application of these concepts, see Kenneth Burke, *Permanence and Change* (New York: New Republic, 1935), pp. 50 ff.; Daniel Warnotte, "Bureaucratie et Fonctionnarisme," *Revue de l'Institut de Sociologie*, XVII (1937), 245.
9. *Ibid.*, pp. 58–59.
10. *Ibid.*, p. 70.
11. This process has often been observed in various connections. Wundt's *heterogony of ends* is a case in point; Max Weber's *Paradoxie der Folgen* is another. See also MacIver's observations on the transformation of civilization into culture and Lasswell's remark that "the human animal distinguishes himself by his infinite capacity for making ends of his means." See R. K. Merton, "The Unanticipated Consequences of Purposive Social Action," *American Sociological Review*, I (1936), 894–904. In terms of the psychological mechanisms involved, this process has been analyzed most fully by Gordon W. Allport, in his discussion of what he calls "the

functional autonomy of motives." Allport emends the earlier formulations of Wood-worth, Tolman, and William Stern, and arrives at a statement of the process from the standpoint of individual motivation. He does not consider those phases of the social structure which conduce toward the "transformation of motives." The formula-tion adopted in this paper is thus complementary to Allport's analysis: the one stressing the psychological mechanisms involved, the other considering the constraints of the social structure. The convergence of psychology and sociology toward this central concept suggests that it may well constitute one of the conceptual bridges between the two disciplines. See Gordon W. Allport, *Personality* (New York: Henry Holt & Co., 1937), chap. 7.

12. See E. C. Hughes, "Institutional Office and the Person," *American Journal of Sociology*, XLIII (1937), 404–413; R. K. Merton, "Social Structure and Anomie." *American Sociological Review*, III (1938), 672–681; E. T. Hiller, "Social Structure in Relation to the Person." *Social Forces*, XVI (1937), 34–44.

13. Mannheim. *Ideology and Utopia*, p. 106.

14. Quoted from the *Chicago Tribune* (June 24, 1931, p. 10) by Thurman Arnold, *The Symbols of Government* (New Haven: Yale University Press. 1935), pp. 201–2. (My italics.)

15. Mannheim. *Mensch und Gesellschaft*, pp. 32–33. Mannheim stresses the importance of the "Lebensplan" and the "Amtskarriere." See the comments by Hughes, *op. cit.*, 413.

16. A. L. Lowell. *The Government of England* (New York, 1908), I, 189 ff.

17. For an instructive description of the development of such a defensive organization in a group of workers, see F. J. Roethlisberger and W. J. Dickson, *Management and the Worker* (Boston: Harvard School of Business Administration, 1934).

18. E. C. Hughes, "Personality Types and the Division of Labor," *American Journal of Sociology*, XXXIII (1928), 754–768. Much the same distinction is drawn by Leopold von Wiese and Howard Becker, *Systematic Sociology* (New York: John Wiley & Sons, 1932), pp. 222–25 *et passim*.

19. Hughes recognizes one phase of this process of sanctification when he writes that professional training "carries with it as a by-product assimilation of the candidate to a set of professional attitudes and controls, a *professional conscience and solidarity. The profession claims and aims to become a moral unit.*" Hughes, *op. cit.*, p. 762, (italics inserted). In this same connection, Sumner's concept of *pathos*, as the halo of sentiment which protects a social value from criticism, is particularly relevant, inasmuch as it affords a clue to the mechanism involved in the process of sanctifica-tion. See his *Folkways* (Boston: Ginn & Co., 1906), pp. 180–181.

20. " 'They treat you like a lump of dirt they do. I see a navvy reach across the counter and shake one of them by the collar the other day. The rest of us felt like cheering. Of course he lost his benefit over it. . . . But the clerk deserved it for his sassy way.' " (E. W. Bakke, *The Unemployed Man*, New York: Dutton, 1934, pp. 79–80). Note that the domineering attitude was *imputed* by the unemployed client who is in a state of tension due to his loss of status and self-esteem in a society where the ideology is still current that an "able man" can always find a job. That the imputa-tion of arrogance stems largely from the client's state of mind is seen from Bakke's own observation that "the clerks were rushed, and had no time for pleasantries, but there was little sign of harshness or a superiority feeling in their treatment of the men." Insofar as there is an objective basis for the imputation of arrogant behavior to bureaucrats, it may possibly be explained by the following juxtaposed statements. "Auch der moderne, sei es öffentliche, sei es private, Beamte erstrebt immer und geniesst meist den Beherrschten gegenüber eine spezifisch gehobene, 'ständische' soziale Schätzung." (Weber, *op. cit.*, 652.) "In persons in whom the craving for prestige is uppermost, hostility usually takes the form of a desire to humiliate others." (K. Horney, *The Neurotic Personality of Our Time*, New York: Norton, 1937, pp. 178–79).

21. In this connection, note the relevance of Koffka's comments on certain features of

the pecking-order of birds. "If one compares the behavior of the bird at the top of the pecking list, the despot, with that of one very far down, the second or third from the last, then one finds the latter much more cruel to the few others over whom he lords it than the former in his treatment of all members. As soon as one removes from the group all members above the penultimate, his behavior becomes milder and may even become very friendly. . . . It is not difficult to find analogies to this in human societies, and therefore one side of such behavior must be primarily the effects of the social groupings, and not of individual characteristics." K. Koffka, *Principles of Gestalt Psychology* (New York: Harcourt, Brace, 1935), pp. 668–9.

22. At this point the political machine often becomes functionally significant. As Steffens and others have shown, highly personalized relations and the abrogation of formal rules (red tape) by the machine often satisfy the needs of individual "clients" more fully than the formalized mechanism of governmental bureaucracy. See the slight elaboration of this as set forth in Chapter I.

23. As one of the unemployed men remarked about the clerks at the Greenwich Employment Exchange: "'And the bloody blokes wouldn't have their jobs if it wasn't for us men out of a job either. That's what gets me about their holding their noses up.'" Bakke, *op. cit.*, p. 80.

24. The diagnostic significance of such linguistic indices as epithets has scarcely been explored by the sociologist. Sumner properly observes that epithets produce "summary criticisms" and definitions of social situations. Dollard also notes that "epithets frequently define the central issues in a society," and Sapir has rightly emphasized the importance of context of situations in appraising the significance of epithets. Of equal relevance is Linton's observation that "in case histories the way in which the community felt about a particular episode is, if anything, more important to our study than the actual behavior. . . ." A sociological study of "vocabularies of encomium and opprobrium" should lead to valuable findings.

25. *Cf.* Ellsworth Faris, *The Nature of Human Nature* (New York: McGraw-Hill, 1937), pp. 41 ff.

26. Community disapproval of many forms of behavior may be analyzed in terms of one or the other of these patterns of substitution of culturally inappropriate types of relationship. Thus, prostitution constitutes a type-case where coitus, a form of intimacy which is institutionally defined as symbolic of the most "sacred" primary group relationship, is placed within a contractual context, symbolized by the exchange of that most impersonal of all symbols, money. See Kingsley Davis, "The Sociology of Prostitution," *American Sociological Review*, II (1937), 744–55.


# METAPHYSICAL PATHOS AND THE THEORY OF BUREAUCRACY * (*Gouldner*)

The conduct of a polemic focusses attention on the differences between two points of view to the neglect of their continuity and convergences. No modern polemic better exemplifies this than the controversy between the proponents of capitalism and of socialism. Each tends to define itself as the antithesis of the other; even the uncommitted bystander, rare though he be, is likely to think of the two as if they were utterly alien systems.

* Reprinted in part from Alvin W. Gouldner, *American Political Science Review*, 49 (1955), 493–507, by permission of the author and publisher, The American Political Science Association.

There have always been some, however, who have taken exception to this sharp contrast between socialism and capitalism and who have insisted that there are significant similarities between the two. . . .

Without doubt the most sophisticated formulation of this view was that conceived by the German sociologist, Max Weber. To Weber, the distinguishing characteristic of modern capitalism was the "rational organization of free labor." The pursuit of private gain, noted Weber, was well known in many earlier societies; what distinguishes present-day capitalism, he held, is the peculiar organization of the production unit, an organization that is essentially bureaucratic. This conception of capitalism, writes Parsons, "has one important concrete result; in contradistinction to Marx and most 'liberal' theories, it strongly minimizes the differences between capitalism and socialism, emphasizing rather their continuity. Not only would socialistic organization leave the central fact of bureaucracy untouched, it would greatly accentuate its importance."[1]

While Marx had dwelt largely on the interrelations *among* production units, that is, their market ties, Weber focussed on the social relations *within* the industrial unit. If social relations inside of socialist and capitalist factories are fundamentally alike, in that they are both bureaucratic, then, asked Weber, does a socialist revolution yield very much of an improvement for the capitalist proletarian? If Marx argued that the workers of the world had nothing to *lose* by revolting, Weber contended that they really had nothing to *gain*.

It is sometimes assumed today that the Weberian outlook is at bottom anti-socialist. In effect, the argument runs, Weber's viewpoint devitalizes the myth-like appeal of socialism, draining off its ability to muster immense enthusiasms. Weber's theses are therefore held to be an "ideology" serviceable for the survival of capitalism, while Weber himself is characterized as the "Marx of the bourgeoisie."

Now all this may be true, but it is only a partial truth; for, in actuality, Weber's theories cut two ways, not one. If it is correct that his theory of bureaucracy saps the fervor of the socialist offensive, it also undermines the stamina of the capitalist bastions. If socialism and capitalism are similar in being bureaucratic, then not only is there little *profit* in substituting one for the other, but there is also little *loss*.

Considered only from the standpoint of its political consequences then, the Weberian outlook is not anti-socialist alone, nor anti-capitalist alone, it is both. In the final analysis its political slogan becomes "a plague on both your houses." If Weber is to be regarded as an "ideologist," he is an ideologist not of counter-revolution but of quiescence and neutralism. For many intellectuals who have erected a theory of group organization on Weberian foundations, the world has been emptied of choice, leaving them disoriented and despairing.

That gifted historian of ideas, Arthur O. Lovejoy, astutely observed that every theory is associated with, or generates, a set of sentiments which those subscribing to the theory could only dimly sense. Lovejoy called this the "metaphysical pathos" of ideas, a pathos which is "exemplified in any description of the nature of things, any characterization of the world to which one belongs, in terms which, like the words of a poem, evoke through their associations and through a sort of empathy which they engender, a congenial mood or tone of feelings."[2]

As a result, a commitment to a theory often occurs by a process other than the one which its proponents believe and it is usually more consequential than they realize. A commitment to a theory may be made because the theory is congruent with the mood or deep-lying sentiments of its adherents, rather than merely because it has been cerebrally inspected and found valid.

So too is it with the theory of organization. Paradoxically enough, some of the very theories which promise to make man's own work more intelligible to himself and more amenable to his intelligence are infused with an intangible metaphysical pathos which insinuates, in the very midst of new discoveries, that all is lost. For the metaphysical pathos of much of the modern theory of group organization is that of pessimism and fatalism.

## Explanations of Bureaucracy

Among the serious goads to pessimism are theories explaining bureaucracy as the end-product of increased size and complexity in organizations. This is by far the most popular of the interpretations. Marshall Dimock and Howard Hyde, for example, in their report to the Temporary National Economic Committee (TNEC), state: "The broadest structural cause of bureaucracy, whether in business or in government, is the tremendous size of the organization. Thus with capital or appropriations measured in hundreds of millions and in billions of dollars and personnel in tens and hundreds of thousands, it is difficult to avoid the obtrusion of the objectionable features of bureaucracy."[3]

While suggesting varied causes for the development of bureaucracy, Max Weber also interpreted it as a consequence of large size. For example, in discussing the ubiquity of bureaucratic forms, Weber adds: "The same [bureaucratic] phenomena are found in the large-scale capitalistic enterprise; and the larger it is, the greater their role."[4] He underscores the role of size by emphasizing that "only by reversion in every field—political, religious, economic, etc.—to small-scale organization would it be possible to escape its influence."[5] Despite his consideration of other possible sources of bureaucracy, these comments suggest that Weber regarded organizational size as the controlling factor in the development of bureaucracy.

Weber's emphasis on size as the crucial determinant of bureaucratic development is unsatisfactory for several reasons. First, there are historic examples of human efforts carried out on an enormous scale which were not bureaucratic in any serious sense of the term.[6] The building of the Egyptian pyramids is an obvious example. Second, Weber never considers the possibility that it is not "large size" as such that disposes to bureaucracy; large size may be important only because it generates other social forces which, in their turn, generate bureaucratic patterns.

Of course, in every analysis there are always intervening variables— the unknown "x"—which stand between any cause and effect. Scientific progress depends, in part, on moving away from the gross causes and coming closer to those which are more invariably connected with the object of interest. The point is that when a social scientist accepts "size" as an explanatory factor, instead of going on to ask what there is *about size* that makes for bureaucracy, he is making an analytic *decision*. It is not a formulation unavoidably dictated by the nature of the data itself.

Significantly, though, it is a decision that conduces to bleak pessimism. For to inform members of our society that the only way out of the bureaucratic impasse is to return to the historical past and to trade in large- for small-scale organizations is, in effect, to announce the practical impossibility of coping with bureaucracy. Moreover, many people in our society believe that "bigness" symbolizes progress; to tell them that it also creates bureaucracy is to place them on the horns of a dilemma which gores no matter which way they turn. In such a position the most painless response is inaction.

## The Structural-Functionalists

The fuller ramifications of this approach to bureaucracy can best be explained by turning to the analyses of industrial organization made by some of the "structural-functionalists," who are still the dominant, albeit now seriously challenged, school of American sociologists, which has grown directly out of the theories of Durkheim, Weber, and others, and whose most elaborate expression is to be found in the work of Talcott Parsons.

Parsons' recent analyses of industrial bureaucracy are of sufficient importance to be quoted in full. "Though with many individual exceptions [which he does not examine], *technological advance* almost always leads to increasingly *elaborate division of labor* and the concomitant requirement of increasingly elaborate organization." He continues:

> *The fundamental reason for this is, of course, that with elaborate differentiation of functions the need for* minute coordination *of the different functions develops at the same time. . . . There must be a* complex organization of supervision *to make quite sure that exactly the right thing is done. . . . Feeding the various parts into the process, in such a way that a modern assembly line can operate smoothly, requires very* complex organization *to see that they are available in just the right quantities at the right times and places. . . . One of the most important phases of this process of change is concerned with the necessity for* formalization *when certain points of complexity are reached. . . .*
>
> Smaller *and simpler organizations are typically managed with a high degree of particularism (i.e., personal consideration) in the relations of persons in authority to their own subordinates. But when the "distance" between points of decision and of operation increases, and the number of operating units affected by decisions with it, uniformity and coordination can be attained* only *by a high degree of formalization. . . .*[7]

Surprisingly enough, this is an atavistic recurrence of technological determinism in which characteristic bureaucratic traits—such as an elaborate division of labor, complex organization, and formalization—are held to stem directly from technological advance. This is a form of *technological* determinism because bureaucracy is seen as the result of technological change, without inquiring into the motives and meanings which these changes have for the people involved, and without wondering whether technological change would have a different impact on the formal organization of a group that had a high motivation to produce and therefore did not require close supervision. This is a form of technological *determinism,* because no alternative solutions are appraised or deemed possible and coordination is seen as attainable *"only* by a high degree of formalization. . . ."

Here once again we are invited to draw the conclusion that those who want modern technology must be prepared to pay for it with a minute and even stultifying division of labor.

All this, though, is a theoretical tapestry devoid of even the plainest empirical trimmings. Even on logical grounds, however, it is tenuous indeed.

For it is evident that organizational patterns, such as a high division of labor, are found in spheres where modern technology has made comparatively little headway. This, in fact, is a point that Weber was at pains to insist upon. And if, as he maintained, bureaucratic forms are also found in charitable, political, or religious organizations—and not solely in industry—then they certainly cannot be explained as a consequence of modern machine technology.

Beyond these logical considerations, there are some *empirical* grounds for questioning the adequacy of Parsons' analysis. Peter Drucker, for example, became extremely doubtful about the necessity of a minute division of labor while observing large-scale American industry during World War II. (This is crucial for Parsons' argument, because he holds that it is through increased specialization that technology evokes the other elements of bureaucratic organization.) Drucker comments that

> *We have learned that it is neither necessary nor always efficient to organize all mass production in such a manner as to have the majority of workers confine themselves to doing one and only one of the elementary manipulations. . . . It was impossible [because of wartime shortages of skilled labor] to "lay out" the job in the usual assembly-line fashion in which one unskilled operation done by one unskilled man is followed by the next unskilled man. The operation was broken down into its unskilled components like any assembly-line job.* But then the unskilled components were put together again with the result that an unskilled worker actually performed the job of a highly skilled mechanic—*and did it as reliably and efficiently as had been done by skilled men.*[8]

In short, lower degrees of specialization than those normally found in large-scale industry are not necessarily forbidden by modern technology. Drucker's observations must, at the very least, raise the question as to how much of the minute division of labor is attributable to technological causes. Parsons, though, gives no consideration to other factors contributing to an extreme division of labor. However, Carl Dreyfuss, a German industrial sociologist, has advanced an array of keen observations and hypotheses which meet this question directly. He writes: "the artificial complication of the rank order . . . permits numerous employees to feel that they hold high positions and are to a certain extent independent." Moreover, he notes that a complicated division of labor is "with its unwarranted differentiations, telescoped positions, and ramifications, diametrically opposed to efforts of rationalization."[9] In other words, Dreyfuss suggests that much of the com-

plex division of labor today is not to be explained by technological requirements, but rather in terms of the prestige satisfactions, the "psychic income,"
that it presumably provides workers.

In Dreyfuss' view, the "minute division of labor" also stems from management's needs to *control* workers and to make themselves independent of
any specific individual or group of workers. A high division of labor, said
Dreyfuss, means that "individual workers and employees can be exchanged
and replaced at any time."[10] Through its use, "dependence of the employee
upon the employer is greatly increased. It is much more difficult for today's
employee, trained in only one particular function, to find re-employment
than it was for his predecessor, a many-sided, well-instructed business man,
able and fitted to fill a variety of positions."[11]

It is unnecessary for our purpose here to resolve this disparity between
Dreyfuss, on the one hand, and Parsons, on the other. What may be suggested, however, is that there is considerable reason for holding Parsons'
position to be both logically and empirically inadequate and to recognize
that it has, without compelling scientific warrant, accommodated itself to the
metaphyscial pathos of organizational theory, which sees no escape from
bureaucracy.

### The Tradition of Michels

There is another offshoot among the structural-functionalists which is
distinguished by its concern for the problems bequeathed by Robert Michels,
and, as such, it is even more morosely pessimistic than others in the school.
Michels, it will be remembered, focussed his empirical studies on the Social
Democratic parties of pre-World War I Europe. He chose these, quite deliberately, because he wanted to see whether groups which stood for greater
freedom and democracy, and were hostile to authoritarianism, were not
themselves afflicted by the very organizational deformity to which they were
opposed.

Michels' conclusions were, of course, formulated in his "iron law of
oligarchy," in which he maintained that always and everywhere a "system
of leadership is incompatible with the most essential postulates of democracy."[12]

Focussing, as Michels did, on an apparently democratic group, Philip
Selznick examined the TVA, which many Americans had long believed to
be an advanced expression of democratic values. Like Michels, Selznick
assumes that

> *Wherever there is organization, whether formally democratic or not, there is a split between the leader and the led, between the agent and the initiator. The phenomenon of abdication to bureaucratic directives in corporations, in trade unions, in parties, and in cooperatives is so widespread that it indicates a fundamental weakness of democracy.*[13]

Selznick's study concludes that the TVA's emphasis on "decentralization" is to be best understood as a result of that agency's needs to adapt to suspicious local communities and to survive in competition with older governmental agencies based in Washington. "Decentralization" is viewed as a "halo that becomes especially useful in countries which prize the symbols of democracy."[14] In its turn, the TVA's emphasis on "participation" is explained as a catchword, satisfying the agency's needs to transform "an unorganized citizenry into a reliable instrument for the achievement of administrative goals. . . ."[15]

Selznick, like Michels, is impressed with the similarity in the organizational devices employed by different groups, whether they are democratic or authoritarian in ideology. He asserts

> *. . . there seems to be a continuum between the voluntary associations set up by the democratic (mass) state—such as committees of farmers to boost or control agricultural production—and the citizens' associations of the totalitarian (mass) state. Indeed, the devices of corporatism emerge as relatively effective responses to the need to deal with the mass, and in time of war the administrative techniques of avowedly democratic countries and avowedly totalitarian countries tend to converge.*[16]

In Selznick's analysis human action involves a commitment to two sets of interests: first to the *goals* intended, and second to the organizational *instruments* through which these goals are pursued. These tools are, however, recalcitrant; they generate "needs" which cannot be neglected. Hence if men persist in their ends, they are forced to satisfy the needs of their organizational instruments. They are, therefore, as much committed to their tools as to their ends, and "these commitments may lead to unanticipated consequences resulting in a deflection of original ends."[17]

For these reasons, organizational behavior must be interpreted not so much in terms of the *ends* that administrators deliberately seek, as in terms of the organizational "needs" which their pursuit engenders.

> *The needs in question are organizational, not individual, and include: the security of the organization as a whole in relation to social forces in its environment; the stability of the lines of authority and communication; the stability of informal relations within the organization; the continuity of policy and of the sources of its determination; a homogeneity of outlook with respect to the means and role of the organization.*[18]

Selznick chose to focus on those social constraints that *thwart* democratic aspirations, but neglected to consider the constraints that enable them to be *realized*, and that foster and encourage "good will" and "intelligence." Are these, however, random occurrences, mere historic butterflies which flit through events with only ephemeral beauty? Or are they, as much as anything else, often the unanticipated products of our "commitments"? Why is it that "unanticipated consequences" are always tacitly assumed to be destructive of democratic values and "bad"; why can't they sometimes be "good"? Are there no constraints which *force* men to adhere valorously to their democratic beliefs, which *compel* them to be intelligent rather than blind, which leave them *no choice* but to be men of good will rather than predators? The neglect of these possibilities suggests the presence of a distorting pathos.

It is the pathos of pessimism, rather than the compulsions of rigorous analysis, that leads to the assumption that organizational constraints have stacked the deck against democracy. For on the face of it there is every reason to assume that "the underlying tendencies which are likely to inhibit the democratic process" are just as likely to impair authoritarian rule. It is only in the light of such a pessimistic pathos that the defeat of democratic values can be assumed to be probable, while their victory is seen as a slender thing, delicately constituted and precariously balanced.

When, for example, Michels spoke of the "iron law of oligarchy," he attended solely to the ways in which organizational needs inhibit democratic possibilities. But the very same evidence to which he called attention could enable us to formulate the very opposite theorem—the "iron law of democracy." Even as Michels himself saw, if oligarchical waves repeatedly wash away the bridges of democracy, this eternal recurrence can happen only because men doggedly rebuild them after each inundation. Michels chose to dwell on only one aspect of this process, neglecting to consider this other side. There cannot be an iron law of oligarchy, however, unless there is an iron law of democracy.

Much the same may be said for Selznick. He posits certain organizational needs: a need for the *security* of the organization, for *stable* lines of authority and communication, for *stable* informal relationships. But for each of the organizational needs which Selznick postulates, a set of contrary needs can also be posited, and the satisfaction of these would seem to be just as necessary for the survival of an organization. If, as Selznick says, an organization must have security in its environment, then certainly Toynbee's observations that too much security can be stultifying and corrosive is at least as well taken. To Selznick's security need, a Toynbee might counterpose a need for a moderate *challenge* or *threat*.

A similar analysis might also be made of Selznick's postulated need for homogeneity of outlook concerning the means and role of the organization. For unless there is some *heterogeneity* of outlook, then where is an organization to find the tools and flexibility to cope with changes in its environment? Underlying Selznick's need for homogeneity in outlook, is there not another "need," *a need that consent of the governed be given—at least in some measure—to their governors?* Indeed, this would seem to be at the very core of Selznick's empirical analysis, though it is obscured in his high-level theoretical statement of the needs of organizations. And if all organizations must adjust to such a need for consent, is there not built into the very marrow of organization a large element of what we mean by democracy? This would appear to be an organizational constraint that makes oligarchies, and all separation of leaders from those led, no less inherently unstable than democratic organization.[19]

These contrary needs are just as real and just as consequential for organizational behavior as those proposed by Selznick. But they point in a different direction. They are oriented to problems of change, of growth, of challenging contingencies, of provoking and unsettling encounters. Selznick's analysis seems almost to imply that survival is possible only in an icy stasis, in which "security," "continuity," and "stability" are the key terms. If anything, the opposite seems more likely to be true, and organizational survival is impossible in such a state.

Wrapping themselves in the shrouds of nineteenth-century political economy, some social scientists appear to be bent on resurrecting a dismal science. Instead of telling men how bureaucracy might be mitigated, they insist that it is inevitable. Instead of explaining how democratic patterns may, to some extent, be fortified and extended, they warn us that democracy cannot be perfect. Instead of controlling the disease, they suggest that we are deluded, or more politely, incurably romantic, for hoping to control it. Instead of assuming responsibilities as realistic clinicians, striving to further democratic potentialities wherever they can, many social scientists have become morticians, all too eager to bury men's hopes.[20]

REFERENCES

1. Parsons, p. 509. See also the provocative fuller development of this argument as it applies to industrial organization. George C. Homans, "Industrial Harmony as a Goal," in *Industrial Conflict*, eds. Kornhauser, Dubin, and Ross (New York, 1954).
2. Arthur O. Lovejoy, *The Great Chain of Being* (Cambridge, Mass., 1948), p. 11.
3. Monograph # 11, Temporary National Economic Committee, *Bureaucracy and Trusteeship in Large Corporations* (Washington, D.C., 1940), p. 36.
4. *Max Weber: The Theory of Social and Economic Organization*, translated and edited by A. M. Henderson and Talcott Parsons (New York, 1947), p. 334.
5. *Ibid.*, p. 338.
6. See Reinhard Bendix, "Bureaucracy: The Problem and Its Setting," *American Sociological Review*, Vol. 12, pp. 502–7 (Oct., 1947). On the other hand, there are theoretically significant cases of small organizations which are highly bureaucratized, for example, the Boulton and Watt factory in 1775–1805. This "case illustrates the fact that the bureaucratization of industry is not synonymous with the recent growth in the size of business enterprises." Reinhard Bendix, "Bureaucratization in Industry," in *Industrial Conflict*, p. 166.
7. Talcott Parsons, *The Social System* (Glencoe, Illinois, 1951), pp. 507–8. Italics added.
8. Peter Drucker, *Concept of the Corporation* (New York, 1946), pp. 183–84.
9. Carl Dreyfuss, *Occupation and Ideology of the Salaried Employee*, trans. Eva Abramovitch (New York, 1938), p. 17.
10. *Ibid.*, p. 75.
11. *Ibid.*, p. 77.
12. Robert Michels, *Political Parties* (Glencoe, Ill., 1949), p. 400. Michels' work was first published in 1915.
13. Philip Selznick, *TVA and the Grass Roots* (Berkeley and Los Angeles, 1949), p. 9.
14. *Ibid.*, p. 220.
15. *Loc. cit.*
16. *Loc. cit.*
17. *Ibid.*, p. 259.
18. *Ibid.*, p. 252.
19. See Arthur Schweitzer, "Ideological Groups," *American Sociological Review*, Vol. 9, pp. 415–27 (Aug., 1944), particularly his discussion of factors inhibiting oligarchy. For example, "A leadership concentrating all power in its hands creates indifference among the functionaries and sympathizers as well as decline in membership of the organization. This process of shrinkage, endangering the position of the leaders, is the best protection against the supposedly inevitable iron law of oligarchy" (p. 419). Much of the research deriving from the Lewinian tradition would seem to lend credence to this inference.
20. We have sought to develop the positive implications of this approach to bureaucratic organization in *Patterns of Industrial Bureaucracy* (Glencoe, Ill., 1954).

# BUREAUCRACY, BUREAUCRATIZATION, AND DEBUREAUCRATIZATION* (*Eisenstadt*)

## Conditions of Development of Bureaucratic Organizations

We shall start with an analysis of the conditions of development of bureaucratic organizations and see to what extent these conditions can explain the existence of different inherent tendencies in their development and their patterns of activities. . . .

The available material suggests that bureaucratic organizations tend to develop in societies when

1. There develops extensive differentiation between major types of roles and institutional (economic, political, religious, and so forth) spheres.
2. The most important social roles are allocated not according to criteria of membership in the basic particularistic (kinship or territorial) groups, but rather according to universalistic and achievement criteria, or criteria of membership in more flexibly constituted groups such as professional, religious, vocational, or "national" groups.
3. There evolve many functionally specific groups (economic, cultural, religious, social-integrative) that are not embedded in basic particularistic groups, as, for example, economic and professional organizations, various types of voluntary associations, clubs, and so forth.
4. The definition of the total community is not identical with, and consequently is wider than, any such basic particularistic group, as can be seen, for instance, in the definition of the Hellenic culture in Byzantium or of the Confucian cultural order.
5. The major groups and strata in the society develop, uphold, and attempt to implement numerous discrete, political, economic, and social-service goals which cannot be implemented within the limited framework of the basic particularistic groups.
6. The growing differentiation in the social structure makes for complexity in many spheres of life, such as increasing interdependence between far-off groups and growing difficulty in the assurance of supply of resources and services.
7. These developments result to some extent in "free-floating" resources,

* Reprinted in part from S. N. Eisenstadt, *Administrative Science Quarterly*, 4 (1959), 302–320, by permission of the author and the publisher, Cornell University.

i.e., manpower and economic resources as well as commitments for political support which are neither embedded in nor assured to any primary ascriptive-particularistic groups, as, for example, monetary resources, a relatively free labor force, and a free political vote. Consequently, the various institutional units in the society have to compete for resources, manpower, and support for the implementation of their goals and provision of services; and the major social units are faced with many regulative and administrative problems.

The available material suggests that bureaucratic organizations develop in relation to such differentiation in the social system. Bureaucratic organizations can help in coping with some of the problems arising out of such differentiation, and they perform important functions in the organization of adequate services and coordination of large-scale activities, in the implementation of different goals, in the provision of resources to different groups and in the regulation of various intergroup relations and conflicts. Such bureaucratic organizations are usually created by certain elites (rulers, economic entrepreneurs, etc.) to deal with the problems outlined and to assure for these elites both the provision of such services and strategic power positions in the society.

Thus in many historical societies bureaucratic administrations were created by kings who wanted to establish their rule over feudal-aristocratic forces and who wanted, through their administration, to control the resources created by various economic and social groups and to provide these groups with political, economic, and administrative services that would make them dependent on the rulers.

In many modern societies bureaucratic organizations are created when the holders of political or economic power are faced with problems that arise because of external (war, etc.) or internal (economic development, political demands, etc.) developments. For the solution of such problems they have to mobilize adequate resources from different groups and spheres of life.

Obviously, these conclusions have to be tested and amplified. . . .


## Bureaucratization and Debureaucratization

It is through continuous interaction with its environment that a bureaucratic organization may succeed in maintaining those characteristics that distinguish it from other social groups. The most important of these characteristics, common to most bureaucratic organizations and often stressed in the literature, are specialization of roles and tasks; the prevalence of autonomous, rational, nonpersonal rules in the organization; and the general orientation to rational, efficient implementation of specific goals.[1]

These structural characteristics do not, however, develop in a social vacuum but are closely related to the functions and activites of the bureaucratic organization in its environment. The extent to which they can develop and persist in any bureaucratic organization is dependent on the type of dynamic equilibrium that the organization develops in relation to its environment. Basically, three main outcomes of such interaction or types of such dynamic equilibrium can be distinguished, although probably each of them can be further subdivided and some overlapping occurs between them.

The first type of equilibrium is one in which any given bureaucratic organization maintains its autonomy and distinctiveness. The basic structural characteristics that differentiate it from other social groups and in which it implements its goal or goals (whether its initial goals or goals added later) are retained and it is supervised by those who are legitimately entitled to do this (holders of political power, "owners," or boards of trustees).

The second main possibility is that of bureaucratization. This is the extension of the bureaucracy's spheres of activities and power either in its own interest or those of some of its elite. It tends toward growing regimentation of different areas of social life and some extent of displacement of its service goals in favor of various power interests and orientations. Examples are military organizations that tend to impose their rule on civilian life, or political parties that exert pressure on their potential supporters in an effort to monopolize their private and occupational life and make them entirely dependent on the political party.

The third main outcome is debureaucratization. Here there is subversion of the goals and activities of the bureaucracy in the interests of different groups with which it is in close interaction (clients, patrons, interested parties). In debureaucratization the specific characteristics of the bureaucracy in terms both of its autonomy and its specific rules and goals are minimized, even up to the point where its very functions and activities are taken over by other groups or organizations. Examples of this can be found in cases when some organization (i.e., a parents' association or a religious or political group) attempts to divert the rules and working of a bureaucratic organization (school, economic agency, and so forth) for its own use or according to its own values and goals. It makes demands on the members of bureaucratic organizations to perform tasks that are obviously outside the specific scope of these organizations. . . .

Many overlappings between these various tendencies and possibilities may, of course, develop. The tendencies toward bureaucratization and debureaucratization may, in fact, develop side by side. Thus, for instance, a growing use of the bureaucratic organization and the extension of its scope of activities for purposes of political control might be accompanied by deviation from its rules for the sake of political expediency. The possibility of these tendencies occurring in the same case may be explained by the fact that a stable service-oriented bureaucracy (the type of bureaucracy depicted in the Weberian ideal type of bureaucracy) is based on the existence of some equilibrium or *modus vivendi* between professional autonomy and societal (or political) control. Once this equilibrium is severely disrupted, the outcome with respect to the bureaucracy's organization and activity may be the simultaneous development of bureaucratization and debureaucratization in different spheres of its activities, although usually one of these tendencies is more pronounced. . . .

## Some Variables in the Study of Bureaucracy

It is as yet very difficult to propose any definite and systematic hypothesis about this problem since very little research is available that is specifically related to it.[2]

What can be done at this stage is, first, to point out some variables that, on the basis of available material and the preceding discussion, seem central to this problem, and then to propose some preliminary hypotheses, which may suggest directions in which research work on this problem may be attempted.

On the basis of those discussions we would like to propose that (a) the major goals of the bureaucratic organization, (b) the place of these goals in the social structure of the society, and (c) the type of dependence of the bureaucracy on external forces (clients, holders of political power, or other prominent groups) are of great importance in influencing both its internal structure and its relation with its environment. These different variables, while to some extent interdependent, are not identical. Each brings into relief the interdependence of the bureaucratic organization with its social setting from a different point of view.

The bureaucracy's goals, as has been lately shown in great detail by Parsons,[3] are of strategic importance, because they constitute one of the most important connecting links between the given organization and the total social structure in which it is placed. That which from the point of view of the organization is the major goal is very often from the point of view of the total society the function of the organization. Hence the various interrelations between a bureaucratic organization, other groups, and the total society are largely mediated by the nature of its goals. This applies both to the resources needed by the organization and to the products it gives to the society.[4]

But it is not merely the contents of the goals, i.e., whether they are mainly political, economic, cultural, and so forth, that influence the relation of the organization with its environment, but the place of the goals in the institutional structure of the society as well. By the relative place of the specific goals of any given bureaucratic organization within the society we mean the centrality (or marginality) of these goals with respect to the society's value and power system and the extent of legitimation it affords them. Thus there would obviously be many differences between a large corporation with critical products and a small economic organization with marginal products; between a political party close to the existing government performing the functions of a "loyal opposition" and a revolutionary group; between established churches and minority or militant sects; between fully established educational institutions and sectarian study or propaganda groups.

A third variable which seems to influence the bureaucracy's structural characteristics and activities is the extent and nature of its dependence on external resources and power. This dependence or relation may be defined in terms of

1. The chief function of the organization, i.e., whether it is a service, market, or membership recruitment agency. (This definition is closely related to, but not necessarily identical with, its goals.)
2. The extent to which its clientele is entirely dependent upon its products, or conversely, the type and extent of competition between it and parallel agencies.
3. The nature and extent of the internal (ownership) and external control.
4. The criteria used to measure the success of the organization as such and its members' performance, especially the extent of changes in the behavior and membership affiliation of its clients (as, for instance, in the case of a political party).
5. The spheres of life of its personnel that the activities of a given bureaucratic organization encompass.

It is not claimed that this list is exhaustive, but it seems to provide some preliminary clues as to the possible direction of further research on the problem.

All these variables indicate the great interdependence existing between the bureaucratic organization and its social environment. Each variable points to some ways in which a bureaucratic organization attempts to control different parts of its environment and to adapt its goals to changing environment or to different ways in which groups outside the bureaucracy control it and direct its activities. The outcome of this continuous interaction varies continuously according to the constellation of these different variables.

## Conditions of Bureaucratization and Debureaucratization

On the basis of the foregoing considerations and of current research like that of Janowitz,[5] of historical research on which we have reported already, and research in progress on the relations between bureaucratic organization and new immigrants in Israel,[6] we propose several general hypotheses concerning the conditions that promote autonomy or, conversely, bureaucratization or debureaucratization. . . .

The first of these hypotheses proposes that the development of any given bureaucratic organization as a relatively autonomous service agency is contingent upon the following conditions obtaining in its social setting:

1. Relative predominance of universalistic elements in the orientations and goals of the groups most closely related to the bureaucracy.
2. Relatively wide distribution of power and values in the economic, cultural, and political spheres among many groups and the maintenance of continuous struggle and competition among them or, in other words, no monopoly of the major power positions by any one group.
3. A wide range of differentiation among different types of goals.
4. The continuous specialization and competition among different bureaucratic organizations and between them and other types of groups about their relative places with regard to implementation of different goals.
5. The existence of strongly articulated political groups and the maintenance of control over the implementation of the goals by the legitimate holders of political, communal, or economic power.

Thus a service bureaucracy, one that maintains both some measure of autonomy and of service orientation, tends to develop either in a society, such as the "classical" Chinese Empire or the Byzantine Empire from the sixth to the tenth century, in which there exist strong political rulers and some politically active groups, such as the urban groups, aristocracy, and the church in the Byzantine Empire, or the literati and gentry in China, whose aspirations are considered by the rulers.[7] It also tends to develop in a democratic society in which effective political power is vested in an efficient, strong, representative executive. In both cases it is the combination of relatively strong political leadership with some political articulation and activity of different strata and groups (an articulation which necessarily tends to be entirely different in expression in historical empires from modern democracies) that facilitates the maintenance of a service bureaucracy.

In some societies a group may establish a power monopoly over parts of its environment and over the definition and establishment of the society's goals and the appropriation of its resources. This group may use the bureaucracy as an instrument of power and manipulation, distort its autonomous function and service orientation, and subvert some of its echelons through various threats or inducements for personal gratification. Historically the most extreme example of such developments can be found in those societies in which the rulers developed political goals that were strongly opposed by various active groups that they tried to suppress, such as in Prussia in the seventeenth and eighteenth centuries, in many conquest empires such as the Ottoman, or in the periods of aristocratization of the Byzantine Empire.[8] Modern examples of this tendency can be found in totalitarian societies or movements. Less extreme illustrations can also be found in other societies, and it should be a major task of comparative research to specify the different possible combinations of the conditions enumerated above and their influence on the possible development of bureaucratic organizations.

The development of a bureaucratic organization in the direction of debureaucratization seems to be connected mainly with the growth of different types of *direct* dependence of the bureaucratic organization on parts of its clientele. At this stage we may propose the following preliminary hypotheses about the influence that the type of dependency of the bureaucracy on its clients has on some of its patterns of activity. First, the greater its dependence on its clientele in terms of their being able to go to a competing agency, the more it will have to develop techniques of communication and additional services to retain its clientele and the more it will be influenced by different types of demands by the clientele for services in spheres that are not directly relevant to its main goals. Second, insofar as its dependence on its clients is due to the fact that its criteria of successful organizational performance are based on the number and behavior pattern of the organization's members or clients (as is often the case in semipolitical movements, educational organizations, and so forth), it will have to take an interest in numerous spheres of its clients' activities and either establish its control over them or be subjected to their influence and direction. Finally, the greater its *direct* dependence on different participants in the political arena, and the smaller the basic economic facilities and political assurance given by the holders of political power—as is the case in some public organizations in the United States and to some extent also in different organizations in Israel[9]—the greater will be its tendency to succumb to the demands of different political and economic pressure groups and to develop its activities and distort its own rules accordingly.

As already indicated, in concrete cases some overlapping between the tendencies to bureaucratization and debureaucratization may occur. Thus, for instance, when a politically monopolistic group gains control over a bureaucratic organization, it may distort the rules of this organization in order to give special benefits to the holders of political power or to maintain its hold over different segments of the population. On the other hand, when a process of debureaucratization sets in because of the growing pressure of different groups on a bureaucracy, there may also develop within the bureaucratic organization, as a sort of defense against these pressures, a tendency toward formalization and bureaucratization. This shows that the distinctive characteristics of a specific bureaucratic organization and role have been impinged upon in different directions, and one may usually discern which of these tendencies is predominant in different spheres of activity of the bureaucracy. It is the task of further research to analyze these different constellations in greater detail.

REFERENCES

1. See, for instance, P. M. Blau, *Bureaucracy in Modern Society* (New York, 1956). Blau summarizes much of the available literature on this problem.
2. Thus, for instance, in existing literature there is but little distinction between conditions which make for the growth of bureaucracy and those conducive to increasing bureaucratization. Gouldner's polemics against those who foresee the inevitability of bureaucratization are to some extent due to the lack of this distinction in the available literature. See his *Metaphysical Pathos and the Theory of Bureaucracy.*
3. *See* P. Parsons, "Suggestions for a Sociological Approach to the Theory of Organization," I and II, *Administrative Science Quarterly,* 1 (June and Sept. 1956), 63–85, 225–239.
4. For additional discussions of this problem see *Trend Report.*
5. See M. Janowitz, D. Wright, and W. Delany, *Public Administration and the Public— Perspectives towards Government in a Metropolitan Community* (Ann Arbor, 1958), which is one of the few available works that have a bearing on this problem. We would also like to mention the work of J. A. Slesinger, who has worked with Janowitz, and who has recently proposed several hypotheses concerning some of the factors that might influence aspects of the development of bureaucracy that are of interest to us. See Slesinger, "A Model for the Comparative Study of Public Bureaucracies," Institute of Public Administration, University of Michigan, 1957 (mimeo.).
6. See E. Katz and S. N. Eisenstadt, "Some Sociological Observations on the Response of Israeli Organizations to New Immigrants," *Administrative Science Quarterly,* Vol. 5 (1960), pp. 113–33.
7. For a more complete discussion of some of the problems of these societies see the references in note 4.
8. Hans Rosenberg, *Bureaucracy, Aristocracy and Autocracy: The Prussian Experience, 1660–1815* (Cambridge, Mass., 1958); A. Lybyer, *The Government of the Ottoman Empire in the Time of Suleiman the Magnificent* (Cambridge, Mass., 1913); and Eisenstadt, *Internal Contradictions.*
9. See Janowitz *et al., op. cit.,* pp. 107–14, and Katz and Eisenstadt, *op. cit.*

# 12: Alienation and Anomie

The notion of alienation has entered into modern sociology from German idealistic philosophy, especially by way of Hegel and the so-called Young Hegelians. But it was Karl Marx who first made it into a powerful diagnostic tool for sociological inquiry. To Marx alienation means, to quote Erich Fromm, "that man does not experience himself as the acting agent in his grasp of the world, but that the world (nature, others, and himself) remain alien to him. They stand above and against him as objects, even though they may be objects of his own creation." For Marx this process of alienation is expressed most forcefully in work and in the division of labor, but he also speaks of religious alienation, of political forms of alienation, and of alienation from one's fellow men.

Alienation seems to account for a variety of discontents in modern civilization. But its overall appeal may obscure certain difficulties. Melvin Seeman's paper has been reprinted here because it is an important attempt to unravel many meanings commonly associated with alienation. It helps to disentangle various dimensions of phenomena which are only too often confused when the overall concept of alienation is applied in contemporary sociology.

*Anomie* means a condition of normlessness, a moral vacuum, the suspension of rules, a state sometimes referred to as de-regulation. *Anomie* presupposes a prior condition in which behavior is normatively determined. A painful social crisis upsets that equilibrium, disturbs large numbers of people, greatly attenuates the regulative force of tradition, and produces widespread *anomie*.

It is unlikely that anyone has enriched sociological thought more than the incomparable French theorist, Emile Durkheim, and among his many contributions, this concept looms large. It was he who early in his work introduced the term *anomie*. Later he developed it as an explanatory concept in analyzing several concrete social problems. Since then references to *anomie* have gained wide currency.

Durkheim witnessed a major phase of what many observers have since called moral anarchy as it enveloped large sectors of the French Republic. Economic distress and social dislocation, which were to grow even more acute, had already shaken the Western world. One manifestation of the malaise that particularly fascinated Durkheim was a steadily rising suicide rate. He addressed himself to the subject in a classic study that, after more than half a century, still remains a touchstone for all further work. In addition to egoistic or individualistic suicide, the familiar form of self-destruction, and altruistic suicide, a less common inclination to sacrifice one's own life for some higher cause, Durkheim singled out *anomic suicide* for reasons largely explained in the pages reprinted here.

It is not always easy to fructify social science, and although Durkheim supplied a useful lead, it lay dormant for many years. Hence, it is necessary to move forward to the late nineteen thirties, in order to locate a point in American thought at which *anomie* again becomes a vital concept. That point is the famous essay of an eminent American sociologist, Robert K. Merton, entitled "Social Structure and Anomie." Durkheim had theorized that an abrupt and unforeseen growth or diminution of an individual's power and wealth tended to produce *anomie*, and also that in the sphere of business and trade it was a regular, therefore statistically normal, factor. Similarly, Merton defines his aim as that of discovering how "some social structures exert a definite pressure upon certain persons in the society to engage in nonconformist rather than conformist conduct." By refining the analysis of *anomie*, Merton emphasizes the differential impact of culturally defined goals and acceptable modes of obtaining those goals in different segments of the population. *Anomie* with respect to the means used is quite different from *anomie* with respect to the ends in view; it may exist in either one, in neither, or in both means *and* ends. This four-fold division makes it possible to construct the kind of typology which has become Merton's trademark, and as such, opens up new avenues of research.

Talcott Parsons, whose name for at least two decades has been synonymous with sociological theory and who in *The Structure of Social Action* awakened American interest in his towering European predecessors, took up the question of *anomie* in his second comprehensive work, *The Social System*. We have excerpted one relevant portion. There are others. It is perhaps worth quoting one passage from the second chapter of his book: "The polar antithesis of full institutionalization is . . . *anomie*, the absence of structured complementarity of the interaction process or, what is the same thing, the complete breakdown of normative order . . . This is, however, a limiting concept which is never descriptive of a concrete social system. Just as there are degrees of institutionalization so are there also degrees of *anomie*. The one is the obverse of the other." In short, *anomie* is a construct which, with its polar opposite, full institutionalization, may be the basis for a continuum from within which real social predicaments can be usefully studied.

The paper by Richard A. Cloward, takes its departure from Merton's work and extends it further by suggesting a basis for consolidating several major traditions of sociological thought on deviance and nonconformity. The notion of differential opportunity structures developed here is of considerable value in the study of various forms of deviance, which our next chapter will take up in some detail.

Of late, and inevitably, a certain reaction has set in against parts of Merton's analysis, which Merton himself has twice rewritten and further refined in answering his critics. A major contribution to reshaping Merton's powerfully logical essay so as to render its postulates more usable, both speculatively and empirically, has been made by Ephraim Harold Mizruchi in his excellent little book, *Success and Opportunity*, with portions of which we close this section.

# THE NOTION OF ALIENATION * (*Marx*)

Every alienation of man from himself and from Nature appears in the relation which he postulates between other men and himself and Nature. Thus religious alienation is necessarily exemplified in the relation between laity and priest, or, since it is here a question of the spiritual world, between the

* Excerpts from the following three works of Karl Marx, *The German Ideology*, *The Political Economic Manuscripts*, and *Economic Studies from Marx's Notebooks*, reprinted from Karl Marx, *Selected Writings in Sociology and Social Philosophy*, ed. by T. B. Bottomore and Maximilien Rubel, pp. 169–75, by permission of the publishers, Watts and Co., London.

laity and a mediator. In the real world of practice, this self alienation can only be expressed in the real, practical relation of man to his fellow men. The medium through which alienation occurs is itself a practical one. Through alienated labour, therefore, man not only produces his relation to the object, and to the process of production as alien and hostile men; he also produces the relation of other men to his production and his product, and the relation between himself and other men.

. . .

However, alienation shows itself not merely in the result, but also in the *process, of production,* within *productive activity* itself. . . .

In what does this alienation of labour consist? First, that the work is *external* to the worker, that it is not a part of his nature, that consequently he does not fulfil himself in his work but denies himself, has a feeling of misery, not of well-being, does not develop freely a physical and mental energy, but is physically exhausted and mentally debased. The worker therefore feels himself at home only during his leisure, whereas at work he feels homeless. His work is not voluntary but imposed, *forced labour.* It is not the satisfaction of a need, but only a *means* for satisfying other needs. Its alien character is clearly shown by the fact that as soon as there is no physical or other compulsion it is avoided like the plague. Finally, the alienated character of work for the worker appears in the fact that it is not his work but work for someone else, that in work he does not belong to himself but to another person.

Just as in religion the spontaneous activity of human fantasy, of the human brain and heart, reacts independently, that is, as an alien activity of gods or devils, upon the individual, so the activity of the worker is not his spontaneous activity. It is another's activity, and a loss of his own spontaneity.

. . .

The more the worker expends himself in work, the more powerful becomes the world of objects which he creates in face of himself, and the poorer he himself becomes in his inner life, the less he belongs to himself. It is just the same as in religion. The more of himself man attributes to God, the less he has left in himself. The worker puts his life into the object, and his life then belongs no longer to him but to the object. The greater his activity, therefore, the less he possesses. What is embodied in the product of his labour is no longer his. The greater this product is, therefore, the more he himself is diminished. The *emptying* of the worker into his product means not only that his labour becomes an object, takes on its own existence, but that it exists outside him, independently, and alien to him, and that it stands opposed to him as an autonomous power. The life which he has given to the object sets itself against him as an alien and hostile force.

. . .

The object produced by labour, its product, now stands opposed to it as an *alien being,* as a *power independent* of the producer. The product of labour is labour which has been embodied in an object, and turned into a physical thing; this product is an *objectification* (*Vergegenständlichung*) of labour. The performance of work is at the same time its objectification. This performance of work appears, in the sphere of political economy, as a *vitiation* of the worker, objectification as a *loss* and as *servitude to the object,* and appropriation as *alienation.*

. . .

Political economy conceives the *social life of men,* their active *human* life, their many-sided growth towards a communal and genuinely human life, under the form of *exchange* and *trade. Society,* says Destutt de Tacy, is *a series of multilateral exchanges.* It *is* this movement of multilateral integration. According to Adam Smith, *society* is a *commercial enterprise.* Every one of its members is a *salesman.* It is evident how political economy establishes an *alienated* form of social intercourse, as the *true and original* form, and that which corresponds to human nature.

. . .

Mill's description of *money* as the *intermediary* of exchange is an excellent conceptualization of its nature. The nature of money is not, in the first place, that in it property is alienated but that the *mediating activity* of *human* social action by which man's products reciprocally complete each other, is *alienated* and becomes the characteristic of a *material thing,* money, which is external to man. When man exteriorizes this mediating activity he is active only as an exiled and dehumanized being; the *relation* between things, and human activity with them, becomes the activity of a being outside and above man. Through this *alien intermediary*—whereas man himself should be the intermediary between men—man sees his will, his activity and his relation to others as a power which is independent of him and of them. His slavery therefore attains its peak. That this *intermediary* becomes a *real* god is clear, since the intermediary is the *real power* over that which he mediates to me. His cult becomes an end in itself. The objects, separated from this intermediary, have lost their value. Thus they only have value in so far as they represent it, whereas it seemed originally that it only had value in so far as it represented them. This reversal of the original relationship is inevitable. This *intermediary* is thus the exiled, alienated *essence* of private property, *exteriorized* private property, just as it is the *alienated exchange* of human production with human production and the *alienated* social activity of man. All the qualities involved in the production of this activity, which really belong to man, are attributed to the intermediary. Man himself becomes poorer, that is, separated from this intermediary, as the intermediary becomes *richer*.

*Money,* since it has the *property* of purchasing everything, of appropriating objects to itself, is therefore the *object par excellence.* The universal character of this *property* corresponds to the omnipotence of money, which is regarded as an omnipotent essence . . . money is the *pander* between need and object, between human life and the means of subsistence. But *that which* mediates my life, mediates also the existence of other men for me. It is for me the *other* person. . . .

> "Gold? yellow, glittering, precious gold? No, gods,
> I am no idle votarist: roots, you clear heavens!
> Thus much of this will make black white; foul, fair;
> Wrong, right; base, noble; old, young; coward, valiant.
> . . . . . . . . . . Why, this
> Will lug your priests and servants from your sides;
> Pluck stout men's pillows from below their heads:
> This yellow slave
> Will knit and break religions; bless th'accurst;
> Make the hoar leprosy ador'd; place thieves,
> And give them title, knee, and approbation,
> With senators on the bench: this is it
> That makes the wappen'd widow wed again;
> She, whom the spital-house and ulcerous sores
> Would cast the gorge at, this embalms and spices
> To th'April day again. Come, damned earth,
> Thou common whore of mankind, that putt'st odds
> Among the rout of nations, I will make thee
> Do thy right nature."
>
> (*Timon of Athens,* Shakespeare)

Shakespeare attributes to money two qualities:

1. It is the visible deity, the transformation of all human and natural qualities into their opposite, the universal confusion and inversion of things; it brings incompatibles into fraternity.
2. It is the universal whore, the universal pander between men and nations. The power to confuse and invert all human and natural qualities, to

bring about fraternization of incompatibles, the *divine power* of money, resides in its *essence* as the alienated and exteriorized social life of men. It is the alienated *power of humanity*.

What I as a *man* am unable to do, what therefore all my individual faculties are unable to do, is made possible for me by means of *money*. Money therefore turns each of these faculties into something which in itself it is not, into its *opposite*.

. . . .

The division of labour implies from the outset the division of the *prerequisites of labour*, tools and materials, and thus the partitioning of accumulated capital among different owners. This also involves the separation of capital and labour and the different forms of property itself. The more the division of labour develops and accumulation increases, the more sharply this differentiation emerges.

Two facts are revealed here. In the first place, the productive forces appear to be completely independent and severed from the individuals and to constitute a self-subsistent world alongside the individuals. The reason for this is that the individual, whose forces they are, themselves exist separated and in opposition to one another, while on the other hand these forces are only real forces in the intercourse and association of these individuals. Thus there is on the one hand a sum of productive forces which have, as it were, assumed a material form and which are for the individuals concerned the forces, not of these individuals, but of private property, and consequently of the individuals only in so far as they are owners of private property. Never, in any earlier period, did the productive forces assume a form so indifferent to the intercourse of individuals as individuals, because in these periods their intercourse was still limited. On the other hand, confronting these productive forces is the majority of individuals from whom these forces have been sundered and who, robbed in this way of all the real substance of life, have become abstract individuals, but who by this very fact are enabled to enter into relation with each other as individuals.

The only connection which they still have with the productive forces and with their own existence, labour, has lost for them any semblance of personal activity, and sustains their life only while stunting it. While in the earlier periods personal activity and the production of material life were separated in that they devolved upon different persons, and while the production of material life because of the limitations of the individuals themselves was still regarded as a subordinate kind of personal activity, they now diverge to such an extent that material life generally appears as the aim while the production of this material life, labour (which is now the only possible but, as we have seen, negative form of personal activity) appears as the means.

# ON THE MEANING OF ALIENATION* (*Seeman*)

*At the present time, in all the social sciences, the various synonyms of alienation have a foremost place in studies of human relations. Investigations of the "unattached," the "marginal," the "obsessive," the "normless," and the "isolated" individual all testify to the central place occupied by the hypothesis of alienation in contemporary social science.*

So writes Robert Nisbet in *The Quest for Community;*[1] and there would seem to be little doubt that his estimate is correct. In one form or another, the concept of alienation dominates both the contemporary literature and the history of sociological thought. It is a central theme in the classics of Marx, Weber, and Durkheim; and in contemporary work, the consequences that have been said to flow from the fact of alienation have been diverse, indeed.

Ethnic prejudice, for example, has been described as a response to alienation—as an ideology which makes an incomprehensible world intelligible by imposing upon that world a simplified and categorical "answer system" (for example, the Jews cause international war).[2] In his examination of the persuasion process in the Kate Smith bond drive, Merton emphasizes the significance of pervasive distrust: "The very same society that produces this sense of alienation and estrangement generates in many a craving for reassurance, an acute need to believe, a flight into faith"[3]—in this case, faith in the sincerity of the persuader. In short, the idea of alienation is a popular vehicle for virtually every kind of analysis, from the

* This paper is based in part on work done while the author was in attendance at the Behavioral Sciences Conference at the University of New Mexico, in the summer of 1958. The conference was supported by the Behavioral Sciences Division, Air Force Office of Scientific Research, under contract AF 49 (638)–33. The work on alienation was carried out in close conjunction with Julian B. Rotter and Shephard Liverant of The Ohio State University. I gratefully acknowledge their very considerable help, while absolving them of any commitment to the viewpoints herein expressed. Reprinted by permission of the author and *American Sociological Review*, XXIV, December, 1959, copyright, 1959, American Sociological Association.

prediction of voting behavior to the search for *The Same Society*.[4] This inclusiveness, in both its historical and its contemporary import, is expressed in Erich Kahler's remark: "The history of man could very well be written as a history of the alienation of man."[5]

A concept that is so central in sociological work, and so clearly laden with value implications, demands special clarity. There are, it seems to me, five basic ways in which the concept of alienation has been used. The purpose of this paper is to examine these logically distinguishable uasges, and to propose what seems a workable view of these five meanings of alienation. Thus, the task is a dual one: to make more organized sense of one of the great traditions in sociological thought; and to make the traditional interest in alienation more amenable to sharp empirical statement.[6]

I propose, in what follows, to treat alienation from the personal standpoint of the actor—that is, alienation is here taken from the social-psychological point of view. Presumably, a task for subsequent experimental or analytical research is to determine (a) the social conditions that produce these five variants of alienation, or (b) their behavioral consequences. In each of the five instances, I begin with a review of where and how that usage is found in traditional sociological thought; subsequently, in each case, I seek a more researchable statement of meaning. In these latter statements, I focus chiefly upon the ideas of expectation and value.[7]

## Powerlessness

The first of these uses refers to alienation in the sense of *powerlessness*. This is the notion of alienation as it originated in the Marxian view of the worker's condition in capitalist society: the worker is alienated to the extent that the prerogative and means of decision are expropriated by the ruling entrepreneurs. Marx, to be sure, was interested in other alienative aspects of the industrial system; indeed, one might say that his interest in the powerlessness of the worker flowed from his interest in the consequences of such alienation in the work place—for example, the alienation of man from man, and the degradation of men into commodities.

In Weber's work, we find an extension beyond the industrial sphere of the Marxian notion of powerlessness. Of this extension, Gerth and Mills remark:

> *Marx's emphasis upon the worker as being "separated" from the means of production becomes, in Weber's perspective, merely one special case of a universal trend. The modern soldier is equally*

*"separated" from the means of violence; the scientist from the means of enquiry, and the civil servant from the means of administration.*[8]

The idea of alienation as powerlessness is, perhaps, the most frequent usage in current literature. The contributors to Gouldner's volume on leadership, for example, make heavy use of this idea; as does the work of C. Wright Mills—and, I suppose, any analysis of the human condition that takes the Marxist tradition with any seriousness. This variant of alienation can be conceived as *the expectancy or probability held by the individual that his own behavior cannot determine the occurrence of the outcomes, or reinforcements, he seeks.*

Let us be clear about what this conception does and does not imply. First, it is a distinctly social-psychological view. It does not treat powerlessness from the standpoint of the objective conditions in society; but this does not mean that these conditions need be ignored in research dealing with this variety of alienation. These objective conditions are relevant, for example, in determining the degree of realism involved in the individual's response to his situation. The objective features of the situations are to be handled like any other situational aspect of behavior—to be analyzed, measured, ignored, experimentally controlled or varied, as the research question demands.

Second, this construction of "powerlessness" clearly departs from the Marxian tradition by removing the critical, polemic element in the idea of alienation. Likewise, this version of powerlessness does not take into account, as a definitional matter, the frustration an individual may feel as a consequence of the discrepancy between the control he may expect and the degree of control that he desires—that is, it takes no direct account of the value of control to the person.

In this version of alienation, then, the individual's expectancy for control of events is clearly distinguished from (a) the *objective* situation of powerlessness as some observer sees it, (b) the observer's *judgment* of that situation against some ethical standard, and (c) the individual's sense of a *discrepancy* between his expectations for control and his desire for control.

The issues in the philosophy of science, or in the history of science, on which these distinctions and decisions touch can not be debated here. Two remarks must suffice: (1) In any given research, any or all of the elements discussed above—expectancies, objective conditions, deviation from a moral standard, deviation from the actor's standards—may well be involved, and I see little profit in arguing about which is "really" alienation so long as what is going on at each point in the effort is clear. I have chosen to focus on expectancies since I believe that this is consistent with what follows, while it avoids building ethical or adjustmental features into the concept. (2) I do not think that the expectancy usage is as radical a departure from the Marxian legacy as it may appear. No one would deny the editorial character of the Marxian judgment, but it was a judgment about a state of affairs—the elimination of individual freedom and control. My version of alienation refers to the counterpart, in the individual's expectations, of that state of affairs.

Finally, the use of powerlessness as an expectancy means that this version of alienation is very closely related to the notion (developed by Rotter) of "internal *versus* external control of reinforcements." The latter construct refers to the individual's sense of personal control over the reinforcement situation, as contrasted with his view that the occurrence of reinforcements is dependent upon external conditions, such as chance, luck, or the manipulation of others. The congruence in these formulations leaves the way open for the development of a closer bond between two languages of analysis—that of learning theory and that of alienation—that have long histories in psychology and sociology. But the congruence also poses a problem—the problem of recognizing that these two constructs, though intimately related, are not generally used to understand the same things.[9]

In the case of alienation, I would limit the applicability of the concept to expectancies that have to do with the individual's sense of influence over socio-political events (control over the political system, the industrial economy, international affairs, and the like). Accordingly, I would initially limit the applicability of this first meaning of alienation to the arena for which the concept was originally intended, namely, the depiction of man's relation to the larger social order. Whether or not such an operational concept of alienation is related to expectancies for control in more intimate need areas (for example, love and affection; status-recognition) is a matter for empirical determination. The need for the restriction lies in the following convictions: First, the concept of alienation, initially, should not be so global as to make the *generality* of powerlessness a matter of fiat rather than fact. Second, the concept should not be dangerously close to merely an index of personality *adjustment*—equivalent, that is, to a statement that the individual is maladjusted in the sense that he has a generally low expectation that he can, through his own behavior, achieve any of the personal rewards he seeks.[10]

## Meaninglessness

A second major usage of the alienation concept may be summarized under the idea of *meaninglessness*. The clearest contemporary examples of this usage are found in Adorno's treatment of prejudice; in Cantril's *The Psychology of Social Movements*, in which the "search for meaning" is used as part of the interpretive scheme in analyzing such diverse phenomena as lynchings, the Father Divine movement, and German fascism; and in Hoffer's portrait of the "true believer" as one who finds, and needs to find, in the doctrines of a mass movement "a master key to all the world's problems."[11]

This variant of alienation is involved in Mannheim's description of the increase of "functional rationality" and the concomitant decline of "substantial rationality." Mannheim argues that as society increasingly organizes its members with reference to the most efficient realization of ends (that is, as functional rationality increases), there is a parallel decline in the "capacity to act intelligently in a given situation on the basis of one's own insight into the interrelations of events."[12]

This second type of alienation, then, refers to the individual's sense of understanding the events in which he is engaged. We may speak of high alienation, in the meaninglessness usage, when *the individual is unclear as to what he ought to believe—when the individual's minimal standards for clarity in decision-making are not met*. Thus, the post-war German situation described by Adorno was "meaningless" in the sense that the individual could not choose with confidence among alternative explanations of the inflationary disasters of the time (and, it is argued, substituted the "Jews" as a simplified solution for this unclarity). In Mannheim's depiction, the individual cannot choose appropriately among alternative interpretations (cannot "act intelligently" or "with insight") because the increase in functional rationality, with its emphasis on specialization and production, makes such choice impossible.

It would seem, for the present at least, a matter of no consequence what the beliefs in question are. They may, as in the above instance, be simply descriptive beliefs (interpretations); or they may be beliefs involving moral standards (norms for behavior). In either case, the individual's choice among alternative beliefs has low "confidence limits": he cannot predict with confidence the consequences of acting on a given belief. One might operationalize this aspect of alienation by focusing upon the fact that it is characterized by a *low expectancy that satisfactory predicitions about future outcomes of behavior can be made.* Put more simply, where the first meaning of alienation refers to the sensed ability to control outcomes, this second meaning refers essentially to the sensed ability to predict behavioral outcomes.

This second version of alienation is logically independent of the first, for, under some circumstances, expectancies for personal control of events may not coincide with the understanding of these events, as in the popular depiction of the alienation of the intellectual.[13] Still, there are obvious connections between these two forms of alienation: in some important degree, the view that one lives in an intelligible world may be a prerequisite to expectancies for control; and the unintelligibility of complex affairs is presumably conducive to the development of high expectancies for external control (that is, high powerlessness).[14]

## Normlessness

The third variant of the alienation theme is derived from Durkheim's description of "anomie," and refers to a condition of *normlessness*. In the traditional usage, anomie denotes a situation in which the social norms regulating individual conduct have broken down or are no longer effective as rules for behavior. As noted above, Merton emphasizes this kind of rulelessness in his interpretation of the importance of the "sincerity" theme in Kate Smith's war bond drive:

> *The emphasis on this theme reflects a social disorder—"anomie" is the sociological term—in which common values have been submerged in the welter of private interests seeking satisfaction by virtually any means which are effective. Drawn from a highly competitive, segmented urban society, our informants live in a climate of reciprocal distrust which, to say the least, is not conducive to stable human relationships. . . . The very same society that produces this sense of alienation and estrangement generates in many a craving for reassurance. . . .*[15]

Elsewhere, in his well-known paper "Social Structure and Anomie," Merton describes the "adaptations" (the kinds of conformity and deviance) that may occur where the disciplining effect of collective standards has been weakened. He takes as his case in point the situation in which culturally prescribed goals (in America, the emphasis upon success goals) are not congruent with the available means for their attainment. In such a situation, he argues, anomie or normlessness will develop to the extent that "the technically most effective procedure, whether culturally legitimate or not, becomes typically preferred to institutionally prescribed conduct."[16]

Merton's comments on this kind of anomic situation serve to renew the discussion of the expectancy constructs developed above—the idea of meaninglessness, and the idea of powerlessness or internal-external control. For Merton notes, first, that the anomic situation leads to low predictability in behavior, and second, that the anomic situation may well lead to the belief in luck:

> *Whatever the sentiments of the reader concerning the moral desirability of coordinating the goals-and-means phases of the social structure, it is clear that imperfect coordination of the two leads to anomie. Insofar as one of the most general functions of the social structure is to provide a basis for predictability and regularity of social behavior, it becomes increasingly limited in effectiveness as these elements of the social structure become dissociated. . . . The victims of this contradiction between the cultural emphasis on pecuniary ambition and the social bars to full opportunity are not always aware of the structural sources of their thwarted aspirations. To be sure, they are typically aware of a discrepancy between individual worth and social rewards. But they do not necessarily see how this comes about. Those who do find its source in the social structure may become alienated from that structure and become ready candidates for Adaptation V [rebellion]. But others, and this appears to include the great majority, may attribute their difficulties to more mystical and less sociological sources. . . . In such a society [a society suffering from anomie] people tend to put stress on mysticism: the workings of Fortune, Chance, Luck.[17]*

It is clear that the general idea of anomie is both an integral part of the alienation literature, and that it bears upon our expectancy notions. What is not so clear is the matter of how precisely to conceptualize the events to which "anomie" is intended to point. Unfortunately, the idea of normlessness has been over-extended to include a wide variety of both social conditions and psychic states: personal disorganization, cultural breakdown, reciprocal distrust, and so on.

Those who employ the anomie version of alienation are chiefly concerned with the elaboration of the "means" emphasis in society—for example, the loss of commonly held standards and consequent individualism, or the development of instrumental, manipulative attitudes. This interest represents our third variant of alienation, the key idea of which, again, may be cast in terms of expectancies. Following Merton's lead, the anomic situation, from the individual point of view, may be defined as one in which there is a *high expectancy that socially unapproved behaviors are required to achieve given goals*. This third meaning of alienation is logically independent of the two versions discussed above. Expectancies concerning unapproved means, presumably, can vary independently of the individual's expectancy that his own behavior will determine his success in reaching a goal (what I have called "powerlessness") or his belief that he operates in an intellectually comprehensible world ("meaninglessness"). Such a view of anomie, to be sure, narrows the evocative character of the concept, but it provides a more likely way of developing its research potential. This view, I believe, makes possible the discovery of the extent to which such expectancies are held, the conditions for their development, and their consequences either for the individual or for a given social system (for example, the generation of widespread distrust).

The foregoing discussion implies that the means and goals in question have to do with such relatively broad social demands as the demand for success or for political ends. However, in his interesting essay, "Alienation from Interaction," Erving Goffman presents a more or less parallel illustration in which the focus is on the smallest of social systems, the simple conversation:

> *If we take conjoint spontaneous involvement in a topic of conversation as a point of reference, we shall find that alienation from it is common indeed. Conjoint involvement appears to be a fragile thing, with standard points of weakness and decay, a precarious unsteady state that is likely at any time to lead the individual into some form of alienation. Since we are dealing with obligatory involvement, forms of alienation will constitute* misbehavior of a kind that can be called mis-involvement.[18]

Goffman describes four such "mis-involvements" (for example, being too self-conscious in interaction), and concludes: "By looking at the ways in which individuals can be thrown out of step with the sociable moment, perhaps we can learn something about the way in which he can become alienated from things that take much more of his time."[19] In speaking of "misbehavior" or "mis-involvement," Goffman is treating the problem of alienation in terms not far removed from the anomic feature I have described, that is, the expectancy for socially unapproved behavior. His analysis of the social microcosm in these terms calls attention once more to the fact that the five variants of alienation discussed here can be applied to as broad or as narrow a range of social behavior as seems useful.

## Isolation

The fourth type of alienation refers to *isolation*. This usage is most common in descriptions of the intellectual role, where writers refer to the detachment of the intellectual from popular cultural standards—one who, in Nettler's language, has become estranged from his society and the culture it carries.[20] Clearly, this usage does not refer to isolation as a lack of "social adjustment"—of the warmth, security, or intensity of an individual's social contacts.

In the present context, in which we seek to maintain a consistent focus on the individual's expectations or values, this brand of alienation may be usefully defined in terms of reward values: The alienated in the isolation sense are those who, like the intellectual, *assign low reward value to goals or beliefs that are typically highly valued in the given society*. This, in effect, is the definition of alienation in Nettler's scale, for as a measure of "apartness from society" the scale consists (largely though not exclusively) of items that reflect the individual's degree of commitment to popular culture. Included, for example, is the question "Do you read *Reader's Digest*?", a magazine that was selected "as a symbol of popular magazine appeal and folkish thoughtways."[21]

The "isolation" version of alienation clearly carries a meaning different from the three versions discussed above. Still, these alternative meanings can be profitably applied in conjunction with one another in the analysis of a given state of affairs. Thus, Merton's paper on social structure and anomie makes use of both "normlessness" and "isolation" in depicting the adaptations that individuals may make to the situation in which goals and means are not well coordinated. One of these adaptations—that of the "innovator"—is the prototype of alienation in the sense of normlessness, in which the individual innovates culturally disapproved means to achieve the goals in question. But another adjustment pattern—that of "rebellion"—more closely approximates what I have called "isolation." "This adaptation [rebellion] leads men outside the environing social structure to envisage and seek to bring into being a new, that is to say, a greatly modified, social structure. It presupposes alienation from reigning goals and standards."[22]

## Self-Estrangement

The final variant distinguishable in the literature is alienation in the sense of *self-estrangement*. The most extended treatment of this version of alienation is found in *The Sane Society*, where Fromm writes:

> In the following analysis I have chosen the concept of alienation as the central point from which I am going to develop the analysis of the contemporary social character. . . . By alienation is meant a mode of experience in which the person experiences himself as an alien. He has become, one might say, estranged from himself.[23]

In much the same way, C. Wright Mills comments: "In the normal course of her work, because her personality becomes the instrument of an alien purpose, the salesgirl becomes self-alienated;" and, later, "Men are estranged from one another as each secretly tries to make an instrument of the other, and in time a full circle is made: One makes an instrument of himself and is estranged from It also."[24]

There are two interesting features of this popular doctrine of alienation as self-estrangement. The first of these is the fact that where the usage does not overlap with the other four meanings (and it often does), it is difficult to specify what the alienation is *from*. To speak of "alienation from the self" is after all simply a metaphor, in a way that "alienation from popular culture," for example, need not be. The latter can be reasonably specified, as I have tried to do above; but what is intended when Fromm, Mills, Hoffer, and the others speak of self-estrangement?

Apparently, what is being postulated here is some social ideal human condition from which the individual is estranged. This is, perhaps, clearest in Fromm's treatment, for example, in his description of production and consumption excesses in capitalist society: "The *human* way of acquiring would be to make an effort qualitatively commensurate with what I acquire. . . . But our craving for consumption has lost all connection with the real needs of man."[25] To be self-alienated, in the final analysis, means to be something less than one might ideally be if the circumstances in society were otherwise —to be insecure, given to appearances, conformist. Riesman's discussion of other-direction falls within this meaning of alienation; for what is at stake is that the child learns "that nothing in his character, no possession he owns, no inheritance of name or talent, no work he has done, is valued for itself, but only for its effect on others. . . ."[26]

Riesman's comment brings us to the second feature of special interest in the idea of self-alienation. I have noted that this idea invokes some explicit or implicit human ideal. And I have implied that such comparisons of modern man with some idealized human condition should be viewed simply as rhetorical appeals to nature—an important rhetoric for some purposes, though not very useful in the non-analytical form it generally takes. But Riesman's assertion contains, it seems to me, one of the key elements of this rhetoric—one, indeed, that not only reflects the original interest of Marx in alienation but also one that may be specifiable in a language consistent with our other uses of alienation.

I refer to that aspect of self-alienation which is generally characterized as the loss of intrinsic meaning or pride in work, a loss which Marx and others have held to be an essential feature of modern alienation. This notion of the loss of intrinsically meaningful satisfactions is embodied in a number of ways in current discussions of alienation. Glazer, for example, contrasts the alienated society with simpler societies characterized by "spontaneous acts of work and play which were their own reward."[27]

Although this meaning of alienation is difficult to specify, the basic idea contained in the rhetoric of self-estrangement—the idea of intrinsically meaningful activity—can, perhaps, be recast into more manageable social learning terms. One way to state such a meaning is to see alienation as *the degree of dependence of the given behavior upon anticipated future rewards,* that is, upon rewards that lie outside the activity itself. In these terms, the worker who works merely for his salary, the housewife who cooks simply to get it over with, or the other-directed type who acts "only for its effect on others"—all these (at different levels, again) are instances of self-estrangement. In this view, what has been called self-estrangement refers essentially to the inability of the individual to find self-rewarding—or in Dewey's phrase, self-consummatory—activities that engage him.[28]

## Conclusion

I am aware that there are unclarities and difficulties of considerable importance in these five varieties of alienation (especially, I believe, in the attempted solution of "self-estrangement" and the idea of "meaninglessness"). But I have attempted, first, to distinguish the meanings that have been given to alienation, and second, to work toward a more useful conception of each of these meanings.

It may seem, at first reading, that the language employed—the language of expectations and rewards—is somewhat strange, if not misguided. But

I would urge that the language is more traditional than it may seem. Nathan Glazer certainly is well within that tradition when, in a summary essay on alienation, he speaks of our modern ". . . sense of the splitting asunder of what was once together, the breaking of the seamless mold in which *values, behavior,* and *expectations* were once cast into interlocking forms."[29] These same three concepts—reward value, behavior, and expectancy—are key elements in the theory that underlies the present characterization of alienation. Perhaps, on closer inspection, the reader will find only that initial strangeness which is often experienced when we translate what was sentimentally understood into a secular question.

REFERENCES

1. New York: Oxford, 1953, p. 15.
2. T. W. Adorno *et al., The Authoritarian Personality,* New York: Harper, 1950, pp. 617 ff.
3. R. K. Merton, *Mass Persuasion,* New York: Harper, 1946, p. 143.
4. Erich Fromm, *The Sane Society,* New York: Rinehart, 1955.
5. *The Tower and the Abyss,* New York: Braziller, 1957, p. 43.
6. An effort in this direction is reported by John P. Clark in "Measuring Alienation Within a Social System," pp. 849–52 of this issue of the *Review.—The Editor.*
7. The concepts of expectancy and reward, or reinforcement value, are the central elements in J. B. Rotter's "social learning theory"; see *Social Learning and Clinical Psychology,* New York: Prentice Hall, 1954. My discussion seeks to cast the various meanings of alienation in a form that is roughly consistent with this theory, though not formally expressed in terms of it.
8. H. H. Gerth and C. W. Mills, *From Max Weber: Essays in Sociology,* New York: Oxford, 1946, p. 50.
9. Cf. W. H. James and J. B. Rotter, "Partial and One Hundred Percent Reinforcement under Chance and Skill Conditions," *Journal of Experimental Psychology,* 55 (May, 1958), pp. 397–403. Rotter and his students have shown that the distinction between internal and external control (a distinction which is also cast in expectancy terms) has an important bearing on learning theory. The propositions in that theory, they argue, are based too exclusively on experimental studies which simulate conditions of "external control," where the subject "is likely to perceive reinforcements as being beyond his control and primarily contingent upon external conditions" (p. 397). Compare this use of what is essentially a notion of powerlessness with, for example, Norman Podhoretz's discussion of the "Beat Generation": "Being apathetic about the Cold War is to admit that you have a sense of utter helplessness in the face of forces apparently beyond the control of man." "Where is the Beat Generation Going?" *Esquire,* 50 (December, 1958), p. 148.
10. It seems best, in regard to the adjustment question, to follow Gwynn Nettler's view. He points out that the concepts of alienation and anomie should not "be equated, as they so often are, with personal disorganization defined as intrapersonal goallessness, or lack of 'internal coherence' . . . [their] bearing on emotional sickness must be independently investigated." "A Measure of Alienation," *American Sociological Review,* 22 (December, 1957), p. 672. For a contrasting view see Nathan Glazer's "The Alienation of Modern Man," *Commentary,* 3 (April, 1947), p. 380, in which he comments: "If we approach alienation in this way, it becomes less a description of a single specific symptom than an omnibus of psychological disturbances having a similar root cause—in this case, modern social organization."
    With regard to the question of the generality of powerlessness, I assume that high

or low expectancies for the control of outcomes through one's own behavior will (a) vary with the behavior involved—e.g., control over academic achievement or grades, as against control over unemployment; and (b) will be differentially realistic in different areas (it is one thing to feel powerless with regard to war and quite another, presumably, to feel powerless in making friends). My chief point is that these are matters that can be empirically rather than conceptually solved; we should not, therefore, build either "generality" or "adjustment" into our concept of alienation. This same view is applied in the discussion of the other four types of alienation.

11. See, respectively, Adorno *et al., op. cit.;* Hadley Cantril, *The Psychology of Social Movements,* New York: Wiley, 1941; and Eric Hoffer, *The True Believer,* New York: Harper, 1950, p. 90.

12. Karl Mannheim, *Man and Society in an Age of Reconstruction,* New York: Harcourt, Brace, 1940, p. 59.

13. C. Wright Mills' description reflects this view: "The intellectual who remains free may continue to learn more and more about modern society, but he finds the centers of political initiative less and less accessible. . . . He comes to feel helpless in the fundamental sense that he cannot control what he is able to foresee." *White Collar,* New York: Oxford, 1951, p. 157. The same distinction is found in F. L. Strodtbeck's empirical comparison of Italian and Jewish values affecting mobility: "For the Jew, there was always the expectation that everything could be understood, if perhaps not controlled." "Family Interaction, Values and Achievement," in D. C. McClelland *et al., Talent and Society,* New York: Van Nostrand, 1958, p. 155.

14. Thorstein Veblen argues the same point, in his own inimitable style, in a discussion of "The Belief in Luck": ". . . the extra-causal propensity or agent has a very high utility as a recourse in perplexity" [providing the individual] "a means of escape from the difficulty of accounting for phenomena in terms of causal sequences." *The Theory of the Leisure Class,* New York: Macmillan, 1899; Modern Library Edition, 1934, p. 386.

15. Merton, *op. cit.,* p. 143.

16. R. K. Merton, *Social Theory and Social Structure,* Glencoe, Ill.; Free Press, 1949, p. 128.

17. *Ibid.,* pp. 148–149, 138.

18. *Human Relations,* 10 (February, 1957), p. 49 (italics added).

19. *Ibid.,* p. 59. Obviously, the distinction (discussed above under "powerlessness") between objective conditions and individual expectancy applies in the case of anomie. For a recent treatment of this point, see R. K. Merton, *Social Theory and Social Structure,* Glencoe, Ill.: Free Press, 1957 (revised edition), pp. 161–194. It is clear that Srole's well-known anomie scale refers to individual experience (and that it embodies a heavy adjustment component). It is not so clear how the metaphorical language of "normative breakdown" and "structural strain" associated with the conception of anomie as a social condition is to be made empirically useful. It may be further noted that the idea of rulelessness has often been used to refer to situations in which norms are unclear as well as to those in which norms lose their regulative force. I focused on the latter case in this section; but the former aspect of anomie is contained in the idea of "meaninglessness." The idea of meaninglessness, as defined above, surely includes situations involving uncertainty resulting from obscurity of rules, the absence of clear criteria for resolving ambiguities, and the like.

20. Nettler, *op. cit.,* p. 672.

21. *Ibid.,* p. 675. A scale to measure social isolation (as well as powerlessness and meaninglessness) has been developed by Dean, but the meanings are not the same as those given here; the "social isolation" measure, for example, deals with the individual's friendship status. (See Dwight Dean, "Alienation and Political Apathy," Ph.D. thesis, Ohio State University, 1956.) It seems to me now, however, that this is not a very useful meaning, for two reasons. First, it comes very close to being a statement of either social adjustment or of simple differences in associational styles (i.e., some people are sociable and some are not), and as such seems irrelevant to the root historical notion of alienation. Second, the crucial part of this "social isolation"

component in alienation—what Nisbet, for example, calls the "unattached" or the "isolated"—is better captured for analytical purposes, I believe, in the ideas of meaninglessness, normlessness, or isolation, as defined in expectancy or reward terms. That is to say, what remains, after sheer sociability is removed, is the kind of tenuousness of social ties that may be described as value uniqueness (isolation), deviation from approved means (normlessness), or the like.

22. Merton, "Social Structure and Anomie," *op. cit.*, pp. 144–145. Merton is describing a radical estrangement from societal values (often typified in the case of the intellectual)—i.e., the alienation is from reigning *central* features of the society, and what is sought is a "greatly" modified society. Presumably, the "isolation" mode of alienation, like the other versions, can be applied on the intimate or the grand scale, as noted above in the discussion of Goffman's analysis. Clearly, the person who rejects certain commonly held values in a given society, but who values the society's tolerance for such differences, is expressing a fundamental commitment to societal values and in this degree he is not alienated in the isolation sense.

23. Fromm, *op. cit., pp.* 110, 120.

24. Mills, *op. cit.*, pp. 184, 188.

25. Fromm, *op. cit.*, pp. 131, 134 (italics in original).

26. David Riesman, *The Lonely Crowd,* New Haven: Yale University Press, 1950, p. 49. Although the idea of self-estrangement, when used in the alienation literature, usually carries the notion of a generally applicable human standard, it is sometimes the individual's standard that is at issue: to be alienated in this sense is to be aware of a discrepancy between one's ideal self and one's actual self-image.

27. Glazer, *op. cit.*, p. 379.

28. The difficulty of providing intrinsically satisfying work in industrial society, of course, has been the subject of extensive comment; see, for example, Daniel Bell, *Work and Its Discontents,* Boston: Beacon Press, 1956. A similar idea has been applied by Tumin to the definition of creativity: "I would follow Dewey's lead and view 'creativity' as the esthetic experience, which is distinguished from other experiences by the fact that it is self-consummatory in nature. This is to say, the esthetic experience is enjoyed for the actions which define and constitute the experience, whatever it may be, rather than for its instrumental results or social accompaniments in the form of social relations with others." Melvin M. Tumin, "Obstacles to Creativity," *Etc.: A Review of General Semantics,* 11 (Summer, 1954), p. 261. For a more psychological view of the problem of "intrinsically" governed behavior, see S. Koch, "Behavior as 'Intrinsically' Regulated: Work Notes Toward a Pre-Theory of Phenomena Called 'Motivational,'" in M. R. Jones, editor, *Nebraska Symposium on Motivation,* Lincoln: University of Nebraska Press, 1956, pp. 42–87.

29. Glazer, *op. cit.*, p. 378 (italics added).

# ANOMIE AND SUICIDE * (*Durkheim*)

No living being can be happy or even exist unless his needs are sufficiently proportioned to his means. In other words, if his needs require more than can be granted, or even merely something of a different sort, they will be under continual friction and can only function painfully. Movements in-

* Reprinted from *Suicide: A Study in Sociology,* by Emile Durkheim, translated by George Simpson, pp. 246–257, with permission of the publishers, The Free Press, Glencoe, Ill., and Routledge & Kegan Paul Ltd., London. Copyright 1951 by The Free Press, A Corporation.

capable of production without pain tend not to be reproduced. Unsatisfied tendencies atrophy, and as the impulse to live is merely the result of all the rest, it is bound to weaken as the others relax.

In the animal, at least in a normal condition, this equilibrium is established with automatic spontaneity because the animal depends on purely material conditions. All the organism needs is that the supplies of substance and energy constantly employed in the vital process should be periodically renewed by equivalent quantities; that replacement be equivalent to use. When the void created by existence in its own resources is filled, the animal, satisfied, asks nothing further. Its power of reflection is not sufficiently developed to imagine other ends than those implicit in its physical nature. On the other hand, as the work demanded of each organ itself depends on the general state of vital energy and the needs of organic equilibrium, use is regulated in turn by replacement and the balance is automatic. The limits of one are those of the other; both are fundamental to the constitution of the existence in question, which cannot exceed them.

This is not the case with man, because most of his needs are not dependent on his body or not to the same degree. Strictly speaking, we may consider that the quantity of material supplies necessary to the physical maintenance of a human life is subject to computation, though this be less exact than in the preceding case and a wider margin left for the free combinations of the will; for beyond the indispensable minimum which satisfies nature when instinctive, a more awakened reflection suggests better conditions, seemingly desirable ends craving fulfillment. Such appetites, however, admittedly sooner or later reach a limit which they cannot pass. But how determine the quantity of well-being, comfort or luxury legitimately to be craved by a human being? Nothing appears in man's organic nor in his psychological constitution which sets a limit to such tendencies. The functioning of individual life does not require them to cease at one point rather than at another; the proof being that they have constantly increased since the beginnings of history, receiving more and more complete satisfaction, yet with no weakening of average health. Above all, how establish their proper variation with different conditions of life, occupations, relative importance of services, etc.? In no society are they equally satisfied in the different stages of the social hierarchy. Yet human nature is substantially the same among all men, in its essential qualities. It is not human nature which can assign the variable limits necessary to our needs. They are thus unlimited so far as they depend on the individual alone. Irrespective of any external regulatory force, our capacity for feeling is in itself an insatiable and bottomless abyss.

But if nothing external can restrain this capacity, it can only be a source of torment to itself. Unlimited desires are insatiable by definition and insatiability is rightly considered a sign of morbidity. Being unlimited, they constantly and infinitely surpass the means at their command; they cannot be quenched. Inextinguishable thirst is constantly renewed torture. It has been claimed, indeed, that human activity naturally aspires beyond assignable limits and sets itself unattainable goals. But how can such a undetermined state be any more reconciled with the conditions of mental life than with the demands of physical life? All man's pleasure in acting, moving and exerting himself implies the sense that his efforts are not in vain and that by walking he has advanced. However, one does not advance when one walks toward no goal, or—which is the same thing—when his goal is infinity. Since the distance between us and it is always the same, whatever road we take, we might as well have made the motions without progress from the spot. Even our glances behind and our feeling of pride at the distance covered can cause only deceptive satisfaction, since the remaining distance is not proportionately reduced. To pursue a goal which is by definition unattainable is to condemn oneself to a state of perpetual unhappiness. Of course, man may hope contrary to all reason, and hope has its pleasures even when unreasonable. It may sustain him for a time; but it cannot survive the repeated disappointments of experience indefinitely. What more can the future offer him than the past, since he can never reach a tenable condition nor even approach the glimpsed ideal? Thus, the more one has, the more one wants, since satisfactions received only stimulate instead of filling needs. Shall action as such be considered agreeable? First, only on condition of blindness to its uselessness. Secondly, for this pleasure to be felt and to temper and half veil the accompanying painful unrest, such unending motion must at least always be easy and unhampered. If it is interfered with only restlessness is left, with the lack of ease which it, itself, entails. But it would be a miracle if no insurmountable obstacle were never encountered. Our thread of life on these conditions is pretty thin, breakable at any instant.

To achieve any other result, the passions first must be limited. Only then can they be harmonized with the faculties and satisfied. But since the individual has no way of limiting them, this must be done by some force exterior to him. A regulative force must play the same role for moral needs which the organism plays for physical needs. This means that the force can only be moral. The awakening of conscience interrupted the state of equilibrium of the animal's dormant existence; only conscience, therefore, can furnish the means to re-establish it. Physical restraint would be ineffective; hearts cannot be touched by physio-chemical forces. So far as the appetites are not automatically restrained by physiological mechanisms, they can be halted only by a limit that they recognize as just. Men would never consent to restrict their desires if they felt justified in passing the assigned limit. But, for reasons given above, they cannot assign themselves this law of justice. So they must receive it from an authority which they respect, to which they yield spontaneously. Either directly and as a whole, or through the agency of one of its organs, society alone can play this moderating role; for it is the only moral power superior to the individual, the authority of which he accepts. It alone has the power necessary to stipulate law and to set the point beyond which the passions must not go. Finally, it alone can estimate the reward to be prospectively offered to every class of human functionary, in the name of the common interest.

As a matter of fact, at every moment of history there is a dim perception, in the moral consciousness of societies, of the respective value of different social services, the relative reward due to each, and the consequent degree of comfort appropriate on the average to workers in each occupation. The different functions are graded in public opinion and a certain coefficient of well-being assigned to each, according to its place in the hierarchy. According to accepted ideas, for example, a certain way of living is considered the upper limit to which a workman may aspire in his efforts to improve his existence, and there is another limit below which he is not willingly permitted to fall unless he has seriously demeaned himself. Both differ for city and country workers, for the domestic servant and the day-laborer, for the business clerk and the official, etc. Likewise the man of wealth is reproved if he lives the life of a poor man, but also if he seeks the refinements of luxury overmuch. Economists may protest in vain; public feeling will always be scandalized if an individual spends too much wealth for wholly superfluous use, and it even seems that this severity relaxes only in times of moral disturbance.[1] A genuine regimen exists, therefore, although not always legally formulated, which fixes with relative precision the maximum degree of ease of living to which each social class may legitimately aspire. However, there is nothing immutable about such a scale. It changes with the increase or decrease of collective revenue and the changes occurring in the moral ideas of society. Thus what appears luxury to one period no longer does so to another; and the well-being which for long periods was granted to a class only by exception and supererogation, finally appears strictly necessary and equitable.

Under this pressure, each in his sphere vaguely realizes the extreme limit set to his ambitions and aspires to nothing beyond. At least if he respects regulations and is docile to collective authority, that is, has a wholesome moral constitution, he feels that it is not well to ask more. Thus, an end and goal are set to the passions. Truly, there is nothing rigid nor absolute about such determination. The economic ideal assigned each class of citizens is itself confined to certain limits, within which the desires have free range. But it is not infinite. This relative limitation and the moderation it involves, make men contented with their lot while stimulating them moderately to improve it; and this average contentment causes the feeling of calm, active happiness, the pleasure in existing and living which characterizes health for societies as well as for individuals. Each person is then at least, generally speaking, in harmony with his condition, and desires only what he may legitimately hope for as the normal reward of his activity. Besides, this does not condemn man to a sort of immobility. He may seek to give beauty to his life; but his attempts in this direction may fail without causing him to despair. For, loving what he has and not fixing his desire solely on what he lacks, his wishes and hopes may fail of what he has happened to aspire to, without his being wholly destitute. He has the essentials. The equilibrium of his happiness is secure because it is defined, and a few mishaps cannot disconcert him.

But it would be of little use for everyone to recognize the justice of the hierarchy of functions established by public opinion, if he did not also consider the distribution of these functions just. The workman is not in harmony with his social position if he is not convinced that he has his deserts. If he feels justified in occupying another, what he has would not satisfy him. So it is not enough for the average level of needs for each social conditions to be regulated by public opinion, but another, more precise rule, must fix the way in which these conditions are open to individuals. There is no society in which such regulation does not exist. It varies with times and places. Once it regarded birth as the almost exclusive principle of social classification; today it recognizes no other inherent inequality than hereditary fortune and merit. But in all these various forms its object is unchanged. It is also only possible, everywhere, as a restriction upon individuals imposed by superior authority, that is, by collective authority. For it can be established only by requiring of one or another group of men, usually of all, sacrifices and concessions in the name of the public interest.

Some, to be sure, have thought that this moral pressure would become unnecessary if men's economic circumstances were only no longer determined by heredity. If inheritance were abolished, the argument runs, if everyone began life with equal resources and if the competitive struggle were fought out on a basis of perfect equality, no one could think its results unjust. Each would instinctively feel that things are as they should be.

Truly, the nearer this ideal equality were approached, the less social restraint will be necessary. But it is only a matter of degree. One sort of heredity will always exist, that of natural talent. Intelligence, taste, scientific, artistic, literary or industrial ability, courage and manual dexterity are gifts received by each of us at birth, as the heir to wealth receives his capital or as the nobleman formerly received his title and function. A moral discipline will therefore still be required to make those less favored by nature accept the lesser advantages which they owe to the chance of birth. Shall it be demanded that all have an equal share and that no advantage be given those more useful and deserving? But then there would have to be a discipline far stronger to make these accept a treatment merely equal to that of the mediocre and incapable.

But like the one first mentioned, this discipline can be useful only if considered just by the peoples subject to it. When it is maintained only by custom and force, peace and harmony are illusory; the spirit of unrest and discontent are latent; appetites superficially restrained are ready to revolt. This happened in Rome and Greece when the faiths underlying the old organization of the patricians and plebeians were shaken, and in our modern societies when aristocratic prejudices began to lose their old ascendancy. But this state of upheaval is exceptional; it occurs only when society is passing through some abnormal crisis. In normal conditions the collective order is regarded as just by the great majority of persons. Therefore, when we say that an authority is necessary to impose this order on individuals, we certainly do not mean that violence is the only means of establishing it. Since this regulation is meant to restrain individual passions, it must come from a power which dominates individuals; but this power must also be obeyed through respect, not fear.

It is not true, then, that human activity can be released from all restraint. Nothing in the world can enjoy such a privilege. All existence being a part of the universe is relative to the remainder; its nature and method of manifestation accordingly depend not only on itself but on other beings, who consequently restrain and regulate it. Here there are only differences of degree and form between the mineral realm and the thinking person. Man's characteristic privilege is that the bond he accepts is not physical but moral; that is, social. He is governed not by a material environment brutally imposed on him, but a conscience superior to his own, the superiority of which he feels. Because the greater, better part of his existence transcends the body, he escapes the body's yoke, but is subject to that of society.

But when society is disturbed by some painful crisis or by beneficent but abrupt transitions, it is momentarily incapable of exercising this influence;

thence come the sudden rises in the curve of suicides which we have pointed out above.

In the case of economic disaster, indeed, something like a declassification occurs which suddenly casts certain individuals into a lower state than their previous one. Then they must reduce their requirements, restrain their needs, learn greater self-control. All the advantages of social influence are lost so far as they are concerned; their moral education has to be recommenced. But society cannot adjust them instantaneously to this new life and teach them to practice the increased self-repression to which they are unaccustomed. So they are not adjusted to the condition forced on them, and its very prospect is intolerable; hence the suffering which detaches them from a reduced existence even before they have made trial of it.

It is the same if the source of the crisis is an abrupt growth of power and wealth. Then, truly, as the conditions of life are changed, the standard according to which needs were regulated can no longer remain the same; for it varies with social resources, since it largely determines the share of each class of producers. The scale is upset; but a new scale cannot be immediately improvised. Time is required for the public conscience to reclassify men and things. So long as the social forces thus freed have not regained equilibrium, their respective values are unknown and so all regulation is lacking for a time. The limits are unknown between the possible and the impossible, what is just and what is unjust, legitimate claims and hopes and those which are immoderate. Consequently, there is no restraint upon aspirations. If the disturbance is profound, it affects even the principles controlling the distribution of men among various occupations. Since the relations between various parts of society are necessarily modified, the ideas expressing these relations must change. Some particular class especially favored by the crisis is no longer resigned to its former lot, and, on the other hand, the example of its greater good fortune arouses all sorts of jealousy below and about it. Appetites, not being controlled by a public opinion become disoriented, no longer recognize the limits proper to them. Besides, they are at the same time seized by a sort of natural erethism simply by the greater intensity of public life. With increased prosperity desires increase. At the very moment when traditional rules have lost their authority, the richer prize offered these appetites stimulates them and makes them more exigent and impatient of control. The state of de-regulation or *anomie* is thus further heightened by passions being less disciplined, precisely when they need more disciplining.

But then their very demands make fulfillment impossible. Over-weening ambition always exceeds the results obtained, great as they may be, since there is no warning to pause here. Nothing gives satisfaction and all this agitation is uninterruptedly maintained without appeasement. Above all, since this race for an unattainable goal can give no other pleasure but that of the race itself, if it is one, once it is interrupted the participants are left empty-handed. At the same time the struggle grows more violent and painful, both from being less controlled and because competition is greater. All classes contend among themselves because no established classification any longer exists. Efforts grows, just when it becomes less productive. How could the desire to live not be weakened under such conditions?

This explanation is confirmed by the remarkable immunity of poor countries. Poverty protects against suicide because it is a restraint in itself. No matter how one acts, desires have to depend upon resources to some extent; actual possessions are partly the criterion of those aspired to. So the less one has the less he is tempted to extend the range of his needs indefinitely. Lack of power, compelling moderation, accustoms men to it, while nothing excites envy if no one has superfluity. Wealth, on the other hand, by the power it bestows, deceives us into believing that we depend on ourselves only. Reducing the resistance we encounter from objects, it suggests the possibility of unlimited success against them. The less limited one feels, the more intolerable all limitation appears. Not without reason, therefore, have so many religions dwelt on the advantages and moral value of poverty. It is actually the best school for teaching self-restraint. Forcing us to constant self-discipline, it prepares us to accept collective discipline with equanimity, while wealth, exalting the individual, may always arouse the spirit of rebellion which is the very source of immorality. This, of course, is no reason why humanity should not improve its material condition. But though the moral danger involved in every growth of prosperity is not irremediable, it should not be forgotten.

If *anomie* never appeared except, as in the above instances, in intermittent spurts and acute crisis, it might cause the social suicide-rate to vary from time to time, but it would not be a regular, constant factor. In one sphere of social life, however—the sphere of trade and industry—it is actually in a chronic state.

For a whole century, economic progress has mainly consisted in freeing industrial relations from all regulation. Until very recently, it was the function of a whole system of moral forces to exert this discipline. First, the influence of religion was felt alike by workers and masters, the poor and the rich. It consoled the former and taught them contentment with their lot by informing them of the providential nature of the social order, that the share of each class was assigned by God Himself, and by holding out the hope for just compensation in a world to come in return for the inequalities of this world. It governed the latter, recalling that worldly interests are not man's entire lot, that they must be subordinate to other higher interests, and that they should therefore not be pursued without rule or measure. Temporal power, in turn, restrained the scope of economic functions by its supremacy over them and by the relatively subordinate role it assigned them. Finally, within the business world proper, the occupational groups by regulating salaries, the price of products and production itself, indirectly fixed the average level of income on which needs are partially based by the very force of circumstances. However, we do not mean to propose this organization as a model. Clearly it would be inadequate to existing societies without great changes. What we stress is its existence, the fact of its useful influence, and that nothing today has come to take its place.

Actually, religion has lost most of its power. And government, instead of regulating economic life, has become its tool and servant. The most opposite schools, orthodox economists and extreme socialists, unite to reduce government to the role of a more or less passive intermediary among the various social functions. The former wish to make it simply the guardian of individual contracts; the latter leave it the task of doing the collective bookkeeping, that is, of recording the demands of consumers, transmitting them to producers, inventorying the total revenue and distributing it according to a fixed formula. But both refuse it any power to subordinate other social organs to itself and to make them converge toward one dominant aim. On both sides nations are declared to have the single or chief purpose of achieving industrial prosperity; such is the implication of the dogma of economic materialism, the basis of both apparently opposed systems. And as these theories merely express the state of opinion, industry, instead of being still regarded as a means to an end transcending itself, has become the supreme end of individuals and societies alike. Thereupon the appetites thus excited have become freed of any limiting authority. By sanctifying them, to so speak, this apotheosis of well-being has placed them above all human law. Their restraint seems like a sort of sacrilege. For this reason, even the purely utilitarian regulation of them exercised by the industrial world itself through the medium of occupational groups has been unable to persist. Ultimately, this liberation of desires has been made worse by the very development of industry and the almost infinite extension of the market. So long as the producer could gain his profits only in his immediate neighborhood, the restricted amount of possible gain could not much overexcite ambition. Now that he may assume to have almost the entire world as his customer, how could passions accept their former confinement in the face of such limitless prospects?

Such is the source of the excitement predominating in this part of society, and which has thence extended to the other parts. There, the state of crisis and *anomie* is constant and, so to speak, normal. From top to bottom of the ladder, greed is aroused without knowing where to find an ultimate foothold. Nothing can calm it, since its goal is far beyond all it can attain. Reality seems valueless by comparison with the dreams of fevered imaginations; reality is therefore abandoned, but so too is possibility abandoned when it in turn becomes reality. A thirst arises for novelties, unfamiliar pleasures, nameless sensations, all of which lose their savor once known. Henceforth one has no strength to endure the least reverse. The whole fever subsides and the sterility of all the tumult is apparent, and it is seen that all these new sensations in their infinite quantity cannot form a solid foundation of happiness to support one during days of trial. The wise man, knowing how to enjoy achieved results without having constantly to replace them with others, finds in them an attachment to life in the hour of difficulty. But the man who has always pinned all his hopes on the future and lived with his eyes fixed upon it, has nothing in the past as a comfort against the present's afflictions, for the past was nothing to him but a series of hastily experienced stages. What blinded him to himself was his expectation always to find further on the happiness he had so far missed. Now he is stopped in his tracks; from now on nothing remains behind or ahead of him to fix his gaze upon. Weariness alone, moreover, is enough to bring disillusionment, for he cannot in the end escape the futility of an endless pursuit.

We may even wonder if this moral state is not principally what makes economic catastrophes of our day so fertile in suicides. In societies where a man is subjected to a healthy discipline, he submits more readily to the blows of chance. The necessary effort for sustaining a little more discomfort costs him relatively little, since he is used to discomfort and constraint. But when every constraint is hateful in itself, how can closer constraint not seem intolerable? There is no tendency to resignation in the feverish impatience of men's lives. When there is no other aim but to outstrip constantly the point arrived at, how painful to be thrown back! Now this very lack of organization characterizing our economic condition throws the door wide open to every sort of adventure. Since imagination is hungry for novelty, and ungoverned, it gropes at random. Setbacks necessarily increase with risks and thus crises multiply, just when they are becoming more destructive.

Yet these dispositions are so inbred that society has grown to accept them and is accustomed to think them normal. It is everlastingly repeated that it is man's nature to be eternally dissatisfied, constantly to advance, without relief or rest, toward an indefinite goal. The longing for infinity is daily represented as a mark of moral distinction, whereas it can only appear within unregulated consciences which elevate to a rule the lack of rule from which they suffer. The doctrine of the most ruthless and swift progress has become an article of faith. But other theories appear parallel with those praising the advantages of instability, which, generalizing the situation that gives them birth, declare life evil, claim that it is richer in grief than in pleasure and that it attracts men only by false claims. Since this disorder is greatest in the economic world, it has most victims there.

Industrial and commercial functions are really among the occupations which furnish the greatest number of suicides. Almost on a level with the liberal professions, they sometimes surpass them; they are especially more afflicted than agriculture, where the old regulative forces still make their appearance felt most and where the fever of business has least penetrated. Here is best recalled what was once the general constitution of the economic order. And the divergence would be yet greater if, among the suicides of industry, employers were distinguished from workmen, for the former are probably most stricken by the state of *anomie*. The enormous rate of those with independent means (720 per million) sufficiently shows that the pos-sessors of most comfort suffer most. Everything that enforces subordination attenuates the effects of this state. At least the horizon of the lower classes is limited by those above them, and for this same reason their desires are more modest. Those who have only empty space above them are almost inevitably lost in it, if no force restrains them.

REFERENCE

1. Actually, this is a purely moral reprobation and can hardly be judicially implemented. We do not consider any reestablishing of sumptuary laws desirable or even possible.

# SOCIAL STRUCTURE AND ANOMIE * (*Merton*)

A decade ago, and all the more so before then, one could speak of a marked tendency in psychological and sociological theory to attribute the faulty

* Reprinted from *Social Theory and Social Structure* by Robert K. Merton, pp. 125–133, with permission of the publisher, The Free Press, Glencoe, Ill. Copyright, 1949, by The Free Press, A Corporation.

operation of social structures to failures of social control over man's imperious biological drives. The imagery of the relations between man and society implied by this doctrine is as clear as it is questionable. In the beginning, there are man's biological impulses which seek full expression. And then, there is the social order, essentially an apparatus for the management of impulses, for the social processing of tensions, for the "renunciation of instinctual gratifications," in the words of Freud. Nonconformity with the demands of a social structure is thus assumed to be anchored in original nature.[1] It is the biologically rooted impulses which from time to time break through social control. And by implication, conformity is the result of an utilitarian calculus or of unreasoned conditioning.

With the more recent advancement of social science, this set of conceptions has undergone basic modification. For one thing, it no longer appears so obvious that man is set against society in an unceasing war between biological impulse and social restraint. The image of man as an untamed bundle of impulses begins to look more like a caricature than a portrait. For another, sociological perspectives have increasingly entered into the analysis of behavior deviating from prescribed patterns of conduct. For whatever the role of biological impulses, there still remains the further question of why it is that the frequency of deviant behavior varies within different social structures and how it happens that the deviations have different shapes and patterns in different social structures. Today, as a decade ago, we have still much to learn about the processes through which social structures generate the circumstances in which infringement of social codes constitutes a "normal" (that is to say, an expectable) response.[2] This paper is an essay seeking clarification of the problem.

The framework set out in this essay is designed to provide one systematic approach to the analysis of social and cultural sources of deviant behavior. Our primary aim is to discover how some *social structures exert a definite pressure upon certain persons in the society to engage in noncomformist rather than conformist conduct.* If we can locate groups peculiarly subject to such pressures, we should expect to find fairly high rates of deviant behavior in these groups, not because the human beings comprising them are compounded of distinctive biological tendencies but because they are responding normally to the social situation in which they find themselves. Our perspective is sociological. We look at variations in the *rates* of deviant behavior, not at its incidence.[3] Should our quest be at all successful, some forms of deviant behavior will be found to be as psychologically normal as conformist behavior, and the equation of deviation and abnormality will be put in question.

## Patterns of Cultural Goals and Institutional Norms

Among the several elements of social and cultural structures, two are of immediate importance. These are analytically seperable although they merge in concrete situations. The first consists of culturally defined goals, purposes and interests, held out as legitimate objectives for all or for diversely located members of the society. The goals are more or less integrated—the degree is a question of empirical fact—and roughly ordered in some hierarchy of value. Involving various degrees of sentiment and significance, the prevailing goals comprise a frame of aspirational reference. They are the things "worth striving for." They are a basic, though not the exclusive, component of what Linton has called "designs for group living." And though some, not all, of these cultural goals are directly related to the biological drives of man, they are not determined by them.

A second element of the cultural structure defines, regulates and controls the acceptable modes of reaching out for these goals. Every social group invariably couples its cultural objectives with regulations, rooted in the mores or institutions, of allowable precedures for moving toward these objectives. These regulatory norms are not necessarily identical with technical or efficiency norms. Many procedures which from the standpoint of particular individuals would be most efficient in securing desired values—the exercise of force, fraud, power—are ruled out of the institutional area of permitted conduct. At times, the disallowed procedures include some which would be efficient for the group itself—e.g., historic taboos on vivisection, on medical experimentation, on the sociological analysis of "sacred" norms—since the criterion of acceptability is not technical efficiency but value-laden sentiments (supported by most members of the group or by those able to promote these sentiments through the composite use of power and propaganda). In all instances, the choice of expedients for striving toward cultural goals is limited by institutionalized norms.

Sociologists often speak of these controls as being "in the mores" or as operating through social institutions. Such elliptical statements are true enough, but they obscure the fact that culturally standardized practices are not all of a piece. They are subject to a wide gamut of control. They may represent definitely prescribed or preferential or permissive or proscribed patterns of behavior. In assessing the operation of social controls, these variations—roughly indicated by the terms *prescription, preference, permission* and *proscription*—must of course be taken into account.

To say, moreover, that cultural goals and institutionalized norms operate jointly to shape prevailing practices is not to say that they bear a constant relation to one another. The cultural emphasis placed upon certain goals varies independently of the degree of emphasis upon institutionalized means. There may develop a very heavy, at times a virtually exclusive stress upon the value of given goals, involving comparatively little concern with the institutionally prescribed means of striving toward these goals. The limiting case of this type is reached when the range of alternative procedures is governed only by technical rather than by institutional norms. Any and all procedures which promise attainment of the all-important goal would be permitted in this hypothetical polar case. This constitutes one type of mal-integrated culture. A second polar type is found in groups where activities originally conceived as instrumental are transmuted into self-contained practices, lacking further objectives. The original purposes are forgotten and close adherence to institutionally prescribed conduct becomes a matter of ritual.[4] Sheer conformity becomes a central value. For a time, social stability is ensured—at the expense of flexibility. Since the range of alternative behaviors permitted by the culture is severely limited, there is little basis for adapting to new conditions. There develops a tradition-bound, "sacred" society marked by neophobia. Between these extreme types are societies which maintain a rough balance between emphases upon cultural goals and institutionalized practices, and these constitute the integrated and relatively stable, though changing, societies.

An effective equilibrium between these two phases of the social structure is maintained so long as satisfactions accrue to individuals conforming to both cultural constraints, viz., satisfactions from the achievement of goals and satisfactions emerging directly from the institutionally canalized modes of striving to attain them. It is reckoned in terms of the product and in terms of the process, in terms of the outcome and in terms of the activities. Thus continuing satisfactions must derive from sheer participation in a competitive order as well as from eclipsing one's competitors if the order itself is to be sustained. If concern shifts exclusively to the outcome of competition, then those who perennially suffer defeat will, understandably enough, work for a change in the rules of the game. The sacrifices occasionally—not, as Freud assumed, invariably—entailed by conformity to institutional norms must be compensated by socialized rewards. The distribution of statuses through competition must be so organized that positive incentives for adherence to status obligations are provided *for every position* within the distributive order. Otherwise, as will soon become plain, aberrant behavior ensues. It is, indeed, my central hypothesis that aberrant behavior may be regarded sociologically as a symptom of dissociation between culturally prescribed aspirations and socially structured avenues for realizing these aspirations.

Of the types of societies which result from independent variation of cultural goals and institutionalized means, we shall be primarily concerned with the first—a society in which there is an exceptionally strong emphasis upon specific goals without a corresponding emphasis upon institutional procedures. If it is not to be misunderstood, this statement must be elaborated. No society lacks norms governing conduct. But societies do differ in the degree to which the folkways, mores and institutional controls are effectively integrated with the goals which stand high in the hierarchy of cultural values. The culture may be such as to lead individuals to center their emotional convictions about the complex of culturally acclaimed ends, with far less emotional support for prescribed methods of reaching out for these ends. With such differential emphases upon goals and institutional procedures, the latter may be so vitiated by the stress on goals as to have the behavior of many individuals limited only by considerations of technical expediency. In this context, the sole significant question becomes: Which of the available procedures is most efficient in netting the culturally ap-proved value?[5] The technically most effective procedure, whether culturally legitimate or not, becomes typically preferred to institutionally prescribed conduct. As this process of attenuation continues, the society becomes un-stable and there develops what Durkheim called "anomie" ( or normless-ness).[6]

The working of this process eventuating in anomie can be easily glimpsed in a series of familiar and instructive, though perhaps trivial, epi-sodes. Thus, in competitive athletics, when the aim of victory is shorn of its institutional trappings and success becomes construed as "winning the game" rather than "winning under the rules of the game," a premium is implicitly set upon the use of illegitimate but technically efficient means. The star of the opposing football team is surreptitiously slugged; the wrestler inca-pacitates his opponent through ingenious but illicit techniques; university alumni covertly subsidize "students" whose talents are confined to the athletic field. The emphasis on the goal has so attenuated the satisfactions deriving from sheer participation in the competitive activity that only a suc-cessful outcome provides gratification. Through the same process, tension generated by the desire to win in a poker game is relieved by successfully dealing one's self four aces or, when the cult of success has truly flowered, by sagaciously shuffling the cards in a game of solitaire. The faint twinge of uneasiness in the last instance and the surreptitious nature of public delicts indicate clearly that the institutional rules of the game are *known* to those who evade them. But cultural (or idiosyncratic) exaggeration of the success-goal leads men to withdraw emotional support from the rules.[7]

This process is of course not restricted to the realm of competitive sport, which has simply provided us with microcosmic images of the social macrocosm. The process whereby exaltation of the end generates a literal *demoralization*, i.e., a deinstitutionalization, of the means occurs in many[8] groups where the two components of the social structure are ·not highly integrated.

Contemporary American culture appears to approximate the polar type in which great emphasis upon certain success-goals occurs without equivalent emphasis upon institutional means. It would of course be fanciful to assert that accumulated wealth stands alone as a symbol of success just as it would be fanciful to deny that American assign it a place high in their scale of values. In some large measure, money has been consecrated as a value in itself, over and above its expenditure for articles of consumption or its use for the enhancement of power. "Money" is peculiarly well adapted to become a symbol of prestige. As Simmel emphasized, money is highly abstract and impersonal. However acquired, fraudulently or institutionally, it can be used to purchase the same goods and services. The anonymity of an urban society, in conjunction with these peculiarities of money, permits wealth, the sources of which may be unknown to the community in which the plutocrat lives or, if known, to become purified in the course of time, to serve as a symbol of high status. Moreover, in the American Dream there is no final stopping point. The measure of "monetary success" is conveniently indefinite and relative. At each income level, as H. F. Clark has found, Americans want just about twenty-five per cent more (but of course this "just a bit more" continues to operate once it is obtained). In this flux of shifting standards, there is no stable resting point, or rather, it is the point which manages always to be "just ahead." An observer of a community in which annual salaries in six figures are not uncommon reports the anguished words of one victim of the American Dream: "In this town, I'm snubbed socially because I only get a thousand a week. That hurts."[9]

To say that the goal of monetary success is entrenched in American culture is only to say that Americans are bombarded on every side by precepts which affirm the right or, often, the duty of retaining the goal even in the face of repeated frustration. Prestigeful representatives of the society reinforce the cultural emphasis. The family, the school and the workplace—the major agencies shaping the personality structure and goal formation of Americans—join to provide the intensive disciplining required if an individual is to retain intact a goal that remains elusively beyond reach, if he is to be motivated by the promise of a gratification which is not redeemed. As we shall presently see, parents serve as a transmission belt for the values and goals of the groups of which they are a part—above all, of their social class or of the class with which they identify themselves. And the schools are of course the official agency for the passing on of the prevailing values, with a large proportion of the textbooks used in city schools implying or stating explicitly "that education leads to intelligence and consequently to job and money success."[10] Central to this process of disciplining people to maintain their unfulfilled aspirations are the cultural prototypes of success, the living documents testifying that the American Dream can be realized if one but has the requisite abilities. Consider in this connection the following excerpt from the business journal, *Nation's Business*, drawn from a large mass of comparable materials found in mass communications setting forth the values of business class culture.

| The Document (Nation's Business Vol. 27, No. 8, p. 7) | Its Sociological Implications |
|---|---|
| " 'You have to be born to those jobs, buddy, or else have a good pull.' | *Here is an heretical opinion, possibly born of continued frustration, which rejects the worth of retaining an apparently unrealizable goal and, moreover, questions the legitimacy of a social structure which provides differential access to this goal.* |
| "That's an old sedative to ambition. | *The counter-attack, explicitly asserting the cultural value of retaining one's aspirations intact, of not losing "ambition."* |
| "Before listening to its seduction, ask these men: | *A clear statement of the function to be served by the ensuing list of "successes." These men are living testimony that the social structure is such as to permit these aspirations to be achieved, if one is worthy. And correlatively, failure to reach these goals testifies only to one's own per-* |

sonal shortcomings. Aggression provoked by failure should therefore be directed inward and not outward, against oneself and not against a social structure which provides free and equal access to opportunity.

"Elmer R. Jones, president of Wells-Fargo and Co., who began life as a poor boy and left school at the fifth grade to take his first job.

Success prototype I: All may properly have the same lofty ambitions, for however lowly the starting-point, true talent can reach the very heights. Aspirations must be retained intact.

"Frank C. Ball, the Mason fruit jar king of America, who rode from Buffalo to Muncie, Indiana, in a boxcar along with his brother George's horse, to start a little business in Muncie that became the biggest of its kind.

Success prototype II: Whatever the present results of one's strivings, the future is large with promise; for the common man may yet become a king. Gratifications may seem forever deferred, but they will finally be realized as one's enterprise becomes "the biggest of its kind."

"J. L. Bevan, president of the Illinois Central Railroad, who at twelve was a messenger boy in the freight office at New Orleans."

Success prototype III: If the secular trends of our economy seem to give little scope to small business, then one may rise within the giant bureaucracies of private enterprise. If one can no longer be a "king" in a realm of his own creation, he may at least become a "president" in one of the economic democracies. No matter what one's present station, messenger boy or clerk, one's gaze should be fixed at the top.

From divers sources there flows a continuing pressure to retain high ambition. The exhortational literature is immense, and one can choose only at the risk of seeming invidious. Consider only these: The Reverend Russell

H. Conwell, with his *Acres of Diamonds* address heard and read by hundreds of thousands and his subsequent book, *The New Day, or Fresh Opportunities: A Book for Young Men;* Elbert Hubbard, who delivered the famous *Message to Garcia* at Chautauqua forums throughout the land; Orison Swett Marden, who, in a stream of books, first set forth *The Secret of Achievement,* praised by college presidents, then explained the process of *Pushing to the Front,* eulogized by President McKinley and finally, these democratic testimonials notwithstanding, mapped the road to make *Every Man a King.* The symbolism of a commoner rising to the estate of economic royalty is woven deep in the texture of the American culture pattern, finding what is perhaps its ultimate expression in the words of one who knew whereof he spoke, Andrew Carnegie: "Be a king in your dreams. Say to yourself, 'My place is at the top.' "[11]

Coupled with this positive emphasis upon the obligation to maintain lofty goals is a correlative emphasis upon the penalizing of those who draw in their ambitions. Americans are admonished "not to be a quitter" for in the dictionary of American culture, as in the lexicon of youth, "there is no such as word 'fail.' " The cultural manifesto is clear: one must not quit, must not cease striving, must not lessen his goals, for "not failure, but low aim, is crime."

Thus the culture enjoins the acceptance of three cultural axioms: First, all should strive for the same lofty goals since these are open to all; second, present seeming failure is but a way-station to ultimate success; and third, genuine failure consists only in the lessening or withdrawal of ambition.

In rough psychological paraphrase, these axioms represent, first, a symbolic "secondary reinforcement" of incentive; second, curbing the threatened extinction of a response through an associated stimulus; third, increasing the motive-strength to evoke continued responses despite the continued absence of reward.

In sociological paraphrase, these axioms represent, first, the deflection of criticism of the social structure onto one's self among those so situated in the society that they do not have full and equal access to opportunity; second, the preservation of a given structure of social power by having individuals in the lower social strata identify themselves, not with their compeers, but with those at the top (whom they will ultimately join); and third, providing pressures for conformity with the cultural dictates of unslackened ambition by the threat of less than full membership in the society for those who fail to conform.

It is in these terms and through these processes that contemporary American culture continues to be characterized by a heavy emphasis on wealth as a basic symbol of success, without a corresponding emphasis upon the legitimate avenues on which to march toward this goal. How do individuals living in this cultural context respond? And how do our observations bear upon the doctrine that deviant behavior typically derives from biological impulses breaking through the restraints imposed by culture? What, in short, are the consequences for the behavior of people variously situated in a social structure of a culture in which the emphasis on dominant success-goals has become increasingly separated from an equivalent emphasis on institutionalized procedures for seeking these goals?

## REFERENCES

1. See, for example, S. Freud, *Civilization and Its Discontents* (*passim,* and esp. at p. 63); Ernest Jones, *Social Aspects of Psychoanalysis* (London, 1924) p. 28. If the Freudian notion is a variety of the "original sin" doctrine, then the interpretation advanced in this paper is a doctrine of "socially derived sin."

2. "Normal" in the sense of the psychologically expectable, if not culturally approved, response to determinate social conditions. This statement does not, of course, deny the role of biological and personality differences in fixing the *incidence* of deviant behavior. It is simply that *this* is not the problem considered here. It is in the same sense as our own, I take it, that James S. Plant of the "normal reaction of normal people to abnormal conditions." See his *Personality and the Cultural Pattern* (New York, 1937), p. 248.

3. The position taken here has been perceptively described by Edward Sapir. ". . . problems of social science differ from problems of individual behavior in degree of specificity, not in kind. Every statement about behavior which throws the emphasis, explicitly or implicitly, on the actual, integral experiences of defined personalities or types of personalities is a datum of psychology or psychiatry rather than of social science. Every statement about behavior which aims, not to be accurate about the behavior of an actual individual or individuals or about the expected behavior of a physically and psychologically defined type of individual, but which abstracts from such behavior in order to bring out in clear relief certain expectancies with regard to those aspects of individual behavior which various people share, as an interpersonal or 'social' pattern, is a datum, however crudely expressed, of social science." I have here chosen the second perspective; although I shall have occasion to speak of attitudes, values and function, it will be from the standpoint of how the social structure promotes or inhibits their appearance in specified types of situations. See Sapir, "Why Cultural Anthropology Needs the Psychiatrist," *Psychiatry*, 1938, 1, 7–12.

4. This ritualism may be associated with a mythology which rationalizes these practices so that they appear to retain their status as means, but the dominant pressure is toward strict ritualistic comformity, irrespective of the mythology. Ritualism is thus most complete when such rationalizations are not even called forth.

5. In this connection, one sees the relevance of Elton Mayo's paraphrase of the title of Tawney's well-known book. "Actually the problem is *not that of the sickness of an acquisitive society; it is that of the acquisitiveness of a sick society." Human Problems of an Industrial Civilization* (New York, 1933), p. 153. Mayo deals with the process through which wealth comes to be the basic symbol of social achievement and sees this as arising from a state of anomie. My major concern here is with the social consequences of a heavy emphasis upon monetary success a a goal in a society which has not adapted its structure to the implications of this emphasis. A complete analysis would require the simultaneous examination of both processes.

6. Durkheim's resurrection of the term "anomie" which, so far as I know, first appears in approximately the same sense in the late sixteenth century, might well become the

object of an investigation by a student interested in the historical filiation of ideas. Like the term "climate of opinion" brought into academic and political popularity by A. N. Whitehead three centuries after it was coined by Joseph Glanvill, the word "anomie" (or anomy or anomia) has lately come into frequent use, once it was reintroduced by Durkheim. Why the resonance in contemporary society? For a magnificent model of the type of research required by questions of this order, see Leo Spitzer, "*Milieu* and *Ambiance*: An Essay in Historical Semantics," *Philosophy and Phenomenological Research*, 1942, 3, 1–42, 169–218.

7. It appears unlikely that cultural norms, once interiorized, are wholly eliminated. Whatever residuum persists will induce personality tensions and conflict, with some measure of ambivalence. A manifest rejection of the once-incorporated institutional norms will be coupled with some latent retention of their emotional correlates. "Guilt feelings," "a sense of sin," "pangs of conscience" are diverse terms referring to this unrelieved tension. Symbolic adherence to the nominally repudiated values or rationalizations for the rejection of these values constitute a more subtle expression of these tensions.

8. "Many," not all, unintegrated groups, for the reason mentioned earlier. In groups where the primary emphasis shifts to institutional means, the outcome is normally a type of ritualism rather than anomie.

9. Leo C. Rosten, *Hollywood* (New York, 1940), p. 40.

10. Malcolm S. MacLean, *Scholars, Workers and Gentlemen* (Harvard University Press, 1938), p. 29.

11. *Cf.* A. W. Griswold, *The American Cult of Success* (Yale University doctoral dissertation, 1933); R. O. Carlson, "*Personality Schools*": A Sociological Analysis, (Columbia University Master's Essay, 1948).

# SUCCESS AND OPPORTUNITY * (*Mizruchi*)

Although Durkheim has suggested elsewhere (1951, p. 254) that anomie in the economic system is in a *chronic* state, the tone of his more general statements suggests that anomie is primarily an *acute* crisis in a social system or subsystem. Thus in addition to his emphasis upon "abrupt transition," he observed that:

> *Economic progress [i.e., the Industrial Revolution] has mainly consisted in freeing industrial relations from all regulation. Until very recently, it was the function of a whole system of moral forces to exert this discipline. (ibid.)*

He points out that all subsystems of society are powerless to cope with this phenomenon and that, therefore, anomie has extended from the economic system into other parts of the social system.[1]

* Reprinted with permission of The Macmillan Company from *Success and Opportunity: A Study in Anomie*, by Ephraim H. Mizruchi (The Free Press of Glencoe, a Division of The Macmillan Company, 1964), pp. 106–108, 126–133.

[1] Note that Karl Polanyi's *The Great Transformation* (New York: Holt, Rinehart & Winston, Inc., 1944), deals with the disruption of total social systems in industrial societies as a result of the same phenomenon with which Durkheim is concerned in the above quotation.

A stable society is thus characterized by limited aspirations and limited but gratifying attainments. Durkheim views extreme vertical social mobility as symptomatic primarily of acute crisis.

Merton, on the other hand, focuses on a society that is markedly different from that of nineteenth-century France. Durkheim's France was not only emerging as an industrial society, but was also experiencing the progressive breakdown of its highly structured feudal social system, which had suffered three revolutions in less than a century. Although the traditional classes in French society were no longer so rigid as they had once been, Durkheim was still able to observe the remnants of a relatively structured society— including limited classes of artisans, aristocrats, and intellectuals, to name only a few.[2] While extreme social mobility was not a common expectation in nineteenth-century France, it is in twentieth-century America. As we indicated earlier, social mobility is normative in American society, and, consequently, *absence* of social mobility represents a crisis in the social system. Since there are no legitimate aristocracy and no values that support the acceptance of parental or ascribed status, upward social mobility is accepted as a worthy goal and is not interpreted as going beyond one's "rightful place" in society. This unlimited expectation is "built into" the American social system through its values, and it is for this reason that Merton describes anomie as a more *chronic* condition than does Durkheim.

High social mobility thus reflected anomie in nineteenth-century France, while low social mobility reflects anomie in twentieth-century America. The two cases, it should be noted, do not represent two different conditions but two different forms of the anomic condition. The nature of the value system determines the form anomie takes. Social mobility itself, then, is not the central factor but how social mobility is *defined*. And the definitions reflect different kinds of social structures.

More specifically, different orientations to social mobility reflect value systems based on different systems of stratification. In an *estate* system, there would be relatively modest expectations of upward social mobility. *Class* systems, on the other hand, are characterized by expectations of upward social mobility.

The essence of Durkheim's theory, then, is to be found in the norms and values that characterize a given society. Stability is achieved when there are common beliefs and sentiments, by which members of society act. The cultural system and the social system are inextricably intertwined. A

---

[2] The Dreyfus case, in which Durkheim was involved years after the development of his views on anomie, partially reflected the last gasp of the threatened remnants of this feudal hierarchy.

change in values thus reflects itself in changing behavior, and changing behavior is reflected in changing values. We therefore return to our original position that anomie is symptomatic, at least partially, of a disjunction between a social and cultural system that were formerly integrated. We believe that the concept of anomie is sufficiently broad to encompass several types of empirical phenomena. . . .

## Merton's Theory of Social Structure and Anomie

We pointed out earlier that Merton's theory of social structure and anomie has two essential parts: his application of Durkheim's essential concept of anomie and his theory and typology of the consequences of anomie in American society. We tried to make clear that our concern is specifically with Merton's formulation of Durkheim's concept and its application to American society and that we were not attempting to make an empirical assessment of the typology. It follows, however, that, if Merton's application of Durkheim's concept—to explain relatively high crime rates in the lower classes, for example—were not supported by empirical research, then his *explanation* for his typology would be without support. The typology may still, however, have considerable empirical and theoretical merit, even though its explanation may warrant modification or even rejection.

In our test of the Durkheim-Merton hypothesis, we found that anomie had greater effects as we descended the class structure, independently of the degree to which success values were shared by the class groups in our sample. Our interpretation of these findings was that, while there was generally strong evidence to support the hypothesis, blocked efforts to reach socially defined occupational goals provided only a partial explanation for the progressively greater demoralization observed in the lower classes. Our data on the relationships between social class, social participation, and personal demoralization supported our hypothesis that the lower classes are, in addition to being blocked in their success aspirations, cut off from those sources of the community structure that provide both a sense of integration with the community and access to values that motivate striving for life goals. We agree with Robert and Helen Lynd that these segments of the community are "in" but not "of" the community. It seems to us that greater demoralization in the lower classes reflects not only strain associated with disparities between aspiration and achievement but with social integration as well.

We found, further, that there is a tendency for the middle classes to experience the effects of anomie associated with striving toward occupational goals to a degree that was not anticipated in Merton's hypothesis. When occupational achievement is perceived as blocked, the middle classes tend to become more demoralized than do the lower classes. We suggested that the effects of disparity between aspiration and achievement may possibly be smaller in the lower classes than in the higher classes, because there is a greater familiarity with failure among the former and greater opportunity to rationalize. Furthermore, work does not have the same significance for those who are on the lower rungs of the occupational hierarchy. In general, these suggestions were supported by our data.

As a consequence of our findings and our interpretation of them, some modification of Merton's theory is in order. More specifically, our findings suggest that at least two sets of causal factors operate to produce personal demoralization. On this basis, we suggest that there is more than one type of anomie and that different types are reflected in differential class distribution of anomie.

The strains that affect the lower classes include the type of anomie Merton has described. As our analysis of values has shown, there is a disparity between the *success* goals to which those in the lower classes aspire and the values that enhance opportunities to reach these goals. Such opportunities are largely limited by self-imposed barriers based on low valuation of the activities that are most instrumental in the climb to success. There are, of course, also real external limitations that affect the lower classes. Merton's concept of anomie does, however, apply to the lower classes in general and is one type, which we shall call *bondlessness*. Bondlessness represents a type of structured strain in which socially structured goals are incompatible with the various socially structured means by which they may be sought.

We have noted that there is no bond uniting the *cognitive* perception of education as an instrument for seeking success and a correspondingly high *valuation of education*. Our assumption was that awareness of education as a potential instrument for seeking success was inadequate to sustain long-term striving and, therefore, that education must itself be highly *valued* if it is to function effectively as a means. This form of bondlessness, then, results from a disparity between the perceived requirements of socially structured situations and an absence of the socially structured mechanisms necessary to meet such requirements. The suggestion is clear that certain values must occur in clusters, if systemic strains are to be avoided. *Ends-values* without functionally corresponding *means-values* are a critical source of systemic strain. In this particular case, the effect of such strain is greatest in the lower classes.

Still another source of bondlessness is the external obstacles to reaching success goals. The lower the class position, the more obstacles are placed by relatively high classes in the path to attainment of success goals. It has already been recognized that there is discrimination against the lower classes in the public schools, beginning with the primary grades (Warner, *et al.,* 1944). There is clearly a job ceiling for those whose class characteristics fail to conform to middle-class standards of grammar, dress, and manners. Hollingshead, for example, has shown how middle-class adolescents exclude lower-class adolescents from extra-curricular activities in Elmtown (1949, pp. 202–3). This exclusion limits opportunities for association with the middle classes and consequent socialization in middle-class patterns. A very recent study indicates that even among those who have achieved professional positions, in this case engineers, the individual whose class background is relatively low tends to hold a lower-status position in the profession, compared with those whose class background are relatively high (Perrucci, 1961).

Clearly, wherever there are socially structured goals that groups of people strive to reach and socially structured obstacles limiting opportunities for the attainment of these goals, we find effects of the type of anomie we have called *bondlessness.*

The second type of anomie reflected in our data is more closely associated with that aspect of deregulation on which Durkheim placed the greatest emphasis in his explanation of suicide. Since poverty is itself a restraining force, then the kind of anomie characteristic of those who are lower on the social scale—defining "poverty" broadly—is not the same as that characteristic of those higher on the social scale. As Durkheim has so eloquently put it:

> *Poverty protects against suicide because it is a restraint in itself. No matter how one acts, desires have to depend upon resources to some extent; actual possessions are partly the criterion of those aspired to. So the less one has the less he is tempted to extend the range of his needs indefinitely. Lack of power, compelling moderation, accustoms men to it, while nothing excites envy if no one has superfluity. Wealth, on the other hand, by the power it bestows, deceives us into believing that we depend on ourselves only. Reducing the resistance we encounter from objects, it suggests the possibility of unlimited success against them. The less limited one feels, the more intolerable all limitation appears. Not without reason, therefore, have so many religions dwelt on the advantages and moral value of poverty. It is actually the best school for teach-*

*ing self-restraint. Forcing us to constant self-discipline, it prepares us to accept collective discipline with equanimity, while wealth, exalting the individual, may always arouse the spirit of rebellion which is the very source of immorality. This, of course, is no reason why humanity should not improve its material condition. But though the moral danger involved in every growth of prosperity is not irremediable, it should not be forgotten. (1951, p. 254.)*

Merton is inclined to classify this reaction as retreatism, which he defines as an explicitly individual reaction:

*[Retreatism is the mode of adaptation] of the socially disinherited who if they have none of the rewards held out by society also have few of the frustrations attendant upon continuing to seek rewards. It is, moreover, a privatized rather than a collective mode of adaptation. Although people exhibiting this deviant behavior may gravitate toward centers where they come into contact with other deviants and although they may come to share in the subculture of these deviant groups, their adaptations are largely private and isolated rather than unified under the aegis of a new cultural mode. The type of collective adaptation remains to be considered. (1957, p. 155.)*[3]

B. M. Spinley, in a study of a London slum, has made still another observation relevant to explaining the differential effects of limited opportunity:

*To postpone pleasure for a time it is necessary to be certain that ultimate reward will come and will be worth waiting for. [The slum dweller] has no such certainty. He cannot be sure of greater love, longer education, greater economic reward, for he sees that these rewards do not come to his associates, and he is basically insecure. Therefore he takes what he can while he is sure of having it, e.g., a night of fun at the club, a dead-end job, and early marriage. (1953, p. 84.)*

Middle-class anomie, as our data indicate, is much more related to what Durkheim called "aspiring to what is unattainable" than is lower-class anomie. The achievement goals of the middle classes are, by their very nature more difficult to reach than the concrete success goals of the lower

---

[3] Note that Merton's *retreatism* may actually be a collective rather than an individual reaction. Where group sentiment inhibits efforts to seek rewards and where social conditions inhibit the motivation of large segments of the population, it is difficult to think of the process in *individual* terms.

classes. There is no end to achievement, and there may be little recognition or reward for it for at least two reasons. First, *achievement* goals are nebulous and without limit. Even among prominent scientists, there is no limit to the fame or recognition that can be sought. Perusal of the advertisements directed to Americans of all classes—but primarily to those who can afford or who *should be able* to afford the most luxuries—shows that their appeal is geared to desires for more, and larger, and more elegant symbols that reflect achievement in the occupational sphere. In education, a master's degree represents much less achievement than it did in the past.

Second, achievement is very difficult to assess, and indirect, symbolic referents have therefore become the basis for such assessment. These symbols may have little or no relation to actual achievement, yet they assume great importance for the many who crave recognition for their accomplishments.

Veblen, although he was referring to the somewhat different phenomenon of "pecuniary emulation," has provided us with a clear statement about the significance of such rewards for the member of the community:

> *In order to stand well in the eyes of the community, it is necessary to come up to a certain, somewhat indefinite, conventional standard of wealth. . . . Those members of the community who fall short of this . . . suffer in the esteem of their fellowmen; and consequently they suffer also in their own esteem, since the usual basis of self-respect is the respect accorded by one's neighbors. Only individuals with an aberrant temperament can in the long run retain their self esteem in the face of the disesteem of their fellows.* (1953, p. 38.)

We have already shown that college-educated individuals earning relatively low incomes tend to become more demoralized than do those who had less education. The reason is that they need symbols to reflect what they have achieved, symbols that, presumably, only money can buy. In the academic sphere, we observe similar problems. There is no way that outstanding teaching or research can be easily evaluated by one's peers. What one has achieved, then, is symbolized by publications, which in many cases bear little relationship to the significance of one's contributions to knowledge.

Furthermore, we suggested that the American middle classes—to whom consumer credit is etxended with little hesitation—have more occupational and consumption wants than the majority can possibly attain. It is to men garbed in white shirts and ties and driving finance-company-owned automobiles that real-estate men, auto manufacturers, clothiers, and luxury manufacturers, beam their television and radio broadcasts. The "dream houses" in Hollywood movies and television shows have little concrete meaning for the wage-earner, who has difficulty bridging the gap between his awareness of himself as an underdog and the middle-class way of life envisaged in Hollywood productions. The middle-class American, on the other hand, lives by these images. Still, he does not always get ahead. Although the success ideology preaches that every man can receive abundant fruits from his labor, it is only true in a limited sense. Many of the outward *symbols* of success can be attained, but not every employee can become an executive, and not every executive can be president of the firm.[4] In short, the middle classes seem to suffer to a greater extent than the lower classes from what we shall call "the myth of infinite elevation." Many middle-class Americans can be described, in terms Kluckhohn used, as "adrift on a meaningless voyage" (1949, p. 249).[5]

We shall call this type of anomie, characterized by striving for unattainable goals, *boundlessness*. Of the two types we have distinguished, the first is derived from Merton's thinking, while the second is more distinctly Durkheimian.

It is interesting to note too that Abram Kardiner, a distinguished psychoanalyst and social scientist has made a similar observation about American patterns. He suggests that those in the lower reaches of the class structure have limited opportunities for education, for example, while in the middle classes, the greatest stress arises from blocks to self-esteem.

> *We are witnessing the* reductio ad absurdum *of the promises of the liberal way of life in which one is responsible for one's own fate, granted the assumption that the social machinery for implementing these approved goals exists. To make use of this machinery requires planning and the requisite capital, neither of which is available to any but a few. Most people live unplanned lives and improvise as they go along, even if the rate of those who get college education has increased 200 percent in fifty years. Most people do not reach middle classdom, but have to engage in the fringe activities and drudgery. At the same time they are stimulated to need and want things, for they have now become the "consumers." They have*

---

[4] The novels of John P. Marquand portray this problem in a number of settings.

[5] Note that Kluckhohn suggests that this anchorless condition is a major cause of the American's penchant for joining formal associations. See also our excerpt from *The Organization Man* in the introduction to this study.

*learned to live by the religion of things and gadgets, each of which simplifies, adds a small increment of pleasure or triumph. Henry Ford made every man a Columbus and a conqueror. The higher the social stratum, the greater the pressure for accomplishment and the greater the risks to self esteem. A great many give up the fight; it is not, however, a resignation, but a resentful defeat. Life has become harder because there is no ceiling on aspiration, and in the past two generations, from 1914 on, the external barriers to fulfilling life goals have been seriously increased by two world wars and a depression. (In Hook, 1959, p. 99.)*

Our data suggest, then, that the particular type of anomie must be specified within the framework of social structural contexts. In this study, the context is the class structure.

REFERENCES

1. Emile Durkheim, *Suicide*, translated by J. A. Spaulding and George Simpson. New York: The Free Press of Glencoe, 1951.
2. August B. Hollingshead, *Elmtown's Youth*, New York: John Wiley & Sons, Inc., 1949.
3. Sidney Hook, ed., *Psychoanalysis, Scientific Method and Philosophy*, New York: New York University Press, 1959.
4. Clyde Kluckhohn, *Mirror for Man*, New York: McGraw-Hill Book Co., Inc., 1949.
5. Robert K. Merton, *Social Theory and Social Structure*, New York: The Free Press of Glencoe, 1949. Revised, 1957.
6. Robert Perrucci, "The Significance of Intra-Occupational Mobility," *American Sociological Review*, Vol. 27 (December, 1961).
7. B. M. Spinley, *The Deprived and the Privileged*, New York: Humanities Press, 1953.
8. Thorstein Veblen, *The Theory of the Leisure Class*, New York: New American Library of World Literature, Inc., 1953.
9. Lloyd W. Warner, Robert Havighurst, and Martin Loeb, *Who Shall Be Educated?*, New York: Harper & Row, Publishers, 1944.

# INSTITUTIONALIZATION AND ANOMIE * *(Parsons)*

It should immediately be evident on general grounds that the most fundamental mechanisms of social control are to be found in the normal processes of interaction in an institutionally integrated social system. The essentials of these processes have been analyzed and illustrated throughout the earlier chapters of this work. Hence it is necessary here only to add a few points.

* Reprinted from *The Social System* by Talcott Parsons, pp. 301–306, with permission of the publishers, The Free Press, Glencoe, Ill., and Tavistock Publications, Ltd., London. Copyright, 1951, by The Free Press, A Corporation.

The central phenomena are to be found in the institutional integration of motivation and the reciprocal reinforcement of the attitudes and actions of the different individual actors involved in an institutionalized social structure. These considerations apply to any one pattern of role-expectations. But institutionalization has integrative functions on various levels, both with reference to the different roles in which any one actor is involved, and to the coordination of the behavior of different individuals. The latter has been dealt with in a number of contexts.

A few remarks are, however, in order in the former context. The individual engages in a wide variety of different activities and becomes involved in social relationships with a large number of different people whose relations to him vary greatly. One of the primary functions of institutionalization is to help order these different activities and relationships so that they constitute a sufficiently coordinated system, to be manageable by the actor and to minimize conflicts on the social level. There are two particularly interesting aspects of this ordering. One is the establishment of a time schedule so that different times are "set aside" for different activities, with different people. "Time off" from occupational obligations on Sundays, holidays, vacations, etc., is one example. The fact that there is a time for each of many different activities—and also a place—keeps the claims of each from interfering with those of the others. In fact a society so complex as ours probably could not function without relatively rigid time scheduling, and the problem of the cultural values and psychological need-disposition structure of such a time organization is of great importance. We know that in many societies the motivational prerequisites for fitting into such a time-orientation do not exist.

A second major area is the establishment of institutionalized priorities. Especially in a relatively free and mobile society it is inevitable that people should become involved in situations where conflicting demands are made upon them. It is quite obvious that such situations are sources of serious potential conflict. This can be minimized if there is a legitimized priority scale so that in choosing one obligation above the other the individual can in general be backed by the sentiments of a common value system. It is indeed in areas where this scheme of priorities is indefinite or not well integrated that loopholes for deviance are most common. One example of such a potential conflict may be cited. A physician has peculiarly sharply emphasized obligations to his patients. But he also has important obligations to his family. Far more than in most occupations he is often called away at times when the family has important claims on him—meal times, evenings when social engagements may be scheduled, etc. The institutionalized expectation of the priority of the claims of patients is indispensable to the physician in dealing with his wife on such an occasion. As Merton has so well analyzed, the exposure to situations of such conflict without clearly institutionalized priorities of obligations is a very important aspect of *anomie.*

The above considerations do not however concern mechanisms of social control in a strict sense though they describe essential aspects of the background on which we must understand the operation of such mechanisms. When we turn to the consideration of normal social interaction within such an institutionalized framework as a process of mutually influenced and contingent action we see that a process of social control is continually going on. Actors are continually doing and saying things which are more or less "out of line," such as by insinuation impugning someone's motives, or presuming too much. Careful observation will show that others in the situation often without being aware of it, tend to react to these minor deviances in such a way as to bring the deviant back "into line," by tactfully disagreeing with him, by a silence which underlines the fact that what he said was not acceptable, or very often by humor as a tension-release, as a result of which he comes to see himself more nearly as others see him. These minor control mechanisms are, it may be maintained, the way in which the institutionalized values are implemented in behavior. They are, on a certain level, the most fundamental mechanisms of all, and only when they break down does it become necessary for more elaborate and specialized mechanisms to come into play.

Beyond the scope of such mechanisms there are points in the social system at which people are exposed to rather special strains. In a good many such cases we find special phenomena which have been interpreted to function at least in part as mechanisms for "coping" with such strains with a minimum of disruptive consequences for the social system. Two types may be briefly discussed. One is the type of situation where because of uncertainty factors or specially acute adjustment problems there is exposure to what, for the persons concerned, is an unusual strain. In general the field of religion and magic yields many examples of this. The problem of uncertainty in the health field and of bereavement are good examples. The reactions which such unusual strains tend to produce are of the character noted above. They both include potentially disruptive components and are unstructured in relation to the social system. In the case of uncertainty, as in gardening in the Trobriands, one of these may be discouragement, a general tendency to withdrawal. Similarly in the case of bereavement, there may be a loss of incentive to keep on going. Ritual on such occasions serves to organize the reaction system in a positive manner and to put a check on the disruptive tendencies.[1]

One aspect of such ritual patterns is always the permissive one of giving an opportunity for "acting out" symbolically the wishes and emotional tensions associated with the situation of strain. It provides opportunities for a permissive relaxation of some of the disciplines of everyday life which are characterized in part by a relatively strict pressure to reality-orientation. But at the same time it is by no means a completely free and untrammeled opportunity for expression. Action is on the contrary strictly channeled into culturally prescribed forms, which prevent "wandering all over the lot." It is a conspicuous feature of such rituals that they are communally prescribed and thus give the support of emphasizing group concern with the situation. They also symbolically assert the dominant value attitudes, thus in the case of death for instance the importance of the survivors going on living in terms of that value system, redefining the solidarity with the deceased in these terms: it is "what he would have wished."[2]

A slightly different type of structuring of behavior which is certainly in part significant as a mechanism of control is what may be called the "secondary institution." The American youth culture is a good example. Like ritual it has its conspicuous permissive aspect, so much so that it shades over into explicit deviance. In this permissive aspect it also may be regarded as primarily a "safety valve" of the social system in that attempting to keep youth completely in line with adult disciplines would probably greatly increase the strains of their position. But it also has more positive control aspects. One of these is the integration of the youth culture with major institutional structures, mainly in the field of formal education. This not only brings it under direct adult supervision, but it legitimizes some of the patterns, for example athletics and dances. In spite of the deviant fringe, the existence of such a legitimized core undoubtedly keeps down the total amount of deviance.

Finally there are certain "self-liquidating" features of the youth culture which are relatively hard to identify but probably quite important. In a variety of ways, through the experience of youth culture activities and relationships the individual in the optimum case goes through a process of emotional development to the point where he ceases to need youth culture and "graduates" into full adult status. Of course in this as in many features of our social control system there are innumerable "miscarriages." But broadly speaking it is extremely probable that on the whole the net effect tends to be emotionally "maturing." For example, the very insistence on independence from adult control accustoms the individual to take more and more responsibility on his own. In the youth culture phase he tends to substitute dependency on his peer group for that on the parents, but gradually he becomes emancipated from even this dependency. Similarly in the relations of the sexes the youth culture offers opportunities and mechanisms for emotional maturation. The element of rebelliousness against the adult world helps to emancipate from more immature object-attachments, while certain features of the "rating and dating" complex protect the individual during the process of this emancipation from deeper emotional involvements than he is yet able to accept. The very publicity of such relationships within the peer group serves as such a protection. Thus the youth culture is not only projective but also exposes the individual passing through it to positively adjustive influences.[3]

It will be noted that the above mechanisms operate within the framework of socially legitimated interaction. Within the normal processes of nipping of minor deviances in the bud of course no differentiated social structures are involved at all. In the case of "safety-valve" mechanisms like ritual, and of secondary institutional patterns, there are special social structures. These entail a limited permissiveness for modes of behavior and types of emotional expression which would be tabooed in ordinary everyday life, e.g., the display of "grief" at funeral ceremonies. But this permissiveness is rather narrowly limited, and it is of the greatest importance that it operates within a system of interaction which is continuous with the main institutionalized social structure, differing from it only with respect to occasion, or as in the case of the youth culture, to stage in the socialization process. The behavior is emphatically not stigmatized as deviant, but is legitimized for people in the relevant situations. They are treated in the present context because of their relevance to the control of *potentially* deviant motivational elements.

Thus it is clear that some balance of permissiveness and its restriction is maintained. Support is clearly given through the institutionalized legitimation of the patterns in question and the resulting solidarity. Generally speaking, however, there is little conscious manipulation of sanctions.

REFERENCES

1. Almost the classic analysis of this type of function of ritual is Malinowski's analysis of funeral ceremonies in *Magic, Science and Religion*. As Kroeber, *op. cit.*, notes, however, there are still important problems of the universality of the relationship between such strains and ritual which must be further studied.
2. We shall discuss in the next two chapters some of the ways in which the religious orientation of a society can be of the first importance with reference to its general system of values in the secular sphere. The control mechanisms in certain areas of special strain tend in turn to be integrated with both. This is the essential difference

between the view of religion taken here and that of Kardiner in *The Individual and His Society*. The latter tends to treat it overwhelmingly as a "pr⸱jective system" which expresses motivational elements which are blocked by the discipline of secular life. This is undoubtedly *one* major aspect of the matter, but only one.

3. Suggestive evidence of the importance of the youth culture        connection is given in Demareth's study of a sample of schizophrenics. A     ...y "maturity" of interests combined with lack of participation in youth culture activities was highly characteristic of the group. Not one of the 20 had established sa⸱ iactory heterosexual relationships on a youth culture level. It may well be that with    . the youth culture there would be many more schizophrenic breakdowns. See N. J. Demareth, *Adolescent Status and the Individual*, unpublished Ph.D. dissertation, Harvard University, 1942. It is also suggestive that one element of alcoholism for men may be connected with over-involvement in the youth culture and failure to become emancipated from it at the proper time. The alcoholic may be in part an adolescent who is unsuccessfully trying to be an adult.

# ILLEGITIMATE MEANS, ANOMIE, AND DEVIANT BEHAVIOR* (*Cloward*)

## Differentials in Availability of Legitimate Means: The Theory of Anomie

The theory of anomie has undergone two major phases of development. Durkheim first used the concept to explain deviant behavior. He focussed on the way in which various social conditions lead to "overweening ambition," and how, in turn, unlimited aspirations ultimately produce a breakdown in regulatory norms. Robert K. Merton has systematized and extended the theory, directing attention to patterns of disjunction between culturally prescribed goals and socially organized access to them by *legitimate* means. In this paper, a third phase is outlined. An additional variable is incorporated in the developing scheme of anomie, namely, the concept of *differentials in access to success-goals by illegitimate means*.[1]

*Phase I: Unlimited Aspirations and the Breakdown of Regulatory Norms.* In Durkheim's work, a basic distinction is made between "physical needs" and "moral needs." The importance of this distinction was heightened for Durkheim because he viewed physical needs as being regulated automatically by features of man's organic structure. Nothing in the organic structure, however, is capable of regulating social desires; as Durkheim put it, man's "capacity for feeling is in itself an insatiable and bottomless abyss."[2]

* Reprinted by permission of the author and *American Sociological Review*, XXIV, April, 1959, copyright, 1959, American Sociological Association.

If man is to function without "friction," "the passions must first be limited. . . . But since the individual has no way of limiting them, this must be done by some force exterior to him." Durkheim viewed the collective order as the external regulating force which defined and ordered the goals to which men should orient their behavior. If the collective order is disrupted or disturbed, however, men's aspirations may then rise, exceeding all possibilities of fulfillment. Under these conditions, "de-regulation or anomy" ensues: "At the very moment when traditional rules have lost their authority, the richer prize offered these appetites stimulates them and makes them more exigent and impatient of control. The state of de-regulation or anomy is thus further heightened by passions being less disciplined precisely when they need more disciplining." Finally, pressures toward deviant behavior were said to develop when man's aspirations no longer matched the possibilities of fulfillment.

Durkheim therefore turned to the question of *when* the regulatory functions of the collective order break down. Several such states were identified, including sudden depression, sudden prosperity, and rapid technological change. His object was to show how, under these conditions, men are led to aspire to goals extremely difficult if not impossible to attain. As Durkheim saw it, sudden depression results in deviant behavior because "something like a declassification occurs which suddenly casts certain individuals into a lower state than their previous one. Then they must reduce their requirements, restrain their needs, learn greater self-control. . . . But society cannot adjust them instantaneously to this new life and teach them to practice the increased self-repression to which they are unaccustomed. So they are not adjusted to the condition forced on them, and its very prospect is intolerable; hence the suffering which detaches them from a reduced existence even before they have made trial of it." Prosperity, according to Durkheim, could have much the same effect as depression, particularly if upward changes in economic conditions are abrupt. The very abruptness of these changes presumably heightens aspirations beyond possibility of fulfillment, and this too puts a strain on the regulatory apparatus of the society.

. . . . .

In developing the theory, Durkheim characterized goals in the industrial society, and specified the way in which unlimited aspirations are induced. He spoke of "dispositions . . . so inbred that society has grown to accept them and is accustomed to think them normal," and he portrayed these "inbred dispositions": "It is everlastingly repeated that it is man's nature to be eternally dissatisfied, constantly to advance, without relief or rest, toward an indefinite goal. The longing for infinity is daily represented as a mark of moral distinction. . . ." And it was precisely these pressures to strive for "infinite" or "receding" goals, in Durkheim's view, that generate a breakdown in regulatory norms, for "when there is no other aim but to outstrip constantly the point arrived at, how painful to be thrown back!"

*Phase II: disjunction between cultural goals and socially structured opportunity.* Durkheim's description of the emergence of "overweening ambition" and the subsequent breakdown of regulatory norms constitutes one of the links between his work and the later development of the theory by Robert K. Merton. In his classic essay, "Social Structure and Anomie," Merton suggests that goals and norms may vary independently of each other, and that this sometimes leads to malintegrated states. In his view, two polar types of disjunction may occur: "There may develop a very heavy, at times a virtually exclusive, stress upon the value of particular goals, involving comparatively little concern with the institutionally prescribed means of striving toward these goals. . . . This constitutes one type of malintegrated culture."[3] On the other hand, "A second polar type is found where activities originally conceived as instrumental are transmuted into self-contained practices, lacking further objectives. . . . Sheer conformity becomes a central value." Merton notes that "between these extreme types are societies which maintain a rough balance between emphasis upon cultural goals and institutionalized practices, and these constitute the integrated and relatively stable, though changing societies."

Having identified patterns of disjunction between goals and norms, Merton is enabled to define anomie more prescisely: "Anomie [may be] conceived as a breakdown in the cultural structure, occurring particularly when there is an acute disjunction between cultural norms and goals and the socially structured capacities of members of the group to act in accord with them."

Of the two kinds of malintegrated societies, Merton is primarily interested in the one in which "there is an exceptionally strong emphasis upon specific goals without a corresponding emphasis upon institutional procedures." He states that attenuation between goals and norms, leading to anomie or "normlessness," comes about because men in such societies internalize an emphasis on common success-goals under conditions of varying access to them. The essence of this hypothesis is captured in the following excerpt: "It is only when a system of cultural values extols, virtually above all else, certain *common* success-goals for the population at large while the social structure rigorously restricts or completely closes access to approved modes of reaching these goals *for a considerable part of the same population,* that deviant behavior ensues on a large scale." The focus, in short, is on the way in which the social structure puts a strain upon the cultural structure. Here one may point to diverse structural differentials in access to culturally approved goals by legitimate means, for example, differentials of age, sex, ethnic status, and social class. Pressures for anomie or normlessness vary from one social position to another, depending on the nature of these differentials.

. . . .

Merton suggests that differing rates of ritualistic and innovating behavior in the middle and lower classes result from differential emphases in socialization. The "rule-oriented" accent in middle-class socialization presumably disposes persons to handle stress by engaging in ritualistic rather than innovating behavior. The lower-class person, contrastingly, having internalized less stringent norms, can violate convetions with less guilt and anxiety.[4] Values, in other words, exercise a canalizing influence, limiting the choice of deviant adaptations for persons variously distributed throughout the social system.

Apart from both socially patterned pressures, which give rise to deviance, and from values, which determine choices of adaptations, a further variable should be taken into account: namely, *differentials in availability of illegitimate means.*

. . . .

Several sociologists have alluded to such variations without explicitly incorporating this variable in a theory of deviant behavior. Sutherland, for example, writes that "an inclination to steal is not a sufficient explanation of the genesis of the professional thief."[5] Moreover, "the person must be appreciated by the professional thieves. He must be appraised as having an adequate equipment of wits, front, talking-ability, honesty, reliability, nerve and determination." In short, "a person can be a professional thief only if he is recognized and received as such by other professional thieves." But recognition is not freely accorded: "Selection and tutelage are the two necessary elements in the process of acquiring recognition as a professional thief. . . . A person cannot acquire recognition as a professional thief until he has had tutelage in professional theft, *and tutelage is given only to a few persons selected from the total population.*" Furthermore, the aspirant is judged by high standards of performance, for only "a very small percentage of those who start on this process ever reach the stage of professional theft." The burden of these remarks—dealing with the processes of selection, induction, and assumption of full status in the criminal group—is that motivations or pressures toward deviance do not fully account for deviant behavior. The "self-made" thief—lacking knowledge of the ways of securing immunity from prosecution and similar techniques of defense—"would quickly land in prison." Sutherland is in effect pointing to differentials in access to the role of professional thief.

. . . .

The availability of illegitimate means, then, is controlled by various criteria in the same manner that has long been ascribed to conventional means. Both systems of opportunity are (1) limited, rather than infinitely available, and (2) differentially available depending on the location of persons in the social structure.

When we employ the term "means," whether legitimate or illegitimate, at least two things are implied: first, that there are appropriate learning enviornments for the acquisition of the values and skills associated with the performance of a particular role; and second, that the individual has opportunities to discharge the role once he has been prepared. The term subsumes, therefore, both *learning structures* and *opportunity structures*.

A case in point is recruitment and preparation for careers in the rackets. There are fertile criminal learning environments for the young in neighborhoods where the rackets flourish as stable, indigenous institutions. Because these environments afford integration of offenders of different ages, the young are exposed to "differential associations" which facilitate the acquisition of criminal values and skills. Yet preparation for the role may not insure that the individual will ever discharge it. For one thing, more youngsters may be recruited into these patterns of differential association than can possibly be absorbed, following their "training," by the adult criminal structure. There may be a surplus of contenders for these elite positions, leading in turn to the necessity for criteria and mechanisms of selection. Hence a certain proportion of those who aspire may not be permitted to engage in the behavior for which they have been prepared.

This illustration is similar in every respect, save for the route followed, to the case of those who seek careers in the sphere of legitimate business. Here, again, is the initial problem of securing access to appropriate learning environments, such as colleges and post-graduate schools of business. Having acquired the values and skills needed for a business career, graduates then face the problem of whether or not they can successfully discharge the roles for which they have been prepared. Formal training itself is not sufficient for occupational success, for many forces intervene to determine who shall succeed and fail in the competitive world of buisness and industry—as throughout the entire conventional occupational structure.

This distinction between learning structures and opportunity structures was suggested some years ago by Sutherland. In 1944, he circulated an unpublished paper which briefly discusses the proposition that "criminal behavior is partially a function of opportunities to commit specific classes of crimes, such as embezzlement, bank burglary, or illicit heterosexual intercourse."[6] He did not, however, take up the problem of differentials in opportunity as a concept to be systematically incorporated in a theory of deviant behavior. Instead, he held that "opportunity" is a necessary but not sufficient explanation of the commission of criminal acts, "since some persons who have opportunities to embezzle, become intoxicated, engage in illicit heterosexual intercourse or to commit other crimes do not do so." He also noted that the differential association theory did not constitute a full explanation of criminal activity, for, notwithstanding differential association, "it is axiomatic that persons who commit a specific crime must have the opportunity to commit that crime." He therefore concluded that "while opportunity may be partially a function of association with criminal patterns and of the specialized techniques thus acquired, *it is not determined entirely in that manner,* and consequently differential association is not the sufficient cause of criminal behavior." (emphasis not in original)

In Sutherland's statements, two meanings are attributed to the term "opportunity." As suggested above, it may be useful to separate these for analytical purposes. In the first sense, Sutherland appears to be saying that opportunity consists in part of learning structures. The principal components of his theory of differential association are that "criminal behavior is learned," and, furthermore, that "criminal behavior is learned in interaction with other persons in a process of communication." But he also uses the term to describe situations conducive to carrying out criminal roles. Thus, for Sutherland, the commission of a criminal act would seem to depend upon the existence of two conditions: differential associations favoring the acquisition of criminal values and skills, and conditions encouraging participation in criminal activity.

This distinction heightens the importance of identifying and questioning the common assumption that illegitimate means are freely available. We can now ask (1) whether there are socially structured differentials in access to illegitimate learning environments, and (2) whether there are differentials limiting the fulfillment of illegitimate roles. If differentials exist and can be identified, we may then inquire about their consequences for the behavior of persons in different parts of the social structure.

. . . .

### Differentials in Availability of Illegitimate Means: The Subculture Tradition

In their studies of the ecology of deviant behavior in the urban environ-ment, Shaw and McKay found that delinquency and crime tended to be confined to delimited areas and, furthermore, that such behavior persisted despite demographic changes in these areas. Hence they came to speak of "criminal tradition," of the "cultural transmission" of criminal values.[7] As a result of their observations of slum life, they concluded that *particular importance must be assigned to the integration of different age-levels of offenders.* Thus:

> *Stealing in the neighborhood was a common practice among the children and approved by the parents. Whenever the boys got to-gether they talked about robbing. The little fellows went in for petty stealing, breaking into freight cars, and stealing junk. The older guys did big jobs like stick-up, burglary, and stealing autos. The little fellows admired the "big shots" and longed for the day when they could get into the big racket. Fellows who had "done time" were the big shots and looked up to and gave the little fellow tips on how to get by and pull off big jobs.*[8]

In other words, access to criminal roles depends upon stable associations with others from whom the necessary values and skills may be learned. Shaw and McKay were describing deviant learning structures—that is, alternative routes by which people seek acess to the goals which society holds to be worthwhile. They might also have pointed out that, in areas where such learning structures are unavailable, it is probably difficult for many individuals to secure access to stable criminal careers, even though motivated to do so.[9]

The concept of illegitimate means and the socially structured conditions of access to them were not explicitly recognized in the work of Shaw and McKay because, probably, they were disposed to view slum areas as "dis-organized." Although they consistently referred to illegitimate activities as being organized, they nevertheless often depicted high-rate delinquency areas as disorganized because the values transmitted were criminal rather than conventional.

. . . .

Sutherland was among the first to perceive that the concept of social disorganization tended to obscure the stable patterns of interaction among carriers of criminal values. Like Shaw and McKay, he had been influenced by the observation that lower-class areas were organized in terms of both conventional and criminal values, but he was also impressed that these alternative value systems were supported by patterned systems of social relations. He expressly recognized that crime, far from being a random, unorganized activity, was typically an intricate and stable system of human arrangements. He therefore rejected the concept of "social disorganization" and substituted the concept of "differential group organization."

> The third concept, social disorganization, was borrowed from Shaw and McKay. I had used it but had not been satisfied with it because the organization of the delinquent group, which is often very complex, is social disorganization only from an ethical or some other particularistic point of view. At the suggestion of Albert K. Cohen, this concept has been changed to differential group organization, with organization for criminal activities on one side and organization against criminal activities on the other.[10]

Having freed observation of the urban slum from conventional evaluations, Sutherland was able to focus more clearly on the way in which its social structure constitutes a "learning environment" for the acquisition of deviant values and skills. In the development of the theory of "differential association" and "differential group organization," he came close to stating explicitly the concept of differentials in access to illegitimate means. But Sutherland was essentially interested in learning processes, and thus he did not ask how such access varies in different parts of the social structure, nor did he inquire about the consequences for behavior of variations in the accessibility of these means.[11]

William F. Whyte, in his classic study of an urban slum, advanced the empirical description of the structure and organization of illegitimate means a step beyond that of Sutherland. Like Sutherland, Whyte rejected the earlier view of the slum as disorganized:

> It is customary for the sociologist to study the slum district in terms of "social disorganization" and to neglect to see that an area such as Cornerville has a complex and well-established organization of its own. . . . I found that in every group there was a hierarchical structure of social relations binding the individuals to one another and that the groups were also related hierarchically to one another. Where the group was formally organized into a political club, this

> *was immediately apparent, but for informal groups it was no less true.*[12]

Whyte's contribution to our understanding of the organization of illegitimate means in the slum consist primarily in showing that individuals who participate in stable illicit enterprise do not constitute a separate or isolated segment of the community.

.   .   .   .

The description of the organization of illegitimate means in slums is further developed by Solomon Kobrin in his article, "The Conflict of Values in Delinquency Areas."[13] Kobrin suggests that urban slum areas vary in the degree to which the carriers of deviant and conventional values are integrated with one another. Hence he points the way to the development of a "typology of delinquency areas based on variations in the relationship between these two systems," depicting the "polar types" on such a continuum. The first type resembles the integrated areas described in preceding paragraphs. Here, claims Kobrin, there is not merely structural integration between carriers of the two value systems, but reciprocal participation by each in the value system of the other. Thus:

> *Leaders of [illegal] enterprises frequently maintain membership in such conventional institutions of their local communities as churches, fraternal and mutual benefit societies and political parties. . . . Within this framework the influence of each of the two value systems is reciprocal, the leaders of illegal enterprise participating in the primary orientation of the conventional elements in the population, and the latter, through their participation in a local power structure sustained in large part by illicit activity, participating perforce in the alternate, criminal value system.*

Kobrin also notes that in some urban slums there is a tendency for the relationships between carriers of deviant and conventional values to break down. Such areas constitute the second polar type. Because of disorganizing forces such as "drastic change in the class, ethnic, or racial characteristics of its population," Kobrin suggests that "the bearers of the conventional culture and its value system are without the customary institutional machinery and therefore in effect partially demobilized with reference to the diffusion of their value system." At the same time, the criminal "value system remains implicit" since this type of area is "characterized principally by the absence of systematic and organized adult activity in violation of the law, despite the fact that many adults in these areas commit violations."

Since both value systems remain implicit, the possibilities for effective integration are precluded.

. . . .

With respect to the contrasting or "unintegrated area," Kobrin makes no mention of the extent to which learning structures and opportunities for criminal careers are available. Yet his portrayal of such areas as lacking in the articulation of either conventional or criminal values suggests that the appropriate learning structures—principally the integration of offenders of different age levels—are not available. Furthermore, his depiction of adult violative activity as "unorganized" suggests that the illegal opportunity structure is severely limited. Even if youngsters were able to secure adequate preparation for criminal roles, the problem would appear to be that the social structure of such neighborhoods provides few opportunities for stable, criminal careers. For Kobrin's analysis—as well as those of Whyte and others before him—leads to the conclusion that illegal opportunity structures tend to emerge in lower-class areas only when stable patterns of accommodation and integration arise between the carriers of conventional and deviant values. Where these values remain unorganized and implicit, or where their carriers are in open conflict, opportunities for stable criminal role performance are more or less limited.

. . . .

## Some Implications of a Consolidated Approach to Deviant Behavior

It is now possible to consolidate the two sociological traditions described above. Our analysis makes it clear that these traditions are oriented to different aspects of the same problem: differentials in access to opportunity. One tradition focusses on legitimate opportunity, the other on illegitimate. By incorporating the concept of differentials in access to *illegitimate* means, the theory of anomie may be extended to include seemingly unrelated studies and theories of deviant behavior which form a part of the literature of American criminology. In this final section, we try to show how a consolidated approach might advance the understanding of both rates and types of deviant conduct. The discussion centers on the conditions of access to *both* systems of means, legitimate and illegitimate.

*The distribution of criminal behavior.* One problem which has plagued the criminologist is the absence of adequate data on social differentials in criminal activity. Many have held that the highest crime rates are to be found in the lower social strata. Others have suggested that rates in the middle and upper classes may be much higher than is ordinarily thought. The question of the social distribution of crime remains problematic.

In the absence of adequate data, the theorist has sometimes attacked this problem by assessing the extent of pressures toward normative departures in various parts of the social structure. For example, Merton remarks that his "primary aim is to discover how some social structures exert a definite pressure upon certain persons in the society to engage in non-conforming rather than conforming conduct."[14] Having identified structural features which might be expected to generate deviance, Merton suggests the presence of a correlation between "pressures toward deviation" and "rate of deviance."

> *But whatever the differential rates of deviant behavior in the several social strata, and we know from many sources that the official crime statistics uniformly showing higher rates in the lower strata are far from complete or reliable,* it appears from our analysis that the greater pressures toward deviation are exerted upon the lower strata. . . . *Of those located in the lower reaches of the social structure, the culture makes incompatible demands. On the one hand they are asked to orient their behavior toward the prospect of large wealth . . . and on the other, they are largely denied effective opportunities to do so institutionally.* The consequence of this structural inconsistency is a high rate of deviant behavior.[15]

Because of the paucity and unreliability of existing criminal statistics, there is as yet no way of knowing whether or not Merton's hypothesis is correct. Until comparative studies of crime rates are available the hypothesized correlation cannot be tested.

From a theoretical perspective, however, questions may be raised about this correlation. Would we expect, to raise the principal query, the correlation to be fixed or to vary depending on the distribution of access to illegitimate means? The three possibilities are (1) that access is distributed uniformly throughout the class structure, (2) that access varies inversely with class position, and (3) that access varies directly with class position. Specification of these possibilities permits a more precise statement of the conditions under which crime rates would be expected to vary.

If access to illegitimate means is *uniformly distributed* throughout the class structure, then the proposed correlation would probably hold—higher rates of innovating behavior would be expected in the lower class than elsewhere. Lower-class persons apparently experience greater pressures toward deviance and are less restrained by internalized prohibitions from employing illegitimate means. Assuming uniform access to such means, it would therefore be reasonable to predict higher rates of innovating behavior in the lower social strata.

If access to illegitimate means varies *inversely* with class position, then the correlation would not only hold, but might even be strengthened. For pressures toward deviance, including socialization that does not altogether discourage the use of illegitimate means, would coincide with the availability of such means.

Finally, if access varies *directly* with class position, comparative rates of illegitimate activity become difficult to forecast. The higher the class position, the less the pressure to employ illegitimate means; furthermore, internalized prohibitions are apparently more effective in higher positions. If, at the same time, opportunities to use illegitimate methods are more abundant, then these factors would be in opposition. Until the precise effects of these several variables can be more adequately measured, rates cannot be safely forecast.

The concept of differentials in availability of illegitimate means may also help to clarify questions about varying crime rates among ethnic, age, religious, and sex groups, and other social divisions. This concept, then, can be systematically employed in the effort to further our understanding of the distribution of illegitimate behavior in the social structure.

. . . .

## Summary

This paper attempts to identify and to define the concept of differential opportunity structures. It has been suggested that this concept helps to extend the developing theory of social structure and anomie. Furthermore, by linking propositions regarding the accessibility of *both* legitimate and illegitimate opportunity structures, a basis is provided for consolidating various major traditions of sociological thought on nonconformity. The concept of differential systems of opportunity and of variations in access to them, it is hoped, will suggest new possibilities for research on the relationship between social structure and deviant behavior.

REFERENCES

1. "Illegitimate means" are those proscribed by the mores. The concept therefore includes "illegal means" as a special case but is not coterminous with illegal behavior, which refers only to the violation of legal norms. In several parts of this paper, I refer to particular forms of deviant behavior which entail violation of the law and

there use the more restricted term, "illegal means." But the more general concept of illegitimate means is needed to cover the wider gamut of deviant behavior and to relate the theories under review here to the evolving theory of "legitimacy" in sociology.

2. All of the excerpts in this section are from Durkheim, *op. cit.*, pp. 247–257.
3. For this excerpt and those which follow immediately, see Merton, *op. cit.*, pp. 131–194.
4. Merton, *op. cit.*, p. 151.
5. For this excerpt and those which follow immediately, see Sutherland, *The Professional Thief*, pp. 211–213.
6. For this excerpt and those which follow immediately, see Albert Cohen, Alfred Lindesmith and Karl Schuessler, editors, *The Sutherland Papers*, Bloomington: Indiana University Press, 1956, pp. 31–35.
7. See especially *Delinquency Areas*, Chapter 16.
8. Shaw, *The Jack-Roller*, p. 54.
9. We are referring here, and throughout the paper, to stable criminal roles to which persons may orient themselves on a career basis, as in the case of racketeers, professional thieves, and the like. The point is that access to stable roles depends in the first instance upon the availability of learning structures. As Frank Tannenbaum says, "it must be insisted on that unless there were older criminals in the neighborhood who provided a moral judgment in favor of the delinquent and to whom the delinquents could look for commendation, the careers of the younger ones could not develop at all." *Crime and the Community*, New York: Ginn, 1938, p. 60.
10. Cohen, Lindesmith and Schuessler, *op. cit.*, p. 21.
11. It is interesting to note that the concept of differentials in access to *legitimate* means did not attain explicit recognition in Sutherland's work, nor in the work of many others in the "subculture" tradition. This attests to the independent development of the two traditions being discussed. Thus the ninth proposition in the differential association theory is stated as follows:

(9) *Though criminal behavior is an expression of general needs and values, it is not explained by those general needs and values since noncriminal behavior is an expression of the same needs and values.* Thieves generally steal in order to secure money, but likewise honest laborers work in order to secure money. The attempts by many scholars to explain criminal behavior by general drives and values, such as the happiness principle, striving for social status, the money motive, or frustration, have been and must continue to be futile since they explain lawful behavior as completely as they explain criminal behavior.

Of course, it is perfectly true that "striving for status," the "money motive" and similar modes of socially approved goal-oriented behavior do not as such account for both deviant and conformist behavior. But if goal-oriented behavior occurs under conditions of socially structured obstacles to fulfillment by legitimate means, the resulting pressures might then lead to deviance. In other words, Sutherland appears to assume that the distribution of access to success-goals by legitimate means is uniform rather than variable, irrespective of location in the social structure. See his *Principles of Criminology*, 4th edition, pp. 7–8.

12. William F. Whyte, *Street Corner Society* (original edition, 1943). Chicago: The University of Chicago Press, 1955, p. viii.
13. *American Sociological Review*, 16 (October, 1951), pp. 657–658, which includes the excerpts which follow immediately.
14. Merton, *op. cit.*, p. 132.
15. *Ibid.*, pp. 144–145.

# 13: Social Disorganization and Deviance

Often devoid of conceptual clarity but never long neglected, no field has flourished more than the one variously designated as social pathology, social disorganization and deviance, or simply social problems. Every one of these terms has been subject to fierce and continuous criticism, usually with good reason. Pathology suggests organicism; it offers an inadmissible medical analogy to the practitioner of sociological theory; one man's disorganization is another's reorganization; deviance from norms A and B may mean no more than adherence to norms C and D, and there is no consensus in the definition of social problems.

As one term is discarded over a generation or two, and others become fashionable, sociologists agonize over the subject matter that interests many of them, as it does a large general public, most of all. Given the upheaval of a revolutionary age, private administrators, government officials, and plain citizens seek answers to the many bewildering questions that beset them. More than ever, the sociologist is called upon to help men of action. Everywhere he finds himself driven by a sense of urgency about practical matters.

In this setting, the need for substantive theory is very great, and now again that theory begins to exist. Others did much to lay its foundations, but no one more than Emile Durkheim, who was concerned from first to last with the "normal" and the "pathological" manifestations of human behavior. Indeed, by establishing their logical and sociological indissolubility he achieved a kind of Galileian synthesis, comparable to that of Freud. If we have learned, thanks to Freud, that psychopathological acts are merely an extension of "normality" in the individual, our knowledge of the social

569

sphere has been similarly enhanced by Durkheim. His *Rules* make the theoretical point with typical lucidity.

Crime as a universal phenomenon that could never be extirpated (and ought not to be if it could) fascinated Durkheim all his life. He discovered it among aborigines and, even more so, in advanced civilizations, where, however, restitutive justice tended to replace retributive or punitive justice. But the lust for revenge by society against those stigmatized as criminals has disappeared less rapidly than Durkheim assumed. Punitive justice persists— and it is to this theme that George Herbert Mead addressed himself with such insight decades ago. Durkheim, as we would say today, found crime functional as a vehicle for innovation, and Mead found the punishment of crime functional for the affirmation of social solidarity—a remarkably Durkheimian conclusion!

In the twentieth century, criminology as a subdivision of sociology followed an errant course down many a dead end. The most popular path to nowhere is biologism, according to which men violate the criminal code out of a hereditary, constitutional compulsion to do so. This view dies hard despite a hundred years of sterile speculation and misbegotten research. Economism, the theory—in one phrase—that poverty causes crime, is perhaps more plausible, but no more helpful. In a single stroke, Edwin H. Sutherland, dean of American criminology until his death in 1950, dealt a final blow to economism. His reasoning is summarized in the textbook published under his name and that of an important continuator, Donald H. Cressey, from which we have extracted a relevant portion, one that includes the famous *sociological* theory of differential association.

Four sociological "laws" hypothesized by Thomas and Znaniecki are included to indicate the quality of their thinking as of 1918, for they were directly confronted with the disorganization of traditional family forms in their pioneering study of the Polish peasant. These early sociologists understood that there was much more to disorganization and deviance than crime and family instability. They located such problems in a total sociopsychological context. Since their time good work (such as that of Albert K. Cohen, who in 1955 produced at least a minor classic in his *Delinquent Boys*) has been done only within that context. If the old-timers sound a bit dated and simple-minded by comparison with Cohen, we can only rejoice at this sign that theoretical progress has been made in a tricky field and against heavy odds.

By far the most noteworthy recent development of deviance theory has been spearheaded by Howard S. Becker in several books and articles, but most strikingly in his capacity, for several years, as editor of an increasingly significant journal entitled *Social Problems.* Becker revived and elaborated a theory that had lain dormant for many years. The story of its emergence, submergence and re-emergence would make an interesting exercise in the sociology of knowledge. This generation of students interested in deviance taps roots planted by the Chicago school and looks to two books which, though they were grossly neglected when published, now seem to make very good sense. These books are *Crime and the Community* by Frank Tannenbaum, written in 1938 and Edwin H. Lemert's *Social Pathology* of 1951. The pivotal point of these books, as of Becker's, is that society creates deviance by definition. No group, whatever its behavior, is "deviant" until and unless its members have been labeled, branded and stigmatized. By so viewing the matter, Becker and his associates have turned our attention around, causing us to see more clearly what too many theoreticians and practitioners had tended to overlook.

# THE NORMALITY OF CRIME * (*Durkheim*)

If there is any fact whose pathological character appears incontestable, that fact is crime. All criminologists are agreed on this point. Although they explain this pathology differently, they are unanimous in recognizing it. But let us see if this problem does not demand a more extended consideration.

We shall apply the foregoing rules. Crime is present not only in the majority of societies of one particular species but in all societies of all types. There is no society that is not confronted with the problem of criminality. Its form changes; the acts thus characterized are not the same everywhere; but, everywhere and always, there have been men who have behaved in such a way as to draw upon themselves penal repression. If, in proportion as societies pass from the lower to the higher types, the rate of criminality, i.e., the relation between the yearly number of crimes and the population, tended to decline, it might be believed that crime, while still normal, is tending to lose this character of normality. But we have no reason to believe that such a regression is substantiated. Many facts would seem rather to indicate a movement in the opposite direction. From the beginning of the [nineteenth] century, statistics enable us to follow the course of criminality. It has everywhere increased. In France the increase is nearly 300 per cent.

* Reprinted with permission of The Free Press of Glencoe from *The Rules of Sociological Method,* 8th ed., 1938, pp. 65–75. Copyright 1938 by The University of Chicago.

There is, then, no phenomenon that presents more indisputably all the symptoms of normality, since it appears closely connected with the conditions of all collective life. To make of crime a form of social morbidity would be to admit that morbidity is not something accidental, but, on the contrary, that in certain cases it grows out of the fundamental constitution of the living organism; it would result in wiping out all distinction between the physiological and the pathological. No doubt it is possible that crime itself will have abnormal forms, as, for example, when its rate is unusually high. This excess is, indeed, undoubtedly morbid in nature. What is normal, simply, is the existence of criminality, provided that it attains and does not exceed, for each social type, a certain level, which it is perhaps not impossible to fix in conformity with the preceding rules.[1]

Here we are, then, in the presence of a conclusion in appearance quite pathological. Let us make no mistake. To classify crime among the phenomena of normal sociology is not to say merely that it is an inevitable, although regrettable phenomenon, due to the incorrigible wickedness of men; it is to affirm that it is a factor in public health, an integral part of all healthy societies. This result is, at first glance, surprising enough to have puzzled even ourselves for a long time. Once this first surprise has been overcome, however, it is not difficult to find reasons explaining this normality and at the same time confirming it.

In the first place crime is normal because a society exempt from it is utterly impossible. Crime, we have shown elsewhere, consists of an act that offends certain very strong collective sentiments. In a society in which criminal acts are no longer committed, the sentiments they offend would have to be found without exception in all individual consciousnesses, and they must be found to exist with the same degree as sentiments contrary to them. Assuming that this condition could actually be realized, crime would not thereby disappear; it would only change its form, for the very cause which would thus dry up the sources of criminality would immediately open up new ones.

Indeed, for the collective sentiments which are protected by the penal law of a people at a specified moment of its history to take possession of the public conscience or for them to acquire a stronger hold where they have an insufficient grip, they must acquire an intensity greater than that which they had hitherto had. The community as a whole must experience them more vividly, for it can acquire from no other source the greater force necessary to control these individuals who formerly were the most refractory. For murderers to disappear, the horror of bloodshed must become greater in those social strata from which murderers are recruited, but, first it must become greater throughout the entire society. Moreover, the very absence of crime would directly contribute to produce this horror because any sentiment seems much more respectable when it is always and uniformly respected.

One easily overlooks the consideration that these strong states of the common consciousness cannot be thus reinforced without reinforcing at the same time the more feeble states, whose violation previously gave birth to mere infraction of convention—since the weaker ones are only the prolongation, the attenuated form, of the stronger. Thus robbery and simple bad taste injure the same single altruistic sentiment, the respect for that which is another's. However, this same sentiment is less grievously offended by bad taste than by robbery, and since, in addition, the average consciousness has not sufficient intensity to react keenly to the bad taste, it is treated with greater tolerance. That is why the person guilty of bad taste is merely blamed, whereas the thief is punished. But, if this sentiment grows stronger, to the point of silencing in all consciousnesses the inclination which disposes man to steal, he will become more sensitive to the offenses which, until then, touched him but lightly. He will react against them, then, with more energy; they will be the object of greater opprobrium, which will transform certain of them from the simple moral faults that they were and give them the quality of crimes. For example, improper contracts, or contracts improperly executed, which ony incur public blame or civil damages, will become offenses in law.

Imagine a society of saints, a perfect cloister of exemplary individuals. Crimes, properly so called, will there be unknown, but faults which appear venial to the layman will create there the same scandal that the ordinary offense does in ordinary consciousnesses. If, then, this society has the power to judge and punish, it will define these acts as criminal and will treat them as such. For the same reason, the perfect and upright man judges his smallest failings with a severity that the majority reserve for acts more truly in the nature of an offense. Formerly, acts of violence against persons were more frequent than they are today, because respect for individual dignity was less strong. As this has increased, these crimes have become more rare; and also, many acts violating this sentiment have been introduced into the penal law which were not included there in primitive times.[2]

In order to exhaust all the hypotheses logically possible, it will perhaps be asked why this unanimity does not extend to all collective sentiments without exception. Why should not even the most feeble sentiment gather enough energy to prevent all dissent? The moral consciousness of the society would be present in its entirety in all the individuals, with a vitality sufficient to prevent all acts offending it—the purely conventional faults as well as the crimes. But a uniformity so universal and absolute is utterly impossible; for the immediate physical milieu in which each one of us is placed, the hereditary antecedents, and the social influences vary from one individual to the next, and consequently diversify consciousnesses. It is impossible for all to be alike, if only because each one has his own organism and that these organisms occupy different areas in space. That is why even among the lower peoples, where individual originality is very little developed, it nevertheless does exist.

Thus, since there cannot be a society in which the individuals do not differ more or less from the collective type, it is also inevitable that, among these divergences, there are some with a criminal character. What confers this character upon them is not the intrinsic quality of a given act but that definition which the collective conscience lends them. If the collective conscience is stronger, if it has enough authority practically to suppress these divergences, it will also be more sensitive, more exacting, and, reacting against the slightest deviations with the energy it otherwise displays only against more considerable infractions, it will attribute to them the same gravity as formerly to crimes. In other words, it will designate them as criminal.

Crime is, then, necessary; it is bound up with the fundamental conditions of all social life, and by that very fact it is useful, because these conditions of which it is a part are themselves indispensable to the normal evolution of morality and law.

Indeed, it is no longer possible today to dispute the fact that law and morality vary from one social type to the next, nor that they change within the same type if the conditions of life are modified. But, in order that these transformations may be possible, the collective sentiments at the basis of morality must not be hostile to change, and consequently must have but moderate energy. If they were too strong, they would no longer be plastic. Every pattern is an obstacle to new patterns, to the extent that the first pattern is inflexible. The better a structure is articulated, the more it offers a healthy resistance to all modification; and this is equally true of functional, as of anatomical, organization. If there were no crimes, this condition could not have been fulfilled, for such a hypothesis presupposes that collective sentiments have arrived at a degree of intensity unexampled in history. Nothing is good indefinitely and to an unlimited extent. The authority which the moral conscience enjoys must not be excessive; otherwise no one would dare criticize it, and it would too easily congeal into an immutable form. To make progress, individual originality must be able to express itself. In order that the originality of the idealist whose dreams transcend his century may find expression, it is necessary that the originality of the criminal, who is below the level of his time, shall also be possible. One does not occur without the other.

Nor is this all. Aside from this indirect utility, it happens that crime itself plays a useful role in this evolution. Crime implies not only that the way remains open to necessary changes but that in certain cases it directly prepares these changes. Where crime exists, collective sentiments are sufficiently flexible to take on a new form, and crime sometimes helps to determine the form they will take. How many times, indeed, it is only an anticipation of future morality—a step toward what will be! According to Athenian law, Socrates was a criminal, and his condemnation was no more than just. However, his crime, namely, the independence of this thought, rendered a service not only to humanity but to his country. It served to prepare a new morality and faith which the Athenians needed, since the traditions by which they had lived until then were no longer in harmony with the current conditions of life. Nor is the case of Socrates unique; it is reproduced periodically in history. It would never have been possible to establish the freedom of thought we now enjoy if the regulations prohibiting it had not been violated before being solemnly abrogated. At that time, however, the violation was a crime, since it was an offense against sentiments still very keen in the average conscience. And yet this crime was useful as a prelude to reforms which daily became more necessary. Liberal philosophy had as its precursors the heretics of all kinds who were justly punished by secular authorities during the entire course of the Middle Ages and until the eve of modern times.

From this point of view the fundamental facts of criminality present themselves to us in an entirely new light. Contrary to current ideas, the criminal no longer seems a totally unsociable being, a sort of parasitic element, a strange and unassimilable body, introduced into the midst of society.[3] On the contrary, he plays a definite role in social life. Crime, for its part, must no longer be conceived as an evil that cannot be too much suppressed. There is no occasion for self-congratulation when the crime rate drops noticeably below the average level, for we may be certain that this apparent progress is associated with some social disorder. Thus, the number of assault cases never falls so low as in times of want.[4] With the drop in the crime rate, and as a reaction to it, comes a revision, or the need of a revision in the theory of punishment. If, indeed, crime is a disease, its punishment is its remedy and cannot be otherwise conceived; thus, all the discussions it arouses bear on the point of determining what the punishment must be in order to fulfil this role of remedy. If crime is not pathological at all, the object of punishment cannot be to cure it, and its true function must be sought elsewhere.

It is far from the truth, then, that the rules previously stated have no other justification than to satisfy an urge for logical formalism of little practical value, since, on the contrary, according as they are or are not applied, the most essential social facts are entirely changed in character. If the foregoing example is particularly convincing—and this was our hope in dwelling upon it—there are likewise many others which might have been cited with equal profit. There is no society where the rule does not exist that the punishment must be proportional to the offense; yet, for the Italian school, this principle is but an invention of jurists, without adequate basis.[5]

For there criminologists the entire penal system, as it has functioned until the present day among all known peoples, is a phenomenon contrary to nature. We have already seen that, for M. Garafalo, the criminality peculiar to lower societies is not at all natural. For socialists it is the capitalist system, in spite of its wide diffusion, which constitutes a deviation from the normal state, produced, as it was, by violence and fraud. Spencer, on the contrary, maintains that our administrative centralization and the extension of governmental powers are the radical vices of our societies, although both proceed most regularly and generally as we advance in history. We do not believe that scholars have ever systematically endeavored to distinguish the normal or abnormal character of social phenomena from their degree of generality. It is always with a great array of dialectics that these questions are partly resolved.

Once we have eliminated this criterion, however, we are not only exposed to confusions and partial errors, such as those just pointed out, but science is rendered all but impossible. Its immediate object is the study of the normal type. If, however, the most widely diffused facts can be pathological, it is possible that the normal types never existed in actuality; and if that is the case, why study the facts? Such study can only confirm our prejudices and fix us in our errors. If punishment and the responsibility for crime are only the products of ignorance and barbarism, why strive to know them in order to derive the normal forms from them? By such arguments the mind is diverted from a reality in which we have lost interest, and falls back on itself in order to seek within itself the materials necessary to reconstruct its world. In order that sociology may treat facts as things, the sociologists must feel the necessity of studying them exclusively.

The principal object of all sciences of life, whether individual or social, is to define and explain the normal state and to distinguish it from its opposite. If, however, normality is not given in the things themselves—if it is, on the contrary, a character we may or may not impute to them—this solid footing is lost. The mind is then complacent in the face of reality which has little to teach it; it is no longer restrained by the matter which it is analyzing, since it is the mind, in some manner or other, that determines the matter.

The various principles we have established up to the present are, then, closely interconnected. In order that sociology may be a true science of things, the generality of phenomena must be taken as the criterion of their normality.

Our method has, moreover, the advantage of regulating action at the same time as thought. If the social values are not subjects of observation, but can and must be determined by a sort of mental calculus, no limit, so to speak, can be set for the free inventions of the imagination in search of the best. For how may we assign to perfection a limit? It escapes all limitation, by definition. The goal of humanity recedes into infinity, discouraging some by its very remoteness and arousing others who, in order to draw a little nearer to it, quicken the pace and plunge into revolutions. This practical dilemma may be escaped if the desirable is defined in the same way as is health and normality and if health is something that is defined as inherent in things. For then the object of our efforts is both given and defined at the same time. It is no longer a matter of pursuing desperately an objective that retreats as one advances, but of working with steady perseverance to maintain the normal state, of re-establishing it if it is threatened, and of rediscovering its conditions if they have changed. The duty of the statesman is no longer to push society toward an ideal that seems attractive to him, but his role is that of the physician: he prevents the outbreak of illnesses by good hygiene, and he seeks to cure them when they have appeared.[6]

REFERENCES

1. From the fact that crime is a phenomenon of normal sociology, it does not follow that the criminal is an individual normally constituted from the biological and psychological points of view. The two questions are independent of each other. This independence will be better understood when we have shown, later on, the difference between psychological and sociological facts.
2. Calumny, insults, slander, fraud, etc.
3. We have ourselves committed the error of speaking thus of the criminal, because of a failure to apply our rule (*Division du travail social*, pp. 395–96).
4. Although crime is a fact of normal sociology, it does not follow that we must not abhor it. Pain itself has nothing desirable about it; the individual dislikes it as society does crime, and yet it is a function of normal physiology. Not only is it necessarily derived from the very constitution of every living organism, but it plays a useful role in life, for which reason it cannot be replaced. It would, then, be a singular distortion of our thought to present it as an apology for crime. We would not even think of protesting against such an interpretation, did we not know to what strange accusations and misunderstandings one exposes oneself when one undertakes to study moral

facts objectively and to speak of them in a different language from that of the layman.
5. See Garofalo, *Criminologie*, p. 299.
6. From the theory developed in this chapter, the conclusion has at times been reached that according to us, the increase of criminality in the course of the nineteenth century was a normal phenomenon. Nothing is farther from our thought. Several facts indicated by us apropos of suicide (see *Suicide*, pp. 420ff.) tend, on the contrary, to make us believe that this development is in general morbid. Nevertheless, it might happen that a certain increase of certain forms of criminality would be normal, for each state of civilization has its own criminality. But on this, one can only formulate hypotheses.

# THE PSYCHOLOGY OF PUNITIVE JUSTICE * (*Mead*)

A threatened attack upon these values[1] places us in an attitude of defense, and as this defense is largely intrusted to the operation of the laws of the land we gain a respect for the laws which is in proportion to the goods which they defend. There is, however, another attitude more easily aroused under these conditions which is, I think, largely responsible for our respect for law as law. I refer to the attitude of hostility to the lawbreaker as an enemy to the society to which we belong. In this attitude we are defending the social structure against an enemy with all the animus which the threat to our own interests calls out. It is not the detailed operation of the law in defining the invasion of rights and their proper preservation that is the center of our interest but the capture and punishment of the personal enemy, who is also the public enemy. The law is the bulwark of our interests, and the hostile procedure against the enemy arouses a feeling of attachment due to the means put at our disposal for satisfying the hostile impulse. The law has become the weapon for overwhelming the thief of our purses, our good names, or even of our lives. We feel toward it as we feel toward the police officer who rescues us from a murderous assault. The respect for the law is the obverse side of our hatred for the criminal aggressor. Furthermore the court procedure, after the man accused of the crime is put under arrest and has been brought to trial, emphasizes this emotional attitude. The state's attorney seeks a conviction. The accused must defend himself against this attack. The aggrieved person and the community find in this officer of the government their champion. A legal battle takes the place of the former physical struggle which led up to the arrest. The emotions called out are the emotions of battle. The impartiality of the court who sits as the adjudicator

* Reprinted from *The American Journal of Sociology*, March, 1918, pp. 585–592, by permission of the University of Chicago Press.

is the impartiality of the umpire between the contending parties. The assumption that contending parties will each do his utmost to win, places upon each, even upon the state's attorney, the obligation to get a verdict for his own side rather than to bring about a result which will be for the best interests of all concerned. The doctrine that the strict enforcement of the law in this fashion is for the best interest of all concerned has no bearing upon the point which I am trying to emphasize. This point is that the emotional attitude of the injured individual and of the other party to the proceedings—the community—toward the law is that engendered by a hostile enterprise in which the law has become the ponderous weapon of defense and attack.[2]

There is another emotional content involved in this attitude of respect for the law as law, which is perhaps of like importance with the other. I refer to that accompanying stigma placed upon the criminal. The revulsions against criminality reveal themselves in a sense of solidarity with the group, a sense of being a citizen which on the one hand excludes those who have transgressed the laws of the group and on the other inhibits tendencies to criminal acts in the citizen himself. It is this emotional reaction against conduct which excludes from society that gives to the moral taboos of the group such impressiviness. The majesty of the law is that of the angel with the fiery sword at the gate who can cut one off from the world to which he belongs. The majesty of the law is the dominance of the group over the individual, and the paraphernalia of criminal law serves not only to exile the rebellious individual from the group, but also to awaken in law-abiding members of society the inhibitions which make rebellion impossible to them. The formulation of these inhibitions is the basis of criminal law. The emotional content that accompanies them is a large part of the respect for law as law. In both these elements of our respect for law as law, in the respect for the common instrument of defense from and attack upon the enemy of ourselves and of society, and in the respect for that body of formulated custom which at once identifies us with the whole community and excludes those who break its commandments, we recognize concrete impulses—those of attack upon the enemy of ourselves and at the same time of the community, and those of inhibition and restraint through which we feel the common will, in the identity of prohibition and of exclusion. They are concrete impulses which at once identify us with the predominant whole and at the same time place us on the level of every other member of the group, and thus set up that theoretical impartiality and evenhandedness of punitive justice which calls out in no small degree our sense of loyalty and respect. And it is out of the universality that belongs to the sense of common action springing out of these impulses that the institutions of law and of regulative and repressive justice arise. While these impulses are concrete in respect of their immediate object, i.e., the criminal, the values which this hostile attitude toward the criminal protects either in society or in ourselves are negatively and abstractly conceived. Instinctively we estimate the worth of the goods protected by the procedure against the criminal and in terms of this hostile procedure. These goods are not simply the physical articles but include the more precious values of self respect, in not allowing one's self to be overridden, in downing the enemy of the group, in affirming the maxims of the group and its institutions against invasions. Now in all of this we have our backs toward that which we protect and our faces toward the actual or potential enemy. These goods are regarded as valuable because we are willing to fight and even die for them in certain exigencies, but their intrinsic value is neither affirmed nor considered in the legal proceeding. The values thus obtained are not their values in use but sacrifice values. To many a man his country has become infinitely valuable because he finds himself willing to fight and die for it when the common impulse of attack upon the common enemy has been aroused, and yet he may have been, in his daily life, a traitor to the social values he is dying to protect because there was no emotional situation within which these values appeared in his consciousness. It is difficult to bring into commensurable relationship to each other a man's willingness to cheat his country out of its legitimate taxes and his willingness to fight and die for the same country. The reactions spring from different sets of impulses and lead to evaluations which seem to have nothing in common with each other. The type of valuation of social goods that arises out of the hostile attitude toward the criminal is negative, because it does not present the positive social function of the goods that the hostile procedure protects. From the standpoint of protection one thing behind the wall has the same import of anything else that lies behind the same defense. The repect for law as law thus is found to be a respect for a social organization of defense against the enemy of the group and a legal and judicial procedure that are oriented with reference to the criminal. The attempt to utilize these social attitudes and procedures to remove the causes of crime, to assess the kind and amount of punishment which the criminal should suffer in the interest of society, or to reinstate the criminal as a law-abiding citizen has failed utterly. For while the institutions which inspire our respect are concrete institutions with a definite function, they are responsible for a quite abstract and inadequate evaluation of society and its goods. These legal and political institutions organized with reference to the enemy or at least the outsider give a statement of social goods which is based upon de-

fense and not upon function. The aim of the criminal proceeding is to determine whether the accused is innocent, i.e., still belongs to the group or
whether he is guilty, i.e., is put under the ban which criminal punishment
carries with it. The technical statement of this is found in the loss of the
privileges of a citizen, in sentences of any severity, but the more serious
ban is found in the fixed attitude of hostility on the part of the community
toward a jailbird. One effect of this is to define the goods and privileges of
the members of the community as theirs in virtue of their being law-abiding,
and their responsibilities as exhausted by the statutes which determine the
nature of criminal conduct. This effect is not due alone to the logical
tendency to maintain the same definition of the institution of property over
against the conduct of the thief and that of the law-abiding citizen. It is
due in far greater degree to the feeling that we all stand together in the
protection of property. In the positive definition of property, that is in terms
of its social uses and functions, we are met by wide diversity of opinion,
especially where the theoretically wide freedom of control over private
property, asserted over against the thief, is restrained in the interests of
problematic public goods. Out of this attitude toward the goods which the
criminal law protects arises that fundamental difficulty in social reform
which is due, not to mere difference in opinion nor to conscious selfishness,
but to the fact that what we term opinions are profound social attitudes
which, once assumed, fuse all conflicting tendencies over against the enemy
of the people. The respect for law as law in its positive use in defense of
social goods becomes unwittingly a respect for the conceptions of these
goods which the attitude of defense has fashioned. Property becomes sacred
not because of its social uses but because of the community is as one in its
defense, and this conception of property, taken over into the social struggle
to make property serve its functions in the community, becomes the bulwark of those in possession, *beati possidentes*.

Besides property other institutions have arisen, that of the person with its
rights, that of the family with its rights, and that of the government with its
rights. Wherever rights exist, invasion of those rights may be punished, and
a definition of these institutions is formulated in protecting the right against
trespass. The definition is again the voice of the community as a whole proclaiming and penalizing the one whose conduct has placed him under the
ban. There is the same unfortunate circumstance that the law speaking
against the criminal gives the sanction of the sovereign authority of the community to the negative definition of the right. It is defined in terms of its
contemplated invasion. The individual who is defending his own rights
against the trespasser is led to state even his family and more general so-

cial interests in abstract individualistic terms. Abstract individualism and a negative conception of liberty in terms of the freedom from restraints become the working ideas in the community. They have the prestige of battle cries in the fight for freedom against privilege. They are still the countersigns of the descendants of those who cast off the bonds of political and social restraint in their defense and assertion of the rights their forefathers won. Wherever criminal justice, the modern elaborate development of the taboo, the ban, and their consequences in a primitive society, organizes and formulates public sentiment in defense of social goods and institutions against actual or prospective enemies, there we find that the definition of the enemies, in other words, the criminals, carries with it the definition of the goods and institutions. It is the revenge of the criminal upon the society which crushes him. The concentration of public sentiment upon the criminal which mobilizes the institution of justice, paralyzes the undertaking to conceive our common goods in terms of their uses. The majesty of the law is that of the sword drawn against a common enemy. The evenhandedness of justice is that of universal conscription against a common enemy, and that of the abstract definition of rights which places the ban upon anyone who falls outside of its rigid terms.

Thus we see society almost helpless in the grip of the hostile attitude it has taken toward those who break its laws and contravene its institutions. Hostility toward the lawbreaker inevitably brings with it the attitudes of retribution, repression, and exclusion. These provide no principles for the eradication of crime, for returning the delinquent to normal social relations, nor for stating the transgressed rights and institutions in terms of their positive social functions.

On the other side of the ledger stands the fact that the attitude of hostility toward the lawbreaker has the unique advantage of uniting all members of the community in the emotional solidarity of aggression. While the most admirable of humanitarian efforts are sure to run counter to the individual interests of very many in the community, or fail to touch the interest and imagination of the multitude and to leave the community divided or indifferent, the cry of thief or murder is attuned to profound complexes, lying below the surface of competing individual effort, and citizens who have separated by divergent interests stand together against the common enemy. Furthermore, the attitude reveals common, universal values which underlie like a bedrock the divergent structures of individual ends that are mutually closed and hostile to each other. Seemingly without the criminal the cohesiveness of society would disappear and the universal goods of the community would crumble into mutual repellent individual particles. The criminal does not seriously endanger the structure of society by his destructive activities, and on the other hand he is responsible for a sense of solidarity, aroused among those whose attention would be otherwise centered upon interests quite divergent from those of each other. Thus courts of criminal justice may be essential to the preservation of society even when we take account of the importance of the criminal over against society, and the clumsy failure of criminal law in the repression and suppression of crime. I am willing to admit that this statement is distorted, not however in its analysis of the efficacy of the procedure against the criminal, but in its failure to recognize the growing consciousness of the many common interests which is slowly changing our institutional conception of society and its consequent exaggerated estimate upon the import of the criminal. But it is important that we should realize what the implications of this attitude of hostility are within our society. We should especially recognize the inevitable limitations which the attitude carries with it. Social organization which arises out of hostility at once emphasizes the character which is the basis of the opposition and tends to suppress all other characters in the members of the group. The cry of "stop thief" unites us all as property owners against the robber. We all stand shoulder to shoulder as Americans against a possible invader. Just in proportion as we organize by hostility do we suppress individuality. In a political campaign that is fought on party lines the members of the party surrender themselves to the party. They become simply members of the party whose conscious aim is to defeat the rival organization. For this purpose the party member becomes merely a Republican or a Democrat. The party symbol expresses everything. Where simple social aggression or defense with the purpose of eliminating or encysting an enemy is the purpose of the community, organization through the common attitude of hostility is normal and effective. But as long as the social organization is dominated by the attitude of hostility the individuals or groups who are the objectives of this organization will remain enemies. It is quite impossible psychologically to hate the sin and love the sinner. We are very much given to cheating ourselves in this regard. We assume that we can detect, pursue, indict, prosecute, and punish the criminal and still retain toward him the attitude of reinstating him in the community as soon as he indicates a change in social attitude himself, that we can at the same time watch for the definite transgression of the statute to catch and overwhelm the offender, and comprehend the situation out of which the offense grows. But the two attitudes, that of control of crime by the hostile procedure of the law and that of control through comprehension of social and psychological conditions, cannot be combined. To understand is to forgive and the social procedure seems to deny the very responsibility which the law affirms, and on the other hand the pursuit by criminal justice inevitably awakens the hostile attitude in the offender and renders the attitude of mutual comprehension practically impossible. The social worker in the court is the sentimentalist, and the legalist in the social settlement in spite of his learned doctrine is the ignoramus.

REFERENCES

1. Our basic values [editors].
2. I am referring here to criminal law and its enforcement, not only because respect for the law and the majesty of the law have reference almost entirely to criminal justice, but also because a very large part, perhaps the largest part, of civil law proceedings are undertaken and carried out with the intent of defining and readjusting social situations without the hostile attitudes which characterize the criminal procedure. The parties to the civil proceedings belong to the same group and continue to belong to this group, whatever decision is rendered. No stigma attaches to the one who loses. Our emotional attitude toward this body of law is that of interest, of condemnation and approval as it fails or succeeds in its social function. It is not an institution that must be respected even in its disastrous failures. On the contrary it must be changed. It is hedged about in our feelings by no majesty. It is efficient or inefficient and as such awakens satisfaction or dissatisfaction and an interest in the reform which is in proportion to the social values concerned.

# TWO TYPES OF EXPLANATIONS OF CRIMINAL BEHAVIOR * (*Sutherland and Cressey*)

Scientific explanations of criminal behavior may be stated either in terms of the processes which are operating at the moment of the occurrence of crime or in terms of the processes operating in the earlier history of the criminal. In the first case the explanation may be called "mechanistic," "situational," or "dynamic, " in the second, "historical" or "genetic." Both types of explanation are desirable. The mechanistic type of explanation has been favored by physical and biological scientists, and it probably could be the more efficient type of explanation of criminal behavior. However, criminological explanations of the mechanistic type have thus far been notably unsuccessful perhaps largely because they have been formulated in connection with the attempt to isolate personal and social pathologies among criminals. Work from this point of view has, at least, resulted in the conclusion that the

* Reprinted with the permission of the authors and publisher from *Principles of Criminology*, 5th ed. (1955), by Edwin H. Sutherland and Donald R. Cressey, J. B. Lippincott Co., Philadelphia, pp. 76–80.

immediate determinants of criminal behavior lie in the person-situation complex.

The objective situation is important to criminality largely to the extent that it provides an opportunity for a criminal act. A thief may steal from a fruit stand when the owner is not in sight but refrain when the owner is in sight; a bank burglar may attack a bank which is poorly protected but refrain from attacking a bank protected by watchmen and burglar alarms. A corporation which manufactures automobiles seldom or never violates the Pure Food and Drug Law, but a meat-packing corporation might violate this law with great frequency. But in another sense, a psychological or socio- logical sense, the situation is not exclusive of the person, for the situation which is important is the situation as defined by the person who is involved. That is, some persons define a situation in which a fruit-stand owner is out of sight as a "crime-committing" situation, while others do not so define it. Furthermore, the events in the person-situation complex at the time a crime occurs cannot be separated from the prior life experiences of the criminal. This means that the situation is defined by the person in terms of the inclinations and abilities which the person has acquired up to date. For example, while a person could define a situation in such a manner that criminal behavior would be the inevitable result, his past experiences would for the most part determine the way in which he defined the situation. An explanation of criminal behavior made in terms of these past experiences is an historical or genetic explanation.

The following paragraphs state such a genetic theory of criminal behavior on the assumption that a criminal act occurs when a situation appropriate for it, as defined by the person, is present. The theory should be regarded as tentative, and it should be tested by the factual information presented in the later chapters and by all other factual information and theories which are applicable.

## Genetic Explanation of Criminal Behavior

The following statement refers to the process by which a particular person comes to engage in criminal behavior.

1. *Criminal behavior is learned.* Negatively, this means that criminal behavior is not inherited, as such; also, the person who is not already trained in crime does not invent criminal behavior, just as a person does not make mechanical inventions unless he has had training in mechanics.

2. *Criminal behavior is learned in interaction with other persons in a*

*process of communication.* This communication is verbal in many respects but includes also "the communication of gestures."

3. *The principal part of the learning of criminal behavior occurs within intimate personal groups.* Negatively, this means that the impersonal agencies of communication, such as movies and newspapers, play a relatively unimportant part in the genesis of criminal behavior.

4. *When criminal behavior is learning, the learning includes (a) techniques of committing the crime, which are sometimes very complicated and sometimes very simple; (b) the specific direction of motives, drives, rationalizations, and attitudes.*

5. *The specific direction of motives and drives is learned from definitions of the legal codes as favorable or unfavorable.* In some societies an individual is surrounded by persons who invariably define the legal codes as rules to the observed, while in others he is surrounded by persons whose definitions are favorable to the violation of the legal codes. In our American society these definitions are almost always mixed, with the consequence that we have culture conflict in relation to the legal codes.

6. *A person becomes delinquent because of an excess of definitions favorable to violation of law over definitions unfavorable to violation of law.* This is the principle of differential association. It refers to both criminal and anti-criminal associations and has to do with counteracting forces. When persons become criminal, they do so because of contacts with criminal patterns and also because of isolation from anti-criminal patterns. Any person inevitably assimilates the surrounding culture unless other patterns are in conflict; a Southerner does not pronounce "r" because other Southerners do not pronounce "r." Negatively, this proposition of differential association means that associations which are neutral so far as crime is concerned have little or no effect on the genesis of criminal behavior. Much of the experience of a person is neutral in this sense, e.g., learning to brush one's teeth. This behavior has no negative or positive effect on criminal behavior except as it may be related to associations which are concerned with the legal codes. This neutral behavior is important especially as an occupier of the time of a child so that he is not in contact with criminal behavior during the time he is so engaged in the neutral behavior.

7. *Differential associations may vary in frequency, duration, priority, and intensity.* This means that associations with criminal behavior and also associations with anti-criminal behavior vary in those respects. "Frequency" and "duration" as modalities of associations are obvious and need no explanation. "Priority" is assumed to be important in the sense that lawful behavior developed in early childhood may persist throughout life, and also

that delinquent behavior developed in early childhood may persist through-out life. This tendency, however, has not been adequately demonstrated, and priority seems to be important principally through its selective influence. "Intensity" is not precisely defined but it has to do with such things as the prestige of the source of a criminal or anti-criminal pattern and with emo-tional reactions related to the associations. In a precise definition of the criminal behavior of a person these modalities would be stated in quantita-tive form and a mathematical ratio be reached. A formula in this sense has not been developed, and the development of such a formula would be ex-tremely difficult.

8. *The process of learning criminal behavior by association with criminal and anti-criminal patterns involves all the mechanisms that are involved in any other learning.* Negatively, this means that the learning of criminal behavior is not restricted to the process of imitation. A person who is se-duced, for instance, learns criminal behavior by association, but this process would not ordinarily be described as imitation.

9. *While criminal behavior is an expression of general needs and values, it is not explained by those general needs and values since non-criminal be-havior is an expression of the same needs and values.* Thieves generally steal in order to secure money, but likewise honest laborers work in order to secure money. The attempts by many scholars to explain criminal be-havior by general drives and values, such as the happiness principle, striving for social status, the money motive, or frustration, have been and must continue to be futile since they explain lawful behavior as completely as they explain criminal behavior. They are similar to respiration, which is necessary for any behavior but does not differentiate criminal from non-criminal be-havior.

It is not necessary, at this level of explanation, to explain why a person has the associations which he has; this certainly involves a complex of many things. In any area where the delinquency rate is high a boy who is sociable, gregarious, active, and athletic is very likely to come in contact with the other boys in the neighborhood, learn delinquent behavior from them, and become a gangster; in the same neighborhood the psychopathic boy who is isolated, introvert, and inert may remain at home, not become acquainted with the other boys in the neighborhood, and not become delinquent. In another situation, the sociable, athletic, aggressive boy may become a mem-ber of a scout troop and not become involved in delinquent behavior. The person's associations are determined in a general context of social organiza-tion. A child is ordinarily reared in a family; the place of residence of the family is determined largely by family income; and the delinquency rate is in many respects related to the rental value of the houses. Many other factors enter into this social organization, including many of the small personal group relationships.

The preceding explanation of criminal behavior is stated from the point of view of the person who engages in criminal behavior. As indicated earlier, it is possible, also, to state sociological theories of criminal behavior from the point of view of the community, nation, or other group. The problem, when thus stated, is generally concerned with crime rates and involves a comparison of the crime rates of various groups or the crime rates of a particular group at different times. The explanation of a crime rate must be consistent with the explanation of the criminal behavior of the person, since the crime rate is a summary statement of the number of persons in the group who commit crimes and the frequency with which they commit crimes. One of the best explanations of crime rates from this point of view is that a high crime rate is due to social disorganization. The term "social disorganization" is not entirely satisfactory and it seems preferable to substitute for it the term "differential social organization." The postulate on which this theory is based, regardless of the name, is that crime is rooted in the social organization and is an expression of that social organization A group may be organized for criminal behavior or organized against criminal behavior. Most communities are organized both for criminal and anti-criminal behavior and in that sense the crime rate is an expression of the differential group organization. Differential group organization as an expression of variations in crime rates is consistent with the differential association theory of the processes by which persons become criminals.

# FAMILY DISORGANIZATION—"I" ATTITUDES VS. "WE" ATTITUDES *
## (Thomas and Znaniecki)

We can now draw certain general conclusions from our data which we shall hypothetically propose as sociological laws, to be verified by the observation of other societies.

1. The real cause of all phenomena of family disorganization is to be sought in the influence of certain new values—new for the subject—such as:

* Reprinted from The Polish Peasant in Europe and America (2 vols.), New York, Dover Publications, 1927, pp. 1167–1170.

new sources of hedonistic satisfaction, new vanity values, new (individualistic) type of economic organization, new forms of sexual appeal. This influence presupposes, of course, not only a contact between the individual and the outside world but also the existence in the individual's personality of certain attitudes which make him respond to these new values—hedonistic aspirations, desire for social recognition, desire for economic security and advance, sexual instinct. The specific phenomenon of family disorganization consists in a definite modification of those preexisting attitudes under the influence of the new values, resulting in the appearance of new, more or less different attitudes. The nature of this modification can be generally characterized in such a way that, while the attitudes which existed under the family system were essentially "we"-attitudes (the individual did not dissociate his hedonistic tendencies, his desires for recognition or economic security, his sexual needs from the tendencies and aspirations of his family group), the new attitudes, produced by the new values acting upon those old attitudes, are essentially "I"-attitudes—the individual's wishes are separated in his consciousness from those of other members of his family. Such an evolution implies that the new values with which the individual gets in touch are individualistic in their meaning, appeal to the individual, not to the group as a whole; and this is precisely the character of most modern hedonistic, sexual, economic, vanity values. Disorganization of the family as primary group is thus an unavoidable consequence of modern civilization.

2. The appearance of the new individualistic attitudes may be counteracted, like every effect of a given cause, by the effects of other causes; the result is a combination of effects which takes the form of a suppression of the new attitude; the latter is not allowed to remain in full consciousness or to manifest itself in action, but is pushed back into the subconscious. Causes that counteract individualization within the family are chiefly influences of the primary community of which the family is a part. If social opinion favors family solidarity and reacts against any individualistic tendencies, and if the individual keeps in touch with the community, his desire for recognition compels him to accept the standards of the group and to look upon his individualistic tendencies as wrong. But if the community has lost its coherence, if the individual is isolated from it, or if his touch with the outside world makes him more or less independent of the opinion of his immediate milieu, there are no social checks important enough to counterbalance disorganization.

3. The *manifestations* of family disorganization in individual behavior

are the effects of the subject's attitudes and of the social conditions; these social conditions must be taken, of course, with the meaning which they have for the acting individual himself, not for the outside observer. If the individual finds no obstacles in his family to his new individualistic tendencies, he will express the latter in a normal way; disorganization will consist merely in a loss of family interests, in a social, not anti-social action. If there are obstacles, but disorganization of the primary-group attitudes has gone far enough in the individual to make him feel independent of his family and community, the effect will probably be a break of relations through isolation or emigration. If, however, the individual meets strong opposition and is not sufficiently free from the traditional system to ignore it, hostility and anti-social behavior are bound to follow. In the measure that the struggle progresses, the new attitude of revolt becomes a center around which the entire personality of the individual becomes reorganized, and this includes those of his traditional values which are not dropped, but reinterpreted to fit the new tendency and to give a certain measure of justification to his behavior. In the relatively rare cases where both the new attitude is very strong and the obstacles from the old system are powerfully resented and seem insuperable because the individual is still too much dependent on this system to find some new way out of the situation, the struggle leads to an internal conflict which may find its solution in an attempt to remove the persons by whom the old system is represented in this situation rather than in a complete rejection of the system itself.

4. It is evidently impossible to revive the original family psychology after it has been disintegrated, for the individual who has learned consciously to distinguish and to oppose to one another his own wishes and those of other members of his family group and to consider these wishes as merely personal cannot unlearn it and return to the primary "we"-attitudes. Reorganization of the family is then possible, but on an entirely new basis—that of a moral, reflective coordination and harmonization of individual attitudes for the pursuit of common purposes.

# THE STUDY OF SOCIAL DISORGANIZATION AND DEVIANT BEHAVIOR* (*Cohen*)

## Linkages Among Forms of Deviant Behavior

There is a strong tendency for sociologists to treat the various forms of deviant behavior as somehow interrelated—either as protean symptoms or manifestations of a single underlying pathology, or as cause and consequence of one another.

It is true that varieties of deviant behavior may be linked in a number of ways. Various kinds of deviant behavior—for example, aggressive "acting out" and passive withdrawal—may tend to cluster because they represent different ways of coping with the same situation. One kind of deviant behavior may be instrumental to another—as, for example, in the case of the drug addict who is forced to steal in order to maintain his habit. One kind may be a device for evading the consequences of another; for example, the rapist may be a killer because his victim is his witness. Or again, various kinds of deviant specialties may aid and abet one another. Those already involved in deviant behavior exert pressure upon all those who are in a position to affect their operations adversely or to render them services to become their accessories. Thus slot-machine rackets, labor racketeering, political corruption, police graft, and organized gambling tend to encourage one another, to become symbiotically linked, and to come under common control because each serves the interests of the others.

One of the tasks of a sociology of deviant behavior is to classify and elucidate the mechanisms by means of which one kind of deviant behavior generates others. But this is not to say that the sources of deviant behavior are always to be found in the abnormal, the pathological and the deplorable. They may also be found in the institutionally expected and the sacred. Implicit in the very idea of a system is the fact that whatever is found in it is a function of its total structure. The consequences of any particular feature of a system for deviant behavior or conformity depend not on its moral or hygienic status but on its context. The same strains which help to produce deviant behavior also help to produce the behavior we most admire and

* Reprinted from *Sociology Today*, edited by Merton, Bloom, and Cottrell, New York, Basic Books, 1959, pp. 473–483.

applaud. For example, the characteristic American belief that a man should "make something of himself" encourages the hard work, self-discipline, and productivity that we so much admire; at the same time, it makes failure all the more ego-involved and humiliating and, if the writer's analysis[1] is correct, helps to motivate delinquent subcultures in American society. If Kingsley Davis[2] is correct, the sanctity of the marriage institution and the high value placed upon female chastity help to explain prostitution as well as sexual continence. If Chein and Rosenfeld[3] are correct, teen-age drug use may result from the impact upon a certain kind of personality of age-graded expectations which motivate other young people to assume the responsibilities of adulthood. Furthermore; much that is deviant can be largely attributed to efforts, some of them nobly motivated, to control deviant behavior. For example, efforts to prevent the consumption of liquor and narcotics and to prevent gambling have fostered the growth of large-scale criminal organizations for the provision of these goods and services, and these organizations in turn have contributed to the corruption of politics and law enforcement. In short, that which we deplore and that which we cherish are not only part of the same seamless web, they are actually woven of the same fibers.

## Social Disorganization

The sociology of social disorganization is in an even worse state than the sociology of deviant behavior. Few terms in sociology are defined so variously and obscurely as social disorganization. Values intrude themselves so persistently and insidiously into definition and usage that the concept is often regarded as a term of evaluation and therefore unscientific. It is difficult to determine what, if any, is the line of demarcation between social disorganization and deviant behavior. Some sociologists even question whether social disorganization exists and suggest that there are only different kinds of organization. However, we believe that social disorganization can be defined in a way that is value-free, that is independent of the definition of deviant behavior, and that, at the same time, designates a set of crucial theoretical problems. (This definition owes a great deal to a paper by Dr. Harold Garfinkel.[4])

Let us begin by noting what we consider to be some examples of social disorganization. A children's ball game is disrupted when their only ball falls into the creek. A meeting of a learned society is disrupted when some members of the local Chamber of Commerce appear and announce that the room has been reserved for their use during that hour. A military mission is disrupted when the leader is killed and no one steps forward to assume command. In all these situations some activity has been going on and has been disrupted or interrupted. Our task now is to formulate a general definition of an activity or of an interaction system which enables us to mark the boundaries as it were, between one activity and another, to state whether a particular act is or is not constitutive of a particular activity, and to determine whether an activity is or is not in progress, has or has not been disrupted.

DEFINITION

We shall begin, as does Garfinkel, with the game as our paradigm of an activity or interaction system and show that those characterics which define organization and disorganization for a game are equally applicable to non-game activities.

THE GAME

In the first place, the names of games are taken from the language of the participants. They designate sets of events which the participants perceive as belonging together and jointly constituting one thing, a certain kind of game. Therefore, to determine whether a particular kind of game is going on, we must use the participants' own criteria for defining that sort of game.

These criteria are given by the rules of the game, which designate certain classes of events and state the standards for assigning events to these classes. All events which can be so classified and only those events are possible game events. Thus a swing that misses and a hit ball that goes out of bounds both fall in the class "strike" in the game "baseball." Game events may include not only actions of the players but also events in the situation of action. For example, the advent of darkness during a baseball game is a game event if it is anticipated by the rules and a class of situation exists to which it is assigned by the rules.

Furthermore—and this is crucial—the rules specify an order among these classes of events; to constitute the game in question, events must conform to that order. Many concretely different sequences may conform to the order of a given kind of game. At a given stage of the game, a player on second base may steal third or stay on second. He may not proceed directly to bat, for this would not be a game event in the game of baseball. Note that the order of events enters into the definition of an event. For example, whether or not hitting a ball out of bounds is a strike depends on how many strikes a batter already has against him.

The rules also provide a criterion for determining whether the game is in progress or has been interrupted. If the "constitutive order of events"— an order conforming to the constitutive rules—is interrupted, the game is interrupted or, as we shall use the word, disorganized. If the game terminates in accordance with the rules of the game—that is, if it culminates in a state of affairs defined by the rules as "the end of the game"—we simply say that the game is over. But if the constitutive order of events is breached at any other point, if the game is neither over nor in progress, it is disorganized. If, for example, a brawl develops in which all the players become involved, the game is disorganized. (A brawl, in turn, can be regarded as a game subject to disorganization on its own terms; for example, police may break up a "rumble.")

DEVIANT BEHAVIOR AND DISORGANIZATION

A property of the rules of the game which is of the most fundamental importance is the fact that these rules are definitional statements. They do not tell us what is the right or the wrong thing to do; they merely tell us whether what we are doing is part of a given game. There are also rules of right conduct, morality, fair play—what we have called institutionalized expectations. But violations of these rules of right conduct, if they are covered by the rules of the game, are themselves game events and need not constitute a breach in the constitutive order of events. It may, for example, be forbidden to step over a certain line, to strike another player, to spit on the ball. If the constitutive rules designate such events as "fouls" or "cheating" and prescribe a penalty, events and penalty are part of the constitutive order. In short, deviant behavior is not defined by the same rules that define game events and therefore does not, merely by virtue of being deviant, constitute disorganization.

This is not to say that deviant behavior may not precipitate disorganization. If a player, in clear violation of the rules of good sportsmanship, stalks off the field and the constitutive rules have failed to anticipate such situations, if the rules prescribe that there shall be a certain number of players on both sides and there are no replacements available, or if the rules are obscure and there is disagreement as to how the situation is to be defined, the resulting situation is, at worst, meaningless and, at best, ambiguous. In any case, it creates at least temporary disorganization. Deviant behavior, therefore, may or may not precipitate disorganization, but it is not *ipso facto* disorganization.

## GAMES AND NONGAMES

What we have said of games may be said of the nongames activities of everyday life as well, although the constitutive rules are less likely to be labeled rules and codified, and they may not command the same measure of agreement. The set of constitutive rules of a military operation is the plan of the operation. (Many of its details are provided by an implicit context of army regulations, field manuals, and the subculture of the military unit concerned.) This plan sets forth a sequence of events the fulfillment of which constitutes the operation. In like manner, the operations of a railroad, an industrial organization, a public utility, or a family resolve themselves into sets of recurrent and interlocking activities, each of which is defined by its respective constitutive rules. The range of alternatives possible at any given stage of an activity, and therefore the variety of concrete sequences that are compatible with the constitutive rules, varies from one type of activity to another. The definition of a church service, for example, may require adherence to a rather rigid order of events; the definition of a seminar can be met by a wide range of concretely different sequences.

The matter becomes clearer when we consider how the same set of interactions can be analyzed into different activities. In a basketball game, one of the teams may have a particular strategy, a concerted plan which takes certain contingencies into account and prescribes appropriate action for designated players in the event of those contingencies. Such a strategy has the characteristics of the rules of the game. The order prescribed by the strategy may be breached if the opposing team creates a situation that is not contemplated by the plan. In this case, the execution of the strategy has been disorganized. Nothing has happened, however, that is incompatible with the constitutive rules of basketball; the basketball game, therefore, has not been disorganized. Similarly, the strategy of management or of labor in a collective bargaining process may be disorganized without disorganizing the collective bargaining process itself. Again, the disruption of the operations of a commercial firm or even the failure of the firm as a result of unanticipated changes in the market need not imply any interruption in the market as a system defined by its own constitutive rules. It follows, therefore, that in speaking of organization or disorganization we must be careful to specify the game, activity, or interaction system in question.

An activity may consist in an order among lesser or included activities, each of which can be defined in terms of its own constitutive rules and is subject to disorganization on its own terms. Disorganization of one of these included activities, however, may or may not result in disorganization of the constitutive order that defines the more inclusive activity. For example, the operations of one plant of an industrial concern or one unit of a fire department may be disorganized as a result of a natural disaster. If, however, another plant or another unit can be mobilized to do the same job as the disorganized member of the system, there may be no breach of the organization of the larger activity.

Different activities may be interdependent and even interpenetrating in a variety of ways. It is possible to draw up rules for two games to be played simultaneously on the same checkerboard such that every physical event that is a move in one game is a move—that is, a game event—in the other. A winning move in one game may be a losing move in the other, but the continuity of neither game is disorganizing with reference to the other. In a perfectly organized society, all activities would be so organized that every event in one activity would be a possible event in others or would help to create the conditions necessary for the continuity of other activities. As a matter of fact, in every viable social system there must be some approximation to this state of affairs. However, this kind of articulation is always problematical. Every system requires time, space, personnel, and equipment for the unfolding of its constitutive order, but different systems compete for these resources and the availability of these resources to one system may depend upon their denial to another system to which they are equally necessary. Thus, the execution of a business operation or the very survival of a business may depend, on the one hand, upon the continued orderly functioning—that is, functioning in accordance with their own constitutive rules—of the firms from which it buys and sells and, on the other hand, upon the denial to its competitors of the materials and customers upon which their own operations or survival depend.

## Conclusion

The foregoing definition of social disorganization is, we think, congruent with usage. In describing military routs and natural disasters—situations in which there is consensus that the word disorganization is relevant—we say that people "freeze," "panic," "flounder," "give up," "run away," "change their plans," or "stand around helplessly." All these behaviors disrupt or at least threaten the constitutive order of the ongoing activity; therefore, they are themselves or at least they precipitate disorganization—a fact generally recognized by making these behaviors synonymous with disorganization in ordinary English usage.

Disorganization as we have defined it can occur on a less dramatic scale and with less dramatic consequences in any social setting—in the family, on the job, in the classroom. More than this, in every interaction system, no matter how stable and tranquil, the threat of disorganization, like the threat of deviant behavior, is always present, and the mechanisms for averting it and nipping it in the bud pose a problem that is everywhere relevant. As a matter of fact, our definition of organization as an order of events conforming to a set of constitutive rules implies our definition of disorganization as a breach of that order. The two terms, therefore, define a single field—organization-disorganization—as do conformity and deviant behavior.

The poverty of theory in the area of social disorganization reflects the lack of clarity and agreement with respect to the demarcation of the field. For this reason we have devoted a good deal of space to defining disorganization, to clarifying its relationship to deviant behavior, and to showing how the use of the concept as here defined helps us to analyze more rigorously and, we think, more fruitfully the sequences of behavior that are ordinarily described as "social disorganization." The test of any definition, including that presented here, will lie, of course, in the amenability of the field, as demarcated by that definition, to systematic theory.

## THE CONDITIONS OF DISORGANIZATION

Implicit in any definition of a field is a way of formulating its outstanding problems. The problem of clarifying the conditions under which disorganization occurs can be approached by first asking: What are the preconditions of *organization?* If organization is an order of events conforming to a set of constitutive rules, then organization implies two conditions. First, it presupposes that action unfolds in such a way that, at any stage or phase of the system, the situations that the participants confront and the alternative possibilities of action can be defined by the rules. Secondly, it presupposes that the participants are motivated to "play the game"—that is, to assume the perspectives provided by the rules and to select their actions from the constitutive possibilities designated by the rules. Conversely, disorganization must arise when one or both of these two conditions are not satisfied. First, it arises when the situations that the participants confront cannot be defined as system events or when there is no clear definition of the constitutive possibilities of action. This is a situation of normlessness, anomie, or meaninglessness. Secondly, it arises when the participants are not motivated, when their values, interests, and aims are not integrated with the requirements for continuity of the interaction system.

Localized conditions of anomie or failure of motivation, however, are not, in and of themselves, disorganization. Nor do all events which fall outside the constitutive order necessarily breach that order. For example, an individual soldier may panic and start running about wildly, an event which is not contemplated by the plan and which falls outside the scope of the plan. Yet the loss or defection of one soldier may not affect the orderly development called for by the plan. By contrast, however, the failure of one battery in one radio, if that radio is the only means of communication with a command center, may result in complete confusion and disorganization. In the absence of instructions, the situation and the behavior it calls for from each participant cannot be defined. There is a general state of anomie and a complete breach of the constitutive order.

The broader systemic repercussions of an event depend upon the way in which it is articulated with the rest of the system. Local conditions of anomie or failure of motivation may spread, involving more and more areas of the system, until they reach a vital spot and destroy the minimal conditions necessary for the continuity of the events called for by the plan. On the other hand, systems may have mechanisms for walling off the affected areas so that the contagion cannot spread to involve those events that are definitive of the constitutive order. Systems may have mechanisms for restoring organization—for example, by sending in replacements for confused, incompetent, or disaffected personnel—or for reinforcing motivation by bringing powerful sanctions to bear. Systems may have alternative arrangements for producing certain events that are necessary for the constitutive order, which arrangements go into effect when some segment of the system breaks down. All these mechanisms, in turn, depend upon mechanisms for gathering and transmitting information so that incipient or threatening disorganization can be spotted and the appropriate steps taken to halt or avert it.

### ANOMIE AND FAILURE OF MOTIVATION

Anomie and failure of motivation are of such central importance to a theory of disorganization that certain additional comments are called for. Anomie may take a number of forms: confrontation by a situation for which there are no relevant rules, vagueness or ambiguity of the relevant rules, or lack of consensus on which rules are relevant and on the interpretation of rules. However, anomie depends not only on the structure of the set of constitutive rules but also on the situations which the system encounters. No set of rules covers all of the situations which might conceivably arise. The fact that the rules do not cover certain conceivable situations spells anomie only if those situations do in fact arise. Control of anomie, therefore, may depend on one of two conditions. On the one hand, given the situation, it depends upon the existence and clarity of the relevant rules. On the other hand, given the rules, it depends upon the extent to which the system, in interaction with its environment, generates situations for which the constitutive rules provide definitions. This implies that a system capable of maintaining organization only under a narrowly limited set of conditions may nonetheless be very durable, provided that it has sufficient control over its environment to guarantee to itself the conditions it requires, or that some other system, through its functioning, can guarantee those conditions. The "wisdom of the body" in maintaining the constancy of its "internal environment" is an appropriate analogy.

One other property which a system of rules may possess should be noted. When a given situation may be defined in more than one way—that is, when there is more than one relevant rule—the rules themselves may specify priorities among rules or other criteria for resolving the ambiguity. When situations are ambiguous or meaningless, the rules may provide for making rules—for example, by designating leaders whose definitions are, by the rules, authoritative and valid for all participants.

The theoretical problems implied in failure of motivation and in mechanisms for averting that failure also need clarification. Here we shall limit ourselves to some observations on institutional elements in motivation.

Deviant behavior and conformity, we have said, are not definitive of disorganization and organization. This is not to say that moral considerations are not highly revelant to organization and disorganization through the part they play in motivation. It is difficult to conceive of a system in which the incentive to assume one's role and play one's part in accordance with the constitutive rules does not require to some extent at least, the backing of a sense of moral obligation and the assumption that others also feel morally bound. Hobbes' *Leviathan*, the most impressive attempt to conceive such a system, is empirically impossible.

However, a sense of moral obligation is only one factor in motivation. Presumably, even a Nazi concentration camp could not function without some moral discipline among the jailers themselves, but the stability and viability of its constitutive order do not presuppose that the prisoners share the moral sentiments of their jailers. The relevant question for a theory of social disorganization, therefore, is this: How does the relative importance of different types of motivation—for example, moral obligation, force, and coercion—vary with the type of system, the sector within the system, and the situation within which the system functions?

But the relationship between motivation and conformity to institutionalized expectations is more subtle than this. There may well be situations in which deviant behavior is organizing and conformity disorganizing. Under certain conditions, choice of the institutionally sanctioned constitutive possibility may lead to organizational breakdown, and choice of an institutionally condemned alternative can alone avert this breakdown. For example, the procurement of certain supplies may be essential for the continuity of a certain activity. This procurement may be regulated by certain institutionalized expectations which, under the range of conditions ordinarily encountered, serve their purpose quite well. Under other conditions, however, conformity to these institutionally prescribed procedures will not work or will result in fatal delays in procurement. What used to be called "moonlight requisitioning" in the Army was at times the only method of procurement compatible with the execution of a mission or even the routine functioning of some operation. Too delicate a G.I. conscience was destructive to organization.

There is much more to be said about motivation, but our object is only to indicate in a general way the complexity of the relationship of motivation, and especially institutional elements in motivation, to social organization and disorganization, and the nature of the problems to be explored.

RELATED CONCEPTS

In the foregoing, we have implied a number of theoretical problems that have a recognized place in sociology: the problem of order, the functional prerequisites of social systems, the conditions of homeostasis or equilibrium, of boundary maintenance. We shall resist the temptation to discuss at length these concepts and the distinctions among them. It should be pointed out, however, that all of them imply a conception of a social system as a structure of interaction which, despite the buffetings of the environment and internal stresses, manages to preserve certain characteristics. This property is sometimes defined as the ability of the system to maintain constancy with respect to some concrete feature or with respect to the relationships among certain parts of the system or with respect to a direction of movement or change—in other words, the continued adherence of the system to some pattern or model which defines that particular system. One such model is the set of constitutive rules that define, for the participants in the system, the kind of activity in which they are engaged.

All these concepts imply, further, a particular approach to social systems —one that regards them as mechanisms for their own perpetuation. They imply formulation of the problems that systems must solve in order to secure their own viability; they imply classification of the structural features of systems from the standpoint of the part they play in enabling the system to adhere to the model which defines it; they imply classification and analysis of the mechanisms by means of which systems detect conditions that threaten their viability or constancy in some particular respect and meet and counter these threats; and they imply the study of the conditions under which systems break down. These problems exist and are recognized, they constitute a distinct and coherent problem area, and they are implied by our definition of organization-disorganization.

REFERENCES

1. Albert K. Cohen, *Delinquent Boys, The Culture of the Gang,* Free Press, 1955.
2. Kingsley Davis, "The Sociology of Prostitution," *Amer. Social Rev.,* 2 (1937), 744–55.
3. Isidor Chein and Eva Rosenfeld, "Juvenile Narcotics Use," *Law Contemp. Prob.,* 22 (1957) 59–63.
4. Harold Garfinkel, "Trust as a Condition of Stable Concerted Action," paper delivered at the annual meetings of the American Sociological Society, 1957.

# DEVIANCE BY DEFINITION* (*Becker*)

The sociological view I have just discussed defines deviance as the infraction of some agreed-upon rule. It then goes on to ask who breaks rules, and to search for the factors in their personalities and life situations that might account for the infractions. This assumes that those who have broken a rule constitute a homogeneous category, because they have committed the same deviant act.

Such an assumption seems to me to ignore the central fact about deviance: it is created by society. I do not mean this in the way it is ordinarily understood, in which the causes of deviance are located in the social situation of the deviant or in "social factors" which prompt his action. I mean, rather, that *social groups create deviance by making the rules whose infraction constitutes deviance,* and by applying those rules to particular people and labeling them as outsiders. From this point of view, deviance is *not* a quality of the act the person commits, but rather a consequence of the application by others of rules and sanctions to an "offender." The deviant is one to whom

* Reprinted with permission of The Macmillan Company from *Outsiders: Studies in the Sociology of Deviance* by Howard S. Becker (© The Free Press of Glencoe, a Division of The Macmillan Company, 1963).

that label has successfully been applied; deviant behavior is behavior that people so label.[1]

Since deviance is, among other things, a consequence of the responses of others to a person's act, students of deviance cannot assume that they are dealing with a homogeneous category when they study people who have been labeled deviant. That is, they cannot assume that these people have actually committed a deviant act or broken some rule, because the process of labeling may not be infallible; some people may be labeled deviant who in fact have not broken a rule. Furthermore, they cannot assume that the category of those labeled deviant will contain all those who actually have broken a rule, for many offenders may escape apprehension and thus fail to be included in the population of "deviants" they study. Insofar as the category lacks homogeneity and fails to include all the cases that belong in it, one cannot reasonably expect to find common factors of personality or life situation that will account for the supposed deviance.

What, then, do people who have been labeled deviant have in common? At the least, they share the label and the experience of being labeled as outsiders. I will begin my analysis with this basic similarity and view deviance as the product of a transaction that takes place between some social group and one who is viewed by that group as a rule-breaker. I will be less concerned with the personal and social characteristics of deviants than with the process by which they come to be thought of as outsiders and their reactions to that judgment.

Malinowski discovered the usefulness of this view for understanding the nature of deviance many years ago, in his study of the Trobriand Islands:

> *One day an outbreak of wailing and a great commotion told me that a death had occurred somewhere in the neighborhood. I was informed that Kima'i, a young lad of my acquaintance, of sixteen or so, had fallen from a coco-nut palm and killed himself. . . . I found that another youth had been severely wounded by some mysterious coincidence. And at the funeral there was obviously a general feeling of hostility between the village where the boy died and that into which his body was carried for burial.*
>
> *Only much later was I able to discover the real meaning of these events. The boy had committed suicide. The truth was that*

[1] The most important earlier statements of this view can be found in Frank Tannenbaum, *Crime and the Community* (New York: McGraw-Hill Book Co., Inc., 1951), and E. M. Lemert, *Social Pathology* (New York: McGraw-Hill Book Co., Inc., 1951). A recent article stating a position very similar to mine is John Kitsuse, "Societal Reaction to Deviance: Problems of Theory and Method," *Social Problems,* 9 (Winter, 1962), 247–256.

he had broken the rules of exogamy, the partner in his crime being his maternal cousin, the daughter of his mother's sister. This had been known and generally disapproved of but nothing was done until the girl's discarded lover, who had wanted to marry her and who felt personally injured, took the initiative. This rival threatened first to use black magic against the guilty youth, but this had not much effect. Then one evening he insulted the culprit in public—accusing him in the hearing of the whole community of incest and hurling at him certain expressions intolerable to a native.

For this there was only one remedy; only one means of escape remained to the unfortunate youth. Next morning he put on festive attire and ornamentation, climbed a coco-nut palm and addressed the community, speaking from among the palm leaves and bidding them farewell. He explained the reasons for his desperate deed and also launched forth a veiled accusation against the man who had driven him to his death, upon which it became the duty of his clansmen to avenge him. Then he wailed aloud, as is the custom, jumped from a palm some sixty feet high and was killed on the spot. There followed a fight within the village in which the rival was wounded; and the quarrel was repeated during the funeral. . . .

If you were to inquire into the matter among the Trobrianders, you would find . . . that the natives show horror at the idea of violating the rules of exogamy and that they believe that sores, disease and even death might follow clan incest. This is the ideal of native law, and in moral matters it is easy and pleasant strictly to adhere to the ideal—when judging the conduct of others or expressing an opinion about conduct in general.

When it comes to the application of morality and ideals to real life, however, things take on a different complexion. In the case described it was obvious that the facts would not tally with the ideal of conduct. Public opinion was neither outraged by the knowledge of the crime to any extent, nor did it react directly— it had to be mobilized by a public statement of the crime and by insults being hurled at the culprit by an interested party. Even then he had to carry out the punishment himself. . . . Probing further into the matter and collecting concrete information, I found that the breach of exogamy—as regards intercourse and not marriage—is by no means a rare occurrence, and public opinion is lenient, though decidedly hypocritical. If the affair is carried on *sub rosa with a certain amount of decorum, and if no one in particular stirs up trouble—"public opinion" will gossip, but not demand any harsh punishment. If, on the contrary, scandal breaks out—everyone turns against the guilty pair and by ostracism and insults one or the other may be driven to suicide.*[2]

Whether an act is deviant, then, depends on how other people react to it. You can commit clan incest and suffer from no more than gossip as long as no one makes a public accusation; but you will be driven to your death if the accusation is made. The point is that the response of other people has to be regarded as problematic. Just because one has committed an infraction of a rule does not mean that others will respond as though this had happened. (Conversely, just because one has not violated a rule does not mean that he may not be treated, in some circumstances, as though he had.)

The degree to which other people will respond to a given act as deviant varies greatly. Several kinds of variation seem worth noting. First of all, there is variation over time. A person believed to have committed a given "deviant" act may at one time be responded to much more leniently than he would be at some other time. The occurrence of "drives" against various kinds of deviance illustrates this clearly. At various times, enforcement officials may decide to make an all-out attack on some particular kind of deviance, such as gambling, drug addiction, or homosexuality. It is obviously much more dangerous to engage in one of these activities when a drive is on than at any other time. (In a very interesting study of crime news in Colorado newspapers, Davis found that the amount of crime reported in Colorado newspapers showed very little association with actual changes in the amount of crime taking place in Colorado. And, further, that peoples' estimate of how much increase there had been in crime in Colorado was associated with the increase in the amount of crime news but not with any increase in the amount of crime.)[3]

The degree to which an act will be treated as deviant depends also on who commits the act and who feels he has been harmed by it. Rules tend to be applied more to some persons than others. Studies of juvenile delinquency make the point clearly. Boys from middle-class areas do not get as far in the legal process when they are apprehended as do boys from slum areas. The middle-class boy is less likely, when picked up by the police, to be taken

[2] Bronislaw Malinowski, *Crime and Custom in Savage Society* (New York: Humanities Press, 1926), pp. 77–80. Reprinted by permission of Humanities Press and Routledge & Kegan Paul, Ltd.

[3] F. James Davis, "Crime News in Colorado Newspapers," *American Journal of Sociology,* LVII (January, 1952), 325–330.

to the station; less likely when taken to the station to be booked; and it is extremely unlikely that he will be convicted and sentenced.[4] This variation occurs even though the original infraction of the rule is the same in the two cases. Similarly, the law is differentially applied to Negroes and whites. It is well known that a Negro believed to have attacked a white woman is much more likely to be punished than a white man who commits the same offense; it is only slightly less well known that a Negro who murders another Negro is much less likely to be punished than a white man who commits murder.[5] This, of course, is one of the main points of Sutherland's analysis of white-collar crime: crimes committed by corporations are almost always prosecuted as civil cases, but the same crime committed by an individual is ordinarily treated as a criminal offense.[6]

Some rules are enforced only when they result in certain consequences. The unmarried mother furnishes a clear example. Vincent[7] points out that illicit sexual relations seldom result in severe punishment or social censure for the offenders. If, however, a girl becomes pregnant as a result of such activities the reaction of others is likely to be severe. (The illicit pregnancy is also an interesting example of the differential enforcement of results on different categories of people. Vincent notes that unmarried fathers escape the severe censure visited on the mother.)

Why repeat these commonplace observations? Because, taken together, they support the proposition that deviance is not a simple quality, present in some kinds of behavior and absent in others. Rather, it is the product of a process which involves responses of other people to the behavior. The same behavior may be an infraction of the rules at one time and not at another; may be an infraction when committed by one person, but not when committed by another; some rules are broken with impunity, others are not. In short, whether a given act is deviant or not depends in part on the nature of the act (that is, whether or not it violates some rule) and in part on what other people do about it.

Some people may object that this is merely a terminological quibble, that one can, after all, define terms any way he wants to and that if some people want to speak of rule-breaking behavior as deviant without reference to the

---

[4] See Albert K. Cohen and James F. Short, Jr., "Juvenile Delinquency," in Merton and Nisbet, *op. cit.*, p. 87.

[5] See Harold Garfinkel, "Research Notes on Inter- and Intra-Racial Homicides," *Social Forces*, 27 (May, 1949), 369–381.

[6] Edwin H. Sutherland, "White Collar Criminality," *American Sociological Review*, V (February, 1940), 1–12.

[7] Clark Vincent, *Unmarried Mothers* (New York: The Free Press of Glencoe, 1961), pp. 3–5.

reactions of others they are free to do so. This, of course, is true. Yet it might be worthwhile to refer to such behavior as *rule-breaking behavior* and reserve the term *deviant* for those labeled as deviant by some segment of society. I do not insist that this usage be followed. But it should be clear that insofar as a scientist uses "deviant" to refer to any rule-breaking behavior and takes as his subject of study only those who have been *labeled* deviant, he will be hampered by the disparities between the two categories.

If we take as the object of our attention behavior which comes to be labeled as deviant, we must recognize that we cannot know whether a given act will be categorized as deviant until the response of others has occurred. Deviance is not a quality that lies in behavior itself, but in the interaction between the person who commits an act and those who respond to it.

## Whose Rules?

I have been using the term "outsiders" to refer to those people who are judged by others to be deviant and thus to stand outside the circle of "normal" members of the group. But the term contains a second meaning, whose analysis leads to another important set of sociological problems: "outsiders," from the point of view of the person who is labeled deviant, may be the people who make the rules he had been found guilty of breaking.

Social rules are the creation of specific social groups. Modern societies are not simple organizations in which everyone agrees on what the rules are and how they are to be applied in specific situations. They are, instead, highly differentiated along social class lines, ethnic lines, occupational lines, and cultural lines. These groups need not and, in fact, often do not share the same rules. The problems they face in dealing with their environment, the history and traditions they carry with them, all lead to the evolution of different sets of rules. Insofar as the rules of various groups conflict and contradict one another, there will be disagreement about the kind of behavior that is proper in any given situation.

Italian immigrants who went on making wine for themselves and their friends during Prohibition were acting properly by Italian immigrant standards, but were breaking the law of their new country (as, of course, were many of their Old American neighbors). Medical patients who shop around for a doctor may, from the perspective of their own group, be doing what is necessary to protect their health by making sure they get what seems to them the best possible doctor, but, from the perspective of the physician, what they do is wrong because it breaks down the trust the patient ought to put in his physician. The lower-class delinquent who fights for his "turf" is only doing what he considers necessary and right, but teachers, social workers, and police see it differently.

While it may be argued that many or most rules are generally agreed to by all members of a society, empirical research on a given rule generally reveals variation in people's attitudes. Formal rules, enforced by some specially constituted group, may differ from those actually thought appropriate by most people.[8] Factions in a group may disagree on what I have called actual operating rules. Most important for the study of behavior ordinarily labeled deviant, the perspectives of the people who engage in the behavior are likely to be quite different from those of the people who condemn it. In this latter situation, a person may feel that he is being judged according to rules he has had no hand in making and does not accept, rules forced on him by outsiders.

To what extent and under what circumstances do people attempt to force their rules on others who do not subscribe to them? Let us distinguish two cases. In the first, only those who are actually members of the group have any interest in making and enforcing certain rules. If an orthodox Jew disobeys the laws of kashruth only other orthodox Jews will regard this as a transgression; Christians or nonorthodox Jews will not consider this deviance and would have no interest in interfering. In the second case, members of a group consider it important to their welfare that members of certain other groups obey certain rules. Thus, people consider it extremely important that those who practice the healing arts abide by certain rules; this is the reason the state licenses physicians, nurses, and others, and forbids anyone who is not licensed to engage in healing activities.

To the extent that a group tries to impose its rules on other groups in the society, we are presented with a second question: Who can, in fact, force others to accept their rules and what are the causes of their success? This is, of course, a question of political and economic power. Later we will consider the political and economic process through which rules are created and enforced. Here it is enough to note that people are in fact always *forcing* their rules on others, applying them more or less against the will and without the consent of those others. By and large, for example, rules are made for young people by their elders. Though the youth of this country exert a powerful influence culturally—the mass media of communication are tailored to their interests, for instance—many important kinds of rules are made for our youth by adults. Rules regarding school attendance and sex behavior are not drawn up with regard to the problems of adolescence. Rather, adolescents find themselves surrounded by rules about these matters which have been made by older and more settled people. It is considered legitimate to do this, for youngsters are considered neither wise enough nor responsible enough to make proper rules for themselves.

In the same way, it is true in many respects that men make the rules for women in our society (though in America this is changing rapidly). Negroes find themselves subject to rules made for them by whites. The foreign-born and those otherwise ethnically peculiar often have their rules made for them by the Protestant Anglo-Saxon majority. The middle class makes rules the lower class must obey—in the schools, the courts, and elsewhere.

Differences in the ability to make rules and apply them to other people are essentially power differentials (either legal or extralegal). Those groups whose social position gives them weapons and power are best able to enforce their rules. Distinctions of age, sex, ethnicity, and class are all related to differences in power, which accounts for differences in the degree to which groups so distinguished can make rules for others.

In addition to recognizing that deviance is created by the responses of people to particular kinds of behavior, by the labeling of that behavior as deviant, we must also keep in mind that the rules created and maintained by such labeling are not universally agreed to. Instead, they are the object of conflict and disagreement, part of the political process of society.

# 14: Structure and Function

Sociological theorizing in the last few decades has been profoundly influenced by a group of thinkers who have emphasized the so-called "functionalist" or "structural-functional" approach. As some of our selections will illustrate, by no means all of the social scientists who have worked in this tradition are agreed upon the precise denotations or connotations of these terms. We might nevertheless suggest as a point of departure that "structure" in their usage generally refers to a set of relatively stable and patterned relationships of social units, while by "function" they mean those consequences of any social activity which make for the adaptation or adjustment of a given structure or its component parts. In other words, "structure" refers to a system with relatively enduring patterns, and "function" refers to the dynamic process within the structure.

This type of analysis arose out of the need felt by sociologists and anthropologists to develop theoretical and methodological tools adequate for dealing with the interrelatedness of various "traits," institutions, groups, etc., within a total social system, and to overcome certain atomistic and descriptive methods which had prevailed in the nineteenth century.

Functionalism was brought into sociological thought by borrowing directly and developing analogies for concepts in the biological sciences. Biology since the middle of the last century frequently referred to the "structure" of an organism, meaning a relatively stable arrangement of relationships between the different cells, and referred to the consequences of the activity of the various organs in the life process of the organism as their "function." As our excerpt from Herbert Spencer (1820–1903), the great British evolutionary sociologist, will make clear, structure-function theory in sociology was at first conceived not only as pointing to many analogies and similarities between the body social and the biological organism, but as revealing that the same principles, the same "definition of life," applied to both. This early *organicism* has long since been abandoned in sociology. Yet Spencer's contribution, that of having introduced functional types of analysis into sociology, should not be forgotten—as it so often has been.

The first systematic formulation of the logic of a functionalist approach in sociology can be found in the work of Emile Durkheim. Durkheim was no longer intent upon illustrating alleged correspondences between biological and sociological processes, but he made it his task to explore systematically the contributions that particular social factors, such as ritual, crime, punishment, and role differentiation, make to the maintenance or change of given social structures. Our selection from Durkheim illustrates the distinctions he suggests between causal and functional types of analysis and indicates that these two methods, far from being antithetical, are in fact complementary.

Functional analysis in this country was crucially influenced by the work of two British anthropologists, A. R. Radcliffe-Brown and Bronislaw Malinowski. Though an Englishman, trained at Cambridge, Radcliffe-Brown closely followed in the footsteps of Durkheim and his school. Like Durkheim, he was often led, as our selection makes clear, to utilize analogical models imported from biology to illustrate his conceptualization of social function. This tendency probably accounted for his propensity to devote his attention mainly to the function of each element in the maintenance and development of a *total* structure and to neglect the functional consequences of specific elements for differentiated parts of such structures or for their individual components. It is this last distinction, above all, which led Bronislaw Malinowski to distinguish his type of functionalism from that of his eminent colleague. To Malinowski the Durkheimian bent in the work of Radcliffe-Brown led to "a tendency to ignore completely the individual and to eliminate the biological element from the functional analysis of culture." Malinowski proposed "to link up functionally the various types of cultural responses, such as economic, legal, educational, scientific, magic and religious" and then to show that they were all related to the biological needs of individuals. But, whatever the differences between the two eminent anthropologists, and they should not be minimized, it remains true that their life work in anthropological research provides us with splendid illustrations of the fruitfulness of an approach that focuses attention upon the functional interrelatedness of the parts that make a cultural and structural whole. Their work enables one to perceive cultures as single functioning systems interrelated in their component parts, rather than as a patchwork of culture traits, institutions, customs, and norms.

Vilfredo Pareto (1848–1923), the distinguished Italian sociologist, developed a system of analysis which, though it cannot be called "functionalist," nevertheless incorporates many features of functional analysis. Pareto, who had done distinguished work in mathematical economics before he developed an interest in sociological theory, abandoned the biological analogies still so pronounced in the thinkers discussed above in favor of an attempt to build a generalized theory of social systems on the model of mechanics. He saw society as essentially a system in equilibrium, consisting of parts so interdependent that every change in each part will necessarily affect all other parts as well as the system as a whole. While Pareto's world view is now generally considered to be of relatively limited usefulness, there are elements in it, such as the classification of logical and non-logical actions and the differentiation between objective end and subjective purpose, that seem to present fruitful leads for functional analysis. In fact, Merton's later distinction between latent and manifest functions would seem to be foreshadowed in these pages.

Our final selection, from the work of Robert K. Merton, is part of a larger study in which the whole functionalist school, its assumptions and its shortcomings, are discussed in detail. This seems to us the most sophisticated treatment of the functionalist approach now available. Merton introduces a number of important new concepts into functional analysis, such as the concept of *functional alternatives* and the distinction between *latent* and *manifest* functions. In addition, he provides us with a tentative codification for functional analysis which is as invaluable for the judgment of past theory as it is for the development of future research and theory.

Space does not permit us to present samples of the work of other significant contributors to functional theory in contemporary sociology. We can merely mention the names of Talcott Parsons, Marion J. Levy, Jr., and Kingsley Davis. Yet many of the selections in other parts of this book reflect, directly or indirectly, a functionalist orientation, and thus may be said to supplement the selections in this section.

# SOCIAL STRUCTURE AND SOCIAL FUNCTION * (*Spencer*)

## Social Structures

In societies, as in living bodies, increase of mass is habitually accompanied by increase of structure. Along with that integration which is the primary trait of evolution, both exhibit in high degrees the secondary trait, differentiation.

The association of these two characters in animals was described in the *Principles of Biology.* . . .

So, too, is it with societies. As we progress from small groups to larger; from simple groups to compound groups; from compound groups to doubly compound ones; the unlikenesses of parts increase. The social aggregate, homogeneous when minute, habitually gains in heterogeneity along with each increment of growth; and to reach great size must acquire great complexity. Let us glance at the leading stages.

Naturally in a state like that of the Cayaguas or Wood Indians of South America, so little social that "one family lives at a distance from another," social organization is impossible; and even where there is some slight association of families, organization does not arise while they are few and wandering. Groups of Esquimaux, of Australians, of Bushmen, of Fuegians, are without even that primary contrast of parts implied by settled chieftainship. Their members are subject to no control but such as is temporarily acquired by the stronger, or more cunning, or more experienced: not even a permanent nucleus is present. Habitually where larger simple groups exist, we find some kind of head. Though not a uniform rule (for, as we shall hereafter see, the genesis of a controlling agency depends on the nature of the social activities), this is a general rule. The headless clusters, wholly ungoverned, are incoherent, and separate before they acquire considerable sizes; but along with maintenance of an aggregate approaching to, or exceeding, a hundred, we ordinarily find a simple or compound ruling agency—one or more men claiming and exercising authority that is natural, or supernatural, or both. This is the first social differentiation. Soon after it there frequently comes another, tending to form a division between regulative and operative

---

* Abridged from Herbert Spencer, *The Principles of Sociology*, Vol. I, pp. 471–489. New York, Appleton-Century-Crofts, Inc., 1897.

parts. In the lowest tribes this is rudely represented only by the contrast in status between the sexes: the men, having unchecked control, carry on such external activities as the tribe shows us, chiefly in war; while the women are made drudges who perform the less skilled parts of the process of sustentation. But that tribal growth, and establishment of chieftainship, which gives military superiority, presently causes enlargement of the operative part by adding captives to it. This begins unobtrusively. While in battle the men are killed, and often afterwards eaten, the non-combatants are enslaved. Patagonians, for example, make slaves of women and children taken in war. Later, and especially when cannibalism ceases, comes the enslavement of male captives; whence results, in some cases, an operative part clearly marked off from the regulative part. Among the Chinooks, "slaves do all the laborious work." We read that the Beluchi, avoiding the hard labour of cultivation, impose it on the Jutts, the ancient inhabitants whom they have subjugated. Beecham says it is usual on the Gold Coast to make the slaves clear the ground for cultivation. And among the Felathahs "slaves are numerous: the males are employed in weaving, collecting wood or grass, or on any other kind of work; some of the women are engaged in spinning . . . in preparing the yarn for the loom, others in pounding and grinding corn, etc."

Along with that increase of mass caused by union of primary social aggregates into a secondary one, a further unlikeness of parts arises. The holding together of the compound cluster implies a head of the whole as well as heads of the parts; and a differentiation analogous to that which originally produced a chief, now produces a chief of chiefs. Sometimes the combination is made for defence against a common foe, and sometimes it results from conquest by one tribe of the rest. In this last case the predominant tribe, in maintaining its supremacy, develops more highly its military character: thus becoming unlike the others.

After such clusters of clusters have been so consolidated that their united powers can be wielded by one governing agency, there come alliances with, or subjugations of, other clusters of clusters, ending from time to time in coalescence. When this happens there results still greater complexity in the governing agency, with its king, local rulers, and petty chiefs; and at the same time, there arise more marked divisions of classes—military, priestly, slave, etc. Clearly, then, complication of structure accompanies increase of mass.

This increase of heterogeneity, which in both classes of aggregates goes along with growth, presents another trait in common. Beyond unlikenesses of parts due to development of the co-ordinating agencies, there presently follow unlikenesses among the agencies co-ordinated—the organs of alimentation, etc., in the one case, and the industrial structures in the other.

When animal-aggregates of the lowest order unite to form one of a higher order, and when, again, these secondary aggregates are compounded into tertiary aggregates, each component is at first similar to the other components; but in the course of evolution dissimilarties arise and become more and more decided. . . . It is thus with the minor social groups combined into a major social group. Each tribe originally had within itself such feebly-marked industrial divisions as sufficed for its low kind of life; and those were like those of each other tribe. But union facilitates exchange of commodities; and if, as mostly happens, the component tribes severally occupy localities favourable to unlike kinds of production, unlike occupations are initiated, and there result unlikenesses of industrial structure. Even between tribes not united, as those of Australia, barter of products furnished by their respective habitats goes on so long as war does not hinder. And evidently when there is reached such a stage of integration as in Madagascar, or as in the chief Negro states of Africa, the internal peace that follows subordination to one government makes commercial intercourse easy. The like parts being permanently held together, mutual dependence becomes possible; and along with growing mutual dependence the parts grow unlike.

The advance of organization which thus follows the advance of aggregation, alike in individual organisms and in social organisms, conforms in both cases to the same general law: differentiations proceed from the more general to the more special. First broad and simple contrasts of parts; then within each of the parts primarily contrasted, changes which make unlike divisions of them; then within each of these unlike divisions, minor unlikenesses; and so on continually.

The successive stages in the development of a vertebrate column, illustrate this law in animals. . . . During social evolution analogous metamorphoses may everywhere be traced. The rise of the structure exercising religious control will serve as an example. In simple tribes, and in clusters of tribes during their early stages of aggregation, we find men who are at once sorcerers, priests, diviners, exorcists, doctors,—men who deal with supposed supernatural beings in all the various possible ways: propitiating them, seeking knowledge and aid from them, commanding them, subduing them. Along with advance in social integration, there come both differences of function and differences of rank. In Tanna "there are rain-makers . . . and a host of other 'sacred men;'" in Fiji there are not only priests, but seers; among the Sandwich Islanders there are diviners as well as priests; among the New Zealanders, Thomson distinguishes between priests and sorcerers; and among the Kaffirs, besides diviners and rain-makers, there are two classes of doctors who respectively rely on supernatural and on natural agents in curing their patients. More advanced societies, as those of ancient America, show us still greater multiformity of this once-uniform group. In Mexico, for example, the medical class, descending from a class of sorcerers who dealt antagonistically with the supernatural agents supposed to cause disease, were distinct from the priests, whose dealings with supernatural agents were propitiatory. Further, the sacerdotal class included several kinds, dividing the religious offices among them—sacrificers, diviners, singers, composers of hymns, instructors of youth; and then there were also gradations of rank in each. This progress from general to special in priesthoods, has, in the higher nations, led to such marked distinctions that the original kinships are forgotten. The priest-astrologers of ancient races were initiators of the scientific class, now variously specialized; from the priest-doctors of old have come the medical class with its chief division and minor divisions; while within the clerical class proper, have arisen not only various ranks from Pope down to acolyte, but various kinds of functionaries—dean, priest, deacon, chorister, as well as others classed as curates and chaplains. Similarly if we trace the genesis of any industrial structure; as that which from primitive blacksmiths who smelt their own iron as well as make implements from it, brings us to our iron-manufacturing districts, where preparation of the metal is separated into smelting, refining, puddling, rolling, and where turning this metal into implements is divided into various businesses.

The transformation here illustrated is, indeed, an aspect of that transformation of the homogeneous into the heterogeneous which everywhere characterizes evolution; but the truth to be noted is that it characterizes the evolution of individual organisms and of social organisms in especially high degrees. . . . .

## Social Functions

Changes of structures cannot occur without changes of functions. Much that was said in the last chapter might, therefore, be said here with substituted terms. Indeed, as in societies many changes of structure are more indicated by changes of function than directly seen, it may be said that these last have been already described by implication.

There are, however, certain functional traits not manifestly implied by traits of structure. To these a few pages must be devoted.

If organization consists in such a construction of the whole that its parts can carry on mutually-dependent actions, then in proportion as organization is high there must go a dependence of each part upon the rest so great that separation is fatal; and conversely. This truth is equally well shown in the individual organism and in the social organism.

The lowest animal-aggregates are so constituted that each portion, similar to every other in appearance, carries on similar actions; and here spontaneous or artificial separation interferes scarcely at all with the life of either separated portion. When the faintly-differentiated speck of protoplasm forming a Rhizopod is accidentally divided, each division goes on as before. . . . The like happens for the like reason with the lowest social aggregates. A headless wandering group of primitive men divides without any inconvenience. Each man, at once warrior, hunter, and maker of his own weapons, hut, etc., with a squaw who has in every case the like drudgeries to carry on, needs concert with his fellows only in war and to some extent in the chase; and, except for fighting, concert with half the tribe is as good as concert with the whole. Even where the slight differentiation implied by chieftainship exists, little inconvenience results from voluntary or enforced separation. Either before or after a part of the tribe migrates, some man becomes head, and such low social life as is possible recommences.

With highly-organized aggregates of either kind it is very different. We cannot cut a mammal in two without causing immediate death. Twisting off the head of a fowl is fatal. Not even a reptile, though it may survive the loss of its tail, can live when its body is divided. And among annulose creatures it similarly happens that though in some inferior genera, bisection does not kill either half, it kills both in an insect, an arachnid, or a crustacean. If in high societies the effect of mutilation is less than in high animals, still it is great. Middlesex separated from its surroundings would in a few days have all its social processes stopped by lack of supplies. Cut off the cotton-district from Liverpool and other ports, and there would come arrest of its industry followed by mortality of its people. Let a division be made between the coal-mining populations and adjacent populations which smelt metals or make broadcloth by machinery, and both, forthwith dying socially by arrest of their actions, would begin to die individually. Though when a civilized society is so divided that part of it is left without a central controlling agency, it may presently evolve one; yet there is meanwhile much risk of dissolution, and before re-organization is efficient, a long period of disorder and weakness must be passed through.

So that the consensus of functions becomes closer as evolution advances. In low aggregates, both individual and social, the actions of the parts are but little dependent on one another; whereas in developed aggregates of both kinds, that combination of actions which constitutes the life of the whole, makes possible the component actions which constitute the lives of the parts.

Another corollary, manifest a priori and proved a posteriori, must be named. Where parts are little differentiated, they can readily perform one another's functions; but where much differentiated they can perform one another's functions very imperfectly, or not at all. . . .

In social organisms, low and high, we find these relatively great and relatively small powers of substitution. Of course, where each member of the tribe repeats every other in his mode of life, there are no unlike functions to be exchanged; and where there has arisen only that small differentiation implied by the barter of weapons for other articles, between one member of the tribe skilled in weapon-making and others less skilled, the destruction of this specially-skilled member entails no great evil; since the rest can severally do for themselves that which he did for them, though not quite so well. Even in settled societies of considerable sizes, we find the like holds to a great degree. Of the ancient Mexicans, Zurita says—"Every Indian knows all handicrafts which do not require great skill or delicate instruments;" and in Peru each man "was expected to be acquainted with the various handicrafts essential to domestic comfort:" the parts of the societies were so slightly differentiated in their occupations, that assumption of one another's occupations remained practicable. But in societies like our own, specialized industrially and otherwise in high degrees, the actions of one part which fails in its function cannot be assumed by other parts. Even the relatively-unskilled farm labourers, were they to strike, would have their duties very inadequately performed by the urban population; and our iron manufactures would be stopped if their trained artisans, refusing to work, had to be replaced by peasants or hands from cotton factories. Still less could the higher functions, legislative, judicial, etc., be effectually performed by coal-miners and navvies.

Evidently the same reason for this contrast holds in the two cases. In proportion as the units forming any part of an individual organism are limited to one kind of action, as that of absorbing, or secreting, or contracting, or cenveying an impulse, and become adapted to that action, they lose adaptation to other actions; and in the social organism the discipline required for effectually discharging a special duty, causes unfitness for discharging special duties widely unlike it.

Beyond these two chief functional analogies between individual organisms and social organisms, that when they are little evolved, division or mutilation causes small inconvenience, but when they are much evolved it causes great perturbation or death, and that in low types of either kind the parts can assume one another's functions, but cannot in high types; sundry consequent functional analogies might be enlarged on did space permit.

There is the truth that in both kinds of organisms the vitality increases as fast as the functions become specialized. In either case, before there exist structures severally adapted for the unlike actions, these are ill-performed; and in the absence of developed appliances for furthering it, the utilization of one another's services is but slight. But along with advance of organization, every part, more limited in its office, performs its office better; the means of exchanging benefits become greater; each aids all, and all aid each with increasing efficiency; and the total activity we call life, individual or national, augments.

# CAUSAL AND FUNCTIONAL ANALYSIS* (Durkheim)

Most sociologists think they have accounted for phenomena once they have shown how they are useful, what role they play, reasoning as if facts existed only from the point of view of this role and with no other determining cause than the sentiment, clear or confused, of the services they are called to render. That is why they think they have said all that is necessary to render them intelligible, when they have established the reality of these services and have shown what social needs they satisfy.

Thus Comte traces the entire progresive force of the human species to this fundamental tendency "which directly impels man constantly to ameliorate his condition, whatever it may be, under all circumstances,"[1] and Spencer relates this force to the need for greater happiness. It is in accordance with this principle that Spencer explains the formation of society by the alleged advantages which result from co-operation; the institution of government, by the utility of the regularization of military co-operation;[2] the transformations through which the family has passed, by the need for reconciling more and more perfectly the interests of parents, children, and society.

But this method confuses two very different questions. To show how a fact is useful is not to explain how it originated or why it is what it is. The uses which it serves presuppose the specific properties characterizing it but do not create them. The need we have of things cannot give them existence,

---

* Reprinted from *The Rules of Sociological Method* by Emile Durkheim, pp. 89–97, with permission of the publisher, The Free Press, Glencoe, Ill. Copyright, 1938, by The Free Press, A Corporation.

nor can it confer their specific nature upon them. It is to causes of another sort that they owe their existence. The idea we have of their utility may indeed motivate us to put these forces to work and to elicit from them their characteristic effects, but it will not enable us to produce these effects out of nothing. This proposition is evident so long as it is a question only of material, or even psychological, phenomena. It would be equally evident in sociology if social facts, because of their extreme intangibility, did not wrongly appear to us as without all intrinsic reality. Since we usually see them as a product purely of mental effort, it seems to us that they may be produced at will whenever we find it necessary. But since each one of them is a force, superior to that of the individual, and since it has a separate existence, it is not true that merely by willing to do so may one call them into being. No force can be engendered except by an antecedent force. To revive the spirit of the family, where it has become weakened, it is not enough that everyone understand its advantages; the causes which alone can engender it must be made to act directly. To give a government the authority necessary for it, it is not enough to feel the need for this authority; we must have recourse to the only sources from which all authority is derived. We must, namely, establish traditions, a common spirit, etc., and for this it is necessary again to go back along the chain of causes and effects until we find a point where the action of man may be effectively brought to bear.

What shows plainly the dualism of these two orders of research is that a fact can exist without being at alle useful, either because it has never been adjusted to any vital end or because, after having been useful, it has lost all utility while continuing to exist by the inertia of habit alone. There are, indeed, more survivals in society than in biological organisms. There are even cases where a practice or a social institution changes its function without thereby changing its nature. The rule, *Is pater quem justae nuptiae declarant*[3] has remained in our code essentially the same as it was in the old Roman law. While its purpose then was to safeguard the property rights of a father over children born to the legitimate wife, it is rather the rights of children that it protects today. The custom of taking an oath began by being a sort of judiciary test and has become today simply a solemn and imposing formality. The religious dogmas of Christianity have not changed for centuries, but the role which they play is not the same in our modern societies as in the Middle Ages. Thus, the same words may serve to express new ideas. It is, moreover, a proposition true in sociology, as in biology, that the organ is independent of the function—in other words, while remaining the same, it can serve different ends. The causes of its existence are, then, independent of the ends it serves.

Nevertheless, we do not mean to say that the imperative needs, and desires of men never intervene actively in social evolution. On the contrary, it is certain that they can hasten or retard its development, according to the circumstances which determine the social phenomena. Apart from the fact that they cannot, in any case, make something out of nothing, their actual intervention, whatever may be its effects, can take place only by means of efficient causes. A deliberate intention can contribute, even in this limited way, to the production of a new phenomenon only if it has itself been newly formed or if it is itself a result of some transformation of a previous intention. For, unless we postulate a truly providential and pre-established harmony, we cannot admit that man has carried with him from the beginning— potentially ready to be awakened at the call of circumstances—all the intentions which conditions were destined to demand in the course of human evolution. It must further be recognized that a deliberate intention is itself something objectively real; it can, then, neither be created nor modified by the mere fact that we judge it useful. It is a force having a nature of its own; for that nature to be given existence or altered, it is not enough that we should find this advantageous. In order to bring about such changes, there must be a sufficient cause.

For example, we have explained the constant development of the division of labor by showing that it is necessary in order that man may maintain himself in the new conditions of existence as he advances in history. We have attributed to this tendency, which is rather improperly named the "instinct of self-preservation," an important role in our explanations. But, in the first place, this instinct alone could not account for even the most rudimentary specialization. It can do nothing if the conditions on which division of labor depends do not already exist, i.e., if individual differences have not increased sufficiently as a consequence of the progressive disintegration of the common consciousness and of hereditary influences.[4] It was even necessary that division of labor should have already begun to exist for its usefulness to be seen and for the need of it to make itself felt. The very development of individual differences, necessarily accompanied by a greater diversity of tastes and aptitudes, produced this first result. Further, the instinct of self-preservation did not, of itself and without cause, come to fertilize this first germ of specialization. We were started in this new direction, first, because the course we previously followed was now barred and because the greater intensity of the struggle, owing to the more extensive consolidation of societies, made more and more difficult the survival of individuals who continued to devote themselves to unspecialized tasks. For such reasons it became necessary for us to change our mode of living. Moreover, if our ac'' ·· has been turned toward a constantly more developed division of labor,      because this was also the direction of least resistance. The other possible solutions were emigration, suicide, and crime. Now, in the average case the ties attaching us to life and country and the sympathy we have for our fellows are sentiments stronger and more resistant than the habits which could deflect us from narrower specialization. These habits, then, had inevitably to yield to each impulse that arose. Thus the fact that we allow a place for human needs in sociological explanations does not mean that we even partially revert to teleology. These needs can influence social evolution only on condition that they themselves, and the changes they undergo, can be explained solely by causes that are deterministic and not at all purposive.

But what is even more convincing than the preceding considerations is a study of actual social behavior. Where purpose reigns, there reigns also a more or less wide contingency, for there are no ends, and even fewer means, which necessarily control all men, even when it is assumed that they are placed in the same circumstances. Given the same environment, each individual adapts himself to it according to his own disposition and in his own way, which he prefers to all other ways. One person will seek to change it and make it conform to his needs; another will prefer to change himself and moderate his desires. To arrive at the same goal, many different ways can be and actually are followed. If, then, it were true that historic development took place in terms of ends clearly or obscurely felt, social facts should present the most infinite diversity, and all comparison should be almost impossible.

To be sure, the external events which constitute the superficial part of social life vary from one people to another, just as each individual has his own history, although the bases of physical and moral organization are the same for all. But when one comes in contact with social phenomena, one is, on the contrary, surprised by the astonishing regularity with which they occur under the same circumstances. Even the most minute and the most trivial practices recur with the most astonishing uniformity. A certain nuptial ceremony, purely symbolical in appearance, such as the carrying-off of the betrothed, is found to be exactly the same wherever a certain family type exists; and again this family type itself is linked to a whole social organization. The most bizarre customs, such as the couvade, the levirate, exogamy, etc., are observed among the most diverse peoples and are symptomatic of a certain social state. The right to make one's will appears at a certain phase of history, and the more or less important restrictions limiting it offer a fairly exact clue to the particular stage of social evolution. It would be easy to multiply examples. This wide diffusion of collective forms would be inexplicable if purpose or final causes had the predominant place in sociology that is attributed to them.

*When, then, the explanation of a social phenomenon is undertaken, we must seek separately the efficient cause which produces it and the function it fulfils.* We use the word "function," in preference to "end" or "purpose," precisely because social phenomena do not generally exist for the useful results they produce. We must determine whether there is a correspondence between the fact under consideration and the general needs of the social organism, and in what this correspondence consists, without occupying ourselves with whether it has been intentional or not. All these questions of intention are too subjective to allow scientific treatment.

Not only must these two types of problems be separated, but it is proper, in general, to treat the former before the latter. This sequence, indeed, corresponds to that of experience. It is natural to seek the causes of a phenomenon before trying to determine its effects. This method is all the more logical since the first question, once answered, will often help to answer the second. Indeed, the bond which unites the cause to the effect is reciprocal to an extent which has not been sufficiently recognized. The effect can doubtless not exist without its cause; but the latter, in turn, needs its effect. It is from the cause that the effect draws its energy, but it also restores it to the cause on occasion, and consequently it cannot disappear without the cause showing the effects of its disappearance.[5]

For example, the social reaction that we call "punishment" is due to the intensity of the collective sentiments which the crime offends, but, from another angle, it has the useful function of maintaining these sentiments at the same degree of intensity, for they would soon diminish if offenses against them were not punished.[6] Similarly, in proportion as the social milieu becomes more complex and more unstable, traditions and conventional beliefs are shaken, become more indeterminate and more unsteady, and reflective powers are developed. Such rationality is indispensable to societies and individuals in adapting themselves to a more mobile and more complex environment.[7] And again, in proportion as men are obliged to furnish more highly specialized work, the products of this work are multiplied and are of better quality; but this increase in products and improvement in quality are necessary to compensate for the expense which this more considerable work entails.[8] Thus, instead of the cause of social phenomena consisting of a mental anticipation of the function they are called to fill, this function, on the contrary, at least in a number of cases, serves to maintain the pre-existent cause from which they are derived. We shall, then, find the function more easily if the cause is already known.

If the determination of function is thus to be delayed, it is still no less necessary for the complete explanation of the phenomena. Indeed, if the usefulness of a fact is not the cause of its existence, it is generally necessary that it be useful in order that it may maintain itself. For the fact that it is not useful suffices to make it harmful, since in that case it costs effort without bringing in any returns. If, then, the majority of social phenomena had this parasitic character, the budget of the organism would have a deficit and social life would be impossible. Consequently, to have a satisfactory understanding of the latter, it is necessary to show how the phenomena comprising it combine in such a way as to put society in harmony with itself and with the environment external to it. No doubt, the current formula, which defines social life as a correspondence between the internal and the external milieu, is only an approximation; however, it is in general true. Consequently, to explain a social fact it is not enough to show the cause on which it depends; we must also, at least in most cases, show its function in the establishment of social order.

REFERENCES

1. *Cours de philosophie positive*, IV, 262.
2. *Principles of Sociology*, II, 247.
3. Legal marriage with the mother establishes the father's rights over the children.
4. *Division du travail*, Book II, chaps. iii and iv.
5. We do not wish to raise here questions of general philosophy, which would not be in place. Let us say, however, that, if more profoundly analyzed, this reciprocity of cause and effect might furnish a means of reconciling scientific mechanism with the teleology which the existence, and especially the persistence, of life implies.
6. *Division du travail social*, Book II, chap. ii, notably pp. 105 ff.
7. *Ibid.*, pp. 52–53.
8. *Ibid.*, pp. 301 ff.

# STRUCTURE AND FUNCTION IN PRIMITIVE SOCIETY * (*Radcliffe-Brown*)

## On the Concept of Function in Social Science

The concept of function applied to human societies is based on an analogy between social life and organic life. The recognition of the analogy and

* Reprinted from the *American Anthropologist*, Vol. XXXVII, 1935, and as reprinted in *Structure and Function in Primitive Society*, copyright by Cohen & West (London); by permission of both publishers and the author.

of some of its implications is not new. In the nineteenth century the analogy, the concept of function, and the word itself appear frequently in social philosophy and sociology. So far as I know the first systematic formulation of the concept as applying to the strictly scientific study of society was that of Emile Durkheim in 1895. (*Règles de la Méthode Sociologique.*)

Durkheim's definition is that the 'function' of a social institution is the correspondence between it and the needs (*besoins* in French) of the social organism. This definition requires some elaboration. In the first place, to avoid possible ambiguity and in particular the possibility of a teleological interpretation, I would like to substitute for the term "needs" the term "necessary condition of existence," or, if the term "need" is used, it is to be understood only in this sense. It may be here noted, as a point to be returned to, that any attempt to apply this concept of function in social science involves the assumption that there *are* necessary conditions of existence for human societies just as there are for animal organisms, and that they can be discovered by the proper kind of scientific enquiry.

For the further elucidation of the concept it is convenient to use the analogy between social life and organic life. Like all analogies it has to be used with care. An animal organism is an agglomeration of cells and interstitial fluids arranged in relation to one another not as an aggregate but as an integrated living whole. For the biochemist, it is a complexly integrated system of complex molecules. The system of relations by which these units are related is the organic structure. As the terms are here used the organism is *not* itself the structure; it is a collection of units (cells or molecules) arranged in a structure, i.e., in a set of relations; the organism *has* a structure. Two mature animals of the same species and sex consist of similar units combined in a similar structure. The structure is thus to be defined as a set of relations between entities. (The structure of a cell is in the same way a set of relations between complex molecules, and the structure of an atom is a set of relations between electrons and protons.) As long as it lives the organism preserves a certain continuity of structure although it does not preserve the complete identity of its constituent parts. It loses some of its constituent molecules by respiration or excretion; it takes in others by respiration and alimentary absorption. Over a period its constituent cells do not remain the same. But the structural arrangement of the constituent units does remain similar. The processs by which this structural continuity of the organism is maintained is called life. The life-process consists of the activities and interactions of the constituent units of the organism, the cells, and the organs into which the cells are united.

As the word function is here being used the life of an organism is conceived as the *functioning* of its structure. It is through and by the continuity of the functioning that the continuity of the structure is preserved. If we consider any recurrent part of the life-process, such as respiration, digestion, etc., its *function* is the part it plays in, the contribution it makes to, the life of the organism as a whole. As the terms are here being used a cell or an organ has an *activity* and that activity has a *function*. It is true that we commonly speak of the secretion of gastric fluid as a "function" of the stomach. As the words are here used we should say that this is an "activity" of the stomach, the "function" of which is to change the proteins of food into a form in which these are absorbed and distributed by the blood of the tissues.[1] We may note that the function of a recurrent physiological process is thus a correspondence between it and the needs (i.e., necessary conditions of existence) of the organism.

If we set out upon a systematic investigation of the nature of organisms and organic life, there are three sets of problems presented to us. (There are, in addition, certain other sets of problems concerning aspects or characteristics of organic life with which we are not here concerned.) One is that of morphology—what kinds of organic structures are there, what similarities and variations do they show, and how can they be classified? Second are the problems of physiology—how, in general, do organic structures function, what, therefore, is the nature of the life-process? Third are the problems of evolution or development—how do new types of organisms come into existence?

To turn from organic life to social life, if we examine such a community as an African or Australian tribe we can recognize the existence of a social structure. Individual human beings, the essential units in this instance, are connected by a definite set of social relations into an integrated whole. The continuity of the social structure, like that of an organic structure, is not destroyed by changes in the units. Individuals may leave the society, by death or otherwise; others may enter it. The continuity of structure is maintained by the process of social life, which consists of the activities and interactions of the individual human beings and of the organised groups into which they are united. The social life of the community is here defined as the *functioning* of the social structure. The *function* of any recurrent activity, such as the punishment of a crime, or a funeral ceremony, is the part it plays in the social life as a whole and therefore the contribution it makes to the maintenance of the structural continuity.

The concept of function as here defined thus involves the notion of a structure consisting of a set of relations amongst unit entities, the continuity of the structure being maintained by a life-process made up of the activities of the constituent units.

If, with these concepts in mind, we set out on a systematic investigation of the nature of the human society and of social life, we find presented to us three sets of problems. First, the problems of social morphology—what kinds of social structures are there, what are their similarities and differences, how are they to be classified? Second, the problems of social physiology—how do social structures function? Third, the problems of development—how do new types of social structure come into existence?

Two important points where the analogy between organism and society breaks down must be noted. In an animal organism, it is possible to observe the organic structure to some extent independently of its functioning. It is therefore possible to make a morphology which is independent of physiology. But in human society the social structure as a whole can only be observed in its functioning. Some of the features of social structure, such as the geographical distribution of individuals and groups can be directly observed, but most of the social relations which in their totality constitute the structure, such as relations of father and son, buyer and seller, ruler and subject, cannot be observed except in the social activities in which the relations are functioning. It follows that a social morphology cannot be established independently of a social physiology.

The second point is that an animal organism does not, in the course of its life, change its structural type. A pig does not become a hippopotamus. (The development of the animal from germination to maturity is not a change of type since the process in all its stages is typical for the species.) On the other hand a society in the course of its history can and does change its structural type without any breach of continuity.

By the definition here offered "function" is the contribution which a partial activity makes to the total activity of which it is a part. The function of a particular social usage is the contribution it makes to the total social life as the functioning of the total social system. Such a view implies that a social system (the total social structure of a society together with the totality of social usages in which that structure appears and on which it depends for its continued existence) has a certain kind of unity, which we may speak of as a functional unity. We may define it as a condition in which all parts of the social system work together with a sufficient degree of harmony or internal consistency, i.e., without producing persistent conflicts which can neither be resolved nor regulated.[2]

This idea of the functional unity of a social system is, of course, a hypothesis. But it is one which, to the functionalist, it seems worth while to test by systematic examination of the facts.

There is another aspect of functional theory that should be briefly mentioned. To return to the analogy of social life and organic life, we recognise that an organism may function more or less efficiently and so we set up a special science of pathology to deal with all phenomena of disfunction. We distinguish in an organism what we call health and disease. The Greeks of the fifth century B.C. thought that one might apply the same notion to society, to the city-state, distinguishing conditions of *eunomia,* good order, social health, from *dysnomia,* disorder, social ill-health. In the nineteenth century Durkheim, in his application of the notion of function, sought to lay the basis for a scientific social pathology, based on a morphology and a physiology.[3] In his works, particularly those on suicide and the division of labour, he attempted to find objective criteria by which to judge whether a given society at a given time is normal or pathological, eunomic or dysnomic. For example, he tried to show that the increase of the rate of suicide in many countries during part of the nineteenth century is symptomatic of a dysnomic or, in his terminology, anomic, social condition. Probably there is no sociologist who would hold that Durkheim really succeeded in establishing an objective basis for a science of social pathology.[4]

In relation to organic structures we can find strictly objective criteria by which to distinguish disease from health, pathological from normal, for disease is that which either threatens the organism with death (the dissolution of its structure) or interferes with the activities which are characteristic of the organic type. Societies do not die in the same sense that animals die and therefore we cannot define dysnomia as that which leads, if unchecked, to the death of a society. Further, a society differs from an organism in that it can change its structural type, or can be absorbed as an integral part of a larger society. Therefore we cannot define dysnomia as a disturbance of the usual activites of a social type (as Durkheim tried to do).

Let us return for a moment to the Greeks. They conceived the health of an organism and the eunomia of a society as being in each instance a condition of the harmonious working together of its parts.[5] Now this, where society is concerned, is the same thing as what was considered above as the functional unity or inner consistency of a social system, and it is suggested that for the degree of functional unity of a particular society it may be possible to establish a purely objective criterion. Admittedly this cannot be done at present; but the socience of human society is as yet in its extreme infancy. So that it may be that we should say that, while an organism that is attacked by a virulent disease will react thereto, and, if its reaction fails, will die, a society that is thrown into a condition of functional disunity or inconsistency (for this we now provisionally identify with dysnomia) will not die, except in such comparatively rare instances as an Australian tribe, overwhelmed by the white man's destructive force, but will continue to struggle toward some sort of eunomia, some kind of social health, and may, in the course of this, change its structural type. This process, it seems, the "functionalist" has ample opportunities of observing at the present day, in native peoples subjected to the domination of the civilised nations, and in those nations themselves.[6]

Space will not allow a discussion here of another aspect of functional theory, viz. the question whether change of social type is or is not dependent on function, i.e., on the laws of social physiology. My own view is that there is such a dependence and that its nature can be studied in the development of the legal and political institutions, the economic systems and the religions of Europe through the last twenty-five centuries. For the preliterate societies with which anthropology is concerned, it is not possible to study the details of long processes of change of type. The one kind of change which the anthropologist can observe is the disintegration of social structures. Yet even here we can observe and compare spontaneous movements towards reintegration. We have, for instance, in Africa, in Oceania, and in America the appearance of new religions which can be interpreted on a functional hypothesis as attempts to relieve a condition of social dysnomia produced by the rapid modification of the social life through contact with white civilization.

The concept of function as defined above constitutes a "working hypothesis" by which a number of problems are formulated for investigation. No scientific enquiry is possible without some such formulation of working hypothesis. Two remarks are necessary here. One is that the hypothesis does not require the dogmatic assertion that everything in the life of every community has a function. It only requires the asumption that it may have one, and that we are justified in seeking to discover it. The second is that what appears to be the same social usage in two societies may have different functions in the two. Thus the practice of celibacy in the Roman Catholic Church of today has very different functions from those of celibacy in the early Christian Church. In other words, in order to define a social usage, and therefore in order to make valid comparisons between the usages of different peoples or periods, it is necessary to consider not merely the form of the usage but also its function. On this basis, for example, belief in a Supreme Being in a simple society is something different from such a belief in a modern civilised community.

The acceptance of the functional hypothesis or point of view outlined above results in the recognition of a vast number of problems for the solution of which there are required wide comparative studies of societies of many diverse types and also intensive studies of as many single societies as possible. In field studies of the simpler peoples it leads, first of all, to a direct study of the social life of the community as the functioning of a social structure, and of this there are several examples in recent literature. Since the function of a social activity is to be found by examining its effects upon individuals, these are studied, either in the average individual or in both average and exceptional individuals. Further, the hypothesis leads to attempts to investigate directly the functional consistency or unity of a social system and to determine as far as possible in each instance the nature of that unity. Such field studies will obviously be different in many ways from studies carried out from other points of view, e.g., the ethnological point of view that lays emphasis on diffusion. We do not have to say that one point of view is better than another, but only that they are different, and any particular piece of work should be judged in reference to what it aims to do.

If the view here outlined is taken as one form of "functionalism," a few remarks on Dr. Lesser's paper become permissible. He makes reference to a difference of "content" in functional and non-functional anthropology. From the point of view here presented the "content" or subject-matter of social anthropology is the whole social life of a people in all its aspects. For convenience of handling it is often necessary to devote special attention to some particular part or aspect of the social life, but if functionalism means anything at all it does mean the attempt to see the social life of a people as a whole, as a functional unity.

Dr. Lesser speaks of the functionalist as stressing "the psychological aspects of culture," I presume that he here refers to the functionalists' recognition that the usages of a society work or "function" only through their effects in the life, i.e., in the thoughts, sentiments and actions of individuals.

The "functionalist" point of view here presented does therefore imply that we have to investigate as thoroughly as possible all aspects of social life, considering them in relation to one another, and that an essential part of the task is the investigation of the individual and of the way in which he is moulded by or adjusted to the social life.

Turning from content to method Dr. Lesser seems to find some conflict between the functional point of view and the historical. This is reminiscent of the attempts formerly made to see a conflict between sociology and history. There need be no conflict, but there is a difference.

There is not, and cannot be, any conflict between the functional hypothesis and the view that any culture, any social system, is the end-result of a unique series of historical accidents. The process of development of the race-horse from its five-toed ancestor was a unique series of historical accidents. This does not conflict with the view of the physiologist that the horse of today and all the antecedent forms conform or conformed to physiological laws, i.e., to the necessary conditions of organic existence. Palaeontology and physiology are not in conflict. One "explanation" of the race-horse is to be found in its history—how it came to be just what it is and where it is. Another and entirely independent "explanation" is to show how the horse is a special exemplification of physiological laws. Similarly one "explanation" of a social system will be its history, where we know it—the detailed account of how it came to be what it is and where it is. Another "explanation" of the same system is obtained by showing (as the functionalist attempts to do) that it is a special exemplification of laws of social physiology or social functioning. The two kinds of explanation do not conflict, but supplement one another.[7]

The functional hypothesis is in conflict with two views that are held by some ethnologists, and it is probably these, held as they often are without precise formulation, that are the cause of the antagonism to that approach. One is the "shreds and patches" theory of culture, the designation being taken from a phrase of Professor Lowie[8] when he speaks of "that planless hodgepodge, that thing of shreds and patches called civilisation." The concentration of attention on what is called the diffusion of culture-traits tends to produce a conception of culture as a collection of disparate entities (the so-called traits) brought together by pure historical accident and having only accidental relations to one another. The conception is rarely formulated and maintained with any precision, but as a half-unconscious point of view it does seem to control the thinking of many ethnologists. It is, of course, in direct conflict with the hypothesis of the functional unity of social systems.

The second view which is in direct conflict with the functional hypothesis is the view that there are no discoverable significant sociological laws such as the functionalist is seeking. I know that some two or three ethnologists say that they hold this view, but I have found it impossible to know what they mean, or on what sort of evidence (rational or empirical) they would base their contention. Generalisations about any sort of subject matter are of two kinds: the generalisations of common opinion, and generalisations that have been verified or demonstrated by a systematic examination of evidence afforded by precise observations systematically made. Generalisations of the latter kind are called scientific laws. Those who hold that there are no laws of human society cannot hold that there are no generalisations about human society because they themselves hold such generalisations and even make new ones of their own. They must therefore hold that in the field of social phenomena, in contradistinction to physical and biological phenomena, any attempt at the systematic testing of existing generalisations or towards the discovery and verification of new ones, is, for some unexplained reason, futile, or, as Dr. Radin puts it, "crying for the moon." Argument against such a contention is unprofitable or indeed impossible.

REFERENCES

1. The insistence on this precise form of terminology is only for the sake of the analogy that is to be drawn. I have no objection to the use of the term "function" in physiology to denote both the activity of an organ and the results of that activity in maintaining life.
2. Opposition, i.e., organised and regulated antagonism, is, of course, an essential feature of every social system.
3. For what is here called dysnomia Durkheim used the term "anomia" (*anomie* in French). This is to my mind inappropriate. Health and disease, eunomia and dysnomia, are essentially relative terms.
4. I would personally agree in the main with the criticism of Roger Lacombe (*La Méthode Sociologique de Durkheim*, 1926, ch. iv) on Durkheim's general theory of social pathology, and with the criticisms of Durkheim's treatment of suicide presented by Halbwachs, *Les Causes du Suicide*.
5. See, for example, the Fourth Book of Plato's *Republic*.
6. To aviod misunderstanding it is perhaps necessary to observe that this distinction of eunomic and dysnomic social conditions does not give us any evaluation of these societies as "good" or "bad." A savage tribe practicing polygamy, cannibalism, and sorcery can possibly show a higher degree of functional unity or consistency than the United States of 1935. This objective judgment, for such it must be if it is to be scientific, is something very different from any judgment as to which of the two social systems is the better, the more to be desired or approved.
7. I see no reason at all why the two kinds of study—the historical and the functional—should not be carried on side by side in perfect harmony. In fact, for fourteen years I have been teaching both the historical and geographical study of peoples under the name of ethnology in close association with archaeology, and the functional study of social systems under the name of social anthropology. I do think that there are many disadvantages in mixing the two subjects together and confusing them. See 'The Methods of Ethnology and Social Anthropology' (*South African Journal of Science*, 1923, pp. 124–47).
8. *Primitive Society*, p. 441. A concise statement of this point of view is the following passage from Dr. Ruth Benedict's "The Concept of the Guardian Spirit in North America" (*Memoirs*, American Anthropological Association, 29, 1923), p. 84: "It is, so far as we can see, an ultimate fact of human nature that man builds up his culture out of disparate elements, combining and recombining them; and until we have abandoned the superstition that the result is an organism functionally interrelated, we shall be unable to see our cultural life objectively, or to control its manifestations." I think that probably neither Professor Lowie nor Dr. Benedict would, at the present time, maintain this view of the nature of culture.

# FUNCTIONALISM IN ANTHROPOLOGY*
(*Malinowski*)

*The Functional Analysis of Culture.*   This type of theory aims at the explanation of anthropological facts at all levels of development by their function, by the part which they play within the integral system of culture, by the manner in which they are related to each other within the system, and by the manner in which this system is related to the physical surroundings. It aims at the understanding of the nature of culture, rather than at conjectural reconstructions of its evolution or of past historical events.

Two factors contribute toward the development of the functional point of view. The modern specialist field-worker soon recognises that in order to *see* the facts of savage life, it is necessary to understand the nature of the cultural process. Description cannot be separated from explanation, since in the words of a great physicist, "explanation is nothing but condensed description." Every observer should ruthlessly banish from his work conjecture, preconceived assumptions and hypothetical schemes, but not theory.

Modern field work thus regards a theory as purely empirical, never going beyond inductive evidence, serving only to gain an insight into the mechanism of culture in its various phases: social organisation, belief and material outfit. The field-worker who lives among savages soon discards the antiquarian outlook. He sees every implement constantly used; every custom backed up by strong feeling and cogent ideas; every detail of social organisation active and effective. He perceives that culture, above all, provides primitive man with the means of satisfying his wants, and of mastering his surroundings. The functional view of culture insists therefore upon the principle that in every type of civilisation, every custom, material object, idea and belief fulfills some vital function, has some task to accomplish, represents an indispensable part within a working whole.

It keeps always in mind the biological basis of human civilisation, the correlation of culture to human wants, hence to human instincts and emotional dispositions. Instincts, emotions and ideas cannot, however, be treated by biology alone but must be approached through the study of mental proc-

* By Bronislaw Malinowski, reprinted from "Anthropology," *Encyclopaedia Britannica,* first supplementary volume, 1936, pp. 132–139, with permission of the publisher.

ess. Psychology, therefore, is indispensable for due understanding of culture.

At the same time the functional view teaches that man in the very fact of culture transcends his biological outfit. In his implements, weapons, clothes and ornaments he extends his anatomical endowment, whether to protect his life, to charm his fellow-beings or to procure his nourishment. Knowledge supplies man with responses which go far beyond anything implied in instinct. In dogmatic belief we have a new type of mental attitude not observed in animals. Biology is therefore not enough to explain human adjustments through culture. Psychology again is not sufficient, for man does all important business in common, while every individual contribution has to be translated into cultural fact, imprinted upon material objects and linked with social organisation. The other approach to the functional method is from the evolutionary point of view, nowadays generally discredited and discarded, yet fundamentally sound when correctly set forth. The development of culture consists in the gradual crystallisation of well-defined institutions out of mixed and non-specialised behaviour. The essential features of each institution remain permanent while the less relevant ones change considerably. In order to understand, however, what is essential and what is not, it is necessary to define each institution and custom by its function. Again since the essence of evolution consists not in a sequence of different forms changing one into another, but in a better adaptation of an institution to its function, the more precise way of posing the evolutionary problem leads inevitably to the functional point of view.

The functional view of culture can be traced back to the inchoate but stimulating writings of A. Bastian, to the suggestions of Lazarus and Steinthal, to the work of E. B. Tylor and W. Robertson Smith. It is implied in the best achievements of modern field-work (notably of the American anthropologists, F. Boas; J. W. Fewkes; C. Wissler; A. Fletcher and La Flèche; A. E. Jenks; A. L. Kroeber; Elsie C. Parsons; J. R. Swanton, P. E. Goddard; J. O. and G. A. Dorsey; R. H. Lowie; F. C. Cole; P. Radin; E. Sapir; Ruth Benedict). It has been active in the work of the French school, where it is constantly gaining ground (compare the latest publications of MM. Davy, Fauconnet, Granet, Mauss and Rivet). Functional interpretations will be found predominant among the soundest theories of the comparative school (Brinton; H. Schurtz; W. Wundt; J. G. Frazer; H. Webster; E. A. Crawley; Westermarck; Van Gennep; Marett). The comparative school however has allowed the evolutionary view to overshadow the functional method, while most American anthropologists have failed to disentangle the empirical interpretation of culture in terms of function from reconstruction in terms of conjectural history. They have thus lapsed into a type of explanation which at its best belongs to archaeology, and thus have greatly sterilised their otherwise splendid field-work and stimulating theory.

Recently, however, and among a small number of anthropologists only, the functional method has been applied systematically and exclusively in field-work and theory (W. Hoernlé; B. Malinowski; A. Radcliffe-Brown; Richard Thurnwald).

The functional method, by showing what culture does for a primitive community, establishes its value and thus utters a warning against too hasty interference with native belief and institution and too wasteful an exploitation of native labour and resources. By demonstrating how primitive custom and law work, it furnishes the administrator with practical hints of how to frame and administer native regulations. By inquiring into savage economic organisation, the functional method can teach how to manage indigenous labour and how to trade with the natives. By a sympathetic study of early belief and ritual, it can instruct the missionary how to graft a new creed upon the old one without destroying what is good and sound in it.

The functional method, concerned as it is with the actual working and mechanism of primitive culture, supplies the right theoretical foundation for the practical application of anthropology (*see* ANTHROPOLOGY, APPLIED), for which mere antiquarian reconstructions, whether historical or evolutionary, are irrelevant.

The following analysis of concrete problems is carried out from a functional point of view.

## The Cultural Function of Marriage and Family

This is perhaps the most debated and the most instructive of all anthropological problems.

*The institutions of marriage and family.* Careful inductive comparison reveals one important indication: marriage and family are almost universal, and can be traced through all types and levels of culture. Their universality can be accounted for by the functional analysis of these institutions. Two functions of paramount importance are fulfilled by any institution which regulates mating and propagation; the maintenance of racial quality and the maintenance of the continuity of culture. Sociological considerations prove that the individual family based on monogamous marriage provides the best opportunities for effective sexual selection. It also supplies the best training for the future cultural work and sociological orientation of the young individual (Lowie, Kroeber, E. C.

Parsons). The importance of the family as the early social and cultural pattern for later life has been independently established by anthropology and psychoanalysis (A. Radcliffe-Brown, J. C. Flügel). The family is the link between instinctive endowment and the acquisition of cultural inheritance, in that it permits the biological bonds between parent and infant gradually to ripen into social ties. It also eliminates a number of dangers due to the disruptive factors of the sexual instinct.

*Regulated licence.* This phenomenon does not allow of a simple and satisfactory solution. As culture advances and larger numbers of men and women come into contact, the experimental component of the sexual instinct drives people to indiscriminate mating. Freedom in pre-nuptial intercourse, festive licence, religious prostitution, lewd marriage ceremonies are the rule in savage and barbarous communities, with the exception perhaps of those on the lowest level (Schmidt and Koppers). Again, in some tribes the institution of marriage suffers temporary obliteration in the form of wife-lending or exchange, *jus primae noctis*, sexual over-rights of chiefs and magicians and similar relaxations of the matrimonial type. These customs have been explained as "survivals of primitive promiscuity." That such an explanation is untenable has been convincingly shown by Westermarck. There are two ways of regulating the intercourse between the sexes: either by suppressing all irregular mating, or by allowing a well-defined and limited licence. Biology and psycho-analytic theory teach that stern repression and rigid sex morals are not a complete solution of the problems here involved. Anthropology, moreover, shows that this problem is especially present at low levels of culture. According to some authorities, a regulated and limited licence should be considered as an imperfect but effective way of dealing with the disruptive forces of sex. Such regulation, moreover, is in no savage tribe found to be subversive to the fundamental institutions of marrige and the family which exist in spite of it everywhere.

At the same time, there is not one single tribe where sexual licence is found untrammelled, where anything approaching promiscuity obtains. Two forms of regulation are found everywhere: the strict prohibition of the wife's adultery safeguards the bonds of marriage and is only now and then overruled by exceptional customs; the prohibition of incest within the household safeguards the integrity of the family. This is very often extended to exogamy which embraces the whole clan.

*The clan.* The clan and the classificatory principle of kinship appear on a closer sociological analysis not to be substitutes for the family and household, but the outcome of more extended co-operation in matters other than sexual mating and the rearing of children (A. Radcliffe-Brown, A. L.

Kroeber, Thurnwald). The clan functions principally in economic, legal, and above all, in ceremonial matters. It is also closely connected with age-grades, secret societies and men's clubs wherever these exist; with the ceremonial distributions of wealth (the *kula,* the *potlatch* or the *hakari*), with magical specialisation and co-operation. Thus, in its functional definition, the clan represents the non-sexual and non-genetic extension of the kinship principle beyond the household and above the natural function of the family. Exogamy again appears as an additional bond of solidarity—a natural extension of the principle of incest running side by side with the extension of the kinship principle. As the link between the individual family and the wider groupings of local and political type, the clan is of special importance.

The clan is always due to the over-emphasis of one side of kinship—an over-emphasis necessary to eliminate any ambiguity in the transmissions of heredity rights and obligations. This has been aptly summed up by Dr. Lowie in his terminology of bilateral and unilateral kinship. The clan appears therefore as the natural result of the two influences which come into the foreground as culture advances: the continuity of tradition on the one hand and the extension of co-operation on the other. The clan allows of the establishment of greater cohesion within each generation and across succeeding generations. The explanation here given accounts for the institution, neither by an accident nor by specific ideas, nor by a hypothetical primitive communism in sexual matters, but by reference to certain deep-seated influences of cultural progress working before our very eyes. With all this, although the clan is of great benefit for society and culture, it never becomes an absolute necessity like the family. It is rather a symptom of advancing social differentiation than its inevitable effect. Thus, although the family and marriage are found to be universal, there exist tribes without any subdivisions into clans, moieties or matrimonial classes. Further, since the clan is associated with the general scheme of development, it cannot be regarded as a fortuitous index of this or that culture.

*Mother-right and father-right.* The correlated phenomenon of unilateral kinship also plays a very important part in diffusionist schemes. Mother-right and father-right respectively have been taken by Ankermann, Graebner, Rivers, W. Schmidt and Koppers as principal indices in their classification of cultures. But the question arises, is either mother-right or father-right an independent element, or are they both always correlated? It seems, however, that mother-right and father-right are never found in isolation, but always co-exist—one of them emphasised by the tribal law and the economic arrangements, the other, though subordinate, never completely absent. Until the problem thus raised has been solved, until the proof is given that mother-right and father-right can exist as exclusive, sharply defined stages or sociological principles, their use as indices of culture, and evidence of its spread must remain meaningless. Here again, functional analysis of the methods of reckoning descent leads to a clear definition of such concepts, indispensable for their use in any speculative constructions.

*Problem of sex.* Thus the family, the clan, sexual restrictions, as well as sexual liberties, are not the stages of a transformation nor fortuitous indices of cultural type or cultural stratum, but correlated, component parts of one big institution: the institution which controls the mating of sexes, the pro-creation of offspring and the education of the young, and fulfills the integral function of racial and cultural continuity. The nature of its component elements is explained by the part which they play within this integral scheme. The functional method might also be extended to all the other aspects of organisation—territorial, political, legal and economic. Each is related to an essential need of human society and culture, distribution over its locality, defence, maintenance of order, and the production of necessaries and values.

## Economic Organisation

Until the researches of anthropologists in Melanesia, in New Zealand, in North-West America, in Africa, and in Micronesia revealed a wealth of material, and theoretical students laid stress on the cultural importance of primitive economics, there reigned in anthropology the simple, occupational view of primitive husbandry. Schemes of occupational stages or types, the collecting of food, hunting, fishing, the tending of herds, the raising of crops and industrial production were set forward as the only subject matter of descriptive or analytical economics, as it is called.

In all such views, primitive man is regarded as having but simple elementary needs, and proceeding reasonably and naturally to satisfy them. The little spare time he has left over he devotes to the casual production of superfluities, and to the satisfaction of his hobbies, which latter activities, however, are usually placed outside the domain of economics. Thus we read in an authoritative work, *Notes and Queries in Anthropology:* "The first essential of maintenance is a supply of food; and in many simple communities the actual food quest and operations arising from it . . . . occupy by far the greater part of the people's time and energy, leaving little opportunity for the satisfaction of any lesser needs." And again, we are told by another writer (Buxton) that generally the savage "has no means to acquire more wealth than he can carry about on his person or on the persons of his family." The main questions cut short by such *a priori* assumptions are those of the incentives to production, of the organisation of labour and of the primitive forms of the apportionment of wealth.

*The economic motive.* Is it true then that primitives work only to satisfy their primary needs? In the lowest stages of culture people are ready to endure thirst and hunger, but bent upon stimulants or narcotics. We know of tribes without clothing, but of none without ornaments. There are natives without fixed habitations, yet keen on display of such wealth as they possess. At higher levels, under more favourable conditions, certain commodities are actually produced far in excess of actual needs. And this is not done "in exchange for food or for the means of obtaining it," as runs the usual opinion (*Notes and Queries*).

Nor is it carried out through economic foresight. Large quantities of accumulated food and wealth are employed instead for festive display, for ceremonial yet useless donations, sometimes even for mere destruction, often on a gigantic scale. All such customs serve merely for the manifestation of the wealth of the owner, of his generosity, of his economic power. In the South Seas, the accumulated food is employed for the production of objects of value by the feeding of artisans, who devote themselves to the polishing of axe-blades, to carving, to the making of shell ornaments or of mats (Thurnwald, Müller-Wissmar). Some of these early forms of valuable tokens of wealth have a distinctly religious character, serve in ritual ceremonies, are associated with belief and possess elaborate mythical pedigrees (Mauss). Finally, there is one very important fact which contradicts the merely utilitarian view of primitive economic incentives: the products of savage industries in general, far from being made with the minimum of effort required for their utility, show a lavishness of artistic detail, of decoration and pedantic finish, which often put to shame any civilised artisan. The joy in the work, the satisfaction of perfect craftsmanship, the artistic passion for the general appearance of the finished product dominate savage industries and enterprise.

It is clear from this evidence that the "first essentials of maintenance," the primary needs and the requirements of practical utility, do not exclusively control the economic effort of primitive man. Nor is their aim always to achieve the utilitarian maximum of effect by the minimum of effort. To understand the driving forces of early production, it is, therefore, not sufficient to make reference to man's animal needs. It is necessary to realise also the native ideas of value: their pleasure in the integral effect of their work in which artistic, sporting, social and even religious motives are mixed with those of pure utility.

*The character of early production.* The well-known scheme of K. Buecher, who would place the whole range of primitive husbandry within the limits of the "individual search for food" and of "closed household economy" is the clearest expression of the view that primitive man works for himself and his family alone, and that he knows no production on a wider, a communal or tribal scale.

A fuller insight into the nature of primitive labour reveals the existence of organisation. Even in the lowest cultures there are tasks which transcend the forces of one individual or of one family—the felling of trees, drive-hunting, the very collecting of food. At higher stages, such pursuits as communal hunting and fishing, the making of gardens, the construction of houses and canoes require some type of organised labour. This points to a definite specialisation, distribution and synchronisation in time, a division of functions, an integration of the individual contributions to the common end. If we enquire what are the elements of the economic organisation, it soon becomes clear that we must distinguish between moral or persuasive, and social or coercive factors. K. Buecher in a later work (*Arbeit und Rhythmus*) has drawn attention to the great importance of rhythm for successful work. Many other stimulants and incentives could be mentioned, the most efficient of which is unquestionably work in company. Conversation, jokes, mutual assistance and interest relieve the tedium of solitary labour, while emulation, example and the satisfaction of pride are under primitive conditions possible only in communal work. The best worker is always recognized as such among savages, and his leadership is followed. Much more important, however, is the moral prestige enjoyed by supernatural expert knowledge which, in the form of magic, always controls vital and difficult economic pursuits. Marking the dates, inaugurating the successive stages, imposing periods of rest and setting the time limits, it acts as an organising, co-ordinating influence.

Social coercion is the other important force of economic organisation. As soon as distinctions of rank and power arise they are used as means of extorting labour, while, on the other hand, economic inequalities function as indices of social status.

*Primitive ownership.* This economic problem has been discussed with some detail by anthropology. But while, on the one hand, the writers, who, like Buecher, assume an atomised economic production, admit only of individual or personal ownership, those following Morgan, and influenced by a strong socialistic bent, Engels, Bebel, Cunow, make the savage into a communist. As a matter of fact, property, which is but one form of legal relationship, is neither purely individualistic nor communal, but always mixed (*cf. Nature,* Supplement, Feb. 1926, on "Law and Order").

The misuse of such conceptions as "communism," associated with an incorrect application of the concept of "money" may be exemplified on a scheme recently put forward by the late Dr. Rivers. Dr. Rivers designates certain forms of valuables found in Melanesia, such as mats, arrows, pigs' jawbones and, above all, shell discs, as "money," following the usage of white traders, missionaries and planters. Dr. Rivers, to justify the use of this word, insists that these objects "are used for no other purpose" and "have a very definite scale of value," but he gives in other contexts a definite and concrete account of several ways in which these objects are used "for other purposes," and thus stultifies his first criterion. The second criterion is obviously insufficient for identifying a commodity as "money." All objects have in our economy "a very definite scale of value," yet we do not apply the word money to a pair of slippers, a motor-car or a picture by Raphael, nor use these things as such.

Now the taking of terminological liberties with well-defined concepts has its dangers. "Money" has no sooner been introduced into the argument than communism crops up and the two are related by a remarkable piece of reasoning:

> *The subject of communism in property is closely connected with that of money. A thoroughly communistic people can have no use for money among themselves. If they possess anything which can be regarded as currency, it can only be used in transaction with other peoples. The use of money should therefore be associated with the disappearance of communism; if it can be shown that Melanesian money is due to immigrant influence, and especially to that of the Kava people, we shall have gone far to establish the conclusions already suggested.* (History of Melanesian Society, vol. 2, p. 385.)

And again:

> *A thoroughly communistic people would have no need for money, and any explanation of the communism of Polynesia will therefore furnish also the explanation of the absence of money* (p. 392).

And as an "historical explanation" of these facts:

> *The explanation of the absence of money in Polynesia and of the communism of its people is to be found in the special mode of settlement of the Kava people* (p. 393).

These passages furnish a conspicuous example of how ill-defined concepts lead to far-fetched schemes and unsound constructions.

*Summary.*  To sum up briefly, it is incorrect to assume that man for a long time has lived in a semi-natural primitive stage of individual acquisition of food and primary utilities. Equally untrue is the correlated assumption that he lifted himself out of this condition by the gradual application of the economic principle of maximum of effect for the minimum of effort. Instead, from the outset, artificial, cultural, non-instinctive aims have been indispensable to him and his culture. Early types of value and symbols of wealth have spurred him from the outset to economic effort. This effort is organised and standardised by tradition. The real problem, therefore, consists in gaining insight into the primitive forms of condensed wealth, into the mixture of motives and impulses which drive man; and in studying the manner in which these primitive incentives control organised effective effort. All the conclusions arrived at show that for the discussion of economic problems it is necessary to consider the relation of early wealth to religion and to magic as well as its function in primitive social structure.

The borderland questions—the influence of economics on social structure; the problem of wealth as the foundation of rank, power and status; the rule of give-and-take in social obligations; ceremonial distribution of goods and its economic importance—are gradually coming into the forefront of anthropological interest, and open up entirely new horizons in theory and observances. They bring it into close contact with the disciplines of economics, history and sociology (Buecher, Schwiedland, M. Weber, K. Lamprecht).

The relation between the various larger aspects of culture opens a new type of problem. Social organisation is largely dependent upon economic foundations, while economics cannot be studied without a knowledge of the various groups within the tribe. Religion and magic are not independent, but are intimately associated with economic pursuits, with power and prestige, with domestic life and everyday necessities.

## The Supernatural

Here the functional view is put to its acid test. What can be the function of primitive belief and superstition, of animism considered as valueless, crude and mistaken, of magic, regarded as a spurious and fallacious pseudoscience, of totemism, of barbarous burial ceremonies and of cruel initiation rites? And yet the method here set forth stands and falls with the possibility of defining the whole of the supernatural. It is bound to show in what way belief and ritual work for social integration, technical and economic efficiency, for culture as a whole—indirectly therefore for the biological and mental welfare of each individual member.

*The current theories.*   Most modern theories in fact come near to the posing of this problem and to its solution. It is implied in the whole structure of Frazer's *Golden Bough,* in the contributions of Westermarck to the moral side of religion, in Durkheim's analysis of the integrative function of public ceremonial, in the additions of Hubert and Mauss to his theories, in Marett's analysis of magic, in Crawley's vitalistic view of religion, above all, in the analysis of Andaman belief and ceremonial by A. Radcliffe-Brown. But too often the functional view is still smothered by evolutionary or historical discussions—as to whether magic preceded religion, as to what was the primitive form of religion, and so on.

*Magic.*   The great number of modern theories dealing with magic range between two apparently opposed views, which label magic as primitive science or primitive stupidity (*Urdummheit*) respectively. We must reject the implication of the first theory, that magic preceded science, and that it once did fulfill that function. It must be placed to the credit of this theory, however, that it does full justice to the practical context of magic. The second theory emphasising the central conception of impersonal ubiquitous force—*mana, orenda, wakan* rightly appreciates the difference between belief and knowledge; and brings out the mystical character of magic (Marett, Hubert and Mauss, Preuss).

The functional theory reconciles both points of view. Let us start from the close association of magic with practical activities. First, every practical pursuit amongst savages is always primarily based upon knowledge and is never exclusively controlled by magic. There are in all savage cultures certain activities in which technical ability, guided by knowledge, completely suffices. In others, the help of magic is also invoked. What are the respective contributions of knowledge and of magic to such a mixed activity? In its essentials the division of function between the two is very simple: as far as his knowledge goes, as far as he can safely rely on experience, reason and technical ability, the native—whether in his gardening or fishing, in the building of craft, in warfare or sailing—does not use magic. No savage has ever been observed to select the tree for his dug-out by divination, to bring forth seedlings by formulae without having planted them. Only where, in spite of knowledge and effort, the results still turn unaccountably against him, only when forces completely beyond his mental grasp and practical control baffle him—in dealing with garden pests, with the supply of fish and animals, in securing wind or weather, in preventing disaster at sea or in war, above all, in dealing with bodily decay, disease or personal accidents—does the savage resort to supernatural means of filling the lacunae in his practical power.

The type of belief met in magic is always an affirmation of man's power to deal with the situation by a rite or spell. This belief simply repeats in a standardised manner, what hope all the time has whispered within the individual's own mind. Again, the rite repeats in a fixed, definite form what the natural expression of emotions already contains, only, as a rite, it is carried out with a purpose and with the conviction that it is a means to an end.

When we compare the forms of the fixed magical ritual, they are remarkably akin to the response of upset equilibrium occurring under similar conditions. Black magic, which corresponds to the sentiment of hate, and which replaces the outbursts of impotent rage, contains in its most typical ritual of stabbing, pointing the bone, mimic destruction, in the text of its formulae, a reproduction of the various gestures, words and types of behaviour, which we can watch in the natural vent of the emotions. Exorcism of evil powers repeats in word and deed the reactions of fear.

In all practical activities, the successful ends, which hope vividly brings before the mental vision at moments of uncertainty and suspense, are connected in such ritual, which bridges over the fateful moments. Sir J. Frazer's apposite term of "imitative magic" and his exhaustive illustrations of his point of view illustrate also the present theory. Here it is only suggested that the association of "ideas," designated by Frazer as the cause of "imitative magic," can only be accounted for by our theory of imperfect biological adjustment induced by culture. Baffled instinct arouses emotional tension as well as a conflict of ideas and an impasse in conduct. Through magic, culture prescribes the adequate ideas, standardises the valuable emotional tone and establishes a line of conduct which carries man over the dangerous moment.

This new type of explanation, based on the functional method, shows how cultural behaviour, in the very act of bestowing immense benefits and advantages on man, also opens up new problems and creates new needs. To satisfy these a new type of behaviour, ritual practices and a new mental adjustment, faith or mystical outlook, come into being, thus providing an answer to the question which is always essential: What actual benefit does magic confer upon man, what is its positive contribution to culture? It is a remedy for specific maladjustments and mental conflicts, which culture creates in allowing man to transcend his biological equipment.

*Social consequences.*   In its traditional aspect, magic leads to important social consequences. It is the essence of magical lore that every word of a formula must be spoken correctly without omission or alteration, every detail of the rite performed. Since magical knowledge can live only in man's memory, the correct transmission, the legitimate filiation of magic are essential to man's confidence in its efficiency. The inheritance of magic is always one of the most important problems of descent and of the modes of reckoning kinship. As a rule, magic is handed on within the family circle.

In this connection it is important to stress that *all* forms of magic usually perform an important social rôle. No magic can be regarded as anti-social in the sense in which Durkheim and his school attempt to define it. Even sorcery or black magic functions as a legitimate though dangerous weapon, of which one of the main uses is in the enforcing of an established power and the biddings of law. The actual manner in which magic is connected with practical activities makes it, as we have seen, into the very skeleton of economic organisation. It supplies most of the co-ordinating and driving forces of labour, it develops the qualities of forethought, of order, of steadiness and punctuality, which are essential to all successful enterprise. Thus magic fulfils an indispensable function within culture. It satisfies a definite need which cannot be satisfied by any other factor of primitive civilisation.

*Totemism.* Totemism is a belief which affirms an intimate bond between a group of men and an animal or vegetable species, sometimes a class of objects. It raises therefore two problems, the first as to the nature of the belief, the second as to the social organisation with which it is linked.

Most theories saw its origin in some small or accidental detail of social organisation or belief, as in nicknames, guardian spirits, transmigration of souls and, recently, in the Freudian theory of parricide. To the functional theory the real problem, however, is: what is the function of a type of belief which affirms the affinity between man and animal, is correlated with clan organisation and leads to moral and ritual rules associated with the multiplication, killing and eating of animals?

Man's interest in his surroundings is primarily practical. He has to collect food, construct his dwelling, roam about his district to hunt or fish. In the forefront of importance are the animals in his territory—those which feed him, those whose skins clothe him, whose feathers, teeth and claws supply him with ornaments and those which threaten his safety or comfort. Hence the whole of animal life has an intense interest and significance for him.

Now in dealing with the animal kingdom, in obtaining the useful species to eat, in defending himself against the dangerous or repulsive ones, primitive man, where his natural means fail him, has recourse to supernatural ones. The magical claims over any aspect of nature lead always to an assertion of a sort of affinity or kinship between the magician and the object controlled. Indeed most magic implies mythological descent from animals or affiliation to them. Thus we see that the native's practical interest in the animal or vegetable kingdom leads through magic directly to the assertion of a mutual bond.

Magic has a tendency to become specialised and departmental, exclusive and hereditary in a kinship group or clan. The subdivision of the tribe into totemic clans seems to be best explained, therefore, by the hypothesis that such clans were originally magical bodies engaged in controlling, through spell and rite, certain animal or vegetable species for the welfare of the tribe.

*Summary.* In recent work (Frazer, Crawley, Van Gennep, Miss Jane Harrison) much stress has been laid upon the association of religion with the crises of life. In fact in most religions, savage or civilised, the main phases of human life history—conception and pregnancy, birth and puberty, marriage and death—are associated with belief, ritual and mythological stories. Religion therefore fulfils at vital crises an indispensable function in the scheme of human culture.

Culture entails a transformation of direct instinctive response into a mode of behaviour governed by purposive ends, that is, by cultural values. The super-instinctive type of behaviour leads man into impasses and difficulties out of which he can be extricated only by rules of thought and of behaviour which also have to be supplied by culture. In practical pursuits magic helps man over the difficulties. The rôle of religion consists in the establishment of spiritual ends, dogmatic realities and moral rules of conduct. In totemism, which sacralises important factors of the environment; in the belief in immortality and in the associated ideas about communion with spirits and their influence on human fate; in the consecration of food and of indispensable elements of culture, such as fire, standard implements, tokens of wealth; in surrounding tribal tradition and order by the halo of sanctity, religion is the source of social and cultural values.

# OBJECTIVE END AND SUBJECTIVE PURPOSE * (*Pareto*)

Every social phenomenon may be considered under two aspects: as it is in reality, and as it presents itself to the mind of this or that human being. The first aspect we shall call *objective*, the second *subjective*. Such a division is necessary, for we cannot put in one same class the operations performed by a chemist in his laboratory and the operations performed by a person practising magic; the conduct of Greek sailors in plying their oars to drive their ship over the water and the sacrifices they offered to Poseidon to make sure of a safe and rapid voyage. In Rome the Laws of the XII Tables punished anyone casting a spell on a harvest. We choose to distinguish such an act from the act of burning a field of grain.

We must not be misled by the names we give to the two classes. In reality both are subjective, for all human knowledge is subjective. They are to be distinguished not so much by any difference in nature as in view of the greater or lesser fund of factual knowledge that we ourselves have. We know, or think we know, that sacrifices to Poseidon have no affect whatsoever upon a voyage. We therefore distinguish them from other acts which (to our best knowledge, at least) are capable of having such effect. If at some future time we were to discover that we have been mistaken, that sacrifices to Poseidon are very influential in securing a favourable voyage, we should have to reclassify them with actions capable of such influence. All that of course is pleonastic. It amounts to saying that when a person makes a classification, he does so according to the knowledge he has. One cannot imagine how things could be otherwise.

There are actions that use means appropriate to ends and which logically link means with ends. There are other actions in which those traits are missing. The two sorts of conduct are very different according as they are considered under their objective or their subjective aspect. From the subjective point of view nearly all human actions belong to the logical class. In the eyes of the Greek mariners sacrifices to Poseidon and rowing with oars were equally logical means of navigation. To avoid verbosities which could only prove annoying, we had better give names to these types of con-

---

* Reprinted from *The Mind and Society* by Vilfredo Pareto, Vol. I, pp. 76–79, copyright, 1935, by Harcourt, Brace and Company, Inc. Reprinted by permission of the publishers.

duct.[1] Suppose we apply the term *logical actions* to actions that logically conjoin means to ends not only from the standpoint of the subject performing them, but from the standpoint of other persons who have a more extensive knowledge—in other words, to actions that are logical both subjectively and objectively in the sense just explained. Other actions we shall call *non-logical* (by no means the same as "illogical"). This latter class we shall subdivide into a number of varieties.

A synoptic picture of the classification will prove useful:

The ends and purposes here in question are immediate ends and purposes. We choose to disregard the indirect. The objective end is a real one, located within the field of observation and experience, and not an imaginary end, located outside that field. An imaginary end may, on the other hand, constitute a subjective purpose.

## *Genera and Species*
### *Have the Actions Logical Ends and Purposes:*

|  | OBJECTIVITY? | SUBJECTIVITY? |
|---|---|---|
| CLASS I: LOGICAL ACTIONS (The objective end and the subjective purpose are identical.) | | |
|  | Yes | Yes |
| CLASS II: NON-LOGICAL ACTIONS (The objective end differs from the subjective purpose.) | | |
| Genus 1 | No | No |
| Genus 2 | No | Yes |
| Genus 3 | Yes | No |
| Genus 4 | Yes | Yes |

SPECIES OF THE GENERA 3 AND 4

| 3a, 4a | The objective end would be accepted by the subject if he knew it. |
|---|---|
| 3b, 4b | The objective end would be rejected by the subject if he knew it. |

Logical actions are very numerous among civilized peoples. Actions connected with the arts and sciences belong to that class, at least for artists and scientists. For those who physically perform them in mere execution of orders from superiors, there may be among them non-logical actions of our II-4 type. The actions dealt with in political economy also belong in very great part in the class of logical actions. In the same class must be located, further, a certain number of actions connected with military, political, legal, and similar activities.

So at the very first glance induction leads to the discovery that non-logical actions play an important part in society. Let us therefore proceed with our examination of them.

First of all, in order to get better acquainted with these non-logical actions, suppose we look at a few examples. Many others will find their proper places in chapters to follow. Here are some illustrations of actions of Class II:

Genera 1 and 3, which have no subjective purpose, are of scant importance to the human race. Human beings have a very conspicuous tendency to paint a varnish of logic over their conduct. Nearly all human actions therefore work their way into genera 2 and 4. Many actions performed in deference to courtesy and custom might be put in genus 1. But very very often people give some reason or other to justify such conduct, and that transfers it to genus 2. Ignoring the indirect motive involved in the fact that a person violating common usages incurs criticism and dislike, we might find a certain number of actions to place in genera 1 and 3.

Says Hesiod:[2] "Do not make water at the mouth of a river emptying into the sea, nor into a spring. You must avoid that. Do not lighten your bowels there, for it is not good to do so." The precept not to befoul rivers at their mouths belongs to genus 1. No objective or subjective end or purpose is apparent in the avoidance of such pollution. The precept not to befoul drinking-water belongs to genus 3. It has an objective purpose that Hesiod may not have known, but which is familiar to moderns: to prevent contagion from certain diseases.

It is probable that not a few actions of genera 1 and 3 are common among savages and primitive peoples. But travellers are bent on learning at all costs the reasons for the conduct they observe. So in one way or another they finally obtain answers that transfer the conduct to genera 2 and 4.

REFERENCES

1. As we have already said (sections 116 f.), it would perhaps be better to use designations that have no meanings in themselves, such as letters of the alphabet. On the other hand, such a system would impair the clarity of our argument. We must therefore resign ourselves to using terms of ordinary speech; but the reader must bear in mind that such words, or their etymologies, in no way serve to describe the things they stand for. Things have to be examined directly. Names are just labels to help us keep track of them (section 119).
2. *Opera et dies,* vv. 757–58.

# A PARADIGM FOR FUNCTIONAL ANALYSIS IN SOCIOLOGY * (*Merton*)

As an initial and admittedly tentative step in the direction of codifying functional analysis in sociology, we set forth a paradigm of the concepts and problems central to this approach. As will become at once evident, the chief components of this paradigm have progressively emerged in the foregoing pages as we have critically examined the vocabularies, postulates, concepts and ideological imputations now current in the field. The paradigm brings these together in compact form, thus permitting simultaneous inspection of the major requirements of functional analysis and serving as an aid to self-correction of provisional interpretations, a result difficult to achieve when concepts are scattered and hidden in page after page of discursive exposition.[1] The paradigm presents the hard core of concept, procedure and inference in functional analysis.

Above all, it should be noted that the paradigm does not represent a set of categories introduced *de novo*, but rather a *codification* of those concepts and problems which have been forced upon our attention by critical scrutiny of current research and theory in functional analysis. (Reference to the preceding sections of this chapter will show that the groundwork has been prepared for every one of the categories embodied in the paradigm.)

## Paradigm for Functional Analysis in Sociology

1. *The item(s) to which functions are imputed*
   *The entire range of sociological data can be, and much of it has been, subjected to functional analysis. The basic requirement is that the object of analysis represent a standardized* (i.e. *patterned and repetitive) item, such as social roles, institutional patterns, social processes, cultural pattern, culturally patterned emotions, social norms, group organization, social structure, devices for social control, etc.*

   *Basic query: what must enter into the protocol of observation*

* Reprinted from *Social Theory and Social Structure* by Robert K. Merton, pp. 49–61, with permission of the publisher. The Free Press, Glencoe, Ill. Copyright, 1949, by The Free Press, A Corporation.

*of the given item if it is to be amenable to systematic functional analysis?*

2. *Concepts of subjective dispositions ( motives, purposes )*

At some point, functional analysis invariably assumes or explicitly operates with some conception of the motivation of individuals involved in a social system. As the foregoing discussion has shown, these concepts of subjective disposition are often and erroneously merged with the related, but different, concepts of objective consequences of attitude, belief and behavior.

Basic query: in which types of analysis is it sufficient to take observed motivation as data, as given, and in which are they properly considered as problematical, as derivable from other data?

3. *Concepts of objective consequences ( functions, dysfunctions )*
We have observed two prevailing types of confusion enveloping the several current conceptions of "function":

(1) the tendency to confine sociological observations to the positive contributions of a sociological item to the social or cultural system in which it is implicated; and

(2) the tendency to confuse the subjective category of motive with the objective category of function.

Appropriate conceptual distinctions are required to eliminate these confusions. The first problem calls for a concept of multiple consequences and a net balance of an aggregate of consequences.

Functions *are those observed consequences which make for the adaptation or adjustment of a given system; and* dysfunctions, *those observed consequences which lessen the adaptation or adjustment of the system. There is also the empirical possibility of* non-functional *consequences, which are simply irrelevant to the system under consideration.*

In any given instances, an item may have both functional and dysfunctional consequences, giving rise to the difficult and important problem of evolving canons for assessing the net balance of the aggregate of consequences. ( This is, of course, most important in the use of functional analysis for guiding the formation and enactment of policy.)

The second problem ( of confusion between motives and functions) requires us to introduce a conceptual distinction between the cases *in which the subjective aim-in-view coincides with the objective consequence, and the cases in which they diverge.*

Manifest functions *are those objective consequences contributing to the adjustment or adaptation of the system which are intended and recognized by participants in the system;*

Latent functions, *correlatively, being those which are neither intended nor recognized.*[2]

> Basic query: *what are the effects of seeking to transform a previously latent function into a manifest function (involving the problem of the role of knowledge in human behavior and the problems of "manipulation" of human behavior)?*

4. *Concepts of the unit subserved by the function*

We have observed the difficulties entailed in confining *analysis to functions fulfilled for "the society," since items may be functional for some individuals and subgroups and dsyfunctional for others. It is necessary, therefore, to consider a* range *of units affected by the given item: individuals in diverse statuses, subgroups, the larger social system and culture systems. (Terminologically, this implies the concepts of psychological function, group function, societal function, cultural function, etc.)*

5. *Concepts of functional requirements (needs, prerequisites)*

*Embedded in every functional analysis is some conception, tacit or expressed, of functional requirements of the system under observation. As noted elsewhere,*[3] *this remains one of the cloudiest and empirically most debatable concepts in functional theory. As utilized by sociologists, the concept of functional requirement tends to be tautological or* ex post facto; *it tends to be confined to conditions of "survival" of a given system; it tends, as in the work of Malinowski, to include biological as well as social "needs." This involves the difficult problem of establishing types of functional requirements (universal vs. highly specific); procedures for validating the assumption of these requirements; etc.*

> Basic query: *what is required to establish the validity of such an intervening variable as "functional requirement" in situations where rigorous experimentation is impracticable?*

6. *Concepts of the mechanisms through which functions are fulfilled*

*Functional analysis in sociology, as in other disciplines like physiology and psychology, calls for a "concrete and detailed" account of the mechanisms which operate to perform a given function. This refers, not to psychological, but to social, mechanisms (e.g., role-segmentation, insulation of institutional demands, hierarchic ordering of values, social division of labor, ritual and ceremonial enactments, etc.).*

>  *Basic query: what is the presently available inventory of social mechanisms corresponding, say, to the large inventory of psychological mechanisms? What are the methodological problems entailed in discerning the operation of these social mechanisms?*

7. *Concepts of functional alternatives (functional equivalents or substitutes)*

   *As we have seen, once we abandon the gratuitous assumption of the functional indispensability of given social structures, there is immediately required some concept of functional alternatives, equivalents, or substitutes. This focusses attention on the range of possible variation in the items which can, in the given instance, subserve a functional requirement. It unfreezes the identity of the existent and the inevitable.*

   >  *Basic query: since scientific proof of the equivalence of an alleged functional alternative ideally requires rigorous experimentation, and since this is not often practicable in large-scale sociological situations, which practicable procedures of inquiry most nearly approximate the logic of experiment?*

8. *Concepts of structural context (or structural constraint)*

   *The range of variation in the items which can fulfill designated functions within a given instance is not unlimited (and this has been repeatedly noted in our foregoing discussion). The interdependence of the elements of a social structure limit the effective possibilities of change or functional alternatives. The concept of structural constraint corresponds, in the area of social structure, to Goldenweiser's "principle of limited possibilities" in a broader sphere. Failure to recognize the relevance of interdependence and attendant structural restraints leads to utopian thought in which it is tacitly assumed that certain elements of a social system can be eliminated without affecting the rest of that system. This consideration is recognized by both Marxist social scientists (e.g., Karl Marx) and by non-Marxists (e.g., Malinowski).[4]*

Basic query: how narrowly does a given structural context limit the range of variation in the items which can effectively satisfy functional requirements? Do we find, under conditions yet to be determined, an area of indifference, in which any one of a wide range of alternatives may fulfill the function?

9. *Concepts of dynamics and change*

We have noted that functional analysts tend to focus on the statics of social structure and to neglect the study of structural change. The concept of dysfunction, which implies the concept of strain, stress and tension on the structural level, provides an analytical approach to the study of dynamics and change. How are observed dysfunctions contained within a given structure, so that they do not produce instability? Does the accumulation of stresses and strains produce pressure for change in such directions as are likely to lead to their reduction?

Basic query: does the prevailing concern among functional analysts with the concept of social equilibrium *divert attention* from the phenomena of social disequilibrium? Which available procedures will permit the sociologist most adequately to gauge the accumulation of stresses and strains in a given social system? To what extent does the structural context permit the sociologist to anticipate the most probable directions of social change?

10. *Problems of validation of functional analysis*

Throughout the paradigm, attention has been called repeatedly to the specific points at which assumptions, imputations and observations must be validated.[5] This requires, above all, a rigorous statement of the sociological procedures of analysis which most nearly approximate the logic of experimentation. It requires a systematic review of the possibilities and limitations of comparative (cross-cultural and cross-group) analysis.

Basic query: to what extent is functional analysis limited by the difficulty of locating adequate samples of social systems which can be subjected to comparative (quasi-experimental) study?[6]

11. *Problems of the ideological implications of functional analysis*

It has been emphasized in a preceding section, that functional analyisis has no intrinsic commitment to a given ideological position. This does not gainsay the fact that particular func-

*tional analysis and* particular *hypotheses advanced by functionalists may have an identifiable ideological role. This, then, becomes a specific problem for the sociology of knowledge: to what extent does the social position of the functional sociologist (e.g., vis-à-vis a particular "client" who has authorized a given research) evoke one rather than another formulation of a problem, affect his assumptions and concepts, and limit the range of inferences drawn from his data?*

*Basic query: how does one detect the ideological tinge of a given functional analysis and to what degree does a particular ideology stem from the basic assumptions adopted by the sociologist? Is the incidence of these assumptions related to the status and research role of the sociologist?*

Before proceeding to a more intensive study of some parts of this paradigm, let us be clear about the uses to which it is supposed the paradigm can be put. After all, taxonomies of concepts may be multiplied endlessly without materially advancing the tasks of sociological analysis. What, then, are the purposes of the paradigm and how might it be used?

PURPOSES OF THE PARADIGM

The first and foremost purpose is to supply a provisional codified guide for adequate and fruitful functional analysis. This objective evidently implies that the paradigm contains the minimum set of concepts with which the sociologist must operate in order to carry through an adequate functional analysis and, as a corollary, that it can be used here and now as a guide for the critical study of existing analyses. It is thus intended as an all-too-compact and elliptical guide to the formulation of researches in functional analysis and as an aid in locating the distinctive contributions and deficiencies of earlier researches. Limitations of space will permit us to apply only limited sections of the paradigm to a critical appraisal of a selected list of cases in point.

Secondly, the paradigm is intended to lead directly to the postulates and (often tacit) assumptions underlying functional analysis. As we have found in earlier parts of this chapter, some of these assumptions are of central importance, others insignificant and dispensable, and still others, dubious and even misleading.

In the third place, the paradigm seeks to sensitize the sociologist not only to the narrowly scientific implications of various types of functional analysis, but also to their political and sometimes ideological implications.

The points at which a given functional analysis presupposes an implicit political outlook and the points at which it has bearing on "social engineering" are concerns which find an integral place in the paradigm.

It is obviously beyond the limits of this chapter to explore in detail the large and inclusive problems involved in the paradigm. This must await fuller exposition in a volume devoted to this purpose. We shall, therefore, confine the remainder of the present discussion to brief applications of only the first parts of the paradigm to a severely limited number of cases of functional analysis in sociology. And, from time to time, these few cases will be used as a springboard for discussion of special problems which are only imperfectly illustrated by the cases in hand.

## Items Subjected to Functional Analysis

At first glance, it would appear that the sheer *description* of the item to be analyzed functionally entails few, if any, problems. Presumably, one should describe the item "as fully and as accurately" as possible. Yet, at second thought, it is evident that this maxim provides next to no guidance for the observer. Consider the plight of a functionally oriented neophyte armed only with this dictum as an aid to answering the question: *what* am I to observe, *what* am I to incorporate into my field notes, and *what* may I safely omit?

Without assuming that a detailed and circumstantial answer can now be supplied to the field worker, we can nevertheless note that the question itself is legitimate and that *implicit* answers have been partly developed. To tease out these implicit answers and to codify them, it is necessary to approach cases of functional analysis with the query: *what kinds of data have been consistently included, no matter what the item undergoing analysis, and why have these rather than any other data been included?*

It soon becomes apparent that the functionalist orientation largely determines what is included in the description of the item to be interpreted. Thus, the description of a magical performance or a ceremonial is not confined to an account of the spell or formula, the rite and the performers. It systematically includes a systematic account of the people participating and the onlookers, of the types and rates of interaction among performers and audience, of changes in these patterns of interaction in the course of the ceremonial. Thus, describing Hopi rain ceremonials, for example, entails describing more than the actions seemingly oriented toward the intervention of the gods in meteorological phenomena. It involves a report of *who* is variously involved in the pattern of behavior. And the description of the participants (and onlookers) is in *structural terms,* that is, in terms of locating these people in their inter-connected social statuses.

Brief excerpts will illustrate how functional analyses begin with a systematic inclusion (and, preferably, charting) of the statuses and social inter-relations of those engaging in the behavior under scrutiny.

> Chiricahua puberty ceremonial for girls: the extended domestic family (*parents and relatives financially able to help*) *bear the expense of this four-day ceremony. The parents select the time and place for the ceremonial.* "All the members of the girl's encampment *attend and nearly all the* members of the local group. A goodly sprinkling of visitors from *other local groups and some* travelers from outside bands *are to be seen, and their numbers increase as the day wears on." The* leader of the local group *to which the girl's family belongs speaks, welcoming all visitors. In short, this account explicitly calls attention to the following statuses and groups variously involved in the ceremonial: the girl; her parents and immediate family; the local group, especially through its leader; the band represented by members of outside local groups, and the "tribe by members of other bands."*[7]

As we shall see in due course, but it bears stating at this point, *the sheer description* of the ceremony (partly) in terms of the statuses and group affiliations of those variously involved *provides a major clue to the functions* performed by this ceremonial. In a word, we suggest that structural description of participants in the activity under analysis provides hypotheses for subsequent functional interpretations.

Another illustration will again indicate the nature of such descriptions in terms of role, status, group affiliation and the interrelations among these.

> Patterned responses to mirriri (hearing obscenity directed at one's sister) *among the Australian Murngin: the standardized pattern must be all too briefly described: when a husband swears at his wife in the presence of her brother, the brother engages in the seemingly anomalous behavior of throwing spears at the wife (not the husband) and her sisters. The description of this pattern goes on to include status descriptions of the participants. The* sisters *are members of the brother's* clan; *the husband comes from another* clan.
>
> *Note again that participants are* located *within social structures and this location is basic to the subsequent functional analysis of this behavior.*[8]

But these are cases drawn from non-literate society, and it may be assumed that this and other requirements for description are peculiar to non-literate materials. Turning to other instances of functional analyses of patterns found in modern Western society, we shall find this same requirement as well as additional guides to "needed descriptive data."

> The "romantic love complex" in American society: *although all societies recognize "occasional violent emotional attachments," contemporary American society is among the few which capitalize upon romantic attachments and in popular belief, at least, makes these the basis for choice of a marriage partner. This characteristic pattern of choice minimizes or eliminates the selection of one's mate by parents or the wider kinship group.*[9]

Note that the emphasis upon one pattern of choice of mates thereby excludes alternative patterns of choice known to occur elsewhere. This case suggests a *second* desideratum for a type of data to be included in the account of the item subjected to functional analysis. In describing the characteristic (modal) pattern for handling a standardized problem (choice of marriage-partner), the observer, wherever possible, indicates the alternatives which are thereby excluded. This, as we shall see, provides direct clues to the structural context of the pattern and, by suggesting pertinent comparative materials, points toward the validation of the functional analysis.

A *third* integral element of the description of the problematical item preparatory to the actual functional analysis—a further requirement for preparing the specimen for analysis, so to speak—is to include the *"meanings"* (or cognitive and affective significance) of the activity or pattern for members of the group. In fact, as will become evident, a fully circumstantial account of the meanings attached to the item goes far toward suggesting appropriate lines of functional analysis. A case drawn from Veblen's many functional analysis serves to illustrate the general thesis:

> The cultural pattern of conspicuous consumption: *the conspicuous consumption of relatively expensive commodities "means" (symbolizes) sufficient wealth to "afford" such expenditures and wealth in turn is honorific. Persons engaging in conspicuous consumption not only derive gratification from the direct consumption but also from the heightened status reflected in the attitudes and opinions of others who observe this consumption. This pattern is most notable among the leisure class, i.e., those who can and largely do refrain from productive labor [this is the status or role component*

*of the description]. However, it diffuses to other strata who seek to emulate the pattern and who likewise experience pride in "wasteful" expenditures. Finally, consumption in conspicuous terms tends to crowd out other criteria for consumption (e.g., "efficient" expenditure of funds)—[This is an explicit reference to alternative modes of consumption obscured from view by the cultural emphasis on the pattern under scrutiny.]*[10]

As is well known, Veblen goes on to impute a variety of functions to the pattern of conspicuous consumption—functions of aggrandizement of status, of validation of status, of "good repute," of display of pecuniary strength (p. 84)—which go far toward explaining the continuance of the pattern. *The clues to the imputed functions are provided almost wholly by the description of the pattern itself* which includes explicit references to (1) status of those differentially exhibiting the pattern, (2) known alternatives to the pattern of consuming in terms of display and "wastefulness" rather than in terms of private and "intrinsic" enjoyment of the item of consumption; and (3) the divers meanings culturally ascribed to the behavior of conspicuous consumption by participants in and observers of the pattern.

These three prerequisites for the description of the specimen to be analyzed are by no means exhaustive. A full descriptive protocol, adequate for subsequent functional analysis, will inevitably spill over into a range of immediate psychological and social consequences of the behavior. But these may be more profitably examined in connection with the concepts of function. It is here only necessary to repeat that the description of the item does not proceed according to whim or intuition, but must include at least these three characteristics of the item, if the preanalytical descriptive protocol is to be of optimum value for functional analysis. Though much remains to be learned concerning desiderata for the descriptive phase of the total analysis, this brief presentation of models for descriptive content may serve to indicate that procedures for functional analysis *can* be codified—ultimately to the point where the sociological field worker will have a chart of observation.

Another case illustrates a further desideratum for the description of the item to be analyzed.

> Taboo on out-marriage: *the greater the degree of group solidarity, the more marked the sentiment adverse to marriage with people outside the group. "It makes no difference what is the cause of the desire for group solidarity. . . ." Out-marriage means either losing one's group-member to another group or incorporation in one's*

*own group of individuals who have not been thoroughly socialized
in the values, sentiments and practices of the in-group.*[11]

This suggests a *fourth* type of datum to be included in the description of
the social or cultural specimen, prior to functional analysis. Inevitably, participants in the practice under scrutiny have *some* array of motives for conformity or for deviation. *The descriptive account should, so far as possible,
include an account of these motivations, but these motives must not be
confused, as we have seen, with (a) the objective pattern of behavior or
(b) with the social functions of that pattern.* Inclusion of motives in the
descriptive account helps explain the *psychological* functions subserved by
the pattern and often proves suggestive with respect to the social functions.

Thus far, we have been considering items which are clearly patterned
practices or beliefs, patterns recognized as such by participants in the society. Thus, members of the given society can, in varying degrees, describe
the contours of the Chiricahua puberty ceremony, of the Murngin mirriri
pattern, the choice of mates on the basis of romantic attachments, the concern with consuming conspicuously and the taboos on out-marriage. These
are all parts of the overt culture and, as such, are more or less fully known
to those who share in this culture. The social scientist, however, does not
confine himself to these overt patterns. From time to time, he uncovers a
covert cultural pattern, a set of practices or beliefs which is as consistently
patterned as overt patterns, but which is not regarded as a normatively
regulated pattern by the participants. Examples of this are plentiful. Thus,
statistics show that in a quasi-caste situation such as that governing Negro-
white relations in this country, the prevailing pattern of interracial marriage
(when it occurs) is between white females and Negro males (rather than
between Negro females and white males). This pattern, which we may call
caste hypogamy, is not institutionalized but it is persistent and remarkably
stable.[12]

Or, to take another instance of a fixed but apparently unrecognized pattern. Malinowski reports that Trobrianders cooperatively engaged in the
technological task of building a canoe are engaged not only in that explicit
technical task but also in establishing and reinforcing interpersonal relations
among themselves in the process. Much of the recent data on those primary
groups called "informal organizations," deals with these patterns of relations
which are observed by the social scientist but unrecognized, at least in their
full implications, by the participants.[13]

All this points to a *fifth* desideratum for the descriptive protocol: regularities of behavior *associated* with the nominally central activity (although

not part of an explicit culture pattern) should be included in the protocols of the field worker, since these *unwitting regularities* often provide basic clues to distinctive functions of the total pattern. As we shall see, the inclusion of these "unwitting" regularities in the descriptive protocol directs the investigator almost at once to analysis of the pattern in terms of what we have called latent functions.

In summary, then, the descriptive protocol should, so far as possible, include:

1. location of participants in the pattern within the social structure—differential participation;
2. consideration of alternative modes of behavior excluded by emphasis on the observed pattern (*i.e.* attention not only to what occurs but also to what is omitted by virtue of the existing pattern);
3. the emotive and cognitive meanings attached by participants to the pattern;
4. a distinction between the motivations for participating in the pattern and the objective behavior involved in the pattern;
5. regularities of behavior not recognized by participants but which are nonetheless associated with the central pattern of behavior.

That these desiderata for the observer's protocol are far from complete is altogether likely. But they do provide a tentative step in the direction of *specifying* points of observation which facilitate subsequent functional analysis. They are intended to be somewhat more specific than is ordinarily found in such general statements of procedure as those advising the observer to be sensitive to the "context of situation."

REFERENCES

1. For a brief statement of the purpose of analytical paradigms such as this, see the note on paradigms elsewhere in *Social Theory and Social Structure.*
2. The relations between the "unanticipated consequences" of action and "latent functions" can be clearly defined, since they are implicit in the foregoing section of the paradigm. The unintended consequences of action are of three types:
   (1) those which are functional for a given system, and these comprise the latent functions;
   (2) those which are dysfunctional for a given system, and these comprise the latent dysfunctions; and
   (3) those which are irrelevant to the system which they affect neither functionally nor dysfunctionally, i.e., the pragmatically unimportant class of non-functional consequences.

   For a preliminary and now-outmoded statement, see R. K. Merton, "The unanticipated consequences of purposive social action," *American Sociological Review,* 1936, 1, 894–904.
3. R. K. Merton, "Discussion of Parsons' 'Position of Sociological Theory,'" *American Sociological Review,* 1949, 13:164–168.

**4.** Previously cited excerpts from Marx document this statement, but these are, of course, only a few out of many places in which Marx in effect stresses the importance of taking account of the structural context. In *A Contribution to the Critique of Political Economy* (appearing in 1859 and republished in Karl Marx, *Selected Works, op. cit.*, I, 354–371), he observes for example: "No social order ever disappears before all the productive forces for which there is room in it have been developed; and new higher relations of production never appear before the material conditions of their existence have matured in the womb of the old society itself. Therefore, mankind always sets itself only such tasks as it can solve; since, looking at the matter more closely, we will always find that the task itself arises only when the material conditions necessary for its solution already exist or are at least in the process of formation." (p. 357) Perhaps the most famous of his many references to the constraining influence of a given social structure is found in the second paragraph of *The Eighteenth Brumaire of Louis Napoleon:* "Man makes his own history, but he does not make it out of whole cloth: he does not make it out of conditions chosen by himself, but out of such conditions as he finds close at hand." (From the paraphrase of the original as published in Marx, *Selected Works*, II, 315.) To my knowledge, A. D. Lindsay is the most perceptive among the commentators who have noted the theoretic implications of statements such as these. See his little book, *Karl Marx's Capital: An Introductory Essay* (Oxford University Press, 1931), esp. at 27–52.

And for other language with quite different ideological import and essentially similar theoretic implications, see B. Malinowski, "Given a definite cultural need, the means of its satisfaction are small in number, and therefore the cultural arrangement which comes into being in response to the need is determined within narrow limits." "Culture," *Encyclopedia of the Social Sciences, op. cit.*, 626.

**5.** By this point, it is evident that we are considering functional analysis as a method for the *interpretation* of sociological data. This is not to gainsay the important role of the functional orientation in sensitizing sociologists to the *collection of* types of data which might otherwise be neglected. It is perhaps unnecessary to reiterate the axiom that one's concepts *do* determine the inclusion or exclusion of data, that, despite the etymology of the term, *data* are not "given" but are "contrived" with the inevitable help of concepts. In the process of evolving a functional interpretation, the sociological analyst invariably finds it necessary to obtain data other than those initially contemplated. Interpretation and the collection of data are thus inextricably bound up in the array of concepts and propositions relating these concepts. For an extension of these remarks, see my paper on "Sociological Theory" in the present volume.

**6.** Inspection of the book by George P. Murdock, *Social Structure* (New York, Macmillan, 1949), is enough to show that procedures such as those involved in the cross-cultural survey hold large promise for dealing with certain methodological problems of functional analysis.

**7.** Morris E. Opler, "An Outline of Chiricahua Apache Social Organization," in Fred Eggan ed. *Social Anthropology of North American Tribes* (Chicago, University of Chicago Press, 1937), 173–239, esp. at 226–230 [italics supplied].

**8.** W. L. Warner, *A Black Civilization—A Social Study of an Australian Tribe* (New York, Harper & Bros., 1937), 112–113.

**9.** For various approaches to a functional analysis of the "romantic love complex," see Ralph Linton, *Study of Man* (New York, D. Appleton-Century Co., 1936), 174–5; T. Parsons, "Age and Sex in the Social Structure of the United States," *American Sociological Review*, Oct. 1942, 7, 604–616, esp. at 614–15; T. Parsons, "The Kinship System of the Contemporary United States," *American Anthropologist*, 1943, 45, 22–38, esp. at 31–32, 36–37, both reprinted in his *Essays in Sociological Theory, op. cit.;* T. Parsons, "The Social Structure of the Family," in Ruth N. Anshen ed., *The Family: Its Function and Destiny* (New York, Harper, 1949), 173–201; R. K. Merton, "Intermarriage and the Social Structure," *Psychiatry*, 1941, 4, 361–74, esp. at 367–8; and Isidor Thorner, "Sociological Aspects of Affectional Frustration," *Psychiatry*, 1943, 6, 157–173, esp. at 169–172.

**10.** Thorstein Veblen, *The Theory of the Leisure Class* (New York, Vanguard Press, 1928), esp. chapters 2–4.

11. Romanzo Adams, *Interracial Marriage in Hawaii,* esp. at 197–204; Merton, "Intermarriage . . . ," *op. cit.,* esp. at 368–9; K. Davis "Intermarriage in Caste Societies," *American Anthropologist,* 1941, 43, 376–395.

12. *Cf. Merton,* "Intermarriage . . . ," *op. cit.;* Otto Klineberg ed. *Characteristics of the American Negro* (New York, Harper, 1943).

13. The rediscovery of the primary group by those engaged in sociological studies of industry has been one of the chief fillips to the functional approach in recent sociological research. Reference is had here to the work of Elton Mayo, Roethlisberger and Dickson, William Whyte, and Burleigh Gardner, among many others. There remain, of course, the interesting differences in *interpretation* to which these data lend themselves.

# 15: Social Evolution and Social Change

Attempts at a sociological explanation of social change are as old as the discipline itself. In particular, most major nineteenth century sociologists, under the stimulus of evolutionary thinking in the biological sciences, attempted to trace the evolution of mankind through a series of stages and states.

Powerfully influenced by the heritage of eighteenth century Enlightenment thought and the theory of progress in such key figures as Turgot and Condorcet, Auguste Comte, originated most modern evolutionary thinking in the social sciences when he enunciated his well-known "law of three stages." (See Chapter 1.) It was his contention that all of mankind gradually evolved from a theological, to a metaphysical and finally to a positive (i.e., scientific) state. Gradually freeing itself from the remnants of theology and metaphysics, mankind was now about to be ushered into a state in which scientific rationality would be the reigning mode of thought. While Comte saw the evolution of mankind as predominantly determined by the evolution of sets of ideas, he was by no means inattentive, as our excerpt makes clear, to other determinants, such as the gradual increase in the density of population. His great French successor, Emile Durkheim, was later to develop the notion that demographic density is a major determinant of societal evolution.

Karl Marx's general theory of the evolution of mankind, which he developed in dialectical opposition to the pan-logical theory of his one-time mentor Hegel, rejected the Comtean and Hegelian schemes, concerned as they were primarily with sets of ideas and world views. He focused instead, on the development of productive forces and resources in their relation to specific forms of productive and property relations. Ideas, Marx argued, were but ephiphenomenal reflections of the modes of relations which men instituted among themselves in accord with specific economic conditions. The Asiatic, the ancient, the feudal and the modern capitalist modes of production were the main stages, Marx contended, in man's evolutionary development.

Herbert Spencer was undoubtedly the most powerful evolutionary thinker of the nineteenth century. His doctrine dominated social thought in the late nineteenth and early twentieth century. Building upon the earlier biological evolutionism of Jean Baptiste Lamarck and later incorporating Darwinian conceptualizations, Spencer sought to present a unified evolutionary scheme encompassing both organic and inorganic evolution as well as the evolution of mankind.

The very appeal of the Spencerian system, its attempt to supply a kind of a master key to all the riddles of the universe, proved its undoing. Beginning in the years immediately preceding the first World War, a number of scholars questioned Spencer's methodology, in particular his tendency to fit innumerable isolated facts into a preconceived scheme. Others pointed out that he simply postulated evolutionary sequences without being able to show actual historical connections. Others again claimed that, far from following a predetermined path from one stage to another, actual societies had often skipped stages or had been powerfully changed by the diffusion of cultural traits from one cultural area to another. Under the blows of these criticisms the Spencerian system soon lost its appeal and was for long considered a historical curiosity of no real use in the analysis of social change. In the thirties most sociologists would have agreed with Talcott Parsons when he opened his *The Structure of Social Action* with the rhetorical question, "Who now reads Spencer?"—implying, of course, that nobody did.

Yet, in one of those curious reversals of which intellectual history abounds, Talcott Parsons has been instrumental during the last ten years in the revival of evolutionary thought in American sociology. Actuated perhaps by the sense that his previous theorizing in the structural-functional manner did not allow him to come to grips with social dynamics, Parsons deliberately turned to the thought of Spencer and other evolutionary thinkers in articulating his own distinctive scheme, one in which a progressive differentiation of human institutions in the course of evolution is crucial. A few years before Parson's work, the anthropologists Sahlins and Service, who had been students of Leslie White (an upholder of Marxian and Durkheimian notions of evolutionary development when practically all his colleagues had scoffed at them) renewed evolutionary thought in anthropology by rejecting unilinear development while pointing up the crucial differences between general and specific evolution. Still more recently, S. N. Eisenstadt followed the lead of Parsons but moved from the lofty level of abstraction on which Parsons dwelled to a more detailed investigation of those processes which favored societal differentiation and those which impeded it. In Eisenstadt's hands evolutionary theory became a rather flexible instrument which did not commit the scholar to any rigid sequence of development but did sensitize him to the many obstacles to evolutionary development which societies in the process of "modernization" are likely to encounter.

Finally, Wilbert Moore, one of our foremost scholars in the area of economic and social development, contributed a number of papers, one of which we reprint, in which he urged a sceptical attitude toward any mono-causal theory of social change, arguing that scientific progress in this sphere was more likely to come from the integration and mutual fructification of a variety of sociological theories.

# POPULATION INCREASE AND THE LAW OF THREE STAGES * (*Comte*)

Another cause which affects the rate of progress is the natural increase of population, which contributes more than any other influence to accelerate the speed. This increase has always been regarded as the clearest symptom of the gradual amelioration of the human condition; and nothing can be more unquestionable when we take the whole race into the account; or at least, all the nations which have any mutual interest: but this is not the view with which my argument is concerned. I have to consider only the progressive condensation of our species as a last general element concurring in the regulation of our rate of social progress. It is clear that by this condensation, and especially in its early stages, such a division of employments is favoured as could not take place among smaller numbers: and again, that the faculties of individuals are stimulated to find subsistence by more refined methods; and again, that society is obliged to react with a firmer and better concerted energy against the expansion of individual divergences. In view of these considerations, I speak, not of the increase of the numbers of mankind, but

* From *The Positive Philosophy of August Comte*, freely translated and condensed by Harriet Martineau, vol. III, pp. 305–308. London, Bell, 1896.

of their concentration upon a given space, according to the special expression which I have made use of, and which is particularly applicable to the great centres of population, whence, in all ages, human progression has started. By creating new wants and new difficulties, this gradual concentration develops new means, not only of progress but of order, by neutralizing physical inequalities, and affording a growing ascendency to those intellectual and moral forces which are suppressed among a scanty population. If we go on to inquire into the effect of a quicker or slower concentration, we shall perceive that the social movement is further accelerated by the disturbance given to the old antagonism between the conservative and the innovating instincts, the last being strongly reinforced. In this sense the sociological influence of a more rapid increase of population is in analogy with that which we have just been considering in regard to the duration of life; for it is of little consequence whether the more frequent renewal of individuals is caused by the short life of some, or the speedier multiplication of others; and what was said in the former case will suffice for the latter. It must be observed, however, that if the condensation and rapidity were to pass beyond a certain degree, they would not favour, but impede this acceleration. The condensation, if carried too far, would render the support of human life too difficult; and the rapidity, if extreme, would so affect the stability of social enterprises as to be equivalent to a considerable shortening of our life. As yet, however, the increase of population has never nearly reached the natural limits at which such inconveniences will begin; and we have really no experience of them, unless in a few exceptional cases of disturbance caused by migrations, ill-managed as to their extent of numbers and of time. In an extremely distant future, our posterity will have to consider the question, and with much anxiety; because, from the smallness of the globe, and the necessary limitation of human resources, the tendency to increase will become extremely important, when the human race will be ten times as numerous as at present, and as much condensed everywhere as it now is in the west of Europe. Whenever that time comes, the more complete development of human nature, and the more exact knowledge of the laws of human evolution, will no doubt supply new means of resistance to the danger; means of which we can form no clear conception, and about which it is not for us to decide whether they will, on the whole, afford a sufficient compensation. . . .

Though the elements of our social evolution are connected, and always acting on each other, one must be preponderant, in order to give an impulse to the rest, though they may, in their turn, so act upon it as to cause its further expansion. We must find out this superior element, leaving the lower degrees of subordination to disclose themselves as we proceed: and we have not to search far for this element, as we cannot err in taking that which can be best conceived of apart from the rest, notwithstanding their necessary connection, while the considerations of it would enter into the study of the others. This double characteristic points out the intellectual evolution as the preponderant principle. If the intellectual point of view was the chief in our statical study of the organism, much more must it be so in the dynamical case. If our reason required at the outset the awakening and stimulating influence of the appetites, the passions, and the sentiments, not the less has human progression gone forward under its direction. It is only through the more and more marked influence of the reason over the general conduct of Man and of society, that the gradual march of our race has attained that regularity and persevering continuity which distinguish it so radically from the desultory and barren expansion of even the highest of the animal orders, which share, and with enhanced strength, the appetites, the passions, and even the primary sentiments of Man. If the statical analysis of our social organism shows it resting at length upon a certain system of fundamental opinions, the gradual changes of that system must affect the successive modifications of the life of humanity: and this is why, since the birth of philosophy, the history of society has been regarded as governed by the history of the human mind. As it is necessary, in a scientific sense, to refer our historical analysis to the preponderant evolution, whatever it may be, we must in this case choose, or rather preserve, the general history of the human mind as the natural guide to all historical study of humanity. One consequence of the same principle,—a consequence as rigorous but less understood,—is that we must choose for consideration in this intellectual history, the most general and abstract conceptions, which require the exercise of our highest faculties. Thus it is the study of the fundamental system of human opinions with regard to the whole of phenomena, in short, the history of Philosophy, whatever may be its character, theological, metaphysical, or positive,—which must regulate our historical analysis. No other department of intellectual history, not even the history of the fine arts, including poetry, could, however important in itself, be employed for this object; because the faculties of expression, which lie nearer to the affective faculties, have always, in their palmiest days, been subordinated, in the economy of social progress, to the faculties of direct conception. The danger (which is inherent in every choice, and which is least in the choice that I have made), of losing sight of the interconnection of all the parts of human development, may be partly guarded against by frequently comparing them, to see if the variations in any one corresponds with equivalent variations in the others. I believe we shall find that this confirmation is eminently obtainable by my method of historical analysis. This will be proved at once if we find that the development of the highest part of human interests is in accordance with that of the lowest,—the intellectual with the material. If there is an accordance between the two extremes, there must be also between all the intermediate terms.

We have indicated the general direction of the human evolution, its rate of progress, and its necessary order. We may now proceed at once to investigate the natural laws by which the advance of the human mind proceeds. The scientific principle of the theory appears to me to consist in the great philosophical law of the succession of the three states:—the primitive theological state, the transient metaphysical, and the final positive state,—through which the human mind has to pass, in every kind of speculation. This seems to be the place in which we should attempt the direct estimate of this fundamental law, taking it as the basis of my historic analysis, which must itself have for its chief object to explain and expand the general notion of this law by a more and more extended and exact application of it in the review of the entire past of human history.


# PRODUCTIVE FORCES AND RELATION OF PRODUCTION * (Marx)

The first work undertaken for the solution of the question that troubled me, was a critical revision of Hegel's "Philosophy of Law"; the introduction to that work appeared in the "Deutsch-Französische Jahrbücher," published in Paris in 1844. I was led by my studies to the conclusion that legal relations as well as forms of state could neither be understood by themselves, nor explained by the so-called general progress of the human mind, but that they are rooted in the material conditions of life, which are summed up by Hegel after the fashion of the English and French of the eighteenth century under the name "civic society"; the anatomy of that civic society is to be sought in political economy. . . . The general conclusion at which I arrived and which, once reached, continued to serve as the leading thread in my studies, may be briefly summed up as follows: In the social production which men carry on they enter into definite relations that are indispensable

---

* Reprinted from Karl Marx, A Contribution to the Critique of Political Economy, pp. 11–13. Chicago, Charles H. Kerr, 1904.

and independent of their will; these relations of production correspond to a definite stage of development of their material powers of production. The sum total of these relations of production constitutes the economic structure of society—the real foundation, on which rise legal and political super-structures and to which correspond definite forms of social consciousness. The mode of production in material life determines the general character of the social, political and spiritual processes of life. It is not the consciousness of men that determines their existence, but, on the contrary, their social existence determines their consciousness. At a certain stage of their de-velopment, the material forces of production in society come in conflict with the existing relations of production, or—what is but a legal expression for the same thing—with the property relations within which they had been at work before. From forms of development of the forces of production these relations turn into their fetters. Then comes the period of social revolution. With the change of the economic foundation the entire immense super-structure is more or less rapidly transformed. In considering such trans-formations the distinction should always be made between the material transformation of the economic conditions of production which can be determined with the precision of natural science, and the legal, political, religious, aesthetic or philosophic—in short ideological forms in which men become conscious of this conflict and fight it out. Just as our opinion of an individual is not based on what he thinks of himself, so can we not judge of such a period of transformation by its own consciousness; on the contrary, this consciousness must rather be explained from the contradictions of material life, from the existing conflict between the social forces of produc-tion and the relations of production. No social order ever disappears before all the productive forces, for which there is room in it, have been developed; and new higher relations of production never appear before the material conditions of their existence have matured in the womb of the old society. Therefore, mankind always takes up only such problems as it can solve; since, looking at the matter more closely, we will always find that the prob-lem itself arises only when the material conditions necessary for its solution already exist or are at least in the process of formation. In broad outlines we can designate the Asiatic, the ancient, the feudal, and the modern bourgeois methods of production as so many epochs in the progress of the economic formation of society. The bourgeois relations of production are the last antagonistic form of the social process of production—antagonistic not in the sense of individual antagonism, but of one arising from conditions surrounding the life of individuals in society; at the same time the productive forces developing in the womb of bourgeois society create the material

670 SOCIAL EVOLUTION AND SOCIAL CHANGE

conditions for the solution of that antagonism. This social formation constitutes, therefore, the closing chapter of the prehistoric stage of human
society.


# PROGRESS: ITS LAW AND CAUSE *
(*Spencer*)

The current conception of progress is shifting and indefinite. Sometimes it
comprehends little more than simple growth—as of a nation in the number
of its members and the extent of territory over which it spreads. Sometimes
it has reference to quantity of material products—as when the advance of
agriculture and manufactures is the topic. Sometimes the superior quality
of these products is contemplated; and sometimes the new or improved appliances by which they are produced. When, again, we speak of moral or
intellectual progress, we refer to states of the individual or people exhibiting
it; while, when the progress of Science, or Art, is commented upon, we have
in view certain abstract results of human thought and action. *Not only,
however, is the current conception of progress more or less vague, but it is
in great measure erroneous. It takes in not so much the reality of progress
as its accompaniments—not so much the substance as the shadow.* That
progress in intelligence seen during the growth of the child into the man,
or the savage into the philosopher, is commonly regarded as consisting in
the greater number of facts known and laws understood; whereas, the
actual progress consists in those internal modifications of which this larger
knowledge is the expression. *Social progress is supposed to consist in the
making of a greater quantity and variety of the articles required for satisfying men's wants; in the increasing security of person and property; in
widening freedom of action; whereas, rightly understood, social progress
consists in those changes of structure in the social organism which have
entailed these consequences. The current conception is a teleological one.*
The phenomena are contemplated solely as bearing on human happiness.
Only those changes are held to constitute progress which directly or indirectly tend to heighten human happiness; and they are thought to constitute progress simply *because* they tend to heighten human happiness. But
rightly to understand progress, we must learn the nature of these changes,
considered apart from our interests. Ceasing, for example, to regard the

* Herbert Spencer, "Progress: Its Law and Cause," from Vol. I of *Essays: Scientific,
Political and Speculative*, New York, Appleton, 1915. First published in 1857.

successive geological modifications that have taken place in the Earth, as modifications that have gradually fitted it for the habitation of Man, and as *therefore* constituting geological progress, we must ascertain the character common to these modifications—the law to which they all conform. And similarly in every other case. Leaving out of sight concomitants and beneficial consequences, let us ask what progress is in itself.

In respect to that progress which individual organisms display in the course of their evolution, this question has been answered by the Germans. The investigations of Wolff, Goethe, and von Baer have established the truth that the series of changes gone through during the development of a seed into a tree, or an ovum into an animal, constitute an advance from homogeneity of structure to heterogeneity of structure. In its primary stage, every germ consists of a substance that is uniform throughout, both in texture and chemical composition. The first step is the appearance of a difference between two parts of this substance; or, as the phenomenon is called in physiological language, a differentiation. Each of these differentiated divisions presently begins itself to exhibit some contrast of parts: and by and by these secondary differentiations become as definite as the original one. This process is continuously repeated—is simultaneously going on in all parts of the growing embryo; and by endless such differentiations there is finally produced that complex combination of tissues and organs constituting the adult animal or plant. This is the history of all organisms whatever. It is settled beyond dispute that organic progress consists in a change from the homogeneous to the heterogeneous.

*Now, we propose in the first place to show that this law of organic progress is the law of all progress.* Whether it be in the development of the Earth, in the development of Life upon its surface, in the development of Society, of Government, of Manufactures, of Commerce, of Language, Literature, Science, Art, this same evolution of the simple into the complex, through successive differentiations, holds throughout. From the earliest traceable cosmical changes down to the latest results of civilization, we shall find that the *transformation of the homogeneous into the heterogeneous is that in which progress essentially consists.* . . .

Whether an advance from the homogeneous to the heterogeneous is or is not displayed in the biological history of the globe, it is clearly enough displayed in the progress of the latest and most heterogeneous creature— Man. It is true alike that, during the period in which the Earth has been peopled, the human organism has grown more heterogeneous among the civilized divisions of the species; and that the species, as a whole, has been growing more heterogeneous in virtue of the multiplication of races and the differentiation of these races from each other. . . .

On passing from Humanity under its individual form, to Humanity as socially embodied, we find the general law still more variously exemplified. The change from the homogeneous to the heterogeneous is displayed in the progress of civilization as a whole, as well as in the progress of every nation; and is still going on with increasing rapidity. As we see in existing barbarous tribes, society in its first and lowest form is a homogeneous aggregation of individuals having like powers and like functions: the only marked difference of function being that which accompanies difference of sex. Every man is warrior, hunter, fisherman, tool-maker, builder; every woman performs the same drudgeries. Very early, however, in the course of social evolution, there arises an incipient differentiation between the governing and the governed. Some kind of chieftainship seems coeval with the first advance from the state of separate wandering families to that of a nomadic tribe. The authority of the strongest or the most cunning makes itself felt among a body of savages as in a herd of animals, or a posse of schoolboys. At first, however, it is indefinite, uncertain; is shared by others of scarcely inferior power; and is unaccompanied by any difference in occupation or style of living: the first ruler kills his own game, makes his own weapons, builds his own hut, and, economically considered, does not differ from others of his tribe. Gradually, as the tribe progresses, the contrast between the governing and the governed grows more decided. Supreme power becomes hereditary in one family; the head of that family, ceasing to provide for his own wants, is served by others; and he begins to assume the sole office of ruling. At the same time there has been arising a co-ordinate species of government—that of Religion. As all ancient records and traditions prove, the earliest rulers are regarded as divine personages. The maxims and commands they uttered during their lives are held sacred after their deaths, and are enforced by their divinely-descended successors; who in their turns are promoted to the pantheon of the race, here to be worshipped and propitiated along with their predecessors: the most ancient of whom is the supreme god, and the rest subordinate gods. For a long time these connate forms of government—civil and religious—remain closely associated. For many generations the king continues to be the chief priest, and the priesthood to be members of the royal race. For many ages religious law continues to include more or less of civil regulation, and civil law to possess more or less of religious sanction; and even among the most advanced nations these two controlling agencies are by no means completely separated from each other. Having a common root with these, and gradually diverging from them, we find yet another controlling agency—that of Ceremonial usages. All titles of honour are originally the names of the god-king; afterwards of the god and the king; still later of persons of high rank; and finally come, some of them, to be used between man and man. All forms of complimentary address were at first the expressions of submission from prisoners to their conqueror, or from subjects to their ruler, either human or divine—expressions which were afterwards used to propitiate subordinate authorities, and slowly descended into ordinary intercourse. All modes of salutation were once obeisances made before the monarch and used in worship of him after his death. Presently others of the god-descended race were similarly saluted; and by degrees some of the salutations have become the due of all.[1] Thus, no sooner does the originally-homogeneous social mass differentiate into the governed and the governing parts, than this last exhibits an incipient differentiation into religious and secular—Church and State; while at the same time there begins to be differentiated from both, that less definite species of government which rules our daily intercourse— a species of government which, as we may see in heralds' colleges, in books of the peerage, in masters of ceremonies, is not without a certain embodiment of its own. Each of these is itself subject to successive differentiations. In the course of ages, there arises, as among ourselves, a highly complex political organization of monarch, ministers, lords and commons, with their subordinate administrative departments, courts of justice, revenue offices, &c., supplemented in the provinces by municipal governments, county governments, parish or union governments—all of them more or less elaborated. By its side there grows up a highly complex religious organization, with its various grades of officials, from archbishops down to sextons, its colleges, convocations, ecclesiastical courts, &c.; to all which must be added the ever-multiplying independent sects, each with its general and local authorities. And at the same time there is developed a highly complex aggregation of customs, manners, and temporary fashions, enforced by society at large, and serving to control those minor transactions between man and man which are not regulated by civil and religious law. Moreover, it is to be observed that this increasing heterogeneity in the governmental appliances of each nation, has been accompanied by an increasing heterogeneity in the assemblage of governmental appliances of different nations: all nations being more or less unlike in their political systems and legislation, in their creeds and religions institutions, in their customs and ceremonial usages.

[1] For detailed proof of these assertions see essay on "Manners and Fashion."

Simultaneously there has been going on a second differentiation of a more familiar kind; that, namely, by which the mass of the community has been segregated into distinct classes and orders of workers. While the governing part has undergone the complex development above detailed, the governed part has undergone an equally complex development, which has resulted in that minute division of labour characterizing advanced nations. It is needless to trace out this progress from its first stages, up through the caste-divisions of the East and the incorporated guilds of Europe, to the elaborate producing and distributing organization existing among ourselves. It has been an evolution which, beginning with a tribe whose members severally perform the same actions each for himself, ends with a civilized community whose members severally perform different actions for each other; and an evolution which has transformed the solitary producer of any one commodity into a combination of producers who, united under a master, take separate parts in the manufacture of such commodity. But there are yet others and higher phases of this advance from the homogeneous to the heterogeneous in the industrial organization of society. Long after considerable progress has been made in the division of labour among different classes of workers, there is still little or no division of labour among the widely separated parts of the community: the nation continues comparatively homogeneous in the respect that in each district the same occupations are pursued. But when roads and other means of transit become numerous and good, the different districts begin to assume different functions, and to become mutually dependent. The calico manufacture locates itself in this country, the woollen-cloth manufacture in that; silks are produced here, lace there; stockings in one place, shoes in another; pottery, hardware, cutlery come to have their special towns; and ultimately every locality becomes more or less distinguished from the rest by the leading occupation carried on in it. This subdivision of functions shows itself not only among the different parts of the same nation, but among different nations. That exchange of commodities which free-trade is increasing so largely, will ultimately have the effect of specializing, in a greater or less degree, the industry of each people. So that, beginning with a barbarous tribe, almost if not quite homogeneous in the functions of its members, the progress has been, and still is, towards an economic aggregation of the whole human race; growing ever more heterogeneous in respect of the separate functions assumed by separate nations, the separate functions assumed by the local sections of each nation, the separate functions assumed by the many kinds of makers and traders in each town, and the separate functions assumed by the workers united in producing each commodity.

The law thus clearly exemplified in the evolution of the social organism, is exemplified with equal clearness in the evolution of all products of human thought and action; whether concrete or abstract, real or ideal. . . .

. . .

And now, must not this uniformity of procedure be a consequence of some fundamental necessity? May we not rationally seek for some all-pervading principle which determines this all-pervading process of things? *Does not the universality of the* law *imply a universal* cause?

That we can comprehend such cause, noumenally considered, is not to be supposed. To do this would be to solve that ultimate mystery which must ever transcend human intelligence. But it still may be possible for us to reduce the law of all progress, above set forth, from the condition of an empirical generalization, to the condition of a rational generalization. Just as it was possible to interpret Kepler's laws as necessary consequences of the law of gravitation; so it may be possible to interpret this law of progress, in its multiform manifestations, as the necessary consequence of some similarly universal principle. As gravitation was assignable as the *cause* of each of the groups of phenomena which Kepler generalized; so may some equally simple attribute of things be assignable as the cause of each of the groups of phenomena generalized in the foregoing pages. We may be able to affiliate all these varied evolutions of the homogeneous into the heterogeneous, upon certain facts of immediate experience, which, in virtue of endless repetition, we regard as necessary.

The probability of a common cause, and the possibility of formulating it, being granted, it will be well, first, to ask what must be the general characteristics of such cause, and in what direction we ought to look for it. We can with certainty predict that it has a high degree of abstractness, seeing that it is common to such infinitely varied phenomena. We need not expect to see in it an obvious solution of this or that form of progress; because it is equally concerned with forms of progress bearing little apparent resemblance to them: its association with multiform orders of facts involves its dissociation from any particular order of facts. Being that which determines progress of every kind—astronomic, geologic, organic, ethnologic, social, economic, artistic, &c.—it must be involved with some fundamental trait displayed in common by these; and must be expressible in terms of this fundamental trait. The only obvious respect in which all kinds of progress are alike, is, that they are modes of *change;* and hence, in some characteristic of changes in general, the desired solution will probably be found. We may suspect *a priori* that in some universal law of change lies the explanation of this universal transformation of the homogeneous into the heterogeneous.

Thus much premised, we pass at once to the statement of the law, which is this:—*Every active force produces more than one change—every cause produces more than one effect.* . . .

If the advance of Man towards greater heterogeneity is traceable to the production of many effects by one cause, still more clearly may the advance of Society towards greater heterogeneity be so explained. Consider the growth of an industrial organization. When, as must occasionally happen, some member of a tribe displays unusual aptitude for making an article of general use—a weapon, for instance—which was before made by each man for himself, there arises a tendency towards the differentiation of that member into a maker of such weapon. His companions—warriors and hunters all of them,—severally feel the importance of having the best weapons that can be made; and are therefore certain to offer strong inducements to this skilled individual to make weapons for them. He, on the other hand, having not only an unusual faculty, but an unusual liking, for making such weapons (the talent and the desire for any occupation being commonly associated), is predisposed to fulfil each commission on the offer of an adequate reward: especially as his love of distinction is also gratified and his living facilitated. This first specialization of function, once commenced, tends ever to become more decided. On the side of the weapon-maker practice gives increased skill—increased superiority to his products. On the side of his clients, cessation of practice entails decreased skill. Thus the influences which determine this division of labour grow stronger in both ways; and the incipient heterogeneity is, on the average of cases, likely to become permanent for that generation if no longer. This process not only differentiates the social mass into two parts, the one monopolizing, or almost monopolizing, the performance of a certain function, and the other losing the habit, and in some measure the power, of performing that function; but it tends to initiate other differentiations. The advance described implies the introduction of barter,—the maker of weapons has, on each occasion, to be paid in such other articles, as he agrees to take in exchange. He will not habitually take in exchange one kind of article, but many kinds. He does not want mats only, or skins, or fishing-gear, but he wants all these, and on each occasion will bargain for the particular things he most needs. What follows? If among his fellows there exist any slight differences of skill in the manufacture of these various things, as there are almost sure to do, the weapon-maker will take from each one the thing which that one excels in making: he will exchange for mats with him whose mats are superior, and will bargain for the fishing-gear of him who has the best. But he who has bartered away his mats or his fishing-gear, must make other mats or fishing-gear for himself; and in so doing must, in some degree, further develop his aptitude. Thus it results that the small specialities of faculty possessed by various members of the tribe, will tend to grow more decided. And whether or not there ensue distinct differentiations of other individuals into makers of particular articles, it is clear that incipient differentiations take place throughout the tribe: the one original cause produces not only the first dual effect, but a number of secondary dual effects, like in kind, but minor in degree. This process, of which traces may be seen among schoolboys, cannot well produce lasting effects in an unsettled tribe, but where there grows up a fixed and multiplying community, such differentiations become permanent, and increase with each generation. The enhanced demand for every commodity, intensifies the functional activity of each specialized person or class; and this renders the specialization more definite where it already exists, and establishes it where it is but nascent. By increasing the pressure on the means of subsistence, a larger population again augments these results; seeing that each person is forced more and more to confine himself to that which he can do best, and by which he can gain most. Presently, under these same stimuli, new occupations arise. Competing workers, ever aiming to produce improved articles, occasionally discover better processes or raw materials. The substitution of bronze for stone entails on him who first makes it a great increase of demand; so that he or his successor eventually finds all his time occupied in making the bronze for the articles he sells, and is obliged to depute the fashioning of these articles to others; and, eventually, the making of bronze, thus differentiated from a pre-existing occupation, becomes an occupation by itself. But now mark the ramified changes which follow this change. Bronze presently replaces stone, not only in the articles it was first used for, but in many others—in arms, tools, and utensils of various kinds: and so affects the manufacture of them. Further, it affects the processes which these utensils subserve, and the resulting products, modifies buildings, carvings, personal decorations. Yet again, it sets going manufacturers which were before impossible, from lack of a material fit for the requisite implements. And all these changes react on the people—increase their manipulative skill, their intelligence, their comfort, refine their habits and tastes. Thus the evolution of a homogeneous society into a heterogeneous one, is clearly consequent on the general principle, that many effects are produced by one cause.

# THE LAW OF EVOLUTIONARY POTENTIAL* (*Sahlins*)

In order to test our ability to explain and predict the evolutionary progress of specific populations and cultures, we must first define the expectable results of the various evolutionary processes in their interaction. Once these relationships have been discussed generally we shall attempt various interpretations with them. The illustrations will range diversely from some simple anthropological problems of the primitive world to the complex question of the modern and future world and America's place in it.

One of the virtues of the evolutionary view is that, more than any other perspective, it makes the concerns of cultural anthropology directly relevant to modern life and to the future. As Tylor once put it, it is the "knowledge of man's course of life, from the remote past to the present," the study of the *evolution* of culture, that will enable us to forecast the future. The modern social sciences, now that they are almost exclusively nontemporal, or functional, have not been able to help us to judge the future and thus guide our actions and deliberations in relation to modern political problems. The past-as-related-to-the-future has long since been left to dogmatic Marxists or to the more respectable but nevertheless equally non-scientific "universal" historians such as Brooks Adams, Spengler, Huntington, and Toynbee.

Let us briefly review those characteristics of evolution that we now want to consider as interrelated phenomena. First, it has been noted that evolution can be regarded as a double-faceted phenomenon. On the one hand any given system—a species, a culture, or an individual—improves its chances for survival, progresses in the efficiency of energy capture, by increasing its adaptive specialization. This is specific evolution. The obverse is directional advance or progress stage by stage, measured in absolute terms rather than by criteria relative to the degree of adaptation to particular environments. The systems also are assigned to stages irrespective of their phylogenetic relationship. A man is higher than an armadillo; yet they are each adapted differently and are contemporary species and members of different lines of descent. This is general evolution.

---

* Reprinted from Thomas G. Harding *et al.*, *Evolution and Culture*, ed. by D. Sahlins and Elman R. Service, University of Michigan Press, Ann Arbor, with permission of the publisher.

We have also seen that there is a limiting factor inherent in specific evolution. This has been called the Principle of Stabilization, and it occurs as an end product of adaptation. Specific evolution means increasing adaptation to an environment, which is to say that it ultimately becomes non-progressive. Because adaptation is self-limiting at some point, if all of the forms of life and culture were to become fully adapted, evolution, whether viewed specifically or generally, would halt.

The fact of the matter is, of course, that evolution continues precisely because new forms come into being which are *not* highly specialized. Some of these more generalized mutants have a potential for new kinds of adaptation or adaptation to new kinds of environments. Thus we have the contradictory-sounding propositions: the evolution of species takes place *because* of adaptation; the evolution of the total system of life takes place *in spite of* adaptation.

Another factor, the dominance which a higher species may exert over lower species, tends to be the most effective inhibitor of any potential that may reside in an unspecialized species. Much of the struggle and warfare that is endemic in both the world of biology and of culture can be interpreted as the contest between the dominance factor and the potentiality factor. This also may be phrased in contradictory-sounding statements: specific evolution is a movement from homogeneity to heterogeneity, from few to more species; yet one of the frequent consequences of evolution is the movement from heterogeneity toward homogeneity, as a higher dominant form such as man spreads at the expense of lower forms.

These ideas should not be unfamiliar to anyone conversant with recent literature on biological evolution. Julian Huxley, in particular, has pointed out that evolution is not a straight line of progress from one highly developed species to the next highest but that it proceeds in zigzag fashion as advances are countered by stabilization or dominance, that limitation is as likely as improvement. Most relevant to the present discussion is the recognition that what Simpson has called "opportunism" for evolutionary advance exists as a better possibility for a more generalized form than for the specialized, well-adapted and therefore stabilized one. As Huxley put it: ". . . the further a trend toward specialization has proceeded, the deeper will be the biological groove in which [the species] has thus entrenched itself."[1] Or again: ". . . there is no certain case on record of a line showing a high degree of specialization giving rise to a new type. All new types which

[1] Huxley, Julian, 1943, *Evolution*, N.Y. and London, Harper, p. 500.

themselves are capable of adaptive radiation seem to have been produced by relatively unspecialized ancestral lines."[2]

One of the main purposes of this chapter is to show that this characteristic of biological evolution is expectable in the evolution of culture as well. Further, we wish to state the proposition in the form of a law—that is, to affirm its generality as explicitly as possible. It has been introduced in the context of biological evolution in order to argue for its acceptability as an idea; evolutionary ideas expressed in biological terms seem to find readier acceptance than they do in cultural terms. But this should not be taken to mean that the idea began in biology and that now it is simply being carried over into the cultural context. As we shall see, there are evidences of its prior realization, incipiently at least, by students of cultural phenomena.

The law, which may be called The Law of Evolutionary Potential, is a simple one: The more specialized and adapted a form in a given evolutionary stage, the smaller is its potential for passing to the next stage. Another way of putting it . . . is: Specific evolutionary progress is inversely related to general evolutionary potential.

It is important to remember that because of the stabilization of specialized species and because new advances occur in less specialized species, over-all progress is characteristically irregular and discontinuous rather than a direct line from one advanced species to its next descendant. Instead of continuing the advance related species diverge as they specialize and adapt. This discontinuity, which now seems obvious. has been usually overlooked as a significant feature of the evolutionary process. Evolution is usually diagrammed as a tree with the trunk representing the "main line" of progress, as though the advance from the highest form at one stage to the new form at the next were phylogenetically continuous. It is an inappropriate and misleading picture, however, and the recognition of the discontinuity of advance is an important element in the understanding of some major problems.

We are not sure where the lineal view of evolution came from, but it has been a mischievous one. . . . Hegel's "dialectical" conception of evolution is a special version of the lineal view and when it was adopted by Marx and Engels and ultimately became part of a political dogma, the error was widespread as well as resistant to any arguments against it. According to Hegel, *everything*, including society and even human nature, is in a state of evolution; everything carries within itself the forces which change it. Never mind the famous "negations" that cause the revolutionary leaps; what is at issue now is Hegel's "flux," the idea that each and every system of things

[2] *Ibid.*, p. 562.

THE LAW OF EVOLUTIONARY POTENTIAL / SAHLINS 681

evolves as a self-contained unit. There is no phylogenetic discontinuity and no sound idea of variable potentiality in the Hegelian view. This fault is what led Marx, Engels, and others to presume that the revolution which would usher in the new stage of industrial socialism would occur in the most *advanced* industrial countries—that evolution proceeds from the most advanced form on to the next level. But when the Bolsheviks won in Russia, a most unlikely place from the Hegel-Marx point of view, the Marxists became confused. When expediency led Lenin and then Stalin to retain power in Russia no matter what the theory said, many others, "pure Marxists," rejected the Bolsheviks and formed the numerous splinter parties that exist to this day as opponents of Stalinism. What a lot of assassinations a mere theory can cause! Perhaps this is a sufficient answer to those who say that evolutionary laws are so general that they are meaningless.

In order to emphasize the nonlineal nature of progress, we shall state two new principles, obvious aspects of the law of potential. One could be called the Phylogenetic Discontinuity of Progress. It would mean only what was stated above, that an advanced form does not normally beget the next stage of advance; that the next stage begins in a different line.

Because species tend to occupy a given territory continuously, another obvious derivative principle suggests itself. This may be called the Local Discontinuity of Progress. It means merely that if successive stages of progress are not likely to go from one species to its next descendant, then they are not likely to occur in the same locality. As we shall see, this principle is especially appropriate for studies of cultural evolution because we so frequently name a culture after the territory in which it is found.

No one has completely or succinctly formulated any of these laws but several writers have come close. Two in particular have discussed and used rather similar ideas in specific interpretations. They are Thorstein Veblen and Leon Trotsky.

Veblen's anaysis of Imperial Germany makes considerable use of two ideas reminiscent of the above discussion. One is that Germany became more efficient industrially than her predecessor, England, because of "the merits of borrowing"; the other is that England, conversely, was finally less efficient than Germany because of "the penalty of taking the lead."[3] Later, Trotsky, in his *History of the Russian Revolution* formulated the idea somewhat more aptly. He used one particularly luminous phrase: "the privilege of historic backwardness." In the context of his discussion this means that an "under-

[3] Veblen, Thorstein, *Imperial Germany and The Industrial Revolution.* 1915, N.Y. Macmillan; esp. Chapters II–IV.

developed" civilization has certain evolutionary potentials that an advanced one lacks. He put it this way:

> *Although compelled to follow after the advanced countries, a backward country does not take things in the same order. The privilege of historic backwardness and such a privilege exists—permits, or rather compels, the adoption of whatever is ready in advance of any specified date, skipping a whole series of intermediate stages.*[4]

Trotsky went on to develop his idea and to formulate it as The Law of Combined Development

> *The law of combined development reveals itself most indubitably . . . in the history and character of Russian industry. Arising late, Russian industry did not repeat the development of the advanced countries, but inserted itself into this development, adapting their latest achievements to its own backwardness. Just as the economic evolution of Russia as a whole skipped over the epoch of craft-guilds and manufacture, so also the separate branches of industry made a series of special leaps over technical productive stages that had been measured in the West by decades. Thanks to this, Russian industry developed at certain periods with extraordinary speed.*[5]

Several writers prior to Veblen and Trotsky, including Lewis H. Morgan, had remarked on the tendency of backward societies to skip over whole stages of development by borrowing from the culture of advanced societies, but no one has been so explicit as Trotsky about the *potentiality* of backwardness, nor so daring as to propose it as a scientific law. The emphasis on diffusion in Trotsky's argument (as suggested in the phrase "combined development") and in Veblen's idea of the "merits of borrowing" calls attention to an important feature of the evolutionary process in culture which does not have its analogue in biological evolution. The lack of any possible connection between species except the genetic makes convergence in biological evolution a rarer phenomenon, and also makes specific evolution a slower, more gradual, and more connected series of changes than in the diffusional continuum of culture. This difference, nevertheless, does not alter the applicability of the law of evolutionary potential to both biology and culture.

Other writers have commented on the converse of the notion of the privi-

---

[4] Trotsky, Leon. *The History of the Russian Revolution*. Ann Arbor, University of Michigan Press, nd., 4–5.

[5] *Ibid.*, p. 9.

lege of backwardness, that there is a stagnation and lack of potentiality inherent in highly developed cultures.

That very wise Frenchman, Alexis de Tocqueville, over 100 years ago made an interesting statement concerning the potentiality of the U.S.A. and Russia as compared with the stabilization of the more developed nations. He wrote:

> *There are at the present time two great nations in the world which seem to tend toward the same end, although they started from different points; I allude to the Russians and the Americans. Both of them have grown up unnoticed; and while the attention of mankind was directed elsewhere, they have suddenly assumed a prominent place among the nations; and the world learned their existence and their greatness at almost the same time. All other nations seem to have nearly reached their natural limits . . . but these are still in the act of growth; all others are stopped, or continue to advance with extreme difficulty. . . .*[6]

Arnold Toynbee is also concerned with this historical stop-and-go, leap-frogging character of progress and addresses it as a central problem, but his anthropocentric, psychologistic perspective prevents him from seeing any nonmental process at work. All of the historians concerned with the phenomenon usually called "the rise and fall of civilizations" could have made good use of the law of evolutionary potential. It could have, for example, made Spengler's and Brooks Adams' conceptions of "decline" and "decay" more comprehensible.

Another historian, H. Stuart Hughes, has written a provocative essay called "The Twentieth Century Byzantium,"[7] expanding the subject of cultural stabilization and conservatism. Hughes says (as others have) that the U.S.A. is to Western Europe as Rome was to Greece; that as a later but more primitive offshoot of an older civilization, the U.S.A., like Rome, raised certain aspects of that civilization to new levels of efficiency and specialization. He then goes on to stress that the U.S.A. is now stabilized and coming to occupy a conservative position in the world, more like the later Byzantium than Rome itself. One wishes that Professor Hughes had formulated his idea in more general evolutionary terms. As it is, the law of evolutionary potential is practically at the point of his pen.

[6] de Tocqueville, Alexis, *Democracy in America*, 1954, 2 vols., New York, Vintage ed., 1952, vol. 2, p. 452.
[7] Hughes, H. Stuart, *An Essay for our Times*, 1949, N.Y., Knopf.

The failure of so many historians, including such anthropological culture-historians as A. L. Kroeber, to formulate such a law even when they seem to be purposely seeking a general statement is probably because they *are* historians, by profession and commitment nonevolutionists, whereas the explanation for the variable potentiality for civilizational advance among different kinds of cultures stems logically only from evolutionary theory. Happily for this argument, both Veblen and Trotsky can be considered evolutionists.

One feels a little foolish in proclaiming a scientific law inasmuch as it is done so frequently as a form of humor. There are certain advantages to this procedure, however, which are greater than the risks. But first it must be admitted that all of the illustrations to follow, and a thousand more, would not prove that the law of evolutionary potentials is "true." A law states a relationship between two (or more) classes of phenomena, as this one has done with respect to general evolution and specific adaptation, but always it must be understood that other factors are regarded as constant. In nature, however, there are no constants. A law can be proved true only with laboratory apparatus which can keep all factors controlled, and of course many scientific laws cannot be submitted to laboratory tests. The criterion in these cases becomes not truth in the absolute sense, but their explanatory value. A law is a law if it is useful, if it renders particular events more understandable by showing them to be instances of an already comprehended general phenomenon. As Morris Cohen put it, "the repeatable escapes us if it is not identified."

# EVOLUTIONARY UNIVERSALS IN SOCIETY* (*Parsons*)

Slowly and somewhat inarticulately, emphasis in both sociological and anthropological quarters is shifting from a studied disinterest in problems of social and cultural evolution to a "new relativity" that relates its universals to an evolutionary framework.

The older perspectives insisted that social and cultural systems are made up of indefinitely numerous discrete "traits," that "cultures" are totally separate, or that certain broad "human" universals, like language and the

* Reprinted from *The American Sociological Review*, Vol. 29, 3 (June 1964), pp. 339–357 with permission of the American Sociological Association and the author.

incest taboo, should be emphasized. Varied as they are, these emphases have in common the fact that they divert attention from specific *continuities* in patterns of social change, so that either traits or culture types must be treated as discretely unique and basically unconnected, and a pattern, to be considered universal, must be equally important to *all* societies and cultures. Despite their ostentatious repudiation of "culture-boundness," these perspectives have been conspicuously anthropocentric in setting off problems of man's modes of life so sharply from questions of continuity with the rest of the organic world. But the emphasis on human universals has also had a kind of "levelling" influence, tending to restrict attention to what is generally and essentially human, without considering gradations within the human category.

The "new relativity" removes this barrier and tries to consider human ways in direct continuity with the sub-human. It assumes that the watershed between subhuman and human does not mark a cessation of developmental change, but rather a stage in a long process that begins with many pre-human phases and continues through that watershed into our own time, and beyond. Granting a wide range of variability of types at all stages, it assumes that levels of evolutionary advancement may be empirically specified for the human as well as the pre-human phases.

## Evolutionary Universals

I shall designate as an evolutionary universal any organizational development sufficiently important to further evolution that, rather than emerging only once, it is likely to be "hit upon" by various systems operating under different conditions.

In the organic world, vision is a good example of an evolutionary universal. Because it mediates the input of organized information from the organism's environment, and because it deals with both the most distant and the widest range of information sources, vision is the most generalized mechanism of sensory information. It therefore has the greatest potential significance for adaptation of the organism to its environment.

The evidence is that vision has not been a "one shot" invention in organic evolution, but has evolved independently in three different phyla—the molluscs, the insects, and the vertebrates. A particularly interesting feature of this case is that, while the visual organs in the three groups are anatomically quite different and present no evolutionary continuity, biochemically all use the same mechanism involving Vitamin A, though there is no evidence that it was not independently "hit upon" three times.[1] Vision, whatever its mechanisms, seems to be a genuine prerequisite of *all* the higher levels of organic evolution. It has been lost only by very particular groups like the bats, which have not subsequently given rise to important evolutionary developments.

With reference to man and his biological potential for social and cultural evolution, two familiar evolutionary universals may be cited, namely the hands and the brain. The human hand is, of course, the primordial general-purpose tool. The combination of four mobile fingers and an opposable thumb enables it to perform an enormous variety of operations—grasping, holding, and manipulating many kinds of objects. Its location at the end of an arm with mobile joints allows it to be maneuvered into many positions. Finally, the pairing of the arm-hand organs much more than doubles the capacity of each one because it permits cooperation and a complex division of labor between them.

It is worth noting that the development of the hands and arms has been bought at a heavy cost in locomotion: man on his two legs cannot compete in speed and maneuverability with the faster four-legged species. Man, however, uses his hands for such a wide range of behavior impossible for handless species that the loss is far more than compensated. He can, for instance, protect himself with weapons instead of running away.

The human brain is less nearly unique than the hand, but its advantages over the brains of even anthropoids is so great that it is man's most distinctive organ, the most important single source of human capacity. Not only is it the primary organ for controlling complex operations, notably manual skills, and coordinating visual and auditory information, but above all it is the organic basis of the capacity to learn and manipulate symbols. Hence it is the organic foundation of culture. Interestingly, this development too is bought at the sacrifice of immediate adaptive advantages. For example the brain occupies so much of the head that the jaws are much less effective than in other mammalian species—but this too is compensated for by the hands. And the large brain is partly responsible for the long period of infantile dependency because the child must learn such a large factor of its effective behavior. Hence the burden of infant care and socialization is far higher for man than for any other species.

With these organic examples in mind, the conception of an evolutionary universal may be developed more fully. It should, I suggest, be formulated

---

[1] George Wald, "Life and Light," *Scientific American*, 201 (October, 1959), pp. 92–108.

with reference to the concept of adaptation, which has been so fundamental to the theory of evolution since Darwin. Clearly, adaptation should
mean, not merely passive "adjustment" to environmental conditions, but
rather the capacity of a living system[2] to cope with its environment. This
capacity includes an active concern with mastery, or the ability to change
the environment to meet the needs of the system, as well as an ability to
survive in the face of its unalterable features. Hence the capacity to cope
with broad *ranges* of environmental factors, through adjustment or active
control, or both, is crucial. Finally, a very critical point is the capacity to
cope with unstable relations between system and environment, and hence
with *uncertainty*. Instability here refers both to predictable variations, such
as the cycle of the seasons, and to unpredictable variations, such as the sudden appearance of a dangerous predator.

An evolutionary universal, then, is a complex of structures and associated
processes the development of which so increases the long-run adaptive capacity of living systems in a given class that only systems that develop the
complex can attain certain higher levels of general adaptive capacity. This
criterion, derived from the famous principle of natural selection, requires
one major explicit qualification. The relatively disadvantaged system not
developing a new universal need not be condemned to extinction. Thus some
species representing all levels of organic evolution survive today—from the
unicellular organisms up. The surviving lower types, however, stand in a
variety of different relations to the higher. Some occupy special "niches"
within which they live with limited scope, others stand in symbiotic relations
to higher systems. They are not, by and large, major threats to the continued existence of the evolutionarily higher systems. Thus, though infec-
tious diseases constitute a serious problem for man, bacteria are not likely
to replace man as the dominant organic category, and man is symbiotically
dependent on many bacterial species.

Two distinctions should be made here, because they apply most generally
and throughout. The first is between the impact of an innovation when it is
*first* introduced in a given species or society, and its importance as a continuing component of the system. Certain evolutionary universals in the social
world, to be discussed below, initially provide their societies with major
adaptive advantages over societies not developing them. Their introduction
and institutionalization have, to be sure, often been attended with severe
dislocations of the previous social organization, sometimes resulting in short-

---

[2] Note that the species rather than the individual organism is the major system of
reference here. See George Gaylord Simpson, *The Meaning of Evolution,* New Haven:
Yale University Press, 1950.

run losses in adaptation. Once institutionalized, however, they tend to become essential parts of later societies in the relevant lines of *development* and are seldom eliminated except by regression. But, as the system undergoes further evolution, universals are apt to generate major changes of their own, generally by developing more complex structures.

Unlike biological genes, cultural patterns are subject to "diffusion." Hence, for the cultural level, it is necessary to add a second distinction, between the conditions under which an adaptive advantage can develop for the first time, and those favoring its adoption from a source in which it is already established.

## Prerequisites of the Evolution of Culture and Society

From his distinctive organic endowment and from his capacity for and ultimate dependence on generalized learning, man derives his unique ability to create and transmit *culture*. To quote the biologist Alfred Emerson within a major sphere of man's adaptation, the "gene" has been replaced by the "symbol."[3] Hence, it is not only the genetic constitution of the species that determines the "needs" confronting the environment, but this constitution *plus* the cultural tradition. A set of "normative expectations" pertaining to man's relation to his environment delineates the ways in which adaptation should be developed and extended. Within the relevant range, cultural innovations, especially definitions of what man's life *ought* to be, thus replace Darwinian variations in genetic constitution.

Cultural "patterns" or orientations, however, do not implement themselves. Properly conceived in their most fundamental aspect as "religious," they must be articulated with the environment in ways that make effective adaptation possible. I am inclined to treat the entire orientational aspect of culture itself, in the simplest, least evolved forms, as directly synonymous with *religion*.[4] But since a cultural system—never any more an individual matter than a genetic pattern—is shared among a plurality of individuals, mechanisms of *communication* must exist to mediate this sharing. The fundamental evolutionary universal here is language: no concrete human group lacks it. Neither communication nor the learning processes that make it possible, however is conceivable without determinately organized relations among those who teach and learn and communicate.

[3] Alfred Emerson, "Homeostasis and Comparison of Systems" in Roy R. Grinker (ed.), *Toward a Unified Theory of Behavior,* New York: Basic Books, 1956.
[4] Cf. Emile Durkheim, *The Elementary Forms of the Religious Life,* London: Allen and Unwin, 1915.

The evolutionary origin of *social organization* seems to be kinship. In an evolutionary sense it is an extension of the mammalian system of bisexual reproduction. The imperative of socialization is of course a central corollary of culture, as is the need to establish a viable social system to "carry" the culture. From one viewpoint, the core of the kinship system is the incest taboo, or, more generally, the rules of exogamy and endogamy structuring relations of descent, affinity, and residence. Finally, since the cultural level of action implies the use of brain, hands, and other organs in actively coping with the physical environment, we may say that culture implies the existence of technology, which is, in its most undifferentiated form, a synthesis of empirical knowledge and practical techniques.

These four features of even the simplest action system—"religion," communication with language, social organization through kinship, and technology—may be regarded as an integrated set of evolutionary universals at even the earliest human level. No known human society has existed without *all* four in relatively definite relations to each other. In fact, their presence constitutes the very minimum that may be said to mark a society as truly human.

Systematic relations exist not only among these four elements themselves, but between them and the more general framework of biological evolution. Technology clearly is the primary focus of the organization of the adaptive relations of the human system to its physical *environment*. Kinship is the social extension of the individual *organism's* basic articulation to the species through bisexual reproduction. But, through plasticity and the importance of learning, cultural and symbolic communications are integral to the human level of individual *personality* organization. *Social* relations among personalities, to be distinctively human, must be mediated by linguistic communication. Finally, the main *cultural patterns* that regulate the social, psychological, and organic levels of the total system of action are embodied (the more primitive the system, the more exclusively so) in the religious tradition, the focus of the use of symbolization to control the variety of conditions to which a human system is exposed.

### Social Stratification

Two evolutionary universals are closely interrelated in the process of "breaking out" of what may be called the "primitive" stage of societal evolution. These are the development of a well-marked system of social stratification, and that of a system of explicit cultural legitimation of differentiated societal functions, preeminently the political function, independent of kinship. The two are closely connected, but I am inclined to think that stratification comes first and is a condition of legitimation of political function.

The key to the evolutionary importance of stratification lies in the role in primitive societies of *ascription* of social status to criteria of biological relatedness. The kinship nexus of social organization is intrinsically a "seamless web" of relationships which, in and of itself, contains no principle of boundedness for the system as distinguished from certain subgroups within it. Probably the earliest and most important basis of boundedness is the political criterion of territorial jurisdiction. But the economic problem of articulation with the environment, contingent on kinship as well as other groups, is also prominent in primitive societies. In the first instance this is structured primarily through place of residence, which becomes increasingly important as technological development, notably of "settled agriculture," puts a premium on definiteness and permanence of location.

For present purposes, I assume that in the society we are discussing, the population occupying a territorial area is generally endogamous, with marriage of its members to those of other territorial groups being, if it occurs, somehow exceptional, and not systematically organized.[5] Given a presumptively endogamous territorial community, comprising a plurality of purely local groups, certain general processes of internal differentiation of the society can be explained. One aspect of this tends to be a prestige difference between central or "senior" lineage groups and "cadet" groups, whether or not the differentiation is on the basis of birth.[6] Quite generally, the latter must accept less advantageous bases of subsistence including place of residence, than the former. At least this is apt to be the case where the residence groups become foci for the control of resources and as such are sharply differentiated from more inclusive political groupings. Thus a second aspect of an increased level of functional differentiation among the structures of the society tends to be involved.

Typically, I think, kinship status, in terms of both descent criteria and relative prestige of marriage opportunities is highly correlated with relative economic advantage and political power. This is to say that, under the conditions postulated, a tendency toward *vertical* differentiation of the society as a system overrides the pressure of the seamless web of kinship to

[5] See W. Lloyd Warner, *A Black Civilization* (2nd ed.), New York: Harper, 1958, for an analysis showing that such boundedness can be problematic.

[6] This analysis has been suggested in part by Charles Ackerman who bases himself on a variety of the recent studies of kinship systems, but, perhaps, particularly on Rodney Needham's studies of the Purums, *Structure and Sentiment,* Chicago: University of Chicago Press, 1960.

equalize the status of all units of equivalent *kinship* character. This tendency is the product of two converging forces.

On the one hand, relative advantages are differentiated: members of cadet lineages, the kinship units with lesser claims to preferment, are "forced" into peripheral positions. They move to less advantaged residential locations and accept less productive economic resources, and they are not in a position to counteract these disadvantages by the use of political power.[7]

On the other hand, the society as a system gains functional advantages by concentrating responsibility for certain functions. This concentration focuses in two areas, analytically, the political and the religious. First, the increased complexity of a society that has grown in population and probably territory and has become differentiated in status terms raises more difficult problems of internal order, e.g., controlling violence, upholding property and marriage rules, etc., and of defense against encroachment from outside. Second, a cultural tradition very close to both the details of everyday life and the interests and solidarities of particular groups is put under strain by increasing size and diversity. There is, then, pressure to centralize both responsibility for the symbolic systems, especially the religious, and authority in collective processes, and to redefine them in the direction of greater generality.

For the present argument, I assume that the tendencies to centralize political and religious responsibility need not be clearly differentiated in any immediate situation. The main point is that the differentiation of groups relative to an advantage-disadvantage axis tends to converge with the functional "need" for centralization of responsibility. Since responsibility and prestige seem to be inherently related in a system of institutionalized expectations, the advantaged group tends to assume, or have ascribed to it, the centralized responsibilities. It should be clear that the problem does not concern the balance between services to others and benefits accruing to the advantaged group, but the convergence of *both* sets of forces tending to the same primary structural outcome.

The development of written language can become a fundamental accelerating factor in this process, because in the nature of the case literacy cannot

---

[7] I am putting forward this set of differentiating factors as an ideal type. Of course, in many particular cases they may not all operate together. For example, it may frequently happen that the outer lands to which cadet lineages move are more productive than the old ones. The net effect of these discrepancies is probably a tendency toward diversity of lines of development rather than the extinction of the main one sketched here. Indeed we can go farther and say that unless this advantage of economic resources comes to be combined with such structural advantages as incorporation in a stratification system it will not lead to further evolutionary developments.

immediately be extended to total adult populations, and yet it confers enormous adaptive advantages. It also has a tendency to favor cultural or religious elements over the political.[8]

The crucial step in the development of a stratification system occurs when important elements in the population assume the prerogatives and functions of higher status and, at least by implication, exclude all other elements. This creates an "upper," a "leading" or, possibly, a "ruling" class set over against the "mass" of the population. Given early, or, indeed, not so early conditions, it is inevitable that membership in this upper class is primarily if not entirely based on kinship status. Thus, an individual military or other leader may go far toward establishing an important criterion of status, but in doing so he elevates the status of his lineage. He cannot dissociate his relatives from his own success, even presuming he would wish to.

Stratification in the present sense, then, is the differentiation of the population on a prestige scale of kinship units such that the distinctions among such units, or classes of them, become hereditary to an important degree. There are reasons to assume that the early tendency, which may be repeated, leads to a *two*-class system. The most important means of consolidating such a system is upper-class endogamy. Since this repeats the primary principle which, along with the territoriality, delineates the boundaries of early societies, the upper class constitutes a kind of subsociety. It is not a class, however, unless its counterpart, the lower class, is clearly included in the *same* societal community.

From this "primordial" two-class system there are various possibilities for evolutionary change. Probably the most important leads to a four-class system.[9] This is based on the development of urban communities in which political-administrative functions, centralized religious and other cultural activities, and territorially specialized economic action are carried on. Thus, generalized "centers" of higher-order activity emerge, but the imperatives of social organization require that these centers, as local communities— including, e.g., "provincial" centers—cannot be inhabited exclusively by upper-class people. Hence the urban upper class tends to be differentiated from rural upper class,[10] and the urban from the rural lower class. When this occurs there is no longer a linear rank-order of classes. But so long as hereditary kinship status is a primary determinant of the individual's access

[8] See Talcott Parsons, *Societies: Comparative and Evolutionary Perspectives,* Englewood, N.J.: Prentice-Hall, 1964.

[9] Cf. Gideon Sjoberg, *The Preindustrial City,* Glencoe, Ill.: The Free Press, 1960, ch 5.

[10] The upper class will be primarily rural in societies that take a more or less feudal direction.

to "advantages," we may speak of a stratified society; beyond the lowest level of complexity, every society is stratified.

Diffuse as its significance is, stratification is an *evolutionary* universal because the most primitive societies are not in the present sense stratified, but, beyond them, it is on two principal counts a prerequisite of a very wide range of further advances. First, what I have called a "prestige" position is a generalized prerequisite of responsible concentration of leadership. With few exceptions, those who lack a sufficiently "established" position cannot afford to "stick their necks out" in taking the responsibility for important changes. The second count concerns the availability of resources for implementing innovations. The dominance of kinship in social organization is inseparably connected with rigidity. People do what they are required to do by virtue of their kinship status. To whatever degree kinship is the basis of solidarity *within* an upper class, closure of that class by endogamy precludes kinship from being the basis of upper-class claims on the services and other resources of the lower groups. So long as the latter are genuinely within the same society, which implies solidarity across the class line, relations of mutual usefulness (e.g., patron-client relationships across class lines) on non-kin bases are possible—opening the door to universalistic definitions of merit as well as providing the upper groups with the resources to pursue their own advantages.

Social stratification in its initial development may thus be regarded as one primary condition of releasing the process of social evolution from the obstacles posed by ascription. The strong emphasis on kinship in much of the sociological literature on stratification tends to obscure the fact that the new mobility made possible by stratification is due primarily to such breaks in kinship ascription as that across class lines. . . .

## Cultural Legitimation

Specialized cultural legitimation is, like stratification, intimately involved in the emergence from primitiveness, and certainly the two processes are related. Legitimation could, perhaps, be treated first; in certain crucial respects it is a prerequisite to the establishment of the type of prestige position referred to above. The ways in which this might be the case pose a major problem for more detailed studies of evolutionary processes. Our task here, however, is much more modest, namely to call attention to the fact that without both stratification and legitimation no major advances beyond the level of primitive society can be made.

The point of reference for the development of legitimation systems is the cultural counterpart of the seamless web of the kinship nexus with its presumptive equality of units. This is the cultural definition of the social collectivity simply as "we" who are essentially human or "people" and as such are undifferentiated, even in certain concepts of time, from our ancestors—except in certain senses for the mythical "founders"—and from contemporary "others." If the others are clearly recognized to be others (in an ideal type seamless web they would not be; they would be merely special groups of kin), they are regarded as not "really human," as strange in the sense that their relation to "us" is not comprehensible.

By explicit cultural legitimation, I mean the emergence of an institutionalized cultural definition of the society of reference, namely a referent of "we" (e.g., "We, the Tikopia" in Firth's study) which is differentiated, historically or comparatively or both, from other societies, while the merit of we-ness is asserted in a normative context. This definition has to be religious in some sense, e.g., stated in terms of a particular sacred tradition of relations to gods or holy places. It may also ascribe various meritorious features to the group, e.g., physical beauty, warlike prowess, faithful trusteeship of sacred territory or tradition, etc.

This usage of the term legitimation is closely associated with Max Weber's analysis of political authority. For very important reasons the primary focus of early stages beyond the primitive is political, involving the society's capacity to carry out coordinated collective action. Stratification, therefore, is an essential condition of major advances in political effectiveness, because, as just noted, it gives the advantaged elements a secure enough position that they can accept certain risks in undertaking collective leadership.

The differentiation inherent in stratification creates new sources of strain and potential disorganization, and the use of advantaged position to undertake major innovations multiplies this strain. Especially if, as is usually the case, the authors of major social innovation are already advantaged, they require legitimation for both their actions and their positions. Thus, a dynamic inherent in the development of cultural systems[11] revolves about the cultural importance of the question *why*—why such social arrangements as prestige and authority relations, and particular attendant rewards and deprivations, come about and are structured as they are. This cultural dynamic converges with the consequences of the stratification developments already outlined. Hence the crucial problem here is distributive, that of justifying advantages and prerogatives *over against* burdens and depriva-

[11] Claude Lévi-Strauss, *Totemism*, Boston: Beacon Paperbacks, 1963.

tions. Back of this, however, lies the problem of the meaning of the societal enterprise as a whole.

As the bases of legitimation are inherently cultural, meeting the legitimation need necessarily involves putting some kind of a premium on certain cultural services, and from this point of view there is clearly some potential advantage in specializing cultural action. Whether, under what conditions, and in what ways political and religious leadership or prestige status are differentiated from each other are exceedingly important general problems of societal evolution, but we cannot go into them here. A "God-King" may be the primary vehicle of legitimation for his own political regime, or the political "ruler" may be dependent on a priestly class that is in some degree structurally independent of his regime. But the main problems have to do with explicating the cultural basis of legitimation and institutionalizing agencies for implementing that function.

The functional argument here is essentially the same as that for stratification. Over an exceedingly wide front and relatively independently of particular cultural variations, political leaders must on the long run have not only sufficient power, but also legitimation for it. Particularly when bigger implementive steps are to be legitimized, legitimation must become a relatively explicit and, in many cases, a socially differentiated function. The combination of differentiated cultural patterns of legitimation with socially differentiated agencies is the essential aspect of the evolutionary universal of legitimation.

As evolutionary universals, stratification and legitimation are associated with the developmental problems of breaking through the ascriptive nexus of kinship, on the one hand, and of "traditionalized" culture, on the other. In turn they provide the basis for differentiation of a system that has previously, in the relevant respects, been undifferentiated. Differentiation must be carefully distinguished from segmentation, i.e., from either the development of undifferentiated segmental units of any given type within the system, or the splitting off of units from the system to form new societies, a process that appears to be particularly common at primitive levels. Differentiation requires solidarity and integrity of the system as a whole, with both common loyalties and common normative definitions of the situation. Stratification as here conceived is a hierarchical status differentiation that cuts across the overall seamless web of kinship and occurs definitely within a single collectivity, a "societal community." Legitimation is the differentiation of cultural definitions of normative patterns from a completely embedded, taken-for-granted fusion with the social structure, accompanied by institutionalization of the explicit, culture-oriented, legitimizing function in subsystems of the society. . . .

## Bureaucratic Organization

A second pair of evolutionary universals develop, each with varying degrees of completeness and relative importance, in societies that have moved considerably past the primitive stage, particularly those with well-institutionalized literacy.[12] These universals are administrative bureaucracy, which in early stages is found overwhelmingly in government, and money and markets. I shall discuss bureaucracy first because its development is likely to precede that of money and markets.

Despite the criticisms made of it, mainly in the light of the complexities of modern organizations, Weber's ideal type can serve as the primary point of reference for a discussion of bureaucracy.[13] Its crucial feature is the institutionalization of the *authority of office*. This means that both individual incumbents and, perhaps even more importantly, the bureaucratic organization itself, may act "officially" for, or "in the name of," the organization, which could not otherwise exist. I shall call this capacity to act, or more broadly, that to make and promulgate binding decisions, *power* in a strict analytical sense.[14]

Although backed by coercive sanctions, up to and including the use of physical force, *at the same time* power rests on the consensual solidarity of a system that includes both the users of power and the "objects" of its use. (Note that I do not say *against* whom it is used: the "against" may or may not apply.) Power in this sense is the capacity of a unit in the social system, collective or individual, to establish or activate commitments to performance that contributes to, or is in the interest of, attainment of the goals of a collectivity. It is not itself a "factor" in effectiveness, nor a "real" output of the process, but a medium of mobilization and acquisition of factors and outputs. In this respect, it is like money.

Office implies the differentiation of the role of incumbent from a person's

[12] As a predominantly cultural innovation, literacy is not discussed here. Cf. Parsons, *Societies, op. cit.*, ch. 1.

[13] See "The Analysis of Formal Organizations," Part I of my *Structure and Process in Modern Societies*, Glencoe, Ill.: The Free Press, 1960; Peter M. Blau, "Critical Remarks on Weber's Theory of Authority," *American Political Science Review*, 57 (June, 1963), pp. 305–316, and *The Dynamics of Bureaucracy* (2nd ed.) Chicago: University of Chicago Press, 1963; Carl J. Friedrich (ed.), *Authority* (Nomos I), Cambridge: Harvard University Press, 1958, especially Friedrich's own contribution, "Authority and Reason."

[14] Cf. Talcott Parsons, "On the Concept of Political Power," *Proceedings of the American Philosophical Society*, 107 (June, 1963), pp. 232–262.

other role-involvements, above all from his kinship roles. Hence, so far as function in the collectivity is defined by the obligations of ascriptive kinship status, the organizational status cannot be an office in the present sense. Neither of the other two types of authority that Weber discusses—traditional and charismatic—establishes this differentiation between organizational role and the "personal" status of the incumbent. Hence bureaucratic authority is always rational-legal in type. Weber's well-known proposition that the top of a bureaucratic structure cannot itself be bureaucratic may be regarded as a statement about the modes of articulation of such a structure with other structures in the society. These may involve the ascribed traditional authority of royal families, some form of charismatic leadership, or the development of democratic associational control, to be discussed briefly below.

Internally, a bureaucratic system is always characterized by an institutionalized hierarchy of authority, which is differentiated on two axes: *level* of authority and "sphere" of competence. Spheres of competence are defined either on segmentary bases, e.g., territorially, or on functional bases, e.g., supply vs. combat units in an army. The hierarchical aspect defines the levels at which a higher authority's decisions, in case of conflict, take precedence over those of a lower authority. It is a general bureaucratic principle that the higher the level, the smaller the relative number of decision-making agencies, whether individual or collegia, and the wider the scope of each, so that at the top, in principle, a single agency must carry responsibilty for *any* problems affecting the organization. Such a hierarchy is one of "pure" authority only so far as status within it is differentiated from other components of status, e.g., social class. Even with rather clear differentiation, however, position in a stratification system is likely to be highly correlated with position in a hierarchy of authority. Seldom, if ever, are high bureaucratic officials unequivocally members of the lowest social class.[15]

Externally, two particularly important boundaries pose difficulties for bureaucracies. The first has to do with recruiting manpower and obtaining facilities. In ideal type, a position in a bureaucratic organization constitutes an occupational role, which implies that criteria of eligibility should be defined in terms of competence and maximal responsibility to the organization, not to "private" interests independent of, and potentially in conflict with,

---

[15] The Ottoman Empire, where many high officials were "slaves" of the Sultan, is not an exception. In such circumstances slaves took on the status of their master's "household," and hence were outside the normal stratification system. See H.A.R. Gibb, *Studies on the Civilization of Islam,* Boston: Beacon Press, 1962.

those of the organization. Thus high aristocrats may put loyalty to their lineage ahead of the obligations of office, or clergymen in political office may place loyalty to the church ahead of obligation to the civil government. Also, remunerating officials and providing facilities for their functions presents a serious problem of differentiation and hence of independence. The "financing of public bodies," as Weber calls it,[16] cannot be fully bureaucratic in this sense unless payment is in money, the sources of which are outside the control of the recipients. Various forms of benefices and prebends only very imperfectly meet these conditions, but modern salaries and operating budgets approximate them relatively closely.[17]

The second boundary problem concerns political support. An organization is bureaucratic so far as incumbents of its offices can function independently of the influence of elements having special "interests" in its output, except where such elements are properly involved in the definition of the organization's goals through its nonbureaucratic top. Insulation from such influence, for example through such crude channels as bribery, is difficult to institutionalize and, as is well known, is relatively rare.[18]

In the optimal case, internal hierarchy and division of functions, recruitment of manpower and facilities, and exclusion of "improper" influence, are all regulated by universalistic norms. This is implicit in the proposition that bureaucratic authority belongs to Weber's rational-legal type. Of course, in many concrete instances this condition is met very imperfectly, even in the most highly developed societies.

· · · ·

[16] Max Weber, "The Financing of Political Bodies," in *The Theory of Social and Economic Organization*, Glencoe, Ill.: The Free Press, 1947, pp. 310 ff.

[17] Problems of this type have been exceedingly common over wide ranges and long periods. Eisenstadt gives many illustrations of the loss of fluidity of resources through aristocratization and similar developments. A very important one is the ruralization of the Roman legions in the later imperial period—they became essentially a border militia. At a lower level, a particularly good example is the difficulty of institutionalizing the differentiation of occupational from familial roles for the industrial labor force. S. N. Eisenstadt, *The Political Systems of Empires*, New York: The Free Press of Glencoe, 1963, especially ch. 3; Martin P. Nilsson, *Imperial Rome*, New York: Harcourt, Brace, 1926; Neil J. Smelser, *Social Change in the Industrial Revolution*, Chicago: University of Chicago Press, 1959.

[18] The difficulty of mobilizing political support for bureaucratic regimes is exemplified by the particularly important case of the struggle between monarchs and aristocracies in early modern Europe. In spite of the obvious dangers of absolutism to the freedoms of the urban classes, the alliance between them and the monarchs was an essential way of developing sufficient support to counteract the traditionalizing influence of the aristocracies. The special place of the latter in military organization made the task of monarchies more difficult. Max Beloff, *The Age of Absolutism*, New York: Harper Torchbooks, 1962; John B. Wolf, *The Emergence of the Great Powers*, New York: Harper Torchbooks, 1962; especially chs. 4 and 7.

The basis on which I classify bureaucracy as an evolutionary universal is very simple. As Weber said, it is the most effective large-scale administrative organization that man has invented, and there is no direct substitute for it.[19] Where capacity to carry out large-scale organized operations is important, e.g., military operations with mass forces, water control, tax administration, policing of large and heterogeneous populations, and productive enterprise requiring large capital investment and much manpower, the unit that commands effective bureaucratic organization is inherently superior to the one that does not. It is by no means the only structural factor in the adaptive capacity of social systems, but no one can deny that it is an important one. Above all, it is built on further specializations ensuing from the broad emancipation from ascription that stratification and specialized legitimation make possible.

## Money and the Market Complex

Immediate effectivenes of collective function, especially on a large scale, depends on concentration of power, as noted. Power is in part a function of the mobility of the resources available for use in the interests of the collective goals in question. Mobility of resources, however, is a direct function of access to them through the market. Though the market is the most general means of such access, it does have two principal competitors. First is requisitioning through the direct application of political power, e.g., defining a collective goal as having military significance and requisitioning manpower under it for national defense. A second type of mobilization is the activation of nonpolitical solidarities and commitments, such as those of ethnic or religious membership, local community, caste, etc. The essential theme here is, "as one of us, it is your duty . . ."

The political power path involves a fundamental difficulty because of the role of explicit or implied coercion—"you contribute, or else . . ."—while the activation of non-political commitments, a category comprising at least two others, raises the issue of alternative obligations. The man appealed to in the interest of his ethnic group, may ask, "what about the problems of my family?" In contrast, market exchange avoids three dilemmas: first, that I must do what is expected or face punishment for noncompliance; second, if I do not comply, I will be disloyal to certain larger groups, identification with which is very important to my general status; third, if I do not comply,

[19] Weber, *The Theory of Social and Economic Organization, op. cit.,* p. 377.

I may betray the unit which, like my family, is the primary basis of my immediate personal security.

Market exchange makes it possible to obtain resources for future action and yet avoid such dilemmas as these, because money is a generalized resource for the consumer-recipient, who can purchase "good things" regardless of his relations to their sources in other respects. Availability through the market cannot be unlimited—one should not be able to purchase conjugal love or ultimate political loyalty—but possession of physical commodities, and by extension, control of personal services by purchase, certainly can, very generally, be legitimized in the market nexus.

As a symbolic medium, money "stands for" the economic utility of the real assets for which it is exchangeable, but it represents the concrete objects so abstractly that it is neutral among the competing claims of various other orders in which the same objects are significant. It thus directs attention away from the more consummatory and, by and large, immediate significance of these objects toward their *instrumental* significance as potential means to further ends. Thus money becomes the great mediator of the instrumental use of goods and services. Markets, involving both the access of the consuming unit to objects it needs for consumption and the access of producing units to "outlets" that are not ascribed, but contingent on the voluntary decisions of "customers" to purchase, may be stabilized institutionally. Thus this universal "emancipates" resources from such ascriptive bonds as demands to give kinship expectations priority, to be loyal in highly specific senses to certain political groups, or to submit the details of daily life to the specific imperatives of religious sects.

In the money and market system, money as a medium of exchange and property rights including rights of alienation, must be institutionalized. In general it is a further step that institutionalizes broadly an individual's contractual right to sell his services in a labor market without seriously involving himself in diffuse dependency relationships, which at lower status levels are usually in some ways "unfree." Property in land, on a basis that provides for its alienation, presents a very important problem. Its wide extension seems, except in a very few cases, to be a late development. The institution of contract in exchange of money and goods is also a complex area of considerable variation. Finally, money itself is by no means a simple entity, and in particular the development of credit instruments, banking and the like, has many variations.[20]

[20] A useful typology of the organization of economic exchange relations, from an evolutionary point of view, is given by Neil J. Smelser, *The Sociology of Economic Life*, Englewood Cliffs, N.J.:Prentice-Hall, 1963; pp. 86–88.

EVOLUTIONARY UNIVERSALS IN SOCIETY / PARSONS 701

These institutional elements are to a considerable degree independently variable and are often found unevenly developed. But if the main ones are sufficiently developed and integrated, the market system provides the operating units of the society, including of course its government, with a pool of disposable resources that can be applied to any of a range of uses and, within limits, can be shifted from use to use. The importance of such a pool is shown by the serious consequences of its shrinkage for even such highly organized political systems as some of the ancient empires.[21]

Modern socialist societies appear to be exceptional because, up to a point, they achieve high productivity with a relatively minimal reliance on monetary and market mechanisms, substituting bureaucracy for them. But too radical a "demonetization" has negative consequences even for such an advanced economy as that of the Soviet Union.

A principal reason for placing money and markets after bureaucracy in the present series of evolutionary universals is that the conditions of their large-scale development are more precarious. This is particularly true in the very important areas where a generalized system of universalistic norms has not yet become firmly established. Market operations, and the monetary medium itself, are inevitably highly dependent on political "protection." The very fact that the mobilization of political power, and its implementation through bureaucratic organization, is so effective generates interests against sacrificing certain short-run advantages to favor the enhanced flexibility that market systems can provide. This has been a major field of conflict historically, and it is being repeated today in underdeveloped societies. The strong tendency for developing societies to adopt a "socialistic" pattern reflects a preference for increasing productivity through governmentally controlled bureaucratic means rather than more decentralized market-oriented means.[22] But in general the money and market system has undoubtedly made a fundamental contribution to the adaptive capacity of

[21] S. N. Eisenstadt, op. cit. for example, makes a great deal of this factor, particularly in accounting for the gradual decline of the political power of the Byzantine Empire. This analysis is also closely related to Weber's thesis in his famous essay on the decline of the Roman Empire. Weber, however, particularly emphasized the mobility of manpower through slavery. Max Weber, "The Social Causes of the Decay of Ancient Civilization," Journal of General Education (October, 1950).

[22] See Gregory Grossman, "The Structure and Organization of the Soviet Economy" in the Slavic Review, 21 (June, 1962), pp. 203–222. The constriction of the market system may also have been a major factor in the difficulties suffered by the Chinese Communist regime in connection with the "Great Leap Forward" of 1958 and subsequent years. Audrey Donnithorne, "The Organization of Rural Trade in China Since 1958," China Quarterly, No. 8 (October–December, 1961), pp. 77–91, and Leo A. Orleans, "Problems of Manpower Absorption in Rural China," China Quarterly, No. 7 (July–September, 1961), pp. 69–84.

the societies in which it has developed; those that restrict it too drastically are likely to suffer from severe adaptive disadvantages in the long run.

## Generalized Universalistic Norms

A feature common to bureaucratic authority and the market system is that they incorporate, and are hence dependent on, universalistic norms. For bureaucracy, these involve definitions of the powers of office, the terms of access to it, and the line dividing proper from improper pressure or influence. For money and markets, the relevant norms include the whole complex of property rights, first in commodities, later in land and in monetary assets. Other norms regulate the monetary medium and contractual relations among the parties to transactions. Here relations between contracts of service or employment and other aspects of the civil and personal statuses of the persons concerned are particularly crucial. . . .

Although it is very difficult to pin down just what the crucial components are, how they are interrelated, and how they develop, one can identify the development of a general legal system as a crucial aspect of societal evolution. A general legal system is an integrated system of universalistic norms, applicable to the society as a whole rather than to a few functional or segmental sectors, highly generalized in terms of principles and standards, and relatively independent of both the religious agencies that legitimize the normative order of the society and vested interest groups in the operative sector, particularly in government.

The extent to which both bureaucratic organization and market systems can develop *without* a highly generalized universalistic normative order should not be underestimated. Such great Empires as the Mesopotamian, the ancient Chinese, and, perhaps the most extreme example, the Roman, including its Byzantine extension, certainly testify to this. But these societies suffered either from a static quality, failing to advance beyond certain points, or from instability leading in many cases to retrogression.[23] Although many of the elements of such a general normative order appeared in quite highly developed form in earlier societies, in my view their crystallization into a coherent system represents a distinctive new step, which more than the industrial revolution itself, ushered in the *modern* era of social evolution.[24]

The clear differentiation of secular government from religious organization has been a long and complicated process, and even in the modern world

[23] Eisenstadt, *op. cit.,* pp. 349 ff.
[24] Parsons, *Societies, op. cit.*

its results are unevenly developed. It has perhaps gone farthest in the sharp separation of Church and State in the United States. Bureaucracy has, of course, played an important part in this process. The secularization of government is associated with that of law, and both of these are related to the level of generality of the legal system.

Systems of law that are *directly* religiously sanctioned, treating compliance as a religious obligation, also tend to be "legalistic" in the sense of emphasizing detailed prescriptions and prohibitions, each of which is given specific Divine sanction. Preeminent examples are the Hebrew law of Leviticus, the later developments in the Talmudic tradition, and Islamic law based on the Koran and its interpretations. Legal decisions and the formulation of rules to cover new situations must then be based as directly as possible on an authoritative sacred text.

Not only does religious law as such tend to inhibit generalization of legal principle, but it also tends to favor what Weber called *substantive* over *formal* rationality.[25] The standard of legal correctness tends to be the implementation of religious precepts, not procedural propriety and consistency of general principle. Perhaps the outstanding difference between the legal systems of the other Empires, and the patterns that were developed importantly in Roman law, was the development of elements of formal rationality, which we may regard as a differentiation of legal norms out of "embeddedness" in the religious culture. The older systems—many of which still exist—tended to treat "justice" as a direct implementation of precepts of religious and moral conduct, in terms of what Weber called *Wertrationalität*, without institutionalizing an independent system of *societal* norms, adapted to the function of social control at the societal level and integrated on its own terms. The most important foci of such an independent system are, first, some kind of "codification" of norms under principles not *directly* moral or religious, though they generally continue to be grounded in religion, and, second, the formalization of procedural rules, defining the situations in which judgments are to be made on a societal basis. Especially important is the establishment of courts for purposes other than permitting political and religious leaders to make pronouncements and "examples."[26]

Something similar can be said about what I have called operative vested interests, notably government. Advantages are to be gained, on the one hand, by binding those outside the direct control of the group in question

25 Weber, *The Theory of Social and Economic Organization, op. cit.,* pp. 184 ff, and *Max Weber on Law in Economy and Society,* Cambridge: Harvard University Press, 1954, ch. 8.
26 Weber, *Max Weber on Law in Economy and Society, op. cit.*

with detailed regulation, while, on the other hand, leaving maximum free-dom for the group's leadership. This duality Weber made central to his concept of traditional authority, with its sphere of traditionalized fixity, on the one hand, and that of personal prerogative, reaching its extreme form in "sultanism," on the other.[27] Both aspects are highly resistant to the type of rationalization that is essential to a generalized universalistic legal system.

Though the Chinese Empire, Hindu law (*Manu*), Babylonia, and to some extent, Islam made important beginnings in the direction I am dis-cussing, the Roman legal system of the Imperial period was uniquely ad-vanced in these respects. Though the early *jus civilis* was very bound religiously, this was not true to the same extent of the *jus gentium*, or of the later system as a totality. While a professional judiciary never developed, the jurisconsults in their "unofficial" status did constitute a genuine pro-fessional group, and they systematized the law very extensively, in the later phases strongly under the influence of Stoic Philosophy.[28]

Though Roman law had a variety of more or less "archaic" features, its "failure" was surely on the level of institutionalization more than in any intrinsic defect of legal content. Roman society of that period lacked the in-stitutional capacity, through government, religious legitimation, and other channels, to integrate the immense variety of peoples and cultures within the Empire, or to maintain the necessary economic, political, and administra-tive structures.[29] Roman law remained, however, the cultural reference point of all the significant later developments.

The next phase, of course, was the development of Catholic Canon Law, incorporating much of Roman law. A major characteristic of the Western Church, Canon law was not only very important in maintaining and con-solidating the Church's differentiation from secular government and society, but, with the Justinian documents, it also preserved the legal tradition.

The third phase was the revival of the study of Roman secular law in Renaissance Italy and its gradual adoption by the developing national states of early modern Europe. The result was that the modern national state developed as, fundamentally, a *Rechtsstaat*. In Continental Europe, however, one fundamental limitation on this development was the degree to which the law continued to be intertwined and almost identified with gov-ernment. For example, most higher civil servants were lawyers. One might

[27] Weber, *The Theory of Social and Economic Organization, op. cit.*
[28] A handy summary of Roman legal development is "The Science of Law" by F. de Zulueta in Cyrus Balley (ed.), *The Legacy of Rome,* London: Oxford University Press, 1923.
[29] Weber, "The Social Causes of the Decay of Ancient Civilization," *op. cit.*

ask whether this represented a "legalization of bureaucracy" or a bureaucratization of the law and the legal profession. But with elaborate bodies of law, law faculties as major constituents of every important university, and the prominence of university-trained legal professions, Continental European nations certainly had well institutionalized legal systems. . . .

The development of English Common Law, with its adoption and further development in the overseas English-speaking world, not only constituted the most advanced case of universalistic normative order, but was probably decisive for the modern world. This general type of legal order is, in my opinion, the most important single hallmark of modern society. So much is it no accident that the Industrial Revolution occurred first in England, that I think it legitimate to regard the English type of legal system as a fundamental prerequisite of the first occurrence of the Industrial Revolution.[30]

## The Democratic Association

A rather highly generalized universalistic legal order is in all likelihood a necessary prerequisite for the development of the last structural complex to be discussed as universal to social evolution, the democratic association with elective leadership and fully enfranchised membership. At least this seems true of the institutionalization of this pattern in the governments of large-scale societies. This form of democratic association originated only in the late 18th century in the Western world and was nowhere complete, if universal adult suffrage is a criterion, until well into the present century. Of course, those who regard the Communist society as a stable and enduring type might well dispute that democratic government in this sense is an evolutionary universal. But before discussing that issue, I will outline the history and principal components of this universal.

Surely it is significant that the earliest cases of democratic government were the *poleis* of classical antiquity, which were also the primary early sources of universalistic law. The democratic *polis*, however, not only was small in scale by modern standards (note Aristotle's belief that a citizen body should never be too large to assemble within earshot of a given speaker, of course without the aid of a public address system), but also its democratic associational aspects never included a total society. It is esti-

[30]It is exceedingly important here once more to distinguish the first occurrence of a social innovation from its subsequent diffusion. The latter can occur without the whole set of prerequisite societal conditions necessary for the former. Cf. my *Structure and Process in Modern Societies, op. cit.*, ch. 3.

mated that during the Periclean age in Athens, only about 30,000 of a total population of about 150,000 were citizens, the rest being metics and slaves. And, of course, citizen women were not enfranchised. Thus even in its democratic phase the *polis* was emphatically a two-class system. And under the conditions of the time, when Roman society increased in scale away from the *polis* type of situation, citizenship, at least for large proportions of the Empire's population, was bound to lose political functions almost in proportion to its gains in legal significance.

The basic principle of democratic association, however, never completely disappeared. To varying degrees and in varying forms, it survived in the *municipia* of the Roman Empire, in the Roman Senate, and in various aspects of the organization of the Christian Church, though the Church also maintained certain hierarchical aspects. Later the collegial pattern, e.g., the *college* of Cardinals, continued to be an aspect of Church structure. In the Italian and North European city-states of the late Middle Ages and early modern period, it had its place in government, for example in "senates," which though not democratically elected, were internally organized as democratic bodies. Another important case was the guild, as an association of merchants or craftsmen. In modern times there have, of course, been many different types of private association in many different fields. It is certainly safe to say that, even apart from government, the democratic association is a most prominent and important constituent of modern societies.

At the level of national government, we can speak first of the long development of Parliamentary assemblies functioning as democratic associations and legislating for the nation, whose members have been to some degree elected from fairly early times. Secondly, there has been a stepwise extension of both the franchise for electing legislative representatives and the legislative supremacy of their assemblies, following the lead of England, which developed rapidly in these respects after 1688. Later, the French and American Revolutions dramatized the conception of the total national community as essentially a democratic association in this sense.

There are four critically important components of the democratic association. First is the institutionalization of the leadership function in the form of an elective office, whether occupied by individuals, executive bodies, or collegial groups like legislatures. The second is the franchise, the institutionalized participation of members in collective decision-making through the election of officers and often through voting on specific policy issues. Third is the institutionalization of procedural rules for the voting process and the determination of its outcome and for the process of "discussion" or campaigning for votes by candidates or advocates of policies. Fourth is the institutionalization of the nearest possible approximation to the voluntary principle in regard to membership status. In the private association this is fundamental—no case where membership is ascribed or compulsory can be called a "pure" democratic association. In government, however, the coercive and compulsory elements of power, as well as the recruitment of societal communities largely by birth, modify the principle. Hence universality of franchise tends to replace the voluntary membership principle.

Formalization of definite procedural rules governing voting and the counting and evaluation of votes may be considered a case of formal rationality in Weber's sense, since it removes the consequences of the act from the control of the particular actor. It limits his control to the specific act of casting his ballot, choosing among the alternatives officially presented to him. Indirectly his vote might contribute to an outcome he did not desire, e.g., through splitting the opposition to an undesirable candidate and thus actually aiding him, but he cannot control this, except in the voting act itself.

Besides such formalization, however, Rokkan has shown in his comparative and historical study of Western electoral systems, that there is a strikingly general tendency to develop three other features of the franchise.[31] The first of these is universality, minimizing if not eliminating the overlap between membership and disenfranchisement. Thus property qualifications and, most recently, sex qualifications have been removed so that now the main Western democratic polities, with minimal exceptions, have universal adult suffrage. The second is equality, eliminating "class" systems, like the Prussian system in the German Empire, in favor of the principle, one citizen, one vote.[32] Finally, secrecy of the ballot insulates the voting decision from pressures emanating from status superiors or peers that might interfere with the expression of the voter's personal preferences.

Certain characteristics of elective office directly complementary to those of the franchise can be formulated. Aside from the ways of achieving office and the rules of tenure in it, they are very similar to the pattern of bureaucratic office. The first, corresponding to the formalization of electoral rules, is that conduct in office must be legally regulated by universalistic norms.

[31] Stein Rokkan, "Mass Suffrage, Secret Voting, and Political Participation," *The European Journal of Sociology*, 2 (1961), pp. 132–152.

[32] The recent decisions of the U.S. Supreme Court on legislative reapportionment also constitute an important step in this process. In the majority opinion of the decision outlawing the Georgia county unit system of voting, Justice Douglas explicitly stated that this was a direct application of the Constitutional principle of equal protection of the laws. See *The New York Times*, March 19, 1963.

Second, corresponding to the universality of the franchise, is the principle of subordinating segmental or private interests to the collective interest within the sphere of competence of the office. Third, corresponding to equality of the franchise, is the principle of accountability for decisions to a total electorate. And finally, corresponding to secrecy of the ballot, is the principle of limiting the powers of office to specified spheres, in sharp contrast to the diffuseness of both traditional and charismatic authority.

The adoption of even such a relatively specific pattern as equality of the franchise may be considered a universal tendency, essentially because, under the principle that the membership rightfully chooses both the broad orientations of collective policy and the elements having leadership privileges and responsibilities, there is, among those with minimal competence, no universalistic basis for discriminating among classes of members. As a limitation on the hierarchical structure of power within collectivities, equality of franchise is the limiting or boundary condition of the democratic association, corresponding to equality of opportunity on the bureaucratic boundary of the polity.[33]

Especially, though not exclusively, in national territorial states, the stable democratic association is notoriously difficult to institutionalize. Above all this seems to be a function of the difficulty in motivating holders of immediately effective power to relinquish their opportunities voluntarily despite the seriousness of the interest at stake—relinquishment of control of governmental machinery after electoral defeat being the most striking problem.[34] The system is also open to other serious difficulties, most notably corruption and "populist" irresponsibility, as well as *de facto* dictatorship. Furthermore, such difficulties are by no means absent in private associations, as witness the rarity of effective electoral systems in large trade unions.[35]

The basic argument for considering democratic association a universal, despite such problems, is that, the larger and more complex a society becomes, the more important is effective political organization, not only in its administrative capacity, but also, and not least, in its support of a universalistic legal order. Political effectiveness includes both the scale and

[33] Cf. Parsons, "On the Concept of Political Power," *op. cit.* and John Rawls, *loc. cit.*

[34] In the 1920's and 30's the late Professor H. J. Laski was fond of saying that no "ruling class" would *ever* relinquish its position peacefully. Yet, in the late 1940's, the British Labor government both introduced the "welfare state" and set India free without a Conservative *coup d'état* occurring against them.

[35] Seymour Martin Lipset, Martin Trow, and James Coleman, *Union Democracy,* Glencoe, Ill.: The Free Press, 1956.

operative flexibility of the organization of power. Power, however, precisely as a generalized societal medium, depends overwhelmingly on a consensual element,[36] i.e., the ordered institutionalization and exercise of influence, linking the power system to the higher-order societal consensus at the value level.[37]

No institutional form basically different from the democratic association can, *not* specifically *legitimize* authority and power in the most general sense, but *mediate consensus in its exercise* by particular persons and groups, and in the formation of particular binding policy decisions. At high levels of structural differentiation in the society itself and in its governmental system, generalized legitimation cannot fill this gap adequately. Providing structured participation in the selection of leaders and formation of basic policy, as well as in opportunities to be heard and exert influence and to have a real choice among alternatives, is the crucial function of the associational system from this point of view.

. . . .

## Conclusion

This paper is not meant to present even the schematic outline of a "theory" of societal evolution. My aim is much more limited: I have selected for detailed attention and illustration an especially important type of structural innovation that has appeared in the course of social change. I have attempted to clarify the concept "evolutionary universal" by briefly discussing a few examples from organic evolution, namely, vision, the human hands, and the human brain. I have interpreted these as innovations endowing their possessors with a very substantial increase in generalized adaptive capacity, so substantial that species lacking them are relatively disadvantaged in the major areas in which natural selection operates, not so much for survival as for the opportunity to initiate further major developments.

Four features of human societies at the level of culture and social organization were cited as having universal and major significance as prerequisites for socio-cultural development: technology, kinship organization based on an incest taboo, communication based on language, and religion. Primary attention, however, was given to six organizational complexes that develop

[36] Parsons, "On the Concept of Political Power," *loc. cit.*
[37] Parsons, "On the Concept of Influence," *Public Opinion Quarterly*, 27 (Spring, 1963), pp. 37–62.

mainly at the level of social structure. The first two, particularly important for the emergence of societies from primitiveness, are stratification, involving a primary break with primitive kinship ascription, and cultural legitimation, with institutionalized agencies that are independent of a diffuse religious tradition.

Fundamental to the structure of modern societies are, taken together, the other four complexes: bureaucratic organization of collective goal-attainment, money and market systems, generalized universalistic legal systems, and the democratic association with elective leadership and mediated membership support for policy orientations. Although these have developed very unevenly, some of them going back a very long time, all are clearly much more than simple "inventions" of particular societies.

Perhaps a single theme tying them together is that differentiation and attendant reduction in ascription has caused the initial two-class system to give way to more complex structures at the levels of social stratification and the relation between social structure and its cultural legitimation. First, this more complex system is characterized by a highly generalized universalistic normative structure in all fields. Second, subunits under such normative orders have greater autonomy both in pursuing their own goals and interests and in serving others instrumentally. Third, this autonomy is linked with the probability that structural units will develop greater diversity of interests and subgoals. Finally, this diversity results in pluralization of scales of prestige and therefore of differential access to economic resources, power, and influence.

Comparatively, the institutionalization of these four complexes and their interrelations is very uneven. In the broadest frame of reference, however, we may think of them as together constituting the main outline of the structural foundations of modern society. Clearly, such a combination, balanced relative to the exigencies of particular societal units, confers on its possessors an adaptive advantage far superior to the structural potential of societies lacking it. . . .

# SOCIAL CHANGE, DIFFERENTIATION AND EVOLUTION * (*Eisenstadt*)

Evolutionary theory dominated sociological thought in the 19th and early 20th centuries, but since about 1920 interest in it has, on the whole, given way to preoccupation with systematic analysis of social systems, analysis of broad social and demographic trends, and investigation of the social determinants of behavior. The recent tentative revival of interest in an evolutionary perspective is closely related to growing interest in historical and comparative studies. It does not, of course, denote a mere "return" to the assumptions of the older schools, but it does imply revision and reappraisal of evolutionary theory in the light of recent advances in sociological theory and research.

The older evolutionary models broke down mainly on two stumbling blocks. The first was the assumption that the development of human societies is unilinear, and the major "stages" of development universal.[1] The second stumbling block was the failure to specify fully the systemic characteristics of evolving societies or institutions, as well as the mechanisms and processes of change through which the transition from one "stage" to another was effected. Most of the classical evolutionary schools tended, rather, to point out general causes of change (economic, technological, spiritual, etc.) or some general trends (e.g., the trend to complexity) inherent in the development of societies. Very often they confused such general tendencies with the causes of change or assumed that the general tendencies explain concrete instances of change.[2]

* Reprinted from *The American Sociological Review*, Vol. 29, 3 (June 1964) pp. 373–386 with permission of the American Sociological Association and the author.

[1] One of the best expositions of the strength and limitations of the classical evolutionary approach was written by a prominent contemporary sociologist identified with that approach. See Morris Ginsberg, "On the Concept of Evolution in Sociology" in *idem, Essays on Sociology and Social Philosophy*, Vol. I, London: William Heinemann, 1957, and *idem, Diversity of Morals*, London: William Heinemann, 1956, chs. 11 and 12. For a more recent summary, see T. B. Bottomore, *Sociology, A Guide to Problems and Literature*, London: Unwin University Books, 1962, chs. 7 and 16.

[2] See Kenneth E. Bock, "Evolution, Function and Change," *American Sociological Review*, 28 (April, 1963), pp. 229–237. The use of general causes or trends for explanation of evolution can be found also in Marshall D. Sahlins and Elman R. Service (eds.), *Evolution and Culture*, Ann Arbor, Mich.: University of Michigan Press, 1960, who follow Leslie A. White, *The Evolution of Culture*, New York: McGraw-Hill, 1959. However, their distinction between general and specific evolution indicates that they are aware at least of some of the difficulties in such an assumption.

Hence, reappraisal of an evolutionary perspective is contingent on systematic explanation of the processes of change within a society, the processes of transition from one type of society to another, and especially the extent to which such transition may crystallize into different types or "stages" that evince some basic characteristics common to different societies. Despite contrary claims, the conceptual tools recently developed for the analysis of systematic properties of societies and social institutions may be used to analyze the concrete processes of change within them.

First, tendencies to change are inherent in all human societies, because they face basic problems to which no overall continuous solutions exist. These problems include uncertainties of socialization, perennial scarcity of resources relative to individual aspirations and different, contrasting, types of social orientation or principles of social organization (e.g., *Gemeinschaft* vs. *Gesellschaft*) within the society.[3] Second, specific processes of change in any concrete society are closely related to the specific characteristics of its institutional structure and can be explained largely in terms of the crystallization of this structure and the problem of maintaining it. Moreover, the directions of change in any given society are greatly influenced and limited by its basic systematic characteristics and by the specific problems resulting from its institutionalization.[4]

From the point of view of reappraising evolutionary theory, however, the more crucial problem concerns the extent to which change from one type of society to another is not accidental or random but evinces overall evolutionary or "developmental" trends in the society's adaptability to an extending environment. In other words, the main problem here is the extent to which such changes may be envisaged as crystallizing into developmental "stages" —the key concept in classical evolutionary thought.

In the older evolutionary school such stages have been construed mostly in terms of "specialization" and "complexity." In recent works these concepts have been to a large extent replaced by that of "differentiation."[5] This replacement is not merely semantic: it reflects an important theoretical advance in the study of society—an advance that greatly facilitates critical re-evaluation of the evolutionary perspective in the social sciences.

---

[3] See Wilbert E. Moore, "A Reconsideration of Theories of Social Change," *American Sociological Review*, 25 (December, 1960), pp. 817 ff.

[4] See Shmuel N. Eisenstadt, "Institutionalization and Change," *American Sociological Review*, 29 (April, 1964), pp. 49–59.

[5] See, for instance, Robert M. MacIver and Charles Page, *Society*, New York: Rinehart, 1947; Talcott Parsons, *The Social System*, Glencoe, Ill.: The Free Press, 1951, chs. 4, 5; and Marion J. Levy, Jr., *The Structure of Society*, Princeton: Princeton University Press, 1952, especially ch. 7.

Differentiation is, like complexity or specialization, first of all a classificatory concept. It describes the ways through which the main social functions or the major institutional spheres of society become disassociated from one another, attached to specialized collectivities and roles, and organized in relatively specific and autonomous symbolic and organizational frameworks within the confines of the same institutionalized system.

In broad evolutionary terms, such continuous differentiation has been usually conceived as a continuous development from the "ideal" type of the primitive society or band in which all the major roles are allocated on an ascriptive basis, and in which the division of labor is based primarily on family and kinship units.[6] Development proceeds through various stages of specialization and differentiation.

Specialization is manifest first when each of the major institutional spheres develops, through the activities of people placed in strategic roles within it, its own organizational units and complexes, and its specific criteria of action. The latter tend to be more congruent with the basic orientations of a given sphere, facilitating the development of its potentialities—technological innovation, cultural and religious creativity, expansion of political power or participation, or development of complex personality structure.[7]

Secondly, different levels or stages of differentiation denote the degree to which major social and cultural activities, as well as certain basic resources —manpower, economic resources, commitments—have been disembedded or freed from kinship, territorial and other ascriptive units. On the one hand, these "free-floating" resources pose new problems of integration, while on the other they may become the basis for a more differentiated social order which is, potentially at least, better adapted to deal with a more variegated environment.

## Differentiation and Problems of Integration

The more differentiated and specialized institutional spheres become more interdependent and potentially complementary in their functioning within the same overall institutionalized system. But this very complementarity creates more difficult and complex problems of integration. The growing

[6] For a recent discussion of primitive societies from an evolutionary point of view, see Elman R. Service, *Primitive Social Organization, An Evolutionary Perspective*, New York: Random House, 1962.

[7] For an earlier approach, see Pitirim A. Sorokin, *Society, Culture and Personality*, New York: Harper, 1947, and for one of the fullest recent analytic approaches, see Talcott Parsons and Edward A. Shils (eds.), *Toward a General Theory of Action*, Cambridge, Mass.: Harvard University Press, 1951, p. 2.

autonomy of each sphere of social activity, and the concomitant growth of interdependence and mutual interpretation among them, pose for each sphere more difficult problems in crystallizing its own tendencies and potentialities and in regulating its normative and organizational relations with other spheres.[8] And at each more "advanced" level or stage of differentiation, the increased autonomy of each sphere creates more complex problems of integrating these specialized activities into one systemic framework.[9]

Continuous regulation of these more specialized units and of the flow of "free-floating" resources among them necessitates the institutionalization of certain symbolic, normative and organizational patterns[10]—written language, generalized legal systems, and various types of complex social organization—which evince, at each more complex level of differentiation, a greater scope of generalization.

Perhaps the best indication of the importance of these macrosocietal integrative problems is the emergence of a "center," on which the problems of different groups within the society increasingly impinge.[11] The emergence of a political or religious "center" of a society, distinct from its ascriptive components, is one of the most important break-throughs of development from the relatively closed kinship-based primitive community. In some of the archaic societies of the ancient Near East, Pre-Han China, and various preliminary stages of City States, the center in these first stages of differentiation was not only structurally differentiated from the major ascriptive groups but also distinct from them, being largely identical with relatively closed but already differentiated higher-status groups.

With growing differentiation in later city states and in feudal and centralized Imperial systems, impingement of the broader groups and strata on

[8] For an analysis of these problems in one major cultural and social sphere, see Robert N. Bellah's companion article in this issue on evolution in religion.

[9] For an analysis of one such case see Shmuel N. Eisenstadt, *The Political Systems of Empires,* New York: The Free Press, 1963.

[10] Talcott Parsons describes these as "evolutionary universals" in his companion article in this issue.

[11] On the concept of "center of society" and on the problems of macrosociological analysis, see Edward A. Shils, "Epilogue," in Talcott Parsons, Edward A. Shils, Kaspar D. Naegele, and Jesse R. Pitts (eds.), *Theories of Society,* New York: The Free Press, 1961, Vol. 2, especially pp. 1441–1445. For special developments in modern societies see Daniel Lerner, *The Passing of Traditional Society,* Glencoe, Ill.: The Free Press, 1958; Talcott Parsons, *Structure and Process in Modern Societies,* Glencoe, Ill.: The Free Press, 1960, ch. 4; Edward A. Shils, *Political Development in New States,* The Hague: Mouton, 1963; and Shmuel N. Eisenstadt, *Modernization, Growth and Diversity,* The Carnegie Faculty Seminar on Political and Administrative Development, Indiana University, Bloomington, Ind., 1963.

the center increased somewhat. This is most clearly visible at the onset of modernization, when broader groups and strata tend to be drawn into the center, demanding greater participation.

Recognition of the integrative problems that are attendant on new levels of differentiation constitutes the main theoretical implication of the concept of differentiation. How does this analytical implication affect the possibility of reappraising the evolutionary perspective in sociological theory?

Such a reappraisal is contingent on the explication of three major problems. First, the occurrence of changes that facilitate growing differentiation must be explained. Second, we must understand the conditions that ensure institutionalization of more differentiated, generalized, and adaptable systems, and third, the possibility that parallel systems will develop within different societies should be evaluated. We are as yet far from any definitive answers to these questions, but at least we can point out some of the most important problems.

The passage of a given society from one stage of differentiation to another is contingent on the development within it of certain processes of change which create a degree of differentiation that cannot be contained within the pre-existing system. Growing differentiation and the consequent structural break-throughs may take place through a secular trend of differentiation, or through the impact of one or a series of abrupt changes, or both. These tendencies may be activated by the occupants of strategic roles within the major institutional spheres as they attempt to broaden the scope and develop the potentialities of their respective spheres. The extent to which these changes are institutionalized, and the concrete form they take in any given society, necessarily depend on the basic institutional contours and premises of the pre-existing system, on its initial level of differentiation, and on the major conflicts and propensities for change within it.[12]

But we need not assume that all changes in all societies necessarily increase differentiation. On the contrary, the available evidence shows that many social changes do not give rise to overall changes in the scope of differentiation, but instead result mainly in changes in the relative strength and composition of different collectivities or in the integrative criteria of a particular institutional sphere. Largely because the problem has not yet been fully studied we do not know exactly what conditions facilitate or precipitate these different types of change in different societies.[13]

[12] See Eisenstadt, "Institutionalization and Change," *op. cit.*

[13] But see Fred Eggan, "Cultural Drift and Social Change," *Current Anthropology,* 4 (October 1963), pp. 347–360. For a preliminary attempt to analyze this problem in one case, see Eisenstadt, *The Political Systems of Empires, op. cit.,* ch. 12.

Similarly we need not assume that the successful, orderly institutionalization of a new, more differentiated social system is a necessary outcome of every instance of social change or of increased social differentiation within a society. Moreover, the concrete contours of such institutionalization may greatly vary among different societies at similar or parallel stages of differentiation.

The degree of differentiation refers mainly to the "division of labor" in any social system. It denotes the extent to which a society has been transformed from something approximating Durkheim's "mechanical" model to a potentially more "organic" one; it also denotes the extent to which new regulative or integrative problems cannot be dealt with by pre-existing institutions. Growing differentiation entails extension of the scope and depth of internal problems and of external environmental exigencies to which any social system is sensitive and with which it may or may not be able to deal.

The growing autonomy of the different institutional spheres, and the extension of their organizational scope, not only increases the range and depth of "social" and human problems, but it opens up new possibilities for development and creativity—for technological development, expansion of political power or rights, or cultural, religious, philosophical, and personal creativity. Growing differentiation also enhances systemic sensitivity to a much wider physical-technical environment and to more comprehensive intersocietal relations. But the growth of systemic sensitivity to a broader and more variegated environment, to new problems and exigencies, does not necessarily imply the development of the ability to deal with these problems, nor does it indicate the ways in which these problems may be solved. At any given level of differentiation, an institutional sphere may or may not achieve an adequate degree of integration, and the potentialities unfolded through the process of differentiation may be "wasted"—i.e., fail to become crystallized into an institutional structure.

## Responses to Growing Differentiation

The possibility that similar processes of change and institutionalization of different levels of differentiation may occur in different societies can be explained only so far as the available evidence bears out the assumption that the tendencies of major social spheres to autonomy and some of the basic potentialities for development in these spheres are characteristic of all societies.

Unlike the classical evolutionary writers, however, most "recent" theorists, from Weber on, do not assume that the types of social system characteristic of a given level of differentiation take on the same concrete institutional contours in all societies.[14] But the implications of this position have not yet been fully explicated.

At any level of development, response to the problems created by the process of differentiation may take one of several different forms. The most extreme outcome is failure to develop any adequate institutional solution to the new problems arising from growing differentiation. Aside from biological extinction, the consequences may be total or partial disintegration of the system, a semi-parasitic existence at the margin of another society, or total submersion within another society.

Thus, for instance, the Greek City States at the end of the Periclean period—in contrast to the late Roman Republic—did not produce a political leadership capable of building new types of political regime; as distinct socio-political units they became extinct. Similarly, many societies undergoing modernization lack the ability to crystallize new, viable regimes in the economic, political or cultural fields. In Bulgaria, for instance, Gerschenkron has analyzed an interesting case of what he calls "missed opportunity." The Congo constitutes perhaps the most extreme instance of this problem among contemporary new states.[15]

A less extreme type of response tends to lead to "regression," i.e., to the institutionalization of less differentiated systems. Examples include the establishment of small patrimonial or semi-feudal chiefdoms on the ruins of the Ahmenid Empire, the development of dispersed tribal-feudal systems at the downfall of the Roman Empire, and similar developments on the ruins of Greek City States.[16] Many such regressive developments are only partial in the sense that within some parts of the new institutional structure some nuclei of more differentiated and creative orientations may survive or even develop. Sometimes, but certainly not always, these nuclei "store" entrepreneurial ability for possible—but not inevitable—future developments.

[14] See Max Weber, *The Theory of Social and Economic Organization*, London: William Hodge, 1941, especially ch. 3. More recent works dealing with these problems include Robert Redfield, *The Primitive World and Its Transformations*, Ithaca, N.Y.: Cornell University Press, 1953; MacIver and Page, *op. cit.*, especially chs. 2 and 3; Talcott Parsons, *Structure and Process in Modern Societies, op. cit.*, ch. 3; and Verne F. Ray (ed.), *Intermediate Societies, Social Mobility and Communication*, Proceedings of the 1959 Annual Spring Meeting of the American Ethnological Society, Seattle: University of Washington Press, 1959.

[15] See Alexander A. Gerschenkron, *Economic Backwardness in Historical Perspective*, Cambridge, Mass.: Harvard University Press, 1962, ch. 8, and also Shmuel N. Eisenstadt, "Breakdowns of Modernization," *Economic Development and Cultural Change*, forthcoming.

[16] For analysis of some of the relevant societies, see Eisenstadt, *The Political Systems of Empires, op. cit.*, including full bibliographical references.

Another possibility, which perhaps overlaps with the last one but is not always identical to it, is the development of a social system in which the processes of differentiation and change go on relatively continuously in one part or sphere of a society without yet becoming fully integrated into a stable wider framework. In such situations a continuous process of unbalanced change may develop, resulting either in a breakdown of the existing institutional framework, or in stabilization at a relatively low level of integration.

Perhaps the best examples of such developments can be found in various dual conquest societies (e.g., conquest of the sedentary population by nomads in the Mongol Empire) and especially in the pre-independence stages of modern colonial societies. In the colonial societies, changes in the "central" areas have not been congruent with changes at the local level. Most changes introduced either directly or indirectly by the colonial powers have been focused on the central political or economic institutions of the society. Central political structures and orientations have been greatly altered by the introduction of unitary systems of administration, the unification or regularization of taxation, the establishment of modern court procedures, and at later stages, the introduction of limited types of representation. Similarly, many changes have been effected in the economy, notably the change to a market economy.

At the same time, however, the colonial powers (or indigenous traditional rulers) saw it as part of their task to effect these changes only within the limits set by the existing institutions and their own interests. The rulers tried to contain the changes taking place in the local rural and urban communities within the pre-existing traditional systems, and at the local level most of their administrative efforts were aimed at strengthening existing organizations and relations, maintaining peace and order, and reorganizing the system of taxation. Thus, while the administration attempted to introduce innovations—particularly new taxes and improved methods of revenue administration—it did so within a relatively unchanged social setting, with the implicit goal of limiting changes to technical matters.

These processes of uneven changes in colonial societies, unlike parallel but less intensive and continuous processes in the older conquest societies, could not be frozen at a given stage. Attempts at indirect rule, on the one hand, and the widespread efforts of indigenous rulers to limit changes to purely technical matters, on the other, reflect attempts to stop development at a particular stage, but such devices did not usually succeed for long. The economic needs of the colonial powers or the indigenous ruling groups, their growing dependency on continuously changing international markets and international political organization, precluded any freezing of development, and tended to draw wider strata of the colonial societies into the orbit of modern institutional settings. This in turn facilitated the development of social movements that tended to focus on solidary symbols to the exclusion of other problems.[17]

A fourth, and perhaps the most variegated, type of response to growing differentiation consists of some structural solution which is on the whole congruent with the relevant problems. But within this broad type a wide variety of concrete institutional arrangements is possible. Such different solutions usually have different structural results and repercussions. Each denotes a different structure crystallized according to different criteria, and different modes of interpenetration of the major social spheres.

Thus, drawing again on examples from the great centralized Empires, we see that although the initial stages of socio-economic differentiation were relatively similar in Byzantium, in the later (Abbasside) Caliphate, and in post-Han China, each of these societies developed different overall institutional structures. The Byzantine Empire became a highly militarized and politically oriented system, while in the Caliphate a theocratic structure, based on continuous attempts to institutionalize a new type of universalistic politico-religious community, developed. China developed a centralized system based, at the center, on the power of the Emperor and the bureaucracy, and at the local level, on the relative predominance of the gentry. The selective channels of the examination and the literati were the major mechanisms integrating the local and central levels.[18]

Among modern and modernizing societies an even wider variety of concrete institutional types can be found at all stages of modernization. Modern societies differ, as is well known, not only in the degree of economic or political differentiation, but also in the basic integrative criteria and symbols in the political, economic or cultural spheres. At each level of differentiation a great variety of institutional patterns occurs.[19]

[17] On the Nomad Empires, see Owen Lattimore, *Studies in Frontier History*, London: Oxford University Press, 1962, especially chs. 3 and 4. On the process of unbalanced change in colonial societies see Shmuel N. Eisenstadt, *Essays on Sociological Aspects of Political and Economic Development*, The Hague: Mouton, 1961.

[18] See Eisenstadt, *The Political Systems of Empires, op. cit.*

[19] On the varieties of modern societies see Parsons, *Structure and Process in Modern Societies, op. cit.*, ch. 3, and "A Revised Analytical Approach to the Theory of Social Stratification," in *Essays in Sociological Theory* (rev. ed.), Glencoe, Ill.: The Free Press, 1954, pp. 386–441; Clifford Geertz (ed.), *Old Societies and New States*, New York: The Free Press, 1963; and Eisenstadt, *Modernization, Growth and Diversity, op. cit.*

One very interesting and intriguing possibility is the development of a relatively stable system in which the major institutional spheres vary in degree of differentiation. One of the most important examples of such variation occurs in feudal systems, which are characterized by a relatively high degree of differentiation in some of the central cultural roles as against a much smaller degree of differentiation in the economic and political roles.[20] Similar instances of "uneven" differentiation which have not yet crystallized into stable overall institutional systems exist in some of the more differentiated tribal and patrimonial societies.

One interesting aspect of uneven differentiation is that the more differentiated units of such related societies (e.g., the church in feudal or patrimonial systems) develop a sort of international system of their own apart from that of their "parent" societies.

Similarly, various aspects of modernization may develop in different degrees in the major spheres of modernizing societies. As one example, in many new states today—especially in Africa but also in Asia—we witness a continuous extension of political modernization, which is not usually accompanied by anything approaching a similar degree of development in the economic sphere, even where economic development is an important slogan. In many of these societies these varying degrees of modernization seem to coalesce into ongoing social and political systems, though at a minimal level of efficiency and integration.[21] This structural type may sometimes be similar to, or a derivative of, the product of continuous "unbalanced" change described above. But much more research is needed to elucidate the exact relations between the two.

The variety of integrative criteria and institutional contours at any level of differentiation is, of course, not limitless. The very notion of interdependence among major institutional spheres negates the assumption that any number of levels of differentiation in different institutional spheres can coalesce into a relatively stable institutionalized system. The level of differentiation in any one sphere necessarily constitutes, within broad limits, a pre-condition for the effective institutionalization of certain levels of differentiation in other social spheres. But within these broad limits of mutual pre-conditioning a great deal of structural variety is possible.

[20] See Otto Hintze, "Wesen und Verbreitung des Feudalismus," *Sitzungsberichte der Preussischen Akademie der Wissenschaften, Phil. Hist. Klasse*, 1929, 5, 321–347, and Rushton Coulborn (ed.), *Feudalism in History*, Princeton: Princeton University Press, 1956, p. 1. C. L. Cahen, "Réflexions sur L'usage du mot de 'Féodalite,'" *Journal of the Economic and Social History of the Orient*, 3 (April, 1960), pp. 1–20.
[21] See Eisenstadt, *Modernization, Growth and Diversity, op. cit.*

## Constricted Development

Not only may different institutional contours and integrative mechanisms develop at each level of differentiation, but each such structure, once institutionalized, creates its own boundary-maintaining mechanisms, its own directions of change, and its potential for further development or for breakdown and regression. Each such institutional system tends to develop specific tendencies toward "de-differentiation," or the constriction of the new potentialities for further development. The growing differentiation and increasing interdependence among the various more autonomous and diversified institutional spheres increases the probability that one sphere will attempt to dominate the other coercively, by restricting and regimenting their tendencies toward autonomy.

This probability is especially strong with respect to the political and religious (or value) spheres, because these spheres are especially prone to "totalistic" orientations that tend to negate the autonomy of other spheres. Religious and political elites may attempt to dominate other spheres, imposing rigid frameworks based on their own criteria. The aim of such policies is usually an effective de-differentiation of the social system, and they may result in rigidity and stagnation, or precipitate continual breakdown of the system. These tendencies to de-differentiation are usually very closely related to the specific processes of change that may develop within any institutionalized system.

Thus, in the Byzantine Empire, the centralistic tendencies of the monarchs and the Church alternated with the more centrifugal tendencies of the aristocracy and some peasant groups, while the relatively high levels of political commitment demanded by the polity conflicted with the strong tendencies toward passivity and "other-worldliness" among elements within the Church. In the long run, the predominance of the latter alternatives contributed to the downfall of the Byzantine Empire and the "ossification" of the Eastern Church.

This outcome was also facilitated by the weakness of later Emperors who oscillated between repressive policies and giving in to the aristocratic forces, in both cases without developing a consistent new institutional framework.

The situation was different in the early Caliphate. On the one hand there was a strong universalistic emphasis on the state as the framework of the religious community but in a way subordinate to it. On the other hand, no comprehensive, independent, and cohesive organization of the religious groups and functionaries developed. Political participation was confined mostly to court cliques, and neither participation in the bureaucracy nor the religious check on political authority was effective because no machinery other than revolt existed to enforce it. Indeed, various religious sects and movements continually arose, very often contributing to the downfall of the state.

This aspect of the early Caliphates gave rise to a continual oscillation between "totalistic" political-religious movements, aiming at the total transformation of the political regime through various illegitimate means— assassinations, rebellions—and an other-worldly passivity that only helped to maintain the despotic character of the existing political regimes.

In the later Caliphate, various sects tried to overthrow the more differentiated polity and establish simple, de-differentiated political communities; these attempts alternated with military-bureaucratic usurpations. These movements, which often overlapped, blocked further political development.[22]

Similarly, breakdowns of relatively differentiated frameworks and attempts to "de-differentiate" have also occurred in various modern modernizing societies. In the more recent period such processes have developed in several "new states" like Burma, Indonesia or Pakistan. These developments are not entirely dissimilar from other less recent examples. The initial modernization of China, so often used as a negative example in comparison with the more successful initial modernization of Japan, comes to mind here. Similarly, the long histories of several Latin American countries represent a similar process. Although in many of them only the very minimal structural or sociodemographic features of modernization developed over a very long time, in other cases, as in Chile and especially in pre-Peron Argentina, evident progress toward modernization was halted or reversed.

Lastly, the rise of militarism in Japan and especially the European Fascism and Nazism of the twenties and thirties should be mentioned here as perhaps the most important case of a breakdown of modernization at a much more advanced level of development.

In each of these cases we witness the breakdown of a relatively differentiated and modern framework, the establishment of a less differentiated framework or the development of blockages and eruptions leading to institutionalized stagnation, rigidity, and instability.[23]

Thus, specific processes of institutional change open up some potentialities

[22] See Eisenstadt, *The Political Systems of Empires, op. cit.*, and "Institutionalization and Change," *op. cit.*
[23] See Eisenstadt, "Breakdowns of Modernization," *op. cit.*

but may block others, and in some cases the institutionalization of a given solution may "freeze" further development or give rise to stagnation or continual breakdown. In these cases the new systems are unable to adapt effectively to the wider and more variegated environments to which they became exposed as a result of the differentiation they have undergone.[24]

## Causes of Different Evolutionary Paths

The great variety of institutional and integrative contours of different societies arriving at similar levels or stages of differentiation may be due to several different, yet interconnected, reasons. First, different societies arrive at the same level of differentiation through different historical paths and through a variety of concrete structural forms. Thus, for instance, the political systems of centralized Empires could develop from city states, or from patrimonial or feudal regimes. These different antecedents greatly affected the social composition and the concrete organization of the new centralized structure as well as the basic orientations and problems of its rulers.

Similarly, the process of modernization may begin in tribal groups, in caste societies, in different types of peasant society, and in societies with different degrees and types of prior urbanization. These groups differ greatly with regards to resources and abilities for setting up and implementing relatively differentiated goals, and for regulating the increasingly complex relations among different parts of the society.

One aspect of the variety among these antecedents of differentiation is of special interest. Within many relatively undifferentiated societies exist enclaves of much more differentiated and specialized activities, especially in the economic and cultural spheres. Thus, cities function in many societies not only as administrative or cultural centers but very often as distinct entities, to some extent separated from the rest of society evincing a much higher degree of differentiation and specialization in the cultural or economic field. Similarly, monasteries and monastic orders, sects and academies, and very often special ethnic and religious minorities and special religious-tribal federations, may to some extent be detached from the wider society and evince, at least in certain spheres, a higher degree of differentiation. In

[24] One of the most interesting recent comparative analyses of the development of different institutional structures and different potentialities for further change, at a similar level of differentiation is Marshal D. Sahlins, "Poor Man, Rich Man, Big Man, Chief: Political Types in Melanesia and Polynesia," *Comparative Studies in Society and History,* 5 (April, 1963), pp. 285–304.

more modern times various political, religious and intellectual sects and elites may constitute important enclaves of more differentiated activities.[25]

Very often enclaves of this sort constitute parts of an international system of their own which transcends, at any given time, the confines of the total society to which they belong as well as its own international system.

Such enclaves may be very important sources of innovation within a society. Their presence or absence in any "antecedent" stage may greatly influence the scope and nature of the different integrative solutions that may be institutionalized at a later stage of differentiation.

Third, the variability of institutional contours at the same level of differentiation also stems from differences among predominant elites. Elites may develop either in different institutional spheres or in the same sphere but with different ideologies and orientations of action. Some of them may be more influential than others in establishing the detailed contours of the new institutional system.

Thus, to return to our earlier example, the major differences in the institutional contours among the Chinese, Byzantine and Abbaside Empires has been to no small degree influenced by the different types of predominant elites—the bureaucratic-literati in China, the separate military and religious elites in Byzantium and the militant sectarian elite in the Caliphate.

Similarly, Shils' analysis of the different institutional patterns of modern and modernizing societies—political democracy, tutelary democracy, modernizing oligarchy, totalitarian oligarchy and traditional oligarchy—shows how the crystallization of each such type is influenced not only by the broad structural conditions of these societies but also, to a very large degree, by the composition and orientation of the leading elites in each type of society.[26] Kerr and associates have shown in a recent analysis that different modernizing elites tend to develop different strategies with regard to some major problems of social and economic policy, such as the pace of industrialization, sources of funds, priorities in development, pressures on enterprises and managers, the educational system, policies of agriculture, methods of allocation of labor and many others.[27]

[25] For an analysis of some modern intellectual sectarian groups see, in addition to Weber's classical analysis of the Protestant Ethic, Franco Venturi, *Roots of Revolution*, New York: Alfred A. Knopf, 1960; Vladimir C. Nahirny, "The Russian Intelligentsia From Men of Ideas to Men of Convictions," *Comparative Studies in Society and History*, 4 (July, 1962), pp. 403–436; Harry J. Benda, "Non-Western Intelligentsia as Political Elites," in John H. Kautsky (ed.), *Political Change in Underdeveloped Countries, Nationalism and Communism*, New York: Wiley, 1962, pp. 235–252.

[26] Shils, *Political Development in the New States, op. cit.*

[27] Clark Kerr, *et al., Industrialism and Industrial Man*, Cambridge, Mass.: Harvard University Press, 1960.

## Innovating Elites

These considerations—especially recognition of the complex relations between the processes of social change and structural differentiation, on the one hand, and viable institutionalization of different types of structure, on the other—are crucial to the critical re-evaluation of the evolutionary perspective in the social sciences.

How can we explain the variability of institutionalized solutions to the problems arising from the development of a given level of structural differentiation? We must first recognize that the emergence of a solution, i.e., the institutionalization of a social order congruent with the new range of problems, is not necessarily given in the process of differentiation. We must discard the assumption—underlying, even if only implicitly, many studies of comparative institutions in general and of modernization in particular—that the conditions giving rise to structural differentiation, and to "structural sensitivity" to a greater range of problems, also create the capacity to solve these problems or determine the nature of such solutions.

The crucial problem is the presence or absence, in one or several institutional spheres, of an active group of special "entrepreneurs," or an elite able to offer solutions to the new range of problems. Among modern sociologists Weber came closest to recognizing this problem when he stressed that the creation of new institutional structures depends heavily on the "push" given by various "charismatic" groups or personalities and that the routinization of charisma is critical for the crystallization and continuation of new institutional structures. The development of such "charismatic" personalities or groups constitutes perhaps the closest social analogy to "mutation."

A number of questions pertaining to such elites and their relation to the broader social strata and structure in which they operate should be considered here, as possible guides to further research.

First, under what conditions do leaders or entrepreneurs with the requisite vision and organizational ability appear at all? Second, what is the nature of this "vision," or the proposed institutional solution to the problems attendant on growing differentiation? This problem has two aspects. One has to do with the particular institutional sphere within which an elite develops and is most active, or the values and orientations it especially emphasizes and attempts to institutionalize or "impose" as the dominant values of the new social structure. The other aspect is the nature of the concrete solution that the emerging elite proposes within this particular institutional framework. At any level of differentiation, a given social sphere contains not one but several, often competing, possible orientations and potentialities for de-velopment. Again, Weber saw this most clearly when he showed that re-ligious institutions may take several forms, often contradictory, at any level of differentiation of the religious sphere from other institutions. Thus, at the stage when autonomous religious orientations and organizations break away from the relatively closed "primitive" community, prophets or mystagogues may arise, and at higher levels of differentiation, sectarian developments may compete with tendencies to establish Churches, or strong "other-worldly" orientations, with "this-worldly" ones.[28]

Finally, we should consider readiness of competing elites and various wider segments of the society to accept the new elite's solutions, i.e., to pro-vide at least the minimal resources necessary for the institutionalization of the proposed solutions. Within broad limits, the degree of correspondence between the elite's "vision" and the needs of other groups varies; it is not fully determined by the existing or developing level of differentiation.

As yet, we know little about the specific conditions, as distinct from the more general trend to structural differentiation, that facilitate the rise of new elites, and which influence the nature of their basic orientations, on the one hand, and their relations with broader strata, on the other. Available indi-cations, however, are that factors beyond the general trend to differentiation are important. For example, various special enclaves, such as sects, monas-teries, sectarian intellectual groups or scientific communities, play an im-portant role in the formation of such elites. And a number of recent studies have indicated the importance of certain familial, ideological and educa-tional orientations and institutions.[29]

Within this context the whole problem of the extent to which institutional patterns are crystallized not through "independent invention" within a so-ciety but through diffusion from other societies, should be reexamined. Cases

[28] See Max Weber, The Sociology of Religion, translated by Ephraim Fischoff, Boston: Beacon Press, 1963, especially chs. 4, 10, 11. For an interesting modern case study bear-ing on this problem see Ernest Gellner, "Sanctity, Puritanism, Secularism and National-ism in North Africa," Archives de Sociologie des Religions, 15 (Janvier-Juin, 1963), pp. 71–87.

[29] See David C. McClelland, The Achieving Society, Princeton, N.J.: Van Nostrand, 1960, and "National Character and Economic Growth in Turkey and Iran," in Lucien W. Pye (ed.), Communication and Political Development, Princeton, N.J.: Princeton Uni-versity Press, 1963, pp. 152–182; and Everett Hagen, On the Theory of Social Change, Homewood, Ill.: The Dorsey Press, 1962; Clifford Geertz, "Modernization in Moslem Society: The Indonesian Case," in Cultural Motivation to Progress and the Three Great World Religions in South and South East Asia, An International Seminar sponsored by the University of the Philippines, Manila, and The Congress for Cultural Freedom, Manila, 1963 (mimeo.), and idem. Peddlers and Princes, Chicago; University of Chicago Press, 1963.

of diffusion might be partially due to the successful "importation," by entrepreneurial groups on the margins of a given society, of acceptable solutions to latent problems or "needs" within that society.

Thus, at any given level of differentiation the crystallization of different institutional orders is shaped by the interaction between the broader structural features of the major institutional spheres, on the one hand and, on the other hand, the development of elites or entrepreneurs in some of the institutional spheres of that society, in some of its enclaves, or even in other societies with which it is in some way connected.

The variability in the concrete components of such interaction helps to explain the great—but not limitless—variety of structural and integrative forms that may be institutionalized at any given level of differentiation. It indicates also that while different societies may arrive at broadly similar stages of evolution in terms of the differentiation of the major institutional and symbolic spheres, yet the concrete institutional contours developed at each such step, as well as the possible outcomes of such institutionalization in terms of further development, breakdown, regression or stagnation, may greatly differ among them.

## Summary

The considerations presented above constitute the background for a reappraisal of the evolutionary perspective within the framework of recent sociological theory. An evolutionary perspective makes sense, as we have seen, only so far as at least some of the processes of change that are inherent in the very nature of any social system, create the potentialities for institutionalization of more differentiated social and symbolic systems. But recognition of the relation between such changes and institutionalization of more differentiated social orders must be tempered by several systematic considerations.

First, the preceding analysis does not imply that all processes of social change necessarily give rise to changes in overall institutional systems. While the potentialities for such systematic changes (as distinct from changes in patterns of behavior, or in the composition of sub-groups, or in the contents of the major integrative criteria of different spheres), exist in all societies, the tempo and direction of such changes vary.

Second, we need not assume that all systematic changes that alter the scope of differentiation within the major spheres of a society necessarily result in the institutionalization of a new, more differentiated social order, better adapted to a wider and more variegated environment. Under certain circumstances, differentiation may also lead to "regression," stagnation, attempts to differentiate, or breakdown.

Third, even when structural differentiation is institutionalized, the concrete contours of the new institutional and symbolic structure may greatly vary; many concrete structural and cultural crystallizations are possible at each "stage" of differentiation.

Thus, the degree of differentiation within a given society or institutional field does not in itself determine the concrete contours of the system. The institutionalization of greater ranges of differentiation, of a wider scope of autonomy for each major social sphere, and the successful regulation of free-floating resources may rise to new types of social, political or cultural structure, each of which has different potentialities for further change, for break-down or for development.

The concepts of differentiation and of "stages" are important guides for identifying the crucial break-throughs at which different spheres of social and cultural activity are freed from various ascriptive frameworks, and the potential for crystallization of more differentiated social and symbolic systems is enhanced. But these concepts neither describe nor explain the concrete crystallizations that appear at these junctures.[30]

Because the conditions giving rise to structural differentiation differ from those that encourage the formation of new elites who can provide solutions for the problems attendant on such differentiation, the assumption that evolution is undirectional at any given stage of differentiation is untenable.

These different types of concrete institutional crystallization are not, however, entirely random. Study of the interaction between processes of differentiation and the formation and activities of different elites may help to explain systematically the possibilities for institutionalization of such different integrative principles and concrete structures at a given level of societal differentiation. Systematic analysis of the interaction between these different types of condition may provide an approach to the explanation of specific historical constellations. But in this endeavour broad evolutionary con-

[30] The distinction between general and specific evolution, as laid out by Sahlins and Service, *Evolution and Culture, op. cit.*, is in some ways similar to the point of view taken up here. But their insistence on the preponderance of technological factors in evolution leads them to neglect the internal dynamics of change in different social and cultural systems. Even more questionable, from the point of view of the present discussion, is their assumption—as phrased by Eggan—"that these specific, particular developments necessarily add up to the succession of culture through stages of overall progress, which is general evolution." See F. Eggan, "Cultural Drift and Social Change," *op. cit.*, p. 355.

siderations only indicate ranges of possibilities and types of potential break-throughs.

# A RECONSIDERATION OF THEORIES OF SOCIAL CHANGE * (*Moore*)

The mention of "theory of social change" will make most social scientists appear defensive, furtive, guilt-ridden, or frightened. Yet the source of this unease may be in part an unduly awe-stricken regard for the explicitly singular and implicitly capitalized word "Theory." The several social scientific disciplines, and notably economics and sociology, do provide some fairly high-level, empirically-based, and interdependent propositions concerning social change.

The present paper presents some suggested conceptual organization of the problem, and some illustrations of interrelated propositions. The exposition is taxonomic and programmatic rather than discursive. Many of the alleged propositions are hypothetical, but any resemblance between them and real data, living or dead, would be comforting.

## *The Possibility and Scope of Theories*

The current anxious pessimism concerning the topic of social change can be readily traced to several related sources. One such source is clearly the downfall or slight acceptability of global, simplifying theories. Sweeping evolutionary or cyclical doctrines have provided a relatively poor fit to data. Even where generalization may have been "justified," the loss of information in the process of abstraction has resulted in relevance to only minute segments of observed changes, or, in other words, in low predictive power.

Against this background of critical examination and rejection of general theories, the major and rather successful positive effort of social scientists over recent decades has been directed to static, cross-sectional, or "structural-functional" analysis. Now structures and functions, paraphrased as "patterns" and "consequences," are not inherently static. However, the theorists who have been most explicit about their concepts, assumptions, and

* Reprinted from the *American Sociological Review* Vol. 25, 6 (December 1960), pp. 810–818 with permission of the American Sociological Association and the author.

specific theoretical problems have provided little guidance to the orderly transformation of social systems. Wherever an implicit "equilibrium" model is used, changes in patterns of action and their relationships tend to be viewed as deriving from "external" sources, and thus in some sense accidental. The system is viewed as reacting to change either by returning to the *status quo ante* or, more probably, by establishing a new equilibrium. Thus *given* a specifiable change in any component of the system, both the processes and results of social transformation may be traced. But this frame of reference provides little guidance to the occurrence of the initial change, save in the concept of "dysfunction" as a challenge to the notion of perfect integration.

The abandonment of "the quest for origins" in functional analysis—following the dictum that each item of culture or social action is to be explained by the rest of the system—has also meant, commonly, an abandonment of concern for sequences and transformations. It is noteworthy that historical relativism, although nominally rejected by sociologists as unnecessary defeatism, is closely akin to extreme cultural relativism, which implies a rejection of *both* static and dynamic laws of any substantial generality.

The pessimism about laws of social change is scarcely warranted. Scholars and textbook writers (not elsewhere classified) would do well to re-read the works of those theorists who exhibit a more than casual concern for the past and the future as well as for the current state of affairs. Among contemporary theorists, Sorokin[1] and MacIver[2] stand out as scholars who show a major and insistent concern for change as a part of the very nature of social existence, rather than as a regrettable disturbance in the normally placid interdependence of self-equilibrating systems.

Between the global theories, which explain too little because they attempt too much, and the relativistic position that views all change as unique, there is a large middle territory. Within that spacious terrain one may note the standardized internal dynamics of groups of various types, and identify the sources, forms, directions, and rates of change in types and segments of social systems. If the resulting theory is not exactly simple, neither is it wholly simple-minded.

[1] See especially Pitirim A. Sorokin, *Social and Cultural Dynamics*, New York: American Book, 1937–1941, 4 vols.; also, the one-volume edition (the one cited hereafter), Boston: Porter Sargent, 1957; Sorokin, *Society, Culture and Personality*, New York: Harper, 1947.
[2] See Robert M. MacIver, *Social Causation*, Boston: Ginn, 1942; MacIver and Charles H. Page, *Society*, New York: Rinehart, 1949, Chapters 22–29.

## The Sources of Change

Perhaps the most outstanding progress in the theory of social change has been made in the identification and analysis of the sources of change. In very general terms, this progress has resulted from the abandonment of causes primarily external to social systems and of single-factor explanations, with the correlative acceptance of "immanent" change[3] as the prime mover in social dynamics.

*Various determinisms.* The long search for a singular cause of social change is understandable if regrettable. Simplicity is always an aim in theoretical work. If a single factor external to the social system could be identified as the source of change, simplicity would be further aided by avoidance of any confusion or uncertainty about the direction of the causal influence.[4] That comfortable position had to be abandoned, however, in view of several basic difficulties:

1. Climatic trends, physiographic features, and biological characteristics change very slowly relatively to the social dynamics for which causes are sought. A constant cannot explain a variable in any system of logic.

2. The purity of the causal direction is spurious. Human activity alters climate, topography, and human biology. "Natural selection" in the human species is always "social selection." Population changes are by no means independent of social structures.

3. The relevance of human heredity and the non-human environment is always conditional and relative to the technology, social organization, and cultural values of human societies.

The abandonment of "external" causes in favor of causes of change within the system gains little if the theorist clings to a single "determinism." Among the many difficulties, extensively analyzed by Sorokin,[5] the principal ones include, first, the conceptual confusion in identifying the leading variable, so that, for example, technology is equated with "material culture" rather than with a set of applicable scientific principles, or the "economic factor" subsumes such normative elements as property codes; second, the failure to

---

[3] *Social and Cultural Dynamics,* Chapters 38 and 39.

[4] See Newell Le Roy Sims, *The Problem of Social Change,* New York: Crowell, 1939, Chapters 4–6, and pp. 250–280.

[5] See especially *Society, Culture, and Personality,* Chapter 44. The persistence of the "culture lag" hypothesis and its variants in the face of Sorokin's devastating criticism (as well as criticisms by others) is itself an interesting example of resistance to change, or a "lag" not explainable by the hypothesis.

avoid interdependence of variables in functional systems and, therefore, third, a complete failure to find empirical confirmation of alleged principles.

*Adaptation to external events.* Some of the literature on social change essentially avoids questions of primacy of sources, and attends rather to the consequences of external events. Thus shifts and crises deriving from climatic change or physiographic events leave the sources of change largely unpredicted and uncontrolled, but still influential on social systems. Detection of standardized consequences, or a typology of them, however, may still be possible without prediction of the initial events. Even if such external sources of change are beyond the reach of sociological theory, they may still be left within the analytical system if the consequences have sufficient pattern to warrant generalization.

The theoretical situation is not essentially different if the "external" source of change is another "society" or "culture." The literature on acculturation, or contact and diffusion, generally does not predict the occurrence of contact, but rather classifies types of contact and types of consequences.[6] Here, however, the sources of change are not beyond the theoretical limits of sociological inquiry, but rather beyond the actual limits of reliable research.

Two generalizations appear justified with reference to adaptation to "external" events or influences. Both are of the long-term and largely undirectional or cumulative character.[7] With reference to "natural" influences, accumulated knowledge of methods of prediction and control, together with an increased independence of social systems from the non-human environment, serves more and more to cushion (but not to eliminate) the impact of shifts and crises. With reference to inter-system contacts, on the other hand, the multiplication of agencies of communication serves to reduce the isolation and thus the autonomy of societies, to increase the proportion and rate of changes from external sources, and thereby to increase "cultural" interdependence and even homogeneity.[8]

[6] See Sims, *op. cit.*, pp. 244–245, 250–257; Sorokin, *Society, Culture, and Personality,* Chapter 38.

[7] Sorokin's rejection of any "ever-linear" change, although perhaps technically correct, does not rest upon historical grounds, but rather upon "logical" grounds and the appeal to a remote future when the sun's cooling results in an era of human "decline" before the final end of history. He concedes three long-term historically cumulative trends: in population size, knowledge, and social specialization. These, of course, are in some measure interrelated, but it is not clear that finite limits to population size (whether from the purely spatial standpoint or the problem of subsistence under deteriorating environmental conditions) have any necessary consequences for the cumulation of knowledge. Knowledge, translated into the technology, say, of space colonization, may avoid even the remote limits set by the natural environment. (See *Social and Cultural Dynamics,* pp. 664–669).

[8] See Wilbert E. Moore, "Creation of a Common Culture," *Confluence,* 4 (July, 1955), pp. 229–238.

*Resolution of human problems.* If the search for sources of change turns inward to social systems themselves, it becomes apparent that there are persistent problems of the "human condition" that seem to be universal potential sources of positive human effect. Assuming that there are common "functional requisites of any society,"[9] these may be viewed as providing minimal rather than ideal or stable conditions for the survival of systems. Although the translation of functions into values has been strongly criticized by Sorokin and others,[10] it does appear empirically that at least a partial translation is tenable. For example, it is doubtful that health, longevity, and improved material conditions of life have ever been neglected or rejected by any substantial number of the population in any historical or contemporary culture. The virtually universal contemporary acceptance of the "gospel and economic development," despite the documented diversity of cultural values, can scarcely be understood otherwise.[11] Incidentally, this illustration does not imply a baldly "materialistic interpretation": there are many other problems of the human condition, such a normative conformity and the search for "meaning" in a super-empirical sense, that also provide the basis for recurrent social innovation.

On a less general level, and consistent with diversity of cultural values, one may still find prevalent inconsistencies between ideal values and patterned social behavior, inconsistencies that provide a potential, and probable, basis for efforts at closer approximation.

Sorokin is undoubtedly correct in insisting upon the uneven attention given to empirical science and rational technology through time and space.[12] Yet, he is also correct in noting the long-term linear "growth of human knowledge and inventions."[13] The explanation of the cumulative trend seems clear. In the attempt to solve human problems, empirically verifiable knowledge and techniques of rational intervention in the natural or social order do not suffer long-term defeats in the face of competing systems of ex-

---

[9] Marion J. Levy, Jr., *The Structure of Society*, Princeton: Princeton University Press, 1952, Chapter 4.

[10] *Society, Culture, and Personality*, pp. 338–339.

[11] Moore, *op. cit.;* Arnold S. Feldman and Wilbert E. Moore, "Commitment of the Industrial Labor Force," in Feldman and Moore, editors, *Labor Commitment and Social Change in Developing Areas*, New York: Social Science Research Council, 1960, Chapter 1.

The position I have taken here appears consistent with that of MacIver; see his *Social Causation*, Chapter 10. This is a position I previously, and erroneously, criticized in "Sociology of Economic Organization," in G. Gurvitch and W. E. Moore, editors, *Twentieth Century Sociology*, New York: Philosophical Library, 1945, p. 460.

[12] *Social and Cultural Dynamics*, especially Chapters 13–23.

[13] *Ibid.*, p. 667. The difference in Sorokin's two positions is presumably a function of divergent time-and-space specifications.

planation and control. This interpretation argues that persistent problems provide challenges to social innovation, and the secular growth of science and technology implies that rational, secular solutions have a higher probability of acceptance and retention than any alternatives.[14] It may be suggested, in fact, that a rational, technical orientation to the natural or social order is an essentially irreversible intellectual revolution.[15]

*Flexibilities in the system.*   A number of characteristics of human societies assure the probability of change, but without substantial guidance as to form, direction, or rate. Two principal systematic flexibilities are especially noteworthy: uncertainties in socialization, and role ranges and deviations.

To say that children are born into a society or culture is elliptical. They are normally born into a family unit, which in turn can be expected to be only partially representative of a generalized and uniform set of values and normative and cognitive orientations. The universality of social differentiation structurally precludes exact uniformity in family position. Even when they occupy similar positions in the social structure, it is extremely unlikely that families will follow exactly uniform patterns of child care and rearing, or indeed that the same family will exhibit uniform behavior in the intimate interaction with successive offspring. Thus biological individual differences interact with diverse personality and structural factors to provide a rather wide range of possible variation. On a strictly actuarial view of socialization, uniformities are somewhat more remarkable than variations.

The uncertainties of socialization are given added point by the virtual impossibility of absolute role specification, even in a "tightly integrated" social system. Granting the probability of ranges of tolerable conduct within recurrent patterns of social relations, the opportunity if not the certainty of innovation exists.

*Strains inherent in the system.*   The conception of an "integrated" social system, which informs much of the writing in contemporary sociology— often implicity—is a model useful for many purposes, but is clearly contrary to fact. The use of some such model provides a first approximation to the systematic tracing of consequences of given changes, but does not ac-

[14] This interpretation is consistent with the distinction between "civilization" (knowledge and technique, which are cumulative) and "culture" (values and norms, which are "optional" and noncumulative). See, e.g., MacIver and Page, *op. cit.*, pp. 498–506.

[15] See Wilbert E. Moore, "Measurement of the Organizational and Institutional Implications of Changes in Productive Technology," in International Social Science Council, *Social, Economic and Technological Change: A Theoretical Approach*, Paris: 1958, pp. 229–259, where this intellectual revolution is referred to as "the rise of the rational spirit."

count for change itself. For the latter, a somewhat different analytical model is appropriate, namely, one that permits identification of internal or immanent[16] sources of change, including inherent strains.

Several types of inherent strains in ongoing societies are identifiable. Three may be noted as especially significant: demographic imbalances, universal scarcity situations, and the "dialectic" conflict between normative alternatives.

Although the conception of population changes as being essentially "biological" variables, external to social systems, is untenable,[17] it remains true that demographic behavior is extremely unlikely to provide a precise total and differential control of fertility and mortality. In other words, precise stability of population size through time is unlikely, as is, *a fortiori,* precise maintenance of existing numerical distributions among social categories.

Over the short run for most areas of the world and for most periods of history, demographic imbalances probably have resulted in "fluctuations" and adjustments. Over the long run it appears clear that human populations have grown, although most rapidly in the modern era. The modern era has been characterized by a fairly standard sequence, probably unique for any given population,[18] but repeated through space: the "demographic transition" from high fertility and mortality to low vital rates, with rapid intervening growth owing to mortality decline prior to fertility decline. As fertility is brought under deliberate and relatively effective control, its short-run fluctuations closely approximate various changes in levels of economic activity. The negative correlation between the number of children and the family's capacity to support them tends to be reduced or to disappear entirely. Still, no population reproduces its contemporary social differentials precisely. Moreover, the future consequences of current fertility behavior may exhibit, for example, substantial lack of "phasing" of labor supplies and labor demand.

The conception of universal scarcities is in effect a necessary extension of an assumption underlying much of economics. Not only are goods and services, or their monetary representation, likely to be scarce relative to human "wants," but so are time and loyalty (or "affective energy"). These three

16 *Social and Cultural Dynamics,* Chapter 38. Sorokin's explanation of immanent change is on a somewhat more abstract, "philosophical" plane than the present discussion.

17 See Kingsley Davis, *Human Society,* New York: Macmillan, 1949, Chapter 20; also, Wilbert E. Moore, "Sociology and Demography," in P. M. Hauser and O. D. Duncan, editors, *The Study of Population,* Chicago: University of Chicago Press, 1959, Chapter 33.

18 The conventional view of the demographic transition for one western nation, at least, is questioned by William Petersen in "The Demographic Transition in the Netherlands," *American Sociological Review,* 25 (June, 1960), pp. 334–347.

scarcities are often interrelated, so that allocations of loyalty may be indicated by allocation of time or treasure or both. However, they are analytically distinct. Any viable social system requires norms that determine allocation of these scarcities, but the latter remain omnipresent sources of potential strain in individual behavior and in the relations between and among various groups and social categories.

It is *not* suggested that the strains owing to scarcities form the basis for, say, the empirically untenable Marxian theory of "class struggle." But such strains would appear to be a pregnant source of competition within and among social groupings, and accordingly of normative innovation in the attempt to maintain order *and equity.* The equity of any system of differential allocation of scarce values is subject to challenge as to both principles and results. The same is true of any attempt at equalization. To assume that a system of undifferentiated equality in claims and rewards would be more stable (or equitable) than a differential system is pure prejudice.

A final immanent source of change may be suggested. The literature of sociology abounds with dichotomous classifications, ranging from culture-types through forms of social cohesion or relationship, to paired normative alternatives. Although such modes of classification are "primitive" in the sense that they attempt analysis in terms of attributes rather than variables, they are not useless. It is the beginning of wisdom to identify the dichotomies as polar extremes on a range of variation, and the pursuit of wisdom to note that "pure" types do not concretely exist. A very considerable gain in wisdom results, however, from recognizing the paired alternatives as conflicting principles of social organization and regulation, both of which are persistent in the system. Predominant institutionalization of one alternative does not dispel or dismiss its counterpart.[19]

A few illustrations of this essentially "dialectical" view of social systems may serve to indicate its possible value in resolving some theoretical difficulties that stem from the alternative notions of stable "integration." Sociologists have noted, for example, that "achieved status" systems retain elements of "ascription," and conversely. Although not so commonly noted, it is doubtful that predominant attention to common descent as the strongest bond in the "consanguine" kinship system entirely dispels the probable affective bonds arising in the "conjugal" relation, and conversely. The persistence of various reciprocities among adult siblings and between adult

[19] This view has been developed independently, but without primary application to social change, by Reinhard Bendix and Bennett Berger in "Images of Society and Problems of Concept Formation in Sociology," in Llewellyn Gross, editor, *Symposium on Sociological Theory,* Evanston: Row, Peterson, 1959, Chapter 3.

generations despite various inequalities in the mobility of the nuclear family is by this view not anachronistic. The more probable prediction is that of continued persistence if not actual increase in such phenomena, with all the strains that are thus entailed.

Similarly, Parsons' list of "pattern variables" (for example, universalism-particularism, diffuseness-specificity)[20] seem more useful as identifications of conflicting principles actually and always present than simply as concepts available to the observer to remind him that other situations are different.

This view of social dynamics is consistent with Sorokin's position with reference to "immanent change" and the "principle of limit,"[21] but is not repetitive of his position. When Sorokin discusses alternative forms of social relationship (familistic, contractual, compulsory[22]) or forms of government (authoritarian, democratic[23]) he describes them as forms that "fluctuate" in their predominance through time. It appears more useful, and more consistent with the data, to account for such "fluctuations" by the continued presence of competing principles.

What the dialectic principle and other sources of change permit is a theoretical point of view that voids the inhibitions of a static equilibrium model, as well as a partial "accounting" for observed changes. The identification of common sources of change does not, however, uniformly aid in generalization about the direction and rate of change. The notion of successive approximations in the solution of human problems does invite a suggested relation with the apparently cumulative character of knowledge, as noted above. And the dialectic principle of normative alternatives does invite speculation about possible repetitive cycles (of the pendulum-swing variety). But the latter speculation has scant empirical basis and would require careful methodological formulation for reliable testing.

## The Form and Direction of Change

A "pure" theory of social change might be viewed as concerned with any alterations in social phenomena (however defined) through time, with sole concern for such questions as form, sequence, direction, and rate. Such a mode of abstraction is analogous to the "pure" theory of "formal" sociology, which attends to the forms or types of social relations or interaction, in

20 See Talcott Parsons, *The Social System,* Glencoe, Ill.: Free Press, 1951; esp. pp. 180 ff.; see also Parsons, "Pattern Variables Revisited: A Response to Robert Dubin," *American Sociological Review,* 25 (August, 1960), pp. 467–483.

21 *Social and Cultural Dynamics,* Chapters 38 and 39.

22 *Society, Culture, and Personality,* Chapters 5 and 29.

23 *Ibid.,* Chapter 30.

abstraction from the functional or meaningful content of such relations.

Some basis for such a "pure" theory exists, crudely in the common distinction between "evolutionary" and "cyclical" theories, more elaborately in detailed distinctions among forms of change. It may be useful in the present context to note some of the possible formal models of the direction of social change, for such models can be employed for purposes of identification and classification even when the starting point is substantive rather than formal.

Sorokin identifies three principal "patterns of direction" of change: linear—subdivided as unilinear, oscillating, spiral, and branching; cyclical; and variably or creatively recurrent direction, which may be approximately paraphrased as "cycles with trend."[24]

Several methodological points now may be appropriately noted.[25] First, the form and direction of change clearly are in part a function of the time periods and observational units. Second, the shape of a curve fitted to trend data accordingly depends in part on the detail demanded—for example, a curvilinear trend may be made rectilinear by greater generalization (and consequent loss of information or "goodness of fit"). Third, wherever reliable quantities are available, the available mathematical alternatives in curve-fitting are much more numerous than Sorokin's or similar alternatives. Fourth, the possible formal models are further multiplied if "interaction in process" or other complicating features are introduced.

In addition, it should be remembered that not all changes are necessarily directional in any significant sense, or perhaps even consequential for the social analyst. For some changes Sorokin's neutral term "fluctuations" seems to be appropriate. Others may be regarded as "variations on themes." Persons, including scholarly persons, living through large and obvious changes in the conditions of life may have the impression that all is flux, if not chaos. Yet some generalities and some particulars remain remarkably constant. It is presumably unnecessary here to enter an extended discussion of the theory of social structure, but a few reminders may be in order. First, fair agreement obtains among analysts concerning the functions essential for the survival of any society. These functions do not *determine* appropriate structures, but they obviously *limit* them. Thus many changes involve ranges of *structural substitutability* for constant ends and functions. Second, the specification of a number of characteristics of the particular type of society or the special characteristics of one system radically limits the range

24 *Ibid.*, Chapter 45.
25 An extensive unpublished manuscript by Otis Dudley Duncan, "The Study of Social Change," 1958, has proved very useful in the following discussion.

of potential substitution, but does not eliminate variation that, within these limits, may be "random."

These methodological points are of some consequence in view of the probability that increased attention to the phenomena of change will be accompanied by increased emphasis on "measurement."[26] They do not insure "good" theory, since that is first of all a matter of asking the right questions, but they do warn of some analytical options and hazards.

In view of the great diversity of social phenomena, it would probably be possible to illustrate each of the principal directional forms. Such illustration is not attempted here. Rather, two varieties of change are added to the previous list, each of some consequence in the analysis of major contemporary social transformations.

Some sequences (not "cycles") are apparently unique in given systems, but are partially repeated in space, through time. The "demographic transition" is noted above; at an even more general level, "economic modernization" or "industrialization" is another illustration. History of course does not precisely repeat itself either in time or "laterally" in space, but sufficient common elements appear to warrant generalization.

A more complex form of change involves "interaction in process." This may be identified by the rather cumbersome designation, "cumulative, retroactive evolution." The essentials of the pattern are segmental changes that cannot continue until later "stages" react back on the initial ones. The simplest illustrations are the first and second "agricultural revolutions," separated in time by intervening industrialization, each step being essential. Similarly, it appears probable that "automation" requires not only its technological foundations as such, but the intervening and interactive development of manifold managerial and professional services, made possible in turn by earlier gains in technical productivity.[27]

## Unequal Probability and Rate

Theoretically, innovation may occur at any point in the social structure; functional theory and various "equilibrium" models do not tell us where or when it is most likely. And although functional theory, or "systems" analysis, starts from the assumption that any change has repercussions throughout the system, we do not in fact know either this assumption to be true in

[26] Wilbert E. Moore, "A Note on the Measurement of Social Change," Social Science Research Council, Items, 12 (December, 1958), pp. 42–43.

[27] This principle is elaborated in a paper by Arnold S. Feldman and Wilbert E. Moore, "Moot Points in the Theory," in Moore and Feldman, op. cit., Chapter 20.

detail or the path, rate, and degree of dependent change. The rejection of uniform "determinisms" does not necessarily imply the alternative of "equal probability." A more systematic inquiry into the principal sources of change, whether at the general level used here or with reference to more particular social systems, would seem to be the proper course of future inquiry with respect to "lead" and "lags." The grain of truth in technological determinism, for example, appears to be the likelihood that innovation occurs with disproportionate frequency in the means for accomplishing seemingly standard ends, with frequently unanticipated repercussions. This sequence may give rise to the sequential alternation of innovation and accommodation. The possibility of rapid spread and acceptance of new cultural values and ideologies, however, provides a suitably chastening warning against simplification.

## The Possibilities of "Integrated" Theory

Although a "pure" theory of social change can be contemplated, this is not viewed as the preferable path of progress. Even if change is the first criterion of selection for such a theory, nothing of empirical consequence can be said without specification of what is changing. The "structural-functionalists" are thus technically correct in maintaining that statics must *precede* dynamics.[28] But it is equally true that quite unrealistic static propositions may be produced unless statics *is followed by* dynamics.

The conventional organization of general sociological treatises relegates the topic of social change to the final chapter(s). Surely there is an alternative approach.[29] This would be to adopt some modest variant of the standard sociological or anthropological ways of identifying and ordering the principal segments of social systems. Most social science of whatever discipline consists of structural-functional analysis—asking what are the patterns, what are their interrelations? To these would be added several insistent questions: (1) What are the intrinsic dynamics of this segment? Examples might include the tendency of bureaucracies to proliferate offices, or the complex sequence in competitive structures of instrumental innovation, conservative reaction, and additional regulation. (2) What changes are the orderly consequences of intersegment functional interaction? Here, the interpenetration of occupational interest groups like unions, and complex work organizations like corporations afford illustrations. (3) What are the predictable

---

[28] Levy, *op. cit.*, pp. 43–45, 72–76; see also Parsons, *The Social System*, Chapter 11.
[29] The balance of this paragraph follows, with only slight change, the article cited in footnote 26.

leads, lags, tensions—such as the lead of deliberate change and the lag of adversely affected interests? (4) What are the reliable consequences for whole societies of these trends and interplays? An example is the pushing of common values to higher, indeed rarefied, levels of generalization while primary-group values may be intensified and particularized. (5) What can be painted with a broad brush on large canvases about inter-society relations and the trend of human kind generally? An important example is provided by the creation of common material standards of life without effective agreement on an equitable rationale for actual inequalities or even on the more ultimate values of human existence.

In sum, an "integrated" theory of social change will be as singular or plural as sociological theory as a whole, and will include about the same subdivisions and topics. It is not only later than we think, as always, but we are also nearer home.

# Index